Kate F. Parker.

A.
Merry Christmas
1888.

JANE WELSH CARLYLE.

From a miniature in possession of J. A. Froude, Esq.

JANE WELSH CARLYLE.

From a miniature in possession of J. A. Froude, Esq.

LETTERS AND MEMORIALS

OF

JANE WELSH CARLYLE

PREPARED FOR PUBLICATION

BY

THOMAS CARLYLE

EDITED BY

JAMES ANTHONY FROUDE

TWO VOLUMES IN ONE

VOL. I

NEW YORK

HARPER & BROTHERS, FRANKLIN SQUARE

1883

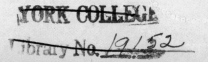

Stereotyped and Printed by the Chas. M. Green Printing Company.

PREFACE.

THE LETTERS which form these volumes were placed in my
hands by Mr. CARLYLE in 1871. They are annotated throughout
by himself. The few additional observations occasionally required
are marked with my initials.

I have not thought it necessary to give an introductory narrative
of Mrs. Carlyle's previous history, the whole of it being already
related in my account of the 'first forty years' of her husband's
life. To this I must ask the reader who wishes for information to
be so good as to refer.

Mr. Carlyle did not order the publication of these Letters, though
he anxiously desired it. He left the decision to Mr. Forster, Mr.
John Carlyle, and myself. Mr. Forster and Mr. John Carlyle
having both died in Mr. Carlyle's lifetime, the responsibility fell
entirely upon me. Mr. Carlyle asked me, a few months before
his end, what I meant to do. I told him that, when the 'Reminiscences' had been published, I had decided that the Letters might
and should be published also.

Mr. Carlyle requested in his will that my judgment in the matter should be accepted as his own.

J. A. FROUDE.

5 ONSLOW GARDENS:
    February 28, 1883.

LETTERS AND MEMORIALS

OF

JANE WELSH CARLYLE.

LETTER I.

'TUESDAY, June 10, 1834,' it appears, was the date of our alighting, amid heaped furniture, in this house, where we were to continue for life. I well remember bits of the drive from Ampton Street; what damp-clouded kind of sky it was; how, in crossing Belgrave Square, *Chico*, her little canary-bird, whom she had brought from Craigenputtock in her lap, burst out into singing, which we all ('Bessy Barnet,' our romantic maid, sat with us in the old hackney-coach) strove to accept as a promising omen. The business of sorting and settling, with two or three good carpenters, &c., already on the ground, was at once gone into, with boundless alacrity, and (under such management as hers) went on at a mighty rate; even the three or four days of quasi-camp life, or gypsy life, had a kind of gay charm to us; and hour by hour we saw the confusion abating, growing into victorious order. Leigh Hunt was continually sending us notes; most probably would in person step across before bedtime, and give us an hour of the prettiest melodious discourse. In about a week (it seems to me) all was swept and garnished, fairly habitable; and continued incessantly to get itself polished, civilised, and beautified to a degree that surprised me. I have elsewhere alluded to all that, and to my little Jeannie's conduct of it: heroic, lovely, pathetic, mournfully beautiful, as in the light of eternity, that little scene of time now looks to me. From birth upwards she had lived in opulence; and now, for my sake, had become poor—so nobly poor. Truly, her pretty little brag (in this letter) was well founded. No such houses, for beautiful thrift, quiet, spontaneous, nay, as it were, unconscious—minimum of money reconciled to human comfort and human dignity—have I anywhere looked upon where I have been.

From the first, or nearly so, I had resolved upon the 'French Revolution,' and was reading, studying, ransacking the Museum (to little purpose) with all my might. Country health was still about me; heart and strength still fearless of any toil. The weather was very hot; defying it (in hard, almost brimless hat, which was *obbligato* in that time of slavery) did sometimes throw me into colic; the Museum collection of 'French Pamphlets,' the completest of its sort in the world, did, after six weeks of baffled wrestle, prove inaccessible to me; and I had to leave them there—so strong was Chaos and Co. in that direction. Happily, John Mill had come to my aid, and the Paris 'Histoire Parlementaire' began to appear. Mill had himself great knowledge of the subject. He sent me down all his own books on the subject (almost a cartload), and was generously profuse and unwearied in every kind of furtherance. He had taken a great attachment to me (which lasted about ten years, and then suddenly ended, I never knew how); an altogether clear, logical, honest, amicable, affectionate young man, and respected as such here, though sometimes felt to be rather colourless, even aqueous—no religion in almost any form traceable in him. He was among our chief visitors and social elements at that time. Came to us in the evenings once or twice a week; walked with me on Sundays, &c.; with a great deal of discourse not worthless to me in its kind. Still prettier were Leigh Hunt's little nights with us; figure and bearing of the man, of a perfectly graceful, spontaneously original, dignified and attractive kind. Considerable sense of humour in him; a very pretty little laugh, sincere and cordial always; many tricksy turns of witty insight, of intellect, of phrase; countenance, tone and eyes well seconding; his voice, in the finale of it, had a kind of musical warble ('chirl' we vernacularly called it) which reminded one of singing-birds. He came always rather scrupulously, though most simply and modestly, dressed. 'Kind of Talking Nightingale,' we privately called him—name first due to her. He enjoyed much, and with a kind of chivalrous silence and respect, her Scotch tunes on the piano, most of which he knew already, and their Burns or other accompaniment: this was commonly enough the wind-up of our evening; 'supper' being ordered (uniformly 'porridge' of Scotch oatmeal), most likely the piano, on some hint, would be opened, and continue till the 'porridge' came—a tiny basin of which Hunt always took, and ate with a teaspoon, to sugar, and many praises of the excellent frugal and noble article. It seems to me, in our long, dim-lighted, perfectly neat and quaint room, these 'evening parties' of three were altogether human and beautiful; perhaps the best I anywhere had before or since! Allan Cunningham occasionally walked down; pleasant enough to talk with—though the topic was sure to be Nithsdale (mainly Nithsdale fun), and nothing else. Mrs. Austin, Mrs. Buller, Darwin, Wedgwood, &c., &c. (of this or shortly posterior dates), I do not mention. I was busy; she still more hopefully and gaily so; and in what is called 'society,' or London interests for us, there was no lack.—Of all which, these 'Letters,' accidental *waifs* among such multitudes as have carelessly perished, are now the only record.

I perfectly recollect the day this following letter describes, though I could not have given the date, even by year. 'Macqueen and Thomson' were two big graziers of respectability, Macqueen a native of Craigenputtock, Thomson, from near Annan, had been a school-fellow of mine. They had called here without very specific errand; and I confess what the letter intimates (of my silent wish to have evaded such interruption, &c., &c.) is the exact truth.

'*Traiked*' means *perished*, contemptuous term, applied to cattle,

&c. '*Traik*' = German '*Dreck*.' To '*bankrape*' is to '*bankrupt*' (used as a verb passive). 'And then he bankrapit, and geed out o' sicht:' a phrase of my father's in the little sketches of Annandale biography he would sometimes give me. During two wholly wet days, on my last visit to Scotsbrig in 1830, he gave me a whole series of such; clearest brief portraiture and life-history of all the noteworthy, vanished figures whom I had known by look only, and now wished to understand. Such a set of *Schilderungen* (human delineations of human life), so admirably brief, luminous, true, and man-like, as I never had before or since. I have heard Wordsworth, somewhat on similar terms (twice over had him in a corner engaged on this topic, which was his *best*); but even Wordsworth was inferior.—T. C.

To Mrs. Carlyle, Scotsbrig.

Chelsea: Sept. 1, 1834.

My dear Mother,—Could I have supposed it possible that any mortal was so stupid as not to feel disappointed in receiving a letter from *me* instead of my husband, I should have written to you very long ago. But while this humility becomes me, it is also my duty (too long neglected) to send a little adjunct to my husband's letter, just to assure you ' with my own hand ' that I continue to love you amidst the hubbub of this ' noble city ' [1] just the same as in the quiet of Craigenputtock, and to cherish a grateful recollection of your many kindnesses to me; especially of that magnanimous purpose to ' sit at my bedside ' through the night preceding my departure, ' that I might be sure to sleep!' I certainly shall never forget that night and the several preceding and following; but for the kindness and helpfulness shown me on all hands, I must have *traiked*, one would suppose. I had every reason to be thankful then to Providence and my friends, and have had the same reason since.

All things, since we came here, have gone more smoothly with us than I at all anticipated. Our little household has been set up again at a quite moderate expense of money and trouble; wherein I cannot help thinking, with a *chastened vanity*, that the superior shiftiness and thriftiness of the Scotch character has strikingly manifested itself. The English women turn up the whites of their eyes, and call on the ' good heavens ' at the bare idea of enterprises which seem to me in the most ordinary course of human affairs. I told Mrs. Hunt, one day, I had been very busy *painting*. ' What?' she asked, ' is it a portrait?' ' Oh! no,' I told her, ' something of more

---

[1] Phrase of Basil Montague's.

importance—a large wardrobe.' She could not imagine, she said,
' how I could have patience for such things?' And so, having no
patience for them herself, what is the result? She is every other
day reduced to borrow my tumblers, my teacups; even a cupful
of porridge, a few spoonfuls of tea, are begged of me, because
' Missus has got company, and happens to be out of the article;'
in plain unadorned English, because ' missus' is the most wretched
of managers, and is often at the point of having not a copper in her
purse. To see how they live and waste here, it is a wonder the
whole city does not ' bankrape, and go out o' sicht' ;—flinging
platefuls of what they are pleased to denominate ' crusts' (that is
what I consider all the best of the bread) into the ashpits! I often
say, with honest self-congratulation, ' In Scotland we have no such
thing as " crusts."' On the whole, though the English ladies seem
to have their wits more at their finger-ends, and have a great advantage over me in that respect, I never cease to be glad that I was
born on the other side of the Tweed, and that those who are nearest
and dearest to me are Scotch.

I must tell you what Carlyle will not tell of himself—that he is
rapidly mending of his Craigenputtock gloom and acerbity. He is
really at times a tolerably social character, and seems to be regarded
with a feeling of mingled terror and love in all companies; which I
should expect the diffusion of Teufelsdröckh will tend to increase.

I have just been called away to John Macqueen, who was followed by a Jack Thomson, of Annan, whom I received in my
choicest mood, to make amends for Carlyle's unreadiness—who was
positively going to let him leave the door without asking him in; a
neglect which he would have reproached himself with after.

My love to all. Tell my kind Mary to write to me; she is the
only one that ever does.

Your affectionate
JANE W. CARLYLE.

LETTER 2.

Mournfully beautiful is this letter to me; a clear little household light shining, pure and brilliant, in the dark obstructive places
of the past!

The 'two East Lothian friends' are George Rennie, then sculptor, and his pretty sister, Mrs. Manderston, wife of an ex-Indian
ship captain.

' Eliza Miles' and ' the Mileses' are the good people in Ampton
Street with whom we lodged; Eliza, their daughter, felt quite

captivated with my Jane, and seems to have vowed eternal loyalty to her almost at first sight; was for coming to be our servant at Craigenputtock (actually wrote proposing it then—a most tempting offer to us, had not the rough element and the delicate aspirant been evidently irreconcilable!). She continued to visit us here, at modest intervals; wrote me, after my calamity befel, the one letter of condolence I could completely read (still extant, and almost worth adjoining here), she was a very pretty and, to us, interesting specimen of the London maiden of the middle classes; refined, polite, pious, clever both of hand and mind; no gentlewoman could have a more upright, modest, affectionate and unconsciously high demeanour. Her father had long been in prosperous upholsterer business ('*Miles* and Edwards,' as we sometimes heard), but the firm had latterly gone awry, and poor Miles now went about as a 'traveller' (showing specimens, &c.), where he had formerly been one of the commanders-in-chief. He was a very good-natured, respectable man; quietly much sympathised with in his own house. Eliza, with her devout temper, had been drawn to Edward Irving; went daily, alone of her family, to his chapel, in those years 1831–2, and was to the last one of his most reverent disciples. She did, in her soft loyal way, right well in the world; married poorly enough, but wisely, and is still living, a now rich man's wife, and the mother of prosperous sons and daughters.

'Buller's Radical meeting,' had one an old newspaper, would give us an exact date: it was the meeting, privately got up by C. Buller, but ostensibly managed by others, which assembled itself largely and with emphasis in the London Tavern, to say what it thought on the first reappearance of Peel and Co. after the Reform Bill, '*first* Peel Ministry,' which lasted only a short time. I duly attended the meeting (never another in my life); and remembered it well. Had some interest, not much. The 2,000 human figures, wedged in the huge room into one dark mass, were singular to look down upon, singular to hear their united voice, coming clearly as from one heart; their fiery 'Yes,' their sternly bellowing 'No.' (Camille Desmoulins in the Palais-Royal Gardens, not long afterwards![1]) I could notice, too, what new *laws* there were of speaking to such a mass; no matter how intensely consentaneous your 2,000 were, and how much you *agreed* with every one of them; you must likewise *begin* where they began, follow pretty exactly their *sequence* of thoughts, or they lost sight of your intention; and, for noise of contradiction to you and to one another, you could not be heard at all. That was new to me, that second thing; and little or nothing else was. In the speeches I had no interest, except a phenomenal; indeed, had to disagree throughout, more or less with every part of them. Roebuck knew the art best; kept the 2,000 in constant reverberation, more and more rapturous, by his adroitly *correct* series of commonplaces; John Crawfurd, much more original, lost the series, and had to sit down again

---

[1] 'Afterwards:' when Carlyle came to write about Camille in the *French Revolution.*—J. A. F.

unheard—ignominiously unheard. *Ohe jam satis est.* I walked briskly home, much musing; found her waiting, eager enough for any news I had.—T. C.

To Mrs. Carlyle, Scotsbrig.

Chelsea: End of November [Nov. 21], 1834.[1]

My dear Mother,—Now that franks are come back into the world, one need not wait for an inspired moment to write; if one's letter is worth nothing, it costs nothing—nor will any letter that tells you of our welfare and assures you of our continual affection, be worth nothing in your eyes, ever destitute of news or anything else that might make it entertaining.

The weather is grown horribly cold, and I am chiefly intent, at present, on getting my winter wardrobe into order. I have made up the old black gown (which was dyed puce for me at Dumfries), with my own hands; it looks twenty per cent. better than when it was new; and I shall get no other this winter. I am now turning my pelisse. I went yesterday to a milliner's to buy a bonnet: an old, very ugly lady, upwards of seventy, I am sure, was bargaining about a cloak at the same place; it was a fine affair of satin and velvet; but she declared repeatedly that ' it had *no air*,' and for her part she could not put on such a thing. My bonnet, I flatter myself, has an *air;* a little brown feather nods over the front of it, and the crown points like a sugar-loaf! The diameter of the fashionable ladies at present is about three yards; their bustles (false bottoms) are the size of an ordinary sheep's fleece. The very servant-girls wear bustles: Eliza Miles told me a maid of theirs went out one Sunday with three kitchen dusters pinned on as a substitute.

The poor Mileses are in great affliction. Mr. Miles, about the time we came to London, got into an excellent situation, and they

---

[1] About a month before this date, Edward Irving rode to the door one evening, came in and stayed with us some twenty minutes, the one call we ever had of him here—his farewell call before setting out to ride towards Glasgow, as the doctors, helpless otherwise, had ordered. He was very friendly, calm and affectionate; spoke, chivalrously courteous, to her (as I remember): 'Ah, yes,' looking round the room, You are like an Eve, make every place you live in beautiful!' He was not sad in manner, but was at heart, as you could notice—serious, even solemn. Darkness at hand, and the weather damp, he could not loiter. I saw him mount at the door, watched till he turned the first corner (close by the rector's garden-door), and had vanished from us for altogether. He died at Glasgow before the end of December coming.

were just beginning to feel independent, and looked forward to a comfortable future, when one morning, about a week ago, Mr. Miles, in walking through his warerooms, was noticed to stagger; and one of the men ran and caught him as he was falling: he was carried to a public-house close by (his own house being miles off), and his wife and daughter sent for. He never spoke to them; could never be removed; but there, in the midst of confusion and riot, they sat watching him for two days, when he expired. I went up to see them so soon as I heard of their misfortune. The wife was confined to bed with inflammation in her head. Poor Eliza was up, and resigned-looking, but the picture of misery. 'A gentleman from Mr. Irving's church' was with her, saying what he could.

A brother and sister, the most intimate friends I ever had in East Lothian, live quite near (for London), and I have other East Lothian acquaintances. Mrs. Hunt I shall soon be quite terminated with, I foresee. She torments my life out with borrowing. She actually borrowed one of the brass fenders the other day, and I had difficulty in getting it out of her hands; irons, glasses, tea-cups, silver spoons, are in constant requisition; and when one sends for them the whole number can never be found. Is it not a shame to manage so, with eight guineas a week to keep house on! It makes me very indignant to see all the waste that goes on around me, when I am needing so much care and calculation to make ends meet. When we dine out, to see as much money expended on a dessert of fruit (for no use but to give people a colic) as would keep us in necessaries for two or three weeks! My present maid has a grand-uncle in town with upwards of a hundred thousand pounds, who drives his carriage and all that; at a great dinner he had, he gave five pounds for a couple of pineapples when scarce; and here is his niece working all the year through for eight, and he has never given her a brass farthing since she came to London.

My mother gave a good account of your looks. I hope you will go and see her again for a longer time. She was so gratified by your visit. I have just had a letter from her, most satisfactory, telling me all she knows about any of you. She gives a most wonderful account of some transcendentally beautiful shawl which Jane had made her a present of. I am sure never present gave more contentment.

Carlyle is going to a Radical meeting to-night, but there is no fear of his getting into mischief. Curiosity is his only motive—

and I must away to the butcher's to get his dinner. I wish you may be able to read what I have written. I write with a steel pen, which is a very unpliable concern, and has almost cut into my finger. God bless you all. A kiss to Mary's new baby when you see it.

Yours affectionately,

JANE CARLYLE.

LETTER 3.

Postscript to some letter of mine, announcing brother John's speedy advent from Italy, and visit to Scotsbrig as his next step.

The 'wee *wains*' (weans) are sister Mary's, sister Jean's, and brother Alick's; 'wee Jane,' her namesake, is brother Alick's eldest. 'Mighty nation' had this origin (derived by tradition of mine): My mother, in the act of removing from Ecclefechan, to Mainhill (in 1816), which was a serious new adventure to the family and her, had, as she privately told me, remembered vividly the first time she came *down* that road, riding towards Ecclefechan, as a little girl behind her father—towards an aunt, and unknown fortune in that new country—and how she could now piously say of herself, like Jacob, 'Now hath the Lord made of me a great nation.' Good dear mother!

I almost think this promised visit to Scotland did not take effect —John's own part of it having failed, and general uncertainty having thereupon supervened. I was myself in dreadful struggle [1] with the burnt first volume of 'French Revolution;' miserable accident which had befallen three months before this date; but which (having persisted to finish 'Book i. Vol. II.,' before turning back) I had now first practically grappled with, and found how near it bordered on the absolutely insuperable! certainly the impossiblest-looking literary problem I ever had: 'resembles swimming in an element not of water, but of quasi-vacuum,' said I mournfully, almost desperately: 'by main force, impossible, I find!'—and so had flung it all by, about this date; and for four weeks was reading the trashiest heap of novels (Marryat's, &c.) to hush down my mind, and, as it were, bury the disaster under ashes for a time. About July I cautiously, gingerly, stept up to the affair again, and gradually got it done. How my darling behaved under all this, with what heroism and what love, I have mentioned elsewhere. I find she renounced Scotland for this year, and instead appointed her mother to come and visit *us* here, which did take effect, as will be seen.—T. C.

---

[1] I may mention here a fact connected with the burning of this MS. Mill had borrowed it to read, and when in his hands it was in some way destroyed: he came himself to Cheyne Row to confess what had happened. He sat three hours trying to talk of other subjects. When he went away at last, Mrs. Carlyle told me that the first words which Carlyle spoke were: 'Well! Mill, poor fellow, is very miserable; we must try to keep from him how serious the loss is to us.'—J. A. F.

To Mrs. Carlyle, Scotsbrig.

Chelsea: May 2, 1835.

I too am coming, dear mother, and expect a share of the welcome! For though I am no son, nor even much worth as a daughter, you have a heart where there is '*coot and coom again.*'[1] I think of nothing so much at present as this journey to Scotland; all the sea-sickness and fatigues of my former journeys do not damp my ardour for this one.

Carlyle has not told you a piece of news we heard yesterday, so curious as to be worth recording. Mrs. Badams, who a year and a half ago made such outrageous weeping and wailing over the death of her husband, is on the eve of a second marriage (has been engaged for months back) to a Frenchman who is—her own half-nephew! ! ! the son of a sister who was daughter to the same father by a former wife! Such things, it seems, are tolerated in France; to us here it seems rather shocking. Such is the upshot of all poor Badam's labours and anxieties, and sacrifices of soul and body, in amassing money! Himself lies killed, with brandy and vexation, in a London churchyard; and the wreck of his wealth goes to supply the extravagances of a rabble of French who have neither common sense nor common decency.

I have just had a call from an old rejected lover, who has been in India these ten years: though he has come home with more thousands of pounds than we are ever likely to have hundreds, or even scores, the sight of him did not make me doubt the wisdom of my preference. Indeed, I continue quite content with my bargain; I could wish him a little *less yellow,* and a little more *peaceable;* but that is all.

What a quantity of wee *wains* I shall have to inspect! though I doubt if any of them will equal the first wee Jane, whom I hope they are not suffering to forget me. Truly you are become 'a mighty nation'! God prosper it!

Your affectionate
JANE WELSH CARLYLE.

LETTER 4.

Susan Hunter of St. Andrews, now and long since Mrs. Stirling of Edinburgh, was daughter of a Professor Hunter in St. Andrews

---

[1] 'The grace of God, brethren,' said some (mythical) Methodist, 'is like a round of beef; there is *coot* and,' &c.

University, and granddaughter of a famous do. do., whose editions of Virgil, and various other Latin classics, all excellently printed in the little county town of Cupar, Fife, are held in deserved esteem, not among ourselves only, but in Germany itself, by the best judges there.

To an elder sister of this Susan the afterwards famous Francis Jeffrey, then a young Edinburgh advocate, had been wedded, and was greatly attached; but she soon died from him and left him a childless widower. A second sister of Susan's, I believe, had married John Jeffrey, younger and only brother of Francis; but she too had died, and there were no children left. John Jeffrey followed no profession, had wandered about the world, at one time been in America, in revolutionary France, but had since settled pleasantly in Edinburgh within reach of his brother, and was a very gentle, affectionate, pleasantly social and idly ingenious man. I remember Susan and her one younger sister as living often with John Jeffrey; I conclude it was at Craigcrook, at Francis Jeffrey's that we had made acquaintance with her. She was a tall, lean, cleanly trim and wise-looking, though by no means beautiful woman, except that her face and manners expressed nothing that was not truthful, simple, rational, modest though decided. Susan and a brother of hers, John, who sometimes visited here in after times, and is occasionally mentioned in these letters, had a great admiration and even affection for Leigh Hunt, to whom John was often actually *subventive*. Susan's mild love for poor Hunt, sparkling through her old-maidish, cold, still, exterior, was sometimes amusingly noticeable.—T. C.

To Miss Hunter, Millfield House, Edmonton.

5 Cheyne Row, Chelsea: June 1835.

My dear Susan Hunter,—What an infidel you are to dream of my ever forgetting either your existence or your kindness! Woman though I be, and though Mr. John Jeffrey once said of me (not in my hearing) that I was ' distinguished as a flirt ' in my time, I can tell you few people are as steady in their attachments. That I was attached to you, a person of your quick penetration could hardly fail to observe.

You were very kind to me; and that was not all; you were several things that women rarely are, straightforward and clear-sighted, among the rest, and so I liked you, and have continued to like you to this hour. Never have I thought of Edinburgh since we left it without thinking of you and the agreeable evenings I spent with you.

Such being the case, you may believe it is with heartfelt gladness that I find you are again within reach. Do come to-morrow evening or Thursday, whichever suits you best, and know that we possess the rarest of London accommodations, a spare bed; so that if you consider the thing in the same reasonable light that I do, you will undoubtedly stay all night.

My dear Susan (do let me dispense with formalites), I am so glad that I have not even taken time to mend my pen.

Your affectionate friend

JANE CARLYLE.

LETTER 5.

Letter to John Sterling; probably her first. Our acquaintance then was but of few weeks' standing. This letter and all the following to the same address were carefully laid together under sealed cover 'Aug. 14, 1845,' in Sterling's still steady hand; and mournfully came back to us in the course of a few weeks longer.— T. C.

To the Rev. John Sterling, Herstmonceux.

5 Cheyne Row, Chelsea: Thursday, June 15, 1835.

My dear Sir,—You did kindly to send the little separate note. The least bit 'all to myself,' as the children say, was sure to give me a livelier pleasure than any number of sheets in which I had but a secondary interest; for, in spite of the honestest efforts to annihilate my *I-ety*, or merge it in what the world doubtless considers my better half, I still find myself a self-subsisting, and, alas! self-seeking *me*. Little Felix, in the 'Wanderjahre,' when, in the midst of an animated scene between Wilhelm and Theresa, he pulls Theresa's gown, and calls out, 'Mama Theresa, I too am here!' only speaks out with the charming trustfulness of a little child what I am perpetually feeling, though too sophisticated to pull people's skirts or exclaim in so many words, 'Mr. Sterling, I too am here.'

But I must tell you I find a grave fault in that note—about the last fault I should have dreamt of finding in any utterance of yours—it is not believing, but faithless! In the first place, the parenthesis ('if ever') seems to me a wilful questioning of the goodness of Providence. Then you say, if in some weeks I can bring myself to think of you with patience, &c., &c. Now both the 'if' and 'perhaps' displease me. Only the most inveterate sceptic could, with your fineness of observation, have known me for two weeks without certifying himself that my patience is infinite, inexhaustible! that, in fact, I, as well as yourself, combine 'the wisdom of Solomon with the patience of Job!' Far from being offended by your dissertation on the ' Sartor,' [1] I think it the best that has been said or sung of him. Even where your criticism does not quite fall in with my humble views, I still love the spirit of the critic. For instance, I am loth to believe that I have married a Pagan; but I approve entirely of the warmth with which you warn your friend against the delusion of burning pastilles before a statue of Jupiter, and such like extravagances. I suppose it is excessively heterodox, and in a Catholic country I should be burnt for it, but to you I may safely confess that I care almost nothing about what a man believes in comparison with how he believes. If his belief be correct it is much the better for himself; but its intensity, its efficacy, is the ground on which I love and trust him. Thus, you see, I am capable of appreciating your fervour in behalf of the Thirty-nine Articles, without being afflicted because my husband is accused of contumacy against them.

But what do you mean by speaking of 'a few weeks ? When you went, you said, with an appearance at least of good faith, that you would be back in London in three weeks; and one week and half of another is already gone. I hope you will keep your time for several reasons: chiefly for this one, that our continuance in London has, of late days, become more uncertain, the American speculation having suddenly received a more practical form; and if we depart for Scotland without seeing you any more, and afterwards our good or evil star actually shoots over the Atlantic, surely, to some of us at least it will be a matter of regret rather than of self-congratulation that our acquaintance should have begun.

I have seen your mother twice. She is very good to me. I have, moreover, been reviving one of my young lady accomplishments for her sake; painting flowers on a portfolio, to keep those verses in, which she was so troubled about losing. Your father has been here since I began writing, to ask us to dinner on Saturday. We played a drawn game at chess, and Carlyle and he debated, more loudly than logically, on the subject of Napoleon's morality. He is just gone to inquire about the house in Cheyne Walk, in which good work I was meaning to have forestalled him, and communicated the result in my letter. If a fairy would grant me three wishes this evening, my first would be that we might remain where we are, my second that you might be settled in Cheyne Walk, and the third, like a thrifty Scotchwoman, I would beg leave to lay by

---

[1] Herstmonceux, May 29, 1835 (*Life of Sterling*, 1864 edit., p. 274).

in reserve for future need.   And now I must go and array myself
with all possible splendour for a rout at Mrs. Buller's,[1] where
O'Connell is to be, and all the earth—that is to say, all the Radical
earth.   Wish me good speed.   May I offer my good wishes, and
prospective regards to your wife?

Affectionately yours,
JANE W. CARLYLE.

LETTER 6.

To Miss Hunter, Millfield House, Edmonton.

5 Cheyne Row, Chelsea: Thursday [July?] 1835.

Dear,—I am too essentially Scotch not to give due heed to the
proverb 'it is good to make hay while the sun shines,' which
means, in the present case, it is good to catch hold of a friend
while she is in the humour.   But I have been provokingly hindered
from acting up to my principle by the prolonged absence of my
usual domestic, which has kept us until the present day in 'the
valley of the shadow' of charwoman; and, thoroughgoing as I
know you to be, I feared to invite you to participate therein.
Now, however, I have got the deficiency supplied, after a more
permanent and comfortable fashion, and make haste to say 'come
and stay.'   Come, dear Susan, and let us make the best of this
'very penetrating world'—as a maid of my mother's used to call it
in vapourish moods—come and wind me up again, as you have
often done before when I was quite run down, so that, from being
a mere senseless piece of lumber, I began to tick and tell people what
o'clock it was.   Will you come in the ensuing week?   Name your
own time, only remember the sooner the better,

My kind regards to Mr. John when you write, and to your sister.
Do you remember her physiological observation on hens?[2]

I hear nothing of his lordship,[3] but the fault is my own.

Yours affectionately,
JANE CARLYLE,

Do not be after thinking that I have lost the power to write more
legibly.   I am just out of one of my headaches—my hand shakes.

---

[1] I remember this 'Buller Soirée,' with 'O'Connell and all the Radical
earth' there; good enough for looking at slightly, as in a menagerie.   O'Connell I had already seen the figure of, heard the voice of, somewhere; speak to
him I never did, nor, in the end, would have done.

[2] Lost to me, or gone to the remnant of an indistinguishable shadow (1873).

[3] Lord-Advocate Jeffrey.

No Miss ——,[1] however, stept in out of space to drive me to extremity. Oh, the horror of that moment!

LETTER 7.

Mrs. Welsh was to come about the end of August. I was now getting tolerably on with my 'burnt MS.,' and could see the blessed end of it lying ahead—had, probably, myself resolved on a run to Annandale, by way of bonfire on that victorious event. At least, I did go for a week or two, it appears, and brought up an Annan maidservant with me, one 'Anne Cook,' who proved peaceable and obedient for a year or more afterwards. The continual trouble my brave little woman bore—all of it kept quiet from me, result quasiperfect, of his own accord, when it came to me—is now, to look back upon, tragically beautiful! That 'miraculous Irish Roman Catholic' proved utterly a failure before long.

The Wilsons of the 'Madeira hamper,' and of many other kind procedures and feelings towards us, were an opulent brother and sister of considerably cultivated and most orthodox type (especially the sister), whom we had met with at Henry Taylor's, and who held much to us for many years—indeed, the sister did (though now fallen deaf, &c.) till my dear one was snatched away. I think they both yet live (2 Upper Eccleston Street), but I shudder to call, and shall likely see them no more. Many dinners—James Spedding, Reverend Maurice, John Sterling (once or twice), James Stephen (afterwards Sir James), Perrot of Edinburgh (who was the brother of 'Tom Wilson's' Cambridge old friend), &c., &c.—many dinners brilliantly complete, and with welcome glad and hearty, at which, however, I would rather not have been.

The coterie-speech abounds in this letter; more witty and amusing, much, very much, to the first reader than it can now ever be to another. Explanation I must add at any rate. 'Blessings &c. over my head:' Extempore public prayer: 'Lord, we thank Thee for the many blessings Thou art making to pass over our heads.' 'Encouragement:' Cumberland man (to me), concerning a squire whose son and he had quite quarrelled: 'Feayther gives him nea encouragement.' 'Arnot,' a little laird, come almost to starvation by drinking, &c. A poor creditor, unpayable, overheard Mrs. A. whispering, 'Let us keep,' &c. 'Victualling:' Old Johnnie Maccaw (McCall), a strange old Galloway peasant of our Craigenputtock neighbourhood, who witnessed the beginning of settlement in 1834, had asked my sister Mary, 'D'ye victual a' thae folk? Ai what a victualling they wull tak!'

I recollect the evening with the Degli Antonis—that evening! all gone, all gone! (Dumfries, August 16, 1868).—T. C.

---

[1] A rather bouncing young Edinburgh lady, daughter of ——, not in the highest esteem everywhere. Her 'stepping in' (two years ago, in the Edinburgh winter) I have forgotten.

To Mrs. Aitken, Dumfries.

Chelsea: Aug. 1885.

My dear Jane,—Even the doubt expressed in your last letter about the durability of my affection was more agreeable to me than the brief notice which you usually put me off with, 'remember us to Mrs. Carlyle,' or still worse, 'remember us to your lady.' I have told you often that it afflicts me to be always, in the matter of correspondence with you, obliged, like the Annandale man, to thank God 'for the blessings made to pass over my head.' It ought not, perhaps, to make any difference whether your letters be addressed to him or me, but it does. You never in your life answered a letter of mine (and I have written you several), except little business notes from Dumfries, which could not be considered any voluntary expression of kind remembrance. Had you even expressed a wish to hear from me since I came here, I would nevertheless have written, being of a disposition to receive thankfully the smallest mercies when greater are denied; but, as I said, you have always put me off with a bare recognition of my existence, which was small 'encouragement.' The fact is, we are both of us, I believe, too proud. We go upon the notion of 'keeping up our dignity, Mr. Arnot.' You have it by inheritance from your mother, who (as I have often told herself) with a great profession of humility is swallowed up in this sin; and I have possibly been seduced into it by her example, which I was simple enough to consider a safe one to imitate in all respects.

For my part, however, I am quite willing to enter into a compact with you henceforth to resist the devil, in so far as he interferes with our mutual good understanding; for few things were more pleasant for me than to 'tell you sundry news [1] of every kind,' nay, rather 'every thought which enters within this shallow mind,' had I but the least scrap of assurance of your contentment therewith.

Now that my mother is actually coming, I am more reconciled to my disappointment about Scotland. Next year, God willing, I shall see you all again. Meanwhile, I am wonderfully well hefted here; the people are extravagantly kind to me, and in most respects my situation is out of sight more suitable than it was at Craigenputtock. Of late weeks Carlyle has also been getting on better with his writing, which has been uphill work since the burning of the first manuscript. I do not think that the second version is on the

---

[1] Some old *child's verses* of this same ' *Craw* Jean' (considerably laughed at and admired by us in their time).

whole inferior to the first; it is a little less vicacious, perhaps, but better thought and put together. One chapter more brings him to the end of his second 'first volume,' and then we shall sing a *Te Deum* and get drunk—for which, by the way, we have unusual facilities at present, a friend (Mr. Wilson) having yesterday sent us a present of a hamper (some six or seven pounds' worth) of the finest old Madeira wine. These Wilsons are about the best people we know here; the lady, verging on oldmaidenism, is distinctly the cleverest woman I know.

Then there are Sterlings, who, from the master of the house down to the footman, are devoted to me body and soul; it is between us as between 'Beauty and the Beast':—

> Speak your wishes, speak your will,
> Swift obedience meets you still.

I have only to say 'I should like to see such a thing,' or 'to be at such a place,' and next day a carriage is at the door, or a boat is on the river to take me if I please to the ends of the earth. Through them we have plumped into as pretty an Irish connection as one would wish. Among the rest is a Mr. Dunn, an Irish clergyman, who would be the delight of your mother's heart—a perfect personification of the spirit of Christianity. You may take this fact to judge him by, that he has refused two bishoprics in the course of his life, for conscience sake. We have also some Italian acquaintances. An Italian Countess Clementina Degli Antoni is the woman to make my husband faithless, if such a one exist—so beautiful, so graceful, so melodious, so witty, so everything that is fascinating for the heart of man. I am learning from her to speak Italian, and she finds, she says, that I have a divine talent (*divino talento*). She is coming to tea this evening, and another Italian exile, Count de Pepoli, and a Danish young lady, 'Singeress to the King of Denmark,' and Mr. Sterling and my old lover George Rennie. 'The victualling' of so many people is here a trifle, or rather a mere affair of the imagination: tea is put down, and tiny biscuits; they sip a few drops of tea, and one or two sugar biscuits 'victuals' a dozen ordinary eaters. So that the thing goes off with small damage to even a long-necked purse. The expenditure is not of one's money, but of one's wits and spirits; and that is sometimes so considerable as to leave one too exhausted for sleeping after.

I have been fidgeted with another change of servants. The woman recommended to me by Mrs. Austin turned out the best servant I had ever had, though a rather unamiable person in temper, &c. We got on, however, quite harmoniously, and the affairs of the house were conducted to my entire satisfaction, when suddenly she was sent for home to attend a sick mother; and, after three weeks' absence, during which time I had to find a charwoman to supply her place, she sent me word, the other day, that, in the state of uncertainty she was kept in she could not expect her place to remain longer vacant for her. The next day I lighted on an active, tidy-looking Irish Roman Catholic in a way so singular that I could not help considering her as intended for me by Providence, and boding well of our connection. She is not come yet, but will be here on Wednesday; and in the meanwhile my charwoman, who has her family in the workhouse, does quite tolerably.

One comfort is, that I have not to puddle about myself here, as I used to have with the ' soot drops ' at Craigenputtock; the people actually do their own work, better or worse. We have no bugs yet, to the best of my knowledge; and I do not know of one other house among all my acquaintance that so much can be said for. For all which, and much more, we have reason to be thankful.

I must not finish without begging your sympathy in a disaster befallen me since I commenced this letter—the cat has eaten one of my canaries! Not Chico, poor dear; but a young one which I hatched [1] myself. I have sent the abominable monster out of my sight for ever—transferred her to Mrs. Hunt.

With kindest regards to every one of you, prattlers included,

Yours affectionately,

JANE CARLYLE.

LETTER 8.

To Miss Hunter, Millfield House, Edmonton.

5 Cheyne Row, Chelsea: Sunday, Sept. 22, 1835.

My dear Friend,—I have been hindered from writing to you all this while by the same cause which has hindered me from doing almost everything on earth that I ought to have done these last six weeks—continued illness, namely, taking one day the form of intolerable headache; another day of equally intolerable colic; and many days together animating me with a noble disposition to hang or drown myself. Since you left me especially, I have been at the

---

[1] *Assisted* in hatching, or, bringing from the shell! Chico was a very bad husband and father.

right pitch of suffering for entitling me to Mr. Jeffrey's warmest sympathy—confined to bed, and not out of danger of 'going to the undertaker' (the cockney idea of a future state).

My projected visit to Herstmonceux did not take effect, my mother arriving[1] on the very day we should have set out. It seemed when I had received her in a perpendicular posture, and seen her fairly established in the house, that I had nothing more to do, for I made no more fight with destiny, but quietly took to bed.

When I was a little recovered, Mrs. Sterling, who would not give up the fancy for taking me out of town, carried me to her brother's for a few days—about twenty-five miles from London,[2] a perfect Paradise of a place—peopled, as every Paradise ought to be, with angels. There I drank warm milk and ate new eggs, and bathed in pure air, and rejoiced in cheerful countenances, and was as happy as the day was long; which I should have been a monster not to have been, when everybody about me seemed to have no other object in life but to study my pleasure. I returned in high feather—to be sick again the very next day.

Now I am but just arisen from another horrible attack, which being the worst, I fondly flatter myself may be the *finale* to the business for this time.

I long very much to see you again, and have too much confidence in your kindness of nature to dread that my inability to make your last visit agreeable, or even decently comfortable, will deter you from giving me again the pleasure which I always have in your company, sick or well.

Carlyle expects to be at the end of his vexatious task this blessed day,[3] and in a week or ten days will probably depart for Scotland. There has been much solicitation on my mother's part that I would go also, and get myself plumped up into some sort of world-like rotundity. But man nor woman lives not by bread alone, nor warm milk, nor any of these things; now that she is here, the most that Dumfriesshire could do for me is already done, and country air and country fare would hardly counterbalance country dulness for me. A little exciting talk is many times, for a person of my temperament, more advantageous to bodily health than either

---

[1] Came Aug. 31. Herstmonceux, where John Sterling still was, had been the kind project of his mother for behoof of my poor suffering Jeannie.

[2] Near Watford (Mr. Cunningham, who tragically died soon after).

[3] Just about to finish his re-writing of Vol. I. *French Revolution*, a task such as he never had before or since!

judicious physicking or nutritious diet and good air. Besides, nobody wasever less than I a partaker in the curse of the man who was 'made like unto a wheel.' I have no taste whatever for loco- motion, by earth, air, or sea (by the way, did you hear that the aërial ship has been arrested for debt?).

Will you come a while in Carlyle's absence, and help to keep my mother and me from wearying? I think I may safely engage to be more entertaining than you found me last time; and one thing you are always sure of, while I keep my soul and body together—an affectionate welcome. For the rest, namely, for external accommo- dations, you, like the rest of us, will be at the mercy of another distracted Irishwoman, or such successor as Heaven in its mercy, or wrath, may provide, for this one also is on the 'move.' My husband, God willing, will bring me a sane creature of the servant sort from Scotland with him; for it is positively a great crook in my present lot to have so much of my time and thought occupied with these mean perplexities.

Your friend Mr. Craik was here lately; he seems a good-hearted pleasant man.

Carlyle unites with me in kind love. My mother also begs her remembrances. Forgive scrawling, and many things besides— poverty in the article of paper among others. Remember me to Mr. John and your sister when you write, and believe me always

Your affectionate and amiable

JANE CARLYLE.

LETTER 9.

'Sereetha': in the interval of servants (rebellious Irishwoman packed off, and Anne Cook not yet come with me), I remember this poor little Chelsea specimen, picked out as a stop-gap from some of the neighbouring huts here—a very feeble though willing little girl, introduced by the too romantic-looking name 'Seraether'—which, on questioning her little self, I discovered to be Sarah Heather (Sar' 'Eather)! much to our amusement for the moment! 'Pees- weep' is peewit, lapwing; with which swift but ineffectual bird Sereetha seemed to have similarity.

'The kindness of these people!' 'I'm sure the,' &c., (inter- jectional in this fashion) was a phrase of her mother's.

'Beats the world.' Annandale form of speech which she had heard without forgetting from my sister Mary.

'Garnier,' big German refugee, dusty, smoky, scarred with duel- cuts; had picked up considerable knowledge in his wanderings, was of intelligent, valiant, manful character; wildly independent, with tendency to go mad or half-mad—as he did by-and-by. Il

Conte 'Pepoli' was from Bologna, exile and dilettante, a very pretty man; married, some years hence, Elizabeth Fergus of Kirk-caldy (elderly, moneyed, and fallen in love with the romantic in distress); and now, as widower, lives in Bologna again.—T. C.

To T. Carlyle, Esq., Scotsbrig.[1]

Chelsea: Oct. 12, 1835.

Dearest,—A newspaper is very pleasant when one is expecting nothing at all; but when it comes in place of a letter it is a positive insult to one's feelings. Accordingly your first newspaper was received by me in choicest mood; and the second would have been pitched in the fire, had there been one at hand, when, after having tumbled myself from the top story at the risk of my neck, I found myself deluded with 'wun penny'm.' However, I flatter myself you would experience something of a similar disappointment on receiving mine; and so we are quits, and I need not scold you. I have not been a day in bed since you went—have indeed been al-most free of headache, and all other aches; and everybody says Mrs. Carlyle begins to look better—and what everybody says must be true. With this improved health everything becomes tolerable, even to the peesweep Sereetha (for we are still without other help). Now that I do not see you driven desperate with the chaos, I can take a quiet view of it, and even reduce it to some degree of order. Mother and I have fallen naturally into a fair division of labour, and we keep a very tidy house. Sereetha has attained the un-hoped-for perfection of getting up at half after six of her own accord, lighting the parlour-fire, and actually placing the breakfast things (*nil desperandum me duce!*). I get up at half after seven, and prepare the coffee and bacon-ham (which is the life of me, making me always hungrier the more I eat of it). Mother, in the interim, makes her bed, and sorts her room. After breakfast, mother descends to the inferno, where she jingles and scours, and from time to time scolds Sereetha till all is right and tight there. I, above stairs, sweep the parlour, blacken the grate—make the room look cleaner than it has been since the days of Grace Macdonald;[2] then mount aloft to make my own bed (for I was resolved to enjoy the privilege of having a bed of my own); then clean myself (as the servants say), and sit down to the Italian lesson. A bit of meat

---

[1] Carlyle had gone to Annandale at the beginning of October.—J. A. F.

[2] The Edinburgh servant we brought with us to Craigenputtock; the skil-fullest we ever had anywhere.

roasted at the oven suffices two days cold, and does not plague us
with cookery. Sereetha can fetch up tea-things, and the porridge is
easily made on the parlour-fire; the kitchen one being allowed to
go out (for economy), when the Peesweep) retires to bed at eight
o'clock.

That we are not neglected by the public, you may infer from the
fact that, this very night, Peesweep fetched up four tea-cups on the
tray; and when I asked the meaning of the two additional, she inquired, with surprise, ' Were there to be no gentlemen?' In fact,
' the kindness of these people ' ' beats the world.' I had some private
misgiving that your men would not mind me when you were not
here, and I should have been mortified in that case, though I could
not have blamed them. But it is quite the reverse. Little Grant [1]
has been twice to know if he could ' do anything for me.' Garnier
has been twice! The first time by engagement to you; the second
time to meet Pepoli, whom he knew in Paris, and wished to re-know,
and who proved *perfido* on the occasion. Pepoli has been twice,
and is gliding into a flirtation with—*mia madre!* who presented
him, in a manner *molto graziosa*, with her tartan scarf. From John
Miil I have been privileged with two notes, and one visit. He evidently tried to yawn as little as possible, and stayed till the usual
hour, lest, I suppose, he should seem to have missed your conversation. John Sterling and the Stimabile,[2] of course. The latter was
at tea last night to meet Mr. Gibson [3]—one of my fatal attempts at
producing a reunion, for they coincided in nothing but years. The
Stimabile was at Brighton for several days, and goes again next
week, so that he has not been too deadly frequent.

Our visiting has been confined to one dinner and two teas at the
Sterlings', and a tea at Hunt's! You must know, ——— ———
came the day after you went, and stayed two days. As she desired
above all things to see Hunt, I wrote him a note, asking if I might
bring her up to call. He replied he was just setting off to town,
but would look in at eight o'clock. I supposed this, as usual, a

---

[1] Official in the India House, a friend and admirer of John Mill's.

[2] A title we had for John's father. Signora degli Antoni, the Italian in-
structress in these months, setting her pupil an epistolary pattern, had
thrown off one day a billet as if addressed to Edward Sterling, which began
with *Stimabile Signor.*

[3] Was a massive, easy, friendly, dull person, physically one of the best
washed I ever saw; American merchant, ' who had made, and again lost,
three fortunes '; originally a Nithsdale pedlar boy, ' Black Wull,' by title;
' Silver-headed Packman,' he was often called here.

mere off-put; but he actually came—found Pepoli as well as Miss
———, was amazingly lively, and very lasting, for he stayed till
near twelve. Between ourselves, it gave me a poorish opinion of
him, to see how uplifted to the third heaven he seemed by ———'s
compliments and sympathising talk. He asked us all, with enthusiasm, to tea the following Monday. ——— came on purpose, and
slept here. He sang, talked like a pen-gun,[1] ever to, ———, who
drank it all in like nectar, while my mother looked cross enough,
and I had to listen to the whispered confidences of Mrs. Hunt. But
for me, who was declared to be grown 'quite prim and elderly,' I
believe they would have communicated their mutual experiences in
a retired window-seat till morning. 'God bless you, Miss ———,'
was repeated by Hunt three several times in tones of ever-increasing
pathos and tenderness, as he handed her downstairs behind me.
———, for once in her life, seemed past speech. At the bottom of
the stairs a demur took place. I saw nothing; but I heard, with
my wonted glegness—what think you?—a couple of handsome
smacks! and then an almost inaudibly soft 'God bless you, Miss
———!'

Now just remember what sort of looking woman is ——— ———;
and figure their transaction! If he had kissed me, it would have
been intelligible, but ——— ———, of all people! By the way,
Mr. Craik[2] is immensely delighted with you, and grateful to Susan
for having brought you together. Mrs. Cole[3] came the other day,
and sat an hour waiting for me while I was out, and finally had to
go, leaving an obliging note offering me every assistance in procuring a servant.

Mrs. John Sterling takes to me wonderfully; but John, I perceive,
will spoil all with his innocence. He told her the other day, when
she was declaring her wish that he would write on theology rather
than make verses, that she 'might fight out that matter with Mrs.
Carlyle, who, he knew, was always on the side of the poetical.'
He (Sterling) has written a positively splendid poem of half-an-
hour's length—an allegorical shadowing of the union of the ideal
and actual. It is far the best thing he ever did—far beyond anything I could have supposed him capable of. He said, when he

---

[1] *Scoticè*, gun made of quill-barrel for shooting peas (and 'cracking,' which
also means pleasantly conversing).
[2] *Useful Knowledge* Craik, poor fellow!
[3] The now thrice-notable 'Crystal Palace,' 'Brompton Boilers,' &c., &c.,
Henry Cole's wife.

was writing it, he thought sometimes, ' Carlyle will be pleased with that.'

To descend to the practical, or, I should rather say ascend, for I have filled my whole paper with mere gossip. I think you seem, so far as human calculations avail, to have made a good hit as to the servant; character is not worth a straw; but you say she looks intelligent and good-humoured, is young and willing.[1] Fetch her, then, in God's name, and I will make the best I can of her. After all, we fret ourselves too much about little things; much that might be laughed off, if one were well and cheerful as one ought to be, becomes a grave affliction from being too gravely looked at. Remember also meal, and oh, for goodness sake, procure a dozen of bacon-hams! There is no bottom to my appetite for them. Sell poor Harry, by all means, or shoot him. We are too poor to indulge our fine feelings with keeping such large pets (especially at other people's expense). What a pity no frank is to be got! I have told you nothing yet. No word ever came from Basil Montague. I have translated four songs into Italian—written a long excessively *spirituosa* letter to ' mia adorabile Clementina,'[2] and many *graziose cartucie* besides. In truth, I have a *divino ingegno !*

You will come back strong and cheerful, will you not? I wish you were come, anyhow. Don't take much castor; eat plenty of chicken broth rather. Dispense my love largely. Mother returns your kiss with interest. We go on tolerably enough; but she has vowed to hate all my people except Pepoli. So that there is ever a ' dark brown shadd ' in all my little reunions. She has given me a glorious black-velvet gown, realising my *beau idéal* of Putz!

Did you take away my folding penknife? We are knifeless here. We were to have gone to Richmond to-day with the Silverheaded; but, to my great relief, it turned out that the steamboat is not running.

God keep you, my own dear husband, and bring you safe back to me. The house looks very empty without you, and my mind feels empty too.

Your JANE.

LETTER 10.

Beautiful Poverty, when so triumphed over, and victoriously bound under foot. Oh, my heroine, my too unacknowledged heroine! I was in the throes of the ' French Revolution ' at this time, heavy-laden in many ways and gloomy of mind.—T. C.

---

[1] Anne Cook (got for me by sister Mary, at Annan).   [2] Degli Antoni.

T. Carlyle, Esq., Scotsbrig.

Chelsea: Oct. 26, 1835.

Caro e rispettabile il mio Marito!—Mi pare, che voi siete assai irre-cordevole della vostra povera piccola! Questi i vostri lunghi silenzi, questa la vostra lunga assenza mi divengono noiosa. Ritornate, mio Marito, ritornate, in nome di Dio, alla vostra casa! In vano stima-bili Signori vengono in gran numero mi far' adorazione! In vano mangio carne di porco, e ricomincio esser una bella Gooda! In vano mi sforzo m' occupare, mi divertire, mi fare contenta! Nell' assenza del mio Marito rimango sempre inquieta, sempre perduta! Se però voi trovatevi meglio nel' paese, se la preziosa vostra sanità diviene più forte, la vostra anima più chiara più tranquilla, non avete pensiero di me. Bisogna ch' io sottometta la mia voglia alla vostra prosperità ; e farò il più meglio possibile d'esser paziente.

Ecco come sono stata studiosa, mio Marito! Questa bellissima Italiana è scritta senza dizionario, senza studio, con penna corrente. Il Conte di Pepoli si maraviglia al divino mio talento; lascia i suoi alti complimenti ; e dice solamente in sotto voce, 'Ah graziosa! Ah bella bella! Ah, ah!'

Dear my husband,—You have probably enough of this, as well as I; so now in English I repeat that I expect with impatience the letter which is to fix your return. So long, I have reason to be thankful that I have been borne through with an honourable through-bearing.[1] Except for two days before your last letter arrived, I flatter myself I have been conducting myself with a quite exemplary patience and good nature towards all men, women, and inanimate things. *Ecco la bella prova di che, Sereetha sta sempre quì, e la mia Madre ed io non siamo ancor imbrogliate.*

What a world of beautiful effort you have had to expend on this matter of the servant! Heaven grant it may be blessed to us! I do not know well why; but I like the abstract idea of this woman[2] now much better than the other. It seemed to me rather an objection to the other that she had a brother a baker. The bakers, you know, trade in servants here, and he would probably have soon been recommending her into more exalted place. Moreover, it was thought displeasing to me that she had been educated in the school of country gigmanism. Macturkdom-ism, and Gillenbie-rig-ism[3] is

---

[1] Helpless phrase of a certain conceited extempore preacher.

[2] Anne Cook.

[3] Annandale 'genteel' places or persons.

just as hateful or more hateful to me than Devonshire-house-ism. The '*uzing*' woman, of tarnished virtue,[1] will suit, I think, much better. In fact, it would be difficult for me to say that an Annandale woman's virtue is the worse for a misfortune. I am certain that, in their circumstances, with their views and examples, I should have had one too, if not more! And now that the best is done which could be done, let us quiet ourselves, and look with equanimity towards the issue. If she does not do better than those that have gone before, if no grown servant any longer exists on this earth, why, we can certainly manage with an ungrown one. Sereetha has hardly been a fair trial of the little-girl plan; but she has been a trial, and I am confident of being able to get on quite peaceably with one of such little girls as, I doubt not, are to be found in plenty; with only a giving up of a few hours of my own time, which might easily be worse spent, and the sacrifice of the beauty and ladylikeness of my hands. For economy, little, I find, is to be gained by the substitution of a child for a woman. The washing runs away with all the difference in wages, and their consumption of victual is much the same. But then the things are washed beautifully; and I clean beautifully when you do not dishearten me with hypercriticism. So never fear, dearest! Never fear about that, or anything else under heaven. Try all that ever you can to be patient and good-natured with your *povera piccola Gooda*,[2] and then she loves you, and is ready to do anything on earth that you wish; to fly over the moon, if you bade her. But when the *signor della casa* has neither kind look nor word for me, what can I do but grow desperate, fret myself to fiddlestrings, and be a torment to society in every direction?[3]

Poiche i giorni divengono sì freddi, la rispettabile mia Signora Madre diviene infelice assai, e di molto cattivo umore. Ma io sono a presente d'un umore divino! et tutto va mediocremente bene! Mr. Gibson comes to-morrow to take me—to prison. I believe the

---

[1] Appears to have had what they call a 'misfortune' there. The *uzing*, some misfeature of pronunciation, which I have now forgotten.

[2] Goody, with diminutives 'Goodykin,' &c., the common name she had from me.

[3] A poor, but lively and healthy, half-idiot and street beggar, in Birmingham, whom I had grown used to, the dirtiest and raggedest of human beings (face never washed, beard a fortnight old, knee-breeches slit at the sides, and become knee-*aprons*, flapping to and fro over bare, dirty legs), said, one day, under my window, while somebody was vainly attempting to chafe him, 'Damn thee, I's an ornament to society in every direction.'—T. C.

King's Bench, &c. *Quello Signor è, per mia Madre, il solo angelo di bontà quì, nella nobile città. Tutti i miei signori e signore (a meno il leggiàdro Conte*[1]) *sono per lei fastidiose persone.* Other sights we have seen none, except the British Museum and the King and Queen. Their majesties very opportunely came to visit the College,[2] and the fact being made known to me by the beggar-woman from New Street (with the cobweb shawl), I hurried off my mother to the place, where, without being kept waiting above five minutes, we saw them walk past our very noses.

My mother's enthusiasm of loyalty on the occasion was a sight for sore eyes! 'Poor Queen, after all!'[3] She looked so frost-bitten and anxious! curtsied, with such a cowering hurriedness, to the veriest rabble that ever was seen. I was wae to look at her, wae to think of her, when I heard that the very same night they hissed her at one of the theatres! Poor thing! She would have done rather well, I do believe, looking after the burning of her cinders![4] But a Queen of England in these days! The British Museum charmed my mother, and I myself was affected beyond measure by the Elgin marbles. We went after to lunch with the Donaldsons.[5] 'The kindness of these people!'[6]

On that day I came, saw, and bought—a sofa! It is my own purchase, but you shall share the possession. Indeed, so soon as you set eyes on it and behold its vastness, its simple greatness, you will perceive that the thought of you was actively at work in my choice. It was neither dear nor cheap,[7] but a bargain nevertheless, being second-hand; and so good a second-hand one is not, I should think, often to be met. Oh, it is so soft! so easy! and one of us, or both, may sleep in it, should occasion require—I mean for

---

[1] Pepoli. [2] Chelsea Hospital.

[3] 'Poor fellow, after all!' a phrase of brother John's.

[4] William IV., soon after his accession, determined one day to see his cellar-regions at Windsor, came upon a vast apartment filled merely with waste masses of cinders: 'What are these?' asked his Majesty astonished. Attendant officials obsequiously explained. 'It seems to me those would burn!' said his Majesty, kicking the cinders with his boot; and walked on.—*Newspaper of the time.*

[5] A Haddington family. Dr. Donaldson (of Cambridge celebrity, &c.) eldest son then. [6] Phrase of Irving's.

[7] Melancholy shopkeeper in Lamb's Conduit Street (in 1831, whom she ever afterwards dealt with, for what he sold) had stated, in answer to a puppy-kind of customer, the how-much of something. Puppy replied: 'D'you call that cheap?' Whereupon answer, in a tone of mournful indifference: 'I call it neither cheap nor dear; but just the price of the article.'

all night. It will sell again at any time; it is so sufficient an article.
With my velvet gown, I shall need no great outlay for *Putz* this
winter, so I thought I might fairly indulge ourselves in a sofa at
last.

The *Stimabile* conducts himself in a quite exemplary manner
since you went, coming but once, or at most twice, in the week.
I fear, however, we must not give him too much credit for his self-
denial; but rather impute it, in part, to his impossibility of getting
at ease with my mother, and also to some rather violent political
arguments which he has had of late with myself. All the men
take fright sooner or later at my violence—*tant mieux!* John I
seldom see; he is so occupied in waiting upon his wife. He came
one night last week with his mother to meet the Cunninghams.
Mrs. S. wished to know Allan. It went off wonderfully well, considering Sereetha was our sole waiter!

There is nothing in the note.[1] Miss Elliot's address was written
on it in pencil, which I interpreted to express an expectation that
you would call for her. I wrote her, therefore, a courteous little
note, stating that you were in Scotland, &c., &c.; that I, &c., &c.,
would be glad to see her here, &c., &c.

Mother's love, of course. Can you bring her from Duncan,
Dumfries, one gross of pills? He has her prescription. My head
has troubled me a little of late days, but I continue generally much
better. Special love to your mother, and a kiss to my Jane's *piccola!*[2] Mill told me it was next to impossible for him to realise a
frank, so I need not waste time sending him this. I have hardly
room to send love to them all; and to you, dear, kisses *senza mi-
sura!* Mrs. Cole came for a day; her husband in the evening;
talkative, niceish people.

My dressing-gown 'likes me very much.' A thousand thanks!
And the hams! Oh, I am glad of them! This one is near done.
Think you one could have a little keg of salt herrings sent at the
same time?

[No signature. These last little paragraphs are crowded in upon
every margin and vacant space, so that there is not a bit of blank
more.—T. C.]

---

[1] Note inclosed, from Miss Elliot, an acquaintance of Lady Clare's and my
brother's.

[2] The now 'Annie Aitken,' I suppose.

LETTER 11.

Mrs. Welsh came to us in the last days in August, by an Edin-burgh steamer. I was waiting at the St. Katherine Dock, in a bright afternoon; pleasant meeting, pleasant voyage up the river in our wherry; and such a welcome here at home as may be fancied. About the end of next month I had finished my burnt MS.; and seem then to have run for Scotsbrig, and been there perhaps three weeks (scarcely a detail of it now clear to me) in October following. I was sickly of body and mind, felt heavy-laden, and without any hope but the 'desperate' kind, which I always did hold fast. Our Irish Catholic housemaid proved a mutinous Irish savage (had a fixed persuasion, I could notice, that our poor house and we had been made for *her*, and had gone awry in the process). One even-ing, while all seated for supper, Eliza Miles and we too, the indig-nant savage, jingling down her plates as if she had been playing quoits, was instantaneously dismissed by me ('To your room at once; wages to-morrow morning; disappear!'), so that the bring-ing of a Scotch servant was one of my express errands. 'Anne Cook,' accordingly, and the journey with her by steamer from An-nan, by 'Umpire coach' from Liverpool, some forty or fifty hours, all in a piece, is dismally memorable! Breakfast at Newport Pag-nell (I had given Anne the inside place, night being cold and wet); awkward, hungry Anne would hardly even eat, till bidden and directed by me. Landing in Holborn, half dead, bright Sunday afternoon, amidst a crowd of porters, cabmen, hungry officials, some seven or ten of them, ravenous for sixpences and shillings, till at length I shut the cab-door. 'To no person will I pay any-thing more at this time!' and drove off, amid a general laugh, not ill-humoured, from the recognising miscellany. Drive home, sur-rounded by luggage, and with Anne for company, seemed endless. I landed at this door in a state of misery, more like mad than sane; but my darling was in the lobby; saw at a glance how it was, and almost without speaking, brought me to my room, and with me a big glass, almost a goblet, of the best sherry: 'Drink that, dear, at a draught!' Never in my life had I such a medicine! Shaved, washed, got into clean clothes, I stepped down quite new-made, and thanking Heaven for such a doctor.

Mrs. Welsh went away a few weeks after to Liverpool, to her brother John's there—favourite and now only brother—a brave and generous man, much liked by all of us.

John Sterling had turned up in the early part of this year, John Sterling, and with him all the Sterlings, which was an immense acquisition to us for the ten years that followed, as is abundantly betokened in the letter that now follows.—T. C.

To Mrs. Carlyle, Scotsbrig.

Chelsea: Dec. 23, 1835.

My dear Mother,—You are to look upon it as the most positive proof of my regard that I write to you in my present circumstances; that is to say, with the blood all frozen in my brains, and my brains turned to a solid mass of ice; for such has, for several days, been the too cruel lot of your poor little daughter-in-law at *Lunnon;* the general lot indeed of all *Lunnon*, so far as I can observe. When the frost comes here, 'it comes,' as the woman said with the four eggs[1]; and it seems to be somehow more difficult to guard against it here than elsewhere; for all the world immediately takes to coughing and blowing its nose with a fury quite appalling. The noise thus created destroys the suffering remnant[2] of senses spared by the cold, and makes the writing of a letter, or any other employment in which thought is concerned, seem almost a tempting of Providence. Nevertheless, I am here to tell you that we are still in the land of the living, and thinking of you all, from yourself, the head of the nation, down to that very least and fattest child, who, I hope, will continue to grow fatter and fatter till I come to see it with my own eyes. I count this fatness a good omen for the whole family; it betokens good-nature, which is a quality too rare among us. Those 'long, sprawling, ill-put-together'[3] children give early promise of being 'gey ill to deal wi'.'[4]

That one of them who is fallen to my share conducts himself pretty peaceably at present; writing only in the forenoons. He has finished a chapter much to my satisfaction; and the poor book begins to hold up its head again. Our situation is farther improved by the introduction of Anne Cook into the establishment, instead of the distracted Roman Catholics and distracted Protestants who preceded her. She seems an assiduous, kindly, honest, and thrifty creature; and will learn to do all I want with her quite easily. For the rest, she amuses me every hour of the day with her perfect incomprehension of everything like ceremony. I was helping her

---

[1] 'When I come,' I come, laying down her gift of four eggs.

[2] 'Suffering Remnant,' so the Cameronians called themselves in Claverhouse's time.

[3] 'A lank, sprawling, ill-put-together thing.' Such had been my mother's definition to her of me as a nurseling.

[4] 'Thou's gey' (pretty, pronounced *gyei*) 'ill to deal wi' '—mother's allocution to me once, in some unreasonable moment of mine.

to wring a sheet one day, while she had the cut finger, and she
told me flatly it was 'clean aboon my fit' (ability). 'I shall get at
it by practice,' said I; 'far weaker people than I have wrung
sheets.' 'May be sae,' returned she very coolly; 'but I ken-na
where ye'll find ony weaker, for a weaklier-like cretur I never saw
in a' my life.' Another time, when Carlyle had been off his sleep
for a night or two, she came to me at bedtime to ask, 'If Mr. Carlyle bees ony uneasy through the nicht, and's ga'an staiverĕn[1] aboot
the hoose, will ye bid him gae us a cry[2] at five in the morning?'

We may infer, however, that she is getting more civilisation,
from the entire change in her ideas respecting the handsome Italian
Count[3]; for, instead of calling him 'a fley (fright)-some body' any
longer, she is of opinion that he is 'a real fine man, and nane that
comes can ever be named in ae day with him.' Nay, I notice that
she puts on a certain net cap with a most peculiar knot of ribbons
every time she knows of his coming. The reward of which act is
an 'I weesh you good day' when she lets him out. So much for
poor Anne, who, I hope, will long continue to flourish in the land.

I am much better off this winter for society than I was last.
Mrs. Sterling makes the greatest possible change for me. She is
so good, so sincerely and unvaryingly kind, that I feel to her as to
a third mother. Whenever I have blue devils, I need but put on
my bonnet and run off to her, and the smile in her eyes restores me
to instant good humour. Her husband would go through fire and
water for me; and if there were a third worse element, would go
through that also. The son is devoted to Carlyle, and makes him a
real friend, which, among all his various intimate acquaintances and
well-wishers, he cannot be said ever to have had before: this family,
then, is a great blessing to us. And so has been my study of
Italian, which has helped me through many dullish hours. I never
feel anything like youth about me except when I am learning something; and when I am turning over the leaves of my Italian dic-
tionary, I could fancy myself thirteen: whether there be any good
in fancying oneself thirteen after one is turned of thirty, I leave
your charity to determine.

We sit in hourly, nay, in momentary, expectation of the meal,
&c., which has not yet arrived, but will soon, I am sure; for I
dreamt two nights since that I saw them fetching it out of the waggon: meanwhile, we sup on arrowroot and milk; the little bag
being done.

---

[1] Stumbling.   [2] Awaken us.   [3] Count Pepoli.

Dear mother, excuse all this blash[1] in consideration that I really have a very bad cold, which I am resolved, however, to be rid of on Christmas Day (the day after to-morrow) on which I am engaged to dine at the Sterlings'. Ever since I killed the goose at Craigen-puttock (with the determination to make a Christmas pie in spite of nature and fate), and immediately thereupon took a sore throat, my Christmas days have found me ill, or in some way unlucky. Last year I was lying horizontal with my burnt foot; this year, then, I am very desirous to break the spell, and Mrs. Sterling makes a ploy for the purpose.

God keep you all, and make your new year no worse, and, if may be, better, than all that have preceded it.

Your affectionate
JANE CARLYLE.

[That 'sore foot of Christmas last,' which has never otherwise been forgotten by me, now dates itself. She was in the kitchen one evening, upon some experiment or other; pouring or being poured to from a boiling kettle, got a splash on her poor little foot, instantly ran with it to the pump (following some recent precept in the newspapers), and then had it pumped upon till quite cold, which, indeed, 'cured' it for about four-and-twenty hours; and then it began anew, worse than ever. It seems to me to have lasted for weeks. Never did I see such patience under total lameness and imprisonment. Hurt was on the instep. No doctor's advice had been dreamt of; 'a little wound, don't hurt it, keep it clean; what more?'—and it would not heal. For weeks I carried her upstairs nightly to her bed—ever cheerful, hopeful one. At length, one Willis, a medical acquaintance, called; found that it needed only a bandage—bandaged it there and then; and in two days more it was as good as well, and never heard of again. Oh, my poor little woman!—become 'poor' for me!]—T. C.

LETTER 12.

Helen Welsh was the daughter of John Welsh, of Liverpool, Mrs. Carlyle's uncle on her mother's side. See an account of him in the 'Reminiscences,' vol. 2, p. 142.—J. A. F.

To Miss Helen Welsh, Liverpool.

Chelsea: April 1, 1836.

My dear Cousinkin,—I am charmed to notice in you the rapid growth of a virtue, which for the most part only develops itself in mature age, after many and hard experiences; but which is, never-

---

[1] Watery stuff.

theless, highly necessary at all ages, in this world of sin and misery. I mean the virtue of toleration. Rarely is one edified by the spectacle of so young a lady, meekly acknowledging her own transgressions and shortcomings, when, with perfect justice, she might have adopted rather the tone of accusation. Continue, my sweet little cousin, to cultivate this engaging disposition; this beautiful sensibility to your own imperfections, and beautiful insensibility to the imperfections of your neighbour, and you will become (if indeed you are not such already) an ornament to your sex, and a credit to 'the name of Welsh' (which my mother talks about so proudly; I could never tell precisely why).

In truth you will have added a new lustre of virtue to that name, which I never hoped to see it brightened with; for, as my Penfillan grandfather's physiological observations on his stock had led him to the conclusion that it was capable of producing rascals and vagabonds enough, but not one solitary instance of a blockhead, so mine had hitherto tended to certify me that 'the name of Welsh' had something in it wholly and everlastingly antipathetical to patience and toleration, and was no more capable of coalescing with it than fire with water.

The box came safe, as did also the herrings and the brandy; shame to me that I should be now for the first time acknowledging them all in the lump! But I trust that my mother reported my thanks, as she was charged to do; and that however much you may all have blamed my laziness, you have not suspected me of the atrocious sin of ingratitude, 'alike hateful to gods and men:' at least it used to be so; but now that it is so common in the world, people are getting into the way of regarding it, I suppose, as they do other fashionable vices, 'with one eye shut and the other not open' (as an Irish author said to me the other day in describing his manner of reading a certain journal). Rogers, the poet, who professed to be a man of extensive beneficence, and to have befriended necessitous persons without number in the course of his long life, declares that he never met with gratitude but in three instances. I have a mind to ask him to do something for me, just that he may have the pleasure of swelling his beggarly list of grateful people to four. 'For the name of Welsh,' I flatter myself, cherishes the old Athenian notions about gratitude.

We are labouring under a visitation of rain here, which seems to portend the destruction of the world by deluge.

One feels soaked to the very heart; no warmth or pith remaining in one. As one fire is understood to drive out another, I thought one water might drive out another also; and so this morning I took a shower-bath, and have shivered ever since, 'Too much water hadst thou, poor Ophelia!'

O Helen! what a fearful recollection I have at this instant of your shower-bathing at Moffat! It was indeed the sublime of shower-bathing, the human mind stands astonished before it, as before the Infinite. In fact, you have ever since figured in my imagination as a sort of Undine.

Barring the weather, everything goes on here in the usual way: people eat eight o'clock dinners together; talk politics, philosophy, folly together; attend what they call their business at 'the House,' or where else it may happen to be; and fill up the intervals with vapours, and something that goes by the name of 'checked perspiration;' but I can give you no idea of what that precisely means; it seems to comprehend every malady that flesh is heir to; and for my part, as the cockney said to Allan Cunningham of the lottery, 'I am deadly sure there is a do at the bottom on it!'

We expect John Carlyle in some ten days; for this time his lady will surely, for decency's sake, stick to her purpose, lady of quality though she be! I am afraid he is not a man for grappling in a cunning manner with 'checked perspiration;' and accordingly, that there is small hope of his getting into profitable employment here as a doctor. We do not know even yet if he will try; but time will settle that and much else that waits to be settled. In the meanwhile there were no sense in worrying over schemes for a future, which we may not live to see. 'Sufficient for the day is the evil thereof'—at present more than sufficient.

Two of our dearest friends are dangerously ill; John Mill, whom you have often heard me speak of, and John Sterling, whose novel, 'Arthur Coningsby,' I think I lent you at Templand.

My husband is anything but well, nor likely to be better till he have finished his 'French Revolution,' of which there is still a volume to write: he works beyond his strength.

I myself have been abominably all winter, though not writing, so far as I know, for the press. And more evil still is lying even now while I write, at the bottom of my pocket, in shape of a letter from Annan, requiring me to send off, without delay, the servant whom Carlyle so bothered himself to fetch me: her mother being at the point of death, and 'will not,' says the letter-writer, 'leave the charge of the house to any other than her dear Anne'! What is to be the consequence if Anne do not obey this hurried summons, the letter-writer does not state. One is left to conjecture that the poor woman will either take the house along with her, or stay where she is till she can get it settled to her mind; in which last case it is better for all parties that my maid should stay where she is. I am excessively perplexed. Happy cousinkin, that hast, as yet, no household imbroglios to fetter thy glad movement through life. My husband sends affectionate regards, to be distributed along with mine at your discretion. You may also add a few kisses on my account.

Yours affectionately,
JANE CARLYLE.

[Soon after the date of the last letter Mrs. Carlyle became extremely ill. June brought hot weather, and she grew worse and worse. Carlyle was working at the 'French Revolution.' His 'nervous system' was 'in a flame.' At such times he could think of nothing but the matter which he had in hand, and a sick wife was a bad companion for him. She felt at last that unless 'she could get out of London she would surely die,' and she escaped to Scotland to her mother. She went by Liverpool, and thence for economy she intended to go on by steamer to Annan. At sea she suffered more than most people. Her Liverpool uncle paid her fare in the mail to Dumfries, gave her a warm handsome shawl as a birthday present (July 14), and sent her forward under better auspices. Mrs. Welsh was waiting to receive her at the Dumfries Coach Office—'such an embracing and such a crying,' she said, 'the very "boots" was affected with it and spoke in a plaintive voice all the morning after." At Templand she met the warmest welcome. Mrs. Welsh gave her (for her birthday also) a purse of her own working, filled with sovereigns. She had all the care and nursing which affection could bestow, but sleeplessness, cough, and headache refused to leave hold of her. Her health scarcely mended, and after two months' trial 'desperate of everything here below,' she returned to Cheyne Row, in August. She came back, as she described herself, 'a sadder and a wiser woman,' to find recovered health at home. 'I ought not to regret my flight into Scotland,' she wrote to Miss Hunter, 'since it has made me take with new relish to London. It is a strange praise to bestow on the Metropolis of the world, but I find it so delightfully still here! not so much as a cock crowing to startle nervous subjects out of their sleep; and during the day no inevitable Mrs. this or Miss that, brimful of all the gossip for twenty miles around, interrupting your serious pursuits (whatever they may be) with calls of a duration happily unknown in cities. The feeling of calm, of safety, of liberty which came over me on re-entering my own house was really the most blessed I had felt for a great while. Soon, through the medium of this feeling, the house itself and everything about it, even my Annandale maid, presented a sort of earnest classic appearance to my first regards, which is hardly yet worn off."

It was the dead season; but there were a few persons still in London, who came occasionally to Cheyne Row, one of them a remarkable man of a remarkable family, who, for several years was very intimate there, and was then in exile for conspiracy against Louis Philippe. Mrs. Carlyle thus describes him:—

' We have another foreigner who beats all the rest to sticks, a French Republican of the right thorough-going sort, an "accusé d'Avril," who has had the glory of meriting to be imprisoned and nearly losing his head; a man with that sort of dark half-savage beauty with which one paints a fallen angel, who fears neither heaven nor earth, for aught one can see, who fights and writes with the same passionate intrepidity, who is ready to dare or suffer, to live or to die without disturbing himself much about the matter; who defies all men and honours, all women, and whose name is Cavaignac' (Godefroi, brother of the future President.—J. A. F.]

LETTER 13.

To Mrs. Welsh, Maryland Street, Liverpool.

Chelsea: Sept. 5, 1836.

My dear Aunt,—Now that I am fairly settled at home again, and can look back over my late travels with the coolness of a spectator, it seems to me that I must have tired out all men, women, and children that have had to do with me by the road. The proverb says ' there is much ado when cadgers ride.' I do not know precisely what ' cadger ' means, but I imagine it to be a character like me, liable to headache, to sea-sickness, to all the infirmities ' that flesh is heir to,' and a few others besides; the friends and relations of cadgers should therefore use all soft persuasions to induce them to remain at home.

I got into that Mail the other night with as much repugnance and trepidation as if it had been a Phalaris' brazen bull, instead of a Christian vehicle, invented for purposes of mercy—not of cruelty. There were three besides myself when we started, but two dropped off at the end of the first stage, and the rest of the way I had, as usual, half of the coach to myself. My fellow-passenger had that highest of all terrestrial qualities, which for me a fellow-passenger can possess—he was silent. I think his name was Roscoe, and he read sundry long papers to himself, with the pondering air of a lawyer.

We breakfasted at Lichfield, at five in the morning, on muddy coffee and scorched toast, which made me once more lyrically recognise in my heart (not without a sigh of regret) the very different coffee and toast with which you helped me out of my headache. At two there was another stop of ten minutes, that might be employed in lunching or otherwise. Feeling myself more fevered than hungry, I determined on spending the time in combing my hair and washing my face and hands with vinegar. In the midst of this solacing operation I heard what seemed to be the Mail running its rapid course, and quick as lightning it flashed on me, 'There it goes! and my luggage is on the top of it, and my purse is in the pocket of it, and here am I stranded on an unknown beach, without so much as a sixpence in my pocket to pay for the vinegar I have already consumed!' Without my bonnet, my hair hanging down my back, my face half dried, and the towel, with which I was drying it, firm grasped in my hand, I dashed out—along, down, opening wrong doors, stumbling over steps, cursing the day I was born, still more the day on which a took I notion to travel, and arrived finally at the bar of the Inn, in a state of excitement bordering on lunacy. The barmaids looked at me 'with weender and amazement.' 'Is the coach gone?' I gasped out. 'The coach? Yes!' 'Oh! and you have let it away without me! Oh! stop it, cannot you stop it?' and out I rushed into the street, with streaming hair and streaming towel, and almost brained myself against—the Mail! which was standing there in all stillness, without so much as horses in it! What I had heard was a heavy coach. And now, having descended like a maniac, I ascended again like a fool, and dried the other half of my face, and put on my bonnet, and came back 'a sadder and a wiser' woman.

I did not find my husband at the ' Swan with Two Necks ;' for we were in a quarter of an hour before the appointed time. So I had my luggage put on the backs of two porters, and walked on to Cheapside, where I presently found a Chelsea omnibus. By and by, however, the omnibus stopped, and amid cries of ' No room, sir,' ' Can't get in,' Carlyle's face, beautifully set off by a broad-brimmed white hat, gazed in at the door, like the Peri, who, ' at the Gate of Heaven, stood disconsolate.' In hurrying along the Strand, pretty sure of being too late, amidst all the imaginable and unimaginable phenomena which the immense thoroughfare of a street presents, his eye (Heaven bless the mark!) had lighted on my trunk perched on the top of the omnibus, and had recognised it. This seems to me one of the most indubitable proofs of genius which he ever manifested. Happily, a passenger went out a little further on, and then he got in.

My brother-in-law had gone two days before, so my arrival was most well-timed. I found all at home right and tight; my maid seems to have conducted herself quite handsomely in my absence; my best room looked really inviting. A bust of Shelley (a present from Leigh Hunt), and a fine print of Albert Dürer, handsomely framed (also a present) had still further ornamented it during my absence. I also found (for I wish to tell you all my satisfaction) every grate in the house furnished with a supply of coloured clippings, and the holes in the stair-carpet all darned, so that it looks like new. They gave me tea and fried bacon, and staved off my headache as well as might be. They were very kind to me, but, on my life, everybody is kind to me, and to a degree that fills me with admiration. I feel so strong a wish to make you all convinced how very deeply I feel your kindness, and just the more I would say, the less able I am to say anything.

God bless you all. Love to all, from the head of the house down to Johnny.

Your affectionate
JANE W. CARLYLE.

LETTER 14.

This 'Fairy Tale' I have never yet seen; must have been destroyed by her afterwards. Next bit of MS. sent (Dialogue &c., much admired by Sterling) is still here, and shall be given at the due place.—T. C.

To John Sterling, Esq., Floriac, Bordeaux.

Feb. 1, 1837.

My ever dear John Sterling,—Here are thirty-three pages of writing for you, which would divide into ten letters of the usual size, so that you see I discharge my debt to you handsomely enough in the long run. But even if you should not be complaisant enough to accept a nonsense fairy-tale in lieu of all the sense-letters I ought to have sent you, still you must not be after saying or thinking that 'Mrs. Carlyle has cut you acquaintance.' John Sterling 'is a man of sense' (as Mrs, Buller, one day, in Carlyle's hearing, said patronisingly of the Apostle Paul), and must know that Mrs. Carlyle is a woman of sense by this token, that she perceived him, John Sterling, the very first time she ever set eyes on him, to be no humbug, after all that had been said and sung about him, but the very sort of man one desires to see, and hardly ever succeeds in seeing in this make-believe world! Now I put it to your candour, whether any women of sense, in her right senses, having found a pearl of great price, would dream of dissolving it in a tumbler of water and swallowing it all at one gulp ? For such, in highly figurative language, would be the foolish use I should have made of your friendship, provided it were true, as you wrote, that I had already cut your acquaintance! Oh, no! you have only to take a just view of your own merits and mine, to feel as convinced as though I had sworn it before a magistrate that my long silence had proceeded from some ' crook in the lot,' and not in the mind.

The fact is, since I became so sick and dispirited I have contracted a horror of letter-writing, almost equal to the hydrophobia horror for cold water. I would write anything under heaven—fairy-tales, or advertisements for Warren's Blacking even—rather than a letter! A letter behoves to tell about oneself, and when oneself is disagreeable to oneself, one would rather tell about anything else; for, alas! one does not find the same gratification in dwelling upon one's own sin and misery, as in showing up the sin and misery of one's neighbour. But if ever I get agreeable to myself again, I swear to you I will then be exceedingly communicative, in preparation for which desirable end I must set about getting into better health, and that I may get into better health I must begin by growing wise, which puts me in mind of a boy of the ' English Opium-Eater's,' who told me once he would begin Greek presently; but his father wished him to learn it through the medium of Latin, and he was not entered in Latin yet because his father wished to teach him from a grammar of his own, which he had not yet begun to write!

For the present we are all in sad taking with influenza. People speak about it more than they did about cholera; I do not know whether they die more from it. Miss Wilson, not having come to close quarters with it, has her mind sufficiently at leisure to make philosophical speculations about its gender! She primly promulgates her opinion that influenza is masculine. My husband, for the sake of argument I presume, for I see not what other interest he has in it, protests that influenza is feminine; for me, who have been laid up with it for two weeks and upwards, making lamentations of Jeremiah (not without reason), I am not prejudiced either way, but content myself with sincerely wishing it were neuter. One great comfort, however, under all afflictions, is that ' The French Revolution' is happily concluded; at least, it will be a comfort when one is delivered from the tag-raggery of printers' devils, that at present drive one from post to pillar. *Quelle vie!* let no woman who values peace of soul ever dream of marrying an author! That is to say, if he is an honest one, who makes a conscience of doing the thing he pretends to do. But this I observe to you in confidence; should I state such a sentiment openly, I might happen to get myself torn in pieces by the host of my husband's lady admirers, who already, I suspect, think me too happy in not knowing my happiness. You cannot fancy what way he is making with the fair intellects here! There is Harriet Martineau presents him with her ear-trumpet with a pretty blushing air of coquetry, which would almost convince me out of belief in her identity! And Mrs. Pierce Butler bolts in upon his studies, out of the atmosphere as it were, in riding-habit, cap and whip (but no shadow of a horse, only a carriage, the whip I suppose being to whip the cushions with, for the purpose of keeping her hand in practice)—my inexperienced Scotch domestic remaining entirely in a nonplus whether she had let in 'a leddy or a gentleman'! And then there is a young American beauty—such a beauty! 'snow and rose-bloom' throughout, not as to clothes merely, but complexion also; large and soft, and without one idea, you would say, to rub upon another! And this charming creature publicly declares herself his 'ardent admirer,' and I heard her with my own ears call out quite passionately at parting with him, 'Oh, Mr. Carlyle, I want to see you to talk a long long time about— "Sartor"'! 'Sartor,' of all things in this world! What could such a young lady have got to say about 'Sartor,' can you imagine? And Mrs. Marsh, the moving authoress of the 'Old Man's Tales,' reads 'Sartor' when she is ill in bed; from which one thing at least may be clearly inferred, that her illness is not of the head. In short, my dear friend, the singular author of 'Sartor' appears to me at this moment to be in a perilous position, inasmuch as (with the innocence of a sucking dove to outward appearance) he is leading honourable women, not a few, entirely off their feet. And who can say that he will keep his own? After all, in sober earnest, is it not curious that my husband's writings should be only completely understood and adequately appreciated by women and mad people? I do not know very well what to infer from the fact.

Mr. Spedding is often to be heard of at Miss Wilson's (not that I fancy anything amiss in that quarter, only I mentioned him because he is your friend). Mr. Maurice we rarely see, nor do I greatly regret his absence; for, to tell you the truth, I am never in his company without being attacked with a sort of paroxysm of mental cramp! He keeps one always, with his wire-drawings and paradoxes, as if one were dancing on the points of one's toes (spiritually speaking). And then he will help with the kettle, and never fails to pour it all over the milk-pot and sugar-basin! Henry Taylor draws off into the upper regions of gigmanity. The rest, I think, are all as you left them.

Your mother was here last night, looking young and beautiful, with a new bonnet from Howel and James's. Your brother is a great favourite with Carlyle, and with me also, only one dare not fly into his arms as one does into yours. Will you give my affectionate regards to your wife, and a kiss for me to each of the children? Ask your wife to write a postscript in your next letter; I deserve some such sign of recollection from her, in return for all the kind thoughts I cherish in her. I wish to heaven you were all back again. You make a terrible chasm in our world, which does not look as if it were ever going to get closed in. You will write to me? You will be good enough to write to me after all? There is nothing that I do not fancy you good enough for. So I shall confidently expect a letter. God bless you, and all that belongs to you.

I am, ever affectionately yours,
JANE W. CARLYLE.

Carlyle has made every exertion to get you a printed copy of the 'Diamond Necklace,' but it is not to be got this day. He adds his brotherly regards.

LETTER 15.

Early in January 1837 it must have been when book on 'French Revolution' was finished. I wrote the last paragraph of it here (within a yard of where I now am) in her presence one evening after dinner. Damp tepid kind of evening, still by daylight, read it to her or left her to read it; probably with a 'Thank God, it is done, Jeannie!' and then walked out up the Gloucester Road towards Kensington way: don't remember coming back, or indeed anything quite distinct for three or four months after. My thoughts were by no means of an exultant character: pacifically gloomy rather, something of sullenly contemptuous in them, of clear hope (except in the 'desperate' kind) not the smallest glimpse. I had said to her, perhaps that very day, 'I know not whether this book is worth anything, nor what the world will do with it, or misdo, or entirely forbear to do (as is likeliest), but this I could tell the world: You have not had for a hundred years any book that came more direct and flamingly sincere from the heart of a living man;

do with it what you like, you——!' My poor little Jeannie and me, hasn't it nearly killed us both? This also I might have said, had I liked it, for it was true. My health was much spoiled; hers too by sympathy, by daily helping me to struggle with the intolerable load. I suppose by this time our money, too, was near done: busy friends, the Wilsons principally, Miss Martineau, and various honourable women, were clear that I ought now to lecture on 'German Literature,' a sure financial card, they all said; and set to shaping, organising, and multifariously consulting about the thing; which I unwillingly enough, but seeing clearly there was no other card in my hand at all, was obliged to let them do. The printing of 'French Revolution,' push as I might, did not end till far on in April—'Lectures,' six of them, of which I could form no image or conjecture beforehand, were to begin with May.—T. C.

To John Welsh, Esq., Liverpool.

5 Cheyne Row; March 4, 1837.

Dearest Uncle of me,—'Fellow-feeling makes us wondrous kind'! You and my aunt have had the influenza: I also have had the influenza: a stronger bond of sympathy need not be desired: and so the spirit moves me to write you a letter; and if you think there is no very 'wondrous kindness' in that, I can only say you are mistaken, seeing that I have had so much indispensable writing to do of late days that, like a certain Duchess of Orleans I was reading about the other week, 'when night comes, I am often so tired with writing, that I can hardly put one foot before the other'!

But with respect to this influenza, uncle, what think you of it? above all how is it, and why is it? For my part, with all my cleverness, I cannot make it out. Sometimes I am half persuaded that there is (in Cockney dialect) 'a do at the bottom on it'; medical men all over the world having merely entered into a tacit agreement to call all sorts of maladies people are liable to, in cold weather, by one name; so that one sort of treatment may serve for all, and their practice be thereby greatly simplified. In more candid moments, however, I cannot help thinking that it has something to do with the 'diffusion of useful knowledge': if not a part of that knowledge, at least that it is meant as a counterpoise; so that our minds may be preserved in some equilibrium, between the consciousness of our enormous acquirements on the one hand, and on the other the generally diffused experience that all the acquirements in the world are not worth a rush to one, compared with the blessedness of having a head clear of snifters! However it be, I am thankful to Heaven that I was the chosen victim in this house, instead of my

husband. For, had he been laid up, at present, there would have
been the very devil to pay. He has two printers on his book, that
it may, if possible, be got published in April; and it will hardly be
well off his hands, when he is to deliver a course of Lectures on
German Literature to 'Lords and Gentlemen,' and 'honourable
women not a few.' You wonder how he is to get through such a
thing? So do I, very sincerely. The more, as he proposes to speak
these lectures extempore, Heaven bless the mark! having, indeed,
no leisure to prepare them before the time at which they will be
wanted.

One of his lady-admirers (by the way he is getting a vast number
of lady-admirers) was saying the other day that the grand danger
to be feared for him was that he should commence with 'Gentlemen and Ladies,' instead of 'Ladies and Gentlemen,' a transmuta-
tion which would ruin him at the very outset. He vows, however,
that he will say neither the one thing nor the other, and I believe him
very secure on that side. Indeed, I should as soon look to see gold
pieces, or penny loaves drop out of his mouth, as to hear from it
any such humdrum unrepublican-like commonplace. If he finds it
necessary to address his audience by any particular designation, it
will be thus—'Men and Women'! or perhaps, in my Penfillan
grandfather's style, 'Fool-creatures come here for diversion.' On
the whole, if his hearers be reasonable, and are content that there
be good sense in the things he says, without requiring that he
should furnish them with brains to find it out, I have no doubt but
his success will be eminent. The exhibition is to take place in
Willis's Rooms; 'to begin at three, and end at four precisely'; and
to be continued every Monday and Friday through the first three
weeks of May. 'Begin precisely' it may, with proper precautions
on my part to put all the clocks and watches in the house half-an-
hour before the time; but, as to 'ending precisely'! that is all to be
tried for! There are several things in this world, which, once set
a-going, it is not easy to stop; and the Book is one of them. I have
been thinking that perhaps the readiest way of bringing him to a
cetera desunt (conclusion is out of the question) would be, just as
the clock strikes four, to have a lighted cigar laid on the table before
him—we shall see!

The 'French Revolution' done, and the lectures done, he is
going somewhere (to Scotland most probably) to rest himself
awhile; to lie about the roots of hedges, and speak to no man,
woman, or child except in monosyllables! a reasonable project

enough, considering the worry he has been kept in for almost three years back. For my part, having neither published nor lectured, I feel no call to refresh myself by such temporary descent from my orbit under the waves; and in Shakespearean dialect, I had such a ' belly-full' of travelling last year as is likely to quell my appetite, in that way, for some time to come. If I had been consulted in the getting up of the Litany, there would have been particular mention made of steamboats, mail-coaches, and heavy coaches, among those things from which we pray to be delivered; and more emphatic mention made of ' such as travel by land or sea.'

My mother writes to me from Dabton, where she is nursing the Crichtons. In my humble opinion she is (as my mother-in-law would say) 'gey idle o' wark.' I have expended much beautiful rhetoric in trying to persuade her hitherward, and she prefers nursing these Crichtons! Well! there is no accounting for taste! She will come, however, she says, when you have been there, but not sooner; so I hope you will pay your visit as early in the season as you can, for it would be a pity if she landed as last time, after all the fine weather was gone, and the town emptied. Give my kindest love to my kind aunt, and kisses to all the children. I owe my cousin Helen a letter, and will certainly be just after having been generous. My husband sends his affectionate regards, and hopes you received the copies of two articles, which he sent.

Mr. Gibson has not been here for some weeks; he begins to look stiffish, and a little round at the shoulders, otherwise as heretofore. God bless you all, my dearest uncle.

Yours

JANE WELSH CARLYLE.

LETTER 16.

Monday, May 1, 1837, in Willis's Rooms is marked as date of my first lecture. It was a sad planless jumble, as all these six were, but full enough of new matter, and of a furious determination on the poor lecturer's part not to break down. Plenty of incondite stuff accordingly there was; new, and in a strangely new dialect and tone; the audience intelligent, partly fashionable, was very good to me, and seemed, in spite of the jumbled state of things, to feel it entertaining, even interesting. I pitied myself, so agitated, terrified, driven desperate and furious. But I found I had no remedy, necessity compelling; on the proceeds we were financially safe for another year, that was my one sanction in the sad enterprise.

Mrs. Welsh from Templand was certainly with us a second time

at present. Returning to dinner from that first Monday's performance I gave to my darling and her, from some of the gold that had
been handed me, a sovereign each 'to buy something with, as
handsel of this novelty,' which little gift created such pleasure in
these generous two as is now pathetic to me, and a kind of blessing
to remember. When this second visit of our kind mother's began,
or how long it lasted, I have no recollection. I left her here for
company, in setting out for Annandale, whither I made all haste,
impatient for shelter and silence as soon as the hurlyburly could
be got to end. One wish I had—silence! silence! In the latter
half of June, I got thither. My health had suffered much by
'French Revolution' and its accompaniments, especially in the
later months, when I used to ask myself, Shall I ever actually get
this savagely cruel business flung off me, then, and be rid of it?—a
hope which seemed almost incredible.

Mind and body were alike out of order with me, my nervous system must have been in a horrible state. I remember, in walking up
from the Liverpool-Annan steamboat with brother Alick, Alick had
to call for a moment in some cottage at Landhead, and I waited
looking back towards Annan and the unrivalled prospect of sea and
land which one commands there, leaning on a milestone which I
knew so well from my school-days; and looking on Solway Sea to
St. Bee's Head, and all the pretty Cumberland villages, towns, and
swelling amphitheatre of fertile plains and airy mountains, to me
the oldest in the world, and the loveliest. What a changed meaning in all that! Tartarus itself and the pale kingdoms of Dis could
not have been more preternatural to me, and I felt that they could
not have been more so. Most stern, gloomy, sad, grand, yet terrible, steeped in woe! This was my humour while in Annandale.
Except riding down to Whinnyrigg for a plunge in the sea (seven
miles and back) daily when tide would serve, I can recollect nothing that I did there. All speech (except, doubtless, with my
mother), I did my utmost to avoid. Some books I probably had—
'Pickwick' and 'Johannes Müller' (in strange combination, and
'Pickwick' the preferable to me!) I do partly remember, but the
reading of them was as a mere opiate. In this foul torpor, like flax
thrown into the steeping pool, I seem to have stayed above two
months—stayed, in fact, till ashamed to stay longer. As for recovery, that had not yet considerably—in truth, it never fairly—
came at all.

Of my darling's beautiful reception of me when I did return, all
speech is inadequate, for now in my sad thoughts it is like a little
glimpse of Heaven in this poor turbid earth. I am too unworthy
of it; alas! how thrice unworthy! A day or two ago I discovered,
crowded into my first letter from Chelsea, as her postscript, these
bright words, touching and strange to me [T. C.]:—

To Mrs. Carlyle, Scotsbrig.

Chelsea: Sept. 22, 1837.

My dear Mother,—You know the saying, 'it is not lost which a
friend gets,' and in the present case it must comfort you for losing

him. Moreover, you have others behind, and I have only him, only him in the whole wide world to love me and take care of me, poor little wretch that I am. Not but that numbers of people love me after their fashion far better than I deserve; but then his fashion is so different from all these, and seems alone to suit the crotchety creature that I am. Thank you then for having, in the first place, been kind enough to produce him into this world, and for having, in the second place, made him scholar enough to recognize my various excellencies; and for having, in the last place sent him back to me again to stand by me in this cruel east wind. . . . God bless you all. I will write you a letter all to yourself before long, God willing.

J. W. C.

LETTER 17.

'More Dialogue' is more of 'Watch and Canary-bird' ('Chico' his name). I had been in Scotland lately, or was still there. The admired little Dialogue I never could get sight of, while she had keeping of it!—T. C.

To the Rev. John Sterling, Blackheath.

Chelsea: Sept.-Oct., 1837.

My dear Friend,—Being a sending of more dialogue, it were downright extravagance to send a letter as well. So I shall merely say (your father being sitting impatiently beating with his stick) that you are on no account to understand that by either of these dialogians I mean to shadow forth my own personality. I think it is not superfluous to give you this warning, because I remember you talked of Chico's philosophy of life as my philosophy of life, which was a horrible calumny.

You can fancy how one must be hurried when your father is in the case.

God bless you.

Always yours,
JANE W. CARLYLE.

DIALOGUE I.

The Bird and the Watch.

Watch. 'Chirp, chirp, chirp;' what a weariness thou art with thy chirping! Does it never occur to thee, frivolous thing, that life is too short for being chirped away at this rate?

Bird. Never. I am no philosopher, but just a plain canary-bird.

Watch. At all events, thou art a creature of time that hast been hatched, and that will surely die. And, such being the case, methinks thou art imperatively called upon to think more and to chirp less.

Bird. I 'called upon to think'! How do you make that out? Will you be kind enough to specify how my condition would be improved by thought? Could thought procure me one grain of seed or one drop of water beyond what my mistress is pleased to give? Could it procure me one eighth of an inch, one hair's-breadth more room to move about in, or could it procure me to be hatched over again with better auspices, in fair green wood beneath the blue free sky? I imagine not. Certainly I never yet betook myself to thinking instead of singing, that I did not end in dashing wildly against the wires of my cage, with sure loss of feathers and at the peril of limb and life. No, no, Madam Gravity, in this very conditional world, depend upon it, he that thinks least will live the longest, and song is better than sense for carrying one handsomely along.

Watch. You confess, then, without a blush, that you have no other aim in existence than to kill time?

Bird. Just so. If I were not always a killing of time, time, I can tell you, would speedily kill me. Heigh ho! I wish you had not interrupted me in my singing.

Watch. Thou sighest, 'Chico;' there is a drop of bitterness at the bottom of this froth of levity. Confess the truth; thou art not without compunction as to thy course of life.

Bird. Indeed, but I am, though. It is for the Power that made me and placed me here to feel compunction, if any is to be felt. For me, I do but fulfil my destiny: in the appointing of it, I had no hand. It was with no consent of mine that I ever was hatched; for the blind instinct that led me to chip the shell, and so exchange my natural prison for one made with hands, can hardly be imputed to me as an act of volition; it was with no consent of mine that I was fated to live and move within the wires of a cage, where a fractured skull and broken wings are the result of all endeavour towards the blue infinite, nor yet was it with consent of mine that I was made to depend for subsistence, not on my own faculties and exertions, but on the bounty of a fickle mistress, who starves me at one time and surfeits me at another. Deeply from my inmost soul I have protested, and do and will protest against all this. If, then,

the chirping with which I stave off sorrow and ennui be an offence
to the would-be wise, it is not I but Providence should bear the
blame, having placed me in a condition where there is no alternative but to chirp or die, and at the same time made self-preserva-
tion the first instinct of all living things.

Watch. 'Unhappy Chico![1] not in thy circumstances, but in thyself lies the mean impediment over which thou canst not gain the
mastery.'[2] The lot thou complainest of so petulantly is, with slight
variation, the lot of all. Thou art not free? Tell me who is?
Alas, my bird! Here sit prisoners; there also do prisoners sit.
This world is all prison, the only difference for those who inhabit
it being in the size and aspect of the cells; while some of these
stand revealed in cold strong nakedness for what they really are,
others are painted to look like sky overhead, and open country all
around, but the bare and the painted walls are alike impassable,
and fall away only at the coming of the Angel of Death.

Bird. With all due reverence for thy universal insight, picked up
Heaven knows how, in spending thy days at the bottom of a dark
fob, I must continue to think that the birds of the air, for example,
are tolerably free; at least, they lead a stirring, pleasurable sort of
life, which may well be called freedom in comparison with this of
mine. Oh that, like them, I might skim the azure and hop among
the boughs; that, like them, I might have a nest I could call my
own, and a wife of my own choosing, that I might fly away from,
the instant she wearied me! Would that the egg I was hatched
from had been addled, or that I had perished while yet unfledged!
I am weary of my life, especially since thou hast constituted thyself
my spiritual adviser. *Ay de mi!* But enough of this: it shall
never be told that I died the death of Jenkin's hen.[3] 'Chico,
point de faiblesse.'[4]

Watch. It were more like a Christian to say, 'Heaven be my
strength.'

Bird. And pray what is a Christian? I have seen poets, phi-
losophers, politicians, bluestockings, philanthropists, all sorts of
notable people about my mistress; but no Christian, so far as I am
aware.

Watch. Bird! thy spiritual darkness exceeds belief. What can I
say to thee? I wish I could make thee wiser, better!

---

[1] The name was of my giving.   [2] Goethe's *Wilhelm Meister.*
[3] Annandale comic proverb, originating I know not how.
[4] ' *Danton, point de,*' &c.

Bird. If wishes were saws, I should request you to saw me a passage through those wires; but wishes being simply wishes, I desire
to be let alone of them.

Watch. Good counsel at least is not to be rejected, and I give the
best, wouldst thou but lay it to heart. Look around thee, Chico—
around and within. Ascertain, if thou canst, the main source of
thy discontent, and toward the removal of that direct thy whole faculties and energies. Even should thy success prove incomplete, the
very struggle will be productive of good. 'An evil,' says a great
German thinker, ' ceases to be an evil from the moment in which we
begin to combat it.' Is it what you call loss of liberty that flings the
darkest shadow over your soul? If so, you have only to take a correct and philosophical view of the subject instead of a democratic
sentimental one, and you will find, as other captives have done,
that there is more real freedom within the walls of a prison than in
the distracting tumult without. Ah, Chico, in pining for the pleasures and excitements which lie beyond these wires, take also into
account the perils and hardships. Think what the bird of the air
has to suffer from the weather, from boys and beasts, and even
from other birds. Storms and snares and unknown woes beset it at
every turn, from all which you have been mercifully delivered in
being once for all cooped up here.

Bird. There is one known woe, however, from which I have not
been delivered in being cooped up here, and that is your absolute
wisdom and impertinent interference, from which same I pray
Heaven to take me with all convenient speed. If ever I attain to
freedom, trust me, the very first use I shall make of it shall be to fly
where your solemn prosy tick shall not reach me any more for ever.
Evil befall the hour when my mistress and your master took it into
their heads to 'swear eternal friendship,' and so occasion a juxta-
position betwixt us two which nature could never have meant.

Watch. 'My master'? Thou imbecile. I own no master;
rather am I his mistress, of whom thou speakest. Nothing can he
do without appealing to me as to a second better conscience, and it
is I who decide for him when he is incapable of deciding for himself. I say to him, It is time to go, and he goeth; or, There is time
to stay, and he stayeth. Hardly is he awake of a morning when I
tick authoritatively into his ear, *'Levez-vous, monsieur! Vous avez
des grandes choses à faire;'* [1] and forthwith he gathers himself to-

---

[1] St. Simon (he of 1825, n. b. !).

gether to enjoy the light of a new day—if no better may be. And is not every triumph he ever gained over natural indolence to be attributed to my often-repeated remonstrance, ' Work, for the night cometh ' ? Ay, and when the night is come, and he lays himself down, I take my place at his bed-head, and, like the tenderest nurse, tick him to repose.

Bird. And suppose he neglected to wind thee up, or that thy mainspring chanced to snap? What would follow then? Would the world stand still in consequence? Would thy master—for such he is to all intents and purposes—lie for ever in bed expecting thy *Levez-vous?* Would there be nothing in the wide universe besides thee to tell him what o'clock it was? Impudent piece of mechanism! Thing of springs and wheels, in which flows no life-blood, beats no heart! Depend upon it, for all so much as thou thinkest of thyself, thou couldst be done without. *Il n'y a point de montre nécessaire !* [1] The artisan who made thee with files and pincers could make a thousand of thee to order. Cease, then, to deem thyself a fit critic and lawgiver for any living soul. Complete of thy kind, tick on, with infallible accuracy, sixty ticks to the minute, through all eternity if thou wilt and canst; but do not expect such as have hearts in their breasts to keep time with thee. A heart is a spontaneous, impulsive thing, which cannot, I would have thee know, be made to beat always at one measured rate for the good pleasure of any time-piece that ever was put together. And so good day to thee, for here comes one who, thank Heaven, will put thee into his fob, and so end our *tête-à-tête.*

Watch. (With a sigh.) ' The living on earth have much to bear!'

J. W. C.

This is the piece mentioned in *Sterling's Life*, p. 304 (he had seen it; I never did till now, she refusing me, as usual; nor did I know for certain that it was in existence still). ' Chico ' (*Tiny*, in Spanish) was our canary bird, brought from Craigenputtock hither on her knee. The ' Watch' had been her mother's; it is now (August, 1866) her mother's niece's (Maggie Welsh's, for two months back). A ' Remonstrance,' now placed here, is from the same ' Watch,' probably several years later. Or perhaps this is the ' farther sending' letter referred to in Letter No. 39 (1837) vaguely as in second bit of dialogue? No ' second' otherwise, of any kind, is now discoverable. (August 15, 1869, my last day at present on this sad and sacred task).—T. C. *insomnis* (as to much).

---

[1] ' . . . *point d'homme,*' . . . Napoleon used to say.

I.—3

Remonstrance of my Old Watch.

What have I done to you, that you should dream of 'tearing out my inside' and selling me away for an old song? Is your heart become hard as the nether millstone, that you overlook long familiarity and faithful service, to take up with the new-fangled gimcracks of the day? Did I ever play thee false? I have been driven with you, been galloped with you over the roughest roads; have been 'jolted' as never watch was; and all this without 'sticking up' a single time, or so much as lagging behind! Nay, once I remember (the devil surely possessed you at that moment) you pitched me out of your hand as though I had been a worthless pincushion; and even that unprecedented shock I sustained with unshaken nerves! Try any of your new favourites as you have tried me; send the little wretch you at present wear within your waistband smack against a deal floor, and if ever it stirred more in this world, I should think it little less than a miracle.

Bethink you then, misguided woman, while it is yet time! If not for my sake, for your own, do not complete your barbarous purpose. Let not a passing womanish fancy lead you from what has been the ruling principle of your life—a detestation of shams and humbug. For, believe me, these little watches are arrant shams, if ever there was one. They are not watches so much as lockets with watch faces. The least rough handling puts them out of sorts; a jolt is fatal; they cost as much in repairs every year as their original price; and when they in their turn come to have their insides torn out, what have you left? Hardly gold enough to make a good-sized thimble.

But if you are deaf to all suggestions of common-sense, let sentiment plead for me in your breast. Remember how daintily you played with me in your childhood, deriving from my gold shine your first ideas of worldly splendour. Remember how, at a more advanced age, you longed for the possession of me and of a riding habit and whip, as comprising all that was most desirable in life! And when at length your mother made me over to you, remember how feelingly (so feelingly that you shed tears) I brought home to your bosom the maxim of your favourite Goethe, 'The wished-for comes too late.' And oh! for the sake of all these touching remembrances, cast me not off, to be dealt with in that shocking manner; but if, through the caprice of fashion, I am deemed no longer fit to be seen, make me a little pouch inside your dress, and I am a much mistaken watch if you do not admit in the long run that my solid merit is far above that of any half-dozen of these lilliputian upstarts.

And so, betwixt hope and fear, I remain,

Your dreadfully agitated,

WATCH.

I find so much reason as well as pathos and natural eloquence in the above that I shall proceed no further with the proposed exchange.

JANE.

LETTER 18.

From Phœbe Chorley to Thomas Carlyle, London

(favoured by H. F. Chorley).

Thus to venture unbidden into thy presence may seem somewhat startling to thee in a woman, and a member of the quiet, unobtrusive Society of Friends; but thou must thank the originality, the first-rate talent, the taste, the poetry of thy three wonderful volumes on the French Revolution for drawing on thee the infliction, it may be, of mere commonplace sentences in my endeavour to express, however inadequately, the deep unspeakable interest with which I am perusing thy admirable narrative of the events which astonished and horrified the civilised world forty-five years ago.

The style, described to me before I saw the work, as ' peculiar and uninviting,' I deem of all others calculated to convey the fervour, the fierceness, and the atrocity alternately possessing the feelings of those the chief actors in that most sanguinary drama. So perfectly graphic, too, a painter need desire no better study to improve his art. I can distinctly see the ancient Merovingian kings on their bullock-carts; and the chamber of the dying Louis Quinze with all its accompaniments; and the new Korff berlin, and its wretched, vacillating inmates—the poor queen issuing into the street and lost there. Oh! the breathless anxiety of that journey; how one longed to speed them forward, especially, I think, for her sake, whose curse it was, in a new era, when the light broke through the Cimmerian darkness of ages, to be united to a man of that mediocre sort, who is incapable of reading the fiery language of passing events, and yet not content to be wholly passive. Oh! how the very depths of my heart are stirred up responsive to the humiliations and sufferings of that high-minded, erring woman; she stands there before me in the window at Versailles, the untasted cup of coffee in her hand! A spell is completely cast over me by the waving of the enchanter's wand, given to thee to wield for the instruction of thy less-gifted fellow mortals.

Go on and prosper, saith my whole soul. Such abilities as thine were never designed to be folded in a napkin; use them worthily, and they will bless thyself and thousands. I am truly rejoiced a writer has at last sprung up to do justice to modern history—a greatly neglected species of literature—and to present it in colours so attractive that, as certainly as mind recognises mind, and speaks to it, and is comprehended by it, so certainly will 'The French Revolution' of Thomas Carlyle be read and approved by all men, and all women too, endowed with any of that Promethean fire which he seems to fetch down from heaven at will, and finally win its way through all obstructions to form a part—an important part —of the standard of the English language.

Je le jure (I swear it), Chapter VI., Book i., vol. ii.:—The opening paragraph on Hope is exquisitely constructed. I cannot recall to memory a more felicitous arrangement of words than this paragraph displays. It has become incorporated with the very texture of my thoughts, 'a sacred Constantine's banner written on the eternal skies.'

Henry Chorley, the bearer of this, can tell thee how his own family and my brother and sister Crosfield, all of them people of mind, have been delighted with thy production. Accept my most cordial individual thanks for the rich intellectual banquet thou hast provided. All other books will appear so tame and flat in comparison with these, that I know not what to turn to when I shall have done with the third volume, which travels into the country tomorrow with

Thy sincere friend and admirer,
PHŒBE CHORLEY.

Copied in *her* hand for my mother, after which:

Chelsea: March-April, 1838.

There, dear mother! Pretty fairish for a prim Quakeress, don't you think? Just fancy her speaking all these transcendental flatteries from under a little starched cap and drab-coloured bonnet!

I wonder how old she is; and if she is, or has been, or expects ever to be married? Don't you? Perhaps the spirit may move her to come hither next, and cultivate still more her 'favourable sentiments.' Well, let her! I could pardon her any absurdity almost, in consideration of that beautiful peculiarity she possessed, of admiring his very style, which has hitherto exceeded the capacity of admiration in all men, women, and children that have made the attempt.

An enthusiastic Quaker once gave Edward Irving a gig. I wonder if this enthusiastic Quakeress will give Carlyle one; it would be excessively useful here.

We have fine weather, and I am nearly rid of my cough again. Carlyle has fallen to no work yet; but is absolutely miserable nevertheless. Ellen is pretty strong again, and I hope will be able to 'carry on'—at least, 'till Lonsdale coom.'[1] Chico has got a new cage from a gentleman, not a Quaker. So, you see, all goes tolerably here. Love to Jenny; remember me to Robert.

Your affectionate
JANE CARLYLE.

LETTER 19.

To Miss Helen Welsh, Liverpool.

Chelsea: May 27, 1838.

O Cousin, gracious and benign,—Beautiful is it to see thy tender years bearing such blossoms of tolerance; for tolerance is not in general the virtue of youth, but only of mature or even old age— experienced age, which after long and sore 'kicking against the pricks,' has learned for itself what it would not take on hearsay, that the world we live in is of necessity, and has been, and ever will be, an erring and conditional world; and that in short, all men, women, and children, beginning with ourselves, are shockingly imperfect. So that there is none justified in saying with self-complacency, 'black is the eye' of another. Indeed, I should have felt it

---

[1] Old Cumberland woman, listening as the newspaper was read, full of battling, warring, and tumult all over the world, exclaimed at last: 'Aye, they'll karry on till Lonsdale coom, and he'll soon settle them aw!' A female partner was provided for Chico; on first introducing this latter to me, with what an inimitable air my bright one, recounting her purchase, parodied that Covent Garden chaunt, 'The all-wise, great Creator saw that he . . . !' (See p. 153.)

hard to have been reproached by you for not writing; you, who have health and no cares, cannot at all estimate the effort I make, and doing anything that can be let alone without immediate detriment to the State or the individual.

I have had so much to bear, for a long, long time back, from the derangement of my interior, that when a day of betterness does arrive, I am tempted, instead of employing it in writing letters, or in doing duties of whatever sort, to make a sort of child's play-day of it; and then, when my head is aching, or my cough troublesome—Oh, Helen dear, may you never know by experience how difficult it is in such circumstances, to write a letter all about nothing, even to a sweet-faced, well-beloved cousin!

We were just then in the first ferment of our Lectures,[1] which are still going on, and keeping up an extra degree of tumult within and without us. However, he has been borne through the first eight 'with an honourable through-bearing,' and I dare say will not break down in the remaining four. The audience is fair in quantity (more than fair, considering that he is a lecturer on his own basis, unconnected with any 'Royal Institution,' or the like); and in quality it is unsurpassable; there are women so beautiful and intelligent, that they look like emanations from the moon; and men whose faces are histories, in which one may read with ever new interest. On the whole, if he could get sleep at nights, while the lecturing goes forward, and if I might look on without being perpetually reminded by the pain in my head, or some devilry or other, that I am a mere woman, as the Annan Bailie reminded the people who drank his health at a Corporation dinner that he was a mere man—('O gentlemen! remember that I am but a man of like passions with yourselves')—we should find this new trade rather agreeable. In the meanwhile, with all its drawbacks, it answers the end. 'O gloire,' says a French poet, 'donnez-moi du pain!' And glory too often turns a deaf ear to this reasonable request; but she is kind enough to grant it to us in the present instance; so allons, let us 'eat fire,' as Carlyle calls it, since people are disposed to give their money for such exhibition, over and above their applause.

My husband wishes and needs a change; and a climate where I should not need to be confined for months together to the house (I may say to two rooms) were a manifest improvement in my lot. It was dreary work last winter, though by incredible precautions I

---

[1] Second course, delivered in the spring of 1838.

kept myself perpendicular; and the winter before is horrible to think of, even at this date. A single woman (by your leave be it said) may be laid up with comparative ease of mind; but in a country where a man is allowed only one wife, and needs that one for other purposes than mere show, it is a singular hardship for all parties, when she misgives anyhow, so as to be rendered wholly ineffectual.

I had a box from mother the other day, which came, I believe, through you.

> Everything rich, everything rare,
> Save young Nourmahl, was blowing there.

By the way, Carlyle breakfasted with Thomas Moore the other morning, and fancied him.

I hope very sincerely that my aunt is quite well again, and should like to be assured of it by some of you. Give her and uncle, and the whole generation, my warmest affection. Carlyle joins me in good wishes for you all; and behold! I remain your faithful attached, in-spite-of-appearances, cousin,

JANE CARLYLE.

LETTER 20.

This autumn, after lectures, printing of 'Sartor,' &c., I steamered to Kirkcaldy; was in Scotland five or six weeks—to Edinburgh twice or thrice; to Minto Manse (Dr. Aitken's, now married to 'Bess Stoddart,' heiress òf old Bradfute, and very rich); thence, after dull short sojourn, through Hawick, Langholm to Scotsbrig (mother absent in Manchester); to Chelsea again, early in October. Vivid at this hour are all these movements to me; but not worth noting: only the Kirkcaldy part, with the good Ferguses, and, after twenty years of absence, was *melodiously* interesting to me, more or less. *Ay de mi*, all gone, now, all!—T. C.

To T. Carlyle, at Kirkcaldy.

Chelsea: Aug. 30, 1838.

Dear Husband of me,—I was most thankful to hear an articulate cheep (chirp) from you once more, for the little notekin 'did neither ill nor gude.' But this is a clear and comprehensive view of the matter, which may satisfy the female mind, for a time, and deserves a most ample threepenny in return.[1] I would have sat down instantly on receiving it, and made a clean breast of all my thinkings and doings, in the first fervour of enthusiasm, which such a

---

[1] Our name for a post-letter in those days. 'Send him a threepenny, then.'

good letter naturally inspired; but the letter came at one, and at two the carriage was ordered to convey me to pass the day with Mrs. C——; so it was plain, you could not get the 'first rush o' the tea,' without being stinted in quantity. But this morning, I have said it, that nothing short of an earthquake shall hinder me from filling this sheet.

First of all, then, dear Ill,[1] I am, and have been, in perfectly good case so far as the body is concerned. 'Association of Ideas' was like to have played the devil with me at first. The first night after your departure, I slept three hours; the second, forty minutes; and the third, none at all. If I had a cow, I should have bade it 'consider;'[2] having none it was necessary to 'consider' myself. So I applied to Dr. Marshall[3] for any sort of sleeping-draught, which had no opium in it, to break, if possible, this spell at the out-set. He gave me something, consisting of red-lavender and other stimulants, which 'took an effect on me.'[4] Not that I swallowed it! I merely set it by my bedside; and the feeling of lying down under new circumstances, of having a resource in short, put me to sleep! One night, indeed, the imagination was not enough; and I did take the thing into my inside, where it made all 'cosy';[5] and since then I have slept as well as usual; nor did these bad nights do

---

[1] Converse of Goody.

[2] There was a piper had a cow,
     And he had nocht to give her;
     He took his pipes, and played a spring,
     And bade the cow consider.
       The cow considered wi' hersel'
     That mirth [sportful music] wad ne'er fill her:
     'Gie me a pickle pease-strae,
     And sell your wind for siller.'

Old Scotch rhyme, reckoned 'pawky,' clever and symbolical, in this house. *Gloire! donnez-moi du pain!*

[3] Next-door neighbour this Dr. M., faithful but headlong and fanatical. His wife was from Edinburgh, a kind of 'Haddington Wilkie' withal; died not long after. Dr. M., unsuccessful otherwise, then volunteered upon some Philo-Nigger Expedition—scandalously sanctioned by a Government in need of votes, though he considered it absurd—and did die, like the others, a few days after reaching the poisonous, swampy river they were sent to navigate.

[4] Rigorous navy lieutenant: 'Why, Richard, you're drunk!' 'I've 'ad my allowance, sir, and it's took an effect on me,' answered Richard (Richard Kee-vil, a wandering, innocent creature from the Gloucester cloth countries lat-terly, who came to my father's in a starving state, and managed gently to stay five or six months—a favourite, and study, with us younger ones).

[5] 'Mamma, wine makes cosy,' *Reminiscences*, p. 218. Harper's Edition.

me any visible harm. Helen [1] asks me every morning 'if I have no headache yet?' And when I answer, none, she declares it to be quite 'mysterious!' In fact, I believe Mrs. Elliot's cab is of very material service in keeping me well. And I hope you will become a great *Paid*, and then we shall sometimes have a 'bit clatch.' [2] I have driven out most days, from two till four, quite regularly. I also take care to have some dinner quite regularly. And I contrive to sup on Cape Madeira, which seems to be as good for me as porridge, after all. For the rest, my chief study is to keep myself tranquil and cheerful; convinced that I can do nothing so useful, either for myself or others. Accordingly, I read French novels, or anything that diverts me, without compunction; and sew no more, at curtains or anything else, than I feel to be pleasant.

For company, I have had enough to satisfy all my social wants. One visitor per day would content me; and I have often had more. Two tea-shines [3] went off with *éclat*, the more so that the people came, for most part, at their own peril. The first consisted of Mr. and Mrs. Crawfurd, George Rennie and his wife, Mrs. Sterling, Il Conte, Darwin, and Robert Barker, [4] who was up from Northampton on leave of absence. Do you shriek at the idea of all this? You need not. We all talked through other [5] (except Barker, who, by preserving uninterrupted silence, passed for some very wise man); and we were all happy in the consciousness of doing each our part to 'stave off' *ennui*, though it were by nothing better than nonsense. The next was a more rational piece of work; but more 'insipid': [6] Mrs. Rich, [7] and her two sisters, the Marshalls, Mrs. Sterling, and the always to be got Darwin. We talked about the condition of the poor, &c., &c., one at a time; and I am sure the saints think that, all this while, my light has been hid under a bushel—that, in fact, they have 'discovered me.' They kissed me all over, when they went away, and would have me out to Plumstead Common. Then I had Mr. C—— one night, to whom I prated

---

[1] Helen was a new maid, of whom more hereafter.

[2] Brother James's name for a humble gig, or the like. To 'clatch' is to drag lumberingly.

[3] Scotch peasant's term for such phenomena.

[4] Amiable Nithsdale gentleman, a lieutenant of foot, who had seen service, nearly killed at New Orleans, &c.

[5] German, *durch einander*.   [6] Servant Helen's term.

[7] Daughter of Sir James Mackintosh; among other elderly religious ladies, was a chief admirer of Rev. A. Scott, now nestled silently at Plumstead (died recently professor in Owens College, Manchester).

so cleverly about domestic service, and all that, that his eyes twinkled the purest admiration, through his spectacles; and, two days after, he returned with Mrs. C——! to hear me again on the same topics. But catch me flinging my pearls before swine! But, oh, dear me, dearest, how the paper is getting covered over with absolute nothings; and I have really something to tell.

I have to tell you one very wonderful thing indeed, which brought a sort of tears into my eyes. The first money from F. R.[1] is come to hand, in the shape of a bill of exchange for fifty pounds, inclosed in a short business letter from Emerson. He says: 'An account has been rendered to me, which, though its present balance is in our favour, is less than I expected; yet, as far as I understand, it agrees well with all that has been promised. At least, the balance in our favour, when the edition is sold, which the booksellers assure me will undoubtedly be done within a year from the publication, must be 760 dollars, and whatever more Heaven and the subscribers may grant.' You are to know, dear, fifty pounds is exactly $224.22, the rate of exchange being 9 per cent. He says nothing more, except that he will send a duplicate of the bill by next packet; and that 'the Miscellanies is published in two volumes, a copy of which goes to you immediately; 250 copies are already sold.' So you see, dear, here is Fortune actually smiling on you over the seas, with her lap full of dollars. Pray you, don't you be bashful; but smile on her in return. Another bit of good luck lies in the shape of a little hamper, full of Madeira, the Calvert wine—I have not unpacked it yet; but I guess it holds a dozen. I too am to have some wine given me. John Sterling has desired his wine merchant, on receiving a certain basketful of Malmsey from Madeira for him, to send some fraction of it to me.

He himself, John Sterling, you will be surprised to hear, is off this day for good. He spends a week in settling his family at Hastings, and then proceeds to Italy. Such is the order of Sir James Clark, and his own whim! He breakfasted with me this morning, to take leave; apparently in perfect health, and almost too good spirits, I think. I told him, he seemed to me a man who had a diamond given him to keep, which he was in danger of breaking all down into sparks, that everyone might have a breastpin of it. He looked as Edward Irving used to do. I do not think that, morally, he is at all in a good way—too much of virtue 'and all that' on the lips. Woe to him if he fall into the net of any beautiful Italian!

---

[1] *French Revolution.*

People who are so dreadfully 'devoted' to their wives are so apt, from mere habit, to get devoted to other people's wives as well!

Except Emerson's, there have been no letters for you; and of threepennies, only one of apology from Wilson, along with that *Globe;* and one from your namesake,[1] wanting letters to 'Germany, with which he wants to acquaint himself'—or rather, in the language of truth, where he is going as a missionary (so Dr. Marshall tells me). I answered it politely.

I must not conclude without telling you a most surprising purpose I have in my head, which, if you have heard of O'Connell's late visit to a La Trappean Monastery, you will not be quite incredulous of. I am actually meditating to spend a week with— Miss Wilson at Ramsgate!! To do penance for all the nonsense I speak, by dooming myself, for one whole week, to speak nothing but real sense, and no mistake! She wrote me the most cordial invitation, and not to me only, but to Helen, whom she knew I did not like to leave; for three weeks I was to come. I answered in a long letter, which you would have liked amazingly, if you had had the good luck to hear it, that when I heard from John,[2] if there was time before his arrival, I would absolutely accept. I have had another letter from her since, gracious beyond expression; and am really meaning to lock up, and go with Helen for a week, if John does not come all the sooner. Address to me always here, however; as Dr. Marshall will send on my letters *instanter.* They are touchingly kind to me, these good Marshalls;—got up a dinnerchen, &c., &c. Everybody is kind to me. Only I have put the Stimabile in a great fuff—purposely, that I might not have him dangling here in your absence. Thus it is impossible for me to get a frank. But you will not grudge postage, even for this worthless letter, since it is mine.

I have not heard from my mother, nor written to her yet, so I know not where she is. I have forgot a thousand things. Madame Marcet has not been yet;—is to come,[3]—a friend from Paris has deprived her of the pleasure, &c. Cavaignac was here last Friday. Edgeworth has been; wanted me out to Windsor. The blockhead Hume[4] came to tea one night! No Americans! No strangers! Darwin is going off to the Wedgewoods with Mrs. Rich. Thank you for the particulars to Helen. Yes, try and see her mother.

---

[1] Angel, at Albury, editor of the *Globe* newspaper.
[2] John Carlyle, then expected in London.
[3] Never did, I think.   [4] Ambitious thickhead.

She is very kind to me. Get very very well; and come back so good! and so pooty.

Say all that is kind and grateful from me to the good Ferguses. And tell Elizabeth I will write her a long letter one of these days —to be also in no sorrow about Pepoli. He is merely lackadaisical. God bless you, dearest. Do not, I beseech you, soil your mind with a thought of postage; but write again quick. Be sure you go to Minto.[1]   J. W. C.

LETTER 21.

To T. Carlyle, Esq., Scotsbrig.

Chelsea: Sunday, Sept. 10, 1838.

Thou precious cheap!—I am rejoiced to find you working out your plan so strenuously and steadily. That is really one kind of virtue which does seem to me always its own reward. To have done the thing one meant to do, let it turn out as it may, 'is a good joy.'[2] You will come home to me 'more than plumb,' with conscious manhood, after having reaped such a harvest of 'realised ideals.'

For me, I am purposely living without purpose, from hand to mouth, as it were, taking the good the gods provide me, and, as much as possible, shirking the evil—a manner of existence which seems to suit my constitution very well, for I have not had a single headache these three weeks, nor any bodily ailment, except occasional touches of that preternatural intensity of sensation, which, if one did not know it to be the consequence of sleeplessness, would pass for perfection of health rather than ailment; and which I study to keep down with such dullifying appliances as offer themselves, in dearth of 'a considerable bulk of porridge.' The people are very attentive to me—almost too attentive; for they make me talk more than is for the good of my soul, and go through a power of my tea and bread and butter! Nay, Cavaignac was found sitting yesterday when I came home from my drive, and said, with all the cold-bloodedness imaginable, ' *Voulez-vous me donner à dîner, madame?* '—an astounding question to a woman whose whole earthly prospects in the way of dinner were bounded there and then to one fried sole and two *pommes de terre!* And

---

[1] To the manse there (reverend couple being old acquaintances of both of us).

[2] One of Leigh Hunt's children, on the sight of flowers.

when this sumptuous repast was placed on the table, with the addition of a spoonful of improvised hash, he sat down to it exclaiming, *à plusieurs reprises:* ' *Mon Dieu, comme j'ai faim, moi!* ' However, as Helen remarked, ' It's nae matter what ye gie him; for he can aye mak the bread flee! '

Our first two volumes of the 'Miscellanies' are published. I have sent you a copy. The edition consists of 1,000 copies; of these 500 are bound, 500 remain in sheets. The title-pages, of course, are all printed alike; but the publishers assure me that new title-pages can be struck off at a trifling expense, with the imprint of Saunders and Otley. The cost of a copy in sheets or 'folded' is 89 cents, and bound is $1.15 cents. The retail price is $2.50 cents a copy, and the author's profit is $1.00, and the bookseller's 35 cents per copy, according to my understanding of the written contract. (All of which I have written off with faith and hope, but with infinite *ennui,* not understanding any more of cents than of hieroglyphics.) I think there is no doubt but the book will sell very well there; but if, for the reasons you suggest, you wish any part of it, you can have it as soon as ships can bring your will. We have printed half the matter. I should presently begin to print the remainder, inclusive of the article on Scott in two more volumes; but now I think I shall wait until I hear from you. Of those books we will print a larger edition, say 1,250 or 1,500, if you want a part of it in London; for I feel confident now that our public is a thousand strong. Write me, therefore, by the steam-packet your wishes. So you can ' consider,' cheap![1] and be prepared to answer the letter when I send it in a day or two in the lump.

For my part, I think I should vote for letting these good Americans keep their own wares; they seem to have an art, unknown in our island, of getting them disposed of. I can say nothing of how 'Sartor'[2] poor beast! is going on, only that people tell me, with provoking vagueness, from time to time, that they have read or heard honourable mention of it; but where, or when, or to what possible purport, they seem bound over by oath to be quite silent upon. Mrs. Buller, for example, the other day when I called at her house, said that she was glad to find it succeeding. ' Was it succeeding?' I asked, for I really was quite ignorant. Oh, she had heard and seen the most honourable notice of it. The individual most agog about it seems to be the young Catholic, whose name, I now inform and beg you to remember, is Mr. T. Chisholm Anstey.

---

[1] Converse of ' dear.'   [2] Lately republished from *Fraser's Magazine.*

He sat with me one forenoon, last week, for a whole hour and a half, rhapsodising about you all the while; a most judicious young Catholic, as I ever saw or dreamt of. He had been 'in retreat,' as they call it, for three weeks—that is to say, in some Jesuit *La Trappe* establishment in the north of England—absolutely silent, which he was sure you would be glad to hear; and he is going back at Christmas to hold his peace for three weeks more! He has written an article on you for the 'Dublin Review,' which is to be sent to me as soon as published, and the Jesuits, he says, are enchanted with all they find in you. Your 'opinions about sacrifice, &c., &c., are entirely conformable to theirs!' 'After all,' said Darwin the other day, 'what the deuce is Carlyle's religion, or has he any?' I shook my head, and assuerd him I knew no more than himself. I told Mr. Chisholm Anstey I could not give him the lecture-book, as I was copying it. 'You copying it!' he exclaimed in enthusiasm; 'indeed you shall not have that toil; I will copy it for you; it will be a pleasure to me to write them all a second time!' So you may give him the ten shillings; for he actually took away the book, and what I had done of it, *par vive force!* I wish some other of your admirers would carry off the bed-curtains by *vive forcé*, and finish them also; for, though I have had a sempstress helping me for three days, they are still in hand. Perhaps a Swedenborgian will do that?

Baron von Alsdorf came here the other night, seeking your address, to write to you for a testimonial. 'Such is the lot of celebrity i' the world.'[1] Oh! my 'Revolution' and 'Sartor' are come home, such loves of books! quite beautiful; but such a price! seven shillings per volume! for half-binding! 'Was there ever anything in the least like it?'[2] The Fraserian functionary seemed almost frightened to tell me; but seeing I could make nothing of debating about it, I contented myself with saying: 'Well, "French Revolutions" are not written every day, and the outside should be something worthy of the in.' The man, apparently struck with admiration of my sincerity and contempt of money, bowed involuntarily, and said, 'It is indeed a book that cannot have too much expense put upon it.' 'Why the deuce, then,' I was tempted to answer, 'don't you give us something for it?' The 'German Romance' is to be done in calf at 3*s.* 6*d.* a volume. Do not trouble your head about my investing so much capital in the binding of these books. With such a prospect of cents, it were sheer parsimony not to give them

---

[1] Parodied from Schiller.   [2] Common phrase of her mother's.

a good dress. I have unpacked your wine, and even tasted it; and lo! it proves to be two dozen pint bottles of exquisite port! which disagrees with you. Did you not understand it was to have been Madeira? My Malmsey is not come yet. How I laughed, and how Cavaignac shouted at your encounter with Mrs. 'ickson.'[1] Indeed, your whole letter was most entertaining and satisfactory. Do not be long in sending me another; they are very refreshing, especially when they praise me![2] This is not so good 'a return' as I could wish to make you; but in a single sheet one is obliged to *manger* all superfluous details, though these are more interesting to the absent than more important matter. Robertson called on me the other day, wondering if you were writing anything for him. He has had a splutter with Leigh Hunt—always spluttering. He talked much of Harriet's 'tail of hundreds' at Newcastle[3] till I could not help fancying her as one of those sheep Herodotus tells about. I wonder how many things I have forgotten? Kind regards to them all, and to yourself what you can say of most affectionate. I drive almost every day. Elizabeth's letter is not come yet; but I will write forthwith whether or no.

Your unfortunate

GOODY.

LETTER 22.

A postscript at almost half a year's distance. These are the lecture years, 1837–40; this year's lecture (for it is 'April 12') would be within three weeks.

'First rush o' ye tea,' intelligible now only to myself, was at that time full of mirth, ingenuity, and humour in the quarter it was going to! My mother, many years before, on the eve of an Ecclefechan Fair, happened in the gloaming to pass one Martha Calvert's door, a queer old cripple creature who used to lodge vagrants, beggars, ballad-singers, snap-women, &c., such as were wont, copiously enough (chiefly from the 'Brig-end of Dumfries'), to visit us on these occasions. Two beggar-women were pleasantly chatting, or taking sweet counsel, outside in the quiet summer dusk, when a third started out, eagerly friendly, 'Come awa', haste; t' ye first rush o' ye tea!' (general tea inside, just beginning, first rush of it far superior to third or fourth!)

'God's Providence.' Peg Ir'rin (Irving, a memorable old bread-and-ale woman, extensively prepared to vend these articles at Middlebie Sacrament) could not by entreaty or logic (her husband had fought at Bunker's Hill) extort from the parish official (ruling elder) liberty to use the vacant school-house for that purpose,

---

[1] Hickson, suddenly in Princes Street, Edinburgh, poor woman!
[2] *Vide* Cicero.   [3] Scientific meeting.

whereupon Peg, with a toss of her foolish high head (a loud, absurd, empty woman, though an empty especially of any mischief), 'Ah well; thou canna cut me out of God's Providence.'— T. C.

To Mrs. Carlyle, Scotsbrig, Ecclefechan.

April 12, 1839.

My dear Mother,—It were much pleasanter to write to you if, besides white paper he would leave me something to say. But away he goes, skimming over everything, whipping off the cream of everything, and leaves me nothing but the blue milk to make you a feast of. The much best plan for me were to take the start of him, and have the 'first rush o' ye tea' to myself; as I positively design to do in lecture time, when there will be something worth while to tell.

We see Jeffrey often since he came to London, and he is very friendly still, 'though he could not cut us out of God's Providence.' We had a Roman Catholic Frenchman [1] flying about us, at a prodigious rate, last week, but he has left London for the present. He told us all about how he went to confession, &c., &c., and how he had been demoralised at one period, and was recovered by the spectacle of a holy procession. He seems a very excellent man in his own way, but one cannot quite enter into his ecstasies about white shirts and wax tapers, and all that sort of thing. I hope you are all well, and thinking of me, as heretofore, with kindness; this is cruel weather for Isabella and you and me.

Ever affectionately yours,

JANE CARLYLE.

LETTER 23.

To Mrs. Carlyle, Scotsbrig, Ecclefechan.

Chelsea: May 6, 1839.

My dear Mother,—Our second lecture 'transpired' yesterday, and with surprising success—literally surprising—for he was imputing the profound attention with which the audience listened, to an awful sympathising expectation on their part of a momentary break-down, when all at once they broke into loud plaudits, and he thought they must all have gone clean out of their wits! But, as does not happen always, the majority were in this instance in the

---

[1] A. M. Rio, once very current in London society; vanished now many years ago.

right, and it was he that was out of his wits to fancy himself making a stupid lecture, when the fact is he really cannot be stupid if it were to save his life. The short and long of it was, he had neglected to take a pill the day before, had neglected to get himself a ride, and was out of spirits at the beginning: even I, who consider myself an unprejudiced judge, did not think he was talking his best, or anything like his best; the 'splendids,' 'devilish fines,' 'most trues,' and all that, which I heard heartily ejaculated on all sides, showed that it was a sort of mercy in him to come with bowels in a state of derangement, since, if his faculties had had full play, the people must have been all sent home in a state of excitement bordering on frenzy. The most practical good feature in the business was a considerable increase of hearers—even since last day; the audience seems to me much larger than last year, and even more distinguished. The whole street was blocked up with 'fine yellow' (and all other imaginable coloured) 'deliveries;'[1] and this is more than merely a dangerous flattery to one's vanity, the fashionable people here being (unlike our Scotch gigmen and gigwomen), the most open to light (above all to his light) of any sorts of people one has to do with. Even John Knox, though they must have been very angry at him for demolishing so much beautiful architecture, which is quite a passion with the English, they were quite willing to let good be said of, so that it were indisputably true. Nay, it was in reference to Knox that they first applauded yesterday. Perhaps his being a countryman of their favourite lecturer's might have something to do with it! But we will hope better things, though we thus speak.[2]

You will find nothing about us in the *Examiner* of this week; Leigh Hunt, who writes the notices there, did not arrive at the first lecture in time to make any report of it, having come in an omnibus which took it in its head to run a race with another omnibus, after a rather novel fashion, that is to say, each trying which should be hindmost. We go to lecture this year very commodiously in what is called a fly (a little chaise with one horse), furnished us from a livery-stable hard by, at a very moderate rate. Yesterday the woman who keeps these stables sent us a flunkey more than bargain, in consideration that I was 'such a very nice lady'—showing therein a spirit above slavery and even above livery. Indeed,

---

[1] 'Fine yellow *deliveries* and a'!' exclaimed a goosey maid-servant at Mainhill, seeing a carriage pass in the distance once (in little Craw Jean's hearing).

[2] Common preachers' phrase in Scotland.

as a foolish old woman at Dumfries used to say, 'everybody is kind to me;' and I take their kindness and am grateful for it, without inquiring too closely into their motives. Perhaps I am a genius too, as well as my husband? Indeed, I really begin to think so—especially since yesterday that I wrote down a parrot! which was driving us quite desperate with its screeching. Some new neighbours, that came a month or two ago, brought with them an accumulation of all the things to be guarded against in a London neighbourhood, viz., a pianoforte, a lap-dog, and a parrot. The two first can be borne with, as they carry on the glory within doors; but the parrot, since the fine weather, has been holding forth in the garden under our open windows. Yesterday it was more than usually obstreperous—so that Carlyle at last fairly sprang to his feet, declaring he could 'neither think nor live.' Now it was absolutely necessary that he should do both. So forthwith, on the inspiration of conjugal sympathy, I wrote a note to the parrot's mistress (name unknown), and in five minutes after Pretty Polly was carried within, and is now screeching from some subterranean depth whence she is hardly audible. Now if you will please recollect that, at Comely Bank, I also wrote down an old maid's house-dog, and an only son's pet bantam-cock,[1] you will admit, I think, that my writings have not been in vain.

We have been very comfortable in our household this long while. My little Fifeshire maid grows always the longer the better; and never seems to have a thought of leaving us, any more than we have of parting with her. My kindest love to all the 'great nation' in which you are grown.

Affectionately yours,
JANE CARLYLE.

LETTER 24.

Lectures finished, with again a hint of notice. This was not my last course of lectures; but I infinitely dislike the operation—'a mixture of prophecy and play-acting,' in which I could not adjust myself at all, and deeply longed to see the end of.—T. C.

To Mrs. Carlyle, Scotsbrig, Ecclefechan.

Chelsea: May 20, 1839.

My dear Mother,—The last lecture was indeed the most splendid he ever delivered, and the people were all in a heart-fever over it;

---

[1] True instances both; the first of many hundreds, which lasted till the very end.

on all sides of me people who did not know me, and might therefore be believed, were expressing their raptures audibly. One man (a person of originally large fortune, which he got through in an uncommon way, namely, in acts of benevolence) was saying, 'He's a glorious fellow; I love the fellow's very faults,' &c., &c.; while another answered, 'Aye, faith, is he; a fine, wild, chaotic, noble chap,' and so on over the whole room. In short we left the concern in a sort of whirlwind of 'glory' not without 'bread'; one of the dashing facts of the day being a Queen's carriage at the door, which had come with some of the household. Another thing I noticed, of a counter tendency to one's vanity, was poor Mrs. Edward Irving sitting opposite me, in her weeds, with sorrowful heart enough, I dare say. And when I thought of her lot and all the things that must be passing through her heart, to see her husband's old friend there, carrying on the glory in his turn, while hers—What was it all come to! She seemed to me set there expressly to keep me in mind 'that I was but a woman;'[1] like the skeleton which the old Egyptians placed at table, in their feasts, to be a memorial of their latter end.

My love to them all—and surely I will write a long letter to Jane before long; who is very foolish to imagine I ever had, or could have, any reason for silence towards her, other than my natural dislike to letter-writing.

Ever your affectionate
JANE CARLYLE.

'After lectures,' Carlyle writes, 'and considerable reading for "Cromwell," talking about scheme of London library, struggling and concocting towards what proved "Chartism," and more of the like, we set out together for Scotland by Liverpool about July 2 or 3, for Scotsbrig both of us in the first place, then she to Templand as headquarters, and, after leaving here, then to return to Scotsbrig, all which took effect, my remembrance of it now very indistinct.'

While absent from him, Mrs. Carlyle paid a visit to Ayr. As she was returning in the coach, Carlyle says in a note: 'a fellow-passenger got talking—"So you are from London, ma'am, and know literary people? Leigh Hunt? ah, so," &c., "and do you

---

[1] The Corporate Weavers at Dumfries elected a deacon, or chief of weavers, who was excessively flattered by the honour. In the course of the installation dinner, at some high point of the hep-hep hurrahing, he exclaimed, with sweet pain, 'Oh, gentlemen, remember I am but a man!'—T. C. Mrs. Carlyle tells the story of a Bailie at Annan, see p. 54.—J. A. F.

know anything of Thomas Carlyle?" "Him; right well—I am his wife," which had evidently pleased her little heart.'

The winter which followed, she had a violent chronic cold, sad accompaniment of many winters thenceforth, fiercely torturing nervous headache, continuous sometimes for three days and nights. ' Never,' says her husband, ' did I see such suffering from ill-health borne so patiently as by this most sensitive of delicate creatures all her life long.'

She had an extraordinary power of attaching to her everyone with whom she came in contact. In a letter to her sister-in-law, Mrs. Aitken, written in the midst of her illness, she says: ' My maid[1] is very kind when I am laid up; she has no suggestions or voluntary help in her, but she does my bidding quietly and accurately, and when I am very bad she bends over me in my bed as if I were a little child, and rubs her cheek on mine—once I found it wet with tears—one might think one's maid's tears could do little for a tearing headache, but they do comfort a little.'

During this suffering time she wrote little and briefly. Carlyle was preparing his last course of lectures, the six on Heroes and Hero Worship, which were delivered in the coming season. He had a horse now, which had been presented to him by Mr. Marshall, of Leeds. The riding improved his spirits, but his nerves were always in a state of irritation when he was writing. ' Why do women marry?' she says in a little note to John Forster; ' God knows, unless it be that, like the great Wallenstein, they do not find scope enough for their genius and qualities in an easy life.

Night it must be, ere Friedland's star shall burn!'

In the summer matters were made worse by what to him was a most serious trial, described in the letter which follows. He asked Charles Buller if there were no means by which he could be extricated. Buller said he knew of but one. ' He could register himself as a Dissenting preacher.'—J. A. F.

LETTER 25.

This ' trial by jury' was a Manchester case of patents: patent first, for an improvement on cotton-wool carding machines; patent second, an imitation of that, query theft of it or not? Trial fell in two terms (same unfortunate jury), and lasted three or four days in each. Madder thing I never saw;—clear to myself in the first half-hour (' essential theft '), no advocate doing the least good to it farther, doing harm rather;—and trial costing in money, they said, 1,000l. a day. Recalcitrant juryman (one of the ' Tales ' sort), stupidest-looking fellow I ever saw—it was I that coaxed him round and saved a new trial at 1,000l. a day. Intolerable suffering, rage, almost despair (and resolution to quit London), were, on my part, the consequence of these jury-summonses, which, after this, hap-

---

[1] Kirkcaldy Helen, one of the notabilities, and also blessings, of our existence here.—T. C.

pened to abate or almost cease. On hers, corresponding pity, and
at length no end of amusement over my adventure with that stupidest of jurymen, &c., which she used to narrate in an incomparable manner. Ah me! Ah me!

'Poor fellow, after all!' was very often finish of my brother in
summing up his censures of men—so often that we had grown to
expect it, and banter it.—T. C.

To the Reverend John Sterling, Clifton.

Chelsea: Oct. 5, 1840.

My dear John 'after all,'—In God's name, be 'a hurdy-gurdy,'
or whatever else you like! You are a good man, anyhow, and there
needs not your 'dying' to make me know this at the bottom of my
heart, and love you accordingly. No, my excellent Sir, you are a
blessing which one knows the value of even before one has lost it.
And it is just because I love you better than most people that I
persecute you as I do; that I flare up when you touch a hair of my
head (I mean my moral head). So now we are friends again, are
we not? If, indeed, through all our mutual impertinences, we
have ever been anything else!

You see, I am very lamb-like to-day; indeed, I could neither
'quiz,' nor be 'polite' to you to-day for the whole world. The
fact is, I also have had a fit of illness, which has softened my
mood, even as yours has been softened by the same cause. These
fits of illness are not without their good uses, for us people of too
poetic temperaments. For my part, I find them what the touching
of their mother earth was for the giants of old. I arise from them
with new heart in me for the battle of existence; and you know,
or ought to know, what a woman means by new heart—not new
brute force, as you men understand by it, but new power of loving
and enduring.

We have been in really a rather deplorable plight here for a good
while back, ever since a certain trial about a patent, so strangely
are things linked together in this remarkable world! My poor man
of genius had to sit on a jury two days, to the ruin of his whole
being, physical, moral, and intellectual. And ever since, he has
been reacting against the administration of British justice, to a degree that has finally mounted into influenza. While I, *poverina*,
have been reacting against his reaction, till that malady called by the
cockneys 'mental worry' fairly took me by the throat, and threw
me on my bed for a good many days. And now I am but recovering, as white as the paper I write upon, and carrying my head as

one who had been making a failed attempt at suicide; for, in the ardour of my medical practice, I flayed the whole neck of me with a blister. So you see it is a good proof of affection that I here give you, in writing thus speedily, and so long a note.

God bless you, dear John, and all belonging to you. With all my imperfections, believe me ever faithfully and affectionately,

Yours,

JANE CARLYLE.

No lectures to be this spring, or evermore, God willing.

LETTER 26.

Impossible to date with accuracy; the poor incident I recollect well in all its details, but not the point of time. 'Helen' Mitchell, from Kirkcaldy (originally from Edinburgh), must have come about the end of 1837; she stayed with us (thanks to the boundless skill and patience of her mistress) about eleven years; and was, in a sense, the only servant we ever got to belong to us, and be one of our household, in this place. She had been in Rotterdam before, and found Cheyne Walk to resemble the *Boompjes* there (which it does). Arrived here, by cab, in a wet blustery night, which I remember; seemed to have cared no more about the roar and tumult of huge London all the way from St. Katherine's Docks hither, than a clucking hen would have done, sitting safe in its hand-basket, and looking unconcerned to right and left. A very curious little being; mixture of shrewdness, accurate observancy, flashes of an insight almost genial, with utter simplicity and even folly. A singular humble loyalty and genuine attachment to her mistress never failed in poor Helen as the chief redeeming virtues. Endless was her mistress's amusement (among other feelings) with the talk and ways of this poor Helen; which as reported to me, in their native dialect and manner, with that perfect skill, sportfulness, and loving grace of imitation, were to me also among the most amusing things I ever heard. *E.g.* her criticism of Arthur Helps's book (for Helen was a great reader, when she could snatch a bit of time); criticism of Miss Martineau's (highly didactic) 'Maid of All Work' —and 'a rail insipid trick in Darwin to tell Miss Martno!' &c., &c. Poor Helen, well does she deserve this bit of record from me. Her end was sad, and like a thing of fate; as perhaps will be noticed farther on.

This letter I vaguely incline to date about autumn 1840, though sure evidence is quite wanting.

'Toam tuik ta hint.' Our little Craw Jean had a long, inane, comically solemn dialogue to report of an excellent simple old Mrs. Clough (brother Alick's mother-in-law); of which this about 'Toam' (her own Tom) was a kind of cardinal point or (solemnly inane) corner-stone.

'Stream of time' &c., 'Oh Lord, we're a' sailing down the stream of time into the ocean of eternity: for Christ's sake: Amen,' was the Grace before meat (according to myth) of some extempore Christian suddenly called on, and at a loss for words.

To Mrs. Carlyle, Scotsbrig.

Chelsea: Autumn, 1840.

Dear Mother,—I make no excuse for being so long in complying with your often-repeated hint that I should write to you; it is for the like of ' Tom ' to ' take the hint;' but for me, your highly origi-nal daughter-in-law, I am far beyond hints, or even direct com-mands in the matter of letter-writing. I have now, in fact, no character to lose, and make myself quite comfortable in the reflec-tion that, far from feeling any indignant surprise at my silence, my friends will henceforth receive any communication I may vouch-safe them in the course of years as an unexpected favour for which they cannot be too thankful. What do I do with my time, you wonder? With such 'a right easy seat of it,' one might fancy, I should be glad to write a letter now and then, just to keep the devil from my elbow. But Alick's Jenny and all of you were never more mistaken than when you imagine a woman needs half-a-dozen children to keep her uneasy in a hundred ways without that. For my part, I am always as busy as possible; on that side at least I hold out no encouragement to the devil; and yet, suppose you were to look through a microscope, you might be puzzled to discover a trace of what I do. Nevertheless, depend upon it, my doings are not lost; but, invisible to human eyes, they ' sail down the stream of time into the ocean of eternity,' and who knows but I may find them after many days?

At present, I have got a rather heavy burden on my shoulders, the guarding of a human being from the perdition of strong liquors. My poor little Helen has been gradually getting more and more into the habit of tippling, until, some fortnight ago, she rushed down into a fit of the most decided drunkenness that I ever happened to witness. Figure the head of the mystic school, and a delicate fe-male like myself, up till after three in the morning, trying to get the maddened creature to bed; not daring to leave her at large for fear she should set fire to the house or cut her own throat. Finally we got her bolted into the back kitchen, in a corner of which she had established herself all coiled up and fuffing like a young tiger about to spring, or like the Bride of Lammermoor (if you ever heard of that profane book). Next day she looked black with shame and despair; and the next following, overcome by her tears and promises and self-upbraidings, I forgave her again, very much to my own surprise. About half an hour after this forgiveness had been accorded, I called her to make me some batter; it was long of coming, and I rang the bell; no answer. I went down to the kitchen, to see the meaning of all this delay, and the meaning was very clear, my penitent was lying on the floor, dead-drunk, spread out like the three legs of Man,[1] with a chair upset beside her, and in the midst of a perfect chaos of dirty dishes and fragments of broken crockery; the whole scene was a lively epitome of a place that shall be nameless. And this happened at ten in the morning! All that day she remained lying on the floor insensible, or occasionally sitting up like a little bundle of dirt, executing a sort of whinner; we could not imagine how she came to be so long in sobering; but it turned out she had a whole bottle of whisky hidden within reach, to which she crawled till it was finished throughout the day.

After this, of course, I was determined that she should leave. My friends here set to work with all zeal to find me a servant; and a very promising young woman came to stay with me till a permanent character should turn up. This last scene ' transpired ' on the Wednesday; on the Monday she was to sail for Kirkcaldy. All the intervening days, I held out against her pale face, her tears, her despair; but I suffered terribly, for I am really much attached to the poor wretch, who has no fault under heaven but this one. On the Sunday night I called her up to pay her her wages, and to inquire into her future prospects. Her future prospects! it was enough to break anybody's heart to hear how she talked of them. It was all over for her on this earth, plainly, if I drove her away from me who alone have any influence with her. Beside me, she would struggle; away from me, she saw no possibility of resisting what she had come to regard as her fate. You may guess the sequel: I forgave her a third time, and a last time. I could not deny her this one more chance. The creature is so good otherwise. Since then she has abstained from drink, I believe in every shape, finding abstinence, like old Samuel Johnson, easier than temperance; but how long she may be strong enough to persevere in this rigid course, in which lies her only hope, God knows. I am not very sanguine; meanwhile I feel as if I had adopted a child, I find

---

[1] See any Manx halfpenny, common similitude on those coasts.

it necessary to take such an incessant charge of her, bodily and mentally; and my own body and soul generally keep me in work enough, without any such additional responsibility.

Carlyle is reading voraciously, great folios, preparatory to writing a new book. For the rest, he growls away much in the old style; but one gets to feel a certain indifference to his growling; if one did not, it would be the worse for one. I think he committed a great error in sending away his horse; it distinctly did him good: and would have done him much more good if he could have ' damned the expense.' Even in an economical point of view, he would have gained more in the long run by increased ability to work than he spent in making himself healthier; but a wilful man will have his way.

My kind love to Isabella, and all of them; I hope she is stronger now—it was all she seemed to want, to be a first-rate wife. I never forgot her kindness to me last year; though I do not write to her any more than to others.

Affectionately yours,

JANE W. CARLYLE.

LETTER 27.

To Mrs. Stirling,[1] Cottage, Dundee.

5 Cheyne Row, Chelsea: Jan. 8, 1841.

My dear Susan,—I always thought you a woman of admirable good sense; and I rejoice to see that marriage has not spoiled you. This speaks well for your husband too; for I defy any woman, unless she be no better than a stone, to hinder herself from taking something of the colour of the man she lives beside all days of the year. We women are naturally so impressible, so imitative! the more shame to men if we have all the failings they charge us with! Our very self-will, I believe, which they make such a fuss about, is, after all, only a reflex of their own! I find in your letter no less than three several proofs of this admirable good sense; first, you love me the same as ever—that is highly sensible in you; secondly, you improve in admiration of my husband's writings—that also is highly sensible; thirdly, you understand that my silence means nothing but—that I am silent, and that (to use my mother's favourite phrase) is sensible to ' a degree.' Indeed, if my silence is

---

[1] Susan Hunter, now married.

indicative of anything at all, dear Susan, it indicates more trust in your steady sentiments of kindness towards me than I have in the generality of people who profess to love me best. If I thought that you imagined me forgetful, when I am only not making periodical affirmations of my remembrance of you, and that you were to cast me out of your remembrance in consequence, I would write certainly—would conquer my growing repugnance to letter-writing, rather than risk the loss of your affection; but I should not feel so grateful to you as now, with the assurance I have, that I may give way to my indolence, and keep your affection nevertheless.

In fact, in my character of Lion's Wife here, I have writing enough to do, by constraint, for disgusting even a Duchess of Orleans—applications from young ladies for autographs; passionate invitations to dine; announcements of inexpressible longings to drink tea with me;—all that sort of thing, which, as a provincial girl, I should have regarded perhaps as high promotion, but which at this time of day I regard as very silly and tiresome work; fritters away my time in fractionary writing, against the grain, and leaves me neither sense nor spirit for writing the letters which would suggest themselves in course of nature. Dear Susan, I am sorry to say this world looks always the more absurd to me the longer I live in it! But, thank Heaven, I am not the shepherd set over them; so let them go their way: while we, who are a little higher than the sheep, go ours! Now don't be fancying that I am growing into a ' proud Pharisee,' which were even a degree worse than a sheep! Not at all ! I have a bad nervous system, keeping me in a state of greater or less physical suffering all days of my life, and that is the most infallible specific against the sin of spiritual pride that I happen to know of.

I am better this winter, however, than I have been for the last four winters. Only the confinement (I never get across the threshold in frost) is rather irksome, and increases my liability to headache; but it is a great improvement to have no cough and to be able to keep in the perpendicular.

For my husband, he is as usual; never healthy, never absolutely ill; protesting against ' things in general ' with the old emphasis; with an increased vehemence just at present, being in the agonies of getting under way with another book. He has had it in his head for a good while to write a ' Life of Cromwell,' and has been sitting for months back in a mess of great dingy folios, the very look of which is like to give me locked-jaw.

I never see Mrs. Empson; she lives at a distance from me, in another sphere of things. Her being here, however, is an advantage to me, in bringing her father oftener to London; and he does what he can to seem constant. I shall always love him, and feel grateful to him; all my agreeable recollections of Edinburgh I owe to him directly or indirectly; the delightful evenings at 'Mr. John's,' and so much else.

By the way, Susan, I can never understand what you mean by talking of gratitude to me. The gratitude, it seems to me, should be all on my side. But when people love one another, there is no need of debating such points.

I see Mr. C—— once a week or so; he did seem to get a great good of me (perhaps I should say of us; but it is more sincere as I have written it) for a year or two; but latterly I think he has got some new light, or darkness, or I know not what, which makes him seek my company more from habit than from any pleasure he finds in it—'the *waur*[1] for himsel',' [2]—as they say in Annandale. In London, above all places on earth, '*il n'y a point d'homme nécessaire;*' if one gives over liking you, another begins—that is to say if you be likeable, which I may, without outrage to modesty and probability, infer that I am, since so many have liked me, first and last. There is you, away at Dundee, have gone on liking me without the slightest encouragement, for so many mortal years now! And even 'Mr. John,'[3] could not help liking me, though he met me with prepossession that 'I had been a dreadful flirt;' so at least he told his brother, I remember, who in right brotherly fashion reported it to me the first opportunity. If I had only been still unmarried, and had not been obliged to look sharper to my reputation, I would have made your quiet Mr. John pay for that speech!

What a likeable man, by the way, your brother in Edinburgh is;[4] so intelligent and so unpretentious—a combination not often to be found in Edinburgh; so quietly clever and quietly kind. I love quiet things; and quiet good things will carry me to enthusiasm; though, for the rest, my quality of enthusiasm is pretty well got under.

---

[1] *Waur*, worse. [2] *Sel'*, self. [3] Jeffrey.
[4] John Hunter, a worthy and prosperous law official in Edinburgh, residence Craigcrook (Jeffrey's fine villa), fell weak of nerves and died several years ago (note of 1873).

God bless you, dear. Kind regards to your husband and sister.
Carlyle joins me in all good wishes.

Your affectionate

J. CARLYLE.

LETTER 28.

This of the 'bit of lace' I can throw no light on. Some kindly
gift of Sterling's, thrust in by an unexpected crevice (in which he
had great expertness and still greater alacrity)? The black colour
too suggestive in the place it went to?—T. C.

To the Rev. John Sterling, Penzance.

Chelsea: April 29, 1841.

My dear John,—I do not know whether for you, as for old Bur-
ton, 'a woman in tears be as indifferent a spectacle as a goose going
barefoot!' If so, I make you my compliments, and you need not
read any further. But if you have still enough of human feeling
(or, as my husband would call it, '"Minerva Press" tendency')
about you, to feel yourself commoved by such phenomena, it may
interest you to know that, on opening your letter the other day, and
beholding the little 'feminine contrivance' inside, I suddenly and
unaccountably fell a-crying, as if I had gained a loss. I do not
know what of tender and sad and 'unspeakable' there lay for my
imagination in that lace article, folded up, unskilfully enough, by
man's fingers—your fingers; and wrapt round with kind written
words. But so it was; I wept; and, if this was not receiving your
remembrance in the properest way, I beg of you to read me no lecture on the subject; for your lectures are hateful to me beyond expression, and their only practical result is to strengthen me in my
own course.

My husband is not returned yet, is now at his mother's in
Scotland.[1] He will come, I suppose, the beginning of next week.
These three weeks of solitude have passed very strangely with me.
I have been worn out by what the cockneys call 'mental worry.'
His jury-trials, his influenza, &c., all things had been against me.
For the first time in my life, I could sympathize with Byron's
Giaour ; and, so soon as I had the house all to myself, I flung my-
self on the sofa, with the feeling,

> I would not, if I might, be blest.
> I want no Paradise—but rest!

---

[1] To Milne's, at Fryston, in 1841, afterwards to Scotland.

And accordingly the scope of my being ever since has been to approximate, as nearly as possible, to nonentity. And I flatter myself that my efforts have been tolerably successful. Day after day has found me stretched out on my sofa with a circulating library book in my hand, which I have read, if at all, in Darley's fashion —'one eye shut, and the other not open.' Evening after evening, I have dreamt away in looking into the fire, and wondering to see myself here, in this great big absurdity of a world! In short my existence since I was left alone has been an apathy, tempered by emanations of the 'Minervá Press.' Promising! Well, I shall have to return to my post again presently. One has to die at one's post, has one not? The wonderful thing for me is always the prodigiously long while one takes to die. But

> That is the mystery of this wonderful history
> And you wish that you could tell!

There is a copy of ' Emerson's Essays' come for you here. I wish you good of them. God bless you!

Ever your affectionate
JANE CARLYLE.

LETTER 29.

This letter, which I did not know of before, must have produced the 'Foreign Quarterly Review' article, 'Characteristics of German Genius,' which occupies pp. 382–422 in vol. i. of Hare's Book. A letter which tells its own story; solely, in regard to 'Forster' it should be known that he was yet but a new untried acquaintance, and that our tone towards or concerning him, both as 'critic' and as ever-obliging friend, greatly improved itself, on the ample trial there was.

That of 'worst critic in England but one' was John Mill's laughing deliverance, one evening, as I still remember, imitated from Chamfort's *Dites l'avant-dernier car il y a presse.*—T. C.

To John Sterling, Esq., Falmouth.

Chelsea: Jan. 19, 1842.

My dear Friend,—I find myself engaged to write you a sort of business letter, a thing which lies, one would say, rather out of my sphere. But as I have not troubled you with many letters of late, you need not quarrel with the present, though on a subject as uncongenial to my tastes and habits as it can possibly be to yours, Mr. 'Hurdy-Gurdy.'

There is alive at present in God's universe, and likely to live, a man, Forster by name, a barrister, without practice, residing at number fifty-eight Lincoln's-Inn Fields, not unknown to fame as 'the second worst critic of the age,' who has gained himself a tolerable footing in our house and hearts, by, I cannot precisely say, what merits. Latterly, Carlyle has not thought him 'so very bad a critic;' for he finds him here and there taking up a notion of his own, 'as if he understood it.' For my part, I have always thought rather well of his judgment; for, from the first, he has displayed a most remarkable clear-sightedness, with respect to myself; thinking me little short of being as great a genius as my husband. And you, by you also his character as a critic has deserved to be redeemed from contempt; for he it was who wrote the article in the 'Examiner' in praise of 'The Election.'[1] Well! all this preamble was not essential to the understanding of what is to follow; but at least it will not help to darken it, which is as much as could be expected of a female writer.

This man, then, has been taking counsel with me—me of all people that could have been pitched upon—how to give new life to a dying Review, 'The Foreign,' namely.[2] It has passed into the hands of new publishers, Chapman and Hall, active and moneyed men, who are intent on raising a corps of new worthy contributors, who are somehow (I do not understand that part of it) to kill and devour the old editor, a Dr. Worthington, who has been for a long time 'sitting on it as an incubus.' What they are to do next, that they will arrange, I suppose, among themselves. Meanwhile, of course, they are to be handsomely paid for their pains.

Now, in casting our eyes about for men of genius, fit to infuse new life into dead matter, there naturally slid over my lips your name, 'John Sterling, if the "Review" could be helped by a fifty-page article in rhyme!' 'Why not in prose?' said Forster. 'Ah! that is another question; to persuade him to write prose would not be so easy.' 'At all events,' said Forster, with a burst of enthusiasm, 'he can, and shall, and must be applied to.' And, accordingly, he took your address for that purpose. Having consulted with the publishers, for whom he is acting gratuitously as Prime Minister, for the mere love of humanity and his own inward glory, he finds that it were the most promising way of setting about the thing, to apply to you through some personal friend, and he does

---

[1] Sterling's poem, so named.   [2] *Foreign Quarterly*, that is.

me the honour of taking me for such, in which I hope he is not mistaken.

To-day I have a letter from him, from which I extract the most important paragraph (most important for the business in hand that is, for it contains an invitation to dinner, with bright schemes for going to the play):—'Will you propose the article on Dante to Mazzini, and I want you to write and ask John Sterling (indication of celebrity) to write an article for the next "Foreign Quarterly," placing no restraint on his opinions in any way. If he will but consent to do anything, he may be as radical as he was in his last contribution to Conservatism; you have, if your kindness will take it, full authority from me. This Dr. Worthington, it seems, is to be got rid of, and as speedily as possible. If these two articles are supplied, it is supposed that they will go far towards knocking him on the head—a matter of much desirability. That done, Carlyle must help these active and excellent publishers to a good man.

'Thackeray proposes' (remember all this is strictly private, you who accuse me of blabbing) 'offering to keep a hot kitchen (the grand editorial requisite) on a thousand a year. To that there are one or two objections. But he is going to write an article on France and Louis Philippe, which, if he chooses to take pains, none could do better, &c., &c.

So there you have my story. Can you do anything with it? Even if it were only for my private consolation I would like to see some prose from you once more in this world. Think and answer. There is written on the margin of the letter I have quoted, 'The articles as soon as possible!' To which I answered, 'If John Sterling does the thing at all, to be sure he will do it fast.' Carlyle bids me say that he is purposing to write to you in two days.

Remember me in all kindness to your wife, and believe me,

Ever affectionately yours 'til deth,'

JANE CARLYLE.

I have your little Florentine Villa framed and hung up, and I look at it very often for its own beauty and your sake.[1]

---

[1] It is still here, in my dressing-closet (April, 1869).

LETTER 30.

The enclosed notes, I suppose, are from Forster. Mrs. Taylor, who used to be well known to us, became afterwards John Mill's wife.—T. C.

To John Sterling, Esq., Falmouth.

Chelsea: Thursday, Jan.-Feb. 1842.

My Dear Friend,—The inclosed notes, one to yourself and another to myself, will settle, I hope, the question of the article in a satisfactory manner, without my playing at editors any further, or even dawning further on your astonished sense as the Armida of the 'Foreign Quarterly' (Cavaignac used to call Mrs. Taylor 'the Armida of the "London and Westminster."') I was clearly born for the ornamental rather than the useful, and I have no faith in anything being done by going into the teeth of one's nature.

You ask me how I like your last sendings? In answer I must begin a good way off. When you took it into your head to make a quarrel with me about 'The Election,'[1] actually to complain of me to my husband! (complaining of me to myself would not have been half so provoking); when you thus exposed me to you knew not what matrimonial thunders, which however did not on that occasion so much as begin to rumble, my husband knowing me to be innocent in the transaction as a sucking dove; I was angry, naturally. *Et tu brute!* Had I loved you little, I should not have minded; but loving you much, I regarded myself as a *femme incomprise*, and, what was still worse, maltreated. And so, there and then, 'I registered' (like O'Connell) 'a vow in heaven,' never to meddle or make with manuscript of yours any more, unless at your own particular bidding. Accordingly, these manuscripts, sent to Carlyle, I have not had once in my hands. The best passages that he found in them he read aloud to me; that was his pleasure, and so I felt myself at liberty to hear and admire. But from hearing only the best passages, one can form no true judgment as to the whole, so I am not prepared to offer any. Now that you have asked me my opinion, I should have fallen with all my heart to reading 'Strafford,' which was still here; but Carlyle, I knew, did not like it as a whole, whereas I liked extremely those passages he had read

---

[1] Sterling's poem, some secret about which Sterling supposed Mrs. Carlyle to have revealed.

to me, and I liked better to part with it in the admiring mood than the disparaging one; and who could say, if I read it all, but I should turn to his way of thinking about it? So there you have my confession! Only this I need to tell you—I would not give your last letter to C. for the best drama of Shakespeare! and I care little what comes of John Sterling the poet, so long as John Sterling the man is all that my heart wishes him to be.

God bless you, and remember me always as

Your true friend,

JANE CARLYLE.

Shortly after this letter there came ill news from Templand—ill news, or which to her vigilant affection had an ill sound in them, and which indeed was soon followed by a doleful and irreparable calamity there. Something in a letter of her mother's, touching lightly enough on some disorder of health she was under, and treating the case as common and of no significance, at once excited my poor Jeannie's suspicion, and I had to write to Dr. Russell,[1] asking confidentially, and as if for myself only, what the real state of matters was! The Doctor answered cautiously, yet on the whole hopefully, though not without some ambiguity, which was far enough from quieting our suspicions here; and accordingly, almost by next letter (February 23 or 21 I find it must have been), came tidings of a 'stroke,' apoplectic, paralytic; immediate danger now over, but future danger fatally evident!

My poor little woman instantly got ready. That same night (wild, blustering, rainy night, darkness without us and within), I escorted her to Euston Square for the evening train to Liverpool. She was deaf, or all but deaf, to any words of hope I could urge. Never shall I forget her look as she sat in the railway carriage, seat next the window, still close by me, but totally silent, ———— eyes full of sorrowful affection, gloomy pain, and expectation, gazing steadily forward, as if questioning the huge darkness, while the train rolled away. Alas, at Liverpool, her cousins (Maggie still remembers it here, after twenty-seven years) had to answer, ' All is over at Templand, cousin, gone, gone!' and with difficulty, and with all the ingenuity of love and pity, got her conveyed to bed. February 26, 1842, her mother had departed; that 'first stroke' mercifully the final one. 'Uncle John,' &c., from Liverpool, had found now no sister to welcome him; blithe Templand all fallen dark and silent now; Sister Jeannie, Father Walter, Sister Grizzie also no more there.

I followed to Liverpool two days after (funeral already not to be reached by me), found my poor Jeannie still in bed, sick of body, still more of mind and heart, miserable as I had never seen her. The same night I went by mail-coach (no railway farther for me) to Carlisle, thence through Annan, &c., and was at Templand next

---

[1] Of Thornhill, near Templand.

morning for a late breakfast. Journey in all parts of it still strangely memorable to me. Weather hard, hoar-frosty, windy; wrapt in an old dressing-gown with mackintosh buttoned round it, I effectually kept out the cold, and had a strange night of it, on the solitary coach-roof, under the waste-blowing skies, through the mountains, to Carlisle. It must have been Saturday, I now find, Carlisle market-day. Other side of that city we met groups of market-people; at length groups of Scotch farmers or dealers solidly jogging thither, in some of which I recognized old school-fellows! A certain 'Jock Beattie,' perhaps twelve years my senior, a big good-humoured fellow finishing his arithmetics, &c., who used to be rather good to me, him I distinctly noticed after five-and-twenty years, grown to a grizzled, blue-visaged sturdy giant, sunk in comforters and woollen wrappages, plod-plodding there at a stout pace, and still good-humouredly, to Carlisle market (as a big bacon-dealer, &c., it afterwards appeared), and had various thoughts about him, far as he was from thought of me! Jock's father, a prosperous enough country-carpenter, near by the kirk and school of Hoddam, was thrice-great as a ruling-elder (indeed, a very long-headed, strictly orthodox man), well known to my father, though I think silently not so well approved of in all points. 'Wull Beattie,' was my father's name for him. Jock's eldest brother, 'Sandy Beattie,' a Probationer (Licentiate of the Burgher Church), stepping into our school one day, my age then between seven and eight, had reported to my father that I must go into Latin, that I was wasting my time otherwise, which brought me a Ruddiman's 'Rudiments,' something of an event in the distance of the past. At Annan, in the rimy-hazy morning, I sat gazing on the old well-known houses, on the simmering populations now all new to me—very strange, these old unaltered stone-and-mortar edifices, with their inmates changed and gone!—meanwhile there stalked past, in some kind of rusty garniture against the cold, a dull, gloomy, hulk of a figure, whom I clearly recognized for 'Dr. Waugh,'[1] luckless big goose (with something better in him too, which all went to failure and futility), who is to me so tragically memorable! Him I saw in this unseen manner: him and no other known to me there—him also for the last time. Six miles farther, I passed my sister Mary Austin's farmstead in Cummertrees. Poor kind Mary! little did she dream of me so near! At Dumfries, my sister Jean, who had got some inkling, was in waiting where the coach stopped; she half by force hurried me over to her house, which was near, gave me a hot cup of tea, &c., and had me back again in plenty of time. Soon after 10 A.M. I was silently set down by the wayside, beckoned a hedger working not far off to carry my portmanteau the bit of furlong necessary, and, with thoughts enough articulate and inarticulate, entered the old Templand now become so new and ghastly.

For two months and more I had to continue there, sad but not unhappy. Good John Welsh, with his eldest daughter Helen and a lady cousin of his, good active people, were there to welcome me, and had the house all in order. In about a week these all went, but left an excellent old servant; and for the rest of the time I was as if in perfect solitude—my converse with the mute universe mainly. Much there was to settle, and I had to speak and negotiate with various people, Duke's farm-agents; but that was only at intervals and for brief times; and, indeed, all that could have been finished soon, had the agent people (factor, subfactors, &c., &c.) been definite and alert with me, which they by no means were. Nay, ere long, I myself grew secretly to like the entire seclusion, the dumb company of earth and sky, and did not push as I might have done. Once or twice I drove across the hills to Annandale; had one of my brothers, Jamie or Alick, on this or the other 'errand,' over to me for a day; had my dear old mother for perhaps a week at one time; I had also friendly calls to make (resolutely refusing all dinners); but on the whole felt that silence was the wholesome, strengthening, and welcome element. I walked a great deal, my thoughts sad and solemn, seldom or never meanly painful—sometimes in the great joyless stoicism (great as life itself), sometimes of victorious or high. The figure of the actual terrestrial 'spring' (the first I had seen for years, the last I ever saw) was beautiful, symbolic to me, full of wild grandeur and meanings. By day, now bright sunshine and a tinge of hopeful green, then suddenly the storm-cloud seen gathering itself far up in the centre of the hills, and anon rushing down in mad fury, by its several valleys (Nith, &c., &c., which I could count); a canopy of circular storm, split into *spokes*, and whitening everything with snow! I did not read much—nothing that I now recollect: 'Cromwell' books, which were then my serious reading, were, of course, all in Chelsea. By some accident, now forgotten, I had slid into something of correspondence with Lockhart more than I ever had before or after; three or four altogether friendly, serious, and pleasant notes from him I remember there, which I doubt are not now in existence. A hard, proud, but thoroughly honest, singularly intelligent, and also affectionate man, whom in the distance I esteemed more than perhaps he ever knew. Seldom did I speak to him; but hardly ever without learning and gaining something. From 'Satan Montgomery,' too, I was surprised by a letter or two, invoking me (absurdly enough) to 'review' some new book of his (rhymed rigmarole on 'Luther,' I believe), 'Oh, review it, you who *can;* you who,' &c., &c.! Windy soul, flung aloft by popular delusion, he soon after died with all his vanities and glories!

My plan of business had at first been, 'Let us keep this house and garden as they are, and sublet the land; no prettier place of refuge for us could be in the world!' But my poor darling shrank utterly from that, could not hear of it in her broken heart; which, alas, was natural too; so I had to get the lease valued, cancelled; sell off everything, annihilate all vestige of our past time there, a thing I now again almost regret; and certainly, for the moment, it was in itself a very sad operation. The day of the household sale, which was horrible to me, I fled away to Crawford Churchyard (20 miles off, through the pass of Dalveen, &c.), leaving my brothers in charge of everything; spent the day there by my mother-in-law's grave and in driving thither and back; the day was of bright weather, the road silent and solitary. I was not very miserable; it was rather like a day of religious worship, till in the evening, within short way of Templand again, I met people carrying furniture (Oh heaven; found Templand a ruin, as if sown with salt; and had, from various causes, an altogether sorry night in Thornhill. Tedious pedantic 'factor' still lingering and loitering, I had still to wait at Scotsbrig, with occasional rides across to him, and messages and urgencies, before he would conclude; 'paltry little strutting creature,' thought I sometimes (wrongfully, I have been told; at any rate, the poor little soul is now dead, *requiescat, requiescat!*). It was not till the beginning of May that I got actually back to Chelsea, where my poor sorrow-stricken darling with Jeannie, her Liverpool cousin, had been all this while; and of course, though making little noise about it, was longing to have me back.

Her letters during those two months of absence seem to be all lost. I remember their tone of mournful tenderness; the business part, no doubt, related to the bits of memorials and household relics I was to bring with me, which, accordingly, were all carefully packed and conveyed, and remain here in pious preservation to this day: a poor praying child, some helpless enough rustic carving in funeral jet, commemorative of 'John Welsh'; these and other such things, which had pleased her mother, though in secret not *her*, she now accepted with repentant fondness, and kept as precious. She had great care about matters of that kind; had a real, though unbelieving, notion about omens, luck, 'first foot' on New Year's morning, &c.; in fact, with the clearest and steadiest discerning head, a tremulously loving heart! I found her looking pale, thin, weak; she did not complain of health, but was evidently suffering that way too: what she did feel was of the mind, of the heart sunk in heaviness; and of this also she said little, even to me not much. Words could not avail: a mother and mother's love were gone, irrevocable; the sunny fields of the past had all become sunless, fateful, sorrowful, and would smile no more! A mother dead: it is an epoch for us all; and to each one of us it comes with a pungency as if peculiar, a look as of originality and singularity! Once or oftener she spoke to me in emphatic self-reproach, in vehement repentance about her mother: though seldom had any daughter intrinsically less ground for such a feeling. But, alas, we all have ground for it! could we but think of it sooner; inexpressible the sadness to think of it too late. That little fact of the 'two candles' mentioned above,[1] reserved in sad penitence to be her own death-lights after seven-and-twenty years—what a voice is in that, piercing to one's very soul! All her mother's 'poor people,' poor old half-crazy 'Mary Mills,' and several others (for Mrs. Welsh was ever beneficent and soft of heart), she took the strictest inheritance of, and punctually transmitted from her own small pin-money their respective doles at the due day, till the last of them died and needed no gift more. I well remember, now with emotion enough, the small bank cheques I used to write for her on those occasions,

---

[1] *Reminiscences*, p. 316. Harper's Edition.

always accurately paid me on the spot, from her own small, small fund of pin-money (I do believe, the smallest any actual London lady, and she was ever emphatically such, then had). How beautiful is noble poverty! richer, perhaps, than the noblest wealth! For the rest, I too have my self-reproaches; my sympathy for her, though sincere and honest, was not always perfect; no, not as hers for me in the like case had been. Once, and once only, she even said to me (I forget altogether for what) some thrice-sad words, 'It is the first time you show impatience with my grief, dear'—words which pain my heart at this moment. Ah me! 'too late'; I also too late!

The summer could not but pass heavily in this manner; but it did grow quieter and quieter. Little cousin Jeannie was very affectionate and good; my own return had brought something of light into the household; various kind friends we had, who came about us diligently. Time itself, the grand soother and physician, was silently assuaging—never fails to do so, unless one is oneself too near the *finis!* Towards autumn Mrs. Buller, who had at the first meeting, years ago, recognized my Jeannie, and always, I think, liked her better and better, persuaded her to a visit of some three weeks out to Troston in Suffolk, where Mrs. Buller herself and husband were rusticating with the Rev. Reginald, their youngest son, who was parson there. This visit took effect, and even prospered beyond hope, agreeable in every essential way; entertaining to the parties; and lasted beyond bargain. It was the first reawakening to the sight of life for my poor heavy-laden one; a salutary turning aside, what we call diversion, of those sad currents and sad stagnancies of thought into fruitfuller course; and, I think, did her a great deal of good. Lucid account is given of it in the six following letters which we have now arrived at, which I still recollect right well.—T. C.

[Before these letters, I introduce two of many written in the interval by Mrs. Carlyle to other friends after her mother's death. The first is to the wife of the physician who attended Mrs. Welsh in her last illness.—J. A. F.]

LETTER 31.

To Mrs. Russell, Thornhill.

5 Cheyne Row, Chelsea: Tuesday, April 1842.

My dear Mrs. Russell,—I sit down to write to you at last! But how to put into written words what lies for you in my heart! If I were beside you, I feel as if I should throw myself on your neck, and cry myself to rest like a sick child. At this distance, to ask in cold writing all the heart-breaking things I would know of you, and to say all the kind things I would say for her and myself, is indeed quite impossible for me. You will come and see me, will you not, before very long? I can never go there again; but you will come to me? travelling is made so easy now! And I should feel such gratification in receiving into my own house one who was ever so dearly welcome in hers, and who, of all who loved her, was, by one sad chance and another, the only one whose love was any help to her when she most needed our love! She blessed you for the comfort you gave her, and you shall be blessed for it here and hereafter. The dying blessing of such a pure fervent heart as hers cannot have been pronounced on you in vain; and take my blessing also, 'kind sweet' woman! a less holy one, but not less sincerely given!

Will you wear the little thing I inclose in remembrance of me, and of this time? You will also receive, through my cousin in Liverpool, a little box, and scarf, of hers, which I am sure you will like to have; and along with these will be sent to your care a shawl for Margaret Hiddlestone, who is another that I shall think of with grateful affection, as long as I live, for the comfort which she bestowed on her during the last weeks. I think Dr. Russell has some of her books; I desired that he should have them. He has given me an inestimable gift in that letter; for which I deeply thank him, and for so much else. Remember me to your father. I sent him the poor old *Tablet* last week; I know he used to get it from her. Will you write two or three lines to my Aunt Ann—you sometimes write to her, I believe—and say to her that, although returned to London, and a good deal better in health, I am still incapable of much exertion of any sort, and have not yet set about answering my letters? She sent me a long sermon, to which she has, no doubt, looked for some reply; it was well meant, and I would not offend her, but I am not up to correspondences of that sort just now.

All good be with you all. Think of me, and pray for me; I have much need of more help than lies in myself, to bear up against the stroke that has fallen on me.

Ever affectionately yours,

JANE CARLYLE.

LETTER 32.

To Miss Margaret Welsh,[1] Liverpool.

Chelsea: Friday, July 15, 1842.

My dear Maggie,—It was a good thought in you to send me the little purse, and I feel very grateful to you for it. This last birth-

---

[1] Daughter of John Welsh, sister of Helen.

day was very sad for me, as you may easily suppose, very unlike what it was last year, and all former years; and I needed all the heartening kind souls could give me. But, by your kindness and that of others, the day was got over with less of a forsaken feeling than could have been anticipated. Only think of my husband, too, having given me a little present! he who never attends to such nonsenses as birthdays, and who dislikes nothing in the world so much as going into a shop to buy anything, even his own trowsers and coats; so that, to the consternation of cockney tailors, I am obliged to go about them. Well, he actually risked himself in a jeweller's shop, and bought me a very nice smelling-bottle![1] I cannot tell you how *wae* his little gift made me, as well as glad; it was the first thing of the kind he ever gave to me in his life. In great matters he is always kind and considerate; but these little attentions, which we women attach so much importance to, he was never in the habit of rendering to anyone; his up-bringing, and the severe turn of mind he has from nature, had alike indisposed him towards them. And now the desire to replace to me the irreplaceable, makes him as good in little things as he used to be in great.

Helen's box arrived this morning; so like a Templand box! Alas, alas! those preserves! I had thought about making some all this time, and never could bring myself to set about it. It was not only to make them, but to learn to make them, for me; and I had finally settled it with myself that I must be stronger before I did such out-of-the-way things. So that in every way Helen's present is welcome; most of all welcome for the kind consideration it shows for my helplessness, and the quantity of really disagreeable labour she has imposed on herself for my sake. Give her my kindest love, and say I will write in a day or two to herself. I have been meaning to write to her every day this week back, but the pigs have always run through the good intention.

Jeannie expresses surprise at the fancy of 'sending coffee to Chelsea;' but, for my share, I find the 'fancy' extremely reasonable, considering that when I was in Liverpool I brought coffee from there to Chelsea, and a very good speculation it turned out.

Thank my uncle for his golden kiss. I am thinking seriously what to do with it, as I never eat snaps; and besides would rather

---

[1] Carlyle never forgot her birthday afterwards. Regularly, as July came round, I find traces of some remembrance—some special letter with some inclosed present.—J. A. F.

invest such an amount of capital in something of a permanent character, that might remind me of him more agreeably than by an indigestion; but, for my life, I cannot fix upon anything that I need, and to buy something that I feel to be superfluous is so little in my way! I think I shall let it be in the purse for good luck till winter, and then buy something particularly cosy to put about my throat.

As to 'Miss Jeannie's' return, I can only tell you that neither I nor anybody else hereabouts show any symptoms of 'tiring of her;' the first person to tire, I imagine, will be herself. Her picture is come home from the frame-maker, and looks very fine indeed in its gilt ornamentality. I think it perfectly like, and a beautiful little picture withal, wherein, however, I differ from many persons, who say it 'is not flattered enough'; as if a picture must needs be flattered to be what it ought to be.

We went down the water last night to take tea with the Chaplain of Guy's Hospital; found him and his wife in the country, and had to return tea-less, rather belated, and extremely cold; the consequence of which *bêtise* is, that to-day I am hoarse, with a soreish head and soreish throat; so you will excuse my horrible writing. God bless you all.

Ever your affectionate Cousin,
Jane Carlyle.

LETTER 33.

The Buller family consisted of three sons: Charles, M.P. &c., a man of distinguished faculties and qualities, who was now at length rising into recognition, influence, and distinction; and might have risen far, had his temper of mind been more stubbornly earnest; perhaps I may say, had his bodily constitution been more robust! For he was of weak health, lamed of a leg in childhood; had an airy winged turn of thought, flowing out in lambencies of beautiful spontaneous wit and fancy, which were much admired in society, and too much attracted him thither; so that, with all his integrity, cleverness, and constant veracity of intellect and of character, he did not, nor ever could, as a 'reformer,' so much express his inborn detestation of the base and false by practically working to undo it, as by showering witty scorn upon it; in which, indeed, I never saw his rival, had that been the way to do good upon it. Poor Charles, only five years afterwards he died, amid universal regret, which did not last long, nor amount to anything! He had procured for his younger brother Arthur, who was my other pupil, some law appointment in Ceylon, which proved sufficient; and for his youngest brother Reginald (who used to dine with me in Edinburgh in the tutor times, an airy, pen-drawing, skipping clever enough little creature then) a richish country living; where, as utterly stupid somnolent 'Reverend Incumbent,' he placidly vegetated thence-forth, and still vegetates. Thackeray the novelist had been a college companion of his own; that perhaps is now his chief distinction.

Mr. and Mrs. Charles Buller, senior, who now lead a somewhat nomadic life, in the manner of ex-Indians of distinction, were superior people both; persons of sound judgment, of considerable culture and experience, of thoroughly polite manners (Madam considerably in the Indian style, as ex-'queen of Calcutta,' which she was, with a great deal of sheet-lightning in her ways). Charles, senior, was considerably deaf, a real sorrow to one so fond of listening to people of sense; for the rest, like his wife, a person of perfect probity, politeness, truthfulness, and of a more solid type than she; he read (idly, when he must), rode for exercise, was, above all, fond of chess, in which game he rarely found his superior. Intrinsically these excellent people had from the first, and all along, been very good to me; never boggled at my rustic outside or melancholic dyspeptic ways, but took, with ardent welcome, whatever of best they could discern within—over-estimating all, not under-estimating—especially not 'the benefit,' &c. Charles, junior, was getting of me. Indeed, talent of all real kinds was dear to them (to the lady especially); and at bottom the measure of human worth to both. Nobody in London, accordingly, read sooner what my rural Jeannie intrinsically was; discerned better what graces and social resources might lie under that modest veiling; or took more eagerly to profiting by these capabilities whenever possible. Mrs. Buller was, by maiden name, Kirkpatrick, a scion of the Closeburn (Dumfriesshire) people, which, in its sort, formed another little tie.—T. C.

To T. Carlyle, Esq., Chelsea.

Troston, near St. Edmundsbury, Suffolk: Friday, Aug. 11, 1842.

Here I am then, dearest, established at Troston Rectory, my clothes all in the drawers; one night over; and for the rest, the body and soul of me 'as well as can be expected.' The journey was less fatiguing than we had supposed; the coach got into Bury at three instead of five; and Mr. Buller and the carriage revealed themselves immediately to my searching eyes. Except my parasol, I committed no further stupidity. At eleven o'clock I ate a small Ghent loaf, or the greater part of it (and a very good little loaf it proved to be), a small biscuit, and a bit of Jeannie's barley-sugar; and at two I ate the Ghent . . . . proved to be grey rye with currants in it. I had also, through the politeness of the gentleman in the grey jacket, a glass of water, slightly flavoured with onions. We did not sit in coach on the railway; they put us into a railway carriage, only leaving the luggage in the coach. The country, most part of the way, reminded me of East Lothian; hereabouts it is richer, and better wooded. The harvest was going on briskly —this to show you that I did not sit 'with my eyes on the apron of the gig.'

My reception here was most cordial: Mrs. Buller met me with open arms (literally), and called me 'dear, *dear* Mrs. Carlyle'; which, from a woman so little expansive, was highly flattering. She looks dreadfully ill; as if she were only kept alive by the force of her own volition; and is more out of spirits than I ever saw her. No wonder! for little Theresa is gone away, and they feel her loss as much as if she had been their real child. Theresa's mother has fallen ill—of consumption, the doctors say—and is ordered to the South of France, as the only means of prolonging her life for a year or so. She wished to have her child go with her, and Mrs. Buller could not resist her wishes, under the circumstances; so the little thing was sent off to her, attended by a governess, three days ago. The mother is a most amiable and unfortunate woman, Mrs. Buller says; and she seems to have been on the most intimate terms with her. But Mrs. Buller reads George Sand, like me.

This rectory is a delightful place to be in, in warm weather; but in winter, it must be the reverse of comfortable; all the room-windows opening as doors into the garden, vines hanging over them, &c., &c. It is a sort of compromise between a country parsonage, and an aristocratic cottage; and compromises never are found to answer, I think, in the long run. It stands in the midst of green fields and fine tall trees; with the church (if such an old dilapidated building can be called a church) within a bowshot of it. Around the church is a little quiet-looking church-yard, which, with the sun shining on it, does not look at all sad. A foot-path about half-a-yard wide, and overgrown with green, and strewn with fallen apples, cuts across the bit of green field between the church and the rectory, and being the only road to the church, one may infer from it several things!

I went into the church last night with Reginald, while Mrs. Buller was having her drive; and when I looked at *him* and *it*, and thought of the four hundred and fifty living souls who were to be saved through such means, I could almost have burst into tears. Anything so like the burial-place of revealed religion you have never seen, nor a rector more fit to read its burial-service! The church-bell rings, night and morning, with a plaintive clang. I asked, 'Was it for prayers?' 'No, it was to warn the gleaners that it was their time to go out and to come in.' ' *Monsieur, cela vous fera un*,' &c.[1]

Let no mortal hope to escape night-noises so long as he is above ground! *Here*, one might have thought that all things, except perhaps the small birds rejoicing, would have let one alone, and the fact is that, with one devilry after another, I have had hardly any sleep, for all so dead-weary as I lay down. Just as I was dropping asleep, between eleven and twelve, the most infernal serenade commenced, in comparison of which the shrieking of Mazeppa[2] is soothing melody. It was an ass, or several asses, braying as if the devil wère in them, just under my open window! It ceased after a few minutes, and I actually got to sleep, when it commenced again, and I sprang up with a confused notion that all the Edinburgh watchmen wère yelling round the house, and so on all night! An explosion of ass-brays every quarter of an hour! Then, about four, commenced never so many cocks, challenging each other all over the parish, with a prodigious accompaniment of rooks cawing; ever and anon enlivened by the hooing and squealing of a child, which my remembrance of East Lothian instructed me was some vermin of a creature hired to keep off the crows from the grain. Of course, to-day I have a headache, and if succeeding nights are not quieter, or if I do not use to the noise, my stay will not be very long. I am now writing in my own room (which is very pleasant to sit in), taking time by the forelock, in case my head should get worse instead of better, and then, if you were cut out of your letter, 'you would be vaixed.'[3] The post leaves Ixworth in the evening, but it is two miles to Ixworth, and the letters get there as they can; Mrs. Buller generally takes her afternoon drive in that direction. Letters come in the morning, and this morning I found the French newspaper on the table for me.

I breakfast with Mr. Buller and Reginald at nine, preferring that to having it brought to my room as Mrs. Buller recommended.

I will not write any more to-day, but take care of my head, which needs it. So you must give my love to Jeannie, and a kiss, and bid her do the best she can on that short common till I am rested. God bless you, my dear husband. I hope you are rested,

---

[1] *Grand plaisir*, perhaps.

[2] A wild horse, which we sometimes hear stamping, &c., here.

[3] A foolish, innocent old Scotch lady's phrase, usually historical or prophetic, and not a little unimportant.

and going to Lady Harriet;[1] and I hope you will think of me a great deal, and be as good to me when I return as you were when I came away—I do not desire any more of you.

Your own

J. C.

LETTER 34.

To T. Carlyle, Esq., Chelsea.

Sunday morning, Aug. 14, 1842.

My Dearest,—There are two notes from you this morning, one on each side of my plate; the first, having the address of Bury, only came along with the third; so be sure you keep by Ixworth in future. As for 'Keeting,' it turned out on investigation to be neither more nor less than Mrs. Buller's way of writing Rectory.

It is much better with me now, and I find myself quite hefted to my new position. But I shall not soon forget the horrors of the first day; feeling myself growing every moment worse; away from you all, and desperated by the notion of confessing myself ill, and going to bed, and causing a fuss among strangers!

After having written to you, I tried sauntering among the trees; tried lying on the sofa in my own room; tried eating dinner (which is rationally served up here at three o'clock), and finally tried a drive in the carriage with Mrs. Buller, all the while saying nothing. But instead of admiring the beauties of Livermere Park, which they took me to see, I was wondering whether I should be able to 'stave off' fainting till I got back. On 'descending from the carriage,'[2] I had finally to tell Mrs. Buller I was ill and would go to bed. She came upstairs after me, and offered me sal volatile, &c.; but seeing that I would have nothing, and wanted only to be let alone, she, with her usual good-breeding, pinned the bell-rope to my pillow, and went away. A while after, feeling myself turning all cold and strange, I considered would I ring the bell; I did not, and what came of me I cannot tell—whether I fainted, or suddenly fell dead-asleep; but when I opened my eyes, as it seemed, a minute or two after, it was quite dark, and a maid was lighting a night lamp at the table! I asked what o'clock it was? 'Half-past eleven! Would I have tea?' No. 'Did I want anything?' No.

---

[1] Lady Harriet Baring, afterwards Lady Ashburton.

[2] '*Scende da carrossa*,' &c., said the Signora degli Antoni, describing the erratic town life of a brilliant acquaintance here.

She was no sooner gone than I fell naturally asleep; and when the cocks awoke me after daylight, I was quite free of pain, only desperately wearied.

The asses did not return the second night, nor last night, and I manage better or worse to weave the dogs, cocks, and rooks into my dreams. My condition has undergone a further amelioration, from having the mattress laid above the down-bed; it was like to choke me, besides that I lately read somewhere horrible things about the 'miasma' contracted by down-beds from all their various occupants through successive generations! and my imagination got disagreeably excited in consequence.

For the rest, nothing can be better suited to my wants than the life one has here; so that I feel already quite at home, and almost wishing that you were Rector of Troston—what a blessed exchange would it be for those poor people, whom I hear this moment singing feckless psalms! I could almost find in my heart to run over to the old tower, and give them a word of admonition myself. Reginald does not preach in the morning, he reads service merely, and preaches in the afternoon; I shall go then to see 'how the cretur gets through with it.' I have not made out yet whether there is a downright want in him, or whether his faculties are sunk in shameful indolence. He is grown very much into the figure of Mr. Ogilvie in miniature; when he speaks I dare not look at his mother, and feel it a mercy for his father that he is so deaf. The old people do not mean to remain here,—the climate does not suit Mrs. Buller in winter; but they have not made up their minds whether to remove altogether or to hire some place during the cold weather. Oh dear me! 'They[1] have trouble that have the worl'

---

[1] In pious Scotland 'the worl',' or 'worl's gear,' signifies riches. Margaret (Smith) Aitken, an Annandale farmer's wife, of small possessions, though of large and faithful soul, had (perhaps a hundred years ago), by strenuous industry and thrift, saved for herself twenty complete shillings—an actual £1 note, wholly her own, to do what she liked with!—and was much concerned to lay it up in some place of absolute safety against a rainy day. She tried anxiously all her 'hussives,' boxes, drawers, a cunning hole in the wall, various places, but found none satisfactory, and was heard ejaculating, to the amusement of her young daughters, who never forgot it, 'They have trouble that hae the worl', and trouble that haena't!' There is a Spanish proverb to the same purpose: 'Cuidados acarrea el oro, y cuidados la falta de él.'

This Margaret Smith, a native of Annan, and, by all accounts, a kinswoman to be proud of (or, silently, to be thankful to heaven for), was my mother's mother. It was my mother (Margaret Aitken Carlyle) who told us this story about her, with a tone of gentle humour, pathos, and heart's love, which we

and trouble that want it.' I do not know whether it be worst to be without the power of indulging one's reasonable wishes or to have the power of indulging one's whims. So many people we know seem to have no comfort with their money, just because it enables them to execute all their foolish schemes.

Jeannie writes to me that when you discovered my parasol [1] you 'crossed your hands in despair' as if you had seen 'the sun's perpendicular heat' already striking down on me. I thought you would be vexing yourself about it; but I have not missed it in the least; the drive here the first day was cold; and since then I have had a parasol of Mrs. Buller's, who rejoices in two. And now goodbye, dearest, I have two nice long letters from Jeannie to return some acknowledgment for.

Your own
JANE C.

LETTER 35.

To T. Carlyle, Esq., Chelsea.

Troston: Monday, Aug. 15, 1842.

Dearest,—It was the stupidest-looking breakfast this morning without any letters!—the absence of the loaf or coffee-pot would have been less sensibly felt! However, there is no redress against these London Sundays.

I went to church yesterday afternoon, according to programme, and saw and heard 'strange things, upon my honour.' [2]

---

were used to on such a subject. I doubt whether I ever saw this good grandmother. A vivid momentary image of some stranger, or, rather, of a formidable glowing chintz gown belonging to some stranger, who might have been she, still rises perfectly certain to me, from my second or third year; but more probably it was her sister, my grand-aunt Barbara, of Annan, with whom I afterwards boarded when at school there (1806–1808), and whom I almost daily heard muttering and weeping about her 'dear Margaret,' and their parting 'at the dyke-end' (near Cargenbridge, Dumfries neighbourhood, I suppose, perhaps six years before), 'sae little thinking it was for the last time!' It is inconceivable (till you have seen the documents) what the pecuniary poverty of Scotland was a hundred years ago; and, again (of which also I, for one, still more indubitably 'have the documents'), its spiritual opulence—opulence fast ending in these years, think some? Californian nuggets *versus* jewels of Heaven itself, that is a ruining barter! I know rather clearly, and have much considered, the history of my kindred for the third and second generations back, and lament always that it is not in my power to speak of it at all to the flunkey populations now coming and come.

[1] Left behind.   [2] Phrase of Mazzini's, frequently occurring.

The congregation consisted of some thirty or forty poor people—chiefly adults; who all looked at me with a degree of curiosity rather 'strong' for the place. Reginald ascended the pulpit in his white vestment, and, in a loud sonorous, perfectly Church-of-England-like tone, gave out the Psalm, whereupon there arose, at the far end of the mouldering church, a shrill clear sound, something between a squeal of agony and the highest tone of a bagpipe! I looked in astonishment, but could discover nothing; the congregation joined in with the invisible thing, which continued to assert its predominance, and it was not till the end of the service that Hesketh[1] informed me that the strange instrument was 'a clarionet'! Necessity is the mother of invention.

The service went off quite respectably; it is wonderful how little faculty is needed for saying prayers perfectly well! But when we came to the sermon!—greater nonsense I have often enough listened to—for, in fact, the sermon (Mrs. Buller, with her usual sincerity, informed me before I went) 'was none of his'; he had scraped together as many written by other people as would serve him for years, 'which was much better for the congregation;' but he delivered it exactly as daft Mr. Hamilton[2] used to read the newspaper, with a noble disdain of everything in the nature of a stop; pausing just when he needed breath, at the end of a sentence, or in the middle of a word, as it happened! In the midst of this extraordinary exhortation an infant screamed out, 'Away, mammy! Let's away!' and another bigger child went off in whooping cough! For my part, I was all the while in a state between laughing and crying; nay, doing both alternately. There were two white marble tablets before me, containing one the virtues of a wife and the sorrow of a husband (Capel Loft), the other a beautiful character of a young girl dead of consumption; and both concluded with the 'hopes of an immortality through Jesus Christ.' And there was an old sword and sword-belt hung on the tomb of another, killed in Spain at the age of twenty-eight; he also was to be raised up through Jesus Christ; and this was the Gospel of Jesus Christ I was hearing—made into something worse than the cawing of rooks. I was glad to get out, for my thoughts rose into my throat at last, as if they would choke me; and I privately vowed never to go there when worship was going on again.

We drove as usual in the evening, and also as usual played the

---

[1] Mr. Buller's butler.   [2] Old Haddington phenomenon.

game at chess—'decidedly improper,' but I could not well refuse.
I sat in my own room reading for two hours after I went upstairs;
slept indifferently, the heat being extreme, and the cocks indefatigable; and now Mrs. Buller has sent me her revised 'Play,'
begging I will read it, and speak again my candid opinion as to its
being fit to be acted. So goodbye, dearest, I shall have a letter to-
morrow. Love to Babbie.[1] I wish she had seen the Queen.

> Affectionately yours,
> JANE CARLYLE.

LETTER 36.

To T. Carlyle, Esq., Chelsea.

Troston: Wednesday, Aug. 17, 1842.

Dearest,—There will be no news from me at Chelsea this day: it
is to be hoped there will not be any great dismay in consequence.
The fact is, you must not expect a daily letter; it occasions more
trouble in the house than I was at first aware of; nobody goes from
here regularly to the Post-office, which is a good two miles off;
only, when there are letters to be sent, Mr. and Mrs. Buller take
Ixworth in their evening drive and leave them at the post-office
themselves. Now, twice over, I have found on getting to Ixworth
that, but for my letters, there would have been no occasion to go
that road, which is an ugly one, while there are beautiful drives in
other directions; besides that, they like, as I observe, to show me
the county to the best advantage. They write, themselves, hardly
any letters; those that come are left by somebody who passes this
way from Ixworth early in the morning. Yesterday after breakfast, Mr. Buller said we should go to Ampton in the evening—a
beautiful deserted place belonging to Lord Calthorpe—'unless,' he
added, raising his eyebrows, 'you have letters to take to Ixworth.'
Of course I said my writing was not so urgent that it could not be
let alone for a day. And to Ampton we went, where Reginald and
I clambered over a high gate, with spikes on the top of it, and enjoyed a stolen march through gardens unsurpassed since the original Eden, and sat in a pavilion with the most Arabian-tale-looking
prospect; 'the Kingdom of the Prince of the Black Islands' it
might have been!—and peeped in at the open windows of the old
empty house—empty of people, that is—for there seemed in it

---

1 Cousin Jeannie.

everything mortal could desire for ease with dignity: such quantities of fine bound books in glass bookcases, and easy-chairs, &c., &c.! And this lovely place Lord Calthorpe has taken some disgust to; and has never set foot in it again! Suppose you write and ask him to give it to us! He is nearly mad with Evangelical religion, they say; strange that he does not see the sense of letting somebody have the good of what he cannot enjoy of God's providence himself! 'Look at this delicious and deserted place, on the one side, and the two thousand people[1] standing all night before the Provost's door, on the other! And yet you believe,' says Mrs. Buller, 'that it is a good spirit who rules this world.'

You never heard such strange discourse as we go on with, during the hour or so we are alone before dinner! How she contrives, with such opinions or no opinions, to keep herself so serene and cheerful, I am perplexed to conceive: is it the old story of the 'cork going safely over the falls of Niagara, where everything weightier would sink?' I do not think she is so light as she gives herself out for—at all events, she is very clever, and very good to me.

On our return from Ampton, we found Mr. Loft waiting to tea with us—the elder brother of the Aids-to-Self-Development Loft—an affectionate, intelligent-looking man, but 'terribly off for a language.'[2] Though he has been in India, and is up in years, he looks as frightened as a hare. There were also here yesterday the grandees of the district, Mr. and the Lady Agnes Byng—one of the Pagets 'whom we all know'—an advent which produced no inconsiderable emotion in our Radical household! For my part, I made myself scarce; and thereby 'missed,' Reginald told me, 'such an immensity of petty talk—the Queen, the Queen, at every word with Lady A.'

---

[1] Paupers, probably, but I have forgotten the incident.

[2] Rev. Dr. Waugh, principal Scotch preacher in London, was noted, among other things, for his kindness to poor incidental Scotchmen, who, in great numbers, applied to him for guidance, for encouragement, or whatever help he could give, in their various bits of intricacies and affairs here. One of these incidental clients, a solid old pedlar ('up on business,' second-hand, most probably) had come one day, and was talking with 'the mistress,' who said, at one point of the dialogue: 'Well, Saunders, how do you like the people here?' 'Oh, very weel, m'em; a nice weel-conditioned people, good-natured, honest, very clever, too, in business things; an excellent people—but terribly aff for a lang-aitch, m'em!' (This story was current in Edinburgh in my young time; Dr. Waugh much the theme in certain circles there.)

I.—5

LETTER 37.

To T. Carlyle, Esq., Chelsea.

Troston: Saturday, Aug. 20, 1842.

Oh dear me! how deceitful are appearances! Who would not say, to look at this place, that it was one of the likeliest places 'here down' on which to be 'poured out of a jug'?[1] and the fact is, that sleep is just the one thing that is not to be had in sufficiency for love or money! Every night brings forth some new variety of assassin to murder sleep! The animals here seem to be continually finding themselves in a new position! And the protests and appeals to posterity[2] that ensue, in shape of braying, lowing, crow-ing, cackling, barking, howling, &c., are something the like of which I have not found in Israel! Last night it was hardly possible for me to close my eyes a minute together, with the passionate wailing of what seemed to be a most ill-used dog, not only (I fancied) excluded from its proper home, but also robbed of its young; another or two other such nights will send me home 'with my finger in my mouth to two people both alike gleg!'[3] For I feel that no country air, or country diet, or country drives, or country anything, can make up for such deprivation of my natural rest. It was horrible really!—an everlasting wail as of 'infants in the porch'[4] mixed up with howls of fury and denunciation, from eleven at night till six in the morning, when I trust in Heaven the

---

[1] Driving up Piccadilly once, on a hot summer day, I had pointed out to her a rough human figure, lying prostrate in the Green Park, under the shade of a tree, and very visibly asleep at a furlong's distance. 'Look at the Irishman yonder; in what a depth of sleep, as if you had poured him out of a jug!' I still remember her bright little laugh.

[2] '*Vous êtes des injustes,*' said a drunken man, whom boys were annoying; '*je m'en appelle à la postérité!*' (One of Cavaignac's stories.)

[3] Wull Maxwell, Alick's ploughman at Craigenputtock, one of the stupidest fellows I ever saw, had been sent on some message down the glen, for behoof of Alick, and 'That'll no duih for an answer,' Wull had said to the be-messaged party; 'what'll a duih wi' that for an answer, and twae men, baith alike gleg' (acute, alert; German, *klug*), 'sitting waiting for me yonder?'

[4] Continuô auditæ voces, vagitus et ingens,
 Infantumque animæ flentes in limine primo;
 Quos dulcis vitæ exsortes, et ab ubere raptos,
 Abstulit atra dies, et funere mersit acerbo.

VIRGIL, *Æneid*, vi. 426-430.

poor brute fell down dead. And no whisper of it has since reached my ears; but

> Once give the fish a frying,
> What helps it that the river run? [1]

All is quiet now externally; but my heart is jumping about in me like Mrs. Grove's frog after the first drop of tea! In the few moments that I slept, I dreamt that my mother came to me, and said that she knew of 'a beautiful place where it was so quiet!'— and she and I would go there by ourselves, for some weeks. But somehow we got into different railway trains; and when I could not find her any more, I screamed out, and awoke,[2] and the dog was giving a long howl.

They are very anxious you would come, 'and bring Miss Jeannie along with you. Regy would be delighted to have a young lady' —more delighted, I imagine, than the young lady would be to have Regy! although he does improve on acquaintance. Laziness, and what his mother calls 'muddling habits,' are the worst things one can charge him with—one of the people who, with the best intentions, are always unfortunate;[3] but he is very sweet-tempered and kindly; deserves really the only epithet that remained to him—seeing that there was already 'the clever Buller' and 'the handsome Buller'—viz.: 'the good Buller.' If he were not so completely the victim of snuff, I should think an attractive Babbie might be beneficial to him; but I would as soon undertake the reformation of a drunkard as of anybody that snuffs as he does.

If it were not for the sleeping part of the business, I would back Mrs. Buller's exhortations to you to come, with my own. But when one of us prospers so badly in that matter, I see not what would become of two! Write a line to Mrs. Buller herself, anyhow, that she may not think her kind invitations quite overlooked.

---

[1]   COMFORTERS.

> 'Oh, cease this well-a-daying,
> Think of the faithful saying,
> "New joy when grief is done!"'

JOB.

> 'To mock me are you trying?
> Once give the fish a frying,
> What helps him that the river run?'

GOETHE.

[2] Ah, me, what a dream!   [3] Phrase of brother John's.

I shall return, I think, the week after next; if this dog goes on, sooner. They do not seem to be at all wearying of me; but it were too long if I waited to see symptoms of that. So far, I am confident I have not been in their way, but quite the reverse; the chess is a great resource for Mr. Buller in the first loneliness occasioned by the loss of little Theresa; and Mrs. Buller seems to get some good of talking with me: as for Reginald, now that he has conquered, or rather that I have conquered, his first terror, he does not seem to have anything to object to me very particularly.

[Last leaf wanting.]

LETTER 38.

To T. Carlyle, Esq., Chelsea.

Troston: Tuesday, Aug. 23, 1842.

My dear Husband,—The pen was in my hand to write yesterday; but nothing would have come out of me yesterday except 'literature of desperation;'[1] and, aware of this, I thought it better to hold my peace for the next twenty-four hours, till a new night had either habilitated me for remaining awhile longer, or brought me to the desperate resolution of flying home for my life. Last night, Heaven be thanked, went off peaceably; and to-day I am in a state to record my last trial, without danger of becoming too tragical, or alarming you with the prospect of my making an unseemly termination of my visit. (Oh, what pens!)

To begin where I left off. On Sunday, after writing to you, I attended the afternoon service! Regy looked so *wae* when I answered his question 'whether I was going?' in the negative, that a weak pity induced me to revise my determination. 'It is a nice pew, that of ours,' said old Mr. Buller; 'it suits me remarkably well, for, being so deep, I am not overlooked: and in virtue of that, I read most part of the *Femme de Qualité* this morning!' 'But don't,' he added, 'tell Mr. Regy this! Had Theresa been there, I would not have done it, for I like to set a good example!' I also turned the depth of the pew to good account; when the sermon began, I made myself, at the bottom of it, a sort of Persian couch out of the praying-cushions; laid off my bonnet, and stretched myself out very much at my ease. I seemed to have been thus just one

---

[1] *Litteratur der Verzweiflung* was Goethe's definition of Victor Hugo and Co.'s new gospel.

drowsy minute when a slight rustling and the words 'Now to Father, Son, and Holy Ghost,' warned me to put on my bonnet, and made me for the first time aware that I had been asleep! For the rest, the music that day ought to have satisfied me; for it seemed to have remodelled itself expressly to suit my taste—Scotch tunes, produced with the nasal discordant emphasis of a Scotch country-congregation, and no clarionet. I noticed in a little square gallery-seat, the only one in the church, a portly character, who acts as blacksmith, sitting with a wand, some five feet long, in his hand, which he swayed about majestically as if it had been a sceptre! On inquiring of our man-servant what this could possibly mean or symbolise, he informed me it was 'to beat the bad children.' 'And are the children here so bad that they need such a function-ary?' 'Ah, they will always, them little 'uns, be doing mischief in the church: it's a-wearisome for the poor things, and the rod keeps them in fear!'

In the evening, t' drive, as always, with this only difference, that on Sunda evenings Mr. Buller only walks the horse, from principle! After this conscientious exercising, the game at chess! My head had ached more or less all day, and I was glad to get to bed, where I was fortunate enough to get to sleep without any violent disturbance. The next day, however, my head was rather worse than better; so that I would fain have 'declined from'[1] calling on Lady Agnes; but Mrs. Buller was bent on going to Livermere, and so, as I did not feel up to walking, it was my only chance of get-ting any fresh air and exercise that day. To Livermere we went, then, before dinner, the dinner being deferred till five o'clock to suit the more fashionable hours of our visitees. 'The Pagets' seem to be extremely like other mortals, neither better nor bonnier nor wiser. To do them justice, however, they might, as we found them, have been sitting for a picture of high life doing the amiable and the rural in the country. They had placed a table under the shadow of a beech-tree; and at this sat Mr. Byng studying the 'Examiner;' Lady Agnes reading—'Oh, nothing at all, only some nonsense that Lord Londonderry has been printing; I cannot think what has tempted him;' and a boy and girl marking for a cricket-party, consisting of all the men-servants, and two older little sons, who were playing for the entertainment of their master and mistress and their own; the younger branches ever and anon clapping their hands, and calling out 'What fun!' I may mention for your con-

---

[1] The phrase of a rustic cousin of ours, kind of solemn pedant in his way.

solation that Mr. Byng (a tall, gentlemanly, *blasé*-looking man) was dressed from head to foot in unbleached linen; while Babbie may take a slight satisfaction to her curiosity *de femme* from knowing how a Paget attires herself of a morning, to sit under a beech-tree —a white-flowered muslin pelisse, over pale blue satin; a black lace scarf fastened against her heart with a little gold horse-shoe; her white neck tolerably revealed, and set off with a brooch of diamonds; immense gold bracelets, an immense gold chain; a little white silk bonnet with a profusion of blond and flowers; thus had she prepared herself for being rural! But, with all this finery, she looked a good-hearted, rattling, clever *haveral* [1] sort of a woman. Her account of Lord Londonderry's sentimental dedication to his wife was perfect—'from a goose to a goose!'—and she defended herself with her pocket handkerchief against the wasps, with an energy. When we had sat sufficiently long under the tree, Mrs. Buller asked her to take me through the gardens, which she did very politely, and gave me some carnations and verbenas; and then through the stables, which were, indeed, the finer sight of the two.

All this sight-seeing, however, did not help my head; at night I let the chess go as it liked; took some medicine, and went early to bed, determined to be well on the morrow. About twelve, I fell into a sound sleep, out of which I was startled by the tolling of the church-bell. The church, you remember, is only a stone-cast from the house; so that, when the bell tolls, one seems to be exactly under its tongue. I sprang up—it was half after three by my watch —hardly light; the bell went on to toll two loud dismal strokes at regular intervals of a minute. What could it be? I fancied fire— fancied insurrection. I ran out into the passage and listened at Regy's door, all was still; then I listened at Mrs. Buller's, I heard her cough; surely, I thought, since she is awake, she would ring her bell if there were anything alarming for her in this tolling, it must be some other noise of the many they 'have grown used to.' So I went to bed again, but, of course, could not get another wink of sleep all night; for the bell only ceased tolling at my ear about six in the morning, and then I was too nervous to avail myself of the silence. 'What on earth was that bell?' I asked Regy the first thing in the morning. 'Oh, it was only the passing bell! It was ordered to be rung during the night for an old lady who died the

---

[1] Good-humoured, foolish person. I should not wonder if it came from Avril (which in old Scotch is corrupted into Averil, and even Haver Hill), and had originally meant 'April fool.'

night before.' This time, however, I had the satisfaction of seeing Mrs. Buller as angry as myself; for she also had been much alarmed.

Of course, yesterday I was quite ill, with the medicine, the sleeplessness, and the fright; and I thought I really would not stay any longer in a place where one is liable to such alarms. But now, as usual, one quiet night has given me hopes of more; and it would be a pity to return worse than I went away. I do not seem to myself to be nearly done; but Mr. Buller is sitting at my elbow with the chess-board, saying, 'When you are ready I am ready.' I am ready. Love to Babbie; I have your and her letter; but *must* stop.

. Ends so, without signature, on inverted top-margin of first leaf. day of the week is Tuesday, date August 23.

LETTER 39.

To T. Carlyle, Esq., Chelsea.

Troston: Thursday, Aug. 25, 1842.

Dear,—I hardly expected my letter from you this morning, so that I was all the gladder to find it beside my plate as usual. Along with it was one from Elizabeth Pepoli; the chief merit of which, besides the kindness of writing at all, is that "it expects no answer."

I hope you have the same refreshing rain in London which is reviving our drooping spirits here; for it is easy to see, although you try to put the best face on everything for me at a distance, that you are suffering horribly from the heat. My only consolation in thinking of your being in the town and I in the country in such weather is, that if you might have felt a less degree of suffocation, sitting out of doors here during the day, certainly the improvement would have been counterbalanced by the superior suffocation of our nights. Even with door and window wide open, it is hardly possible to realise a breath of air; the cottage roof collects and retains the heat so very much more than any other sort of roof I ever lived under. After the first few days, I was obliged to give up remaining during the mornings in my own room; my head got into a swimming condition, as when I poisoned myself with the charcoal.[1] Mrs. Buller, I find, goes out of her room into some back apartment; but even there I am sure the closeness is very hurtful to her. The drawing-

---

[1] Dangerous silent accident at Craigenputtock, in 1828, from stooping to the floor in a room upstairs, where a chauffer was burning against damp.

room is the coolest place, and is left to myself till Mrs. Buller comes down; except for occasional inroads of Mr. Buller and Regy to seek some volume of a French novel, repeated cargoes of which are sent for from Rolandi's. 'A very bad stock, this last,' I observed last night. 'Yes,' says Mr. Buller, raising his eyebrows; 'when French novels are decorous, they are monstrous stupid!'

What do I think of Clifton?[1] What do you think? 'Plunges in the sea'—I am afraid it is not very conveniently situated for that; but if you were there, it would be the easiest thing to run over for a few days to your admiring Welshman,[2] who is really one of the sensiblest admirers you have; a man who expresses his enthusiasm in legs of mutton and peaches, &c., &c. I imagine he would make a better host than you think. Mrs. Buller says it is an excellent scheme, being so very easy to execute; 'nothing would be easier, except staying over September and November here, where I am already, and having you to join me!' With such an extravagant invitation as this, I need not hesitate about staying another week from any apprehension of exhausting their hospitality. She says that she can quite sympathise with your nervous dislike to making up your mind; and what you have to do in such a mood is just to come off without making up your mind at all; the first cool morning to put yourself in the coach, without any previous engagement or determination. The only objection to this is that, without being warned, Mrs. Buller could not meet you at Bury; but there is another coach from London which passes through Ixworth (from which you could walk, being only two miles), 'and a coach,' she says, 'just made for you, being called the Phenomenon!' I deliver all this long message, without the expectation that you will lay it duly to heart. I am thankful to hear that the leg is in reality mending, for it has been a great detriment to my repose of conscience while here; I should never have dreamt of leaving my post if I had foreseen that there was to be such a long puddlement before it healed. I cannot understand how it had gone back, for really it was almost closed when I left.

You may tell Babbie that my ardour for nightcap muslin, that morning, was the most superfluous in nature; for except twice, to mend a hole in my black silk stockings, I have not had a needle in my hand since I left London, nor 'wished to.' Neither have I so

---

[1] Invitation from a friend.
[2] Charles H. Redwood, Esq., Llanblethian, Glamorganshire, called the 'Honest Lawyer' in those parts; a man whom I much esteemed and still regret.

much as wound the skein of silk for my purse. I do little in the way of reading, and of writing as you know, and a great deal of nothing at all. I never weary, and yet there is no company comes, and, except the evening drive and the chess, we have no amuse- ments. The chess, however, is getting into the sphere of a passion. Mr. Buller 'does not remember when he had such good playing as this;' and so, to make hay while the sun shines, he must have a game before dinner as well as the one after tea. Sometimes a game will last two hours, and then there are generally three hours con- sumed in the drive; so that there remains no more time on my hands than I can find ways and means to get rid of without calling in the aid of needlework. Last night we drove to a place called New House; which is in fact a very old house, bearing the date 1612. The wainscoat and floors were polished to such a pitch with wax and turpentine, that I am certain I could have skated on them! The Lady, a married sister of Mr. Loft's, showed me an original portrait of 'Fergusson, the self-taught Philosopher, who had been her mother's preceptor': I was ashamed to ask, 'What does't doe?'[1] I never heard of him in my life. There were various pictures besides—Queen Elizabeth, Charles II., and honourable women not a few. To-night we are to go, if it fairs, to take tea at a show place called The Priory, belonging to 'Squire Cartwright.' Mrs. Buller is infinitely kind in her exertions to find me amuse- ment. Bless thee,

Your own JANE.

[One other letter followed from Troston. In a day or two more I went thither myself; walked about, nothing loth (as far as Thet- ford one day), sometimes with escort, oftener with none. Made at last (mainly by Mrs. Buller's contrivance, and delicate furtherance), 'till Charles should come,' a riding tour into Cromwell's Country; which did me much benefit in the future Book, and was abundantly impressive at the time, as indeed in memory it still is, strangely vivid in all its details at this day. Saw Hinchinbrook for the first time, St. Ives, Godmanchester (Ely, Soham, &c.); from Godman- chester to Cambridge trotted before a thunder cloud, always visible behind, which came down in deluges half a minute after I got into the Hoop Hotel, &c., &c. Can have lasted only about four days (three nights)! Can it be possible? I seem as if almost a denizen of that region, which I never saw before or since.—T. C.]

---

[1] Anne Cook's question, when 'Lord Jeffrey,' having called, she reported him ' Lurcherfield ' (to general amazement!) and, getting rebuked: 'But what *is* a "Looard" then? What diz't *duih?*'

5*

LETTER 40.

Follows Troston, seemingly at short distance. Good old Mr. Dobie's visit (Rev. Emeritus, Mrs. Dr. Russell's father) I remember well, and that it was in her absence. He never ' came back.' Letter is infinitely mournful to me, and beautiful in a like degree.

The ' Margaret' is Margaret Hiddlestone, whom she wanted for a servant, but could not get.—T. C.

To Mrs. Russell, Thornhill.

5 Cheyne Row, Chelsea: Sept. 1842.

My dear Mrs. Russell,—I meant to have written to you yesterday, along with my letter to Margaret;—but how to write to you without mentioning the purport of my writing to her, and how very much I had it at heart that she should come! And then if it so happened that she applied to you for advice, as is likely enough, and that your real opinion was she had better remain with her children? Between the two you were thus, it seemed to me, going to find yourself in a constraint, in which it was hardly fair to place you. But now this morning comes another consideration (I have such a way of tormenting myself with all sorts of out-of-the-way considerations!), viz., that you might think it unkind of me to send a letter to your care without a word, and unkindness towards you is what I could not bear to lie under the smallest suspicion of even for a moment. Oh, no, my dear Mrs. Russell, though I should never see you more, nor hear from you more, I shall think of you, and love you, and be grateful to you as long as I live. But for the knowledge of what you did for her,[1] and how thankfully she felt it, I know not how I should ever have brought myself to think of her last weeks with any degree of composure. As it was, God knows there still remains enough to feel eternal regrets about;—but without a friend like you, to make her feel that she was not quite alone with her sickness and her vexations, it would have been unspeakably worse for her then, and for me now.

How grieved I was that I happened to be absent during your father's stay in London! I felt somehow as if he had come from her—had brought me kind messages from her, and I had missed him! I would have returned immediately on purpose to see him; but they knew that I would, and so did not tell me until it was too late. But he will come again, having found how easy it is, will he

---

[1] She means her mother.

not, and bring you with him? Oh, I should like so well to have you here!

I am always very weakly in health, though better than when I last wrote to you. At present my brother-in-law has put me on a course of blue-pill for pain in my side. But, until I turn what health and strength I have to better account, I have no business to regret that I have not more.

I wish you would write to me some day, and tell me about old Mary and all the people. Thornhill and Templand and everything about there is often as distinct before my eyes as the house and street I am actually living in—but as it was; as it must be now, I can never bring myself to figure it.

Give my kindest regards to your father and husband. If felt your father's letter very kind.

God bless you, dear Mrs. Russell.

Ever your affectionate
JANE W. CARLYLE.

LETTER 41.

Fragment (very mournful), first small half of it lost.

To Mrs. Aitken, Dumfries.

Chelsea: (Early Summer) 1843.

What you say of my coming to Scotland is very kind; Isabella, too, has sent me the heartiest invitations, and I should like so well to see you all again. But when I try to fancy myself on the road, to fancy myself there, everything the same for me there as it used to be—and beyond, nothing of all that used to be—I feel so sick at heart, and so afraid of encountering the pain that seeing all those places again, and going about like a ghost in them, would cause me, that I can do no otherwise but say I will not go. It looks very cowardly to you, this?—perhaps, too, unkind and ungrateful towards the living. But fancy yourself in my place, looking out on the hills, at the back of which there had so lately lain a little loving home for you, where your mother had run to meet you with such joy; and now nothing for you there but the silence of death. If you do not feel that you would be just as weak, at least you will understand how I might be so without unkindness. If I were going beside your mother and all of you, I should think myself bound to be cheerful, and to look as if I were happy among you; and until I know myself up to that, is it not right to stay away? At present it seems to me I could do nothing at Scotsbrig or Dumfries but cry from morning till night. All this is excessively weak; I am quite aware of that, and if anybody will show me a way of being stronger, I will follow it to my best ability: but merely telling me or telling myself to be stronger is of no use.

Ever your affectionate

JANE CARLYLE.

LETTER 42.

To Miss Helen Welsh, Liverpool.

Chelsea: March 1843.

My dearest Helen,—After (in *Dumfries and Galloway-Courier* phraseology) 'taking a bird's-eye view' of all modern literature, I am arrived at the conclusion that, to find a book exactly suited to my uncle's taste, I must write it myself! and, alas, that cannot be done before to-morrow morning!

'La Motte Foqué's "Magic Ring,"' suggests Geraldine[1] (Jewsbury). 'Too mystical! My uncle detests confusion of ideas.' 'Paul de Kock? *he* is very witty.' 'Yes, but also very indecent; and my uncle would not relish indecencies read aloud to him by his daughters.' 'Oh! ah! well! Miss Austin?' 'Too washy; water-gruel for mind and body at the same time were too bad.' Timidly, and after a pause, 'Do you think he could stand Victor Hugo's "Notre Dame"?' The idea of my uncle listening to the sentimental monstrosities of Victor Hugo! A smile of scorn was this time all my reply. But in my own suggestions I have been hardly more fortunate. All the books that pretend to amuse in our day come, in fact, either under that category, which you except against, 'the extravagant, clown-jesting sort,' or still worse, under that of what I should call the galvanised-death's-head-grinning sort. There seems to be no longer any genuine, heart-felt mirth in writers of books; they sing and dance still *vigoureusement*, but one sees always too plainly that it is not voluntarily, but only for halfpence; and for halfpence they will crack their windpipes, and cut capers on the crown of their heads, poor men that they are!

I bethink me of one book, however, which we have lately read here, bearing a rather questionable name as a book for my uncle, but, nevertheless, I think he would like it. It is called 'Passages

---

[1] Miss Geraldine Jewsbury, with whom Mrs. Carlyle had just become acquainted, remained her most intimate friend to the end of her life.—J. A. F.

from the Life of a Radical,' by Samuel Bamford, a silk-weaver of Middleton. He was one of those who got into trouble during the Peterloo time; and the details of what he then saw and suffered are given with a simplicity, an intelligence, an absence of everything like party violence, which it does one good to fall in with, especially in these inflated times.

There is another book that might be tried, though I am not sure that it has not a little too much affinity with water-gruel, 'The Neighbours,' a domestic novel translated from the Swedish by Mary Howitt. There is a 'Little Wife' in it, with a husband whom she calls 'Bear,' that one never wearies of, although they never say or do anything in the least degree extraordinary.

Geraldine strongly recommends Stephen's 'Incidents of Travel in Egypt, Arabia, and Petrea,' as 'very interesting and very short.' Also Waterton's 'Wanderings in South America.' There are two novels of Paul de Kock translated into English, which might be tried at least without harm done, for they are unexceptionable in the usual sense of that term, the 'Barber of Paris,' and 'Sister Anne.'

I have read the last, not the first, and I dare say it would be very amusing for anyone who likes 'Gil Blas,' and that sort of books; for my taste it does not get on fast enough.

There! enough of books for one day. Thank you for your letter, dear. If I had not wee angels to write me consolatory missives at present, I should really be terribly ill off. My maid continues highly inefficient, myself ditto; the weather complicates everything; for days together not a soul comes, and then if the sun glimmers forth a whole rush of people breaks in, to the very taking away of one's breath!

Yesterday, between the hours of three and five, we had old Sterling, Mr. and Mrs. von Glëhen, Mr. and Mrs. Macready, John Carlyle, and William Cunningham. Geraldine professed to be mightily taken with Mrs. Macready, not so much so with 'William! Poor dear William! I never thought him more interesting, however. To see a man, who is exhibiting himself every night on a stage, blushing like a young girl in a private room is a beautiful phenomenon for me. His wife whispered into my ear, as we sat on the sofa together, 'Do you know poor William is in a perfect agony to-day at having been brought here in that great-coat? It is a stage great-coat, but was only worn by him twice; the piece it was made for did not succeed, but it was such an expensive coat,

I would not let him give it away; and doesn't he look well in it? I wish Jeannie had seen him in the coat—magnificent fur neck and sleeves, and such frogs on the front. He did look well, but so heartily ashamed of himself.

Oh, I must tell you, for my uncle's benefit, a domestic catastrophe that occurred last week! One day, after dinner, I heard Helen lighting the fire, which had gone out, in the room above, with a perfectly unexampled vengeance; every stroke of the poker seemed an individual effort of concentrated rage. What ails the creature now? I said to myself. Who has incurred her sudden displeasure? or is it the red herring she had for dinner which has disagreed with her stomach? (for in the morning, you must know, when I was ordering the dinner, she had asked, might *she* have a red herring? 'her heart had been set upon it this a good while back;' and, of course, so modest a petition received an unhesitating affirmative.) On her return to the subterranean, the same hubbub wild arose from below, which had just been trying my nerves from above; and when she brought up the tea-tray, she clanked it on the lobby-table as if she were minded to demolish the whole concern at one fell stroke. I looked into her face inquiringly as she entered the room, and seeing it black as midnight (*morally*, that is), I said very coolly, 'A little less noise, if you please; you are getting rather loud upon us.' She cast up her eyes with the look of a martyr at the stake, as much as to say, 'Well, if I must be quiet, I must; but you little know my wrongs.' By-and-by Geraldine went to the kitchen for some reason; she is oftener in the kitchen in one day than I am in a month; but that is irrelevant. 'Where is the cat?' said she to Helen; 'I have not seen her all night.' She takes a wonderful, most superfluous charge of the cat, as of everything else in this establishment. 'The cat!' said Helen grimly, 'I have all but killed her.' 'How?' said Geraldine. 'With the besom,' replied the other. 'Why? for goodness' sake.' 'Why!' repeated Helen, bursting out into new rage; 'why-indeed? Because she ate my red herring! I set it all ready on the end of the dresser, and she ran away with it, and ate it every morsel to the tail—such an unheard of thing for the brute to do. Oh, if I could have got hold her, she should not have got off with her life!' 'And have you had no dinner?' asked Geraldine. 'Oh, yes, I had mutton enough, but I had just set my heart on a red herring.' Which was the most deserving of having a besom taken to her, the cat or the woman?

My love to Babbie; her letter to-day is most comfortable. Blessings on you all.

Your affectionate cousin,

J. WELSH.

LETTER 43.

To Miss Helen Welsh, Liverpool.

Chelsea: March 1843.

Now, do you deserve that I should send you any letter, any autograph, anything, thou graceless, 'graceful Miss Welsh'? I think not; but 'if everyone had his deserts, which of us should escape whipping?' And besides I see not what virtues remain possible for me, unless it be the passive ones of patience and forgiveness; for which, thank Heaven, there is always open course enough in this otherwise tangled world!

Three of the autographs, which I send you to-day, are first-rate. A Yankee would almost give a dollar apiece for them. Entire characteristic letters from Pickwick, Lytton Bulwer, and Alfred Tennyson; the last the greatest genius of the three, though the vulgar public have not as yet recognised him for such. Get his poems if you can, and read the 'Ulysses,' 'Dora,' the 'Vision of Sin,' and you will find that we do not overrate him. Besides he is a very handsome man, and a noble-hearted one, with something of the gypsy in his appearance, which, for me, is perfectly charming. Babbie never saw him, unfortunately, or perhaps I should say fortunately, for she must have fallen in love with him on the spot, unless she be made absolutely of ice; and then men of genius have never anything to keep wives upon!

JANE CARLYLE.

LETTER 44.

To John Sterling, Esq., Falmouth.

Chelsea: June (?) 1843.

My dear John,—Thank you passionately for giving me *Vittoria Accoramboni;* and thank you even more for knowing beforehand that I should like her. Your presentiment that this was 'a woman exactly after my own heart' so pleases my own heart! proves that I am not universally 'a woman misunderstood.' But you said nothing of the man after my own heart, so that Bracciano took me by surprise, and has nearly turned my head! My very *beau-idéal* of manhood that Paul Giordano; could I hear of the like of him existing anywhere in these degenerate times, I would, even at this late stage of the business—send him—my picture! and an offer of my heart and hand for the next world, since they are already disposed of in this. Ah! what a man that must be, who can strangle his young, beautiful wife with his own hands, and, bating one moment of conventional horror, inspire not the slightest feeling of aversion or distrust! When a man strangles his wife nowadays he does it brutally, in drink, or in passion, or in revenge; to transact such a work coolly, nobly, on the loftiest principles, to strangle with dignity because the woman ' was unworthy of him,' that indeed is a triumph of character which places this Bracciano above all the heroes of ancient or modern times; which makes me almost weep that I was not born two centuries earlier, that I might have been— his mistress—not his wife!

But what think you befel? In the simplicity of my heart I lent the book to a friend, a man of course, whose hitherto version of me has borne a considerable resemblance to the *Santa Maria;* lent it too with all my marginal marks (as Carlyle would say) ' significant of much'! And when the man [1] brought it back he could neither look at me nor speak to me; but blushed and stammered, as if he were in the presence of a new goddess of reason. Disliking all that sort of thing, I asked him plain out, what ailed him? 'The truth is,' said he, ' Mrs. Carlyle, that book' (looking at it askance) ' has confused me! May I ask who recommended to you that book?' ' A clergyman,' said I; for the first and probably the last time in my life recognising your sacred vocation; ' John Sterling gave it to me.' ' The son?' ' Yes, to be sure, the son,' and then I laughed outright, and the man looked at me with a mingled expression of pity and alarm, and changed the subject.

JANE CARLYLE.

Fragments of letters to T. Carlyle, July 1843.

The house in Cheyne Row requiring paint and other re-adjustments, Carlyle had gone on a visit to Wales, leaving his wife to endure the confusion and superintend the workmen, alone with her maid.—J. A. F.

July 4, 1843.—The first night is over, and we are neither robbed nor murdered. I must confess, however, that I observed last night

---

[1] Can't guess what ' man.'

for the first time with what tremendous facility a thief with the average thief agility might swing himself, by laying hold of the spout, off the garden wall into my dressing closet, leaving me no time to spring my rattle, or even unsheath my dagger. 'You must excuse us the day;' I am in a complete mess, and my pen refuses to mark. I shall be in a complete mess for a time, times and a half. I will perhaps go for a few days to the Isle of Wight, for breathing, in the midst of it; but I shall not be done with my work this month to come. You see you do so hate commotion that this house gets no periodic cleanings like other people's and one must make the most of your absence.

July 11.—It has been such a morning as you cannot figure: a painter filling the house with terrific smells, the whitewashers still whitewashing, Pearson and men tearing out the closet, and the boy always grinding with pumice stone. Having been taught politeness to one's neighbours by living next door to Mr. Chalmers, I wrote a note to Mr. Lambert, No. 6, regretting that his and his family's slumbers were probably curtailed by my operations, and promising that the nuisance would have only a brief term. This brought Mr. Lambert upon me (virtue ever its own reward), who stayed for an hour, talking, you know how. Then I. . . . And you do not like my beautiful 'Vittoria'! oh, what want of taste!

July 12.—If you had seen me last night asleep you would have seen a pretty sight. The paint was smelling, of course—one can't make a household revolution, any more than a State one, with rose water; and so this house did not smell of rose water, I can assure you. Old Sterling had said so much about its costing me my life, and the absolute necessity of my at least sleeping at his house, that I did begin to think it my cause me a headache! So I took all wise precautions against it, kept my door carefully shut all day, and slept with both my windows open, so that I really suffered very little inconvenience from the smell. But just when I was going to bed, it occurred to me that in this open state of things, with several ladders lying quite handy underneath the window, 'heavy bodies might,' as Helen phrased it, 'drop in,' and be at my pillow before I heard them; so, feeling it my duty to neglect no proper precaution, I laid my dagger and the great policeman's rattle on the spare pillow and went to sleep quite pleasantly, without any more thought about thieves.

I have got such a pretty writing establishment—a sort of gipsy's tent, which I have mounted in the garden 'with my own hands,' constructed out of the clothes rope and posts and the crumb cloth of the library! I sit under its 'dark brown shade—wh'[1]—the Macready of Nature—an armchair, and the little round table, with my writing msterials, and my watch to keep me in mind that I am in a time world, a piece of carpet under foot, and a foot-stool. Behold all that is necessary for my little garden house! Woman wants but little here below—an old crumb cloth mainly, you perceive. But one has no credit in being jolly in such a pretty bower. By-and-by I shall have to return indoors, 'to come out strong.'

July 17.—*Tout va bien.* The work goes well, and myself goes well. The early rising and the shower-bathing and the having something to look after agrees with me wonderfully. The degree of heat also is exactly suited to my needs. This and the other person drops in and asks me if I do not feel very lonely? It is odd what notions men seem to have of the scantiness of a woman's resources. They do not find it anything out of nature that they should be able to exist by themselves; but a woman must always be borne about on somebody's shoulders, and dandled and chirped to, or it is supposed she will fall into the blackest melancholy. When I answered that question from Arthur Helps yesterday, ' Why should I feel lonely? I have plenty to do, and can see human beings whenever I look out at the window,' he looked at me as if I had uttered some magnanimity worthy to have place in a ' Legitimate Drama,' and said, ' Well, really you are a model of a wife.'

LETTER 45.

To John Welsh, Esq., The Baths, Helensburgh.

Chelsea: July 18, 1843.

Dearest, dear only Uncle of me,—I would give a crown that you could see me at this moment through a powerful telescope! You

---

[1] 'Dark brown shade' was to both of us infinitely ridiculous in this place, though the spirit of it is now fled irrevocably. Dr. Ritchie, divinity professor in Edinburgh, was a worthy, earnest, but somewhat too pompous and consciously eloquent, old gentleman. He had no teeth, a great deal of white hair, spoke in a sonorous, mumbling voice, with much proud, almost minatory, wagging of the head, and to a rhythm all his own, which loved to end always with an emphatic syllable, with victorious grave accent, and a kind of ' wh,' or ' h,' superadded. For confutation of Gibbon, his principal argument—the only one that I can recollect—was that Gibbon in his later years, grown rich, famous, &c., &c., confessed that the end of life to him was involved in a ' dark brown shade—wh.'

would laugh for the next twelve hours. I am doing the rural after a fashion so entirely my own! To escape from the abominable paint-smell, and the infernal noise within doors, I have erected, with my own hands, a gipsy-tent in the garden, constructed with clothes lines, long poles, and an old brown floor cloth! under which remarkable shade I sit in an arm-charm at a small round table, with a hearth rug for carpet under my feet, writing-materials, sewing-materials, and a mind superior to Fate!

The only drawback to this retreat is its being exposed to 'the envy of surrounding nations'; so many heads peer out on me from all the windows of the Row, eager to penetrate my meaning! If I had a speaking trumpet I would address them once for all:— 'Ladies and Gentlemen,—I am not here to enter my individual protest against the progress of civilization! nor yet to mock you with an Arcadian felicity, which you have neither the taste nor the ingenuity to make your own! but simply to enjoy Nature according to ability, and to get out of the smell of new paint! So, pray you, leave me to pursue my innocent avocations in the modest seclusion which I covet!'

Not to represent my contrivance as too perfect, I must also tell you that a strong puff of wind is apt to blow down the poles, and then the whole tent falls down on my head! This has happened once already since I began to write, but an instant puts it all to rights again. Indeed, without counteracting the indoors influences by all lawful means, I could not stay here at present without injury to my health, which is at no time of the strongest. Our house has for a fortnight back been a house possessed by seven devils! a painter, two carpenters, a paper-hanger, two nondescript apprentice-lads, and 'a spy;' all playing the devil to the utmost of their powers; hurrying and scurrying 'upstairs, downstairs, and in my lady's chamber!' affording the liveliest image of a sacked city!

When they rush in at six of the morning, and spread themselves over the premises, I instantly jump out of bed, and 'in wera desperation' take a shower bath. Then such a long day to be virtuous in! I make chair and sofa covers; write letters to my friends; scold the work-people, and suggest improved methods of doing things. And when I go to bed at night I have to leave both windows of my room wide open (and plenty of ladders lying quite handy underneath), that I may not, as old Sterling predicted, 'awake dead' of the paint.

The first night that I lay down in this open state of things, I

recollected Jeannie's house-breaker adventure last year, and, not
wishing that all the thieves who might walk in at my open windows should take me quite unprepared, I laid my policeman's
rattle and my dagger on the spare pillow, and then I went to sleep
quite secure. But it is to be confidently expected that, in a week
or more, things will begin to subside into their normal state; and
meanwhile it were absurd to expect that any sort of revolution can
be accomplished. There! the tent has been down on the top of me
again, but it has only upset the ink.

Jeannie appears to be earthquaking with like energy in Maryland Street, but finds time to write me nice long letters nevertheless, and even to make the loveliest pincushion for my birthday;
and my birthday was celebrated also with the arrival of a hamper,
into which I have not yet penetrated. Accept kisses *ad infinitum*
for your kind thought of me, dearest uncle. I hope to drink your
health many times in the Madeira[1] when I have Carlyle with me
again to give an air of respectability to the act. Nay, on that
evening when it came to hand, I was feeling so sad and dreary
over the contrast between this Fourteenth of July—alone, in a
house like a sacked city, and other Fourteenths that I can never
forget, that I hesitated whether or no to get myself out a bottle of
the Madeira there and then, and try for once in my life the hitherto unknown comfort of being dead drunk. But my sense of the
respectable overcame the temptation.

My husband has now left his Welshman, and is gone for a little
while to visit the Bishop of St. David's. Then he purposes crossing over somehow to Liverpool, and, after a brief benediction to
Jeannie, passing into Annandale. He has suffered unutterable
things in Wales from the want of any adequate supply of tea!
For the rest, his visit appears to have been pretty successful;
plenty of sea-bathing; plenty of riding on horseback, and of lying
under trees! I wonder it never enters his head to lie under the
walnut-tree here at home. It is a tree! leaves as green as any
leaves can be, even in South Wales! but it were too easy to repose
under that: if one had to travel a long journey by railway to it,
then indeed it might be worth while!

But I have no more time for scribbling just now; besides, my
pen is positively declining to act. So, God bless you, dear, and all
of them.   Ever your affectionate
                                   JANE CARLYLE.

---

[1] Present sent from Liverpool.

LETTER 46.

T. Carlyle, Esq., at Llandough, Cowbridge.

Chelsea: July 18, 1843.

Dearest,—I take time by the pigtail, and write at night after post-hours. During the day there is such an infernal noise of pumice-stone, diversified by snatches of 'wild strains;' the youth who is scraping the walls (as if it were a hundred knife-grinders melted into one) consoling himself under the hideous task by striking up every two minutes 'The Red Cross Knight,' or 'Evelyn's Bower,' or some such plaintive melody, which, after a brief attempt to render itself 'predominant,' 'dies away into unintelligible whinner.'[1] Yesterday forenoon Mrs. Chadwick came; and had just seated herself on the sofa beside me, and was beginning to set forth amiabilities; when bang, bang, crash, screech, came the pumice-stone over the room-door, to the tune

Oh rest thee, my darling,
Thy sire is a knight; &c., &c.,

making us both start to our feet with a little scream and then fall back again in fits of laughter. Then the stairs are all flowing with whitewash, and 'altogether' when I fancy you here 'in the midst of it,' I do not know whether to laugh, or to cry, or to shriek.

But it will be a clean pretty house for you to come home to; and should you find that I have exceeded by a few pounds your modest allowance for painting and papering, you will find that I have not been thoughtless nevertheless, when I show you a document from Mr. Morgan,[2] promising to 'indemnify us for the same in the undisturbed possession of our house for five years!' A piece of paper equivalent to a lease of the house for five years, 'with the reciprocity all on one side,' binding him and leaving us free. 'Such a thing,' old Sterling said, who attended me to Pope's Head Alley, 'as no woman but myself would have had the impudence to ask, nor any lawyer in his senses the folly to grant.' I do not see but we might get a lease of the house after all for as long as we pleased,

---

[1] My father's account of a precentor who lost his tune, desperately tried several others, and then 'died away into an,' &c.

[2] Lawyer in the city; virtual proprietor here.

if *I* went about it, instead of the volup*chious* Perry.[1] This was
. one of those remarkable instances of fascination which I exercise
over gentlemen of a 'certain age;' before I had spoken six words
to him it was plain to the meanest capacity that he had fallen over
head and ears in love with me; and if he put off time in writing
me the promise I required, it was plainly only because he could
not bear the idea of my going away again! No wonder! probably
no such beatific vision as that of a real live woman, in a silk bonnet
and muslin gown, ever irradiated that dingy, dusty law-chamber
of his, and sat thereon a three-feet-high stool, since he had held
a pen behind his ear; and certainly never before had either man or
woman, in that place, addressed him as a human being, not as a
lawyer, or he would not have looked at me so struck dumb with
admiration when I did so. For respectability's sake, I said, in
taking leave, that 'my husband was out of town, or he would have
come himself.' 'Better as it is,' said the old gentleman, 'do you
think I would have written to your husband's dictation as I have
done to yours?' He asked me if your name were John or William
—plainly he had lodged an angel unawares.

By the way, that other angel[2] is becoming a bore. Charles
Barton, with whom I dined at Sterling's in returning from
Pope's Head Alley, told me that he had been making quite a
sensation in Berlin, and been invited to a great many places, on the
strength of the 'French Revolution.' He (Charles B.) was asked
to meet him—that is 'Thomas Carlyle, author of "The French
Revolution"' at the Earl of Westmoreland's 'Is *he* here?' said
Charles; 'I shall be delighted to see him, I know him quite well;'
and accordingly, on the appointed day, he 'almost ran into the
arms of the announced Thomas Carlyle, and then retreated with
consternation.' It was so far good that he had an opportunity to
disabuse these people at least by declaring 'that was not Thomas
Carlyle at all!' But is it not a shame in the creature to encourage
the delusion, and let himself be fêted as a man of genius when he is
only a 'crack-brained enthusiastic'?[3]

I have awoke at four every morning since you went away; and
the night before last I slept just half an hour in all; it is always the
effect of finding one's self in a new position. When the workpeo-

---

[1] Pedant carpenter and house agent here; characterised the unthrift of the
poor by that adjective.

[2] 'T. Carlyle,' of the Irvingite Church, long a double-ganger of mine.

[3] My father's epithet for Mrs. Carruthers, long ago.

ple come at six, I get up, which makes a prodigiously long day;
but I do not weary, having so many mechanical things to do. This
morning I took, or rather failed to take, a shower bath; I pulled
with concentrated courage, and nothing would come; determined
not to be quite baffled, however, I made Helen pour a pitcherful of
water on me instead.

Mazzini came this forenoon, for the first time; very pale and
weak, but his face pretty well mended. He was horribly out of
spirits; and no wonder. They have brought out the 'British and
Foreign Review' without his article!! a most untimely *contretemps*
for him, in an economical point of view; and besides very mortifying to him morally, as he is sure it is 'merely because of his being
a foreigner that he is so ill-used.' I was strongly advising him to—
run away, to hide himself from all people, friends and creditors, and
disciples, in Switzerland or some cheap, quiet place; and I should
not wonder if he did some such thing in the end—a man cannot
live 'in a state of crisis' (as he calls it) for ever.

I do not see how I am to get to the Isle of Wight. I cannot
leave the house with workpeople coming and going; and Helen declares, naturally, that without me she could not stay a night in the
house for the whole world. But I daresay I am quite as content
here, studious of household goods, as I should be, dragged about
to look at picturesque views, at the Isle of Wight, or anywhere else
that 'fool[1] creturs go for diversion;' but London, be it e'er so hot,
is ne'er too hot for me![2] To-day we have had the beautifullest soft
rain, to make all fresh again; and on the whole, the weather is
charming; and I never go into the dusty streets on foot. Good
night.

Saturday.—Well! you cannot come back here just now at all
rates, that is flat. What think you of going to this——? Here indeed you would not 'come out strong' under the existing circumstances. It is only I who can be 'jolly' in such a mess of noise,
dirt, and wild dismay! I said to the lad in the lobby this morning, who was filling the whole house with 'Love's young dream:'
'How happy you must feel, that can sing through that horrible
noise you are making!' 'Yes, thank you, ma'am,' says he, 'I am
happy enough so far as I knows; but I's always a-singing any how!
it sounds pleasant to sing at one's work, doesn't it, ma'am?' 'Oh,

---

[1] Definition of poetry, 'Pack o' lies, that fuil craitures write for,' &c.

[2] Mrs. Siddons, replying to her host, apologetic for his salt fish: 'Fish, be it
ne'er so salt,' &c.

very pleasant,' said I, quite conquered by his simplicity, 'but it would be still pleasanter for me, at least, if you would sing a song from beginning to end, instead of bits here and there.' 'Thank you, ma'am,' says he again, 'I will try!' But he does not succeed.

I have the most extraordinary letter from * * *, which I would send, only that it would cost twopence of itself. He writes to tell me that 'he did not like his reception,' that 'often as he came and long as he stayed, I treated him indeed with perfect civility, did not yawn, or appear to be suppressing a yawn; but I seemed to labour under a continual feeling of oppression! and to be thinking all the while of something else!' 'What did I see to offend me in him? 'he asks me with great humility; from what he heard of pre- ferences and saw of my society, he was inclined to suppose that what I objected to in him must be the want of that first great requisite earnestness. But he begged to assure me, &c., &c.—in short, that he had as much earnestness 'as he could bear'!! A letter from a man calling himself bishop to a woman whom he calls infidel, and pleading guilty to her of want of earnestness—Bah! I wish I could snort like Cavaignac.

There, now I must stop. I daresay I have wearied you. God keep you, dear. Be quite easy about me. Ever yours

J. C.

LETTER 47.

Cuttikins (old Scotch word for spatterdashes, 'cuits' signifying feet) means * * * * *, now became 'Bishop,' so-called,' 'of ——' (title we used to think analogous to great Mogul of London?), in whose episcopal uniform, unsuitable to the little bandy-legged man, the *spats* were a prominent item. Indisputable man of talent and veracity, though not of much devoutness, of considerable worldliness rather, and quietly composed self-conceit—gone now, ridiculously, into the figure of 'a bandy-legged black beetle,' as was thought by some.

'Old Morrah,' or Murrough, was an Irish surgeon of much sense and merit, well accepted by the Sterlings and us.

The policeman's 'rattle' was a thing she actually had on her night-table at this time.

T. Carlyle, Esq., at Carmarthen.

Chelsea: Thursday, July 20, 1843.

Dearest,—I quite fretted, last night, at your having been cheated out of your letter. *D'abord,* I had a headache; but that was not the reason, for it was not an even-down headache, under which no woman can write; I could have written, better or worse; but I put

off, thinking always I should get into ' a freer and clearer state '[1] before the post left; and, as the copy-line says, ' procrastination is the
root of all evil.' From two till four I had visitors, and not of free
and easy sort who could be told to go away and return at a more
convenient season; first, Mrs. Prior[2] and her companion Miss
Allan, the primmest pair; but meaning well, and making me a long
first visit of ceremony, in testimony of Mrs. Prior's sense of my
' goodness to her poor brother.'

By the way, I really believe that I have been the instrument,
under Providence, of saving old Sterling's life. I told you how
Dr. Fergusson seemed to me to be ruining him with recommendations of ' a plentiful use of porter, wine, and other stimulants to restore the tone of his nervous system (!) Then he recommended him vapour baths. I saw him after his first bath,
all scarlet as a lobster and pale as milk by turns, and shivering
and burning by turns. I had an uncomfortable feeling about
him all the evening; was not sure whether I ought not to write
to John; he looked to me so much in danger of some sudden
stroke. Two days after, he came and told me he had been twice
cupped; had been so ill that he had himself proposed the thing
to Fergusson, who approved. Now this was quite enough to
show what sort of person this Fergusson must be, feeding a man
up with porter and wine, and cupping him at the same time.
I told Sterling most seriously that he looked to me in a very critical state; and that if he did not go home, and send at once to old
Morrah, who was no quack, and had never flattered his tastes, I
would not answer for his living another week. He was furious at
my suspicion of Fergusson; but on the way home thought better
of it, and did send for Morrah; who immediately proceeded to
scour him with the most potent medicines. Morrah called for me
two days ago, and said that he did not think he could have gone
on another week under Fergusson's system, without a stroke of
apoplexy; that his pulse was a hundred and thirty and his tongue
quite black. Now he is sleeping well, and much better every way.

After Mrs. Prior, came the Dundee Stirlings, and the sister who
is going to India. I liked the big bald forehead and kind eyes of
Stirling very much indeed. He looks a right good fellow. They
are to return to Dundee in a few days. But the most unexpected,
the most stroke-of-thunder visitor I have had was Cuttikins!![3] I

[1] Brother John's favourite phrase.　　[2] Elder Sterling's sister.
[3] See preface to this letter.

I.—6

declare when Helen told me he was below, I almost sprung the rattle. I had not answered his letter, had made up my mind not to answer it at all; a man puts one in quite a false position who demands an explanation of one's coldness—coldness which belongs to the great sphere of silence; all speech about it can only make bad worse. Was he come there because, like ——, he 'had found it so easy' to ask me for an answer? Was the small chimera gone out of his wits? When I came down, though outwardly quite calm, even indifferent, I was in a serious trouble. He put me speedily at ease, however, by telling me that he had been sent for express, to see his aunt, who had thought herself dying (and from whom he has expectations); she was now recovering, and he hoped to be able to go back in a few days—I hope so, too. I said I had not answered his letter, because it seemed to me that was the best way to counteract the indiscretion of his having written it; that, 'although, as a man much older than myself, and a dignitary of the church, he ought to be wiser than I, I could not help telling him that I had learned a thing or two, which he seemed to be still in ignorance of—among the rest, that warmth of affection could not be brought about by force of logic.' He said 'I was right, and he did not design to bore me this thme,' and so we parted with polite mutual tolerance. But you may figure the shock of having that little Cuttikins descend from the blue so suddenly when I was relying on seeing no more of him for three years.

Only think what human wickekness is capable of! Some devils broke into Pearson's workshop the night before last, and stole all the men's tools. The poor creatures are running about, lost, their occupation quite gone. They have never any money laid by, so they cannot buy new tools till they get money, and they cannot make money till they get tools. It is the cruellest of thefts—a man's tools. Last night six or seven pounds' worth of glass was cut out of a new house—out of the windows that is to say.

Your letter is just come; I thank you for never neglecting me. Yesterday looked such a blank day; no letters came, as if in sympathy with your silence. You must feel something of a self-constituted impostor in your present location. I have a good many little things to do, and an engagement with Mrs. Prior, who is to come to take me a drive at two o'clock. Oh, if you could mend me some pens! Bless you, dearest.   Your own

J. C.

LETTER 48.

T. Carlyle, Esq., at Liverpool.

Chelsea: Monday night, July 31, 1843.

Dearest,—The postman presented me your letter to-night in Cheyne Walk, with a bow extraordinary. He is a jewel of a postman; whenever he has put a letter from you into the box, he both knocks and rings, that not a moment may be lost in taking possession of it. In acknowledgment whereof, I crossed the street one day, when Cuttikins, who stayed a week and returned twice, was with me, and at that moment doing the impossible to be entertaining, for the purpose of saluting his (the postman's) baby, which he was carrying out for an airing. The rage of Cuttikins at this interruption was considerable; he looked at me as if he could have eaten me raw, and remarked with a concentrated spleen, 'Well, I must say, never did I see any human being so improved in amiability as you are. Everybody and everything seems to be honoured with a particular affection from you.' 'Everything,' thought I, 'except you;' but I contented myself with saying, 'Isn't it a darling baby?' Poor Cuttikins, his aunt did not die; so he is gone with the prospect of —alas!—of having to return ere long. The last day he can. John Sterling exploded him in a way that would have done your heart good to see. John looked at me as much as to say, 'Does he bore you?' and I gave my shoulders a little shrug in the affirmative, whereupon John jumped to his feet and said in a polite undertone, as audible, however, for the Bishop as for me, 'Well, my good friend, if you cannot keep your engagement with me, I must go by myself—I am too late already.' The cool assurance of this speech was inimitable, for I had no engagement in the world with him; but the bishop, suspecting nothing, sprang to his feet, and was off in a minute with apologies for having detained me.

Well, I actually accomplished my dinner at the Kay Shuttleworths'. Mrs. —— was the only lady at dinner; old Miss Rogers and a young *wersh*-looking [1] person with her, came in the evening; it was a very locked-jaw sort of business. Little Helps was there, but even I could not animate him; he looked pale and as if he had a pain in his stomach. Milnes was there, and 'affable' enough, but evidently overcome with a feeling that weighed on all of us—the feeling of having been dropped into a vacuum. There were

---

[1] *Waterish*, an emphatic Scotch word.

various other men, a Sir Charles Lemon, Cornewall Lewis, and some other half-dozen insipidities, whose names did not fix themselves in my memory. Mrs. —— was an insupportable bore; she has surely the air of a retired unfortunate female; her neck and arms were naked, as if she had never eaten of the Tree of the Knowledge of Good and Evil! She reminded me forcibly of the Princess Huncamunca, as I once saw her represented in a barn. She ate and drank with a certain voracity, sneezed once during the dinner, just like a hale old man, 'and altogether' nothing could be more ungraceful, more unfeminine than her whole bearing. She talked a deal about America and her poverty with exquisite bad taste. Indeed, she was every way a displeasing spectacle to me.

Mazzini's visit to Lady Baring (as he calls her) went off wonderfully well. I am afraid, my dear, this Lady Baring of yours, and his, and John Mill's, and everybody's, is an arch coquette. She seems to have played her cards with Mazzini really too well; she talked to him with the highest commendations of George Sand, expressed the utmost longing to read the new edition of 'Lelia'; nay, she made him 'a mysterious signal with her eyes, having first looked two or three times towards John Mill and her husband,' clearly intimating that she had something to tell him about —— which they were not to hear; and when she could not make him understand, she 'shook her head impatiently, which from a woman, especially in your England, was—what shall I say?—confidential, upon *my* honour.' I think it was. John Mill appeared to be loving her very much, and taking great pains to show her that his opinions were right ones. By the way, do you know that Mill considers Robespierre 'the greatest man that ever lived,' his speeches far surpassing Demosthenes' ? He begins to be too absurd, that John Mill! I heard Milnes saying at the Shuttleworths' that 'Lord Ashley was the greatest man alive; he was the only man that Carlyle praised in his book.' I dare say he knew I was overhearing him.

I am quite rid of the paint-smell now; but I have the whitewasher coming again to-morrow. I could not turn up the low room till the upstairs one was in some sort habitable again, and all last week, nothing could be got on with, owing to Pearson's absence. It is surprising how much easier it is to pull down things than to put them up again.

LETTER 49.

Welsh Tour done. Leaving Liverpool for Scotsbrig I get this.
—T. C.

T. Carlyle, Esq., at Liverpool.

Chelsea: Thursday, Aug. 3, 1843.

Dearest,—If you go on board to-night, this letter will reach you
no sooner than if written to-morrow and addressed to Scotsbrig;
but if you do not, and to-morrow there be a second day for you
without any news, you will be 'vaixed;' and on no account must
you be vaixed if one can possibly help it. I cannot, however, make
much of writing to-day; for it is thundering and raining in a quite
soul-confusing manner; that in the first place, then, in the second,
I have a headache. Last night the Stick-woman, who is always
showing me small civilities, brought me a present of ass's milk
(God knows where she got hold of the ass to milk it!), and she
bade Helen tell me that if I would please to drink it to my supper,
I should feel great benefit in the morning. I drank it, more for
curiosity than for any superiority I could taste in it over cow's
milk; and awoke, after two hours' sleep, with such a headache, and
such a detestation of ass's milk! I was able to get up early to my
breakfast; but am not recovered yet, nor shall be till I have had a
night's sleep. I did myself no good by cleaning the lamp in the
morning. It had ceased to act some time ago, and was beginning
to lie heavy on my conscience, besides that light is one of the things
I do not like to economise in, when I am alone; just the more alone
I am, the more light I need, as I told Darwin, the night he drank
tea with me, and, when the lamp was brought in, remarked that
'it was surely far too much light for a single woman'! Darwin,
by the way, has gone out of sight latterly; it is a fortnight, I am
sure, since he was here; he talked then of paying a visit to his
brother and then going to the Mackintosh's.

I am sitting in the upstairs room now, while the earthquake is
rumbling beneath it, and this and the thunder together are almost
too much for me. They have washed the ceilings, and Helen is
now washing the paint, and doing the impossible to clean the paper
with bread. 'Ah!' it takes such a quantity of labour, for a man
quite inconceivable, to make what is dirty look one shade more near
to clean. But here it is all quite clean, and so pretty! I feel like a
little Queen sitting in it, so far as what Mazzini calls 'the material'

is concerned; indeed, I suppose no Queen ever got half the comfort out of a nice room; Queens being born to them as the sparks fly upwards. There are still some finishing strokes to be given, the book-shelves all to be put up, and the window curtains; and a deal of needlework has to go to the last. But when all is done, it will be such a pleasure to receive you and give you tea in your new library! when you have exhausted the world without.

Thanks for your constant little letters; when you come back, I do not know how I shall learn to do without them, they have come to be as necessary as any part of my 'daily bread.' But, my dear, I must stop, you see that my head is bad, and that I am making it worse.

Bless you,

Yours, J. C.

LETTER 50.

T. Carlyle, Esq., at Scotsbrig.

Pier Hotel, Ryde:[1] Wednesday morning, Aug. 9, 1843.

Dearest,—Here I actually am, and so far as has yet appeared, 'if it had not been for the honour of the thing,' I had better have stayed where I was. The journey hither was not pleasant the least in the world. What journey ever was or shall be pleasant for poor me? But this railway seems to me particularly shaky, and then the steam-boating from Gosport, though it had not time to make me sick —the water, ~~~~ ~over, being smooth as the Thames—still made ~~ ~~ perfectly uncomfortable as need be; a heavy dew was falling; one could not see many yards ahead; everybody on board looked peevish. I wished myself at home in my bed.

We reached Ryde at eight in the evening, and, the second hotel being filled, had to take up our quarters for that night at the first, which 'is the dearest hotel in Europe,' and the hotel in Europe, so far as I have seen, where there is the least human comfort. I had to make tea from an urn the water of which was certainly not 'as hot as one could drink it;'[2] the cream was blue milk, the butter tasted of straw, and the 'cold fowl' was a lukewarm one, and as

---

[1] Mrs. Carlyle had gone to Ryde with old Mr. Sterling.

[2] Lady mistress and guests have sat down to tea; butler is summoned up in haste: 'John, John, how is this? Water in the urn not boiling!' John (attempts to deny, then finding he cannot): 'A weel, me'm; I kenna whether it's a'together *boiling*, A'm sure it's better than you can drink it!' and retires with the feeling of a maltreated man.

tough as leather. After this insalubrious repast—which the Stima-bile,[1] more easily pleased than I, pronounced to be 'infinitely re-freshing, by Jove!'—finding that, beyond sounding the depths of vacuum, there was nothing to be done that night, I retired to my bed. The windows looked over house-roofs and the sea, so I hoped it would be quiet; but, alas, there was a dog uttering a volley of loud barks, about once in the five minutes; and rousing up what seemed to be a whole infinitude of dogs in the distance! Of course, fevered and nervous as I was at any rate from the journey, I could not sleep at all; I do not mean that I slept ill, but I have absolutely never been asleep at all the whole night! So you may fancy the favourable mood I am in towards Ryde this morning! I feel as if I would not pass another night in that bed for a hundred pounds!

Nor shall I need. Clark[2] has been out this morning to seek a lodging; and has found one, he says, very quiet, quite away from the town. If I cannot sleep there, I will return to my own red bed as fast as possible. I did not bind myself for any specified time. To Helen I said I should most likely be back in three or four days; but in my own private mind, I thought it possible I might make out a week. It was best, however, to let her expect me from day to day; both that she might get on faster and that she might suffer less from her apprehension of thieves, for she flattered herself nobody would know I was gone before I should be returned. I left Elizabeth with her, with plenty of needlework to do; alone, she would have gone out of her senses altogether, and most proba-bly succeeded in getting the house robbed.

And now let me tell you something which you will perhaps think questionable, a piece of Hero-Worship that I have been after. My youthful enthusiasm, as John Sterling calls it, is not extinct then, as I had supposed; but must certainly be immortal! Only think of its blazing up for Father Mathew! You know I have always had the greatest reverence for that priest; and when I heard he was in London, attainable to me, I felt that I must see him, shake him by the hand, and tell him I loved him consider-ably! I was expressing my wish to see him, to Robertson, the night he brought the Ballad Collector;[3] and he told me it could be gratified quite easily. Mrs. Hall had offered him a note of intro-duction to Father Mathew, and she would be pleased to include

---

[1] See note p. 21. [2] The valet.
[3] Peter Buchan, poor phantasm!

my name in it. 'Fix my time, then.' 'He was administering the pledge all day long in the Commercial Road.' I fixed next evening.

Robertson, accordingly, called for me at five, and we rumbled off in omnibus, all the way to Mile End, that hitherto for me unimaginable goal! Then there was still a good way to walk; the place, the 'new lodging,' was a large piece of waste ground, boarded off from the Commercial Road, for a Catholic cemetery. I found 'my youthful enthusiasm' rising higher and higher as I got on the ground, and saw the thousands of people all hushed into awful silence, with not a single exception that I saw—the only religious meeting I ever saw in cockneyland which had not plenty of scoffers hanging on its outskirts. The crowd was all in front of a narrow scaffolding, from which an American captain was then haranguing it; and Father Mathew stood beside him, so good and simple-looking! Of course, we could not push our way to the front of the scaffold, where steps led up to it; so we went to one end, where there were no steps or other visible means of access, and handed up our letter of introduction to a policeman; he took it and returned presently, saying that Father Mathew was coming. And he came; and reached down his hand to me, and I grasped it; but the boards were higher than my head, and it seemed our communication must stop there. But I have told you that I was in a moment of enthusiasm; I felt the need of getting closer to that good man. I saw a bit of rope hanging, in the form of a festoon, from the end of the boards; I put my foot on it; held still by Father Mathew's hand; seized the end of the boards with the other; and, somehow, to myself (up to this moment), incomprehensible was flung myself horizontally on to the scaffolding at Father Mathew's feet! He uttered a scream, for he thought (I suppose) I must fall back; but not at all; I jumped to my feet, shook hands with him and said—what? 'God only knows.' He made me sit down on the only chair a moment; then took me by the hand as if I had been a little girl, and led me to the front of the scaffold, to see him administer the pledge. From a hundred to two hundred took it; and all the tragedies and theatrical representations I ever saw, melted into one, could not have given me such emotion as that scene did. There were faces both of men and women that will haunt me while I live; faces exhibiting such concentrated wretchedness, making, you would have said, its last deadly struggle with the powers of darkness. There was one man, in particular, with a baby in his arms; and a young girl that seemed of the 'unfortunate' sort, that gave me an insight into the lot of humanity that I still wanted. And in the face of Father Mathew, when one looked from them to him, the mercy of Heaven seemed to be laid bare. Of course I cried; but I longed to lay my head down on the good man's shoulder and take a hearty cry there before the whole multitude! He said to me one such nice thing. 'I dare not be absent for an hour,' he said; 'I think always if some dreadful drunkard were to come, and me away, he might never muster determination perhaps to come again in all his life; and there would be a man lost!'

I was turning sick, and needed to get out of the thing, but, in the act of leaving him—never to see him again through all time, most probably—feeling him to be the very best man of modern times (you excepted), I had another movement of youthful enthusiasm which you will hold up your hands and eyes at. Did I take the pledge then? No; but I would, though, if I had not feared it would be put in the newspapers! No, not that; but I drew him aside, having considered if I had any ring on, any handkerchief, anything that I could leave with him in remembrance of me, and having bethought me of a pretty memorandum-book in my reticule, I drew him aside and put it in his hand, and bade him keep it for my sake; and asked him to give me one of his medals to keep for his! And all this in tears and in the utmost agitation! Had you any idea that your wife was still such a fool! I am sure I had not. The Father got through the thing admirably. He seemed to understand what it all meant quite well, inarticulate though I was. He would not give me a common medal, but took a little silver one from the neck of a young man who had just taken the pledge for example's sake, telling him he would get him another presently, and then laid the medal into my hand with a solemn blessing. I could not speak for excitement all the way home. When I went to bed I could not sleep; the pale faces I had seen haunted me, and Father Mathew's smile; and even next morning, I could not anyhow subside into my normal state, until I had sat down and written Father Mathew a long letter—accompanying it with your 'Past and Present!' Now, dear, if you are ready to beat me for a distracted Gomeril [1] I cannot help it. All that it was put into my heart to do, *Ich konnte nicht anders.*

When you write, just address to Cheyne Row. I cannot engage for myself being here twenty-four hours longer; it will depend on

---

[1] Scotch for good-natured fool.

how I sleep to-night; and also a little on when I find Elizabeth Mudie [1] will be needed in Manchester. I must be back in time to get her clothes gathered together.

Bless you always. Love to them all.

Your J. C.

I began this in the hotel; but it has been finished in our lodging, which looks quiet and comfortable so far.

LETTER 51.

T. Carlyle, Esq., at Scotsbrig.

Ryde: Friday, Aug. 11, 1843.

Dearest,—The sky-rocket will be off to-morrow morning, on the strength of its own explosiveness; the red-hot poker may stay till it has burnt a hole in its box, if it like! 'Oh! what had I to do for to travel? I was well, I would be better, and I am here!' To be sure, Ryde is a place well worth having seen, and knowing about with a view to future needs; but what I get out of it for the time being, *moi*, is sleeplessness, indigestion, and incipient despair.

I finished my letter to you the first thing I did on taking possession of the lodging. It (the lodging) looked passable enough, so far; a small but neat sitting-room, with two bed-rooms, of which the roomiest was assigned to me—plainly in the expectation that I would modestly prefer the inferior one. But not at all; my modesty remained perfectly passive;—for I knew that he could have had two bed-rooms equally good for two or three shillings a week more; and if he chose to make a sacrifice of comfort for so paltry a saving, I was resolved it should be of his own comfort, not mine.

I went to bed in fear and trembling. I do think another such night as the preceding would have thrown me into brain fever; but I selpt, mercifully, not well, but some. On looking, however, at my fair hand in the morning, as it lay outside the bed-clothes, I perceived it to be all—' what shall I say?' 'elevated into inequalities,' [2] 'significant of much!' Not a doubt of it, I had fallen among

[1] One of two girls in difficult circumstances, for whom, with her sister Juliet, Mrs. Carlyle was endeavouring to provide (see p. 151).—J. A. F.

[2] Euphemism of a certain rustic goose (in our Craigenputtock time) to express the condition of his brow bitten by midges. The preceding locution is established Mazzinian; the following clearly mine.

bugs! My pretty neck too, especially the part of it Babbie used to like to kiss, was all bitten infamously; and I felt myself a degraded Goody, as well as a very unfortunate one. As I sat, exceedingly low, at something which, in the language of flattery, we called breakfast, Clark brought me your letter and one from Babbie and three from Geraldine (who always outdoes you all); administering comfort each after a sort, but Geraldine's most, for they offered me the handsomest pretext for returning home suddenly. One of her letters was to announce the safe arrival of Juliet Mudie, whom she expressed herself outrageously pleased with; the other two were to say that I must get Elizabeth off immediately, as the lady could not wait; and in case of missing me, she had written to this effect to Chelsea and Ryde at the same time. I was not to mind clothing her; all that could be done there; if I was absent, I must employ Mazzini or somebody to see her off. But I was too glad of the excuse, to dream of employing anybody; besides, one always does one's own business best oneself; should she miss the thing, through any interference from the mother or other hindrance which my presence could have obviated, who knows but it might be the losing of her whole chances in life! So I wrote to her instantly to go home and take leave of her mother on receiving my letter (to-day), and make one or two small preparations, which were indispensable unless she should go among strangers like a beggar—which, of course, poor thing, being very handsome or whether or no, she would not like to do; and that I would be there to-morrow, to take her to the railway to-morrow evening. Meanwhile I am getting together one decent suit of clothes for her in the Isle of Wight. That is what I call taking time by the middle.

To-day I have another letter from you, as a sort of marmalade to one's bad bread and tea-urn skimmed-milk tea. Do you know, I pity this poor old man. The notion of saving seems to be growing into a disease with him; and he has still a sufficient natural sense of what looks generous, and even magnificent, to make it a very painful disease. He is really pitiable in every way; and if it were possible for me to stay with him, I would out of sheer charity. He is incapable of applying his mind to reading or writing or any earthly thing. And he cannot move about to 'distract himself' as he used to do, he suffers so much from incessant pain in one of his thighs. He cannot even talk, for every minute needing to roar out, 'This is torture, by Jove!' 'My God, this is agony,' &c. &c. He always will go out to walk, and then for hours after he pays the penalty of it.

I went this morning (while a man was taking down my bedstead to look for the bugs, which were worse last night, of course, having found what a rare creature they had got to eat), and investigated another lodging, which Clark had taken for us, and Sterling gave it up, for no other reason one could imagine, than just because Clark had taken it, and he likes to do everything over again himself. I thought it would be good to know something about lodgings here, in case you might like to try it next time.

Ryde is certainly far the most beautiful sea-bathing place I ever saw; and seems to combine the conveniences and civilisation of town with the purity and quiet of the country in a rather successful manner. The lodging I looked at was quite at the outside of the town: a sitting-room and two bed-rooms, in the house of a single lady; the sitting-room beautiful, the bed-rooms small, but, in compensation, the beds very large; good furniture, and, I should expect, good attendance, 'sitting' in a beautiful garden, villa-wise, rejoicing in the characteristic name of Flora Cottage; and within two minutes' walk of the sea and romantic-looking bushy expanses; a very superior place to Newby, and the cost just the same—two guineas a week. God knows whether there be bugs in it. There is no noise; for the lady remarked to me, *par hasard*, that she sometimes felt frightened in lying awake at night, it was so still; nothing to be heard but the murmuring of the sea. We might 'put this in our pipe' for next year; and I shall look about farther during this my last day. I wonder John never recommended Wight to you with any emphasis; it must surely have some drawback which I have not discovered; for it seems to me a place that would suit even you. And now, dear, if you think my letter hardly worth the reading, remember that I am all bug-bitten and bedevilled and out of my latitude,

Your own
J. C.

Kind remembrances to all; a kiss to my kind, good Jamie.

[We never went to Ryde; we once tried Brighton, once inspected Bournemouth, &c., but the very noises, in all these pretty sea-places, denoted flat impossibility, especially to one of us. How heavenly, salutary, pure is silence; how unattainable in the mad England that now is!—T. C.]

LETTER 52.

T. Carlyle, Esq., at Scotsbrig.

Chelsea: Sunday, Aug. 13, 1843.

Dearest,—I have not for a long time enjoyed a more triumphant moment than in 'descending'[1] from the railway yesterday at Vauxhall, and calling a porter to carry my small trunk and dressing box (of course) to a Chelsea steamer! To be sure, I looked (and felt) as if just returning from the Thirty-years' War. Sleepless, bug-bitten, bedusted and bedevilled, I was hardly recognisable for the same trim little Goody who had left that spot only four days before; but still I was returning *with* my shield, not *on* it. A few minutes more, and I should be purified to the shift, to the very skin—should have absolutely bathed myself with *eau de Cologne*—should have some mutton-broth set before me (I had written from Ryde to bespeak it!), and a silver spoon to eat it with (these four days had taught me to appreciate my luxuries), and prospect of my own red bed at night! That of itself was enough to make me the most thankful woman in Chelsea!

Helen screamed with joy when she saw me (for I was come about an hour sooner than I was expected), and then seized me round the neck and kissed me from ear to ear. Then came Bessie Mudie, with her head quite turned. She could do nothing in the world but laugh for joy, over her own prospects so suddenly brightened for her; and from consciousness of her improved appearance, in a pair of stays and a gown and petticoat which she had got for herself here by my directions. And when I showed her the shawl and other little things I had fetched her from Ryde, she laughed still more, and her face grew so very red that I thought she was going to burst a blood-vessel. She had been home, and had taken leave of her mother—no hindrance there whatever, but was extremely thankful. So all was in readiness for taking her to the railway that evening according to programme.

Mazzini called just when I had finished my dinner to inquire if there had been any news from me; and was astonished to find myself; still more astonished at the extent to which I had managed to ruin myself in so short a time: I looked, he said, 'strange, upon my honor!—most like,' if he might be allowed to say it, 'to Lady Mac-

---

[1] Note, p. 92.

beth in the sleeping scene!' No wonder! Four such nights might have made a somnambulant of a much stronger woman than me, *poverina*.

At half after seven I started with Bessie for Euston Square; committed her to the care of a very fat benevolent-looking old man, who was going all the way; pinned her letter for Geraldine to her stays; kissed the poor young creature, and gave her my blessing; came back wondering whether these two girls that I had launched into the world would live to thank me for it, or not rather wish that I had tied a stone about each of their necks and launched them into the Thames! Impossible to predict! So I went to bed and was asleep in two minutes!

After some hours of the deadest sleep I ever slept on earth, I was wakened with pain in my head; but where I was I could not possibly make out. I sat up in the middle of my bed, to ascertain my locality, and there 'I happened'[1] the oddest mystification you can fancy: I actually lost myself in my bed! could not find the right way of lying down again! I felt about for pillows, none were findable! and I could not get the clothes spread upon me again! They seemed to be fixed down. At last, still groping, with my hand, I felt the footboard at my head! I had lain down 'with my head where my feet should be;' and it was a puzzling business to rectify my position! I went to sleep again, and rose at half after eight; and took my coffee and good bread with such relish! Oh, it was worth while to have spent four days in parsimony; to have been bitten with bugs; to have been irritated with fuss and humbug, and last of all to have been done out of my travelling expenses back! it was worth while to have had all this botheration to refresh my sense of all my mercies. Everything is comparative 'here down;' this morning I need no other Paradise than what I have: cleanness (not of teeth), modest comfort, silence, independence (that is to say, dependence on no other but one's own husband). Yes, I need to be well of my headache, over and above; but that also will come, with more sleep.

I found on my return three book-parcels and your last letter: parcel first, John Sterling's 'Strafford' for myself; you will see a review of it in to-day's 'Examiner,' which will make him desperately angry (Really Fuzz,[2] that brother of ours, improves by keep-

---

[1] Maid at Ampton Street: 'This morning, m'em, I've 'appened a misfortune, m'em' (viz. broken something).

[2] Forster, then editor, or critic, of the *Examiner*.

ing sensible company); second, Varnhagen's three volumes from Lockhart, with a note which I enclose; third, a large showy paper book in three volumes, entitled 'The English Universities,' Hunter and Newman, 'With Mr. James Heywood's compliments' on the the first page. At night another parcel came from Maurice, 'Arnold's Lectures' returned, and Strauss (which latter I purpose reading—I?). I brought with me from Ryde a volume of plays by one Kleist (did you ever hear of him?) which Sterling greatly recommends. The tragedian himself had the most tragic end.[1]

I did not forget about the name of Varnhagen's pamphlet; but at the time you asked it of me it was lying at the bottom of the sofa, with the other books of the low room and Pelion on Ossa on the top of it; to get at it would have cost me an hour's hard work. The name, now it is restored to the upper world, is *Leitfaden zur Nordischen Alterthumskunde*.

I have a negotiation going on about a place for Miss Bölte;[2] but the lady is on the Continent, and it cannot be speedily brought to an alternative. Meanwhile the poor girl is gone to some friend in the country, for a month. I am very sorry indeed for poor Isabella. Give her my kind remembrances—my sympathy, if it could but do anything for her.

Are you—or rather would it be very disagreeable for you—to go to Thornhill, and see the Russells, and Margaret, and old Mary? If you could without finding it irksome, I should like. Oh, to think of your going to Thornhill to see only the Russells![3] Oh, my mother, my own mother.

Monday, Aug. 14.—I had to give up writing yesterday, my head was so woefully bad. But a dinner of roast mutton, with a tumbler of white-wine negus, made me a more effectual woman again; you see I am taking care of myself with a vengeance! But I 'consider it my duty' to get myself made well again—and to tell you the truth I was starved at Ryde, as well as bug-bitten.

In the evening I had Miss Bölte till after ten (I thought she had gone to the country, but she goes to-day), she is really a fine manly

---

[1] Killed himself.

[2] This was a bustling, shifty little German governess, who, in few years, managed to pick up some modicum of money here, and then retired with it to Dresden, wholly devoting herself to 'literature.'

[3] I went duly, sat in poor old Mary Mills's cottage, one morning early, by the side of her turf-pile, &c. She had been on pilgrimage to Crawford churchyard, found the grave; 'It was a' bonnie yonder, vera bonnie,' said she, in her old broken pious tone. I never saw her again.

little creature, with a deal of excellent sense, and not without plenty of German enthusiasm, for all so humdrum as she looks.

This morning I got up immensely better, having had another good sleep; and, in token of my thankfulness to Providence, I fell immediately to glazing and painting with my own hands (not to ruin you altogether). It is now just on post-time. I have had your letter, for consolation in my messy job, and I must send this off; trusting that you found other two letters from me waiting you on coming back; and then return to finish my painting. Pray for me.

Ever your unfortunate,

GOODY.

LETTER 53.

T. Carlyle, Esq., at Scotsbrig.

Chelsea: Thursday, Aug. 17, 1843.

I write to-day, dearest, without any faculty for writing; merely to keep your mind easy, by telling you I have a headache; if I said nothing at all, you might fancy I had something worse. ' Ah'—I could not expect to get off from that vile Wight business so cheaply as with one headache or even two.

Since I wrote last, I have had a sad day in bed, another only a little less sad out of it; besides the pain in my head, such pains in my limbs that I could hardly rise or sit down without screaming. I have taken one blue pill and mean to take another. I am better to-day, though still in a state for which stooping over paper and making the slightest approach to thinking is very bad. So 'you must just excuse us the day.' God bless you. I hope your ' feverish cold' is driven off.

Elizabeth was seeking your address for the Kirkcaldy people, who mean to send you an invitation I suppose. Perhaps it would be your best way of coming back.

Affectionate regards to them all.

Your J. C.

LETTER 54.

T. Carlyle, Esq., at Scotsbrig.

Chelsea: Friday morning, Aug. 18, 1843.

Dearest,—If you expect a spirited letter from me to-day, I grieve that you will be disappointed. I am not mended yet: only mend,

ing, and that present participle (to use Helen's favourite word for the weather) is extremely 'dilatory.' The pains in my limbs are gone, however, leaving only weakness; and my head aches now with 'a certain' moderation! still enough to spoil all one's enjoyment of life—if there be any such thing for some of us—and, what is more to the purpose, enough to interfere with one's 'did intends,' which in my case grow always the longer the more manifold and complicated.

Darwin came yesterday after my dinner-time (I had dined at three), and remarked, in the course of some speculative discourse, that I 'looked as if I needed to go to Gunter's and have an ice!' Do you comprehend what sort of look that can be? Certainly he was right, for driving to Gunter's and having an ice revived me considerably; it was the first time I had felt up to crossing the threshold, since I took Bessie Mudie to the railway the same evening I returned from Ryde. Darwin was very clever yesterday; he remarked, *apropos* of a pamphlet of Maurice's (which by the way is come for you), entitled, 'A Letter to Lord Ashley respecting a certain proposed measure for stifling the expression of opinion in the University of Oxford,' that pamphlets were for some men just what a fit of the gout was for others—they cleared the system so that they could go on again pretty comfortably for a while. He told me also a curious conversation amongst three grooms, at which Wrightson had assisted the day before in a railway carriage, clearly indicating to what an alarming extent the schoolmaster is abroad. Groom the first took a pamphlet from his pocket, saying he had bought it two days ago and never found a minute to read it. Groom the second inquired the subject. First groom: 'Oh, a hit at the Puseyists.' Second groom: 'The Puseyists? Ha, they are for bringing us back to the times when people burnt one another!' First groom (tapping second groom on the shoulder with the pamphlet): 'Charity, my brother, charity!' Third groom: 'Well, I cannot say about the Puseyists; but my opinion is that what we need is more Christianity and less religionism!' Now Wrightson swears that every word of this is literally as the men spoke it—and certainly Wrightson could not invent it.

I had a long letter from old Sterling, which stupidly I flung into the fire in a rage (the fire? Yes, it is only for the last two days that I have not needed fire in the morning!); and I bethought me afterwards that I had better have sent it to you, whom its cool Robert Macaire impudence might have amused. Only fancy his inviting me to come back, and 'this time he would take care that I should have habitable lodgings.' His letter began, 'The last cord which held me to existence here is snapped,'—meaning me! and so on. Oh, 'the devil fly away with' the old sentimental ——!

I had letters from both Mr. and Mrs. Buller yesterday explaining their having failed to invite me; she appears to have been worse than ever, and is likely to be soon here again. Poor old Buller's modest hope that the new medicine 'may not turn Madam blue' is really touching!

Here is your letter come. And you have not yet got any from me since my return! Somebody must have been very negligent, for I wrote to you on Sunday, added a postscript on Monday, and sent off both letter and newspapers by Helen, in perfectly good time. It is most provoking after one has been (as Helen says) 'just most particular' not to *vaix* you, to find that you have been *vaixed* nevertheless.

You ask about the state of the house. Pearson and Co. are out of it. Both the public rooms are in a state of perfect habitableness again; a little to be done in the needle-work department, but 'nothing' (like Dodger's Boy's nose) 'to speak of.' Your bedroom, of which the ceiling had to be whitened and the paint washed, &c., &c., will be habitable by to-morrow. The front bedrooms, into which all the confusion had been piled, are still to clean;—but that will soon be done. My own bedroom also needs to have the carpet beaten, and the bed curtains taken down and brushed; all this would have been completed by this time but for a most unexpected and soul-sickening mess, which I discovered in the kitchen, which has caused work for several days. Only fancy, while I was brightening up the outside of the platter to find in Helen's bed a new colony of bugs! I tell you of it fearlessly this time, as past victory gives me a sense of superiority over the creatures. She said to me one morning in putting down my breakfast, 'My! I was just standing this morning, looking up at the corner of my bed, ye ken, and there what should I see but two bogues! I hope there's na mair.' 'You hope?' said I immediately kindling into a fine phrenzy; 'how could you live an instant without making sure? A pretty thing it will be if you have let your bed get full of bugs again!' The shadow of an accusation of remissness was enough of course to make her quite positive. 'How was she ever to have thought of bogues, formerly? What a thing to think about! But since, she had been just most particular! To be sure, these two must have come off these Mudies' shawls!' I left her protesting and 'appealing to posterity,'[1] and ran off myself to see into the business. She had not so much as taken off the curtains; I tore them off distractedly, pulled in pieces all of the bed that was pullable, and saw and killed two, and in one place which I could not get at without a bed-key, 'beings' (as Mazzini would say) were clearly moving! Ah, mercy mercy, my dismay was considerable! Still it was not the acme of horror this time, as last time, for now I knew they could be annihilated root and branch. When I told her there were plenty, she went off to look herself, and came back and told me in a peremptory tone that 'she had looked and there was not a single bogue there!' It was needless arguing with a wild animal. I had Pearson to take the bed down, and he soon gave me the pleasant assurance that 'they were pretty strong!' Neither did he consider them a recent importation.

Helen went out of the way at the taking down of the bed, not to be proved in the wrong to her own conviction; which was 'probably just as well,' as she might have saved a remnant in her petticoats, being so utterly careless about the article. Pearson, who shared all my own nervous sensibility, was a much better assistant for me. I flung some twenty pailfuls of water on the kitchen floor, in the first place, to drown any that might attempt to save themselves; then we killed all that were discoverable, and flung the pieces of the bed, one after another, into a tub full of water, carried them up into the garden, and let them steep there for two days;— and then I painted all the joints, had the curtains washed and laid by for the present, and hope and trust there is not one escaped alive to tell. *Ach Gott,* what disgusting work to have to do!—but the destroying of bugs is a thing that cannot be neglected. In the course of the bug investigation I made another precious discovery. That the woollen mattress was being eaten from under her with moths. That had to be torn up next, all the wool washed and boiled, and teazed,—and I have a woman here this day making it up into a mattress again. In your bed I had ocular conviction that there were none when it was in pieces; in my own I have inferential conviction, for they would have been sure to bite me the very first Adam and Eve of them; in the front room nothing is discoverable either. But I shall take that bed all down for security's sake before I have done with it;—either that, or go up and sleep in it a night:—but then imagination might deceive me, and even cause spots! 'The troubles that afflict the just,' &c.

---

[1] Note, *supra.*

We have warm weather these two days: not oppressive for me, but more summer-like than any that has been this season.

Oh, I always forgot to tell you that in the railway carriage, going to Ryde, my next neighbour was Robert Owen (the Socialist); he did not know anything of me, so that I had the advantage of him. I found something of old Laing in him, particularly the voice. I like him on the whole, and in proof thereof gave him two carnations.

Your affectionate
GOODY.

I have heard nothing farther of Father Mathew. Knowing how busy he was, and supposing him not much used to corresponding with women of genius, I worded my letter so as to make him understand I looked for no answer. As to the stuffed Pope,[1] I thought of him (or rather of it); but I felt too much confidence in Father Mathew's good sense to fear his being shocked.

LETTER 55.

T. Carlyle, Esq., at Scotsbrig.

Chelsea: Monday, Aug. 21, 1843.

Dearest,—I meant to have written you an exceedingly long and satisfactory letter last evening; but a quite other work was cut out for me, which I cannot say I regret. It is but little good one can do to a sane man, whereas for an insane one much is possible; and I did even the impossible for such a one last night. Poor Garnier[2] walked in at five, and stayed till after nine. And if you had seen the difference in him at his entrance and exit, you would have said that I had worked a miracle!

Poor fellow! they may all abuse him as they like; but I think, and have thought, and will think, well of him: he has a good heart and a good head; only a nervous system all bedevilled, and his external life fallen into a horribly burbled state about him. I gave him tea, and took him a walk, and lent him some music, and soothed the troubled soul of him, and when he went away he said the only civil thing to me he ever said in life. 'I am obliged to you, Mrs. Carlyle; you have made me pass one evening pleasantly; and I came very miserable.' He desired his kind regards to you, and has a scheme, a propagation, of small schools, to propound to

---

[1] In *Past and Present.*   [2] See pages 19 and 142.

you. His uncle in Germany is dead, which will ultimately make an amendment in his economics he seems to say.

I am very quiet at present, so few people are left in town. Even poor Gludder (the infamy of giving a Christian such a name!) has been gone some time to Tottenham Park; but his patience seems near the end of its tether, and he purposes emancipating himself shortly, 'before he loses his faculties altogether.' Then Darwin is always going off on short excursions. The Macready women, however, came the day before yesterday, the first time I had seen them since your departure. And I have something to ask on the part of Mrs. Macready: 'If you could give William any letters of introduction for America, it would be such a favour!' She cannot bear the idea of his 'going merely as a player, without private recommendations.' They looked perfectly heart-broken, these women. The letters to America will be needed within ten days. To Emerson? Who is there else worth knowing in America? I promised to spend a day with them before he went.

Poor Father Mathew, they say, is getting into deep waters here. He does not possess the Cockney strength of silence; his Irish blood gets up when he is angered, and he 'commits himself;' I am all the more pleased at having given him my most sweet voice, for there is plainly a vast deal of party spirit taking the field to put him down. One thing they laugh at him for is, to my thinking, highly meritorious. Somebody trying to stir up the crowd against him, said, 'What good can come to you from that man?—he is only a Popish Monk!' Whereupon Father Mathew burst out, 'And what do you mean by saying no good can come from a I ish Monk? Have you not received just the greatest blessings from Popish Monks? Have you not received Christianity from a Popish Monk? the Reformation from a Popish Monk—Martin Luther?' There was something so delightfully Irish, and liberal at the same time, in this double view of Luther!

No letter from you to-day; but perhaps there will come one in the evening. You cannot be accused of remissness in writing, at all rates, whatever your other faults may be. Oh, no! you need not go to Thornhill.[1] It was a selfish request on my part. I would not go myself for a thousand guineas. But send the five pound for poor old Mary before you leave the country: her money falls entirely done at the end of this month. I computed it quite accurately, when Mrs. Russell wrote that she had still thirty shil-

---

[1] See *supra*, however? I hope devoutly it was that time. Ah, me!

lings. She will not be long to provide for, poor old soul! I have sent the books for Lockhart.

I am busy with a little work just now that makes me so sad. You remember the new curtains that came from Templand. When she made them, she wrote to me, 'they looked so beautiful that she could not find in her heart to hang them up till I should be coming again;' and the first sight I was to have of them was here!—and it was here, not there, that they were to be hung up. It needed a deal of scheming and altering to make them fit our high room; and picking out her sewing has been such sorrowful work for me: still I could not let anybody meddle with them except myself; and to keep them lying there was just as sorrowful. Oh, dear, dear!

I hope you are quite free of your cold; the weather is quite cool again. God bless you.

Your affectionate

JANE CARLYLE.

'Garnier'[1] was from Baden; a revolutionary exile, filled with mutinous confusion of the usual kind, and with its usual consequences; a black-eyed, tall, stalwart-looking mass of a man; face all cut with scars (of duels in his student time), but expressive still of frankness, honesty, ingenuity, and good humour; dirty for most part, yet as it were heroically so: few men had more experience of poverty and squalor here, or took it more proudly. He had some real scholarship, a good deal of loose information; occasionally wrote, and had he been of moderate humour could always have written, with something of real talent. Cole, the now great Cole, of 'the Brompton boilers,' occasionally met him (in the Buller Committee, for instance), and tried to help him, as did I. Together we got him finally into some small clerkship under Cole, Cole selecting the feasible appointment, I recommending to Lord Stanley, who, as 'whipper-in,' had the nomination and always believed what I testified to him. 'You called me a *rhinoceros*' (not to be driven like a tame ox), said Garnier to me on this occasion, pretending, and only pretending, to be angry at me. In a year or two he flung off this harness too, and took to the desert again. Poor soul! he was at last visibly now and then rather mad. In 1848 we heard he had rushed into German whirlpool, and, fighting in Baden, had perished. John Mill, in 1834, had been his introducer here.

'Gludder' was one Plattnauer (still living hereabouts and an esteemed tutor in noble families), whom Cavaignac had (on repeated pressure) lately introduced here, and who has hung about us, lovingly, and much pitied by her. ever since. I never could much take to him, had called him 'Gludder' (a word of my father's) from the sad sound he made in articulating (as if through slush), or get

---

real good of him, nor now can when he has grown so sad to me. On the whole, one rapidly enough perceived that the foreign exile element was not the recommendable one, and, except for her picturesque æsthetic, &c. interest in it, would have been very brief with it here. As indeed I essentially was; nor she herself very tedious. Except with Cavaignac I never had any intimacy, any pleasant or useful conversation, among these people—except for Mazzini, and him any real respect—and from the first dialogue, Mazzini's opinions were to me incredible, and (at once tragically and comically) impracticable in this world. She, too, even of Mazzini, gradually came to that view, though to the last she had always an affection for Mazzini, and for the chivalrous and grandly humorous Cavaignac (and for the memory of him afterwards) still more.—T. C.

LETTER 56.

T. Carlyle, Esq., at Scotsbrig, Ecclefechan.

Chelsea: Sunday night, Aug. 27, 1843.

Dearest,—Another evening, in thought set apart for you, has been eaten up alive by ' rebellious consonants.' I had told Helen to go after dinner and take herself a long walk, assuring her nobody could possibly arrive, for the best of reasons, that ' there was not a human being left in London.' And just when I had fetched up my own tea, and was proceeding to ' enjo-oy it '[1] quite in old-maid style, there arrived Darley,[2] the sight of whom gave me a horrible foretaste of fidgets and nameless woe, which was duly fulfilled to me in good time. However, it is to be hoped that he got a little good for having a mouthful of human (or rather, to speak accurately, inhuman) speech with someone; and in that case one's care being ' the welfare of others,' &c. &c. For myself individually, I feel as if I had spent the evening under a harrow.

I hardly know where a letter now shall find you. But perhaps to-morrow will direct me before sending this away. It is very stupid of the Ferguses—a fact almost as absurd as speaking to Elizabeth of sending us potatoes last year, and never sending them. But if you want to see the battle-ground at Dunbar, I am sure you need not miss it for lack of somewhere to go. The poor Donaldsons—nay, everybody in Haddington—would be so glad to have

---

[1] The good W. Graham, of Burnswark, a true and kind, and very emphatic, friend of mine, had thoughtlessly bragged once (first time she saw him), at a breakfast with us dyspeptics, how he ' enjo-oyed ' this and that.

[2] ' Darley ' (George), from Dublin, mathematician, considerable actually and do. poet, an amiable, modest, veracious, and intelligent man; much loved here, though he stammered dreadfully.

you. The Donaldsons, you know, formerly invited you 'for a month or two' this spring. I cannot detect the association, but it comes in my head at this moment, and I may as well tell you, that the Revd. Candlish is in great raptures over 'Past and Present;' so Robertson told me the last time I saw him. Garnier also told me that the book had a success of an unusual and very desirable kind; it was not so much that people spoke about it, as that they spoke out of it; in these mysterious conventions of his, your phrases, he said, were become a part of the general dialect. The booksellers would not have Garnier's translation: that was the reason of its being given up; not that he was too mad for it. It was *I* who told you about the Lord Dudley Stuart affair; Garnier gave me his own version of it that night, and it seemed quite of a piece with his usual conduct—good intentions, always unfortunate; a right thing wrongly set about.

Well, the Italian 'Movement' has begun; and also, I suppose, ended. Mazzini has been in a state of violent excitement all these weeks, really forcibly reminding one of Frank Dickson's goose with the addle egg. Nothing hindered him from going off to head the movement, except that, unexpectedly enough, the movement did not invite him; nay, took pains to 'keep him in a certain ignorance,' and his favourite conspirator abroad. The movement went into Sicily 'to act there alone,' plainly indicating that it meditated some arrangement of Italy such as they two would not approve, 'something—what shall I say?—constitutional.' He came one day, and told me quite seriously that a week more would determine him whether to go singly and try to enter the country in secret, or to persuade a frigate now here, which he deemed persuadable, to revolt openly and take him there by force. 'And with one frigate,' said I, 'you mean to overthrow the Austrian Empire, amidst the general peace of Europe?' 'Why not? the beginning only is wanted.' I could not help telling him that 'a Harrow or Eton schoolboy who uttered such nonsense, and proceeded to give it a practical shape, would be whipt and expelled the community as a mischievous blockhead.' He was made very angry, of course, but it was impossible to see anybody behaving so like 'a mad,' without telling him one's mind. He a conspirator chief! I should make an infinitely better one myself. What, for instance, can be more out of the *rôle* of conspirator than his telling me all his secret operations, even to the names of places where conspiracy is breaking out, and the names of people who are organising it? *Me*, who do not even ever ask him a question on such matters; who on the contrary evade them as much as possible! A man has a right to put his own life and safety at the mercy of whom he will, but no amount of confidence in a friend can justify him for making such dangerous disclosures concerning others. What would there have been very unnatural, for example, in my sending a few words to the Austrian Government, warning them of the projected outbreaks, merely for the purpose of having them prevented, so as to save Mazzini's head and the heads of the greater number, at the sacrifice of a few? If I had not believed that it would be, like the 'Savoy's Expedition,' stopped by some providential toll-bar, I believe I should have felt it my duty as Mazzini's friend to do this thing. Bologna was the place where they were first to raise their foolscap-standard. The 'Examiner' mentions carelessly some young men having collected in the streets, and 'raised seditious cries, and even fired some shots at the police;' cannon were planted, &c., 'Austrians ready to march'—not a doubt of it; and seditious cries will make a poor battle against cannon. Mazzini is confident, however, that the thing will not stop here; and, if it goes on, is resolute also in getting into the thick of it. 'What do you say of my head? what are results? are there not things more important than one's head?' 'Certainly, but I should say that the man who has not sense enough to keep his head on his shoulders till something is to be gained by parting with it, has not sense enough to manage, or dream of managing, any important matter whatever.' Our dialogues become 'warm,' but you see how much I have written about this, which you will think six words too many for.

Good-night; I must go and sleep.

Monday.

Dearest,—Thanks for your letter, and, oh, a thousand thanks for all this you have done for me! I am glad that you have seen these poor people,[1] that they have had the gladness of seeing you. Poor old Mary! it will be something to talk and think over for a year to come. Your letter has made me cry, to be sure, but has made me very contented nevertheless. I am very grateful to you. Did Mrs. Russell say anything about not having answered my letter? I sent a little shawl, on my last birthday, to Margaret, to Mrs. R.'s care, and a pound of tea (that is money for it) to old Mary, in a letter to Mrs. Russell, and, as I have never heard a word from Thornhill

---

[1] At Thornhill, to which Carlyle had gone, at her request.

I.—7

since, I have sometimes feared the things had been taken by the way; it is very stupid in people not to give one the satisfaction of writing on these little occasions.

I am afraid you will think London dreadfully solitary when you return from the country. Actually there never was so quiet a house except Craigenputtock as this has been for the last fortnight. Darwin finally is off this morning to Shrewsbury for three weeks. He gave me a drive to Parson's Green yesterday; 'wondered if Carlyle would give admiration enough for all my needlework, &c., &c., feared not; but he would have a vague sense of comfort from it,' and uttered many other sarcastic things, by way of going off in good Darwin style. Just when I seemed to be got pretty well through my sewing, I have rushed wildly into a new mess of it. I have realised an ideal, have actually acquired a small sofa, which needs to be covered, of course. I think I see your questioning look at this piece of news: 'A sofa? Just now, above all, when there had been so much else done and to pay for! This little woman is falling away from her hitherto thrifty character, and become downright extravagant.' Never fear! this little woman knows what she is about; the sofa costs you simply nothing at all! Neither have I sillily paid four or five pounds away for it out of my own private purse. It is a sofa which I have known about for the last year and half. The man who had it asked 4*l.* 10*s.* for it; was willing to sell it without mattress or cushions for 2*l.* 10*s.* I had a spare mattress which I could make to fit it, and also pillows lying by of no use. But still, 2*l.* 10*s.* was more than I cared to lay out of my own money on the article, so I did a stroke of trade with him. The old green curtains of downstairs were become filthy; and, what was better, superfluous. No use could be made of them, unless first dyed at the rate of 7*d.* per yard; it was good to be rid of them, that they might not fill the house with moths, as those sort of woollen things lying by always do: so I sold them to the broker for thirty shillings; I do honestly think more than their value; but I higgled a full hour with him, and the sofa had lain on his hands. So you perceive there remained only one pound to pay; and that I paid with Kitty Kirkpatrick's sovereign, which I had laid aside not to be appropriated to my own absolutely individual use. So there is a sofa created in a manner by the mere wish to have it.

Oh, what nonsense clatter I do write to thee! Bless you, dearest, anyhow.   Affectionately your own,

                                        JANE CARLYLE.

I did go to Dunbar battle-field, remember vividly my survey there, my wild windy walk from Haddington thither and back; bright Sunday, but gradually the windiest I was ever out in; head wind (west), on my return, would actually hold my hat against my breast for minutes together. It was days before I got the sand out of my hair again. Saw East Lothian, all become a treeless 'Corn Manchester'—a little more money in its pocket—and of piety, to God or man, or mother-earth, how much left? At Linton in the forenoon, I noticed lying on the green, many of them with Bibles, some 150 decent Highlanders; last remnant of the old 'Highland reapers' here; and round them, in every quarter, all such a herd of miserable, weak, restless 'wild Irish,' their conquerors and successors here, as filled me with a kind of rage and sorrow at once; all in ragged grey frieze, 3,000 or 4,000 of them, aimless, restless, hungry, senseless, more like apes than men; swarming about, leaping into bean-fields, turnip-fields, and out again, asking you 'the toime, sir.'—I almost wondered the Sabbatarian country did not rise on them, fling the whole lot into the Frith. Sabbatarian country never dreamt of such a thing, and I could not do it myself; I merely told them 'the toime, sir.'

The excellent old Misses Donaldson, how kind, how good, and sad; I never saw one of them again. Vacant, sad, was Haddington to me; sternly sad the grave which has now become hers as well! I have seen it twice since.

LETTER 57.

Brother 'John' is on the way to Italy—never one of the quietest of men in this house!—'Time and Space,' &c., is a story of Mrs. Austin's, about two metaphysical spouses (I quite forget whom) on their wedding-day: 'Come, my dear one, and let us have,' &c.

T. Carlyle, Esq., at Scotsbrig.

Chelsea: Thursday, Aug. 31, 1843.

Dearest,—The enclosed note from John arrived last night, along with yours announcing his departure for Liverpool. I wish he had been coming after you, or even with you. I had set my heart on your hanselling the clean house yourself, and that there would have been a few days in peace to inspect its curiosities and niceties before he came plunging in to send all the books afloat, and litter the floors with first and second and third and fourth scrawls of *verfehlt* letters. But, like Mademoiselle L'Espinasse, *son talent est d'être toujours hors de propos!* If he cared about seeing oneself, it would be quite different; but if the house would go on like those charming palaces one reads of in the fairy tales, where clothes are found hanging ready at the fire to be put on by the wearied travel-

ler, and a table comes up through the floor all spread to appease
his hunger, oneself might be a thousand miles off, or, like the
enchanted Princess of these establishments, might be running
about in the shape of a 'little mouse,' without his contentment
being disturbed, or indeed anything but increased, by the blank.
Howsomdever!—Only, when you come, I shall insist on going into
some room with you, and locking the door, till we have had a quiet
comfortable talk about 'Time and Space,' untormented by his
blether. Meanwhile, 'the duty nearest hand' is to get on the stair-
carpet that he may run up and down more softly.

LETTER 58.

From the Dunbar expedition I seem to have gone again to Scotsbrig for a few final days; thence homewards, round by Edinburgh,
by Kirkcaldy, and at length by Linlathen, for the sake of a Dundee steamer, in which I still remember to have come hence. Vivid
enough still that day of my embarkation at Dundee; between Dunbar and that, almost nothing of distinct. 'The good Stirlings' are
Susan Hunter, of St. Andrews, and her husband, a worthy engineer,
now resident at Dundee—pleasant house on the sea-shore, where I
must have called, but found them gone out. The good Susan (I
remember hearing afterwards) had, from her windows, with a pros-
pect-glass, singled me out on the chaotic deck of the steamer about
to leave; and kept me steadily in view for about an hour, in spite
of the crowds and confusions, till we actually steamed away.
Which seemed curious! An hour or two before, in driving thither
from Linlathen, I distinctly recognised, on the pathway, John
Jeffrey ('Frank' or Lord Jeffrey's brother), quiet, amiable man,
with his face (which was towards me, but intent on the constitutional walk only) grown strangely red since I had seen him; the
guest of these Stirlings I could well guess, and indeed not far from
their house. He died soon after; my last sight of him this.

T. Carlyle, Esq., at T. Erskine's, Esq., Linlathen, Dundee.

Chelsea: Sept. 12 (?), 1843.

Dearest,—I could almost have cried, last night, when the letter I
had sent off on Thursday came back to me from Scotsbrig; though
I knew, after receiving yours from Dumfries, that it would not
reach you there, I made sure of their sending it on to Edinburgh,
and that so there would be something for you at the post-office.
But for this fond illusion I should not have let a slight headache,
combined with a great washing of blankets, hinder me from doing
your bidding in that small matter. When you are so unfailing in
writing to me—and such kind, good letters—it were a shame indeed

if I wilfully disappointed you. You will not have been anxious anyhow I hope, for that would be a worse effect of my silence than to have made you angry with me.

All is going on here as well as could be expected; not so comfortably indeed as when I was alone, but I shall 'be good,' you may depend upon it, 'till you come.' John arrived in due course, in a sort of sublimely self-complacent state, enlarging much on his general usefulness wherever he had been! Since then I have had his company at all meals, and he reads in the same room with me, in the evenings, a great many books simultaneously, which he rummages out one after another from all the different places where I had arranged them in the highest order. The rest of his time is spent as you can figure: going out and in, up and down, backwards and forwards; smoking, and playing with the cat in the garden; writing notes in his own room and your room alternately; and pottering about Brompton, looking at Robertson's lodgings and Gambardella's lodgings over and over again, with how much of a practical view no mortal can tell. For just when I thought he was deciding for Gambardella's, he came in and told me that he thought he would have an offer from Lady Clare's brother to go to Italy, and expressed astonishment on my saying that I had understood he did not want to go back to Italy. 'Why not? He could not afford to set up as doctor here, and keep up a large house that would be suitable for the purpose.' That is always a subject of discussion which brings the image of my own noble father before me; making a contrast, under which I cannot argue without losing all temper. So I quitted it as fast as possible, and he has not told me anything more of his views. I should really be sorry for him, weltering 'like a fly among treacle' as he is, if it were not for his self-conceit, which seems to be always saying to one, '—— you, be wae for yourself!'[1]

I have nothing to tell you of the news sort, and of the inner-woman sort; I feel as if I had now only to await your coming in silence. The note from Cole came this morning. Nickison's was returned from Scotsbrig along with my letter last night. Do not forget that we have a cousin in Fife.[2] The thing being a novelty

---

[1] A conceited, quizzing man, to poor Rae, an industrious simpleton, nursing his baby at that moment, on the street of Ecclefechan: 'Rae, I's wae for you.' 'Damn ye, be wae for yersel'!' answered Rae sharply, with laughter from the bystanders. [2] Rev. Walter Welsh, Auchtertool.

might easily slip your memory, and if you go back to Edinburgh do try to see poor Betty,[1] who would be made happy for a year by the sight of any of us. Her address is 15 East Adam Street; my aunts', in case you should have any leisure for them, is 30 Clarence Street. And Sam Aitken?[2]

I do not see how you are to get home by Saturday's steamer, after all. If you go to Dundee, you might spend a day very pleasantly with those good Sterlings, besides there being 'St. Thomas'[3] to see. Do not hurry yourself an hour on my account; all will go well till you come. Remember me kindly to everybody that cares for me; if you have time, look in on Helen's sister,[4] and say I have been very well satisfied with her this long while.

Poor Macready called to take leave of me and to leave with me his 'grateful regards' for you. His little wife, who accompanied him, looked the very picture of woe. I could not help thinking, if he met the fate of Power.[5] And when I bade him farewell I turned quite sick myself in sympathy with the little woman. Garnier was back last night uncommonly sane, with a very bad coat, but clean; had been working very hard, and drinking, I should say, not at all.

God bless you, dear; thank you a thousand times for all that you told me in your last two letters; they were very sad but very precious to me.

Your affectionate

JANE C.

LETTER 59.

To John Forster, Esq., 58 Lincoln's Inn Fields.

Chelsea: Friday morning, Sept. 1843.

Oh, my good Brother,—For two things accept my 'unmitigated' thanks! First for having done the King of Prussia so famously that the innocent heart of old Krazinski leapt for joy;—secondly for a more 'questionable' kindness, viz., having done for Strafford! Hang the 'Legitimate Drammar!' or in my husband's more poetical dialect, 'the devil fly away with it!' I have told him (Sterling)

---

[1] 'Betty' is the old servant at Haddington, now married, in Edinburgh, still living near; one of the most pious, true, and affectionate of women.

[2] Obliging bookseller, successor of Bradfute.

[3] T. Erskine, of Linlathen, to whom I did go. Home thence by steamer.

[4] At Kirkcaldy.

[5] Comic Irish actor, sailed to America, had 'splendid success' there. On the return voyage steamer itself went down; mouse and man never heard of more.

all along that it was poor stuff, and had better not see the light, or at least have the light see it. But, no! it was a great and glorious piece of work in its author's opinion; and I, and all who fail to recognise it for such, were blinded by envy or some other of the evil passions. I was so glad you did not praise it, and so undo all the salutary influence which my abuse of it might ultimately exert on him.

My husband is likely to turn up here in about a week. His shadow (his brother) is cast before him,—arrived last night.

LETTER 60.

I had sent out 'Past and Present' I think in the early part of this summer, and then gone on a lengthened tour of expected 'recreation' into Wales (to my poor friend Redwood at Llandough, Cowbridge, there), thence to Carmarthen (three days) to the Bishop of St. David's here, days mostly wet; thence by Malvern to Liverpool; met my brother, and with him to North Wales (top of Snowdon cloaked in thick mist on our arrival there)—at Beth-gellert and Tremadoc deluges of rain, &c. &c.—back to Liverpool, and thence to Annandale for three weeks; after all which home to Chelsea, as noticed in this letter; all the subsequent details of which rise gradually into clearness, generally of a painful nature to me. The fittings and refittings for me full of loving ingenuity, the musical young lady other side the wall; the general dreary and chaotic state of inward man while struggling to get 'Cromwell' started, all this and the bright ever-cheering presence in it, literally the only cheering element there was, comes back into my heart with a mournful gratitude at this moment.

'The Mudies' were two grown daughters of a Mr. Mudie whom I recollect hearing of about 1818 as a restless, somewhat reckless, and supreme schoolmaster at Dundee. He had thrown up his function there in about 1820, and marched off to London as a liter-ary adventurer. Here for above twenty years he did manage to subsist and float about in the 'mother of dead dogs,' had even con-siderable success of a kind; wrote a great many miscellaneous vol-umes mostly about natural history, I think, which were said to dis-play diligence and merit, and to have brought him considerable sums. But by this time the poor fellow had broken down, had died and left a family, mostly daughters, with a foolish widow, and next to no provision whatever for them. The case was abundantly pite-ous, but it was not by encouragement from me, to whom it seemed from the first hopeless, that my dear one entered into it with such zeal and determination. Her plans were, I believe, the wisest that could be formed, and the trouble she took was very great. I re-member these Mudies—flary, staring, and conceited, stolid-looking girls, thinking themselves handsome, being brought to get-with us here, to get out of the maternal element, while 'places' were being prepared for them; but no amount of trouble was, or could be, of the least avail. The wretched stalking blockheads stalked fate-fully, in spite of all that could be done or said, steadily downwards toward perdition, and sank altogether out of view. There was no want of pity in this house. I never knew a heart more open to the sufferings of others, and to the last she persisted in attempts at little operations for behoof of such; but had to admit that except in one or two small instances she had done no good to the unfortunate objects she attempted to aid.—T. C., March 1873.

Mrs. Aitken, Dumfries.

October 1843.

My dear Jane,—Carlyle returned from his travels very bilious, and continues very bilious up to this hour. The amount of bile that he does bring home to me, in these cases, is something 'aw-fully grand!'[1] Even through that deteriorating medium he could not but be struck with a 'certain admiration' at the immensity of needlework I had accomplished in his absence, in the shape of chair-covers, sofa-covers, window curtains, &c., &c., and all the other manifest improvements into which I had put my whole genius and industry, and so little money as was hardly to be conceived![2] For three days his satisfaction over the rehabilitated house lasted; on the fourth, the young lady next door took a fit of practising on her accursed pianoforte, which he had quite forgotten seemingly, and he started up disenchanted in his new library, and informed heaven, and earth in a peremptory manner that 'there he could neither think nor live,' that the carpenter must be brought back and 'steps taken to make him a quiet place somewhere—perhaps best of all on the roof of the house.' Then followed interminable consultations with the said carpenter, yielding, for some days, only plans (wild ones) and estimates. The roof on the house could be made all that a living author of irritable nerves could desire: silent as a tomb, lighted from above; but it would cost us 120*l.*! Impos-sible, seeing that we may be turned out of the house any year! So one had to reduce one's schemes to the altering of rooms that al-ready were. By taking down a partition and instituting a fire-place where no fire-place could have been fancied capable of existing, it is expected that some bearable approximation to that ideal room in the clouds will be realised. But my astonishment and despair on finding myself after three months of what they call here 'regular

---

[1] Newspaper phrase.

[2] Literally and arithmetically true, thou noble darling! richer to me than all the duchesses of the creation!

mess,' just when I had got every trace of the work-people cleared away, and had said to myself, 'Soul, take thine ease, or at all events thy swing, for thou hast carpets nailed down and furniture rubbed for many days!' just when I was beginning to lead the dreaming, reading, dawdling existence which best suits me, and alone suits me in cold weather, to find myself in the thick of a new 'mess:' the carpets, which I had nailed down so well with my own hands, tumbled up again, dirt, lime, whitewash, oil, paint, hard at work as before, and a prospect of new cleanings, new sewings, new arrangements stretching away into eternity for anything I see! 'Well,' as my Helen says (the strangest mixture of philosopher and perfect idiot that I have met with in my life), 'when one's doing this, one's doing nothing else anyhow!' And as one ought to be always doing something, this suggestion of hers has some consolation in it.

John has got a very pleasant lodging, in the solitude of which it is to be hoped he may discover 'what he wanted and what he wants.'[1] There is an old man who goes about singing here, and accompanying himself on the worst of fiddles, who has a song about Adam that John should lend all his ears to: it tells about all his comforts in Paradise, and then adds that he nevertheless was at a loss; to be sure,

> ' He had all that was pleasant in life,
> But the all-wise, great Creator
> Saw that he wanted a wife!'[2]

But you could form no notion of the impressiveness of this song unless you could hear the peculiar jerk in the fiddle in the middle of the last line, and the old man's distribution of emphasis on the different words of it.

---

[1] Character in one of Zechariah Werner's plays.

[2] In a quiet street near Covent Garden, one sunny day, with a considerable straggle of audience, I found this artist industriously fiddling and singing what seemed to be a succinct doggerel 'History of Man' (in Paradise as yet). Artist was not very old, but wanted the front teeth; was rather dirty, had a beard of three weeks, &c., and for the rest a look of great assiduity and earnestness in his vocation; insisting on longs and shorts, with clear emphasis, by fiddle and voice. These were the words I heard (accentuated as here):—

> ' 'E (Adam evidently) 'ad 'ounds and 'osses for 'unting,
> 'E 'ad all things was pleasant in life;
> The all-wīse grēat Creătŏr [*with a deep scrape of the fiddle*]
> Saw that 'ē wanted a wife.'

Ay de mi! how strange at this moment (April 29, 1869)!

Here is come a son of Mrs. Strachey's, to be talked to; werch enough, but there is no help for it. I do not think you shall have such reason to reproach me again, now that the ice is broken.

Kind regards to your husband. God keep you all.

Affectionately yours,

JANE CARLYLE.

Mrs. Carlyle fills out the picture of the 'domestic earthquake' in a letter to Mrs. Stirling.

'Up went all the carpets which my own hands had nailed down, in rushed the troop of incarnate demons, bricklayers, joiners, white-washers, &c., whose noise and dirt and dawdling had so lately driven me to despair. Down went a partition in one room, up went a new chimney in another. Helen, instead of exerting herself to stave the torrent of confusion, seemed to be struck (no wonder) with temporary idiotcy; and my husband himself, at sight of the uproar he had raised, was all but wringing his hands and tearing his hair, like the German wizard servant who has learnt magic enough to make the broomstick carry water for him, but had not the counter spell to stop it. Myself could have sat down and cried, so little strength or spirit I had left to front the pressure of my circumstances. But crying makes no way; so I went about sweeping and dusting as an example to Helen; and held my peace as an example to my husband, who verily, as Mazzini says of him, 'loves silence somewhat platonically.' It was got through in the end, this new hubbub; but, when my husband proceeded to occupy his new study, he found that devil a bit he could write in it any more than beside the piano; 'it was all so strange to him!' The fact is, the thing he has got to write—his long projected life of Cromwell —is no joke, and no sort of room can make it easy, and he has been ever since shifting about in the saddest way from one room to another, like a sort of domestic wandering Jew! He has now a fair chance, however, of getting a settlement effected in the original library; the young lady next door having promised to abstain religiously from playing till two o'clock, when the worst of his day's work is over. Generous young lady! But it must be confessed, the seductive letter he wrote to her the other day was enough to have gained the heart of a stone.

Alas, one can make fun of all this on paper; but in practice it is anything but fun, I can assure you. There is no help for it, however; a man cannot hold his genius as a sinecure.

LETTER 61.

To John Welsh, Esq., Liverpool.

Chelsea: Tuesday night, Nov. 28, 1843.

Uncle dear!—How are you? I kiss you from ear to ear, and I love you very considerably; 'hoping to find you the same.'

The spirit moves me to write to you just at this unlikeliest moment (for my spirit is a contradictory spirit), when the influenza has left me with scarce faculty enough to spell words of more than one syllable. I caught the horrid thing a week ago, by destiny, through no indiscretion of my own, which is a consolation of a certain sort. For it does form a most 'aggravating' ingredient in one's suffering to be held responsible for it; to be told 'this comes of your going to such a place, or doing such a thing; if you had taken my advice' &c. &c.! But this time I had been going nowhere, doing nothing in the least degree questionable; the utmost lark I had engaged in for months being to descend at Grange's (Babbie knows the place) in the course of my last drive with old Sterling, and there refresh exhausted nature with a hot jelly, and one modest sponge cake. It would have been no harm, I think, had the influenza taken, instead of temperate me, a personage who sat on the next chair to us at the said Grange's, and before whose bottomless appetite all the surrounding platefuls of cakes disappeared like reek! His companion, who was treating him, finally snatched up a large pound-cake, cut it into junks, and handed him one after another on the point of a knife, till that also had gone *ad plura*. The dog, for it was with a dog that I had the honour of lunching that day, appeared to consume pound-cake as my Penfillan grandfather professed to eat cheese, 'purely for diversion!'

By the way, it must have been a curious sight for the starved beggars, who hang about the doors of such places, to see a dog make away with as much cake in five minutes as would have kept them in bread for a week, or weeks! Bad enough for them to see human beings, neither bonnier perhaps, nor wiser, nor, except for the clothes on their backs, in any way better than themselves, eating hot jelly, and such like delicacies, while they must go without the necessaries of life. But a dog! really that was stretching the injustice to something very like impiety, it strikes me.

I should like to know the name of 'the gentleman as belonged to that dog.' He seemed, by his equipment and bearing, a person holding some rank in the world, besides the generical rank of fool; and should one find him some other day maintaining in Parliament that ' all goes well,' it would throw some light on the worth of his opinion to know that his dog may have as much pound-cake at Grange's as it likes to eat!

That however was the last social fact which I witnessed, having been since laid up at home, and part of the time in bed. I do not know why the solitude of a bedroom should be so much more solitary than the solitude of other places, but so I find it. When my husband is at work, I hardly ever see his face from breakfast till dinner; and when it rains, as often even when it does not rain, no living soul comes near me, to speak one cheerful word; yet, so long as I am in, what the French call, my ' room of reception,' it never occurs to me to feel lonely. But, send me to my bedroom for a day, to that great red bed in which I have transacted so many headaches, so many influenzas! and I feel as if I were already half buried! Oh, so lonely! as in some intermediate stage betwixt the living world and the dead!

I sometimes think that, were I to remain there long, I should arrive in the end at prophesying, like my great great ancestors! Solitude has such a power of blending past, present, and future, far and near, all into one confused jumblement, in which I wander about like a disembodied spirit, that has put off the beggarly conditions of time and space: and that I take to be a first development of the spirit of prophecy in one.

The letters of Babbie used to be no small comfort to me when I was ailing; but Babbie, since she went to Scotland, has had other things to do, it would seem, than writing to me. Babbie's beautiful constancy in writing has, like many other beautiful things of this earth, succumbed to the force of circumstances. Ah, yes! what young lady can withstand the force of circumstances?

Circumstances are the young lady's destiny; it is only when she has lived long enough to have tried conclusions with the real destiny that she learns to know the difference, and learns to submit herself peaceably to the one, and to say to the other, that humbug force of circumstances, ' But I will! *je le veux, moi!* ' Oh, it is the grand happiness of existence when one can break through one's circumstances by a strong will, as Samson burst the cords of the Philistines! Isn't it, uncle? You should know, if any man does! you who are—permit me, I mean it entirely in a complimentary sense— so very, very wilful. But as for my sweet Babbie, her volition is not yet adequate to breaking the pack-threads of the Lilliputians, never to speak of cords of the Philistines.

And meanwhile, what can one do for her, but just what poor Edward Irving counselled certain elders to do, who once waited upon him at Annan to complain of the backslidings of their minister, and ask his (Edward's) advice under the same. Edward, having listened to their catalogue of enormities, knit his brows, meditated some moments, and then answered succinctly, 'My good friends, you had best pray for him to the Lord!'

My American was immensely pleased with your reception of him. That is the only American whom I have found it possible to be civil to this great long while.

Oh, such a precious specimen of the regular Yankee I have seen since! Coming in from a drive one forenoon, I was informed by Helen, with a certain agitation, that there was a strange gentleman in the library; 'he said he had come a long way, and would wait for the master coming home to dinner; and I have been,' said she, 'in a perfect fidget all this while, for I remembered after he was in that you had left your watch on the table!'

I proceeded to the library to inspect this unauthorised settler with my own eyes; a tall, lean, red-herring-looking man rose from Carlyle's writing-table, which he was sitting writing at, with Carlyle's manuscripts and private letters all lying about; and running his eyes over me, from head to foot, said, 'Oh, you are Mrs. Carlyle, are you?' An inclination of the head, intended to be hauteur itself, was all the answer he got. 'Do you keep your health pretty well, Mrs. Carlyle?' said the wretch, nothing daunted, that being always your regular Yankee's second word. Another inclination of the head, even slighter than the first. 'I have come a great way out of my road,' said he, 'to congratulate Mr. Carlyle on his increasing reputation, and, as I did not wish to have my walk for nothing, I am waiting till he comes in; but in case he should not come in time for me, I am just writing him a letter, here, at his own table, as you see, Mrs. Carlyle!' Having reseated himself without invitation of mine, I turned on my heel and quitted the room, determined not to sit down in it while the Yankee stayed.

But about half an hour after came Darwin and Mr. Wedgwood; and, as there was no fire in the room below, they had to be shown up to the library, where, on my return, I found the Yankee still seated in Carlyle's chair, very actively doing, as it were, the honours of the house to them. And there he sat upwards of another hour, not one of us addressing a word to him, but he not the less thrusting in his word into all that was said.

Finding that I would absolutely make no answer to his remarks, he poured in upon me a broadside of positive questions.

'Does Mr. Carlyle enjoy good health, Mrs. Carlyle?' 'No!' 'Oh, he doesn't! What does he complain of, Mrs. Carlyle?' 'Of everything!' 'Perhaps he studies too hard;—does he study too hard, Mrs. Carlyle?' 'Who knows?' 'How many hours a day does he study, Mrs. Carlyle?' 'My husband does not work by the clock.' And so on—his impertinent questions receiving the most churlish answers, but which seemed to patter off the rhinoceros-hide of him as though they had been sugar-plums. At length he declared that Mr. Carlyle was really very long of coming; to which I replied, that it would be still longer before he came.

Whereupon, having informed himself as to all the possible and probable omnibuses, he took himself away, leaving my two gentlemen ready to expire of laughter, and me to fall upon Helen at the first convenient moment for not defending better 'the wooden guardian of our privacy.' But really these Yankees form a considerable item in the ennuis of our mortal life. I counted lately fourteen of them in one fortnight, of whom Dr. Russel was the only one that you did not feel tempted to take the poker to.

If Mr. Carlyle's 'increasing reputation' bore no other fruits but congratulatory Yankees and the like, I should vote for its proceeding to diminish with all possible despatch.

Give my love to the children. A hearty kiss to Maggie for her long letter; for which I was also charged by Mrs. Wedgwood to make her grateful acknowledgments. The governess was plainly not at all advanced enough for Mrs. Wedgwood's children; but Maggie's letter was a gratification to us on its own basis.

And now, dear uncle, if I have not wearied you, I have wearied myself, which is not at present hard to do, for although the worst of my cold is over, I suppose, I am as weak as a sparrow.

I wish I knew how you exactly are, and what that little demoralised Babbie is doing; for, although she has left my last letter unanswered for nearly three weeks, I cannot help still retaining a certain tenderness for her. God bless you all.

Ever your affectionate
JANE W. CARLYLE.

Carlyle is over head and ears in Cromwell—is lost to humanity for the time being.

LETTER 62.

To Mrs. Aitken, Dumfries.

5 Cheyne Row: Good Friday, March-April, 1844 [?].

My dear Jane,—It is late to thank you for the pretty little mats, later than even an unusual amount of headaches could have excused, had not Mr. C. in the meanwhile conveyed my 'favourable sentiments.' He has probably told you also the fact of my absence for two weeks. I returned from Addiscombe [1] last Saturday, very little set up either in mind or body by my fortnight of dignified idleness. The coldness of the weather prevented my going much into the open air, and within doors the atmosphere at Addiscombe is much more chilly than at Cheyne Row; but it is morally good for one, now and then, to fling oneself into circumstances in which one must exert oneself, and consume one's own smoke, even under the pressure of physical ailment. The more I see wealthy establishments, however, the less I wish to preside over one of my own. The superior splendour is overbalanced by the inferior comfort, and the only indisputable advantage of a large fortune—the power of helping other people with it—all these rich people, however good and generous their hearts may have been in the beginning, seem somehow enchanted into never availing themselves of.

I found Carlyle in a bad way, complaining of sore throat and universal misery, and in this state nothing I could say hindered him from walking out in the rain, and his throat became so much worse during the night that I was afraid he was going to be as ill as when poor Becker attended him at Comely Bank. He had asked a gentleman to dinner on Sunday, and two more to tea—Dodds, and John Hunter of Edinburgh, and two more came 'on the voluntary principle,' and all these men I had to receive and entertain, on my own basis; and to show me, I suppose, that they were not too much mortified in finding only me, the unfortunate creatures all stayed till eleven at night. Then I put a mustard blister on the man's throat, and put him to bed with apprehensions enough; but, to my astonishment, he went almost immediately to sleep, and slept quite peaceably all night, and next morning the throat was miraculously mended. We kept him in bed to breakfast, almost by main force however, and John told him to live on slops to complete his cure; but he told John in very decided An-

---

[1] Visit to the Barings.

nandale that 'he had a great notion he would follow the direction of Nature in the matter of eating and getting up, and if Nature told him to dine on a chop it would be a clever fellow that should persuade him not to do it.'—[*Remainder lost.*]

LETTER 63.

This summer she ventured on a visit to Liverpool, and friends in that neighbourood. I was immovably imprisoned in Cromwell intricacies. The 'Wedgwood' must have been not Hensleigh (who was familiar here), but an elder brother of his: amiable, polite people all.

'*Mauvais état.*'—*Reçu : un Pape en assez mauvais état,*' certified the French officer at some post in the Alps, as Pio VII. (?) was passing through his hands on way to *Fontainebleau.* (Anecdote of Cavaignac's to us.)

'Came to pass,' &c.—A poor Italian painter, *protégé* of Mazzini's, living in some back street of Chelsea, had by ill luck set his chimney on fire; but, by superhuman efforts, to escape the penalty, got it quenched in time. Still, in time, as he hoped; 'when,' said Mazzini, reporting in Mazzini English, 'there came to pass a sweep' who smelt the soot of him; and extorted from him still a guinea of hush money—the greedy knave.

'Ill na gude' had become proverbial here, on the following account. Emeritus, very ancient Annandale cattle dealer, to topsman of an accidental cattle-drove on the highway (as reported by himself to William Graham and me): '"Beautiful cattle," c'ai (quoth I); "what might cattle o' that kind lie ye a head?" "I can d'ye naither ill na' (nor) guid!"' (by blabbing in your market.)

T. Carlyle, Esq., Chelsea.

Liverpool: Monday, June 25, 1844.

Dearest,—It was impossible for me even to aim at sending you any word last night, for in fact I was here in *assez mauvais état;* in other words, quite beside myself. I had set off on the journey with my imagination in far too lively a state; and accordingly, before I had gone far, 'there came to pass' in me 'something— what shall I say?—strange, upon my honour,' and by the time we had got to Rugby I was in all the agonies of sea-sickness, without the sea! It was a great aggravation being cooped up in that small carriage, so ill, with a man I knew so slightly as Mr. Wedgwood. He behaved very well; 'abstained from no attentions,' and at the same time made no fuss, but still I should have preferred being beside an entire stranger. At Birmingham he pressed me to have some coffee; but 'horrible was the idea to me,' both of that, and of the modest repast which I had in my own bag. I took instead a bottle of soda-water, in hopes it would bring the convulsions of my stomach to a crisis: but it did me 'neither ill nor gude;' and the hope I had been cherishing, of being let lie for half an hour on my back in the ladies' waiting room, also went the way of most of our human hopes, the place being so crowded and the smells from the dining-room so pungent that I was glad to return to the carriage.

Mr. Wedgwood kept insisting to the last moment that I ought to stop at Birmingham, but I knew better than that. Just as the train was starting, the clerk of the station (at least Mr. Wedgwood took him for such) jumped up to the window, touched by compassion for my ghastly appearance, and said to me encouragingly: 'I have told the guard to attend to you, ma'am, and take you out at any station where you may wish to be left!' When Mr. Wedgwood went away I had got over the worst of it, and could laugh at his proposal to ask 'one of some Quakers whom he had seen in a front carriage to take his place in case of my fainting all by myself.' What advantage could there be in providing me with a Quaker, in preference to all others?

The rest of the journey was got over without any more faintings, and I found Helen and Maggie at the station. But, worn out with so much sickness, and having taken nothing from breakfast time but the soda-water, you may fancy I was in no state to resist the horror I had been feeling all the way at the notion of entering this house again[1]; and when the rest came all about me in the passage, instead of being able to feel glad to see them, something twisted itself about my throat and across my breast as if I were going to be strangled, and I could get no breath without screaming. In fact, I suppose I had been in what they call hysterics, for the first time, and I hope the last, in my life; for it is a very ugly thing, I can tell you—must be just the next thing to being hanged. But it is all over now; and my uncle was so very good to me, he who so hates all that sort of thing, that you would have felt, as I do this morning, quite grateful to him. The girls, of course, were equally good, but their patience was more natural. I have got Alick's room, he having gone out to sleep, and it is all made as nice as possible for me; and, though I did not get much sleep last night, I daresay I shall get on well enough in that department when I am once quieted.

Maggie brought me the prettiest little breakfast to my bedroom: a little plate of strawberries and all sorts of dainties, that looked

---

[1] Bringing back remembrance of her mother.

quite like Templand. It was right to come; though yesterday one would have said, I had really run away from you, and was spending money very distractedly for the purpose of getting myself tormented. Now that I am up I feel really as well as before I left London, so do not be anyways anxious about me.

Your own

J. C.

LETTER 64.

To T. Carlyle, Esq., Chelsea.

Liverpool: June 27, 1844.

Thanks, dearest, for your note and the newspaper, which was the best part of my breakfast this morning—not that I had 'lost my happityte.'[1] I slept much better last night, in spite of cocks of every variety of power, a dog, and a considerable rumblement of carts. But the evil of these things is not doubled and tripled for me by the reflection that you were being kept awake by them; and what individual evil there was in them could not get the better of my excessive weariness. I feel as if the out-of-door sounds should not lay hold of my imagination for all the time I am likely to be exposed to them; and within doors all is quiet enough, and they let me go to bed whenever I like.

They are all as kind and considerate as possible—even my uncle, who did not use to make any practical admission that there was such a thing as irritable nerves in the world. I suppose his own illness has taught him sympathy in this matter. I find him looking fully better than I expected, and he does not seem to me worse at walking than when I saw him last; his speech is the worst thing, so thick that I have great difficulty in catching what he says without making him repeat; but this seems as much the result of the loss of his teeth, which he has not supplied, as of anything else. They complain much of his temper; but I have not seen the slight-

---

[1] A patient in the York Asylum (country attorney, I was told), a small, shrivelled, elderly man, sat dining among others, being perfectly harmless, at the governor's table there. He ate pretty fairly; but every minute or two inconsolably flung down his knife and fork, stretched out his palms, and twisting his poor countenance into utter woe, gave a low pathetic howl: 'I've la-ast mi happetayte!' The wretchedest scarecrow of humanity I almost ever saw, who had found *his* 'immeasurable of misery' in that particular 'loss'! Date would be autumn 1819; my first visit to England—not farther south than York as yet.

est trace of ill-temper in him since I came, except for a moment yesterday during dinner, when he said some very sharp words to Jeannie, who provoked them in the first instance, and resented them in the second, in a way that quite astonished me, who had never seen her otherwise than imperturbably good-natured. I am afraid my Babbie has been deteriorating in these latter times; she looks most painfully indolent and young ladyish. I have got into no free communication with her yet; alone with me, she is the same gentle, sweet Babbie as ever, but impenetrable. I shall find out what is at the bottom of all this by-and-by. Helen is grown more like my aunt Jeannie in all respects: a higher praise one cannot give her. The one that pleases me least of all is Alick; his Toryism is perfectly insupportable and seems to be awakening reaction even in my uncle. Even the Letter-business [1] Alick defends, because it is the Minister's pleasure. Not so my uncle, for whom your letter had set the thing in its right light; and who honestly confesses, with all devotion to the powers that be, that 'where such things are doing there must come a breakdown.'

I have not written to Mrs. Paulet yet. A letter from Geraldine, which was lying for me here, informed me that she (Mrs. Paulet) had been salivated through mistake; her doctor, in meaning to give her ipecacuanha four times a day, had been giving her mercury to that extent. Whereupon Geraldine observes, 'if she were an ugly woman one would not mind it so much.'

I hope you will not find the silence too delicious; there is a moderation to be observed in all things. I wish you to be neither quite miserable or quite content in my absence; at all events, as long as you are finding the silence a benefit I shall take precious good care to keep away, as I like to have my human speech duly appreciated.

Give my kind remembrances to Helen,[2] and you may tell her, as a thing she will fully appreciate the distress of, that on the way here I got myself all covered over with oil-paint, Heaven knows how; and it has taken nearly a quart of turpentine to clean me (my clothes, I mean).

The little Scotchwoman I sent here welcomed me as if I were come on purpose to see her; she gives great satisfaction, and is grown into a perfect beauty.

---

[1] Sir James Graham's opening of the Mazzini correspondence, for behoof of Pope and Kaiser, on which I had written something to the *Times*.

[2] The servant.

Do not, I beg of you, work too hard.

How provoking about the fly![1]

Bless you.

J. C.

LETTER 65.

To Thomas Carlyle, Esq., Chelsea.

Liverpool: July 1, 1844.

Dearest,—I was in considerable perplexity how I should manage on Sunday; for you cannot displease my uncle more than by declining to go to church. As early as Saturday morning he was questioning me as to which church I meant to go. By way of compromise, I murmured something about James Martineau.

Providence, however, kindly took the matter into its own hand, and arranged it so that I stayed at home and yet gave no offence. For when the Sunday morning came, I was sufficiently ill of headache to convince all beholders that I really could not get up; and if I could not get up, it followed that I could not go to church. I rose before dinner, in time to address your newspaper, and to-day I am quite well again—that is to say, as well as one can be, living, as I feel to be doing just now, in a sort of exhausted receiver. The manner of being in this house is really—'what shall I say? strange upon my honour.' The preparation and deliberation, and unwearying earnestness with which they all dress themselves three times a day, is a continual miracle for me, combined as it is with total want of earnestness about everything else in heaven or earth. I declare I am heartily sorry for these girls, so good naturally, so gentle, and even intelligent; and in this absurd way 'sailing down the stream of time into the ocean of eternity, for Christ's sake. Amen.'[2] As for Babbie, she is sunk into the merest young lady of them all. Her indolence is absolutely transcendental, and I cannot flatter myself that it is the reaction of any secret grief; the only confession which, with all my surprising[3] quality, I have been able to draw from her is that 'one ought really to have a little excitement in one's life, and there is none to be got here.' How grateful I ought to be to you, dear, for having rescued me out of the young-

---

[1] Had driven home from the station, I suppose, without *me?*—for want of a word or hint in time.

[2] Mythical grace, before meals, of an embarrassed and bashful man: 'Oh, Lord, we're a' sailing,' &c.

[3] Chinese personage, in the *Two Fair Cousins*, who sees almost into millstones.

lady sphere! It is a thing that I cannot contemplate with the proper toleration.

I wonder how you are to-day; and if you made out your visit yesterday? I am sure you are working too hard without the interruptions of your Necessary Evil.[1] Do bid Helen, with my kind regards, get you a good large fowl and boil it in four quarters.

Extracts from Liverpool letters.

July 2.—Indeed, dear, you look to be almost unhappy enough already! I do not want you to suffer physically, only morally, you understand, and to hear of your having to take coffee at night and all that gives me no wicked satisfaction, but makes me quite unhappy. It is curious how much more uncomfortable I feel without you, when it is I who am going away from you, and not, as it used to be, you gone away from me. I am always wondering since I came here how I can, even in my angriest mood, talk about leaving you for good and all; for to be sure, if I were to leave you to-day on that principle, I should need absolutely to go back to-morrow to see how you were taking it.

July 5.—My uncle would not be so bad with his Toryism if it were not for Alick egging him on. His feelings as an honest man are always struggling against his prejudices; but the very misgivings he has about the infallibility of his party make him only an angrier partisan, and nothing can be more provoking than the things he occasionally says. For instance, he told me yesterday that ' Sir James Graham had said he only opened one of Mazzini's letters; if Mazzini said he opened more he was a d——d lying rascal, and everybody knows whether to believe the word of a gentleman like Sir James or of a beggarly refugee turned out of his own country for misconduct. D—— these people! If they got leave to find a shelter here, what right had they to insult the Queen by insulting her allies?' Fancy me swallowing all that without answer! To be sure, the only alternative was to hold my peace altogether, or produce a collision that must have ended in my calling a coach.

July 11, *Seaforth House.*[2]—Mrs. Paulet makes an excellent hostess

---

[1] Herself—the dear one!

[2] Seaforth House is three miles or so down river from Liverpool, Bootleward; a bare kind of big mansion (once Gladstone senior's), in these years rented by the Paulets, extensive merchant people. Paulet was a good, cleverish Genoese; Mrs. Paulet, an early friend of Geraldine Jewsbury, a strange,

(morally speaking). Her *ménage* is certainly susceptible of improvement, especially in the article of cooking; but one would prefer living on any sort of victuals not poisoned in such pleasant company to having preparations of these and stupidity therewith.

A Mrs. D., whom you saw once, came the night before last to stay while I stayed. She seems a sensible gentlewoman enough—a Unitarian without the doctrines.[1] But I could not comprehend at first why she had been brought, till at last Mrs. Paulet gave me to understand that she was there to use up Miss N.[2] 'Not,' she said, 'that my sister is an illiberal person, though she believes in Christ, and all that sort of thing. She is quite easy to live with; but it will be pleasanter for herself as well as for us that she should have somebody to talk with of her own sort—a Catholic or Unitarian, she doesn't mind which.' After this initiation I can hardly look with gravity on these two shaking their heads into one another's faces and bum-bumming away on religious topics, as they flatter themselves.

You ask where I shall be on my birthday. My dear, in what view do you ask? To send me something? Now I positively forbid you to send me anything but a letter with your blessing. It is a positive worry for you, the buying of things. And what is the chief pleasure of a birthday present? Simply that it is evidence of one's birthday having been remembered; and now I know, without any bothering present, that you have been thinking of it, my poor Good,[3] for ever so long before! So write me a longer letter than usual, and leave presents to those whose affection stands more in need of vulgar demonstration than yours does.

July 15, *Seaforth.*—Oh, my darling, I want to give you an emphatic kiss rather than to write! But you are at Chelsea and I at Seaforth, so the thing is clearly impossible for the moment. But I will keep it for you till I come, for it is not with words that I can thank you adequately for that kindest of birthday letters and its small enclosure—touching little key! I cried over it and laughed over it, and could not sufficiently admire the graceful idea—an idea which might come under the category of what Cavaignac used to call '*idées de femme*,' supposed to be unattainable by the coarser sex! And I have put the little key to my chain and shall wear it there till I return.

---

indolently ingenious, artistic, &c., creature, very reverent of *us* at this time. —T. C.

[1] A Lais without the beauty.—C. Lamb.   [2] Mrs. Paulet's sister.

[3] Good is masculine for Goody—my frequent name for her.—T. C.

LETTER 66.

John Forster, Esq., 58 *Lincoln's Inn Fields.*

Chelsea: Wednesday, July 1844.

My dear Mr. Forster,—I understand from my husband that, in the romantic generosity of your own heart, you offered him some books for me, to carry home. 'Ah!' Had you made the proposal to him with a loaded pistol at his breast, he might perhaps have acceded ; but merely in the way of social politeness, and for virtue's own reward, the desperate man that should have stopped him on the streets with the offer of a large paper trunk would have had just the same chance of being listened to. He told you, and had the effrontery to repeat the same excuse to myself, that I seemed to have more books about me than I could read. Women, they say, will always give a varnish of duty to their inclinations. I wonder whether men are any better in always giving to their disinclinations a varnish of justice? What he there told you was true no doubt; but one of those insidious one-sided truths which in the practical application is equivalent to a positive falsehood. I have more books in the house at this moment than I can read; but what did that signify since I have at the same time none that I can read? I have read Milford, partially read Köhle; Mrs. Trollope is impossible, and several others that I have impossible. In fact I am very ill off; and if you will still send me some books by the parcels delivery, they will be a godsend. When I go to the London library, besides it being very difficult for me to get so far, that old white owl bothers me so with his assiduous conversation—which, God knows, one does not go there for—that I quite lose all faculty of choice, and end in bringing away any trash he puts into my hands, generally something which he considers adapted for a lady, and, at the same time, not likely to be inquired for by his other ladies. So you may fancy. Have patience with the trouble I give you.

Always affectionately yours,

JANE CARLYLE.

LETTER 67.

This was my first visit to the Grange—alas, alas, how tragic-looking now! I perfectly remember the bustle there about the belated postman, and my letter home—which I at length wrote in pencil. I stayed about a week. Proof-sheets of Election to the Long Par-

liament; visit to Winchester, &c.—'Fleming' is as yet the incon-
solable attached of the late Charles Buller; afterwards the gossiping
Fribble well known in 'fashionable' society. 'Plattnauer' she had
just rescued from a mad-house, and was (with heroic and successful
charity) quite taming here into his normal state: our perfectly
peaceable guest for about a fortnight! Dismissed, launched again,
with outfit, &c., after my return.—T. C.

To Thomas Carlyle, The Grange.

Chelsea: Sept. 10 (?), 1844.

Dearest,—Your note is as lively a little image of discomfort as
one could wish to have before coffee. Now, however, you have
eaten and slept, and seen the Lady Harriet; and 'all,' I hope, 'will
be well,' as Plattnauer says.

For me, I am worried to the last degree: the painter, preparatory
to the paperer, instead of rendering himself here at six in the morning, has kept me expecting him till now—just when I am going up
to town to 'see after my affairs.' Yesterday was very weary.
Mazzini came, then Darwin, then Mr. Fleming, bringing me Mazzini's bust, which is a horror of horrors (oh, no! you certainly shall
not sit to that man). They were all mortally stupid, especially Mr.
Fleming, of whom one might have carried the simile of the Duck
in Thunder to that still more offensive one of 'Jenkin's hen.'
Plattnauer came home in the midst, in a state of violent talkative-
ness—the whole thing looked like Bedlam. At last they all went
away; and we ate our boiled mutton in silence, somewhat sullen.

In the evening I went to take a walk with him, and met little
B—— a few steps from the door, who accompanied us in the walk,
and came in to tea and sat there gabbing till ten o'clock. Plattnauer was seized with such a detestation of him that he could not
stay in the room for ten minutes together. He told me he had
been 'strongly tempted to seize a poker and dash his brains out,
and so put an end to his eternal clack in that way, since nothing
else could stop it.' I suggested to him somewhat sternly that it
did not become one visitor in a house to dash out the brains of
another—a statement which he at once perceived and admitted the
justice of.

And now good-bye, Mr. Good; for I have *de grandes choses à
faire;* and nothing since yesterday to write about that cannot be
put into three words—God bless you.

Your affectionate

J. C.

LETTER 68.

To Thomas Carlyle, Esq., The Grange.

Chelsea: Tuesday, Sept. 13, 1844.

Dearest,—I have absolutely no composure of soul for writing just now. The fact is, I have undertaken far more this time than human discretion would have dreamt of putting into one week; knowing your horror of sweeps and carpet-beaters and 'all that sort of thing,' I would, in my romantic self-devotion, sweep all the chimneys and lift all the carpets before you came; and had you arrived this day, as you first proposed, you would have found me still in a regular mess, threatening to thicken into 'immortal smash.' But by Thursday I hope to have 'got everything satisfactorily arranged,' as poor Plattnauer is always saying.

And there have been so many other things to take me up, besides the sweeps, &c. Almost every evening somebody has been here. The evening of the Bullers' departure Jenkin's Hen [1] came, pale as a candle, with a red circle round each eye which was very touching; —he had evidently been crying himself quite sick and sore. Lady Lewis [2] had invited him to dine with her; but, 'he could not go there, he could not eat any dinner, he was afraid to go home to his own silent house—he thought I could understand his feelings, and so had come to pass the evening with me.' What a gift of understanding people's feelings I am supposed to have—*moi!* Oh, my dear, the cat produced two kittens in your bed this morning, and we have drowned them—and now she also thinks I can understand her feelings, and is coming about my feet mewing in a way that quite wrings my heart. Poor thing! I never saw her take on so badly before.

Well! but on Saturday night Helen had just gone to seek sugar for the tea when a rap came, which I preferred answering myself to allowing Plattnauer to answer it, and—oh, Heavens!—what should I see in the dark opening? A little human phenomenon, in a triple cornered hat! Bishop * * * again! I screamed, a good, genuine, horrified scream! Whereupon he stept in—and, as the devil would have it—on my bad toe! and then I uttered a series of screams which made Plattnauer savage with him for the rest of the

---

[1] Fleming. To 'die the death of Jenkin's hen' expressed, in Annandale, the maximum of pusillanimity.

[2] The late C. Buller's aunt.

I.—8

evening. He had come up to seek himself a new assistant, the old one being promoted. There is no end to his calls to London! But he was plainly mortally afraid of Plattnauer, who as good as told him he was 'one of the wind-bags,' and will not trouble us again I think while he is here.

Yesterday afternoon came Henry Taylor, but only for a few minutes; he had been unexpectedly 'turned adrift on our shores, and could only wait till a Wandsworth steamer should come up. I was very kind to him, and he looked as if he could have kissed me for being glad to see him—Oh, how odd! I put on my bonnet, and went with him to the boat; and he complimented me on going out without gloves or shawl. I was the first woman he had ever found in this world who could go out of her house without at least a quarter of an hour's preparation! They have taken a house at Mortlake, near Richmond.

But there is no possibility of telling you all the things I have to tell at this writing. They will keep till you come. Only let me not forget to say there is an American letter come for John, which I send on by this day's post.

Your letter, written apparently on Saturday, was not read by me till yesterday afternoon; the postman came so long after twelve when I had been under the imperative necessity to go out. Give my love to Mr. Baring.

Ever your distracted

GOODY.

LETTER 69.

To Mrs. Russell, Thornhill.

Nov. 5, 1844.

My dearest Mrs. Russell,—I suspect that my Man-of-Genius-Husband has forgotten old Mary as completely as if she had never been born, Oliver Cromwell having, as the servants at Craigen-puttock used to say, 'taken the whole gang to himsel'.' The wife of Sir Fowell Buxton has been many times heard to wish that the Blacks (her husband's fixed idea) were all at the bottom of the Red Sea; and I am afraid I have often been undutiful enough, of late months, to wish the memory of Cromwell at the bottom of *Some-thing* where I might hear less about it. It is at the bottom of Rubbish enough, I am sure, to judge from the tremendous ransacking of old folios and illegible manuscripts which Carlyle is still going on with; but still he manages to bring it up, in season and out of season, till I begin to be weary of him (the Protector), great man though he was. But as everything comes to an end with patience, he will probably get himself written at last, and printed, and published; and then my husband will return to a consciousness of his daily life, and I shall have peace from the turmoils of the Commonwealth. For, if Carlyle thinks of nothing else but his Book whilst he is writing it, one has always this consolation, that he is the first to forget it when it is written.

Meanwhile, to return to old Mary, I send an order for three sovereigns from my own 'pin money' (which is ample enough) to keep her poor old soul and body together a little longer. And I shall not tell Carlyle that I have done so, as I know it would vex him that he should have needed to be 'put in mind;'—so that, if he sends another supply shortly, you will understand the mystery of this double sending.

I wonder how you are all at Thornhill. It seems so long since I have heard a word of news from that place, which I think of more than any other in the world; I shall hear from you one of these days, and understand that 'the smallest contributions will be gratefully received.'

I had a letter from Liverpool a week ago, and all was going on well there—my uncle better than he had been some little while before. Jeannie and Maggie are at Auchtertool with Walter, leading a very good-for-nothing life there according to their own account of it—engaged in perpetual tea-drinkings with 'people whom they can take no pleasure in,' and 'making themselves amends in sitting at home with their feet on the fender, talking over the absurdities of the said people.' Whereupon I have written Jeannie a very scolding letter, which, it is to be feared, will share the common fate of all good advice in this world—make her angry at me, without putting a stop either to the tea-drinkings with people, 'one can take no pleasure in,' or the idle practice of sitting with her feet on the fender, and still worse practice of laughing at one's neighbors' absurdities rather than one's own.

We have dreadfully cold weather here, but I have no influenza as yet—am on the whole well enough for all practical purposes.

With kindest regards to your father and husband,

Ever, dear Mrs. Russell,

Affectionately yours,

JANE C.

From Mrs. Carlyle's Note Book.[1]

April 13, 1845.—To-day, oddly enough, while I was engaged in re-reading Carlyle's 'Philosophy of Clothes,' Count d'Orsay walked in. I had not seen him for four or five years. Last time he was as gay in his colours as a humming-bird—blue satin cravat, blue velvet waistcoat, cream-coloured coat, lined with velvet of the same hue, trousers also of a bright colour, I forget what; white French gloves, two glorious breastpins attached by a chain, and length enough of gold watch-guard to have hanged himself in. To-day, in compliment to his five more years, he was all in black and brown—a black satin cravat, a brown velvet waistcoat, a brown coat, some shades darker than the waistcoat, lined with velvet of its own shade, and almost black trousers, one breast-pin, a large pear-shaped pearl set into a little cup of diamonds, and only one fold of gold chain round his neck, tucked together right on the centre of his spacious breast with one magnificent turquoise. Well! that man understood his trade; if it be but that of dandy, nobody can deny that he is a perfect master of it, that he dresses himself with consummate skill! A bungler would have made no allowance for five more years at his time of life; but he had the fine sense to perceive how much better his dress of to-day sets off his slightly enlarged figure and slightly worn complexion, than the humming-bird colours of five years back would have done. Poor D'Orsay! he was born to have been something better than even the king of dandies. He did not say nearly so many clever things this time as on the last occasion. His wit, I suppose, is of the sort that belongs more to animal spirits than to real genius, and his animal spirits seem to have fallen many degrees. The only thing that fell from him to-day worth remembering was his account of a mask he had seen of Charles Fox, 'all punched and flattened as if he had slept in a book.'

Lord Jeffrey came, unexpected, while the Count was here. What a difference! the prince of critics and the prince of dandies. How washed out the beautiful dandiacal face looked beside that little clever old man's! The large blue dandiacal eyes, you would have said, had never contemplated anything more interesting than the reflection of the handsome personage they pertained to in a looking-glass; while the dark penetrating ones of the other had

---

[1] Only fragments of these note-books survive. Most of them were destroyed by Mrs. Carlyle herself.

been taking note of most things in God's universe, even seeing a good way into millstones.

Jeffrey told us a very characteristic trait of Lord Brougham. He (Brougham) was saying that some individual they were talking of would never get into aristocratic society: first, because his manners were bad, and secondly, said Brougham, because there is such a want of truth (!) in him. In aristocratic society there is such a quick tact for detecting everything unveracious that no man who is not true can ever get on in it! 'Indeed!' said Jeffrey, 'I am delighted to hear you give such a character of the upper classes; I thought they had been more tolerant.' 'Oh,' said Brougham, 'I assure you it is the fact: any man who is deficient in veracity immediately gets tabooed in the aristocratic circles.'

The force of impudence could no further go.

April.—After I had been in London a short time my husband advised me—ironically, of course—to put an advertisement in the window 'House of refuge for stray dogs and cats.' The number of dogs and cats in distressed circumstances who imposed themselves on my country simplicity was in fact prodigious. Now it strikes me I might put in the window more appropriately, 'General aduit office for all the miseries of the universe.' Why does every miserable man and woman of my acquaintance come to me with his and her woes, as if I had no woes of my own, nothing in the world to do but to console others? *Ach Gott!* my head is getting to be a perfect chaos of other people's disasters and despairs. Here has been that ill-fated C. J.—Next—but to begin at the beginning—returning from the savings bank I observed in the King's Road a child of 'the lower orders,' about two years old, in the act, it seemed, of dissolving all away into tears. A crowd of tatterdemalion boys had gathered about it; but the genteel of both sexes were passing by on the other side. Of course I stopped and inquired, and learnt from the boys that the child was lost. There was no time for consideration if I meant to save the creature from going all into water, so I took its little hand, and bade it give over crying and I would help it to find its mother. It clung to me quite trustfully and dried itself up, and toddled along by my side. The *cortége* of boys dropped off by degrees, and then I fell to questioning my foundling, but with the blankest result. Of its name it knew not a syllable, nor of the street where it lived. Two words, 'Up here,' 'up here,' seemed to constitute its whole vocabulary. In pursuance of this direction, I led it into Manor street; but in the midst it stood still with a mazed look, and proved that it had yet another monosyllable by screaming 'No, no.' Here we were joined by a lad of fourteen smoking a short pipe, and carrying a baby a degree smaller than mine. He evidently suspected I was stealing the child, and felt it his duty not to lose sight of me and it. Nay, he took its other hand without asking, 'by your leave,' and I, suspecting his intent, though not very flattering to me, did not protest. By-and-by he hailed a bigger lad, and with cockney silence deposited his own baby in the arms of the other, put his short pipe into his pocket (a move which I was really thankful for) and so remained free to devote himself to my baby with heart and hand. By this time my baby was wearied, and so was I, so I begged the boy, since he would accompany me, to carry it to my house, as there was clearly no chance of our discovering its home. In the boy's arms my baby grew a little more expansive. 'Have you a father?' the boy asked it. Answer, an inarticulate sound. 'Is your father living?' asked the boy more loudly. The child smiled sweetly, and said, so that we could understand: 'I have a pretty brother, and they put him in a pretty coffin.' Ah, me! At the bottom of my own street I met two policemen, whom I asked how I should proceed to get the child restored to its family. 'Send it to the police station.' That I would not. 'Then send your address to the police station.' That I would. So I gave the boy sixpence and sent him when he had set down the child at my own door, to the station house with a slip of paper—

'Stray child at Mrs. Carlyle's,
. 'No. 5 Cheyne Row.'

The boy went off with an evident change in his feeling towards me, through the fact, I suppose, of my having spoken to the policeman, and partly perhaps on account of my respectable-looking house, and the sixpence. Helen was at work in the bedrooms, so I was obliged to keep my child in the room with me, that it might not fill the house with wail, to the astonishment and wrath of my husband at his writing, as it would have been sure to do if left all alone in the kitchen.

And now *ecco la combinazióne*. On the table was a note, which had been left, Helen said, by a young lady, who looked so distressed at finding me out that she, Helen, had invited her to come in and wait for me, but she preferred waiting at some shop in the neighbourhood. I opened the note with a presentiment that somebody's 'finer sensibilities of the heart' were about to get me into new trouble, and so it was. This lady, whom I had seen but once in my life, felt it due to herself to make some disclosures to me; in addition to certain awkward disclosures already made to me on her subject, 'and to throw herself on my mercy for advice under a new misfortune.' And the child! I could not refuse to see anyone who had come so great a way, and with such prodigious faith, to 'throw herself on my mercy,' but how to keep the child quiet during her 'disclosures?' I saw only one chance, to give it as much butter and bread and hard biscuit as would suffice to keep it munching for an hour or two: and this was forthwith brought, and with that consideration for *les details,* which Cavaignac used to call my ruling passion, a table-cloth was spread on my new carpet, in the midst of which the child was placed, that whatever mess it might create should be without permanent consequences. My preparations were hardly completed when the lady arrived—how changed since our former interview! I had never before found myself in the presence of a woman in my own sphere of life in such a situation. I have a strong prejudice against women 'in such a situation' in the abstract. It indicates such stupidity. But this poor woman in the concrete, covered with crimson and tears, went to my heart like a knife. Stranger as she was to me, I could 'do no otherwise' bu treceive her into my open arms, not figuratively but literally; and then this reception, 'so different from what she had dared to hope,' produced a sort of hysteric on her part, and she laid her poor face on my lap, and covered my hands with kisses. Oh, mercy! What a false position for one woman to be in towards another! It was a desperate interview. The only comfort was that the child gave us no trouble, but munched away unconscious of the tragic scene, never stirring from its enchanted table-cloth. A greater contrast could not be than betwixt these my two *protégées* for the time being—that two-year-old duddy child, drowning its recent sorrows in bread-and-butter, ignorant that there were such things in the world; and that elegantly dressed young lady living and having her being in sentiment, forgetful apparently that the world contained anything else. At last she went away, consoled a little by my kindness perhaps; but as for my advice,' though I gave her the best, she will not of course follow a syllable of it.

When Carlyle came to dinner, he looked rather aghast at my child. 'Only think,' said I, to enlist his sympathies on its behalf, 'what a state of distraction the poor mother must be in all this while!'

'The poor mother,' repeated he scornfully; 'how do you know that the poor mother did not put it down there in the King's Road for some such simpleton as you to pick it up, and saddle yourself with it for life?'

This was giving me a new idea. I began to look at the child with a mixed feeling of terror and interest: to look at it critically as a possible possession, while little ideas of an educational sort flitted through my brain. This state of uncertainty was cut short, however, by a young woman knocking at the door, and, with many protestations of gratitude, applying for the creature, about five hours after I had found it. The young woman was not the mother, but a grown-up sister. The poor mother was 'at home in fits.' They feared the child had staggered down into the Thames. It evinced no 'fine feelings' at sight of its sister; in fact, it looked with extreme indifference on her and indicated an inclination to remain where it was. But so soon as she took it into her arms, it began to tell her 'its travel's history' with renewed tears, and went off into a new explosion.

April 27.—Last night we had a novelty in the way of society, a sort of Irish *rigg*. Mr. L—— came in before tea with a tail consisting of three stranger Irishmen—real hot and hot live Irishmen, such as I have never before sat at meat with or met ' in flow of soul,' newly imported, with the brogue 'rather exquisite,' and *repale* ' more exquisite still.' They came to adore Carlyle, and also remonstrate with him, almost with tears in their eyes, on his opinion, as stated in his ' Chartism,' that 'a finer people than the Irish never lived; only they have two faults: they do lie and they do steal.' The poor fellows got into a quite epic strain over this most calumnious exaggeration. (Pity but my husband would pay some regard to the sensibilities of 'others,' and exaggerate less!)

The youngest one—Mr. Pigot—a handsome youth of the romantic cast, pale-faced, with dark eyes and hair, and an 'Emancipation of the Species' melancholy spread over him—told my husband, after having looked at and listened to him in comparative silence for the first hour, with 'How to observe' written in every lineament, that now he (Mr. Pigot) felt assured he (my husband) was not in his heart so unjust towards Ireland as his writings led one to suppose, and so he would confess, for the purpose of retracting it, the strong feeling of repulsion with which he had come to him that night. ' Why, in the name of goodness, then, *did* you come?' I could not help asking, thereby producing a rather awkward result. Several awkward results were produced in this 'nicht wi' Paddy.' They were speaking of the Scotch intolerance towards Catholics, and Carlyle as usual took up the cudgels for intolerance. 'Why,' said he, 'how *could* they do otherwise? If one sees one's fellow-creature following a damnable error, by continuing in which the devil is sure to get him at last, and roast him in eternal fire and brimstone, are you to let him go towards such consummation? or are you not rather to use all means to save him?'

'A nice prospect for you to be roasted in fire and brimstone,' I said to Mr. L——, the red-hottest of Catholics. 'For all of us,' said poor L——, laughing good-naturedly; 'we are all Catholics.' Nevertheless the evening was got over without bloodshed; at least, *malice prepense* bloodshed, for a little blood *was* shed involuntarily. While they were all three at the loudest in their defence of Ireland against the foul aspersions Carlyle had cast on it, and 'scornfully' cast on it, one of their noses burst out bleeding. It was the nose of the gentleman whose name we never heard. He let it bleed into his pocket handkerchief privately till nature was relieved, and was more cautious of exciting himself afterwards. The third, Mr. D——, quite took my husband's fancy, and mine also to a certain extent. He is a writer of national songs, and came here to 'eat his terms.' With the coarsest of human faces, decidedly as like a horse's as a man's, he is one of the people that I should get to think beautiful, there is so much of the power both of intellect and passion in his physiognomy. As for young Mr. Pigot, I will here, in the spirit of prophecy, inherited from my great great ancestor, John Welsh, the Covenanter, make a small prediction. If there be in his time an insurrection in Ireland, as these gentlemen confidently anticipate, Mr. Pigot will rise to be a Robespierre of some sort; will cause many heads to be removed from the shoulders they belong to; and will 'eventually' have his own head removed from his own shoulders, Nature has written on that handsome but fatal-looking countenance of his, quite legibly to my prophetic eye, 'Go and get thyself beheaded, but not before having lent a hand towards the great work of "immortal smash."'

All these Irishmen went off without their hats, and had to return into the room to seek them. Two of them found theirs after a moderate search. The third, the one whose nose bled, had hid his under the sofa, where I discovered it by help of my aforementioned second-sight. I have now seen what Sir James Graham would call 'fine foamy patriotism,' *dans sa plus simple expression.*

LETTER 70.

In the summer of 1845 Mrs. Carlyle went alone to Lancashire to stay with her uncle at Liverpool, and with Mrs. Paulet at Seaforth. From thence were written the ensuing letters.—J. A. F.

To T. Carlyle, Chelsea.

First day in Flätz,[1]
Liverpool, July 23, 1845.

Dearest,—It is all as well as could be expected. I arrived without accident, not even much tired, an hour and half before I was looked for—in fact between five and six. Consequently there was nobody to meet me, and I had some difficulty in getting myself a car, and at the same time keeping watch over my trunk and dressing-box; the former indeed was getting itself coolly borne away by a porter amongst some other people's luggage, when I laid my hand on it, and indicated: Thus far shalt thou go but no farther. My uncle I met tumbling downstairs, with what speed he might, prepared for being kissed to death; then came Maggie; and lastly Babbie, flushed and embarrassed, and unsatisfactory-looking; for, alas! she had been all day preserving strawberries, and had not expected me so soon, and was not dressed: to be an unwise virgin, taken with one's lamp untrimmed, means here to be caught in *déshabille*. A—— I have not seen yet—*tant mieux*, for I don't like him 'the least in the world.' Johnnie has sunk away into 'an unintelligible whinner.'[2]

On the whole, there is little 'food for the young soul, Mr. Carlyle!' But *she* (as Mazzini insists on calling the soul, and I think with reason; making the soul into an *it* being—what shall I say ?—a desecration, upon my honour)—'she' can do without visible food, like my leech, for all the while 'she' is to abide in the place. And 'one has always one's natural affections left.' And then to 'give pleasure to others!' The compensation that lies in that under all circumstances! Ah!

I am established in Mary's little room (off my uncle's) which they have made as tidy as possible for me. There is a tradition of 'a little wee wifie that lived in a shoe;' but I am still more curiously lodged, for this room is for all the world like a boot, the bed occupying the heel of it, a little bed like a coffin.

[1] *Attila Schmelze's Journey to Flätz*, by Jean Paul.
[2] Some fool's speech to me, I forget whose.

In so new a predicament, of course, I could not sleep; the best I made of it was a doze from time to time of a few minutes' duration, from which I started up with a sensation of horror, like what must have been felt by the victim of the Iron Shroud. For the rest, there was a cat opera, in which the *prima donna* had an organ that 'bet the worl;'[1] then there are some half-dozen of stout-lunged cocks, and a dog that lyrically recognises every passing event. Perhaps, like the pigs, I shall get used to it; if not I must just go all the sooner to Seaforth, where there is at least a certain quiet.

My coachful of men turned out admirably, as silent as could be wished, yet not deficient in the courtesies of life. The old gentleman with moustachios and a red face was Colonel Cleveland, of the artillery, 'much distinguished in the wars.' There was another old gentleman still more miraculous than Rio;'[2] for he had one eye boiled, the other parboiled, no leg and his mind boiled to jelly, and yet he got to Liverpool just as well as the rest of us. The little man opposite me, who was absorbed in Eugène Sue's female Bluebeard, was a German, and, pleased to see me reading his language, he gave me his pea-jacket to wrap my legs in, for we were all perished with cold. The English dandy with the heaven-blue waistcoat slept the whole way, exactly in the attitude of 'James' waiting for the Sylphide to come and kiss him; but he might sleep long enough, I fancy, before any 'bit of fascination' would take the trouble.

And now you must 'excuse us the day.' After such a night, I can neither 'make wits,'[3] nor, what were more to the purpose, senses, for your gratification. I shall go and walk, and look at the *Great Britain* packet; if one does not enlighten one's mind in the shipping department here, I see not how else one shall enlighten it.

Babbie has just knocked to beg I would give her love to you, and most sincere thanks for the Book,[4] the preface of which I read aloud to my uncle at breakfast; and he pronounced it 'very satirical'—a true speak.

God bless you, dear. I do not wish you to feel lonely, nor will you; and yet I should not precisely like if you missed me none at all. Your distracted JANEKIN.

---

[1] Annandale for 'beat the world.'

[2] Rio, a wandering, rather loud and headlong, but innocent-hearted, French friend, Neo-Catholic, &c. I believe is still living at Paris; a stranger here for twenty-five years now.

[3] Bölte's phrase for the sad operation of being with effort 'witty.'

[4] 'Book,' I suppose will be *Life of Schiller*, 2nd edition.

LETTER 71.

To T. Carlyle, Chelsea.

Liverpool: Friday, July 25, 1845.

Dearest,—You have interpreted the library note too ironically; it is a polite *bonâ-fide* offer of the book to read. I applied for it some six months ago without result; the copy I had was lent to me by Darwin.

Tout va bien ici ; le sommeil manque. The cat-operas are a fixed thing; they too, it would seem, have their Thursday night. Last night it was *Der Freyschütz*, or something as devilish, and the performance did not cease till two in the morning; when the cocks took possession of the stage, 'bits of fascination,'[1] and carried on the glory till breakfast-time. Add to which occasional explosions of bad feeling from the dog, and an incessant braying of carts from early dawn, going to and from the quarry; and through all, the sensation of being pent up in the foot of a boot. You may fancy the difficulty experienced by a finely organised human being, like me, in getting even a Scotch 'poor's'[2] minimum of sleep under such circumstances! Ne rtheless, and although the wind here is constantly in the east, and though the eternal smell of roast meat in this house is oppressive to s al and sense, 'it is but fair to state'[3] that I feel less tendency to 'dee and do nought ava'[4] than when I left London. Elizabeth Pepoli would impute the improvement to 'the greater variety of food'—oh, Heavens!—and above all to the excellent porter. I who, though my Sylphide's wings have long fallen off, can still manage by stilts and other means to keep myself above such depths of prose as that comes to, find 'the solution' elsewhere: namely in 'the great comfort' which it is somehow to

---

[1] Two London mechanics paused at a print-shop window where I was. 'Ha!' said one to the other in a jaunty knowing tone, '*Tag-li-oni !* Bit of fascination there.' Poor Taglioni was, indeed, elastic as india-rubber, but as meaningless too, poor soul.—T. C.

[2] Mazzini's, meaning paupers.

[3] Jeffrey, in *Edinburgh Review*, continually.

[4] Sandy Blackadder, factor at Hoddam (long ago), a heavy, baggy, big long-winded man, was overheard one day, in a funeral company which had not yet risen, discoursing largely in monotonous undertones to some neighbour about the doings, intentions, and manifold insignificant proceedings of some anonymous fellow-man; but at length wound up with 'and then he deed and did nought ava.'

be made sensible from time to time that if oneself is miserable, others are 'perhaps more to be pitied that they are *not* miserable.' Here sufficient for the day is the marketing, and eating, and dressing thereof! And a new satin dress can diffuse perfect beautitude through an immortal soul! The circulating library satisfies all their intellectual wants, and flirtation all the wants of their hearts; it is very convenient to be thus easily satisfied. One looks plump, digests without effort, and sleeps in spite of all the cats and cocks in the world. But somehow 'I as one solitary individual'[1] would rather remain in Hell—the Hell I make for myself with my restless *digging*—than accept this drowsy placidity. Yes, I begin to feel again that I am not *la dernière des femmes*, which has been oftener than anything else my reading of myself in these the latter times; a natural enough reaction against the exorbitant self-conceit which put me at fourteen on setting up for a woman of genius. Now I should be only too pleased to feel myself a 'woman without the genius;' a woman, not a 'chimera,' 'a miserable fatuity.' But this is fully worse than a description of scenery—description of one's own inside! Bah! who likes one well enough to find that other than a bore?

Well, I did the *Great Britain*. It is three hundred and twenty feet long and fifty feet broad, and all of iron, and has six sails, and one pays a shilling to see it, and it was not 'a good joy.' All these prodigious efforts for facilitating locomotion seem to me a highly questionable investment of human faculty; people need rather to be taught to sit still. Yesterday I went with the girls and Mr. Liddle (the man who is so like a doll) to a flower-show in the Botanical Gardens. The flowers were well enough, but few of them—the company shockingly bad; really these Liverpool ladies look, two-thirds of them, improper; the democratic tendency of the age in dress has not penetrated hither, I assure you; not a woman that Helen might not stand in admiration before, and exclaim 'How expensive!'[2]

To-day we are going 'across the water' with my uncle; I make a point of accepting every lark proposed to me, however uninviting. I am here for what Helen calls 'a fine change,' and the more movement the better. If I do not get good of the movement, I shall at least get good of the sitting still after it. My uncle is very kind to me. Alick is rather improved, speaks not at all on politics in

---

my hearing. Johnnie I have found a use for. I play one game at chess with him every night. 'He beats us a' for a deep thought.'[1]
Kind regards to Helen, and compliments to the leech.
Do not work too hard.

Ever your affectionate
JANE W. C.

'Noti bena.[2] I've got no bacca.'

EXTRACTS OF FURTHER LETTERS FROM LIVERPOOL.

To T. Carlyle, Chelsea.

July 27, 1845.—They are all gone to church and I am here alone, enjoying virtue's (Roman virtue's) own reward. My uncle at the last minute came to me in the room where I had fortified myself (morally), and asked with a certain enthusiasm, 'Are you not going to church?' 'No, I have no thought of it.' 'And why not?' (crescendo). 'Because your minister is a ranting jackass, that cracks the drum of one's ears.' 'Who told you that?' (stamping like my grandfather.) 'I do not choose to compromise anyone by naming my authority.' 'And what has that to do with going to a place of worship?' 'Nothing whatever; but it has a great deal to do with staying away from a place that is not of worship.' He looked at me over his spectacles for an instant as if doubtful whether to eat me raw or laugh; and 'eventually, thanks God,'[3] he chose the latter part. The girls, who came in fear and trembling to pick up my fragments, were astonished to find that I had carried the day. We get on famously, my uncle and I, and by dint of defiance, tempered with kisses, I can manage him better than anyone else does.

July 30.—My uncle has enjoyed my visit very much. I wrote to him beforehand on the subject of his 'detestable politics,' and we have had no flares up this time. The only one I have witnessed was last night at cards. He and A—— were playing at *écarté* on a little table in a corner, very silently and amicably to all appearance; the rest of us were sewing or reading. Suddenly the little table flew into the air on the point of my uncle's foot, and a shower of

---

[1] Admiring remark of an Annandale mother about her particularly stupid huge lout of a son.

[2] Dragoon's letter to his beloved in some police report which we had read years ago. 'Happy with you to the end of eternity,' and then this *noti bena*.

[3] Mazzini.

cards fell all over the floor! 'D—— these eternal cards!' said he fiercely, as we all stared up at him in astonishment. 'Hang them! Curse them to hell!' They all looked frightened; for me, the suddenness of the thing threw me into a fit of laughter, in which my uncle himself was the first to join. This morning at breakfast something was said about cards to be taken to Scotland. 'But,' said I, 'I thought they had been all sent last night to hell.' 'Pooh!' said my uncle quite gravely, 'that was only one pack.'

I am not wise in writing on with 'my brains' (as Rio would say) tormenting me in this way. But what to do? One's Good, if not feeling so lonely as might be wished, is in fact lonely enough, and one's self without one's own red bed to retire into. Cannot I stay in my 'boot' and be quiet? No, I get beside myself pent up there; latterly I have been bolting out of it through the men's room, whether they were clothed or no, like a bottle of ginger beer bursting the cork! 'Uncle, I beg your pardon but I must get out!' 'Weel, weel,' hiding himself behind the curtain, 'there is no help for it.'

God bless you, dear. I am in the Devil's own humour to-day if you care to know it—but ever yours, *not* without affection.

July 31.—Yesterday in the evening came Dr. James C——, and a young N——, all in black, this last being just returned from the funeral of his only sister, a promising girl of sixteen, the poor mother's chief comfort of late years. I recollected the time when Mrs. N——, then Agnes L——, consulted me whether she ought to marry J. N——. Where were all these young N——'s then—the lad who sate there looking so sadly, the girl who had just been laid under the earth? Had Agnes L—— lived true to the memory of her first love, would these existences have been for ever suppressed by her act? If her act could have suppressed them, what pretension have they to call themselves immortal, eternal? What comfort is there in thinking of the young girl just laid in her grave? 'My dear, you really ought not to go on with that sort of thing—all that questioning leads to nothing. We know nothing about it and cannot know, and what better should we be if we did?' 'All very true, Mr. Carlyle, but '—at least one cannot accept such solution on the authority of others, even of the wisest— one must have worked it out for oneself. And the working of it out is a sore business, very sore; especially with 'a body apt to fall into holes.'

August 5, *Seaforth.*—Geraldine (Jewsbury) came yesterday after-

noon, looking even better than when in London, and not *triste*, as
R—— expected, by any means. She has brought a good stock
of cigaritos with her, which is rather a pity, as I had just begun to
forget there was such a weed as tobacco in the civilised world.
She is very amusing and good-humoured, does all the 'wits' of the
party: and Mrs. Paulet and I look to the Pure Reason and Practical Endeavour. I fancy you would find our talk amusing if you
could assist at it in a cloak of darkness, for one of the penalties of
being 'the wisest man and profoundest thinker of the age' is the
royal one of never hearing the plain, 'unornamented' truth spok-
en; everyone striving to be wise and profound *invitâ naturâ* in the
presence of such a one, and making himself as much as possible into
his likeness. And this is the reason that Arthur Helps and so many
others talk very nicely to me, and bore you to distraction. With
me they are not afraid to stand on the little 'broad basis' of their
own individuality, such as it is. With you they are always balanc-
ing themselves like Taglioni, on the point of their moral or intellectual great toe.

If I were going 'at my age and with my cough' to take up a
mission, it would be the reverse of F. W——'s. Instead of boiling up individuals into the species I would draw a chalk circle
round every individuality, and preach to it to keep within that,
and preserve and cultivate its identity at the expense of ever so
much lost gilt of other people's 'isms.'

August 10.—'*Monsieur le Président!* I begin to be weary of the
treatment I experience here.'[1] Always my 'bits of letters' and
'bits of letters,' as if I were some nice little child writing in half
text on ruled paper to its God-papa! Since Jeffrey was pleased to
compliment me on my 'bits of convictions,' I have not had my
'rights of woman' so trifled with. He paid the penalty of his assurance in losing from that time my valuable correspondence; with
you I cannot so easily cease to ·correspond 'for reasons which it
may be interesting not to state.' But a woman of my invention can
always find legitimate means of revenging herself on those who do
not treat her with the respect due to genius, who put her off with a
pat on the head or a chuck under the chin when she addresses them
in all the full-grown gravity of five feet five inches and three-quarters without her shoes! So let us hear no more of my 'bits of letters' unless you are prepared to front a nameless retribution.

J. M—— seems to be still fighting it out with his conscience,

---

[1] *French Revolution*—speaker in Jacobin Club, evening of August 10.

abating no jot of heart or hope. If he were beside you I am persuaded he would soon become the sincerest disciple that you ever had; he seems so very near kicking his foot through the whole Unitarian concern already. He was arguing with Geraldine about the 'softening tendencies of our age,' 'the sympathy for knaves and criminals,' 'the impossibility of great minds being disjoined from great morality,' 'the stupidity of expecting to be happy through doing good.'

Nothing could be more orthodox! But what would have 'engrushed' him with you more than anything was in talking of Cromwell's doings in Ireland. 'After all,' he said, ' people make a great deal more outcry over massacres than there is any occasion for; one does not understand that exorbitant respect for human life, in overlooking or violating everything that makes it of any value.

August 14.—A delicate attention! This morning the bell for getting up did not ring. I lay awake till near nine expecting it, and then I thought I might as well dress. When I came down everybody had finished breakfast. 'But the bell did not ring,' said I, quite shocked. 'Oh, no, madam,' said Mr. Paulet; 'they told me you were so witty at dinner yesterday that you had better be let slumber this morning as long as possible, in case of your feeling a little exhausted!' And so actually the bell had not been rung in consideration of my incessant wit.

I had a long and really excellent letter from Helen yesterday, containing a little box of salve for my bunions. She had 'tried it on herself first' and found it quite satisfactory. Tell her that her letter was quite a treat for me, so copious and sensible, and not without wits even! She tells me that 'the child'. (the leech) 'gets always more lively,' and she is becoming 'rather fond of it.' She suggests also, very sensibly, that I should bid you give her timely notice when you leave, ' as she would like to have all your things nice for you, and you might never think of telling her till the very day!'

I have your letter. Sometimes the postman prefers taking them to Dale Street, and I have to wait all day in uncertainty, and then I am 'vaixed.' No address seems able to secure us against this *contretemps.* I wish I were there, dear Good, to *baiser* you *à la front.*' I could not reconcile myself to following my pleasures, or at least my eases, here while you are so hard worked and solitary, if it were not that my health is really improving, and I look forward to being less of an Egyptian skeleton lady for you through the winter by this egoism I am indulging in at present.

Mrs. Buller got no letter from me; what with eating, and sleeping, and walking, and driving, and having my feet rubbed, and settling the general question, I have really no time for writing except to one's Good.

Every night, too, after Mr. Paulet comes home, I play one or more games at chess; which is using him up famously. He is wonderfully patient of us all, and 'not without glimmerings of intelligence'! My paper and everybody's is done; so you must put up with scraps.

Your own
ADORABLE WIFE.

LETTER 72.

To T. Carlyle, Esq., Chelsea.

Liverpool: Saturday, Aug. 16, 1845.

Dearest,—I never know whether a letter is welcomer when it arrives after having been impatiently waited for, or like yesterday's, 'quite promiscuously,' when I was standing 'on the broad basis' of, 'Blessed are they who do not hope, for they shall not be disappointed!' I assure you I am the only person obliged by your writing; it makes a very palpable difference in my amiability throughout the day whether I have a letter to begin it with.

Last night we went, according to programme, to Mrs. A——'s, and 'it is but fair to state' that the drive there and back in the moonlight was the best of it. The party did me no ill, however; it was not a Unitarian crush like the last, but adapted to the size of the room: select, moreover, and with the crowning grace of an open window. There was an old gentleman who did the impossible to inspire me with a certain respect; Y—— they called him, and his glory consists in owning the Prince's Park, and throwing it open to 'poors.'[1] Oh, what a dreadful little old man! He plied me with questions, and suggestions about you, till I was within a trifle of putting 'my finger in the pipy o' 'im.'[2] 'How did Mr. Carlyle treat Oliver Cromwell's crimes?' 'His what?' said I. 'The atrocities he exercised on the Irish.' 'Oh, you mean massacring a

---

[1] Note, p. 180.

[2] Crying baby unappeasable. 'Put your finger in ta pipie o't' (little windpipe), said some Highland body.

garrison or two? All that is treated very briefly.' 'But Mr. Carlyle must feel a just horror of that.' 'Horror? Oh, none at all, I assure you! He regards it as the only means under the circumstances to save bloodshed.' The little old gentleman bounced back in his chair, and spread out his two hands, like a duck about to swim, while there burst from his lips a groan that made everyone look at us. What had I said to their Mr. Y——? By-and-by my old gentleman returned to the charge. 'Mr. Carlyle must be feeling much delighted about the Academical Schools?' 'Oh, no! he has been so absorbed in his own work lately that he has not been at leisure to be delighted about anything.' 'But, madam! a man may attend to his own work, and attend at the same time to questions of great public interest.' 'Do you think so? I don't.' Another bounce on the chair. Then, with a sort of awe, as of a 'demon more wicked than your wife:'[1] 'Do you not think, madam, that more good might be done by taking up the history of the actual time than of past ages? Such a time as this, so full of improvements in arts and sciences, the whole face of Europe getting itself changed! Suppose Mr. Carlyle should bring out a yearly volume about all this?' This was Y——'s last flight of eloquence with me, for catching the eyes of a lady (your Miss L—— of 'The Gladiator') fixed on me with the most ludicrous expression of sympathy, I fairly burst out laughing till the tears ran down; and when I had recovered myself, the old gentleman had turned for compensation to J. M——. J. had reasons for being civil to him which I had not, Mr. Y—— being his landlord; but he seemed to be answering him in his sleep, while his waking thoughts were intent on an empty chair betwixt Geraldine and me, and eventually he made it his own. As if to deprecate my confounding him with these Y——'s, he immediately began to speak in the most disrespectful manner of Mechanics Institutes 'and all that sort of thing;' and then we got on these eternal Vestiges of Creation,[2] which he termed, rather happily, 'animated mud.' Geraldine and Mrs. Paulet were wanting to engage him in a doctrinal discussion, which they are extremely fond of: 'Look at Jane,' suddenly exclaimed Geraldine, 'she is quizzing us in her own mind. You must know' (to M——) 'we cannot get Jane to care a bit about doctrines.' 'I should think not,' said M——, with

---

[1] Peter Nimmo's sermon on Ananias and Sapphira: 'Tempted by some demon more wicked than his wife.'

[2] Dull book (quasi-atheistic), much talked of then.

great vivacity; 'Mrs. Carlyle is the most concrete woman that I have seen for a long while.' 'Oh,' said Geraldine, 'she puts all her wisdom into practice, and so never gets into scrapes.' 'Yes,' said M—— in a tone 'significant of much,' ' to keep out of doctrines is the only way to keep out of scrapes!' Was not that a creditable speech in a Unitarian?

Miss L—— is a frank, rather agreeable, woman, forty or thereabouts, who looks as if she had gone through a good deal of hardship; not 'a domineering genius' by any means,[1] but with sense enough for all practical purposes, such as admiring you to the skies, and Cromwell too. The rest of the people were 'chiefly musical, Mr. Carlyle.' Mrs. A—— is very much fallen off in her singing since last year; I suppose, from squalling so much to her pupils. She is to dine here to-day, and ever so many people besides, to meet these R——'s. Doubtless we shall be 'borne through with an honourable throughbearing;'[2] but quietness is best.

And now I must go and walk, while the sun shines. Our weather here is very showery and cold. I heard a dialogue the other morning betwixt Mr. Paulet and his factotum, which amused me much. The factotum was mowing the lawn. Mr. Paulet threw up the breakfast-room window, and called to him: 'Knolles! how looks my wheat?' 'Very distressed indeed, sir!' 'Are we much fallen down?' 'No, sir, but we are black, very black.' 'All this rain, I should have thought, would have made us fall down?' 'Where the crops are heavy they are a good deal laid, sir, but it would take a vast of rain to lay us!' 'Oh, then, Knolles, it is because we are not powerful enough that we are not fallen down?' 'Sir?' 'It is because we are not rich enough?' 'Beg pardon, sir, but I don't quite understand?' Mr. Paulet shut the window and returned to his breakfast. God keep you, dear.

Your own

J. C.

LETTER 73.

To T. Carlyle, Chelsea.

Aug. 21, 1845.

On our return to the railway, I had got out of the carriage, and was walking backwards and forwards when two gentlemen passed,

---

[1] Jeffrey? 'Pooh! clever enough, but not a domineering genius!' (Poor Gray, of the High School, Edinburgh, thirty years before.)

[2] Burgher minister's thanksgiving on a Sacramental occasion.

one of whom I felt to know quite well, and after a little consideration I decided it was Mr. Storey, of Roseneath. Back I ran and laid my hand on his arm. 'See,' I said, 'how much better my memory is than yours!' 'I know your face quite well,' said he, 'but for my life I cannot tell who you are.' 'Why, I am Jeannie Welsh, to be sure.' If you had only seen the man! His transports were 'rather exquisite.' I do not remember to have seen anybody so outrageously glad to see me in all my life before. It was only after he had played all manner of antics that I recollected he had once been in love with me. He was still with me when Mrs. Paulet and Geraldine made their appearance, and they both perceived in the first instance that the gentleman I introduced to them had once been my lover; two women alike 'gleg.' In consideration of which good taste on his part, Mrs. Paulet on the spot invited him to go home with us to dinner; but that he could not do, was just about starting for London, where he had meant to seek me out. It did me great good to see him, especially as he looked so glad, not for his own sake particularly, but as an authentic piece of old times.

We had not been at home three minutes when J. M—— arrived to early dinner by appointment. I told him to-day quite frankly that he had better cut Unitarianism and come over to us. He asked me who I meant by 'us,' and I said Carlyle. He sighed, and shook his head, and said something about a man being bound to remain in the sphere appointed to him till he was fairly drawn out of it by his conscience.

LETTER 74.

Carlyle was himself coming North; his wife to return to London. She had written him an angry letter about his changes of plan, which had disturbed her own arrangements.—J. A. F.

To T. Carlyle, Chelsea.

Aug. 29.

Dearest,—To-day I am restored to my normal state of amiability through the unassisted efforts of nature. I am sorry now I did not repress my little movement of impatience yesterday; a lover would have found it charming, perhaps more flattering than whole pages of 'wits' and *dolcezze;* but husbands are so obtuse. They do not understand one's movements of impatience; want always 'to be treated with the respect due to genius;' exact common sense of their poor wives rather than 'the finer sensibilities of the heart;'

and so the marriage state [1]—'by working late and early, has come to what ye see'—if not precisely to immortal smash as yet, at least to within a hair's-breadth of it. But the matrimonial question may lie over till I write my book on the Rights of Women and make an *Egyptian* happy.

LETTER 75.

To *Charles Gavan Duffy, Esq., Dublin*

5 Cheyne Row, Chelsea: Sept. 14, 1845.

My dear Sir,—Thank you emphatically for the beautiful little volume you have sent me, 'all to myself' (as the children say). Besides the prospective pleasure of reading it, it is no small immediate pleasure to me as a token of your remembrance; for when one has 'sworn an everlasting friendship' at first sight, one desires, very naturally, that it should not have been on your Irish principle, 'with the reciprocity all on one side.'

The book only reached me, or rather I only reached it, last night, on my return home after an absence of two months, in search of—what shall I say?—a religion? Sure enough, if I were a good Catholic, or good Protestant, or good anything, I should not be visited with those nervous illnesses, which send me from time to time out into space to get myself rehabilitated, after a sort, 'by change of air.'

When are you purposing, through the strength of Heaven, to break into open rebellion? I have sometimes thought that in a civil war I should possibly find my mission'—*moi!* But in these merely talking times, a poor woman knows not how to turn herself; especially if, like myself, she 'have a devil' always calling to her, 'March! march!' and bursting into infernal laughter when requested to be so good as specify whither.

If you have not set a time for taking up arms, when at least are you coming again to 'eat terms' (whatever that may mean)? I feel what my husband would call 'a real, genuine, healthy desire' to pour out more tea for you.

My said husband has finished his 'Cromwell' two weeks ago, then joined me at a place near Liverpool, where he remained a

---

[1] By working late and early
We're come to what ye see,
Although we made our bridal bed
On clean pease strae.

week in a highly reactionary state; and then he went North, and I South, to meet again when he has had enough of peat-bog and his platonically beloved ' silence '—perhaps in three weeks or a month hence. Meanwhile I intend a great household earthquake, through the help of chimney-sweeps, carpet-beaters, and other like products of the fall of our first parents. And so you have our history up to the present moment.

Success to all your wishes, except for the destruction of us Saxons, and believe me

Always very cordially yours,

JANE W. CARLYLE.

LETTER 76.

About the end of August I did come to Seaforth; wearisome journey; bulky dull man, Sir W. B——, as I found, and some Irish admirers talking dull antiquarian pedantries and platitudes all day; I as third party silent, till at length, near sunset, bursting out upon them and their Nennius, to their terror and astonishment and almost to my own. Beautiful reception by Mrs. Paulet and her waiting for me at the station. Alas! alas! how unspeakable now! —T. C.

From Liverpool Carlyle went on by sea to Annan, leaving Mrs. Carlyle to go home to Chelsea.—J. A. F.

To T. Carlyle, Esq., Scotsbrig.

Chelsea: Monday, Sept. 15, 1845.

I was sure you would have a wretched voyage; the very smell of that boat made me sick for all the rest of the evening. We ' *did* intend ' to have waived a handkerchief to you in passing, from the roof of the house; but the fog was too thick ' for anything.'

Great efforts were made to keep me longer, but it is my principle always to go away before having exhausted the desire to keep me; besides that, I pique myself on being a woman of my word, and so *me voici* in Cheyne Row once more.

The journey back was a considerable of a bore; the train I came by starting at eleven, and, supposed by Mr. Paulet to answer to that which leaves here at ten, did not land me at Euston Station till half after nine! And all that while, except a glass of porter and a sandwich, ' the chief characteristic of which was its tenuity,' [1] I

---

[1] Mill's account of some celebrated creature's ' literature.'

had no support to nature, for I saw no sense in dining at Birmingham when I expected to be in London at six. John [1] had sent a note the day before, proposing, as he proposed the senna for Mary's children, that I should appoint him to meet me, ' or perhaps I had better not.' Not having got the letter before setting out, I had, of course, no option; 'which was probably just as well.' Arriving here a quarter after ten, I found poor little Helen half distracted at my lateness; 'if it had been the master, she would never have minded, but *me*, that was always to a moment!' And so she had been taking on at a great rate; and finally, just a few minutes before I arrived, got John despatched to look for me (!) at the station, in case, as he fancied, I had preferred coming by the express train; and, through these good intentions, 'highly unfortunate,' [2] I was kept up till half after one; John not coming back till half after twelve, and I too polite to go to bed without awaiting his coming. Moreover, the carriage I came in had pitched like a ship in a storm; so that I was shaken into an absolute fever; 'the flames of fever had seized on me;' and what with all this fatigue, and the excitement of feeling myself at home, I could not sleep 'the least in the world,' and have not recovered myself to this hour. All is quiet about me as quiet can be, even to John's boots; but what signifies that, if one have, like Anne Cook's soldier, ' palpitation.'

I have found everything here as well or better than could have been expected: the leech alive and ' so happy!' Helen radiant with virtue's own reward; the economical department in a very backward state, but not confused, for it is clear as day that not a single bill has been paid since I left. Helen seems to have had four pounds ten for the incidental expenses, which I shall inclose her account of, to amuse Jamie; and there is a national debt to the butcher, baker, and milkman, amounting to about five pounds. So that the housekeeping, during my absence, has been carried on at some six or seven shillings a week less than if I had been at home, which is all as it should be, for I defy three people to live as we do on less than thirty shillings a week. I do think the little creature is very careful; as for honest, that I have been sure about long ago.

---

[1] John Carlyle, then staying in Cheyne Row.
[2] Phrase of John's.

LETTER 77.

To T. Carlyle, Scotsbrig.

Chelsea: Thursday, Sept. 18, 1845.

My Dear,—I have got quite over the fatigues of my journey, which had been most provokingly aggravated for me by a circumstance 'which it may be interesting not to state;' the last two nights I have slept quite as well as I was doing at Seaforth. The retirement of Cheyne Row is as deep at present as anyone not absolutely a Timon of Athens could desire. 'There is, in the first place' (as Mr. Paulet would say), the physical impossibility (hardly anybody being left in town), and then the weather has been so tempestuous that nobody in his senses (except Mazzini, who never reflects whether it be raining or no) would come out to make visits. He (Mazzini) came the day before yesterday, immediately on receiving notification of my advent, and his doe-skin boots were oozing out water in a manner frightful to behold. He looked much as I left him, and appeared to have made no progress of a practical sort. He told me nothing worth recording, except that he had received the other day a declaration of love. And this he told me with the same *calma* and historical precision with which you might have said you had received an invitation to take the chair at a Mechanics' Institute dinner. Of course I asked 'the particulars.' 'Why not?' and I got them fully, at the same time with brevity, and without a smile. Since the assassination affair,[1] he had received many invitations to the house of a Jew merchant of Italian extraction, where there are several daughters—'what shall I say?—horribly ugly: that is, repugnant for me entirely.' One of them is 'nevertheless very strong in music,' and seeing that he admired her playing, she had 'in her head confounded the playing with the player.' The last of the only two times he had availed himself of their attentions, as they sat at supper with Browning and some others, 'the youngest of the horrible family' proposed to him, in *sotto voce*, that they two should drink 'a goblet of wine' together, each to the person that each loved most in the world. 'I find your toast *unegoist*,' said he, 'and I accept it with pleasure.' 'But,' said she, 'when we have drunk, we will then tell each other

---

[1] Trial (at Paris) of some calumnious fellow, who had accused him of being privy to, &c. &c.

I.—9

to whom?' 'Excuse me,' said he, 'we will, if you please, drink without conditions.' Whereupon they drank; 'and then this girl —what shall I say? bold, upon my honour—proposed to tell me to whom she had drunk, and trust to my telling her after. "As you like." "Well, then, it was to you!" "Really?" said I, surprised, I must confess. "Yes," said she, pointing aloft; "true as God exists." "Well," said I, "I find it strange." "Now, then," said she, "to whom did you drink?" "Ah!" said I, "that is another question;" and on this, that girl became ghastly pale, so that her sister called out, "Nina! what is the matter with you?" and now, thanks God, she has sailed to Aberdeen.' Did you ever hear anything so distracted? enough to make one ask if R—— has not some grounds for his extraordinary ideas of English women.

The said R—— presented himself here, last night, in an interregnum of rain, and found me in my dressing-gown (after the wetting), expecting no such *Himmelssendung.* I looked as beautifully unconscious as I could of all the amazing things I had been told of him at Seaforth. He talked much of a 'dreadful illness;' but looked as plump as a pincushion, and had plenty of what Mr. Paulet calls 'colours in his face.' Hs seemed less distracted than usual, and professed to have discovered, for the first time, 'the infinite blessedness of work,' and also to be 'making money at a great rate—paying off his debt by five or six pounds a week.' I remarked that he must surely have had a prodigious amount of debt to begin with.

Kind regards to your mother and the rest.

                                                            J. C.

LETTER 78.

To T. Carlyle, Scotsbrig.

                                        Tuesday, Sept. 23, 1845.

'Nothink'[1] for you to-day in the shape of inclosure, unless I inclose a letter from Mrs. Paulet to myself, which you will find as 'entertaining' to the full as any of mine. And *nothink* to be told either, except all about the play;[2] and upon my honour, I do not feel as if I had penny-a-liner genius enough, this cold morning, to make much entertainment out of that. Enough to clasp one's hand,

---

[1] Dumfries postmaster of old: 'Nothink for Craigenputtock to-day, me'm!'
[2] Private theatricals got up by Dickens and Forster for some benevolent purpose.—J. A. F.

and exclaim, like Helen before the Virgin and Child, 'Oh, how expensive!' But 'how did the creatures get through it?' Too well; and not well enough! The public theatre, scenes painted by Stansfield, costumes 'rather exquisite,' together with the certain amount of proficiency in the amateurs, overlaid all idea of private theatricals; and, considering it as public theatricals, the acting was 'most insipid,' not one performer among them that could be called good, and none that could be called absolutely bad. Douglas Jerrold seemed to me the best, the oddity of his appearance greatly helping him; he played Stephen the Cull. Forster as Kitely and Dickens as Captain Bobadil were much on a par; but Forster preserved his identity, even through his loftiest flights of Macreadyism; while poor little Dickens, all painted in black and red, and affecting the voice of a man of six feet, would have been unrecognisable for the mother that bore him! On the whole, to get up the smallest interest in the thing, one needed to be always reminding oneself: 'all these actors were once men!'[1] and will be men again to-morrow morning. The greatest wonder for me was how they had contrived to get together some six or seven hundred ladies and gentlemen (judging from the clothes) at this season of the year; and all utterly unknown to me, except some half-dozen.

So long as I kept my seat in the dress circle I recognised only Mrs. Macready (in one of the four private boxes), and in my nearer neighbourhood Sir Alexander and Lady Gordon. But in the interval betwixt the play and the farce I took a notion to make my way to Mrs. Macready. John, of course, declared the thing 'clearly impossible, no use trying it;' but a servant of the theatre, overhearing our debate, politely offered to escort me where I wished; and then John, having no longer any difficulties to surmount, followed, to have his share in what advantages might accrue from the change. Passing through a long dim passage, I came on a tall man leant to the wall, with his head touching the ceiling like a caryatid, to all appearance asleep, or resolutely trying it under most unfavourable circumstances. 'Alfred Tennyson!' I exclaimed in joyful surprise. 'Well!' said he, taking the hand I held out to him, and forgetting to let it go again. 'I did not know you were in town,' said I. 'I should like to know who you are,' said he; 'I

---

[1] Speech of a very young Wedgwood at a Woolwich review: 'Ah, papa, all these soldiers were once men!'

know that I know you, but I cannot tell your name.' And I had actually to name myself to him. Then he woke up in good earnest, and said he had been meaning to come to Chelsea. 'But Carlyle is in Scotland,' I told him with due humility. 'So I heard from Spedding already, but I asked Spedding, would he go with me to see Mrs. Carlyle? and he said he would.' I told him if he really meant to come, he had better not wait for backing, under the present circumstances; and then pursued my way to the Macreadys' box; where I was received by William (whom I had not divined) with a 'Gracious heavens!' and spontaneous dramatic start, which made me all but answer, 'Gracious heavens!' and start dramatically in my turn. And then I was kissed all round by his women; and poor Nell Gwyn, Mrs. M—— G——, seemed almost pushed by the general enthusiasm on the distracted idea of kissing me also! They would not let me return to my stupid place, but put in a third chair for me in front of their box; 'and the latter end of that woman was better than the beginning.' Macready was in perfect ecstasies over the 'Life of Schiller,' spoke of it with tears in his eyes. As 'a sign of the times,' I may mention that in the box opposite sat the Du.. ⸴ Devonshire, with Payne Collier! Next to us were D'Orsay and 'Milady!'

Between eleven and twelve it was all over—and the practical result? Eight-and-sixpence for a fly, and a headache for twenty-four hours! I went to bed as wearied as a little woman could be, and dreamt that I was plunging through a quagmire seeking some herbs which were to save the life of Mrs. Maurice; and that Maurice was waiting at home for them in an agony of impatience, while I could not get out of the mud-water!

Craik arrived next evening (Sunday), to make his compliments. Helen had gone to visit numbers.[1] John was smoking in the kitchen. I was lying on the sofa, headachey, leaving Craik to put himself to the chief expenditure of wind, when a cab drove up. Mr. Strachey? No. Alfred Tennyson alone! Actually, by a superhuman effort of volition he had put himself into a cab, nay, brought himself away from a dinner party, and was there to smoke and talk with me!—by myself—me! But no such blessedness was in store for him. Craik prosed, and John babbled for his entertainment; and I, whom he had come to see, got scarcely any speech with him. The exertion, however, of having to provide him with tea, through my own unassisted ingenuity (Helen being gone for

---

[1] 'No 5,' or the like, denoting maid-servant there.

the evening) drove away my headache; also perhaps a little feminine vanity at having inspired such a man with the energy to take
a cab on his own responsibility, and to throw himself on providence
for getting away again! He stayed till eleven, Craik sitting him
out, as he sat out Lady H——, and would sit out the Virgin Mary
should he find her here.

What with these unfortunate mattresses (a work of necessity)
and other processes almost equally indispensable, I have my hands
full, and feel 'worried,' which is worse. I fancy my earthquake
begins to 'come it rather strong' for John's comfort and ease, but
I cannot help that; if I do not get on with my work, such as it is,
what am I here for?

Yours,

J. C.

LETTER 79.

To T. Carlyle, Esq., Scotsbrig.

Chelsea: Thursday evening, Sept. 25 (?), 1845.

Here is an inclosure that will 'do thee neither ill n'r gude!' It
lay along with two brochures, one blue, one pea-green—the thin-
nest brochures in every sense that ever issued from 'the womb of
uncreated night!' 'the insipid offspring' of that 'crack brained enthusiastic' who calls herself *Henri Paris;* one entitled *Grossmütter-
lein,* in verse, the other—oh, Heavens!—*La femme libre, et l'éman-
cipation de la femme: Rhapsodie à propos des Saint-Simoniens,* in
prose—dead prose.

I have looked into it over my tea, and find that the only emancipation for *femme* lies in her having '*le saint courage de rester
vierge!*' Glad tidings of great joy for—Robertson! '*Guerroyez
donc, si vous pouvez, contre les hommes!*' exclaims the great female
mind in an enthusiasm of platitude. '*Mais pour qu'ils daignent
accepter votre défi, prouvez-leur, avant tout, que vous avez appris
. . . à vous passer d'eux!*'

I rose yesterday morning with an immense desire for 'change of
air.' I had made the house into the liveliest representation of
'Hell and Tommy'[1] (I 'Tommy'), and it struck me that I should
do well to escape from it for some hours; so John and I left to-

---

[1] Buller's definition to me of a Martin picture (engraving rather) on Macready's staircase one gala night. Picture mad—mad as Bedlam, all, and with
one 'small figure' (' Tommy ') notably prominent.

gether. In the King's Road he picked up a cab to take back for
his luggage, and I went on to Clarence Terrace, where I dined,
and by six I was at home again to tea. Mrs. Macready had returned to Eastbourne, having only come up for the day to attend
the play. That I was prepared for, as she had invited me to go
along with her, but I was not prepared to find poor Macready ill
in bed, with two doctors attending him. He had caught a horrible
cold that night, from seeing Mrs. M—— G—— to her carriage
through the rain 'in thin shoes;' had been obliged to break an engagement at Cambridge. Poor Letitia[1] was very concerned about
him, but would still not let me go without some dinner. To-day
she writes to me that he is better. There seemed a good deal of
jealousy in Macreadydom on the subject of the amateur actors. A
'tremendous puff of the thing' had appeared in the *Times*—'more
kind really than ever the *Times* showed itself towards William!'[2]
John, when he came at night to pay 'his compliments of digestion,'
suggested, with his usual originality, 'it was probably that (the
puff) which had made Macready so ill just now!' Forster, it
seems, bears away the palm; but they have all had their share of
praise, 'and are in such a state of excitement, poor things, as
never was seen!' 'It will not stop here,' Miss Macready thinks.

To-day I have not been out at all. I rose at seven, to receive—a
sweep! And have been helping Helen to scrub in the library till
now—seven in the evening. John[3] came rushing in soon after
nine this morning: he had left a breast-pin in the glass-drawer, and
'supposed it would not be lost yet!' Then having found it, he
brought it to me in the library, where I was mounted on the steps,
covered with dust, to ask, whether I thought 'the diamonds real;'
and what I thought 'such a thing would cost.' It was the pin he
got years ago in Italy. I told him I would not take upon me
to value it, but I could learn its value for him. 'From whom?'
'From Collier the jeweller.' 'Where does he live?' (with immense
eagerness.) 'At the top of Sloane Street.' 'But wouldn't he tell
me,—if I asked him? me, myself?' 'I dare say he would,' said I

---

[1] His sister, a very amiable gentlewoman.

[2] 'William' was the good Mrs. M.'s constant designation for her husband.

[3] John's careless, helter-skelter ways had been notable since his boyhood,
and which, taking his ease among us, were frequently an object of satire to
her as to the rest of us. The good, affectionate, honest, and manly character
and fine talents that lay deeper she also knew, as we all of us did, though
with less of *vocal* recognition.

soothingly, for he seemed to be going rapidly out of his wits, with all-absorbing desire to know the value of that pin! If I had not seen him the night before playing with his purse and some sovereigns, I might have thought he was on the point of carrying it to a pawnshop to get himself a morsel of victuals! But when, giving up the diamonds as glass, he passed to the individual value of the turquoise in the middle, flesh and blood could stand it no longer, and I returned to my dusting in silence; whereupon he looked at his watch, and found he 'was obliged to go off to the British Museum.' What in all the world will become of him? He seems to be more than ever without 'fixed point,' without will, without so much as a good wish! unless it be to enjoy a tolerable share of material comfort, without 'Amt,' and as much as possible without 'Geld.' However, now that he has 'concluded with his landlady,' it is no business of mine how he flounders on, 'bating no jot of heart and hope,' as he says. My own life is rather of the floundering sort, only I have the grace to have 'abated heart and hope' in it to such an extent as to think sometimes that, 'if I were dead, and a stone at my head,' perhaps it would be be——ter!'[1]

Not a soul has been here since Alfred Tennyson—except the 'dark-fated' Krasinski,[2] who did not get in. I know his rap, and signified to Helen to say 'I was sick—or dead'—what she liked! So she told him, 'the mistress was bad with her head to-night,' which, if not precisely the naked truth, was a Gambardella 'aspiration' towards it. But besides Miss Macready yesterday I saw Helps, who seems to me 'dwindling away into an unintelligible whinner.' I met him in the King's Road, just as John called his cab, and he walked back part of the way with me, decidedly too solemn for his size!

I get no letters in these days except from you. Geraldine has even fallen dumb; still out of sorts I fancy, or absorbed in her 'one-eyed Egyptian;' perhaps scheming a new 'work!' I care very little which. Kind regards wherever they are due.

J. C.

---

[1] Forlorn old pauper, entering a school-room (to dame and little children):

> 'I'm a poor helpless cratur;
> If I was dead, and a stone at my head,
> I think it would be bey-tur [better]!'

[2] Amiable, mild gentleman, Polish exile; utterly poor; died in Edinburgh ten years afterwards.

LETTER 80.

To T. Carlyle, Scotsbrig.

Wednesday, Oct. 1845 [some evening, about post-time].

Well! now I am subsided again; set in for a quiet evening, at leisure to write, and with plenty to write about. I know not how it is; I seem to myself to be leading a most solitary, and virtuous, and eventless life here, at this dead season of the year; and yet when I sit down to write, I have so many things to tell always that I am puzzled where to begin. Decidedly, I was meant to have been a subaltern of the Daily Press—not ' a penny-lady, '[1] but a penny-a-liner; for it is not only a faculty with me, but a necessity of my nature to make a great deal out of nothing.

To begin with something I have been treasuring up for a week (for I would not holloa till we were out of the wood): I have *put down the dog!*[2] 'The dog! wasn't he put down at Christmas, with a hare?' It seemed so; and ' we wished we might get it!' But on my return I found him in the old place, at the back of the wall, barking 'like—like—anything!' 'Helen!' I said, with the calmness of a great despair, ' is not that the same dog?' ''Deed is it!' said she, ' and the whole two months you have been away, its tongue has never lain! it has driven even me almost distracted!' I said no more, but I had my own thoughts on the subject. Poison? a pistol bullet? the Metropolitan Police? Some way or other that dog—or I—must terminate! Meanwhile I went on cleaning with what heart I could. 'My Dear! Will you hasten to the catastrophe?' I am hastening, slowly—*festina lente.* Bless your heart! ' there's nothing pushing'—'the rowins[3] are a' in the loft' for this night! Well! it was the evening after John's departure. I had been too busy all day to listen; the candles were lit, and I had set myself with my feet on the fender to enjoy the happiness of being let alone, and to——bid myself ' consider.' 'Bow-wow-wow,'

---

[1] In Scotland the ' Penny Ladies ' (extraneously so-called) were busy, ' benevolent ' persons; subscribers of a penny a week for educating, &c. &c., not with much success.

[2] Oh, my heroine! Endless were her feats in regard to all this, and her gentle talent too! I could not have lived here but for that, had there been nothing more.

[3] Saying of my indolent sister-in-law, brother Alick's wife, on one occasion. 'Rowins' are wool completely carded, ready for the wheel when it comes down from ' the loft.'

roared the dog, 'and dashed the cup of fame from my brow!'
'Bow-wow-wow' again, and again, till the whole universe seemed
turned into one great dog-kennel! I hid my face in my hands and
groaned inwardly. 'Oh, destiny accursed! what use of scrubbing
and sorting? All this availeth me nothing, so long as the dog sit-
teth at the washerman's gate!' I could have burst into tears, but I
did not! 'I was a republican—before the Revolution; and I
never wanted energy!' I ran for ink and paper, and wrote:—

'Dear Gambardella,—You once offered to shoot some cocks for
me; that service I was enabled to dispense with; but now I accept
your devotion. Come, if you value my sanity, and ——.' But
here 'a sudden thought struck me.' He could not take aim at the
dog without scaling the high wall, and in so doing he would certainly be seized by the police; so I threw away that first sibylline
leaf, and wrote another—to the washerman! Once more I offered
him 'any price for that horrible dog—to hang it,' offered 'to settle
a yearly income on it if it would hold its accursed tongue.' I implored, threatened, imprecated, and ended by proposing that, in
case he could not take an immediate final resolution, he should in
the interim 'make[1] the dog dead-drunk with a bottle of whiskey,
which I sent for the purpose!' Helen was sent off with the note
and the whiskey; and I sat, all concentrated, awaiting her return,
as if the fate of nations had depended on my diplomacy; and so it
did, to a certain extent! Would not the inspirations of 'the first
man in Europe' be modified,[2] for the next six months at least, by
the fact, who should come off victorious, I or the dog? Ah! it is
curious to think how first men in Europe, and first women too,
are acted upon by the inferior animals!

Helen came, but even before that had 'the raven down of night'
smoothed itself in heavenly silence! God grant this were not mere
accident; oh, no! verily it was not accident. The washerman's
two daughters had seized upon and read the note; and what was
death to me had been such rare amusement to them that they 'fell
into fits of laughter' in the first place; and, in the second place,
ran down and untied the dog, and solemnly pledged themselves
that it should 'never trouble me more!' At Christmas they had
sent it into the country for three months 'to learn to be quiet,'
and then chained it in the old place; now they would take some
final measure. Next morning came a note from the washerman

---

[1] Mark, mark!
[2] *Quiz*, mainly this, and glad mockery of some who deserved it.

himself, written on glazed paper, with a crow-quill, apologizing, promising; he could not put it away entirely; as it was 'a great protection' to him, and 'belonged to a relation' (who shall say where sentiment may not exist!), but he 'had untied it, and would take care it gave me no further trouble,' and he 'returned his grateful thanks for what 'as been sent.' It is a week ago; and one may now rest satisfied that the tying up caused the whole nuisance. The dog is to be seen going about there all day in the yard, like any other Christian dog, 'carrying out' your principle of silence, not merely 'platonically,' but practically. Since that night, as Helen remarks, 'it has not said one word!' So, 'thanks God,' you still have quietude to return to! [1]

I took tea with Sterling on Monday night; walked there, and he sent the carriage home with me. It is very difficult to know how to do with him. He does not seem to me essentially mad; but rather mad with the apprehension of madness; a state of mind I can perfectly understand—*moi*. He forgets sometimes Anthony's name, for example, or mine; or how many children he has; and then he gets into a rage, that he cannot recollect; and then he stamps about, and rings the bell, and brings everybody in the house to 'help him to remember;' and when all will not do, he exclaims: 'I am going mad, by God!' and then he is mad, as mad as a March hare. I can do next to nothing for him, beyond cheering him up a little, for the moment. Yesterday, again, I went a little drive with him; of course, not without Saunders as well as the coachman. He told me that when he heard I had written about him, he 'cried for three days.' Anthony's desertion seems the central point, around which all his hypochondriacal ideas congregate. Anthony has never written him the scrape of a pen, since he left him insensible at Manchester; nor even written about him, so far as himself or his manservant knows.

Whom else have I seen? Nobody else, I think, except Mazzini, whom I was beginning to fancy the Jewess must have made an *enlevement* of; and *enlevé* he had been, sure enough, but not by the Jewess—by himself, and only the length of Oxford; or rather he meant to go only the length of Oxford; but, with his usual practicality, let himself be carried sixty miles further, to a place he called Swinton. [2] Then, that the journey back might have also its share of misadventure, he was not in time to avail himself of

---

[1] Well do I remember that dog, behind the wall, on the other side of the street. Never heard more.   [2] Swindon.

the place he had taken 'in the second class;' but had to jump up, 'quite promiscuously,' beside 'the conductor,' where he had 'all the winds of Heaven blowing on him, and through him;' the result a 'dreadful cold.' Dreadful, it must have been when it confined him to the house. Meanwhile he had had—two other declarations of love!! They begin to be as absurd as the midges in Mr. Fleming's 'right eye.' 'What! more of them?' 'Ah yes! unhappily! they begin to—what shall I say?—rain on me like *sauterelles!*' One was from a young lady in Genoa, who sent him a bracelet of her hair (the only feature he has seen of her); and begged 'to be united to him—in plotting!' 'That one was good, upon my honour.' 'And the other?' 'Ah! from a woman here, married, thanks God; though to a man fifty years more old—French, and sings —the other played, decidedly my love of music has consequences!' 'And how did she set about it?' '*Franchement;* through a mutual friend; and then she sent me an invitation to supper; and I returned for answer that I was going to Oxford; where I still am, and will remain a long, long time!' *Emancipation de la femme!* one would say, it marches almost faster than intellect. And now, if there be not clatter enough for one night, I have a great many half-moons and stars to cut in paper before I go to bed. For what purpose? That is my secret. 'And you wish that you could tell!' Good night. *Schlaf wohl.* J. C.

I told Scott, in a note, to despatch Mrs. Rich's letter immediately.

LETTER 81.

To T. Carlyle, Scotsbrig.

Chelsea: Tuesday, Oct. 7, 1845.

'Ah!' my dear! Yes indeed! 'If I could 'quench the devil' also, you might turn your face homewards with a feeling of comparative security. But Sybilline leaves, whisky, game even, all the means of seduction which I have at my poor command, cannot *gain* him. Still, as in the time of old Dr. Ritchie, 'he goeth about, seeking whom he may devour,' and does not, as Helen was remarking this morning the dog did, ever since it had been set at large, 'behave just like any other rational being.' One must be content to 'stave nim off,' then, better or worse. Against the devil my 'notes' themselves are powerless.[1] But here, on the table before me at this moment, one would say, lay means enough to keep him

---

[1] 'Against stupidity the gods themselves are powerless' (Schiller).

at bay for a while: first, two series of discourses on, first, 'Christian Humiliation'; second, 'The City of God,' by C. H. Terrot, D.D., Bishop of Edinburgh; and secondly, a pair of pistols with percussion-locks.

Are not the Fates kind in sending me two such windfalls in one evening? When I have made myself sufficiently desperate by study of the one, I can blow my brains out with the other. Come what may, one has always one's ' City of God' left and—one's pistols.

Meanwhile, I am going to dine with —— ——. She met Darwin here yesterday, and asked him to fetch me; and though I made great eyes at him, he answered, ' With all the pleasure in life!' And so, for want of moral courage to say *No* on my own basis, I am in for a stupid evening and Italian cookery; but I shall take some sewing with me, and stipulate to be brought away early. I have been all day giving the last finish to the china closet; and am shocked, this moment, by the town clock striking four, before my letter is well begun; I will send it, nevertheless, lest you should 'take a notion' to be anxious.

I am also under the disagreeable necessity of warning you that you must bring some money. 'The thirty pounds I left done already?' No, not done absolutely, but near it; and yet my living has been as moderate as well could be, and my little improvements have all been made off the money that was to have been squandered in Wales. I wish you had had the paying out at the end of the quarter instead of the beginning; it is so provoking, when I wanted so much to have been praised for my economy, to have to say instead, you must bring more money. But just take the trouble to see how it has gone, without any mention of victuals at all:—

	£	s.	d.
Your debt to clear off	4	18	6
Water-rate		6	6
Church-rate		11	3
Rent	8	15	0
Aldin's quarter's account	5	8	0
Taxes	3	2	2½
[1] To Helen of wages	1	0	0
	24	1	5½

After so prosaic a page as that, what more were it possible to write, even if I had the time? *Ach Gott!* Ever yours,

JANE CARLYLE.

---

[1] With the receipts all inclosed. Oh, my ' poverty '! richer to me than the Indies!

LETTER 82.

To T. Carlyle, Scotsbrig.

Sunday, Oct. 12, 1845.

Considering that a letter of twelve pages will reach you in the course of nature to-morrow morning, another for Tuesday morning seems to be about as superfluous as Mr. Kenny's second twin.[1] Nevertheless, to be punctual to orders, this little sheet comes 'hopping to find you in the same.'

I have been from twelve to-day till now (six in the evening) with old Sterling. He came to ask me to drive, and dine with him after, which humble prayer I could comply with in both its branches—the day being Sunday, and nothing particular doing at home. In passing along Brompton Road, he suddenly pulled the check-string and said to me in a solemn voice, ' Now, will you please to accompany me to the regions of the dead?' ' Certainly not,' said I, and called to the coachman, ' Drive on!' ' He is rapidly improving in his physical part; but the head is confused as much as ever. He began crying about his wife to-day; and, after declaring that ' she had reason to be satisfied with his grief for her loss,' finished off with ' and now I say it really and religiously, I have just one hope left, and that is—to be left a widower as soon as possible.'

On my return, I found on the table the cards of Mrs. N—— and Mrs. A——. ' How these two women do hate one another!'[2] But they are now, it would seem, not ashamed to drive out together. I was rather sorry to have missed Mrs. N——. Who should drop in on me yesterday at dinner, but little Bölte, looking fat and almost contented? She was passing through with one of her pupils, whom she had been living with six weeks at Sevenoaks, to be near a doctor ' for diseases of the skin.' She had fallen in there with a fine lady who possessed Mr. Carlyle's works, and said she liked them in many respects, and always took his part in public; that there was one thing about him ' deeply to be deplored.' Bölte asked, ' What?' ' Why, you know, on certain subjects Mr. Carlyle thinks for himself, and that is so very wrong.'

---

[1] Kenny, the playwright, married to the widow of Holcroft (the nervous Irish gentleman, to black French giantess, afraid of nothing) had an important bequest depending ' on the birth of a child.' Twins duly came, whereupon anxious Kenny dropped off to Basil Montague to inquire: ' But will that do? Two instead of one?'

[2] So had some spiteful fellow once whispered her, in some rout, on seeing them together.

LETTER 83.

John Forster, Esq., 58 Lincoln's Inn Fields.

Bay House: Sunday, Dec. 7, 1845.

My dear Mr. Forster,—A woman is constantly getting warned against following 'the impulses of her heart!' Why, I never could imagine! for all the grand blunders I am conscious of having committed in life have resulted from neglecting or gainsaying the impulses of my heart, to follow the insights of my understanding, or, still worse, of other understandings. And so I am now arrived at this with it, that I have flung my understanding to the dogs; and think, do, say, and feel just exactly as nature prompts me. Well, having just finished the reading of your article on 'Cromwell,' nature prompts me to take pen and paper, and tell you that I think it devilishly well done, and quite as meritorious as the book itself; only that there is not so much bulk of it! Now, do not fancy it is my wife-nature that is so excited. I am a bad wife in so far as regards care about what is said of my husband's books in newspapers or elsewhere. I am always so thankful to have them done, and out of the house, that the praise or blame they meet with afterwards is of the utmost insignificance to me. It is not, then, because your article covers him with generous praise that I am so delighted with it; but because it is full of sense, and highmindedness of its own; and most eloquently written. As Mrs. Norton would say, 'I love you for writing it;' only nobody will impute to me a fraudulent use of that word!

My pen—all pens here—refuse to write intelligibly. We are to come home in a fortnight hence, and I hope to see you then.

Ever yours affectionately,

J. C.

Love to the Macreadys.

LETTER 84.

To Mrs. Russell, Thornhill.

5 Cheyne Row, Chelsea: Dec. 30, 1845.

Dearest Mrs. Russell,—We are just returned from our Hampshire visit;[1] and I can answer for one of us being so worn out with

---

[1] After a long visit to Mr. and Lady Harriet Baring, at Bay House, Alverstoke.

'strenuous idleness,' as I do not remember ever to have been before! Six weeks have I been doing absolutely nothing but playing at battledore and shuttlecock, chess, talking nonsense, and getting rid of a certain fraction of this mortal life as cleverly and uselessly as possible; nothing could exceed the sumptuosity and elegance of the whole thing, nor its uselessness! Oh dear me! I wonder why so many people wish for high position and great wealth, when it is such an 'open secret' what all that amounts to in these days, merely to emancipating people from all the practical difficulties, which might teach them the facts of things, and sympathy with their fellow creatures. This Lady Harriet Baring, whom we have just been staying with, is the very cleverest woman, out of sight, that I ever saw in my life (and I have seen all our 'distinguished authoresses'); moreover, she is full of energy and sincerity, and has, I am sure, an excellent heart; yet so perverted has she been by the training and life-long humouring incident to her high position that I question if in her whole life she has done as much for her fellow creatures as my mother in one year, or whether she will ever break through the cobwebs she is entangled in, so as to be anything other than the most amusing and most graceful woman of her time. The sight of such a woman should make one very content with one's own trials even when they feel to be rather hard!

To jump to the opposite ends of creation, how is old Mary? Let her have her usual tokens of remembrance from me, poor old soul!—and Margaret. Say kind words to them both from me; which, I know, is always a pleasant commission to one so kindly disposed as you are.

I have never yet thanked you for your welcome letter; but not the less have I thanked you in my heart. I was just expecting my husband's return when it came; and was busy making all sorts of preparations for him; then, after he came, I was kept in a sort of worry till we got away to Bay House, and in the last six weeks I have never felt to have one minute's leisure, though doing nothing all the while. Now that I am home, I hope to settle down into a more peaceful and reasonable life.

God bless you, dear Mrs. Russell, and your father and husband.

Accept the little New Year's gift, I send you as a token of grateful affection, that will never be less.

Yours,

J. CARLYLE.

LETTER 85.

Spring of 1846, she and a small pretty party were at Addiscombe Farm for several weeks; I, busy with the 'Cromwell' second edition, was obliged to keep working steadily at home; but duly, on the Saturday till Monday, went out. There could be no prettier parties, prettier place or welcome, had these been all the requisites, but in truth they were not. Idleness, it must be owned, did sadly prevail—sadly, and even tragically, as I sometimes thought, on considering our hostess and chief lady there, and her noble talents, natural tendencies and aspirations, 'buried under gold thrones,' as Richter says.—T. C.

Mrs. Aitken, Dumfries.

5 Cheyne Row: Wednesday, April 1846.

My dear Jane,—The spirit moves me to fire off at you a small charitable purchase which I have just made. In the way of suggestion, it may perhaps yield me virtue's own reward!

I am just returned, two days ago, from an aristocratic visit of a month's duration, with the mind of me all churned into froth, out of which, alas, no butter is to be expected! Yes, 'gey idle o' wark' have I been for the last month, 'clatching about the country on cuddy-asses'[1] (figuratively speaking). Seeing 'how they ack' in the upper places does not give me any discontent with the place I am born to, quite the contrary. I, for one solitary individual (as Carlyle says), could not be other than perfectly miserable in idleness, world without end; and for a grand lady, it seems somehow impossible, whatever may be her talents and 'good intentions,' to be other than idle to death. Even children do not find them in occupation and duties. A beautiful Lady Anne, who was at Addiscombe along with me for the last ten days, had been confined just a month before; and her new baby was left with an older one in the care of a doctor and nurses; the mother seeming to be as little aware as all the rest (myself excepted) that any mortal could find anything to object to in such free and easy holding of one's children. But, as your ancestor said long ago, 'they're troubled that hae the world, and troubled that want it.' On the whole, however, the more rational sort of trouble, that which brings least remorse along with it, seems to me to be the 'wanting it.' C. is gone to ride; a little 'ill-haired,' this morning.

Ever your affectionate sister,

JANE CARLYLE.

---

[1] Ejaculation of my mother's after reading a long Roman letter from brother John.

LETTER 86.

After Alverstoke, February 1846, I had rallied to a second edition of Cromwell (first had been published in October preceding), enterprise in which, many new letters having come in, there lay a great deal of drudgery, requiring one's most exquisite talent as of shoe cobbling, really, that kind of talent carried to a high pitch, with which I continued busy all summer and farther. She, in the meanwhile, had been persuaded into Lancashire again; not till late in August could I join her at Seaforth for a little while. Whence into Annandale for another silent six weeks, grown all to grey haze now, except that I did get rid of my horse 'Bobus' there on fair terms, and had no want of mournful reflections (sad as death at times or sadder) on my own and the world's confusion and perversities, and the tragedies there bred for oneself and others. God's mercy, God's pardon, we all of us might pray for, if we could.—T. C.

To Mrs. Russell, Thornhill.

Seaforth House, Liverpool: July 2, 1846.

Dearest Mrs. Russell,—Your note found me again at Seaforth, where I have been for the last week. The great heat of London in the beginning of June had made me quite ill again, and as my husband would not make up his mind yet where to go, or when, I made up my own mind one fine morning, and started off hither, which has become a sort of house of refuge for me of late years. My husband talked of following me in a week or two, and then taking me with him to Scotland; but whether I shall be able to bring my mind to that, when the time comes, Heaven knows. The idea of Scotland under the actual circumstances is so extremely desolate for me that I should need to get a little more strength here, both physical and moral, before it were possible for me to entertain it practically. I fancy it were easier for me to go to Haddington than to Dumfriesshire; I have not been there since it was all changed, and myself become a sort of stranger in it. A family of good women,[1] who were dearly attached to my mother, are very desirous that I should pay them a visit; and I have not yet said positively that I will not. We shall see.

Meanwhile, Tuesday is my birthday, when I must not be forgotten by those who have been used to remember it. I send a little parcel for Margaret,[2] to your kind care; and will thank you to give

---

[1] The Misses Donaldson.
[2] Margaret Hiddlestone, the excellent widow servant.

Mary [1] five shillings for me, or rather lay it out for her on a pair of shoes, or tea, or what you think fittest. I will send a Post-Office order, in repayment, the first day I go to Liverpool

I spent part of the day there yesterday, and saw my uncle, who was absent on my first visit. He looks pretty well, and is very patient under the feebleness of age. My cousins, Helen and Mary, were here on Wednesday, and promise to come and see me often, without taking it ill of me that I prefer staying here in this quiet, roomy, country house, to being cooped up in Maryland Street, which is worse for one's health than Cheyne Row. Margaret [2] goes to Scotland to Walter, on Wednesday.

My kind regards to your husband and father. I could not help smiling when I thought of your father receiving his newspaper [3] all in mourning for—the pope!

Affectionately yours ever,

JANE CARLYLE.

LETTER 87.

To T. Carlyle, Esq., Chelsea.

Seaforth: Tuesday, July 14, 1846.

Oh! my dear husband, fortune has played me such a cruel trick this day! and I do not even feel any resentment against fortune, for the suffocating misery of the last two hours. I know always, when I seem to you most exacting, that whatever happens to me is nothing like so bad as I deserve. But you shall hear how it was.

Not a line from you on my birthday, the postmistress averred! I did not burst out crying, did not faint—did not do anything absurd, so far as I know; but I walked back again, without speaking a word; and with such a tumult of wretchedness in my heart as you, who know me, can conceive. And then I shut myself in my own room to fancy everything that was most tormenting. Were you, finally, so out of patience with me that you had resolved to write to me no more at all? Had you gone to Addiscombe, and found no leisure there to remember my existence? Were you taken ill, so ill that you could not write?

---

[1] Mary Mills, who used to depend on charitable Templand, weeding the garden, &c. To me who know the matter, what a piercing beauty in those rigorously punctual small gifts; sad as death, and grand, too, as death!

[2] 'Maggie' *hodie.*

[3] The (Irish-Catholic) *Tablet*, which came gratis to me (from Lucas, founder and editor, a great 'admirer,' &c.), and was sent regularly till his death.

That last idea made me mad to get off to the railway, and back to London. Oh, mercy! what a two hours I had of it![1]

And just when I was at my wits' end, I heard Julia crying out through the house: 'Mrs. Carlyle, Mrs. Carlyle! Are you there? Here is a letter for you.'

And so there was after all! The postmistress had overlooked it, and had given it to Robert, when he went afterwards, not knowing that we had been. I wonder what love-letter was ever received with such thankfulness! Oh, my dear! I am not fit for living in the world with this organisation. I am as much broken to pieces by that little accident as if I had come through an attack of cholera or typhus fever. I cannot even steady my hand to write decently. But I felt an irresistible need of thanking you, by return of post. Yes, I have kissed the dear little card-case; and now I will lie down awhile, and try to get some sleep. At least, to quiet myself, I will try to believe—oh, why cannot I believe it, once for all—that, with all my faults and follies, I am 'dearer to you than any earthly creature.' I will be better for Geraldine here; she is become very quiet and nice; and as affectionate for me as ever.

Your own
J. C.

Two Extracts.

To T. Carlyle.

Liverpool: July 1846.

July 15.—Jeannie writes to me from Auchtertool that the old minister is suddenly dead, so Walter[2] is now in possession of the appointments of his office. There is something rather shocking in one person's death being necessarily a piece of good fortune for another; but it is all one to the old man himself now, whether they make sad faces at his departure or gay ones. And who knows? 'Perhaps somebody loved that pig,'[3] and will give him a genuine tear or two. 'Poor mortals after all!' what a mighty problem we make about our bits of lives; and death as surely on the way to cut us out of 'all that' at least, whatever may come after. Yes, nobody out of Bedlam, even educated in Edinburgh, can contrive to doubt of death. One may go a far way in scepticism; may get to disbelieve in God and the devil, in virtue and in vice, in love, in one's own soul; never to speak of time and space, progress of the species,

---

[1] Oh, my darling little woman!   [2] Mrs. Carlyle's uncle.
[3] Sentimental cockney (mythical) that, trotting past, saw a clean-washed pig with a ribbon round its neck, and exclaimed, 'Somebody,' &c.—T. C.

rights of women, greatest happiness of the greatest number, 'isms,'
world without end; everything, in short, that the human mind ever
believed in, or 'believed that it believed in;' only not in death. The
most outrageous sceptic—even I, after two nights without sleep—
cannot go ahead against that fact—a rather cheering one on the
whole—that, let one's earthly difficulties be what they may, death
will make them all smooth sooner or later, and either one shall
have a trial at existing again under new conditions, or sleep soundly
through all eternity. That last used to be a horrible thought for
me, but it is not so any longer. I am weary, weary to such a point
of moral exhaustion, that any anchorage were welcome, even the
stillest, coldest, where the wicked should cease from troubling, and
the weary be at rest, understanding both by the wicked and the
weary myself.

Several letters lost, and four dismal weeks of my darling's history
in the world left unrecorded. Ill spirits, ill health. Oh what a
world for her too noble being, and for some others not so noble!
I had left perhaps a week before the date of this letter, sorrowfully
enough, but not guessing at all how ill she was. She had gone to
Geraldine's quiet place in Manchester, rather as in duty bound than
with much hope of solacement or even of greater quietude there;
both of which, however, she found, so beautiful was Geraldine's
affectionate skill with her, delicacy, wise silent sympathy and unwearied assiduity (coming by surprise too), for which she never
forgot Geraldine.—T. C.

Manchester: Aug. 23, 1846.

Geraldine has kept to her purpose of not leaving me a single
vacant minute; and her treatment, I believe, has been the most
judicious that was possible. It has brought back something like
colour into my face, and something like calm into my heart, but
how long I shall be able to keep either the one or the other when
left to my own management, God knows, or perhaps another than
God knows, best.

Nor is it to Geraldine alone that I feel grateful; no words can
express the kindness of her brother. To-night I shall be with all
my family that remains, but that thought cannot keep the tears out
of my eyes in quitting these strangers who have treated me like the
dearest of sisters.

Short while after this I at length roused myself from torpor at
Scotsbrig, and made, still very slowly, for home. Slowly, and with
wide circuit, by Dumfries, Craigenputtock (oh my emotions there
with tenant McQueen in the room which had been our bedroom).
After two hours at Craigenputtock with McQueen, who had now

become a mighty cattle-dealer, famed at Norwich, much more over all these moor countries for his grandeur of procedure (and who in a year or two died tragically, poor man!), I returned to Dumfries, took coach next morning for Ayr, impressive interesting drive all the way, wandered lonesome, manifoldly imagining, all afternoon, over Ayr and environs (Arran from the sea sand, in the hazy east wind nightfall, grand and grim. Twa Brigs, &c.). Ayr was holding some grand market; streets and inn had been chokefull during the sunny hours; in twilight and by lamplight become permeable enough, had not one's heart been so heavy. I stept into a small stationer's shop, and at his counter wrote a poor letter to my mother. Except two words there, and a twice-two at my inn, no speech further in Ayr. After dark, rail to Ardrossan (bright moon on the sandy straggling scene there), step on board the steamer for Belfast, intending a little glimpse of Ireland before Liverpool, Duffy and other young Repealers waiting me there, all on the ship. At Belfast next morning, breakfast, stay few hours, (cold stony town) take coach for Drogheda where Duffy and Mitchell will await, a post-office letter will say in what particular house. Coach roof in the sunny day pleasant enough; country rough and ill-husbandried, but all *new;* Portnadown Bridge (of the great massacre of 1641); Duke of Manchester's house; a merry enough young Dublin gentleman sitting next me occasionally talking merry sense. Potatoes all evidently rotten; every here and there air poisoned with their fateful smell. At Drogheda, dismount. Postmaster has no letter for me; angry old fool reiterates 'None, I tell you!' and Duffy, who was there waiting and had a letter waiting, stayed in vain, and did not return till afternoon next day; would have had the Drogheda official punished (or at least complained of), but I wouldn't. An angry old fool, misanthropic, not dishonest, pleaded I. Rolled into Dublin (to Imperial Hotel) by railway. After sunset, wandered far and wide about the broad pavements, listening to the wild melodies and cries of Dublin (on a Saturday night), went tired to bed, and, in spite of riotous sounds audible, slept well enough.

In Dublin or neighbourhood I continued till Thursday or Friday; saw various persons, places, and things, which had a kind of interest to me. One day saw Conciliation Hall, and the last glimpse of O'Connell, chief quack of the then world—first time I had ever heard the lying scoundrel speak—a most melancholy scene to me altogether. Conciliation Hall something like a decent Methodist chapel; but its audience very sparse, very bad, and blackguard-looking; brazen faces like tapsters, tavern keepers, miscellaneous hucksters and quarrelsome male or female nondescripts, the prevailing type; not one that you would have called a gentleman, much less a man of culture; and discontent visible among them. The speech—on potato rot (most serious of topics)—had not one word of sincerity, not to speak of wisdom in it. Every sentence seemed to you a lie, and even to know that it was a detected lie. I was standing in the area in a small group of non-members and transitory people quite near this Demosthenes of blarney, when a low voice close at my ear whispered in high accent: 'Did you ever hear such damned nonsense in all your life?' It was my Belfast Drogheda coach companion, and I thoroughly agreed with him. Beggarly O'Connell made out of Ireland straightway, and never returned—crept under the Pope's petticoat 'to die' (and be 'saved' from what he had merited)—the eminently despicable and eminently poisonous professor of blarney that he was.

I saw Carleton—Irish novelist (big vulgar kind of fellow, not without talent and plenty of humour); certain young lawyers who have since come to promotion, but were not of moment; certain young writers do. do. Dined at John Mitchell's with a select party one evening, and ate there the last truly good potato I have met with in the world. Mitchell's wife, especially his mother (Presbyterian parson's widow of the best Scotch type), his frugally elegant small house and table, pleased me much, as did the man himself, a fine elastic-spirited young fellow with superior natural talent, whom I grieved to see rushing on destruction, palpable by 'attack of windmills,' but on whom all my dissuasions were thrown away. Both Duffy and him I have always regarded as specimens of the best kind of Irish youth, seduced (like thousands of others in their early day) into courses that were at once mad and ridiculous, and which nearly ruined the life of both, by the Big Beggar-man, who had 15,000l. a year (and *proh pudor!* the favour of English ministers instead of the pillory from them) for professing blarney, with such and still worse results. One of my most impressive days was the Sunday (morrow of my arrival) out at Dundrum waiting for Duffy, who did arrive about night. Beautiful prospect; sea with shore and islets; beautiful leafy lanes; mile on mile in total silence, total solitude. I only met two persons all day: one promenading gently on horseback; the other on foot, from which latter I practically learnt that the 'Hill of Howth' was unknown by that name here, and known only as the 'Hill of Hoath.' My last day there was also pretty; wide sweeping drive with Duffy and Mitchell. Dargle, stream and banks, Powerscourt, gate and oaks, &c., altogether fine; finally to Bray and its fine hotel to dinner, till steamer time came, and they hospitably put me on board. Adieu! adieu! ye well-wishing souls.

Next morning between five and six I was safe seated on my luggage before the door of Maryland Street (Liverpool), smoking a cigar in placid silence till the silent home should awaken, which it somehow did unexpectedly before my cigar was done.—T. C.

LETTER 88.

This and the next four letters give clear account of a sordid form of servile chaos in this house, and how it was administered by one who had the best skill I ever saw in such matters. Helen Mitchell, an innocent-hearted, very ingenious, but practically altogether foolish creature, had, by matchless skill in guiding of her and thorough knowledge of her Scotch character and ways, been trained to great perfection of service, been even cured from a wild habit of occasional drinking, and tamed into living with us, and loyally and faithfully serving us for many years. She was one of the strangest creatures I ever saw; had an intellectual insight almost as of genius, and a folly and simplicity as of infancy: her sayings and observations, her occasional criticisms on men and things translated into the dialect of upstairs, were by far the most authentic table wit I have anywhere heard! This is literally true, though I cannot make it conceivable; the 'beautifully prismatic' medium that conveyed it to me, which was unique in my experience, being gone.

The history of Helen's departure, and of her unspeakable successor's arrival are clearly given in these following letters, and to me at present in spite of their mean elements, have the essential aspect of a queenly tragedy, authentic of its kind!—T. C.

To Mrs. Stirling, Hill Street, Edinburgh.

5 Cheyne Row, Chelsea: Saturday, Sept. 1846.

My dear Susan,—Do you remember saying to me when you were last here, 'should you ever have to part with Helen, and be in want of another Scotch servant, tell me, and perhaps I shall be able to help you to one; for there are still good servants to be got in Dundee'? It is years since you said this; years since we have exchanged words with one another; but I now claim your assistance, with as full assurance as if you had offered it yesterday; for I judge of your friendship by my own; and as time and absence have made no change in my feelings towards you, I fancy that neither has any change been made in yours towards me; and that you are still as ready to take some trouble for me as ever you were. If likings depended on locality in this world, poor mortals would have a sad time of it; seeing how those who like one another are drifted asunder, and kept apart; as much, often, as if they were dead for one another; but where a true regard has once existed, I cannot believe that any 'force of circumstances' ever destroys it. And so, as I have said, I calculate on your being still the same warmhearted friend I ever found you, when our stars brought us together—even though we do not write letters to state the fact.

Alas! of late years my letter-writing propensities have been sorely kept down by the continual consciousness of being grown into a sort of bore; ever ailing, ever depressed in spirits—the consequence, I suppose, of this sort of nervous ailment. What have I to tell anyone that cares for me, which it were any satisfaction to hear? The only thing I would write to you, which were not better unwritten, would be just over and over again, 'My dear Susan, I often think of you, and have the same affection for you that ever I had;'—and that, I flatter myself, you will always take for granted.

But, for the practical business that now puts me on writing to you: you are to know that my poor little Helen has not relapsed into drink again, nor otherwise forsaken the paths of virtue; on the contrary, she has been growing, like wine and a few other things, always the better by keeping. So that at no period of our relation could I have felt more regret at losing her. The only consolation is, that she will find her advantage in the change: at least one tries to hope so. A marriage, you think! No, something even more unthought of has turned up for the little woman. She is going to be made a sort of a lady of! at least, so the matter presents itself to her lively imagination! A brother in Dublin has been rising into great prosperity as a manufacturer of coach-fringe; thanks to the immense consumption of that article on the railways! He is now, by his own showing, a regular gentleman—so far as money goes!—and has 'two hundred girls in his pay.' He looks to me a foolish, flustering sort of incredible creature; but Helen feels no doubt as to the solidity of his basis. Hitherto he has taken no charge of Helen beyond coming to see her for a quarter of an hour when his business called him to London.

LETTER 89.

Helen had usefully and affectionately stayed with us eight years or more. Latterly, a silly snob of a younger brother, setting up, or getting forward, in some small business at Dublin, came once or twice, after total neglect before, opened a 'career of ambition' to the poor creature, and persuaded her over to Dublin to keep house for him. It was well foreseen what this was likely to end in; but there could be no gainsaying. Poor Helen went (and took the consequence, as will be seen); bright breakfast-table report of her strange sayings and ways (gentle, genial lambency of grave humour and intelligence—wittiest of wit that I ever heard was poor in comparison!) ceased altogether then; and to us, also, the consequences for the time were variously sad.

To Mrs. Aitken, Dumfries.

Chelsea: End of Dec. 1846.

My dear Jane,—I am not up to much writing yet; my three weeks' confinement to bed, and the violent medicine that was given me to put down my cough, have reduced me to the consistency of a jelly. But I will not write a long letter, but tell you now in a short one how glad I was of the little token of your kind remembrance, which reached me the other night just when I was trying to sit up for the first time. Your letter made me cry; which is always a good sign of a letter, don't you think? But, my dear, what do you mean by 'forgiving' you? What unkind thing did you ever do to me? I have not the faintest recollection of your ever doing unkindly by me in your life! At Craigenputtock we used to have little squabbles about the servants and 'all that sort of thing'; but in these it strikes me I was always quite as much an aggressor as a sufferer, and on the whole, considering the amount of human imperfection going, and the complexities we had to work in at Craigenputtock, I think we got through that business 'as well as could be expected'; and certainly you did not get through it worst. Believe me, my dear sister, I have none but kind feelings towards you and kind recollections of you. Although we are widely parted now, and although much has changed incredibly since those days at the Hill which you remind me of, the regard I conceived for you then has gone on the same, though so seldom giving any sign of itself.

We are still in a fearful puddle here. Helen's loss has been a serious affair. The temporary servant we have drives Carlyle and my cousin to despair, and I am pretty near despair from seeing them so put about while myself cannot go to the rescue, as I could so well have done but for this dreadful cold. I have no decided prospect yet of anything better. I put an advertisement in the 'Times' newspaper but the only applicant as yet resulting from it was not to be thought of. I will inclose you Dr. Christie's brief account of her. There was a Highland woman offered the other day, whom I mean to inquire further into, though she rather shocked me by having forgotten what part of the Highlands she came from! I will write when I am stronger and tell you what comes of us. It is a great worry my cousin being here when everything is so wretchedly uncomfortable, although I suppose there was absolute need of her while I was confined to bed.

Ever your affectionate

J. C.

Kind regards to James.

LETTER 90.

This is the catastrophe or utter down-break of Pessima, whom I still remember as a handsome, cultivated-looking Edinburgh girl, speaking Scotch like an Edinburgh gentlewoman, and exhibiting a character and style of procedure detestable beyond any previous specimen I had ever known of. She had been carefully trained by pious Edinburgh ladies; was filled with the consciousness of free grace; and, I believe, would have got more real education, as I told her, if she had been left to puddle through the gutters with her neglected fellow brats, by whom she would have been trampled out of the world had she behaved no better than now. Indisputably the worst specimen of Scotch character I have ever seen produced. My brief request to her was to disappear straightway, and in no region of God's universe, if she could avoid it, ever to let me behold her again. The poor devil, I believe, died in a year or two, and did not come upon the streets as predicted of her.

Betty, the old Haddington servant, who had been concerned in the sending or sanctioning of this wretched creature, was deeply grieved and disappointed. The charm for Betty had been the perfect Free Kirk orthodoxy and free grace professions of this Pessima, who, I think, reported at home that she had been obliged to leave us, having actually noticed once or oftener that we 'received' on Sabbath.

The cousin mentioned here is good Helen Welsh, of Liverpool, Maggie's eldest sister, whose amiable behaviour and silent helpfulness in this sordid crisis I still well remember. The improvised old woman, I remember, got the name of slowcoach between us, and continued for perhaps three weeks or more. She was a very white aproned, cleanly old creature, and I once noticed her sitting at some meal in her kitchen, with a neatness of table-cloth and other apparatus, and a serene dignity of composure in her poor old self, that were fairly pathetic to me. For the rest, never did I see so sordid a domestic crisis appointed for such a mistress, in this world! But it had its kind of compensation too; and is now more noble and queenlike to me than all the money in the bank could have made it.

The little creature called Anne did prove a good cockney parallel of Scotch Helen Mitchell, and served us well (with only one follower, our butcher's lad, who came silently, and sat two hours once a week): follower and she were then wedded, went to Jersey, where we heard of their doing well in the butcher's business; but, alas, before long, of poor Anne's falling ill and dying.

Before Anne's quitting us, dottle Helen had finished her ladyhood at Dublin, quarrelled with her fool of a brother there, and retired to Kirkcaldy, signifying the warmest wish to return hither. She did return, poor wretch, but was at once discerned (not by me) to be internally in a state of chaos; and within three months, for open and incurable drunkenness, had to be dismissed. Endless pains were taken about her; new place provided (decent old widow in straitened circumstances, content to accept so much merit in a servant and tried to cure the drunkenness). But nothing whatever could avail; the wretched Helen went down and down in this London element, and at last was sent home to her kindred in Kirkcaldy to die. 'Poor bit dottle,' what a history and tragedy in small!—T. C.

To Mrs. Stirling, Hill Street, Edinburgh.

5 Cheyne Row, Chelsea: Dec. 29, 1846.

My dearest Susan,—I wonder if you are out of anxiety about your sister? I am almost afraid to begin telling you of my own troubles, without being first satisfied of that. But it seems unkind, after all your exertions to provide me with a servant, not to tell you of the catastrophe of the one sent me by Betty! It is only now, for the first time, that I am in a condition to give you the disgusting history; for I was taken ill in the second week of her; have been three weeks confined to bed, and a week more to my bedroom fireside; and am just emerged into the library, between which and my bedroom I look forward with 'a certain resignation' to passing all the rest of the winter.

You would see by my last letter that I was dubious as to the result of that Edinburgh damsel. I tried to hope the best and cultivate patience and cheerfulness; but your notion that she had been too much petted for this situation gained on me every day. She showed no disposition to learn her work; in fact, she became every day more sulky and slovenly; and, on the first washing-day, she burst out on me with a sort of hysterical insolence; declared she 'had never been told by anybody she was to wash;' that 'no one woman living could do my work,' and when I told her the answer to that was, that it had been done by 'one woman' for eleven years, without the slightest complaint, she said, almost screaming, 'Oh yes, there are women that like to make slaves of themselves, and her you had was of that sort, but I will never slave myself for anybody's pleasure.' I asked her if she would be so good as state calmly what she meant to do. To 'go, to be sure.' 'Did she propose repaying me her expenses, then?' 'No, she had no money.' I thought the only way to treat such a creature, who seemed to have no sense of obligation, or anything else but her 'own sweet will,' was to let her depart in peace, and remain a loser of only two guineas, and not of my temper as well. So I told her, well, she might go at the end of her month, only to make no noise, if possible, for the remaining three weeks. But even this was too much to ask. In the second week of her, I was laid up in bed with one of my serious colds, caught by doing the most of her work myself, and exposing myself after quite an unusual fashion; once there, I lay, with a doctor attending me daily; and dosing me with tartar-emetic and opium, till I had hardly any sense left, and was too weak to cough; while Carlyle and my cousin had to shift for themselves and me too, with an occasional helping hand from our postman's wife. Isabella, meanwhile, crying about her 'hands getting all spoilt with dirty work'; and doing nothing she could help; till on Saturday night, just a fortnight after she had come, she sent me word in my bed, that if I did not let her go next day (Sunday !) she 'would take fits, and be laid up in my house a whole year, as happened to her once before in a place where the work was too hard.' Carlyle told her to go in the devil's name; and a little more of his mind he told her; which was a satisfaction for me to have said in his emphatic way, since I was unable to rebuke her myself! But you may fancy the mischief all this did to a poor woman taking tartar-emetic and opium every two hours! When my doctor came next day, he said it 'was well he had not been here at the time, as he would have certainly dashed her brains out!' By that time, however, she was gone; actually rushed off after breakfast on Sunday!—(so much for 'free grace,' of which she professed to be full!)—smartly dressed, and very happy, they told me— off to the 'seven cousins,' with whom I had, more good-naturedly than wisely, permitted her, at her own request, to pass all the previous Sunday; leaving me very ill in bed, and no servant in the house! The day after, she brought an omnibus and a female friend to the door, in the finest spirits, to take away her box; and from that day to this I have heard no more of her! But if such a character as she exhibited here does not lead her to the streets some day, I shall be greatly surprised. Of course her respectable appearance, backed out by the seven cousins, will have got her another place ere now; where, if men-servants be kept, she may exert herself. My doctor said he could tell by her looks, the first day she opened the door to him, that she had then, or had quite lately had, the green sickness, and that I was well rid of her.

And now I might write a few sheets more, of the old half-dead cook, whom a lady who was going to part with her at any rate, on account of her 'shocking bad temper,' obligingly made over to us as 'a temporary,' at an hour's notice. Such as she is, she has been an improvement on Isabella, for she does her best. But oh, what a puddle it has been! and rushing down of an orderly house to chaos! Another fortnight of it would have sent my not too patient husband raving mad! Since I got out of bed I have been seeing all sorts of horrid-looking females 'inquiring after the place;' and two days ago finally settled with one not horrid-looking, but a cheery little 'button' of a creature, with a sort of cockney resemblance to Helen; she has been nearly three years in a similar situation close by, which she has only left in consequence of the mistress having died, and the master going into lodgings. He gave her an excellent character to my cousin; especially for quiet habits. 'She had only one lover who came to see her, and one female friend (happy little woman!), both highly respectable, and not too troublesome.' She is to come on the last night of the year.

This will reach you on the first day of the new year; and I put many good wishes and a kiss into it.

Do write to me how your sister is.

Ever your affectionate

JANE CARLYLE.

LETTER 91.

To Miss Helen Welsh, Liverpool.

Chelsea: Jan. 20, 1847.

Dearest Helen,—One hears much fine talk in this hypocritical age about seeking and even finding one's own happiness in 'the happiness of others;' but I frankly confess to you that I, as one solitary individual, have never been able to confound the two things, even in imagination, so as not to be capable of clearly distinguishing the difference; and if every one would endeavour, as I do, to speak without cant, I believe there would be a pretty general admission on the part of sinful humanity that to eat a comfortable beef-steak when one is hungry yields a satisfaction of a much more positive character than seeing one's neighbour eat it! For the fact is, happiness is but a low thing, and there is a confusion of ideas in running after it on stilts. When Sir Philip Sidney took the water from his own parched lips to give it to the dying soldier, I could take my Bible oath that it was not happiness he felt; and that he would never have done that much admired action if his only compensation had been the pleasure resulting to him from seeing the dying soldier drink the water; he did it because he could not help himself; because the sense of duty, of self-denial, was stronger in him at the moment than low human appetite; because the soul in him said, do it; not because utilitarian philosophy suggested that he would find his advantage in doing it, nor because Socinian dilettanteism required of him a beautiful action!

Well, but if these moral reflections are not a preamble to something more relevant, I find such a commencement of a letter 'what shall I say? strange, upon my honour!' Do you so? my sweet little cousin—be thankful, then! we live in a world of commonplace; a strange letter, a strange woman, so far from being taken sharply to task, should be accepted graciously, as a sort of refreshing novelty.

But if I cannot show you that my moral reflections lead to something, I can show you that something led to them. I had been looking over the last budget of autographs that I had got together for you. Such distinguished names! 'To be sure,' I said to myself, 'these will make her fortune in autographs.' And then I felt a certain self-complacency, a certain presentiment of your satisfaction in seeing your collection swelling into something really worth while; and having the pen in my hand to write to you, I was on the point of putting on the paper some such *fadaise* as this: 'It was a capital thought in me, dearest Helen, the making of this collection for you. My own pleasure in sending you the autographs being greater, I am sure, than any you can feel in receiving them.' But the sentence having reached a full stop, in my head, my better judgment said, 'Bah! Beware of the Socinian jargon, *ma chère*, there is always "a do at the bottom of it!"' and so my pen dashed off, of itself as it were, into a reactionary tirade against 'the welfare-of-others' principle.

I have been long plaguing Carlyle to give me, for you, one of the letters of Varnhagen von Ense; for besides being the autograph of a distinguished author and diplomatist and husband of Rahel, you will find it curious for its perfect beauty. I never saw such writing; and in whatever haste, in sickness or in health, it is always the same.

Carlyle was very grumpy about parting with one of his letters; but, having taken a great deal of trouble for him the other day in seeking out some notes he wanted from his trunk of old papers, he presented me with this one as a reward; and also, I suppose, as an encouragement to future exertions of like utility.

Besides Varnhagen von Ense, you have here Goethe, Sir Walter Scott, Rogers, Sir R. Peel, a whole note from Harriet Martineau (before our friendship), Charles Buller, Count d'Orsay, Milman, a very characteristic note from Mazzini, Lord Stanley, Mrs. Austin, Lockhart, Thackeray (alias Titmarsh), Allan Cunningham.

Tell Jeannie that when I informed Mazzini yesterday that Geraldine was to be here on Monday, he first stared, then said 'Well! after then I come for ten minutes only!' and then, looking into the fire, gave a long, clear whistle! Jeannie can figure the sort of mood in which alone Mazzini could dream of whistling!

But alas! I must go and clean the lamp, a much less agreeable occupation than writing to you, my dear. But such consequences of the fall of Adam will always exist. Nothing will go on any time without human labour.

Ever your affectionate cousin,

J. CARLYLE.

LETTER 92.

To Miss Helen Welsh, Liverpool.

Chelsea: July 15, 1847.

My dearest Helen,—I would have written yesterday, if I could have done anything on earth but cry. I suppose 'the fact is,' as Carlyle says, 'that I am very unwell.' In a general way I can keep from crying at all rates. But this heat is most disorganising and demoralising. And so I fell a-crying in the morning over my gifts, and could not stop myself again.

Carlyle had prepared a cameo-brooch for me, and I cannot tell how it is, but his gifts always distress me more than a scold from him would do. Then the postman handed in your letter and little box, and that brought all sorts of reminiscences of home and of Templand along with it; a beautiful little thing as ever I beheld! but too beautiful and too youthful for the individual intended to wear it. A hat-box from poor Bölte completed the overthrow of my sensibility: it contained an immense bouquet of the loveliest flowers, in the middle of which was stuck—her picture! in water-colours, and gilt-framed, and a note. I shall send you the note, that you may see Bölte in her best phase. People wonder always why I let myself be bored with that woman, but, with all her want of tact in the everyday intercourse of life, she manifests a sentiment on occasions so delicate and deep, that I should be a brute not to be touched by it.

Whose is the hair in the little basket? it looks all one shade.

Thank you, dearest, and the others concerned in that little realised ideal of cousinly remembrance. I have attached it to my bracelet, but it seems almost a pity to wear it there. I was thinking whether I ought not to have my nose pierced and suspend it from that.

Perhaps I shall see you this summer after all. I really am suffering dreadfully from the heat; quite as ill, in a different way, as I was in winter from the cold.

I cannot sleep or eat, can hardly sit upright, and am in a continual high fever, obliged to keep wet cloths on my head all day long. In these astonishing circumstances Carlyle declares I absolutely must go away, and best to Haddington. He will take me there and leave me; so if I go to Haddington I shall surely go to Auchtertool; but I am not there yet. I am to write to Miss Donaldson to-day, to inquire if her house be empty; if the London family are there I shall consider that objection final.

I hope, if I go, I may get off before Geraldine returns, for I am not up to any visitor just now, not even to *an angel awares*.

Kind love to all. I have that letter to Miss Donaldson to write and am already worn out.

Ever your affectionate
JANE CARLYLE.

LETTER 93.

October–November, 1846.—We went for a week to the Grange— old Rogers, &c. My poor Jane's health very feeble. Beginning of December, bothered by various things, change of servants, foolish Helen off to Dublin to a foolish brother there, and to ruin, as it proved. My dear little woman fell quite ill—Dr. Christie attending—and for three weeks was helpless, oftenest in bed, amid these household irritations, now painful to remember. Helen Welsh luckily was here on visit from Liverpool; before New Year's Day the hurly-burly, bad servants, Free Kirk Edinburgh ones, slow coach &c., swept away, and a new good one got; and my darling, once more victorious, seemed to be herself again.

End of January, part of February 1847, at Bay House, Alverstoke; there again, however, she had a miserably bad sore throat, sad to read of in her letters. I idle, lying painfully fallow all this time, brother John busy with his Dante.

August 1847 we go for Matlock, stay about a fortnight. W. E. Forster over from Rawdon (Bradford neighbourhood), loyal cheery ex-Quaker then, Radical politician now, ran over to join us, and, pressingly hospitable, took us home with him. Charming drive to Sheffield from the Peak country. Stay at Rawdon for another fortnight; there part; I for Scotsbrig, my Jeannie for a trial day or two at Barnsley (brother of Mrs. Paulet's there), and so home to Chelsea.—T. C.

To T. Carlyle, Scotsbrig.

5 Cheyne Row: Saturday, Sept. 11, 1847.

Here I am, then, safe and sound! rather tired, and as yellow as saffron with yesterday's journey; but that is all. I left Barnsley at one, and got home at eleven, rather low when I stopped at my own door all alone; but Anne received me with a little outburst of affection, as cheering as it was unexpected. What you will consider more to the purpose, she had everything in the nicest possible

order; seemed really to have exerted herself to the uttermost in
divining and executing my wishes. A better-cleaned house I
never set my foot in: and even her own little person had bloomed
out into new clothes for the occasion. All the carpets have been
not only up, and most effectually cleaned, and nailed down again,
as nobody but myself ever succeeded in nailing them before, but
she has been at the unbargained-for pains to darn them, wherever
they needed it. Nay, she has actually learned to stand on steps,
and dusted every book on the shelves! Mrs. Piper has been at
work like a very Brownie. Postie[1] and she came at four o'clock
one morning, and washed up all the blankets and counterpanes.
And then the little post-woman herself fell upon the chair and
table-covers, and, having washed them quite beautifully, nailed
them all on again; so that the whole house looks as bright as a new
pin. Postie had also helped to beat the carpets, considering that
Eaves[2] was rather slimming them; but he charged Anne to keep
this, and indeed all his doings, a secret from me. To fall to work
messing and painting inside, now that everything is so well
cleaned, and so late in the year, would, I think, be 'very absurd.'[3]
When the parlour is new-papered and painted, it should be done
properly, and proper painting takes a prodigious time; but I will
see somebody to-morrow, to speak at least concerning the outside.

I have not seen John yet, but he will come, I suppose, after his
proofs are corrected. Nobody else knows of my return, and I
shall keep it 'a secret to please him,'[4] till I feel a need of company,
which I fancy will not be for some weeks to come. Meanwhile I
have plenty to employ me, in siding[5] drawers and locked places,
which I left in the disgracefullest confusion; and in re-habilitating
the clothes-department, which has been wonderfully reduced and
dilapidated by these weeks of travel, to say nothing of plenty of
letters lying on my conscience. Did you find at Scotsbrig a letter
from Anthony Sterling announcing his father's death? Anne says
he (Anthony) called here last Saturday to ask the address; and
she gave him the Rawdon one. The poor old man had been quite
insensible for a week before his death; and the week before that,
he had insisted on having himself brought in the carriage to this

---

[1] Our excellent, punctual and obliging postman, for above twenty years.
[2] The ostler, turned out (seven or eight years after) to be a very great scamp.
[3] Brother John's phrase.
[4] 'Ou que manger un hareng? C'est un secret pour lui plaire?'
[5] Lancashire for 'sorting.'

door, though even then he was speechless.   Anne said it was the saddest thing she ever saw; he waved to her to come to him, and made signs as if he were leaving a message for me, pointed repeatedly to his lips, and then to the house, and then shook his head with tears running down.   How often I have made a jest of that old man's affection for me, and now it looks one of the most valuable affections I ever possessed, for he clung to it till his last moment of consciousness.   His nurse, who came with him, told Anne she knew I was not at home, but it was perfectly impossible to hinder his coming.   Anthony, Anne says, seemed 'dreadfully cut up;' he 'could hardly speak to her, for the tears in his throat.'

Your letter was lying for me last night when I came in, and gave me somehow the feeling of a letter written out of Hades.   I hope I shall get another soon.   I hardly supposed your Manchester worshippers, and least of all Geraldine, would let you off on the Tuesday.   As to me, I could not well have got home on the Wednesday, even if much set on it, which I was not.   On Tuesday, Nodes[1] and his wife took me through two immense factories, and a long drive besides in a phaeton.   On the way home I was seized with one of my very worst fainting headaches, and had to be carried from the carriage to bed, where I lay in what they took for a last agony, till midnight.   Nothing could be kinder than Mrs. Newton was, but kindness could do nothing till the time came.   Next day I got up to breakfast, but too brashed to dream of going off to London; so I agreed to stay till Friday.   They would fain have had it Monday, but I could not be so silly as to change my day twice.   My visit was a highly successful one, except for that headache, which might have happened anywhere.   The children are beautiful, lovable children, brought up as children used to be in my time, and no trouble to anybody.   Mrs. Newton herself grows more attractive for me the more I see of her; her quiet good sense and loving-heartedness, and perfect naturalness, are very refreshing to one's world-used soul.   Even poor Nodes is a much more interesting man at the head of his mill and his family than when hanging loose on society in London—but it is twenty minutes after four.   Ever yours,

                                                                            J. C.

---

[1] Nodes Newton, Mrs. Paulet's brother at Barnsley.

LETTER 94.

John Forster, Esq., 58 *Lincoln's Inn Fields.*

5 Cheyne Row, Chelsea: Tuesday, Sept. 14, 1847.

Dear Mr. Forster,—Here I am, then! returned to Chelsea; a sadder and a wiser woman for my five weeks of pursuit of the picturesque under difficulties. My husband and I parted company at Leeds a week ago. He is now in Annandale 'spending his time' (he writes to me) 'chiefly in sleeping and in drinking new milk under various forms!' Rather bilious work, one would say! but every man to his humour! For me, I am spending my time chiefly in loving the devil out of a—Yorkshire kitten! which I have adopted for its inexpressible charm of tigerishness. But a huge brown-paper parcel of MS. lies like an incubus on my free spirit! What is to be done? When and how are we to get through it?

Since I arrived on Friday night, I have spoken with no mortal but my maid, and twice for ten minutes with my brother-in-law. I believe, besides you, there is still a man, or perhaps two, of my acquaintance left. But I feel so mesmerised by the silence and the dimness, that I have no power to announce my return.

Write to me. I am prepared for anything.

Ever yours affectionately,

JANE CARLYLE.

LETTER 95.

To T. Carlyle, Scotsbrig.

Chelsea: Thursday, Sept. 16, 1847.

Here are three notes for you, dear; and I cannot send them without a few lines from myself, though up to the ears in my curtains.

If I had waited patiently a few hours longer yesterday, I might have spared you a shrewing. Your nice long letter came in the evening; and before that, I had also seen John, and been favoured with a reading of your letter to him. I could have found in my heart to box his ears, when I found it had been in his pocket since Monday night, and I only told of it then, at three o'clock on Wednesday, after my remonstrance was gone to the post-office. He did not seem to consider my impatience in the meanwhile 'of the slightest consequence.' In fact, he is, for the moment, 'a miserable

wretch, lost in proof-sheets.'[1] He reminds me of the grey chicken
at Craigenputtock, that went about for six weeks cackling over its
first egg. If everybody held such a racket over his book as he, over
this Dante of his, the world would be perfectly uninhabitable.
But he comes seldom, and has always to 'take the road again' in a
few minutes, so I manage to endure the cackling with a certain
stoicism.

Nothing has happened to me since yesterday, except that in the
evening I was startled, almost terrified, by a knock at the door. It
was Fuz! I had written to him about G.'s[2] manuscript, and he answered my note in person, by return of post. I had expected 'a
gentle and free passage of pennies,' extending through, perhaps, a
fortnight, before a meeting actually came off.

He seemed very strong-hearted for the reading, which could not,
however, be commenced last night, for he had to attend the sale of
Shakespeare's house; but on Sunday evening, 'by all that was
sacred,' we would fall to in earnest, 'trusting in God that on that
night he should find me in good voice.' Meanwhile, 'were there
any books—anything on earth—I wished?' He would send Henry
to-day. He stayed only half-an-hour—very fat!

This morning a still greater terror struck into me when a carriage
stopped at the door while I was sitting at breakfast in my dressing-
gown. It was Anthony Sterling on his way from Headley. He did
not offer at coming in; merely sent the servant to ask if I would
be at home in the afternoon. I am glad he is coming, for I will
get him to send me his painter, the one who was to bring me an
estimate having never returned. I walked up to the Library yesterday to get myself, if possible, something to read. White Owl[3]
expected to-day: library 'too bad for anything;' officials mortal
drunk, or worse—overtaken with incurable idiocy! Not a book one
could touch without getting oneself made filthy. I expressed my
horror of the scene, and was answered: 'Are you aware, ma'am,
of the death of Mrs. Cochrane?' I brought away the last four
numbers of 'Vanity Fair,' and read one of them in bed, during the
night. Very good, indeed, beats Dickens out of the world.

Chalmers is now raising brick fabrics—perfectly incomprehensible

---

[1] 'Lost in statistics,' said old Sterling, of a certain philosopher here.

[2] Geraldine.

[3] Poor old Cochrane, our first librarian of London Library, and essentially
the builder and architect there. The only real bibliographer I have ever met
with in Britain.

in their meaning hitherto [1]—in front of his house.[2] I told old John and the other workmen, yesterday, that there was no longer a doubt that they had all gone perfectly deranged. John shook his head quite sorrowfully, and said 'it was only too true.'

The 'National,' Fuz told me, had started a very feasible idea about the Duke de Praslin's intention, in taking the loaded pistol with him. He had ordered the porter to come half-an-hour sooner than usual, and straight to his bedroom. He meant to shoot the porter, and make him pass for the murderer.

Fuz was awfully excited on the subject of Luzzi.[3]

Ever yours,

J. W. C.

LETTER 96.

To T. Carlyle, Scotsbrig.

Chelsea: Wednesday, Sept. 22, 1847.

You are to know, then, that ever since I wrote the last letter to you, I have had no history 'to speak of,' having been confined pretty constantly to bed. When I wrote the last letter, I was already ill; in fact, I had never felt well from the first day of my return. But at that writing, I perceived I was in for some sort of regular illness. I thought, at first, it was going to be a violent cold, but it has not turned to a cold. I suppose a doctor would call it some sort of bilious or nervous fever. Whatever it has been, I have suffered horribly from irritation, nausea, and languor; but now I am in the way of getting well again. I am out of bed to-day, and able to write to you, as you see. John has been very kind to me, since he knew of my illness, which was not till Sunday afternoon. He has come to see me twice a day; and one time stayed four hours in my bedroom, reading to me, &c. I prohibited him from telling you of it, as I did not want you to be kept anxious. But now I am so much better that there is not the slightest occasion for anxiety; and as to your being there, and not here, I assure you it has been the greatest possible comfort to me that it so happened. I can be twice as patient and composed, I find, when there is nobody put about by my being laid up. Had you been here, I should have struggled on longer without taking to bed, and been in the desperatest haste to get out of it. All the nursing possible has been given

---

[1] Turned out to be a porch and pillars.   [2] Then No. 4, Cheyne Row.
[3] Have forgotten.

me, by Anne and Mrs. Piper; and the perfect quiet of the house could not have been had on other terms, nor could Anne have had time to attend to me as I required, if we had not had the house all to ourselves.

So do not be *vaixed*, and do not be uneasy; I have no ailment now, but weakness, and so soon as I can get into the air, that will wear off.

And now I must stop for this time.

Ever yours,
J. W. C.

Sept. 23.

You must have another little letter to-day, dear, in case you take a notion to fret. I continue to mend rapidly. One of the people who has been kindest to me during my illness is ' old John.'[1] He has actually reduced all the pianos to utter silence. Hearing Anne say that the noise of his ladies was enough to drive her mistress mad, he said, ' I will put a stop to that,' and went immediately himself into the drawing-room, and told the ladies then at the piano, 'he wondered they were not ashamed of themselves, making such a noise, and Mrs. Carlyle at death's door on the other side of the wall.' And there has not been a note struck since—five days ago.

J. C.

LETTER 97.

To T. Carlyle, Scotsbrig.

Chelsea: Friday, Sept. 24, 1847.

You can't be said, dear, to have wasted many letters on me in this absence; but if you 'feel a stop' (Quakerly speaking), best to let it have way; no good comes of forcing nature, in the matter of writing or any other matter.

Meanwhile, I go on mending. I had more sleep last night, and feel strong enough to-day to meditate a short turn in the open air. When John comes, I shall propose it to him. I am not to go to Addiscombe to-morrow. Last night, at ten o'clock, I was just going to bed very tired, John and Mazzini having sat talking 'Dante' beside me, till I had to be struck with a sudden thought that M. would miss the Hoxton omnibus, unless John saw him off instantly,

---

[1] Servant in the adjoining house.

when Anne came to announce the important fact of Mr. Fleming. 'Well,' I said, 'send him away; I cannot receive him at this time of night.' But he would not be sent away. 'He had come charged with a message from Lady Harriet (!), and if I would just see him for five minutes.' The other time he called was with Mr. Baring; changed times for little Mrs. Harris.[1]

The message was, that Lady H. was coming up on Saturday, to dine at Holland House on Sunday; so that she could not send for me on Saturday, according to programme, but would take me down with her on Monday. This she had told him (Fleming) when he was 'seeing her off;' and he would tell her my answer 'when he dined with her at Holland House.' 'How very odd,' I said, 'that you should be acting as Lady H.'s Ariel!' 'Oh, not at all now; we are excellent friends now, since we stayed together at Sir W. Molesworth's; and there is nothing I would not do for her! she is the dearest, playfullest, wittiest creature. I love her beyond everything.' 'Very absurd.'

If I can get off from going now, without discourtesy, I will; for to stay over Tuesday is not worth the fag of going and coming; besides, my painting will terminate, I expect, on Saturday night. And there is yet another thing that takes away my ardour for going. Fleming gravely accused me of having brought on this illness, as I did so many others, by my 'unheard-of imprudence.' 'Lady Harriet assures me that nothing was ever like your indiscretion in diet, and that all these attacks proceed from that cause.' Now, I require to have every furtherance given to any faculty that may lie in me for eating and drinking at present, instead of living and eating in the fear of being thought and published a glutton.[2] The quantity of wine that John prescribes for me might also obtain me the reputation of a drunkard. And I believe it quite necessary, when for days together one's pulse 'could not be counted.' Fleming's 'five minutes' prolonged themselves to half-an-hour, and then I was obliged to tell him that I could sit up no longer. And he went away in his little thunder-and-lightning embroidered shirt, and his little new curled wig, lisping out: 'I shall tell Lady Harriet that I found you in a temperature sufficient to produce a bilious fever.' It was all I could do to keep from summoning all my remaining strength together and 'doubling him

---

[1] He used to come very assiduously hither, poor little soul, but was now rising in the world.

[2] Singular indeed! In this world the force of nonsense could no farther go.

up,'[1] prating in that fashion to me, who had just come through such a week of suffering. Never mind, Chalmers's old John comes to ask after me the first thing every morning; and he keeps all the pianos down. And my maid nurses me with an alacrity and kindness that could not be bought with money; and the more I eat, the better you are always pleased.

Kind regards to them all. I hope your mother don't say every half-hour, 'I wonder how Jane is?'

Yours ever,

J. W. C.

LETTER 98.

To T. Carlyle, Scotsbrig.

Addiscombe [2]: Friday, Oct. 1, 1847.

Just two lines, dear, before starting, in case I arrive, as is likely, with a head too bad for writing from Chelsea, by to-day's post.

My visit here has gone off rather successfully in one sense. I never saw Lady Harriet in such spirits, so talkative and disposed to be talked to. I should have enjoyed being beside her more than usual if I had not felt a need of exerting myself much beyond my strength, as she made a point of ignoring the fact that anything ailed me. I fancy it must be one of her notions about me, that I am hypochondriacal; and to be made well by being treated as though there was not a doubt of it.[3]

Happily, I have got through it without giving any trouble; but shall be glad to get home to-day, where I may have a fire in my room when I am shivering, and a glass of wine when I am exhausted, and may go to bed when my head gets the better of me, without feeling it to be 'a secret to displease her.' Every day here I have had to slip into bed about two, and lie with a dreadful headache till five, when it went suddenly away. And when the housemaid (not Eliza, she is in town) found that I lighted my bedroom fire myself, she carried away the coals; and no bell could bring her; and the room is so cold and damp now there is no sun. And then no dinner till six, and no wine but hock, which makes me ill; and John had bid me take two glasses (no less) of Madeira; and, in short, 'there is no place like home' for being sick in; and I should under-

---

[1] Dickens, 'Dombey's marriage,' man of 'science' contemplating Dombey on that occasion.

[2] On a visit to Lady Harriet Baring.

[3] Patience! patience! but there never was a more complete mistake.

stand this, once for all. I am a little stronger, however, than I came, though I have not had one good night, and I expect to feel the benefit of the change when I return. When I look at my white, white face in the glass, I wonder how anybody can believe I am fancying. Ever yours,

J. C.

LETTER 99.

To T. Carlyle, Scotsbrig.

Chelsea: Saturday, Oct. 2, 1847.

'Thanks God,' dear, I write from home again! I arrived yesterday, much in the state I expected, with a racking headache and faceache, but also with a little 'monarch of all I survey' feeling, which was compensation 'for much'! In my life I think I never did so enjoy giving orders and being waited upon as last night, and being asked what I would like to take, and getting it! And thanks to the considerable mess of porridge, which John inculcated, I had some sleep, and to-day I am quite free of headache, and the faceache is greatly diminished; and I had very nice coffee in bed, and a fire to dress at, and, in short, I feel in a state of luxury perfectly indescribable! Your letter last night, too, was a most agreeable surprise; two letters in one day! That I was not exacting enough to have ever looked for! Lady Harriet spoke of writing to you one of these days. On Monday she comes to town, to go to the Grange on Tuesday, perhaps; for, if Charles Buller comes from Cornwall on Monday, he might like one day at the Cottage before they go, in which case they would put off going to the Grange till Wednesday. Or, perhaps, 'if Mr. Baring wants *two* days in London,' Lady H. would come up with him on Monday and go somewhere (Lord Grey's, I think) over Tuesday. At all events, the Grange, after Wednesday, seemed her probable address. Some time in November she expected to be in town for a week; and after Christmas she wished us to go to Alverstoke. She has got a grey Spanish horse, looked up for her by Mr. Fleming, and a new riding habit and beaver, and is 'going to ride quick now.' The coachman has made a new epigram about you. He was backing out Mr. Baring in trying to persuade her ladyship to ride the 'Kangaroo.' 'Good gracious!' said Lady H., 'do none of you remember how it behaved with Mrs. Carlyle? She could not ride it!' 'Pooh! pooh!' said the old humbug, 'Mrs. Carlyle could have ridden the horse perfectly well; it was not the horse Mrs. Carlyle was afraid of. What she was afraid of was Mr. Carlyle!'

Well, if the coachman don't appreciate you, here is 'a young heart' that does, ' immortal one!'

The note I send is accompanied by a blood-red volume entitled ' Criticisms.' I have looked at the gratitude in the preface—a very grand paragraph indeed about the magnificent Trench! and the colossal Carlyle; one of whom ' reminds us of some gigantic river, now winding,' &c., &c.; ' the other of some tremendous being, struggling with mighty power,' &c., &c. A very tremendous block-head does this writer remind us of!

I can tell you next to nothing of Mazzini. After I had been at home a week I sent him simply my visiting card, which, however, he immediately replied to in person; but when he arrived I had already fallen ill, was just going to bed in a fainting state, and could merely shake hands with him and bid him go away. He sent to ask for me two or three days after, and a week after he came one even-ing when John was here, who kept him all the time talking about Dante, and in an hour I was wearied and sent them away together. That is all I have seen of him; and all he had got to tell me of ' our things' was that he had been for weeks expecting private informa-tion that would take him away at an hour's notice, but that now there seemed no prospect of anything immediate taking effect, and that on the 10th October he would go to Paris for a month, and ' into the valley of Madame Sand.' I asked if he had meant to put himself at the disposal of the Pope. ' Oh, no!' he said; what he aimed at was ' to organise and lead an expedition into Lombardy, which would be better than being an individual under the Pope,' in which words seemed to me to lie the whole secret of Mazzini's ' failed life.' [1]

Kind regards to the others.

Ever faithfully yours,
J. W. C.

LETTER 100.

This is Thomas Spedding's residence. I had halted there for a day or two on my return. Very sad to leave my dear old mother, I can still recollect, and much out of sorts, being still in the dumb state. What did come next of writing after ' Cromwell'? Painter Lawrence was there and James Spedding; both in high spirits.

---

[1] Bölte's translation of *Verfehltes Leben.*

To T. Carlyle, Mirehouse, Keswick.

Chelsea: Saturday, Oct. 9, 1847.

Oh, my dear! my dear! I am so busy! which is better than being 'so sick'! When Mrs. Piper came this morning and found me on the steps she looked quite aghast, and said, 'You will lay yourself up again!' 'Not a bit,' I told her; 'I feel quite strong to-day.' 'I am afraid, ma'm,' suggested the little woman, 'it is not strength, but the false excitement of Mr. Carlyle coming home!' Anne remarked, 'Whatever it was, it was no use stopping Missus if she had anything on her mind. She was an example!' She 'wondered where there was another lady that could stuff chair-cushions, and do anything that was needed, and be a lady too!' So now I think I am strong enough in Anne's respect to even smoke in her presence. The worst of it is that my work in these days has been Cromwellian work—makes no show for the pains, consists chiefly in annihilating rubbish; annihilating worms for one thing. Only think of Henry Taylor's famous chair [1] being partly stuffed with dirty old carpet shorn small, which had generated naturally these hundred thousand millions of 'small beings' (as Mazzini would say). Mrs. Piper saw some of them outside when she washed the covers, and I understood that 'indication' at all events. So I had hair, rubbish, and worms, all boiled together in the cauldron, and then the clean hair picked out, and then I remade the cushions with my own hands.'

Besides this, I have been in a pretty mess with Emerson's bed, having some apprehensions he would arrive before it was up again. The quantity of sewing that lies in a lined chintz bed is something awfully grand! And I have been able to get next to no help, all the sewing women I knew of being unable to come, though 'sorry to disoblige,' &c. One had 'work on her hands for three months'; another was 'under a course of physic'; another 'found it more profitable to sew at home.' Postie realised me a little woman, who, having a baby a month old, could only come for three hours in the day; and one day she came, and had sense more or less, and was to come every day for three hours till we had finished. But on going home she found 'her baby had never cried so much since it was born;' and she came in the evening to say she could leave it no more; so there was nothing for it but to fall on the thing like a tiger myself, and it is now well forward, though I fear it will not be up, as I wished, to delight your eyes when you come.

_____

[1] A gift of his; still here.

For the rest, my life is as still as could be wished.   Mr. Ireland [1] called last night and told me much of your sayings at the Brights. Lady Harriet called on Tuesday afternoon.   She had actually ridden from Addiscombe to London the day before on the Spanish horse. 'The coachman put Mr. Baring on one of the carriage horses,' neither 'the Kangaroo' nor the chestnut being judged safe company. 'He rode half the way on that, and then the helper came up on Muff (the pony), and he got on Muff for the rest of the way.' Good Mr. Baring! I showed Lady H. the book of the 'Young Heart,' and she wrote marginal notes all over it for you, which, she said, along with the list of books she had sent, might stand very well for a letter. I could not but think from her manner that day that she had bethought her I had been rather roughly handled on my last visit. She even offered me a 'tonic,' which had been given to her by Sir J. Clarke.   'Certainly I ought to have something to strengthen me; something to make me eat! She never saw a human creature eat so little!' And a great many more unsayings of things she said at Addiscombe. She was going to dine at the Greys and next morning to the Grange, where were Croker and his women—and Miss Mitford ! ! !

Charles Buller came on Monday, and is going into Normandy. Miss Mitford reminds me of Miss Strickland. Craik, whom I saw yesterday, told me that the book which is the most decided success at present is 'The Queens of England'! Colburn has made some twenty thousand pounds by it! And the authoress too is enriched. She goes to the Duke of Cleveland's, &c., &c. (Lady Clara told John), and is treated there like a high-priestess! everybody deferring to her opinions,

But what is the use of all this writing, and with such a horrid pen, when you are coming so soon? On Monday I hardly expect you. But I shall hear. Thanks for your long letters in such a worry. The Hunts [2] give splendid *soirées*.

Ever yours faithfully,

J. W. C.

---

[1] A Manchester 'editorial gentleman,' &c. &c. He and another took me out one evening to Rochdale, where ensued (not by my blame or seeking) a paltry enough speaking-match with John Bright (topics commonplace, shallow, totally worthless to me), the only time I ever saw that gentleman, whom I seem to have known sufficiently without seeing ever since.

[2] Our neighbours still. I know not why so prosperous at present.

LETTER 101.

John Forster, Esq., 58 *Lincoln's Inn Fields.*

Chelsea: Saturday, Nov. 20, 1847.

Dear Mr. Forster,—Sure enough, we are in the gloomy month of November, when the people of England 'commit suicide' under 'attenuating circumstances.' The expediency, nay necessity, of suiciding myself is no longer a question with me. I am only uncertain as to the manner!

On Thursday I was appointed to go to Notting Hill to see my husband's bust; and had to break my appointment, unfeeling as it looked to let myself be withheld by any weather from going to see my husband's bust. I thought it would be more really unfeeling to risk an inflammation in my husband's wife's chest, which makes my husband's wife such a nuisance as you, an unmarried man, can hardly figure. Since then I have mostly lain on the sofa, under the horse-cloth, reading, 'with one eye shut and the other not open' (as poor Darley used to say), some of those divine volumes you lent me. Surely it was in the spirit of divination that I selected 'The Human Body in Health and Disease'; and the 'Means of Abridging Human Life'; and 'Hints on the Formation of Character.' One has such leisure for forming one's character during a shut-up winter!

You perceive whither all this is tending; and wish that I would hasten to the catastrophe. Well, the catastrophe is—I write it with tears in my eyes—that I cannot venture to the play on Monday night. Even if I did not, as is almost certain I should, bring on my cough, I should pass for capricious, insane; and the worst of it is, C., having no longer a duty to fulfil in promoting my happiness, declares that he won't go either, and that I had best write to you that you may take no seats for us. I do so, unwillingly; for if the weather were to 'go soft,' as Geraldine would say, I might be about again on Monday; and in any case he ought to go to his friend's first night. But there is no rebelling against Providence.

I am also bothered about these proofs;[1] C. has got some furious objection to my meddling with them—even declares that I 'do not know bad grammar when I see it, any better than she does;' that 'if I had any faculty I might find better employment for it,' &c., &c. So, after having written to her that I would do what she wished, I must write again that I am not permitted.

---

[1] Proofs of a novel by Miss Jewsbury.

I do think there is much truth in the Young German idea that marriage is a shockingly immoral institution, as well as what we have long known it for—an extremely disagreeable one.

Please countermand the proofs, for every one that comes occasions a row.

Ever affectionately yours,

J. C.

LETTER 102.

To John Welsh, Esq., Liverpool.

Chelsea: Dec. 13, 1847.

My dearest Uncle,—I write to you *de profundis*, that is to say, from the depths of my tub-chair, into which I have migrated within the last two hours, out of the still lower depths of my gigantic red bed, which has held me all this week, a victim to the 'inclemency of the season'! Oh, uncle of my affections, such a season! Did you ever feel the like of it? Already solid ice in one's water jug! 'poor Gardiners all froz out,' and Captain Sterling going at large in a dress of skins, the same that he wore in Canada! I tried to make head against it by force of volition—kept off the fire as if I had been still at 'Miss Hall's,' where it was a fine of sixpence to touch the hearthrug, and walked, walked, on Carlyle's pernicious counsel (always for me, at least) to 'take the bull by the horns,' instead of following Darwin's more sensible maxim, 'in matters of health always consult your sensations.' And so, 'by working late and early, I'm come to what ye see'! in a tub-chair—a little live bundle of flannel shawls and dressing-gowns, with little or no strength to speak of, having coughed myself all to fiddle-strings in the course of the week, and 'in a dibble of a temper,' if I had only anybody to vent it on!

Nevertheless, I am sure 'I have now got the turn,' for I feel what Carlyle would call 'a wholesome desire to smoke'! which cannot be gratified, as C. is dining with Darwin; but the tendency indicates a return to my normal state of health.

The next best thing I can think of is to write to thee; beside one's bedroom fire, in a tub-chair, the family affections bloom up so strong in one! Moreover, I have just been reading for the first time Harriet Martineau's outpourings in the 'Athenæum,' and 'that minds me,' as my Helen says, that you wished to know if I too had gone into this devilish thing. Catch me! What I think about it were not easy to say, but one thing I am very sure of, that the less one has to do with it the better; and that it is all of one family with witchcraft, demoniacal possession—is, in fact, the selfsame principle presenting itself under new scientific forms, and under a polite name. To deny that there is such a thing as animal magnetism, and that it actually does produce many of the phenomena here recorded, is idle; nor do I find much of this, which seems wonderful because we think of it for the first time, a whit more wonderful than those common instances of it, which never struck us with surprise merely because we have been used to see them all our lives. Everybody, for instance, has seen children thrown almost into convulsions by someone going through the motions of tickling them! Nay, one has known a sensitive uncle shrink his head between his shoulders at the first pointing of a finger towards his neck!

Does not a man physically tremble under the mere look of a wild beast or fellow-man that is stronger than himself? Does not a woman redden all over when she feels her lover's eyes on her? How then should one doubt the mysterious power of one individual over another? Or what is there more surprising in being made rigid than in being made red? in falling into sleep, than in falling into convulsions? in following somebody across a room, than in trembling before him from head to foot? I perfectly believe, then, in the power of magnetism to throw people into all sorts of unnatural states of body; could have believed so far without the evidence of my senses, and have the evidence of my senses for it also.

I saw Miss Bölte magnetised one evening at Mrs. Buller's by a distinguished magnetiser, who could not sound his h's, and who maintained, nevertheless, that mesmerism ' consisted in moral and intellectual superiority.' In a quarter of an hour, by gazing with his dark animal eyes into hers, and simply holding one of her hands, while his other rested on her head, he had made her into the image of death; no marble was ever colder, paler, or more motionless, and her face had that peculiarly beautiful expression which Miss Martineau speaks of, never seen but in a dead face, or a mesmerised one. Then he played cantrups with her arm and leg, and left them stretched out for an hour in an attitude which no awake person could have preserved for three minutes. I touched them, and they felt horrid—stiff as iron, I could not bend them down with all my force. They pricked her hand with the point of a penknife, she felt nothing. And now comes the strangest part of my story. The man, who regarded Carlyle and me as Philistines, said, ' Now are you convinced?' 'Yes,' said Carlyle, 'there is no possibility of doubting but that you have stiffened all poor little Miss Bölte there into something very awful.' 'Yes,' said I pertly, 'but then she wished to be magnetised; what I doubt is, whether anyone could be reduced to that state without the consent of their own volition. I should like for instance to see anyone magnetise me!' 'You think I could not?' said the man with a look of ineffable disdain. 'Yes,' said I, 'I defy you!' 'Will you give me your hand, Miss?' 'Oh, by all means;' and I gave him my hand with the most perfect confidence in my force of volition, and a smile of contempt. He held it in one of his, and with the other made what Harriet Martineau calls some 'passes' over it, as if he were darting something from his finger ends. I looked him defiantly in the face, as much as to say, 'You must learn to sound your h's, sir, before you can produce any effect on a woman like me!' And whilst this or some similar thought was passing through my head—flash there went over me, from head to foot, something precisely like what I once experienced from taking hold of a galvanic ball, only not nearly so violent. I had presence of mind to keep looking him in the face, as if I had felt nothing; and presently he flung away my hand with a provoked look, saying, 'I believe you would be a very difficult subject, but nevertheless, if I had time given me, I am sure I could mesmerise you; at least, I never failed with anyone as yet.'

Now, if this destroyed for me my theory of the need of a consenting will, it as signally destroyed his of moral and intellectual superiority; for that man was superior to me in nothing but animal strength, as I am a living woman! I could even hinder him from perceiving that he had mesmerised me, by my moral and intellectual superiority! Of the clairvoyance I have witnessed nothing; but one knows that people with a diseased or violently excited state of nerves can see more than their neighbours. When my insane friend was in this house he said many things on the strength of his insanity which in a mesmerised person would have been quoted as miracles of clairvoyance.

Of course a vast deal of what one hears is humbug. This girl of Harriet's seems half-diseased, half-make-believing. I think it a horrible blasphemy they are there perpetrating, in exploiting that poor girl for their idle purposes of curiosity! In fact, I quite agree with the girl, that, had this Mrs. Winyard lived in an earlier age of the world, she would have been burned for a witch, and deserved it better than many that were; since her poking into these mysteries of nature is not the result of superstitious ignorance, but of educated self-conceit.

In fact, with all this amount of belief in the results of animal magnetism, I regard it as a damnable sort of tempting of Providence, which I, as one solitary individual, will henceforth stand entirely aloof from.

And now, having given you my views at great length, I will return to my bed and compose my mind. Love to all; thanks to Helen. With tremendous kisses,

Your devoted niece,
JANE CARLYLE.

That wretched little Babbie does not write because I owe her a letter. A letter from her would have been some comfort in these dreary days of sickness; but since she has not bestowed it, I owe her the less thanks.

LETTER 103.

To T. Carlyle, Esq., at Alverstoke.[1]

Chelsea: Monday, Jan. 17, 1848.

Well, dearest, I have written what I have written, and what I have written I will keep to. If I am spared on foot till Thursday, I will go on Thursday, and accept the consequences—if any. This time I am under engagement to go, and it is pitiful to break one's engagement for anything short of necessity. But I will never, with the health I have, or rather have not, engage to leave home for a long fixed period, another winter. One of the main uses of a home is to stay in it, when one is too weak and spiritless for conforming, without effort, to the ways of other houses. Besides, is not home —at least, was it not 'in more earnest times'—'the woman's proper sphere'? Decidedly, if she 'have nothing to keep her at home,' as the phrase is, she should 'find something—or die!' That is my idea in the days of solitary musing. Amusement after a certain age is no go; even when there are no other nullifying conditions, it gets to be merely distraction, in the Gambardella sense; between which and distraction in the general sense there is but a thin partition, so thin that one can hear through it, whenever one likes to listen, the clanking of chains, and the shrieking of 'mads,' as

---

[1] Carlyle on visit there to Mr. and Lady Harriet Baring, has written to press his wife to join him.—J. A. F.

I.—11

plainly as I am hearing at this moment the Chalmers's pianoforte. Ah, yes, I had found out that, 'by my own smartness,' before I took to reading on insanity. To be sure, it is hard on flesh and blood, when one 'has nothing to keep one at home,' to sit down in honest life-weariness, and look out into unmitigated zero; but perhaps it 'would be a great advantage' just to 'go ahead' in that; the bare-faced indigence of such a state might drive one, like the piper's cow, to 'consider,'[1] and who knows but, in considering long enough, one might discover what one 'has wanted,' and what one 'wants'—an essential preliminary to getting it. Meanwhile here is Hare's Sterling book come for you—late, for Miss Wynne had read it four days ago—and 'with the publisher's compliments.' No copy had been sent to Anthony when I saw him; he had bought it, and said if you did not feel yourself bound to place his brother in a true light, he must attempt it himself. By the way, what a fine fellow that Mr. O. Holmes is! a sort of man that one would like to see. And Dr. MacEnnery, did not you find his letter had a sort of Cromwellian sincerity and helplessness 'not without worth'? My head aches a great deal, which is natural, for, except the first night after you went, I have slept little—some three hours a night, and that in small pieces; but I am able to lie quite peaceably, without reading.

LETTER 104.

To T. Carlyle, Esq., at Alverstoke.

Chelsea: Jan. 18, 1848.

Ah, my dear! We are both busy reflecting, it would seem; driven to it, by quite opposite pressures—you by stress of society, and I by stress of solitude. *A la bonne heure!* reflection is golden; provided one 'go into practice with it;' otherwise, if, as in my case, for most part it serves only to make the inward darkness more visible, why, then, as John said of the senna, one had 'better take it, but perhaps one had better not.'

Poor human creatures 'after all'! I am heartily sorry for them, severally, and in the lump; think sometimes it would be 'a great advantage' if we were all 'fed off!' but one thinks many things, in moments of *un*enthusiasm, which one does not authentically mean. To-day, however, is the brightest of sunshiny days; and last night I slept like a Christian, and so I ought to feel better, and shall, perhaps, before evening. No letters but your own, for which I was

---

[1] Note, p. 56.

thankful. There was one last night from Espinasse—too much of Emerson, whom he 'likes much better than he did.' In reply to my charge that Emerson had no ideas (except mad ones) that he had not got out of *you*, Espinasse answers prettily, 'but pray, Mrs. Carlyle, who has?' He (E.) had been discussing you with a 'Bey,' whom he met at Geraldine's, sent by the Egyptian; and the Bey 'had the impudence to say': 'M. Carlyle *n'a pas assez de fond pour l'esprit française.*'

I must not write any more to-day, for that weary head 'likes' writing as ill as Mrs. Howatson's 'disguster' liked ewe cheese.

Faithfully yours,
JANE W. C.

LETTER 105.

To T. Carlyle at Alverstoke.

Chelsea: Jan. 21, 1848.

Well, dear, I have written to Lady Harriet that I am not going at all—the only rational course under the circumstances. So now you are to do what you think best for yourself, without reference to me. You are not to hurry home on my account. I am not so ill as to make that a duty for you; nor so well as to make it a pleasure. But if you continue ill yourself, you will certainly be better in your own nest, with me to tell it to, and all your own way, as far as material things are concerned. Do not be uneasy about me. I should know the ways of this sort of cold by now; and I am sure that with reasonable care it need turn to nothing dangerous, though it might easily be fixed in my lungs by any rashness. John said he would write a note himself. I sent for him to take counsel before I began writing. Some Watts have come to town, with whom he dines, &c.; and it is amazing how, in a few days, he has gone all to smithers (morally). Last night he came, for an hour, before going' to these Watts, and found me lying on the sofa, very much done up, and *coffing* worse than usual. 'How d'ye do?' he said, like Mr. Toots.

Mercy, I am going to be belated.

LETTER 106.

To John Forster, Esq., 58 *Lincoln's-Inn Fields.*

5 Cheyne Row: Saturday, Feb. 1848.

Dear Mr. Forster,—It is too bad to plague you with 'a delicate embarrassment' of mine, when you are overhead in 'earnest work;'

but what can I do? If you do not cut me out, my husband will, at the least, send me to Gehenna; and I would much rather not.

Geraldine writes to me this morning (our correspondence had been at a still-stand ever since that feast of ' meats,'[1] and love, and tobacco, at the Fornisari's) that I may expect a copy of her book next week. I had no notion it would be ready so soon. Well! for the delicate embarrassment—she does not say anything about the dedication to Mrs. Paulet and myself, which her heart was much set on some months ago, and which, that is *my* share in it, I neither positively accorded to, nor positively declined at the time, meaning to revise the question when the book was ready for being dedicated, and to be guided by my husband's authentic feelings in the matter. Knowing his dislike to be connected in people's minds, by even the slightest spider-thread, with what he calls ' George Sandism and all that accursed sort of thing,' I was not sure that the half-toleration he gave when asked about it would not be changed into prohibition, if he found it likely to be acted upon. At the time I sounded his feelings, the book, I was able to assure him, contained nothing questionable. Can I say so now? If anything of the last chapters I read be left in it, not only would he detest a dedication to his wife, but his wife herself would detest it. What I want you to do is, if there be a dedication, to erase my name; and leave it all to Mrs. Paulet, and tell me that you have so done; and I will write to Geraldine an explanation of the fact. If there be no dedication, tell me all the same, and then I shall not need to hurt the poor little soul's sensibilities by a premature refusal. You see how I am situated, wishing not to give pain to Geraldine—still less to give offence to my husband; and least of all, to promenade myself as an ' emancipated' woman. I am still confined to the house—weary work. Ever affectionately yours,

JANE CARLYLE.

Have you the other novels of the Currer Bell people? I should like them any time.

LETTER 107.

To T. Carlyle, Chelsea.

Croydon[2]: Thursday, April 13, 1848.

If better for you in all other respects that I should remain in ' some other part of the country,' my return will have, at least, one

---

[1] Not ' shells ' (Ossian).

[2] Mrs. Carlyle, after three months' illness, was now at Addiscombe.—J. A. F.

comfort in it, that I do serve to 'stave off' the people from you, especially at meal-times? But perhaps it is more the cold than the people that makes you more unwell than usual in these days. I have no people here to worry me, have nothing to complain of as to diet, or hours, or noise; and I have not had one well moment day or night, except that day you came. However, I have always been able to keep on foot, and to put a good face on myself; so I have not had the un-'pleasant additimental' consciousness of being a bore. Mr. Baring has not returned yet. On Tuesday evening, after dinner, Lady Harriet went up to the opera—very rashly, I thought, having risen from her sofa to go; but she returned quite well next day about one o'clock. Mr. Baring is not to come, I believe, till she goes up for the Molesworth dinner on Sunday. The evening I spent here, so unexpectedly, alone, was like a morphia dream. The stillness was something superhuman, for the servants, it seemed to me, so soon as they got their Lady out of the way, went, all but Williams, off into space. While I was upstairs for a moment, light had been brought in; and, an hour after, tea was placed for me in the same invisible manner. I looked, to myself, sitting there, all alone, in the midst of comforts and luxuries not my own, like one of those wayfarers in the fairy tales, who, having left home with 'a bannock' to 'poose their fortune,' and followed the road their 'stick fell towards,' find themselves in a beautiful enchanted palace, where all their wants are supplied to them by supernatural agency;—hospitality of the most exquisite description, only without a host! I had been reading Swift all day; but I found that now too prosaical for my romantic circumstances; and, seeking through the books, I came upon 'The Romance of the Forest,' which I seized on with avidity, remembering the 'tremendous' emotions with which I read it in my night-shift, by the red light of our dying schoolroom fire, nearly half a century ago, when I was supposed to be sleeping the sleep of good children. And over that I actually spent the whole evening; it was so interesting to measure my progress—downwards I must think—by comparing my present feelings at certain well-remembered passages with the past. After all, it might have been worse with my imaginative past. I decidedly like the dear old book, even in this year of grace, far better than 'Rose Blanche,' &c.[1] Execrable, that is; I could not have suspected even the ape of writing anything so silly. Lady H. read it all the way down, and decided it was 'too vulgar

---

[1] G. H. Lewes's novel.

to go on with.' I myself should have also laid it aside in the first half volume if I had not felt a pitying interest in the man, that makes me read on in hope of coming to something a little better. Your marginal notes are the only real amusement I have got out of it hitherto.

My head feels as usual to be full of melted lead, swaying this way and that. There is no walking off the heaviness if walkable off, for the rain is incessant. Tell Anne to bid the confectioner bake half a dozen fresh little cakes for the X——'s. Have patience with them. Are they not seeking, which is next best to having found?

Ever yours,
J. C.

LETTER 108.

John Forster, Esq., 58 Lincoln's Inn Fields.

Chelsea: Thursday morning, April 1849.

Dear Friend,—Your Ganymede found me yesterday in a mortal crisis: in the thick of two afflictions, which put together did not make a consolation. In the first place I had got one of my patent headaches to do, which absolutely could not be put off any longer; and at the same time it was required of me to endure the infinite clatter of an old lady—clack, clack, clack, like pailfuls of water poured all over me, world without end. Nevertheless I showed myself to Ganymede for a moment, and bade him tell you heaven knows what!—that it was ' all right,' or that it was ' all wrong,' or perhaps that it was all right and all wrong in the same breath. I did not know what I was saying. Now that I do, thank you for the books and the veil and the stick. I have forwarded your note to Sterling, and doubt not but it will find the gracious welcome which it deserves;—and nothing earthly or divine shall make me forget! Bless you! I never forget anything, except now and then my veil, and, always and for ever, the multiplication table! I have never, for example, forgotten a single one of all the kindnesses you have shown me! So you may expect us on Thursday, as far as depends on me, with a confidence which has for its basis the laws of nature.

Affectionately yours,
JANE CARLYLE.

LETTER 109.

Poor Helen's Dublin glories ended (the second year, I think) in total wreck—drink, quarrel with her fool of a brother, dismissal home or into outer darkness, and adieu of the *spitfire* kind! From home she sent inquiries hither: old regrets, new alacrities, &c. &c. As our good little Anne was now to be wedded, and go to Jersey with her 'James' (where she did well, but died in a couple of years, poor little soul!), we were glad to hear of Helen again. Helen came, a glad sight of her kind; to my eye nothing was wrong in her, but to *another* better observer (though in strict silence towards me) much, much! Accordingly before long strange faults (even theft, to appearance) began to peer out; and, after perhaps four or five months, came the catastrophe described below!

My darling took all pains with the wretched Helen; got her *placed* once, perhaps twice, candidly testifying to qualities and *faults* alike (drove off with her once in a cab, as I can still pathetically recollect having seen):—but nothing could save Helen! She was once, as we heard, dragged from the river; did die, an outcast, few months afterwards. Naivety and even geniality,—imbecility, obstinacy, and *gin*. Her 'sayings,' as reported to me here, were beyond all Jest-Books,—as gold beyond pinchbeck.

19 *March*, 1849, *Cromwell.*—A Third Edition got done (*i.e.* the MS. &c. *copy* of it) 'this morning.'—*Printing* haggles forward till October or after. Mrs. Buller's death 'week before.'

To Mrs. Aitken, Dumfries.

5 Cheyne Row: Tuesday night, May 1849.

My dear Jane,—Many thanks for your kind letter and 'dainties'; these I only realised to-day—the weather having been bad: and my head not good, and no carriage turning up for me till to-day. I ate a little piece of cake so soon as I got it home, and pronounce it first-rate; the marmalade I have not yet broken into.

For ourselves, we are all going on as much as usual: Mr. C. has not got reconciled to his 'interior,' nor I to my head, with which, indeed, I have had several more terrible bouts lately than ever in my life before, which is much to say! John is excessively kind to me on these occasions; has sat on his knees at my bedside for hours together, holding me down, and being sorry for me, which is just all that can be done in the way of alleviation. 'On earth the living have much to bear;' the difference is chiefly in the manner of bearing, and my manner of bearing is far from being the best.

They would tell you of the final crash of my maid Helen, how, on our return from a visit to Captain Sterling,[1] she first would not open the door; and at last did open it, like a stage ghost very ill got up: blood spurting from her lips, her face whitened with chalk from the kitchen floor, her dark gown ditto, and wearing a smile of idiotic self-complacency. I thought Mr. C. was going to kick his foot through her; when she tumbled down at his touch. If she had been his wife he certainly would have killed her on the spot; but his maid-of-all-work he felt could not be got rid of without his being hanged for her. The young woman whom Providence sent me 'quite promiscuously' within an hour of this consummation has hitherto given us the greatest satisfaction. She is far the most lovable servant I ever had; a gentle, pretty, sweet-looking creature, with innocent winning ways; a very fair worker too, clean, orderly, and 'up to her business.'[2] My only fear about her is that being only four-and-twenty, and calculated to produce an impression on the other sex, she may weary of single service; unless indeed she can get up a sentiment for the butcher's man, who is already her devoted admirer; but 'he is so desperately ugly.'

Meanwhile, I have been busy, off and on, for a great many weeks in pasting a screen with four leaves, five feet high, all over with prints. It will be a charming 'work of art' when finished, but of that there is no near prospect. The prints are most of them very small, and it takes so much pondering to find how to scatter them about to the best advantage.[3] What else I have been doing it were hard to tell. I read very little nowadays; not that my eyes are failed the least in the world, but that books have ceased to take any hold on me; and as for sewing, you know that 'being an only child, I never wished to sew.' Still, I have some inevitable work in that line, as, even if I felt rich enough to have the 'family needlework' done by others, I don't know where to find others to do it for money, without bothering me with their stupidity worse than if I did it myself. But the great business of life for a woman like me in this place is an eternal writing of little unavoidable notes. It falls upon me to answer all the invitations, and make

---

[1] February 1849.

[2] This must have been Elizabeth Sprague, from Exeter, a high-going, shining kind of damsel, who did very well for about two years; but then, like most of the genus, went away, and disappeared. What a province of the 'domesticities' that is at present! Anarchic exceedingly; the funnel-neck of all our anarchies.

[3] Stands here to this day, the beautifullest and cleverest screen I have ever seen. How strange, how mournfully affecting to me now!

lying excuses world without end; so that I sometimes look back with the tear in my eye to the time when we were not celebrated, and were left to provide our own dinners as we could. A French poet dying of hunger, in a novel, calls, 'Oh, Glory, give me bread!' I would call to Glory often enough, 'Give me repose!' only that I know beforehand my sole response from Glory would be, 'Don't you wish you may get it?'

And now, dear, the sun is shining—has actually 'taken a notion' of shining for the first time these many days; and I have need to walk, having been shut up lately till I feel quite moulting. And so I must out into space.

Love to your husband and all the rest. It would be pretty of you to write to me sometimes; for I am always

Very affectionately yours,

JANE W. CARLYLE.

LETTER 110.

Nothing in the way of printing, or nothing in the least considerable, had come from me since 'Cromwell;' but much was fermenting in me, in very painful ways, during four years of silence. Irish Repeal, Paraclete, McHale, Irish Industrial Regiments, newspaper articles on such, &c., &c.,—trifling growls, words idly flung away. In the fourth or third year especially, in the revolutionary 1848, matters had got to a kind of boiling pitch with me, and I was becoming very wretched for want of a voice. Much MS. was accumulating on me, with which I did not know what in the world to do. Nigger question (end of 1849) did get out, and the rest, vividly enough, as Latter-Day Pamphlets (next spring)! Meanwhile, all being dark and dumb, I had decided on a six-weeks' visit to Ireland (Duffy, &c. much pressing me). Record of the tour, written slapdash after my return, is among the worthless MSS. here.[1] Emerson had now left England seven or eight months.

To T. Carlyle, Post Office, Dublin.

Addiscombe: Sunday night, July 2, 1849.

Well! it is a consolation of a sort that I cannot figure you more cold and lonely and comfortless there at sea than myself has been on land, even amidst 'the splendid blandishments' of Addiscombe. When I could not distinguish your white hat any longer I went home, and sat down to cry a little; but Elizabeth put a stop to

---

[1] These Notes were given by Mr. Carlyle to a friend, from whom they passed into the hands of Messrs. Sampson Low & Co., and were published by that firm in the spring of 1882.—J. A. F.

that by coming in with—your plaid over her arm! and expressing
her surprise that master hadn't taken it. The plaid forgotten, and
the day so cold! For one frantic moment I was for running back
to the pier, and plunging into the water on my own basis, and
swimming after you with the plaid in my mouth; but a very little
reflection turned me from this course, and instead I proceeded to
the kitchen, and silently boiled my strawberries, like a practical
woman. Then I stowed away some of the valuables, and dressed
myself; and, no one having come for my portmanteau, I took it
with me in the omnibus to the top of Sloane Street, where I had it
and myself transferred to a cab, for greater dignity's sake! I was
at Bath House five minutes before twelve, shivering with cold, excessively low, and so vexed about the plaid! But 'no sympathy
there, thank God!'—'wits' enough, if that could have helped me.
'You would have the sense to wrap yourself in a sail if you were
cold,' or 'Depend upon it, you would seize on the rugs of all the
other passengers' beds. At all events, you had promised to stay
with them in Scotland, and that would quite set you up if you had
taken cold!' Clearly, I must 'come out of that' if I were going to
do any good; and I did, to appearance; but all day I was fancying
you shivering, like myself. We came here in the open carriage,
having picked up Miss Farrar and Blanche. And here there was
neither fire nor sun to warm one. We were taken to the dairy to
lunch on cold milk and bread from the cold stone tables; and then
to the hay-field to sit on cold hay-cocks; and a very large cold pad-
dock[1] jumped up my leg, good God! and 'it was a bad joy!'
The dinner, at six, put me a little to rights; and I felt still better
when we had put a lucifer to some sticks in the grate. At eleven
we went to bed; 'and the evening and the morning were the first
day!'

To-day, Lord Bath and Bingham Mildmay arrived to breakfast;
Milnes and Poodle an hour later. It has been a warm, fresh-blow-
ing day, and spent almost entirely out of doors, sitting about the
swing, tumbling amongst the hay, walking and driving till eight,
when we dined. And after that, very youthful and uproarious
sports till twelve! I have written this much since coming up to
bed. There is no more paper in my book; so I will now go to bed,
and finish at Chelsea. I hope it has been as warm on the sea.
Blanche —— has confided to me all the secrets of her heart—her

---

[1] Scotch for frog.

ideas about her father and mother and sisters and lovers—and wishes me to save her soul!

We are to dine here before starting, and if I do not send my letter till we get to London, there may be none at the post-office [1] when you first call; and that would be vexatious. But there is no time or composure here by day for writing, so this must go as it is.

We have been in the Archbishop's grounds for three hours. The men are all gone back to town, except Lord Bath, who is at this moment singing with Blanche under my window, distracting me worse than a barrel-organ. Good Heavens! What tearing spirits everybody is in!

The note from Davis [2] came before I left. I did not leave my address, so I don't know what others may have come; one to you from Neuberg I left behind. I ought to acknowledge with thankfulness that I have been less sick since I came. Oh, dear, I wish I heard of your safe delivery out of that ship!

Ever yours,

J. W. C.

LETTER 111.

To T. Carlyle, Imperial Hotel, Dublin, Ireland.

Chelsea: Thursday, July 5, 1849.

I am so glad of your letter this morning! after Miss Wynn's non-sensical preparation, I could not feel at all sure. It sounds bad enough, but it might have been worse: 'kept at sea double the time,' and 'short of provisions;'—that would have been a go!

I am very busy to-day, having written to Mr. Neuberg that the last wild goose will alight at him on Monday,[3] and having a world of things to do in the meantime. And so I must be brief; better perhaps I let alone writing altogether, but then you might be 'vaixed.' Hitherto my time has been chiefly taken up by people. Anthony Sterling came while I was at tea, and presently after, Masson and Mr. Russell [4] from Edinburgh; each of these gentlemen drank four cups of tea! I talked a great deal, having all the responsibility to myself, and 'made so many wits' [5] for them that

---

[1] In Dublin.

[2] One of Robson's printers; did the 'Lists,' &c., in *Cromwell;* a very superior kind of man.

[3] Neuberg, with his sister, then in Nottingham; my poor pilgrim on the road thither, as her first stage.

[4] Son of surgery professor, ended very tragically long after.

[5] Bölte's phrase.

Anthony bolted off at nine, and the others stayed till eleven, evidently quite charmed with me—so differently do 'wits' act upon different characters! Yesterday I rose with a headache, the penalty of all that cleverness; but cold water and coffee staved it off.

Having made an inventory of the plate, and packed it to be sent to Bath House, I went out and transacted a variety of small affairs; dined very slightly in a confectioner's shop—Blanche and Miss Farrar having insisted on coming to tea with me at five o'clock!—and was home just in time to receive them.

No such 'everlasting friendship' has been sworn to me these thirty years as this of Blanche's! She flings herself on my neck, begs me to call her Blanche, says with tears in her eyes, 'Oh! does not everyone love you?' protests that she 'would like to stay with me for ever;' and in fact embarrasses me considerably with a sort of thing I have been quite out of these many years. While we were at tea (and these girls too had each four cups! with cakes and bread-and-butter in proportion), up drove Lady Ashburton, which was great fun for all parties. She was in 'tearing spirits,' and so were we by that time; and the racket that followed for the next hour and half was what Forster[1] might have called 'stupendous! Great God!' She said my picture was the horridest thing she had ever seen, 'like, but so disagreeably like, exactly reminding one of a poor old starved rabbit!' I suppose she has criticised it to N——, for he has sent to beg I will give 'one more' sitting; very inconvenient just now, but I promised to go to-morrow. Lord A. was to return last night, feeling a return of his gout, and wishing to be near Fergusson. My party dismissed in good time. Lady A. went at eight 'to dress for a party at Lady Waldegrave's;' the girls about nine, 'to dress for a ball at Lady Wilton's.' I walked to the cabstand with them;—devoutly imagined to go on and ask for Mrs. Chorley, but was too tired; so I read the new 'Copperfield,' being up to nothing else, and went to bed between ten and eleven. Had again talked too much for sleep, and again rose with a headache, which again yielded to cold water and 'determination of character.'

God bless you ever.

Yours,

JANE C.

---

[1] John, of the *Examiner*, &c. &c.

LETTER 112.

To T. Carlyle, at Galway.

Benrydden: Friday, July 20, 1849.

Oh, my dear, I have been 'packed!' The Doctor proposed to 'pack' me for courtesy, and I, for curiosity, accepted. So at six in the morning, just when I had fallen into sound sleep, I was roused by a bath-woman coming to my bedside, in a huge white flannel gown, and bidding me turn out. I got on to the floor in a very bewildered state, and she proceeded to double back one half of my bed clothes and feather-bed, spread a pair of blankets on the mattress, then a sheet wrung out of cold water; then bade me strip and lie down. I lay down, and she swathed me with the wet sheet like a mummy; then swathed me with the blankets, my arms pinioned down, exactly, in fact, like a mummy; then rolled back the feather-bed and original bed-clothes on the top of me, leaving out the head; and so left me, for an hour, to go mad at my leisure! I had no sooner fairly realised my situation of being bound hand and foot under a heap of things, than I felt quite frantic, cursed my foolish curiosity, and made horrid efforts to release myself; thought of rolling to the bell, and ringing it with my teeth, but could not shake off the feather-bed; did ultimately get one of my hands turned round, and was thankful for even that change of posture. Dr. Nicol says the bath-woman should have stayed with me during the first ' pack,' and put a wet cloth on my head; that it was the blood being sent to my head that 'caused all this wildness.' Whatever it was, I would not undergo the thing again for a hundred guineas. When the bath-woman came back at seven, I ordered her to take me out instantly. 'But the doctor?' The doctor, I told her, had no business with me, I was not a patient. ' Oh! then you have only been packed for foon, have you?' 'Yes; and very bad fun!' So she filled a slipper-bath to 'put me to rights,' and I plunged into that so soon as I was set loose, and she splashed pitcher after pitcher full of water on my head. And this shall be the last of my water-curing, for the present. I feel quite shattered still, with an incipient headache, and am wishing that Forster would come, and take us back to Rawdon.

I suppose Forster has sent you a Bradford paper containing the report of our meeting for ' Roman Liberty.' It went off very successfully as a meeting; but did not bring in to Forster all the ' virtue's own reward' he anticipated, and he was out of humour for twenty-four hours after. In fact, the Bradford gentlemen on the platform were like Bess Stodart's legs, 'no great things.' But the Bradford men, filling the hall to suffocation, were a sight to see! to cry over, 'if one liked' such ardent, earnest, half-intelligent, half-bewildered countenance, as made me, for the time being, almost into a friend of the species and advocate for *fusion de biens.*[1] And I must tell you 'I aye thocht meikle o' you,' but that night I 'thocht mair o' you than eve.'[2] A man of the people mounted the platform, and spoke;—a youngish, intelligent-looking man, who alone, of all the speakers, seemed to understand the question, and to have feelings as well as notions about it. He spoke with a heart-eloquence that 'left me warm.' I never was more affected by public speaking. When he ceased I did not throw myself on his neck, and swear everlasting friendship; but, I assure you, it was in putting constraint on myself that I merely started to my feet, and shook hands with him. Then 'a sudden thought' struck me: this man would like to know you; I would give him my address in London. I borrowed a pencil and piece of paper, and handed him my address. When he looked at it, he started as if I had sent a bullet into him —caught my hand again, almost squeezed it to 'immortal smash,' and said, 'Oh, it is your husband! Mr. Carlyle has been my teacher and master! I have owed everything to him for years and years!' I felt it a credit to you really to have had a hand in turning out this man;—was prouder of that heart-tribute to your genius than any amount of reviewer-praises, or aristocratic invitations to dinner. Forster had him to breakfast next morning. I shall have plenty of things to tell you when we meet at leisure, if I can only keep them in mind; but in this wandering Jew life I feel no time on hand, even for going into particulars.

To-day I am pretty well finished off, for all practical purposes, by that confounded pack. My head is getting every moment hotter and heavier; and the best I can do is to get out on the hillside, and think of nothing! Lucas's[3] father and sister are here: genteel Quakerly people—very lean.

After Monday, address to Auchtertool Manse, Kirkcaldy. I wish to heaven I were fairly there. I could almost lose heart, and turn, and go back to London; but I will go: as I used to say when a

---

[1] The St. Simonian recipe.
[2] John Brown's widow (of her murdered husband) to Claverhouse's soldiers.
[3] Catholic editor, Irish M.P., poor soul!

little child, and they asked if anything was too hard for me, 'Me can do what me's bid.' The difficulty is still chiefly to bid myself—and I have bid myself go to Scotland. Mrs. Paulet is asleep on a sofa beside me, so young and pretty and happy-looking; I wonder at her.

God bless you, dear. When I have 'some reasonably good leisure'[1] again, I will write you better letters; and more legible ones when I get a decent pen. If you saw the stump I am writing with, you would be filled with admiration of my superiority to circumstances. God bless you! All to be said worth the saying lies in that. Your affectionate
JANE W. C.

LETTER 113.

Of Irish journey, summer 1849, I think there is the rough jotting[2] hastily done after my return home. In defect of that, or in supplement to that, here are some dates:

August 6, 7.—Miserable puddle of a night; disembarked at Glasgow; ditto day there, and second night with David Hope—last time I saw him. My Jane at Auchtertool (manse, with cousin). I run for Scotsbrig and its shelter first. Remember Ecclefechan station and my parting with W. E. Forster there.

August 27.—Through Kirkcaldy or Auchtertool for some days, we (Jane's last and probably first time) arrive at Linlathen, where I leave her intending for Haddington. Three days with the Donaldsons (three old ladies, dear friends of Dr. Welsh's family in early days), thence to Scotsbrig, and set out with Farie to Perth, intending for Glen Truin (Spey side) and the Ashburtons. There about a fortnight. Crowded, gypsy existence; everywhere chaos, and rest fled whither? Towards Scotsbrig and way home, September 14 at Edinburgh. See Jeffrey drearily, mournfully, for the last time (next spring he died). Not till last week of September get home, my poor, heavy-laden Jane, from Liverpool a few days before, waiting for me with her sad but welcome face—*Ay de mi!* —towards what a three months of excursion had we treated ourselves ! Physically and spiritually don't remember to have ever suffered more. I had never any health for touring. I should have stayed at home had not, indeed, my 'home' been London, with its summer torments! 'Latter-Day Pamphlets' now close ahead.— T. C.

To T. Carlyle (Galway, Sligo; had followed me to) Scotsbrig.

[3] Haddington: Thursday morning, July 26, 1849.

My dear dear,—I wrote you a long, very long, letter last night at midnight from this same place. But this morning, instead of put-

---

[1] Cromwell. [2] See p. 249.
[3] Mrs. Carlyle had gone to Haddington for the first time since her marriage twenty-three years before.—J. A. F.

ting it in the post-office, I have torn it up. You may fancy what
sort of a letter, 'all about feelings (as Lady A. would say), an excitable character like me would write in such circumstances, after a
long railway journey, and a three hours' pilgrimage all up and down,
and across and round about Haddington. And you can also understand how, after some hours of sleep, I should have reacted
against my last night's self, and thought all that steam best gathered
back into the vale of silence. I have now only time to write the
briefest of notes; but a blessing from here I must send you; to no
other mortal would I, or indeed could I, write from this place at
this moment; but it comes natural to me to direct a letter to you
here, and that is still something, is it not?

I will give you all my news so soon as I have slept a night at
Auchtertool. I expect Walter and Jeannie will meet me at the
station in Edinburgh, where I shall be at a quarter after twelve. I
am not too much tired; my journey has been made as easy for me
as possible. From Rawdon to Morpeth on Tuesday, William Edward most kindly accompanying me there, and seeing me off next
day. 'I looked so horribly helpless,' he said, 'that he could not
reconcile it to his conscience to leave me a chance at losing myself.'

I was wandering about till after dark last night, and out again
this morning at six; but I must leave all particulars till a more leisure moment, and till my heart is calmer than at present. I am so
glad I came here on this *incognito* principle. It is the only way in
which I could have got any good of the dear old place. God bless
it! How changed it is, and how changed am I ! But enough just
now.

Ever your affectionate,
JEANNIE WELSH.

Oh ! what a letter, what a letter, to read again now! (May 27,
1869.)

Much Ado about Nothing.

This is a very interesting little narrative, discovered by me the
other day; I had never heard of it before. The 'Forster' mentioned
in it is William Edward Forster, now M.P. for Bradford, conspicu-
ous in various, to me, rather questionable ways—Nigger-Emanci-
pator, Radical Patriot, &c., &c.; at that time an enthusiastic young
'Wet-Quaker' (had been introduced to me by Sterling), full of
cheery talk and speculation, and well liked by both of us till then.
I was in Ireland, travelling about, mainly with Duffy (so far as
not alone) in those weeks. Forster on quitting her at Morpeth (as

mentioned within) shot off for Ireland, and in the very nick of the moment, the next Sunday morning, intersected Duffy and me at Castlebar (Westport, south-west region) just in the act of starting northward; sprang upon the car along with us, and was of the party till it ended (at Ecclefechan, through Derry and Glasgow, Forster's and my part of it), after which I have seen very little of him, nor did she more.—T. C. August 3, 1866.

On Tuesday, July 24, 1849, I left Rawdon[1] after breakfast, and at five of the afternoon reached Morpeth, where I had decided to pass the night. William Forster escorted me thus far, and stayed to start me by the two o'clock train next day, out of purest charity, having adopted Donovan's[2] theory of me, that I am wholly without observing faculty, with large reflectiveness turned inward; a sort of woman, that, ill-adapted for travelling by railway alone, with two boxes, a writing-case and carpet-bag. Anyhow, I was much the better of such a cheerful companion to stave off the nervousness about Haddington, not to speak of the material comforts—a rousing fire, brandy-negus, &c.—which he ordered for me at the inn, and which I should not have had the audacity to order on my own basis.

After a modest dinner of chops and cherry-tart, we walked by the river-side in a drizzling rain (that was at my suggestion); then back to the 'Phœnix' for tea, chess, and speculative talk till midnight; when I went to bed, expecting no sleep to speak of, and of course slept unusually well; for the surest way to get a thing in this life is to be prepared for doing without it, to the exclusion even of hope.

Next morning was bright as diamonds, and we walked all about the town and neighbouring heights; where, rendered unusually communicative by our isolated position, I informed William Edward that my maternal grandmother was 'descended from a gang of gipsies;' was in fact grand-niece to Matthew Baillie who 'suffered at Lanark,' that is to say was hanged there. A genealogical fact, Forster said, which made me at last intelligible for him, 'a cross betwixt John Knox and a gipsy, how that explained all!' By the way, my uncle has told me since I came here that the wife of that Matthew Baillie, Margaret Euston by name, was the original of Sir W. Scott's 'Meg Merrilies.' Matthew himself was the last of gipsies; could steal a horse from under the owner if he liked, but

---

[1] Near Bradford, Yorkshire.
[2] A quack physiognomist, &c., of the time.

left always the saddle and bridle; a thorough gentleman in his way and six feet four in stature!

But to go back to Morpeth: we again dined at the 'Phœnix'; then Forster put me into my carriage, and my luggage into the van, and I was shot off towards Scotland, while himself took train for Ireland.

From Morpeth to Haddington is a journey of only four hours; again 'the wished-for come too late!'—rapidest travelling to Scotland now, and no home there any more! The first locality I recognised was the Peer Bridge; I had been there once before, a little child, in a post-chaise with my father; he had held his arm round me while I looked down the ravine. It was my first sight of the picturesque that. I recognised the place even in passing it at railway speed, after all these long, long years.

At the Dunbar station an old lady in widow's dress, and a young one, her daughter, got into the carriage, which I had had so far all to myself; a man in yeomanry uniform waiting to see them off. 'Ye'll maybe come and see us the morn's nicht?' said the younger lady from the carriage. 'What for did ye no come to the ball?' answered the yeoman, with a look 'to split a pitcher.' The young lady tchick-tchicked, and looked deprecatingly, and tried again and again to enchain conversation; but to everything she said came the same answer—'What for did ye no come to the ball?' The poor young lady then tried holding her tongue; her lover (only her lover would have used her so brutally) did the same; but rested his chin on the carriage window to scowl at her with more convenience. The interest was rising; but one could see who of them would speak first. 'Oh!' broke out the young lady, 'I'm just mourning!' 'What for?' 'Oh, just that ball!' 'What for then did ye no come?' growled the repeating decimal; 'I waited an oor for ye!' and he got his upper lip over the strap of his cap and champed it—like a horse! Squeal went the engine; we were off; the young lady 'just mourned' for a minute or two, then fell to talking with her mother. For me, I reflected how 'the feelings were just the same there as here,'[1] and the Devil everywhere busy! Before the ladies got out at Drem I had identified the pale, old, shrivelled widow with a buxom, bright-eyed, rosy Mrs. Frank Sheriff of my time. The daughter had not only grown up but got herself born in the interval. What chiefly struck me, however—indeed confounded me—was to be stared at by Mrs. Sheriff as a stranger or

---

[1] My mother, on reading *Wilhelm Meister*.

even foreigner! for, when I asked her some question about the road, she answered with that compassionate distinctness which one puts on with only foreigners or idiots. I began to think my precautions for keeping *incognito* in my native place might turn out to have been superfluous. One of these precautions had the foolishest little consequence. In leaving London, I had written the addresses for my luggage on the backs of other people's visiting-cards, 'without respect of persons'—a stupid practice when one thinks of it!—but at Morpeth I removed three of the cards, leaving one to the carpet-bag, carpet-bags being so confoundable. I was at the pains, how-ever, to rub off my own name from that card, which, for the rest, happened to be Mrs. Humphrey St. John Mildmay's. Well, at Longniddry, where I had to wait some fifteen minutes for the cross-train to Haddington, 'there came to pass' a porter! who helped me with my things, and would not leave off helping me, quite teased me in fact with delicate attentions. At last he made me a low bow and said he was 'not aware that any of the family were in this quarter.' I believe I answered, 'Quite well, I thank you;' for I was getting every instant more excited with my circum-stances. He shut the carriage-door on me, then opened it again and said, with another low bow, 'Excuse me, ma'am; but I was in the service of the brother of Mr. Humphrey St. John Mildmay.' I am positive as to my answer this time, that it was, 'Oh, thank you! —no, I am quite another person!'

A few minutes more and I was at the Haddington station, where I looked out timidly, then more boldly, as my senses took in the utter strangeness of the scene; and luckily I had 'the cares of lug-gage' to keep down sentiment for the moment. No vehicle was in waiting but a dusty little omnibus, licensed to carry any number, it seemed; for, on remarking there was no seat for me, I was told by all the insides in a breath, 'Never heed! come in! that makes no difference!' And so I was trundled to the 'George Inn,' where a landlord and waiter, both strangers to me, and looking half-asleep, showed me to the best room on the first floor, a large, old-fashioned, three-windowed room, looking out on the Fore Street, and, without having spoken one word, shut the door on me, and there I was at the end of it! Actually in the 'George Inn,' Haddington, alone, amidst the silence of death!

I sat down quite composedly at a window, and looked up the street towards our old house. It was the same street, the same houses; but so silent, dead petrified! It looked the old place just as I had seen it at Chelsea in my dreams, only more dream-like! Having exhausted that outlook, I rang my bell, and told the silent landlord to bring tea and take order about my bedroom. The tea swallowed down, I notified my wish to view 'the old church there,' and the keeper of the keys was immediately fetched me. In my part of Stranger in search of the Picturesque, I let myself be shown the way which I knew every inch of, shown 'the school-house' where myself had been Dux, 'the play-ground,' 'the boolin' green,' and so on to the church gate; which, so soon as my guide had unlocked for me, I told him he might wait, that I needed him no further.

The churchyard had become very full of graves; within the ruin were two new smartly got-up tombs. His[1] looked old, old; was surrounded by nettles: the inscription all over moss, except two lines which had been quite recently cleared—by whom? Who had been there before me, still caring for his tomb after twenty-nine years? The old ruin knew, and could not tell me. That place felt the very centre of eternal silence—silence and sadness world without end! When I returned, the sexton, or whatever he was, asked, 'Would I not walk through the church?' I said 'Yes,' and he led the way, but without playing the cicerone any more: he had become pretty sure there was no need. Our pew looked to have never been new-lined since we occupied it; the green cloth was become all but white from age! I looked at it in the dim twilight till I almost fancied I saw my beautiful mother in her old corner, and myself, a bright-looking girl, in the other! It was time to 'come out of that!' Meaning to return to the churchyard next morning, to clear the moss from the inscription, I asked my conductor where he lived —with his key. 'Next door to the house that was Dr. Welsh's' he answered, with a sharp glance at my face; then added gently, 'Excuse me, ma'm, for mentioning that, but the minute I set eyes on ye at the "George," I jaloosed it was her we all looked after whenever she went up or down.' 'You won't tell of me?' I said, crying, like a child caught stealing apples; and gave him half-a-crown to keep my secret, and open the gate for me at eight next morning. Then, turning up the waterside by myself, I made the circuit of the Haugh, Dodds's Gardens and Babbie's Butts, the customary evening walk in my teens; and except that it was perfectly solitary (in the whole round I met just two little children walking hand in hand, like the Babes of the Wood) the whole thing looked

---

[1] Her father's.

exactly as I left it twenty-three years back; the very puddles made
by the last rain I felt to have stepped over before. But where were
all the living beings one used to meet? What could have come to
the place to strike it so dead? I have been since answered—the
railway had come to it, and ruined it. At all rates 'it must have
taken a great deal to make a place so dull as that!' Leaving the
lanes, I now went boldly through the streets, the thick black veil,
put on for the occasion, thrown back; I was getting confident that
I might have ridden like the Lady Godiva through Haddington,
with impunity, so far as recognition went. I looked through the
sparred door of our old coach-house, which seemed to be vacant;
the house itself I left over till morning, when its occupants should
be asleep. Passing a cooper's shop, which I had once had the run
of, I stept in and bought two little quaighs; then in the character
of travelling Englishwoman, suddenly seized with an unaccountable
passion for wooden dishes, I questioned the cooper as to the past
and present of his town. He was the very man for me, being
ready to talk the tongue small in his head about his town's-folks—
men, women, and children of them. He told me, amongst other
interesting things, 'Doctor Welsh's death was the sorest loss ever
came to the place,' that myself 'went away into England and—died
there!' adding a handsome enough tribute to my memory. 'Yes!
Miss Welsh! he remembered her famously, used to think her the
tastiest young lady in the whole place; but she was very—not just
to call proud—very reserved in her company.' In leaving this man
I felt more than ever like my own ghost; if I had been walking
after my death and burial, there could not, I think, have been any
material difference in my speculations.

My next visit was to the front gate of Sunny Bank, where I stood
some minutes, looking up at the beautifully quiet house; not unlike
the 'outcast Peri' done into prose. How would my old godmother
and the others have looked, I wondered, had they known who was
there so near them? I longed to go in and kiss them once more,
but positively dared not; I felt that their demonstrations of affection would break me down into a torrent of tears, which there was
no time for; so I contented myself with kissing the gate (?) and
returned to my inn, it being now near dark. Surely it was the
silentest inn on the planet! not a living being, male or female, to
be seen in it except when I rang my bell, and then the landlord or
waiter (both old men) did my bidding promptly and silently, and
vanished again into space. On my re-entrance I rang for candles,

and for a glass of sherry and hot water; my feet had been wetted amongst the long grass of the churchyard, and I felt to be taking cold; so I made myself negus as an antidote, and they say I am not a practical woman! Then it struck me I would write to Mr. Carlyle one more letter from the old place, after so much come and gone. Accordingly I wrote till the town clock (the first familiar voice I had heard) struck eleven, then twelve, and, near one, I wrote the Irish address on my letter and finally put myself to bed —in the 'George Inn' of Haddington, good God! I thought it too strange and mournful a position for ever falling asleep in; nevertheless I slept in the first instance, for I was 'a-weary, a-weary,' body and soul of me! But, alas! the only noise I was to hear in Haddington 'transpired' exactly at the wrong moment; before I had slept one hour I was awoke by—an explosion of cats! The rest of that night I spent betwixt sleeping and waking, in nightmare efforts to 'sort up my thoughts.' At half after five I put my clothes on, and began the business of the day by destroying in a moment of enthusiasm—for silence—the long letter 'all about feelings' which I had written the night before. Soon after six I was haunting our old house, while the present occupants still slept. I found the garden door locked, and iron stanchions—my heavens!— on the porch and cellar windows, 'significative of much!' For the rest, there was a general need of paint and whitewash; in fact, the whole premises had a bedimmed, melancholy look as of having 'seen better days.'

It was difficult for me to realise to myself that the people inside were only asleep, and not dead—dead since many years. Ah! one breathed freer in the churchyard, with the bright morning sunshine streaming down on it, than near that (so-called) habitation of the living! I went straight from one to the other. The gate was still locked, for I was an hour before my time; so I made a dash at the wall, some seven feet high I should think, and dropt safe on the inside—a feat I should never have imagined to try in my actual phase, not even with a mad bull at my heels, if I had not trained myself to it at a more elastic age. Godefroi Cavaignac's ' *Quoi donc, je ne suis pas mort!*' crossed my mind; but I had none of that feeling—*moi*—was *morte* enough I knew, whatever face I might put on it; only, what one has well learnt one never forgets.

When I had scraped the moss out of the inscription as well as I could with the only thing in my dressing case at all suited to the purpose, namely *his own* button-hook with the mother-of-pearl handle, I made a deliberate survey of the whole churchyard; and most of the names I had missed out of the sign-boards turned up for me once more on the tombstones. It was strange the feeling of almost glad recognition that came over me, in finding so many familiar figures out of my childhood and youth all gathered together in one place; but, still more interesting for me than these later graves were two that I remembered to have wept little innocent tears over before I had a conception what real weeping meant—the grave of the little girl who was burnt to death, through drying her white muslin frock at the fire, and that of the young officer (Rutherford) who was shot in a duel. The oval tablet of white marble over the little girl's grave looked as bright and spotless as on the first day—as emblematic of the child existence it commemorated; it seemed to my somewhat excited imagination that the youthfulness and innocence there buried had impregnated the marble to keep it snow-white for ever!

When the sexton came at eight to let me in, he found me ready to be let out. 'How in the world had I got in!' 'Over the wall!' 'No! surely I couldn't mean that?' 'Why not?' 'Lord's sake then,' cried the man in real admiration, 'there is no end to you!' He told me at parting, 'There is one man in this town, me'm, you might like to see, James Robertson, your father's old servant.' Our own old Jamie! he was waiter at 'The Star.'—Good gracious!—had returned to Haddington within the last year. 'Yes, indeed,' I said, 'he must be sent to me at "The George" an hour hence, and told only that a lady wanted him.'

It was still but eight o'clock, so I should have time to look at Sunny Bank from the back gate, and streamed off in that direction; but passing my dear old school-house, I observed the door a littl̇ ajar, walked in and sat down in my old seat, to the manifest astonishment of a decent woman who was sweeping the floor. *Ach Gott!* our maps and geometrical figures had given place to texts from Scripture, and the foolishest half-penny pictures! It was become an Infant School! and a Miss Alexander was now teacher where Edward Irving and James Brown had taught. Miss A—— and her infants were not, it seemed, early risers, their school-room after eight o'clock was only being swept: it was at seven of the morning that James Brown found me asleep there, after two hours' hard study, asleep betwixt the leaves of the Great Atlas, like a keep lesson! but, 'things have been all going to the devil ever since the Reform Bill'—as my uncle is always telling us. The woman interrupted her sweeping to inform me amongst other things that it was 'a most terrible place for dust,' that 'a deal was put into bairns now, which she *dooted* was *waste wark*,' that 'it was little one got by cleaning after them,' and 'if her husband had his legs, they might have the school that liked.' Not the vestige of a boy or even of a girl was to be seen about the Grammar School either. That school, I afterwards heard from Jamie, 'had gone to just per-fect nonsense.' 'There was a master (one White), but no scholars.' 'How is that?' I asked; 'are there no children here any longer?' 'Why, it's not altogether the want o' children,' said Jamie with his queer old *smudge* of inarticulate fun; 'but the new master is rather severe—broke the jawbone of a wee boy, they tell me; but indeed the whole place is sore gone down.' I should think so! But I am not got to Jamie yet, another meeting came off before that one.

Sunny Bank looked even lovelier 'in the light of a new morning' than it had done in the evening dusk. A hedge of red roses in full blow extended now from the house to the gate; and I thought I might go in and gather one without evoking any—beast. Once in-side the gate, I passed easily to the idea of proceeding as far as the back-door, just to ask the servant how they all were, and leave compliments without naming myself; the servants only would be astir so early. Well! when I had knocked at the door with my finger, 'sharp but mannerly,' it was opened by a tidy maid-servant, exhibiting no more surprise than if I had been the baker's boy!

Strange, was it not, that anybody should be in a calm state of mind, while I was so full of emotions? Strange that the universe should pursue its own course without reference to my presence in Haddington! 'Are your ladies quite well?' I asked nevertheless. 'Miss Jess and Miss Catherine are quite well; Miss Donaldson rather complaining. You are aware, me'm, that Mr. Donaldson is dead.' 'Oh, dear, yes!' I said, thinking she meant Alexander. 'At what hour do your ladies get up?' 'They are up, me'm, and done breakfast. Will you walk round to the front door?' Good-ness gracious! should I 'walk round' or not? My own nerves had got braced somewhat by the morning air; but their nerves!—how would the sight of me thus 'promiscuously' operate on them? 'You had better go round and let me tell the ladies,' put in the ser-vant, as if in reply to my cogitations; 'what name shall I say?' 'None; I think perhaps my name would startle them more than my-self;—tell them some one they will be glad to see.' And so, flinging the responsibility on Providence, who is made for being fallen back

upon in such dilemmas (Providence must have meant me to see
them in raising them out of bed so betimes!), I did 'go round,' with
my heart thumping, 'like, like, like anything.' The maid-servant
met me at the front door, and conducted me to the drawing-room;
where was—nobody, but on a table lay a piece of black bordered
note-paper which explained to me that it was Mr. Donaldson of
London who was dead—the last brother—dead in these very days!
I wish I had not come in, but it was out of time now. The door
opened and showed me Miss Catherine changed into an old woman,
and showed Miss Catherine me changed into one of—a certain age!
She remained at the door, motionless, speechless, and I couldn't
rise off my chair—at least I didn't; but when I saw her eyes staring, 'like watch faces,' I said, 'Oh, Miss Catherine, don't be
frightened at me!'—and then she quite shrieked 'Jeannie! Jeannie!
Jeannie Welsh! my Jeannie! my Jeannie!' Oh, mercy! I shan't
forget that scene in a hurry. I got her in my arms and kissed her
into wits again; and then we both cried a little—naturally; both of
us had had enough since we last met to cry for. I explained to her
'how I was situated,' as Mr. C. would say, and that I was meaning
to visit them after, like a Christian; and she found it all 'most
wisely done, done like my own self.' Humph! poor Miss Catherine! it's little she knows of my own self, and perhaps the less the
better! She told me about their brother's death, which had been
sudden at the last. Supposing me still in London as usual, and
that in London we hear of one another's deaths, they had been saying it was strange I did not write to them, and my godmother
had remarked, 'It is not like her!' just while I was standing at
their gate most likely, for it was 'the evening before, about dark,'
they had been speaking of me.

But again the door opened and showed Miss Jess. *Ach!* she had
to be told who I was, and pretty loudly too; but when she did take
in the immense fact, oh, my! if she didn't 'show feeling enough'
(her own favourite expression of old). Poor Jess after all! We
used to think she showed even more feeling than she felt, and nothing came out on the present emergence to alter our opinion of her.
But enough—the very old, it seems to me, should be admitted by
favour to the privilege of the Dead—have 'no ill' spoken of them
that can possibly be helped.

My 'godmother' was keeping her bed 'with rheumatism' and
grief. As I 'would really come back soon,' it was settled to leave
her quiet. They offered me breakfast, it was still on the table, but

I.—12

'horrible was the thought' to me. It was all so solemn and doleful there that I should have heard every morsel going down
my throat! besides, I was engaged to breakfast with myself at the
'George.' So, with blessings for many days, I slipt away from
them like a knotless thread.

My friend the cooper, espying me from his doorway on the road
back, planted himself firmly in my path; 'if I would just compliment him with my name he would be *terribly* obliged; we had been
uncommon comfortable together, and he must know what they
called me!' I told him, and he neither died on the spot nor went
mad; he looked pleased, and asked how many children I had had.
'None,' I told him. 'None?' in a tone of astonishment verging
on horror. 'None at all? then what on earth had I been doing all
this time?' 'Amusing myself,' I told him. He ran after me to
beg I would give him a call on my return (I had spoken of returning) 'as he might be making something, belike, to send south with
me, something small and of a fancy sort, liker myself than them I
had bought.'

Breakfast stood ready for me at the inn, and was discussed in
five minutes. Then I wrote a note to Mr. C., a compromise betwixt 'all about feelings' and 'the new silent system of the prisons.
Then I went to my bedroom to pack up. The chambermaid came
to say a gentleman was asking for me. 'For me?' 'Yes; he
asked for the lady stopping here' (no influx of company at the
'George' it seemed). 'Did you see him?' I asked, divining
Jamie; 'are you sure it is a *gentleman?*' 'I am sure of his being
put on like one.' I flew down to my parlour and there was Jamie
sure enough, Jamie to the life! and I threw my arms round his
neck—that did I. He stood quite passive and quite pale, with
great tears rolling down; it was minutes before he spoke, and then
he said only, low under his breath, 'Mrs.—Carlyle!' So nice he
looked, and hardly a day older, and really as like 'a gentleman' as
some lords; he had dressed himself in his Sunday clothes for the
occasion, and they were capital good ones. 'And you knew me,
Jamie, at first sight?' I asked. 'Toot! we knew ye afore we seed
ye.' 'Then you were told it was me?' 'No; they told us just we
was to speak to a lady at the "George," and I knew it was Mrs.
Carlyle.' 'But how could you tell, dear Jamie?' 'Hoots! who
else could it be?' Dear, funniest of created Jamies! While he
was ostler at the 'Black Bull,' Edinburgh, 'one of them what-ye-
call bagmen furgotted his patterns' at Haddington, and he (Jamie)

was 'sent to take them up; and falling in talk with him at the "Star," it came out there was no waiter, and so in that way,' said Jamie, 'we came back to the old place.' He told me all sorts of particulars 'more profitable to the soul of man' than anything I should have got out of Mr. Charteris in three years, never to say 'three weeks.' But 'a waggon came in atween ten and eleven, and he must be stepping west.' 'He was glad to have seen me looking so' (dropping his voice) 'stootish.' [I saw him from the omnibus, after unloading the waggon, in his workday clothes almost on the very spot where, for a dozen years, he had helped me in and out of our carriage.]

And now there only remained to pay my bill and await the omnibus. I have that bill of 6s. 6d. in my writing-case, and shall keep it all my days; not only as an eloquent memorial of human change, like grass from graves and all that sort of thing, but as the first inn-bill I ever in my life contracted and paid on my own basis. Another long look from the 'George Inn' window, and then into the shabby little omnibus again, where the faces of a lady next me and a gentleman opposite me tormented my memory without result.

In the railway carriage which I selected an old gentleman had taken his seat, and I recognised him at once as Mr. Lea, the same who made the little obelisk which hangs in my bedroom at Chelsea. He had grown old like a golden pippin, merely *crined*,[1] with the bloom upon him. I laid my hand on his arm, turning away my face, and said: 'Thank God here is one person I feel no difficulty about!' 'I don't know you,' he said, in his old blunt way; 'who are you?' 'Guess!' 'Was it you who got over the churchyard wall this morning? I saw a stranger lady climb the wall, and I said to myself, that's Jeannie Welsh! no other woman would climb the wall instead of going in at the gate. Are you Jeannie Welsh?' I owned the soft impeachment; then such shaking of hands, embracing even! But so soon as things had calmed down a little between us, Mr. Lea laid his hand on my shoulder and said, as if pursuing knowledge under difficulties, 'Now tell me, my dear, why did you get over the wall instead of just asking for the key?' He spoke of William Ainsley's death; I said I had never known him, that he went to India before I could remember. 'Nonsense,' said Mr. Lea; 'not remember William Ainsley? Never knew William Ainsley? What are you thinking of? Why, didn't he wrap

---

[1] *I.e.* shrunk.

you in a shawl and run away with you to our house the very day
you were born, I believe?' I said it might be very true, but that
the circumstance had escaped my recollection. Mr. Lea was left at
Longniddry, where he came daily, he said, to bathe in the sea.
What energy!

While waiting there for the train from London, I saw again my
lady and gentleman of the omnibus, and got their names from Mr.
Lea. They were not people I had ever visited with, but I had
been at school with them both. We passed and repassed one another without the slightest sign of recognition on their side.
George Cunningham, too, was pacing the Longniddry platform, the
boy of our school who never got into trouble, and never helped
others out of it—a slow, bullet-headed boy, who said his lessons
like an eight-day clock, and never looked young; now, on the
wrong side of forty, it might be doubted if he would ever look old.
He came up to me and shook hands, and asked me by name how I
did, exactly as though we met on 'change every day of our lives.
To be sure I had seen him once since we were at school together,
had met him at Craik's some twelve years ago. Such as he was,
we stood together till the train came up, and 'talked of geography,
politics, and nature.'

At Edinburgh Jeannie's[1] sweet little face looked wildly into the
carriage for me, and next minute we were chirping and twittering
together on the platform, whilst the eternal two boxes, writing-
case, and carpet-bag were being once more brought into one focus.
'Look, look, cousin!' said Jeannie, 'there are people who know
you!' And looking as I was bid, who but the pair who had accompanied me from Haddington, with their heads laid together,
and the eyes starting out of them me-ward. The lady, the instant
she saw I noticed them, sprang forward extending her hand; the
husband, 'emboldened by her excellent example,' did the same;
they were 'surprised,' 'delighted,' everything that could be wished;
'had not had a conception of its being me till they saw me smiling.' 'Eh, sirs!' said my mother's old nurse to her after a separation of twenty years, 'there's no a featur o' ye left but just the bit
smile!'

I will call for these Richardsons when I go back to Haddington:
I like their hop-step-and-jump over ceremony, their oblivion in the
enthusiasm of the moment that we had 'belonged to different circles' (Haddington speaking).

---

[1] Cousin from Liverpool (now Mrs. Chrystal).

And now having brought myself to Edinburgh, and under the little protecting wing of Jeannie, I bid myself adieu and 'wave my lily hand.' I was back into the present! and it is only in connection with the past that I can get up a sentiment for myself. The present Mrs. Carlyle is—what shall I say?—detestable, upon my honor.'

Auchtertool Manse: Aug. 2.

LETTER 114.

Sunny Bank (now Tenterfield) is the Donaldsons' residence, a pleasant, most tranquil house and garden in the suburbs of Haddington—to her always a quasi-maternal house. Glen Truin (pronounced Troon) is Lord Ashburton's deer-hunting station in Macpherson of Cluny's country, rented, twice over I think, at the easy rate of 1,000l. a season—intrinsic value, perhaps, from 50l. to 25l. Thither I had passed from Scotsbrig; saw my darling at Linlathen for a day or two in passing (she ill oft, I ditto—much out of sorts both of us); had there, too, a miserable enough hugger-mugger time. My own blame; none others' so much—saw that always.— T. C.

To T. Carlyle, at Glen Truin House.

Sunny Bank, Haddington: Sept. 5, 1849.

It looks a month since we parted at Dundee! I have had so much of both motional and 'emotional culture' since that evening. *Goot look* did not follow me into the Orient[2] by any means. A headache followed me, and stuck by me till the Monday that I left Kirkcaldy; of heartache I will not speak; but there is no reason why I should be silent on the misfortune I happened one hour after my return to Fergus-dom; *that* might have happened to any-one, however little of an egoist. I had lain down on the black coffin-like sofa in my bedroom to try what rest, such as could be had under the circumstances, would do for my head, when I felt something like a blue-bottle creep inside my hand; shook it off, and, oh, my! the next instant I was on foot like 'a mad'—stung by a wasp! Miss Jessie got the sting out, and admired it through her glass, and applied, on my own advice, laudanum and honey; but the pain went up to my shoulder and down to my side, and the swelling and inflammation spread so fast all up my arm, that Miss

---

[1] A Mazzini locution.

[2] *Supra*, Haddington is east. Mrs. Carlyle had returned thither to stay with the Donaldsons.

Jessie could hardly be hindered from running herself for both a doctor and a silversmith; the last to cut a ring that could not be got off; but it was my mother's little pebble ring, and I would not suffer it to be cut, and neither would I be at the cost of a doctor just yet. All that evening I suffered horribly, in silence, and all night 'the trophies of the wasp would not let me sleep,' not one wink. However, I went next day to Auchtertool with my hand in a poultice, being still determined to 'come out of that' on Monday, and unwilling to go without saying farewell to my poor uncle, whom it is likely enough I shall never see again.

On Sunday night the pain was sufficiently abated to let me sleep. So I was up to leaving, according to programme, by the quarter-after-eight train. John and Jessie were up to give me breakfast, and see me off, and Mrs. Nixon gave me a nice little trunk to facilitate my packing. They were really very kind, the poor Ferguses; but somehow or other they are radically uncomfortable people for us to be mixed up with, in spite of their 'good intentions.'

I got to the Princes Street station a little before ten, and found on inquiry that I could have my luggage taken care of for me on paying the sum of sixpence for booking; so I left there everything but my writing-case, in which were my jewels and your manuscript; and with that I got into a cab, having bargained with the cabman for two shillings an hour (I tell you these details for your own guidance in case of your returning by Edinburgh), and drove to Adam Street to Betty.[1]

Of all the meetings I have had in Scotland, that was the most moving, as well as the happiest; was just all but a meeting betwixt mother and child after twenty years' separation. She was on her knees blackleading her grate, all in confusion, poor soul! her little carpet up, everything topsy-turvy, a domestic earthquake having been commenced that very morning in preparation for my coming, Miss Anne having kindly warned her that she might be 'all ready;' but I was too early, and so found her all unready, only her heart as right as could be. Oh, dear me! how she does love me, that woman, and how good and pious-hearted she is! While I sat on her knee, with my arms about her neck, and she called me her 'dear bairn,' and looked at me as if she would have made me welcome to her 'skin,' I felt, as nearly as possible, perfectly happy—

---

[1] The old Haddington servant—almost from my Jeannie's birth—is still living (1869), one of the venerablest and most faithful of women. I never saw such perfection of attachment, and doubt if it exists elsewhere.—T. C.

just fancy that! But I must not get into the details of my visit to her just now; my few days here are so filled up, I have not yet seen half the people I wish to see. She gave me four biscuits wrapt in her best pocket-handkerchief, and promised to see me at my aunt's before I left in the evening; and then I jumped into my cab again, and proceeded to Clarence Street.[1]

A kind note, received at Kirkcaldy from Elizabeth, had prepared me for a rather warmer welcome than I had anticipated, but not for so warm a one as I got; it was a great comfort to me to be so received by my father's sisters, however unlike him. My heart was opened by their kindness to tell them that it was nothing but apprehension of their bothering me about my soul which had estranged me from them so entirely. Anne's reply, given with an arch look and tone, was very nice, ' Indeed, Jeannie, you need not have been afraid of our setting ourselves to reform you; it is plain enough that nothing short of God's own grace can do that, but I won't despair that a time may come, though I am not such a fool as to think that I can hasten it.' Anne went out with me, and we called for Mrs. George[2]—not at home; at the Stoddarts'—the lady in the country, John petrified-looking, either hardened into stone, or quite stunned at seeing me, I could not tell which. On our way to Mrs. Sterling's[3] we met her, and she flew into my arms in the open street, just as she would have done before writing ' Fanny Hervey.' I walked into Marshall the jeweller's, who knew me at once; and a Mrs. Watson, who met me on the bridge, shouted out Jeannie Welsh! But I will tell you all the rest afterwards.

Miss Catherine was waiting for me with a carriage at the Haddington station, told me there was a letter from you here for me, but it proved only the briefest of notes from John. Yours, however, came yesterday forenoon, just when I was sallying out to make calls. I was through all our house yesterday, from garret to kitchen; everybody is so good to me, so very good! Miss Howden brought me a bouquet ' out of your own garden' last night, and Helen Howden has just sent me her children to look at, and you wrote me a nice long letter—so I ought to be thankful. I go back to 10 Clarence Street on Thursday (to-morrow night), and stay with my aunts till Saturday, when I shall go to Scotsbrig. I have written to John.   J. W. C.

No more room; margin itself half full.—T. C.

---

[1] To her aunts, Elizabeth, Ann, and Grace Welsh.
[2] Widow of George Welsh.   [3] Susan Hunter.

LETTER 115.

To T. Carlyle, Scotsbrig.

Maryland Street, Liverpool: Friday, Sept. 14, 1849.

Oh, my dear, my dear! How thankful I may be that I knew nothing of that colic [1] till it was over! A colic in these cholera-times would have alarmed me in any circumstances; but there—remembering, as I still do, 'rather exquisitely,' my own sore throat transacted at Alverstoke three winters ago, and other little attacks of my own, under the same *régime*—how could I have stayed in my skin, with no certainty that you would be able to get so much as a cup of bad tea, never to speak of hot water to your feet, or human sympathy? You were not, it would seem, so wholly left to Providence as I was; still it is a great mercy that you were not long laid up in that house, or any other of their houses. As my aunt Grace told me very often during my bad day: 'There is mercy mixed up with all our afflictions! It is a great comfort to think you are in better hands than ours—I mean in Jesus Christ's.' 'Oh, ay!' said dear Betty, 'Christ has care of my bairn a'wheres, even on the railway! And a great comfort that is for me to think, now that she gangs sae muckle be them!' But of all that, some quiet evening at Chelsea.

I have to tell you now that a note from Elizabeth, lying for me here, stated that she continued better, but not strong yet, and that her sister was still with her, and would stay till I came—a great luck that this sister happened to be out of a place just now. I fancy the poor girl had been in a very dangerous way before we heard of her illness.

Now that I know of this sister being with her, I feel in less breathless haste to fly to her rescue—can yield to Jeannie's wish, which is indeed an obligation of duty on me, with a good grace, that I would stay here over Sunday, to give her my advice about Helen; she (Jeannie) being to arrive from Auchtertool to-morrow night, to look after poor Helen, who has been very ill indeed, and I am afraid has a disease on her that may end fatally, sooner than any of them are aware. I was dreadfully shocked with her shape, and emaciated look; still she can go out for exercise, and protests

---

[1] Got by a too violent excursion to Glen—large miscellaneous party. Lord Ashburton and I rode over stock and stone on Highland ponies.

that she is getting better, but there is death in her face. We wish John to examine into her case; but she is extremely nervous about him, and it must be gone about delicately when Jeannie comes. I am glad dear John came with me.

When I have talked with Jeannie I can be of no further use here, only a trouble in fact; so, on Monday, I mean to go to Manchester, to make amends to Geraldine for the vexation about me, caused by that foolish Harriet Martineau;[1] and to London straight, next day. That is my present programme; if it receive any modification I will write again to Scotsbrig, where I hope this will find you safe and slept. If you get as nice porridge, and nice coffee, and nice everything, with such a seasoning of human kindness, as I got there, you will need no more pity.

John went out with Betsy[2] last night, there being no bed for him here, unless he had chosen to sleep in a little one in my room, which I told him he was welcome to do, if he liked!! But he declined. He promised to come to-day about one, and stay till night. And to-morrow Betsy is to bring the carriage, and take me to Seaforth for a few hours, just to satisfy her that I have not 'registered a vow in Heaven' never to set my foot in her house again. But a few hours will be enough of that. She looks to be more than ever in a state of 'mild delirium.'

And now I must end and go to Helen. Kindest love to your mother and all of them. And tell Isabella I forgot the woodriff; and she must stuff some into your carpet-bag.

If you write on Sunday or Monday, in time for Tuesday morning, address to Geraldine's. You remember Carlton Terrace, Green Heys, Manchester.

Ever affectionately yours,

JANE W. C.

LETTER 116.

To Mrs. Carlyle, Scotsbrig.

5 Cheyne Row: Sunday, Oct. 1849.

My dear Mrs. Carlyle,—If John is not there to talk to you, how you will be needing more than ever to be written to. And I should be very ungrateful for all your affection and kindness if I did not contribute my mite, especially as you are the only person that ever complimented me on my handwriting!

---

[1] Gossip of some kind.   [2] Mrs. Paulet.

The settling down at home after all those wanderings has been a serious piece of work for both Mr. C. and myself; for me, I have only managed it by a large consumption of morphia. At last, however, I begin to sleep, if not like a Christian yet, at least less like a heathen. Mr. C. is at his work again, and my maid is at her work again; and the supernumerary sister is gone away; and now that the house should go on in its old routine there is only needed a cat (the last was drowned for unexampled dishonesty during my absence) to eat the regiments of mice, who have effected a settlement in every part of the house, the parlour not excepted, and who threaten to run up one's very petticoats while one is reading one's book! Mr. C., in the midst of talking to me the other evening, suddenly stamped his foot on the hearth-rug and called out furiously 'Get along, sir!' and he had not gone mad, had merely perceived a mouse at his feet!

I am also terribly ill off for curtains, bugs having invaded the premises as well as mice, and all my curtains having been frantically torn down, and sent to the dyers; not so much to have the colour renewed, as to have the bugs boiled to death.

The middle of next week it is promised I shall have my bed set up again; but in the meanwhile I feel like a poor wretch in an hospital, or a beggar's lodging-house, lying without a rag about me to hide my 'sleeping,' or oftenest sleepless, 'beauties' from the universe! What troubles people have in this world in merely protecting themselves from the inferior animals!

For the rest: London is quiet enough for the most retired taste at present, and I like it best so; there are always some 'dandering individuals' dropping in, to prevent one from growing quite savage, and of excitement I had enough in Scotland to serve me for many months to come. I am very glad I have been in Scotland once more, and seen all those places and people; though it was smashing work at the time! I have brought away many recollections that will be a pleasure for me all my life; and my visit to Scotsbrig was the one in which I had most unmixed satisfaction; for, along with my pleasure at Haddington and Edinburgh, there was almost more pain than I could bear. But you were all so kind to me, and then you were little changed. I had seen you all so much more recently, and, in short, in finding so much to please me at Scotsbrig, I miss nothing I had ever possessed there. In the other places it was far otherwise.

I hope you have the same mild weather that has been here the last few days; that your poor face may be quite mended. We shall be very anxious till we hear that you are in your usual state again, and that Jamie is come home well. I am very sorry about Jamie's ill-health; he seems to deserve more than any of us to be strong, leading the natural, hard-working life that he leads, and manifesting at all times such a manly, patient, steadfast mind.

My love to Isabella, who I hope is not gone with him; for she is not strong enough for encountering agitations of that sort.

Hoping to hear soon good news of you all, I remain, dear Mrs. Carlyle, ever yours

Affectionately,

JANE W. CARLYLE.

LETTER 117.

To Mrs. Aitken, Dumfries.

5 Cheyne Row: Oct. 1849.

My dear Jane,—Your letter was one of the letters that one feels a desire to answer the instant one is done reading it—an out-of-the-heart letter that one's own heart (if one happen to have one) jumps to meet. But writing with Mr. C. waiting for his tea was, as you will easily admit, a moral impossibility; and after tea there were certain accursed flannel shirts (oh, the alterations that have been made on them!) to 'piece;' and yesterday, when I made sure of writing you a long letter, I had a headache, and durst not either write or read for fear of having to go to bed with it. To-day I write; but with no leisure, though I have no 'small clothes' to make, nor any disturbance in that line (better for me if I had); still I get into as great bustles occasionally as if I were the mother of a fine boisterous family. Did you hear that I found bugs in my red bed on my return? I who go mad where a bug is! and that bed 'such a harbour for them,' as the upholsterer said. Of course I had it pulled in pieces at once, and the curtains sent to the dyeing—at immense expense—and ever since I have been lying in the cold nights between four tall bare posts, feeling like a patient in a London hospital. To-day at last two men are here putting up my curtains, and making mistakes whenever I stay many minutes away from them; and as soon as their backs are turned I have to go off several miles in an omnibus to see Thackeray, who has been all but dead, and is still confined to his room, and who has written a line to ask me to come and see him. And I have great sympathy always with, and show all the kindness in my power to, sick people—having so much sickness myself, and knowing how much kindness then is gratifying to me.

So you see, dear, it is not the right moment for writing you the letter that is lying in my heart for you. But I could not, under any circumstances, refrain longer from telling you that your letter was very, very welcome; that the tears ran down my face over it—though Mr. C. was sitting opposite, and would have scolded me for 'sentimentality' if he had seen me crying over kind words merely; and that I have read it three times, and carried it in my pocket ever since I got it, though my rule is to burn all letters. Oh, yes; there is no change in me, so far as affection goes, depend upon that. But there are other changes, which give me the look of a very cold and hard woman generally. I durst not let myself talk to you at Scotsbrig, and now that the opportunity is passed I almost wish I had. But I think it not likely, if I live, that I will be long of returning to Scotland. All that true, simple, pious kindness that I found stored up for me there ought to be turned to more account in my life. What have I more precious?

Please burn this letter—I mean don't hand it to the rest; there is a circulation of letters in families that frightens me from writing often; it is so difficult to write a circular to one.

How glad I am to hear such good news of Jamie.[1] I hope to-night's post will tell us he is safe home. John, I fancy from Jeannie's last letter, does not go back with him, but to Auchtertool for a little longer.

Your poor mother and her face—what a bout she must have had! For me, I am really better; though I may say, in passing, that Mr. C.'s 'decidedly stronger' is never to be depended on in any account he gives of me—as, so long as I can stand on my legs, he never notices that anything ails me; and I make a point of never complaining to him unless in case of absolute extremity. But I have, for the last week, been sleeping pretty well, and able to walk again, which I had not been up to since my return.

About the bonnet: send it by any opportunity you find, just as it is; I can trim very nicely myself, and perhaps might not like Miss Montgomery's colour. But I cannot have it for nothing, dear. If Miss G. won't take money, I must find some other way of paying her. God bless you, dear Jane, and all yours. Remember me to

---

[1] Brother Jamie. Been at Edinburgh for a surgical operation with John.

James; and never doubt my affection for yourself, as I shall never doubt yours for me.

Ever,   J. W. C.

LETTER 118.

John Forster, Esq., 58 *Lincoln's Inn Fields.*

Chelsea: Tuesday evening, Nov. 14, 1849.

God's will be done! dear Mr. Foster. If one said otherwise, it would do itself all the same in spite of our teeth; so best to subscribe with a good grace. I have taken 'a heavy cold'—had not five minutes' sleep all night with it, and am just risen after a feverish day in bed. There is no present prospect of my being up to any sort of pleasure to-morrow; and I think with dismay of Mrs. Dickens brought to meet me, and me not forthcoming. So I write at once that you may if you like put the other female off. But for Mrs. Dickens, who may not perhaps feel so perfectly at home 'in Chambers' as you have taught me to feel, I should have waited till the last moment in hope of a miracle being worked in my favour.

Mr. C. of course will be with you as little too late as possible for a man of his habits.

Affectionately yours,
JANE CARLYLE.

There is a novel I might read if I could get it during this period of sneezing and streaming at the eyes, written by a very young girl of the name of Mulock; not Dickens's 'a young lady grow'd.' I can't remember the name of the book; but the authoress's name is Molock or something very like it, and it is published by Chapman. It must be rather curious to see, for I am told by Madame Pepoli the Molock is eighteen, has read 'absolutely no books,' and seen 'nothing whatever of society;' and the book is coming to a second edition—'circulates in families,' and will yield profit.

LETTER 119.

Poor little Nero, the dog, must have come this winter, or 'Fall' (1849)? Railway Guard (from Dilberoglue, Manchester) brought him in one evening late. A little Cuban (Maltese? and otherwise mongrel) shock, mostly white—a most affectionate, lively little dog, otherwise of small merit, and little or no training. Much innocent sport there rose out of him; much quizzical ingenuous preparation of me for admitting of him: 'My dear, it's borne in upon my mind

that I'm to have a dog!' &c., &c., and with such a look and style!
We had many walks together, he and I, for the next ten years; a
great deal of small traffic, poor little animal, so loyal, so loving, so
naïve and true with what of dim intellect he had! Once, perhaps
in his third year here, he came pattering upstairs to my garret;
scratched duly, was let in, and brought me (literally) the *Gift of a*
HORSE (which I had talked of needing)! Brought me, to wit, a
letter hung to his neck, inclosing on a saddler's card the picture of
a horse, and adjoined to it her cheque for 50*l.*—full half of some
poor legacy which had fallen to her! Can I ever forget such a
thing? I was not slave enough to take the money; and got a
horse next year, on the common terms—but all Potosi, and the dig-
gings new and old, had not in them, as I now feel, so rich a gift!
Poor Nero's last good days were with us at Aberdour in 1859.
Twice or thrice I flung him into the sea there, which he didn't at
all like; and in consequence of which he even ceased to follow me
at bathing time, the very strongest measure he could take—or *pretend* to take. For two or three mornings accordingly I had seen
nothing of Nero; but the third or fourth morning, on striking out
to swim a few yards, I heard gradually a kind of swashing behind
me; looking back, it was Nero out on voluntary humble partner-
ship—ready to swim with me to Edinburgh or to the world's end
if I liked! Fife had done his mistress, and still more him, a great
deal of good. But, alas! in Cook's grounds here, within a month
or two a butcher's cart (in *her* very sight) ran over him neck and
lungs; all winter he wheezed and suffered; 'Feb. 1st, 1860,' he
died (prussic acid, and the doctor obliged at last!)—I could not
have believed my grief then and since would have been the twentieth part of what it was—nay, that the want of him would have been
to me other than a riddance. Our last midnight-walk together
(for he insisted on trying to come), Jan. 31, is still painful to my
thought. 'Little dim-white speck, of Life, of Love, Fidelity and
Feeling, girdled by the Darkness as of Night Eternal!' *Her* tears
were passionate and bitter; but repressed themselves as was fit, I
think the first day. Top of the garden, by her direction, Nero was
put under ground; a small stone tablet with date she also got—
which, broken by careless servants, is still there (a little protected
now).

John Forster, Esq., 58 Lincoln's Inn Fields.

Chelsea: Dec. 11, 1849.

My dear Mr. Forster,—I died ten days ago and was buried at Ken-
sal Green; at least you have no certainty to the contrary: what is
the contrary? Do you mean to fulfil that promise of coming in
the evening?

Do you know Alfred's address? if so, forward the inclosed,
please; it is a piece of a letter that may gratify him a little, and,
though no great hand at the 'welfare of others' business, I don't

mind giving a man a little gratification when it can be done at the small cost of one penny.   Your affectionate

JANE CARLYLE.

Oh, Lord! I forgot to tell you I have got a little dog, and Mr. C. has accepted it with an amiability. To be sure, when he comes down gloomy in the morning, or comes in wearied from his walk, the infatuated little beast dances round him on its hind legs as I ought to do and can't; and he feels flattered and surprised by such unwonted capers to his honour and glory.

LETTER 120.

John Forster, Esq., 58 *Lincoln's Inn Fields.*

Chelsea: Dec. 1849.

My dear Mr. Forster,—I hope the newspaper arrived safe! Henry[1] looked so excited when he heard it was consigned to the Post Office, and exclaimed so wildly, 'I would not for five pounds that it were lost! Mr. Forster would be in such a way,' that I quite trembled with apprehension about it all the evening. Mr. C. put it in with his own hand, and out of his own head.

I am still confined to the house in a very shabby condition indeed, and need cheering spectacles (don't I wish I may get 'em?), a sight of you for example. Meanwhile thanks for Mulock's book, which I read with immense interest. It is long since I fell in with a novel of this sort, all about love, and nothing else whatever. It quite reminds one of one's own love's young dream. I like it, and like the poor girl who can still believe, or even 'believe that she believes,' all that. God help her! She will sing to another tune if she go on living and writing for twenty years!

I am desired by the other Forster,[2] the unreal it must be since you are 'the real,' to forward to you his defence of W. Penn, as if anybody out of the family of Friends cared a doit about W. Penn. For me, I could never get up a grain of interest about any Quaker, dead or alive, except 'Tawell'[3] of the apple pips.[4]

All good be with you.

Yours affectionately,
JANE CARLYLE.

---

[1] Mr. Forster's servant.

[2] William Edward (of Bradford), the ex-Quaker, now Her Majesty's Minister, &c. &c.

[3] Murderer.   [4] Advocate's excuse.

LETTER 121.

Mrs. Russell, Thornhill.

5 Cheyne Row, Chelsea: Dec. 31, 1849.

Dearest Mrs. Russell,—To think that I should never have written you one line since the distracted little note I sent you from Nottingham in July last, and so often I have thought of it too! Nay, I actually began a letter one day in October; I had just been writing Drumlanrig Castle, Thornhill, on the back of a letter to Lady Ashburton, who was on a visit there, and had written me out the address as particularly as if I had never heard of Drumlanrig in my life. And it struck me as something quite unnatural that I should be writing Thornhill after any other name than yours; just as when I first wrote to you I found it so very strange and sad to be writing that place after anyone's name but my mother's And so, by way of making amends to nature, I began a second letter, one to you to go by the same post; but some visitor came in, and what does not get done by me at the right moment is apt to miss getting done altogether.

When I wrote from Nottingham I remember I durst not trust myself to tell you anything about me, even if there had been leisure for it. I was in such a nervous state: promised to Mr. C. and to my own mind to go to Scotland, but afraid to make my purpose known lest, after all, I should shirk it at the last moment, as I had done once before; and, even if I got into Scotland, I could not have told you, for my life, what I was going to do there, where I should go or not go. Sometimes, in brave moments, I thought of visiting Thornhill as well as Haddington; and then it seemed all but impossible for me ever to set foot in either place—and if I did I was not sure that I would show myself to any living person of my friends, in either the one place or the other. So I thought it best to say nothing to you of my intentions till I ascertained, by trying, what part of them I could carry out. It was not till I was in the railway for Haddington that I was sure I was really going there. And I did spend a night there in the principal inn, the windows of which looked out on our old house, without anyone suspecting who I was. I arrived at six in the evening, and left at eleven rext day, after having walked over the whole place, and seen everything I wished to see—except the people. I could not have stood their embraces, and tears, and 'all that sort of thing,' without breaking down entirely; so I left that part of the business till the agitation, caused by the sight of the old place, should have subsided, and I could return with my nerves in good order. Which I did for three days, after having been six weeks in Fife and other places, with which I had no associations either sad or gay. It was the same when I went to Annandale; till the last moment I was not sure I could go, and would not have gone but for the pain I was going to give my husband's family by passing them by. Actually when I left Edinburgh for Ecclefechan, I did not know whether the railway went through Thornhill! had not dared to satisfy myself! and at all the stations after I got into Dumfriesshire I kept my eyes shut, This will sound to you like sheer madness; but it was no more than extreme nervousness, which I could not control, and so must be excused for. I stayed only two days at Scotsbrig, and then hurried on to Manchester, where I was detained by severe illness. Another time it will not be so bad, I hope; and I shall behave more like a rational woman. You may believe I got little good of the country, under such circumstances: I returned to London so ill, and continued so ill, so long a time, that I got into the way of doing nothing I could possibly help; and so it happened that, having lightened my conscience of the half-sovereign which a Miss Skinner undertook to convey to you, I postponed writing till —now!

If anniversaries be, in many respects, painful things, they are useful at least in putting orderly people, like me, on settling up their duties as well as their accounts. And so I am busier this week than for months back, bringing up my correspondences, &c., &c. Fortunately I am on foot, and even able to go out a little in the forenoon, though the frost is hard enough. I seem to have got off, this winter, with only three weeks' confinement. For the rest, the pleasantest fact in my life for a good while is, that I have got a beautiful little dog, that I hope I will not make such a fool of myself with, as Mrs. M—— used to make of herself with—what was the object's name? He is not, of course, either so pretty or so clever as Shandy, and if he were I should not think so; but he is 'better than I deserve,' as Coleridge said of his cold tea; and I like him better than I choose to show publicly. The sad part of the business is that I dare not take him out with me without a chain, for fear of the 'dog-stealers,' who are a numerous and active body.

I am sending you, for good luck, a book, which I hope you will get some amusement out of—perhaps the best New Year's gift one can make—a little amusement I mean.   The two bits of things, for Margaret and Mary, you will give them with my kind remembrance, and the Post-Office Order I need not point out the use of.

God bless you, dear Mrs. Russell, with love to your husband and father.

I am ever your affectionate

JANE CARLYLE.

Please tell me how old Mary stands.   When is her money due? I always forget.

LETTER 122.

'Latter-Day Pamphlets' had at last, winter, 1849, resolved themselves into that form; and were to be published by Chapman; Forster, he, and I walking together (I very sad and heavy) towards Chapman's house, which I did not enter, on cold windy Sunday (Chapman with the rough MSS. in his pocket): this I can still recollect; and that my resolution was taken and Chapman's not doubted of—but not the month or day.   Probably after December, on which day Nigger Question (in 'Fraser') had come out with execrative shrieks from several people—J. S. Mill for one; who indeed had personally quite parted from me, a year or two before, I knew not and to this day know not why; nor in fact ever much inquired, since it was his silly pleasure, poor Mill!

First 'Latter-Day' dated 'Feby 1' had come out January 29 and been sent to me at 'The Grange'; where with Robert Lowe and Delane I recollect being for a day or two—and ultimately having a pleasant wise kind of night with Milnes as the one other guest; 'Boreas' the lady's arch designation for me as we talked!   Pamphlet 1st was read by both the Lady A—— and Milnes next day in the railway as we all journeyed up; remarks few or none.   I was to be very busy thenceforth till the chaos of the MSS. was all got spun out into distinct webs—and after that till I tired, which was soon after, essential impulse being spent there.

In this short absence, I have no letter, except this which Nero wrote me, dear little clever dog!   'Columbine' is the black cat, with whom he used to come waltzing in, directly on the dining-room door opening, in the height of joy; like Harlequin and Columbine, as I once heard remarked and did not forget.   'Mrs. Lindsay,' I believe, is a sister of Miss Wynne's.   'Small beings,' Mazzini's name for two roasted larks she would often dine on, especially when by herself!   For smallness, grace, salubrity and ingenuity, I have never seen such human diners.—T. C.

To T. Carlyle, The Grange, Alresford, Hants.

5 Cheyne Row, Chelsea: Tuesday, Jan. 29, 1850.

Dear Master,—I take the liberty to write to you myself (my mistress being out of the way of writing to you she says) that you may know Columbine and I are quite well, and play about as usual. There was no dinner yesterday to speak of; I had for my share only a piece of biscuit that might have been round the world; and if Columbine got anything at all, I didn't see it. I made a grab at one of two 'small beings' on my mistress's plate; she called them heralds of the morn; but my mistress said, 'Don't you wish you may get it?' and boxed my ears. I wasn't taken to walk on account of its being wet. And nobody came, but a man for 'burial rate'; and my mistress gave him a rowing, because she wasn't going to be buried here at all. Columbine and I don't mind where we are buried.

This is a fine day for a run; and I hope I may be taken to see Mohe and Dumm. They are both nice well-bred dogs, and always so glad to see me; and the parrot is great fun, when I spring at her; and Mrs. Lindsay has always such a lot of bones, and doesn't mind Mohe and Dumm and me eating them on the carpet. I like Mrs. Lindsay very much.

Tuesday evening.

Dear Master,—My mistress brought my chain, and said 'come along with me, while it shined, and I could finish after.' But she kept me so long in the London Library, and other places, that I had to miss the post. An old gentleman in the omnibus took such notice of me! He looked at me a long time, and then turned to my mistress, and said 'Sharp, isn't he?' And my mistress was so good as to say, 'Oh yes!' And then the old gentleman said again, 'I knew it! easy to see that!' And he put his hand in his hind-pocket, and took out a whole biscuit, a sweet one, and gave it me in bits. I was quite sorry to part from him, he was such a good judge of dogs. Mr. Greig from Canadagua and his wife left cards while we were out. Columbine said she saw them through the blind, and they seemed nice people.

Wednesday.

I left off, last night, dear master, to be washed. This morning I have seen a note from you, which says you will come to-morrow. Columbine and I are extremely happy to hear it; for then there will be some dinner to come and go on. Being to see you so soon, no more at present from your

Obedient little dog,

NERO.

LETTER 123.

To Mrs. Russell, Thornhill.

5 Cheyne Row, Chelsea: Wednesday, Feb. 27, 1850.

My dear Mrs. Russell,—Perhaps Mr. C. may be in Scotland this coming month; you may have seen by the newspapers that one party of the Aberdeen students want him for their Lord Rector, the others wanting the Duke of Argyll, who will suit the purpose better, I should think. If Mr. C. be elected, he must, in common civility to his admiring boys, go and make them a speech, and come back again. A long journey for so brief a purpose! and at an inconvenient time, when he is bothering with his pamphlets. So he rather wishes the Duke may be the happy man.

The great delight of my life at present is the little dog I think I told you of. It was stolen for a whole day; but escaped back to me on its own four legs. Mr. C. asked while it was a-missing: 'What will you be inclined to give the dog-stealers, for bringing it back to you?' (dog-stealing being a regular trade here); and I answered passionately with a flood of tears 'my whole half-year's allowance!' So you may fancy the fine way I am in. Lady Ashburton has given me the name of Agrippina; the wit of which you would not see unless I told you my dog's name was Nero.

I want you to do something for me, if you can:—I saw at Auch-tertool, a slip of the Templand sweetbriar, that had taken root finely, brought by one of those ladies I saw. If, at the proper time for slipping, you could get me a little bit and send it by post, I should be very grateful. I brought, or rather had sent, from Haddington, a slip of the jessamine that grew over our dining-room window, and another of a Templand rose, which my mother took with her to Sunny Bank; and both are growing to my great satisfaction.

All good be with you, dear Mrs. Russell.

Your ever affectionate

JANE CARLYLE.

LETTER 124.

Is at Addiscombe, on visit for a few days; returned thence, soon, as will be seen. I was too deep in 'Latter-Day Pamphlets' to accompany. 'Poor orphan' was to me abundantly ridiculous, though lost to any stranger. Willie Donaldson and Mrs (usually called Peg) Irrin, crossing Solway sands, with their small cargo of merchandises in their wheezy little equipage, fancy themselves, at one moment, lost utterly; but are not, and are overheard in dialogue: William: ' O Paig, Paig, a misspaint life!' Peg (as if in soliloquy): ' What'll become of the poor orphin at home?'—their only child ' Bett,' a loudhaveril of a lass, against whom this bit of pathos was remembered.

Willie was an Aberdeen man; probably a carpenter before enlisting; had fought at the Bunker Hill business; was now a pensioner, asthmatically making rakes, used to lend his cart, on bonfire-victory occasions (as if in duty bound) to be whirled rapidly from door to door, over the village in peremptory demand of the fuel necessary.—T. C.

To Master Nero, (under cover to) T. Carlyle, Esq., Chelsea.

Addiscombe: Wednesday, March 20, 1850.

My ' poor orphan!' My dear good little dog! How are you? How do they use you? Above all, where did you sleep? Did they put you to bed by yourself in my empty room, or did you ' cuddle in' with your surviving parent? Strange that amidst all my anxieties about you, it should never have struck me with whom were you to sleep; never once, until I was retiring to bed myself without you trotting at my heels! Still, darling, I am glad I did not take you with me. If there had been nothing else in it, the parrot[1] alone was sufficient hindrance; she pops ' all about;' and for certain you would have pulled her head off; and then it would have been ' all over' with you and me. They would have hated us ' intensely!'

The lady for whom I abandoned you—to whom all family ties yield—is pretty well again, so far as I see. She is very kind, and in good spirits; so my absence from you has all the compensation possible. But I shall be glad to receive your affectionate caresses to-morrow. Kiss your father for me.

Ever your loving

AGRIPPINA.

LETTER 125.

Mrs. Aitken, Dumfries.

Chelsea: Sunday, April 1850.

My dear Jane,—The spirit moves me to write you a letter this morning; if I begin with excuses, the impulse will get overlaid by the difficulty of the thing, and stick short in a mere ' good intention;' so here goes ' quite promiscuously.' I have little to tell you

---

[1] Lady A.'s ' green chimera.'

worth even a penny stamp; oneself—at least myself—is a sort of Irish-bog subject in which one is in danger of sinking overhead; common prudence commands therefore to ' keep out of that,' whatever else; and my days do not pass amidst people and things so interesting, in themselves, as to be worth writing about to one safe and sound on the outside of all that, as you are. What good would it do you, for example, to have given the ' most graphic ' description of the great ' flare up ' we had at the Wedgwoods yesterday—where all the notabilities Mrs. W. had ever got a catch at were hauled in ' at one fell swoop,' making a sort of Tower of Babel concern of it; that has left nothing behind for me, ' as one solitary individual,' but a ringing in my ears, and a dull headache! What a tenacity there must be in human nature, that people can go on to the oldest age with that sort of thing! The young ladies in wreaths and white muslins with ' the world all before them where to choose '—a husband—those one can understand delighting in such gatherings; as a young Irish lady told a friend of mine, ' I go wherever I am invited, however much I may dislike the people who ask me; for nobody knows on whose carpet one's lot may be!' But the people who have already taken up their lot and found it (as who does not?) a rather severe piece of work, what they get or expect in such scenes to compensate the cost and fatigue I have no conception. I was sitting beside old Mrs. Fletcher of Edinburgh last night—she is seventy-four, I believe—when old Sir R. Inglis was brought up to her, ' to renew their acquaintance.' ' I dare hardly say,' said Sir Robert, ' how long I believe it to be since I had last the pleasure of meeting you in society.' ' It is just forty-one years,' replied Mrs. Fletcher! and these two old people did not burst into tears or ' go aboot worship' but fell to talking trivialities just like the young ones! Well I shall be dead before I am anything like as old as Mrs. Fletcher, and I shall not wait till I am dead to retire from public life. My beau-ideal of existence this long while has been growing farther and farther from that ' getting on' or rather ' got on' in society which is the aim of so much female aspiration and effort!

I suppose John will be coming back soon now, and that will be one good thing. I have a little dog that I make more fuss about than beseems a sensible woman. The next time I go to Scotland he shall accompany me, and see if he don't ' ingrush himself with the people'! He walks with me, this creature, and sleeps with me, and sits with me—so I am no longer alone any more than you are with your bairns—though the company is different! mine has one advantage however; it needs no sewing for, and then, too, I am troubled with no anxiety about its prospects in life.

An old East Lothian friend turned up for me lately who comes a great deal and makes terrible long stays. The last time I had seen her she was riding away in bridal finery beside her artillery officer husband; I found her now, after thirty years and odd, without teeth, all wrinkled, in weeds for that same husband, whom, however, she had long been separated from. So goes the world! Here is a specimen of a new sort of lady's work—the embroidery is cut out and stiched on—it is done very fast.

With kind regards to James,

Ever your affectionate

J. C.

LETTER 126.

To Mrs. Russell, Thornhill.

5 Cheyne Row, Chelsea: Monday, July 15, 1850.

My dear Mrs. Russell,—I could give myself a good whipping (with a few side strokes to the getters-up of our new Post Office regulations), for having let the 14th pass without any remembrance of me to old Mary. But it is myself who am the chief delinquent; for I might have sent my packet to you any day of the week, who would not have been too puritanical to transmit it to her on the Sunday. I did not think of that, however, till too late, having not yet got familiarised to these new regulations; it was only on Friday that it struck my stupidity, a letter despatched that night would not be delivered any longer on Sunday. Better late than never, anyhow; so I send to-day five shillings for a pair of new shoes to Mary, or anything else you may please to invest it in, and some lace for Margaret to put on a cap.

Two of the roses you sent me are in a promising way, and also the polyanthuses, but the third rose is clean dead, and the sweetbriar too, I fear, is past hope; it did well at first—too well, I suppose—for it hurried itself to put out leaves when it should have been quietly taking root—a procedure not confined to sweet-briars; one sees many human beings go off in the same fashion.

There has been a dreadful racket here this season—worse, I think, than in any London season I ever lived through—it has seemed to me sometimes as if the town must burst into spontaneous combustion. All the people of my acquaintance who come to

London occasionally, have come this year at one time, spoiling the pleasure I should have had in seeing them individually by presenting themselves all in a rush—in fact, our house, for two months back, has been like an inn, only 'no money taken,' and I feel like a landlady after an election week. And the balls and parties all round one, to certain of which I have had to go, for the sake of what is called 'keeping up one's acquaintance,' have been enough to churn one into a sort of human 'trifle.' Peel's death came like a black cloud over this scene of so-called 'gaieties,' for a few days but only for a few days. Nothing leaves a long impression here. People dare not let themselves think or feel in this centre of frivolity and folly; they would go mad if they did, and universally commit suicide; for to 'take a thocht and mend' is far from their intention.

I don't know what is to be done next, now that the town is emptying, and my husband in the act of finishing his last pamphlet. I suppose he will go away somewhere, but where or when will not be known till the day before he does it. My old Helen (now gone to the dogs) used to beg pathetically that she might be 'told in time to wash all his shirts,' but he couldn't tell what he didn't know himself till the eleventh hour. Probably he will be in Annandale wherever else; for myself, I have an arden tand wholesome desire to get my house cleaned, under my own eyes this year, for doesn't it need it! Besides, I had such a fagging about last year that I feel no need of stirring at all, and London is always pleasantest to me when it is what is called 'empty.' For my health, it is rather better than last year—not much, but I make it do.

All good be with you and yours, dear Mrs. Russell.

Ever your affectionate

JANE CARLYLE.

LETTER 127.

'Latter-Day Pamphlets' finished and safe behind me, I go for Wales, to Redwood, 'last day of July' it would seem, on which evening, till near noon of next day, I was Walter Savage Landor's guest, much taken with the gigantesque, explosive, but essentially chivalrous and almost heroic old man. In his poor lodging, 3 Rivers Street, Bath, and his reception and treatment of me there, I found something which I could call 'ducal' or higher than if he had been a duke, and still palatial. To Bristol, to Cardiff, to good solitary Redwood's country cottage next day. There for perhaps a month—solitary and silent.—T. C.

To T. Carlyle, Cowbridge.

Sunday night, Aug. 4, 1850.

' Oh dear me!' It looks already a month since you went away, counting by the number of things I have pulled to pieces, and the weary hours I have lain awake, and the lonely thoughts that have persecuted me. But to lie awake at nights, and to have lonely thoughts by night and by day is surely nothing new or strange for me, that I should think it worth recording at this date! And for the work, it will not be irksome, but ' a good joy,' such good joy as I am still susceptible of—when it gets into the stage of restoring to order. The house has, in fact, been rushing down towards chaos during the last year ; a certain smoothing of the surface kept up; and underneath, dirt and confusion really too bad. But it is in the way of getting itself rehabilitated now; and I shall try in time coming to be a better housewife at least; that career being always open to talent. I remember, when I was very ill of a sore throat at Craigenputtock, thinking that, if I died, all my drawers would be found in the most perfect order; and there was more satisfaction in the thought than you (a man) can conceive. Curious to think how all would have gone, if I had died then! But you will like better some news than ' bottomless speculations of that sort.'

Well, till Thursday night I had no speech with any mortal; then, about eight o'clock, walked in Mrs. N——,[1] of all undesired people! My first feeling was that I was intruded upon by ' an improper female;' but as the interview proceeded, her calm self-approving manner, and radiant face—radiant as with conscious virtue (!) really—quite subjugated me, and I began to fancy it must be 'all right' for her, though looking so very shocking to me. N—— came to take her home; in tearing spirits. He theatrically kissed the tips of my fingers when I shook hands with him, and then kissed Mrs. N—— on the mouth! and said, 'Well, darling! how did you get here?' A more comfortable well-doing-like pair one could not wish to see!

On Friday night Count Reichenbach came, a shade less silent and woebegone. Then Masson. I am going to take Count Reichenbach to Mrs. Austin's with me, if she permit—will write to-morrow to propose the thing for Wednesday or Thursday (to give myself a

---

[1] G—— N.'s wife. Once a very pretty little woman, but now getting stranded on a most miserable shore! Thanks to ——, &c. &c. Faugh!—T. C.

I.—13

day's recreation from my earthquakery). I am sorry for the man, he looks so lost.

To-day (being Sunday) I told Elizabeth to take herself off for the whole day if she chose, that I might have no proposals to 'go out' during the week, when I intend that she shall work. Most likely no one would come, I thought; and if anyone did, I would simply not open the door. I was standing with hands all over whiting, having just made a brilliant job of the curtain rods, when there came a rap and ring—no reply; I held Nero's nose that he might not bark; again a rap, very loud; then, after a long pause, both together as loud as could be. Decidedly the individual would get in. I kept quite still; 'surely it is over now,' I was just saying when the knocking and ringing recommenced, and went on at intervals for, I am sure, ten minutes! I could hardly help screaming, it made me so nervous. At last all was quiet; and, some quarter of an hour after the uproar, I went to look in the letter-box if the horrid visitor had left a card. When I looked in, I met, oh mercy, a pair of fox-eyes peering at me through the slit. I threw the door open in a rage (my hands had been washed by this time); and a coarse-featured red-haired squat woman exclaimed; 'She will com now, please no to shut; Mees S—— com.' 'What is it?' I asked sharply. 'Oh she sit in so small house at corner! I run! keep open! no shoot!' And off she went; and in three minutes brought back Miss J—— S——.[1] I felt ready to strangle her in the first moment; but she looked so pale and grave, like the widow of Chopin, and was so friendly, and unconscious, to all appearance, of my dislike to her, that I behaved quite amiably after all. She had asked at Chalmers' door if we were all gone; and the manservant said you were gone, that Elizabeth had told him you were to go first to Bath, then to Scotland, then to the Black Sea!! And at the stick-shop at the corner the woman assured her 'I always came home at five to my dinner' (it was then half after four); so she had meant to wait, and sent her maid to keep watch!

A letter for you, from Chorley,[2] not read by me for the world! And an invitation from that barenecked hooing gawk Stewart ——. I might have sent word you were away; but he deserves to be left for speculating, for his impudence—sitting in Sloane Street,

---

[1] A hoarse-voiced, restless, invalid Scotch lady, of some rank, mostly wandering about on the Continent, entertaining lions, and Piano Chopin, &c. &c., but always swooping down upon London and us now and then.

[2] Come back from Spain, I suppose.

and summoning you to him to be presented to his grand-lady wife, as he thinks her; a 'rum' lady that could marry the like of him!

For me a note from Emily Baring, an invitation; very kind; but necessarily answered in the negative. It is too long and expensive a journey for a few days; and in my present complication I could not be absent longer than two or three days. Besides, Geraldine is still hanging in the wind.

Miss W—— likes 'Jesuitism' best of all the pamphlets; so does Masson—'such an admirable summing up;' just what I said. Your mother's copy was sent on Thursday.

Took morphine last night, and slept some. A letter this morning from Mrs. Macready, two little sheets all crossed! inviting me to Lyme Regis. Nero desires his respectful regards.

Ever affectionately yours,

JANE.

LETTER 128.

To T. Carlyle, Cowbridge, Glamorganshire.

Chelsea: Thursday night, Aug. 22, 1850.

Now, dear! I have done a fair day's work (of sewing chiefly), and can sit down with a certain leisure to write you a peaceable little letter. Yes, yes; I have 'composed myself,' am 'quiet.' You shall have no more wail or splutter from me on this occasion. If I had been an able-bodied woman instead of a thoroughly broken-down one, I should surely have had sense and reticence enough not to fret you, in your seclusion, with details of my household 'worry.' But that dreadful Elizabeth [1] 'murdered sleep;' I 'lost my *happetite*,' and became so weak and excited that I was really no more responsible for what I wrote than a person in a brain fever would have been. For the last three nights I have been getting into sleep again without morphia, which had become worse than useless; and for the last three days I have eaten some dinner 'to speak of,' and now I begin to feel sane again, and, as John says, 'to see my way.'

Geraldine left me last night, very unwillingly. A little pressing would have made her throw over Letty [2] altogether, and remain here for an indefinite time. It was not my wish, however, that

---

[1] A servant who had given trouble.

[2] Letty ——, an intrusive, stupid, ugly, fat Berlin Jewess, coursing about on the strength of sending windy gossip to the newspapers then.

she should protract her stay longer than she had already done; the pleasure of having her to talk with, and to rub my feet, was not—at least would not have continued to be—a sufficient compensation for the additional trouble of a visitor in the house, with no servant but a little girl who had 'never been out before,' who could not cook a morsel of food or make a bed, or do any civilised thing, without having me at her heels. One does not like, if one can stand on one's legs at all, to see one's visitor doing servant's work; and besides poor Geraldine can't cook or make a bed any more than the girl who has 'never been out;' and at the same time she is nothing like so indifferent as I am to eating, and 'all that sort of thing.' And then to get on with 'the rowans,' and her here, was impossible. When I was not cooking in the kitchen, or in some way providing for the present moment, I must 'lie down' and have my feet rubbed. By myself I get on quite nicely with the little maid, who, now that I have got her to tidy herself, and that she is no longer frightened, has developed a curious likeness to your sister Jane, which makes me feel quite friendly towards her. Not being to keep her, I put off no time in training her, but use her up to the best advantage. To-day, for example, she has been cleaning out the kitchen, closets, and presses, where many an abomination came to light, showing new cause why the 'no-interference' principle should never more get 'carried out' in this house, or any house of which I am the mistress. To-morrow, or next day, I shall probably hear from Miss Darby something final as to the Essex girl she had in view for me. I feel it very kind of you to offer to take me away, but I am perfectly clear that I should be here rather than anywhere else just now. In the first place, locking up the house would be a foolish risk to run; there are more loose people about here now than when we did so formerly, and we are known now to be better worth robbing than we were formerly thought to be; and even then it was 'a tempting of Providence only to be repeated on necessity. I should like very ill to have the house robbed; there are so many odds and ends in it that no money could replace. Secondly, not foreseeing (how could I?) that I was to be left sole agent of my own will and pleasure, I commenced in the first week of your absence a series of operations, which I feel my housewife honour concerned in bringing, without help or with such help as I can get, to a more or less satisfactory close; what I have tumbled up and pulled down must be restored to at least the habitable state I found it in, and no Brownie, I guess, would do that for me if I put the house-key in my pocket and went away. Thirdly (a woman has always three reasons), flying from the present inconvenience would be only postponing it; a servant must be found and set a-going in ' the right way ' some time; and when better than now, when you are out of the road of being bothered by the initiatory process? Would it be preferable to arrive at home, hungry and travel-wearied, with our door-key, to usher ourselves into a dark, cold, foodless house, and go out the first thing next day to hunt up a servant? If Craik's woman could have been engaged for any particular time, that would have met the last objection. But my belief is that they will take her to Ireland and keep her there as long as she will stay. At all events, I can elicit no particle of certainty about her; and indeed, feel it indelicate to press them on the subject. So now, ' compose yourself,' and trouble your heart no further with my ' difficulties.' When I am not too ill for stirring about, as I have not been to-day, and do not mean to be for some time to come, and when you are not there to be put about by them, I make as light of material difficulties as any woman I know; find them, in fact, rather inspiring; it was entirely the moral disturbance from Elizabeth that agitated me so absurdly at the commencement of the present mess.

Friday morning.—So far I had written last night when the clock struck twelve, and Nero, with his usual good sense, insisted on my going to bed; he had gone half an hour before by himself, and established himself under the bedclothes; but he returned at twelve and jumped till I rose and followed him.

I have hardly anything to tell you of the outer world. Mazzini is back from Paris, was here on Tuesday. The revolution in Paris is postponed for the moment. It was anticipated that the President's reception ' would have been, through—what shall I say?—bribery and so on, more enthusiastic ' ; then the President would have been emboldened to venture his great *coup*, and the Communist party would then have tried conclusions with him. As it is, these ' have nothing to fight against,' which is surely very sad. Another concert [1] had come off the night before, in which, at the hour of commencement, not a performer had arrived, nor for half an hour after. Then all the gas went suddenly out; then 'a very fat—what shall I say?—drunk woman fell on Mazzini's neck and almost stifled him, upon my honour.' Then the principal singer did not come at all, and had

---

[1] In aid of some Mazzini fund, no doubt.

to be brought *par vive force* 'in a state of horrible drunkenness,' and was only sobered by Mazzini's taking his hand and 'appealing to his patriotism.' Then Mario and Grisi arrived for the last act without their music. My late difficulties dwindled into insignificance beside those of Mazzini with that tremendous concert—'but there will be much money.'

Anthony Sterling came up on Wednesday, and took Geraldine to the railway at night, I not feeling at all up to taking her myself. Next morning he was to start for Devonshire to have a week's yachting with Mr. Trelawny.

Count Reichenbach started for Belgium the end of last week, as mournful-looking as he came. I have seen no one else lately except Mrs. and Miss Farrar, who called on Tuesday, I think; the old lady in a state for having her patriotism appealed to (it struck me), and the young one very pale, 'needing some outing,' she said, and was to start on a yachting expedition this day. I never thanked you, I verily believe, for the heather, or the peacock's feather, but they were carefully preserved nevertheless.

I think they must have an empty room at Maryland Street just now, Helen being still in Scotland.

Affectionately yours,
J. C.

I am sure the *Nation*[1] miscarried through no fault of mine. After the fate of the former week's *Leader*, I was very careful to put up the paper firmly, and it was posted in Chelsea on Monday.

LETTER 129.

To T. Carlyle, Cowbridge, S. Wales.

Chelsea: Friday, Aug. 23, 1850.

My dear, my dear, my dear!—I sent a long letter off yesterday, knowing that for the next few days I should have something like the sack of Troy on my hands. The sweeps are here, and the whitewashers, and the carpet-beaters! and myself is at this moment all over breadcrumbs, from cleaning the parlour paper, and—and —and—. Even Nero has the consideration to leave off jumping for things, and has retired into 'a place by himself.'[2]

---

[1] Newspaper (Irish).
[2] Misanthropic joiner in Dumfries, whom we had heard of.

And now 'comes to pass,'[1] a poor son of Adam[2] in want of a bathing-cap 'by return of post,' and none nearer than Albemarle Street will please him! Well, I will go after the cap, his hair being so long; but for writing, it cannot be asked of me under the present distracting circumstances. Only a word of thanks for your long letter. Don't mind length, at least only write longly about yourself. The cocks that awake you; everything of that sort is very interesting. I hasten over the cleverest descriptions of extraneous people and things, to find something 'all about' yourself 'all to myself.' But I must not dawdle.

Your affectionate
JANE CARLYLE.

LETTER 130.

Left Wales, intending Gloucester, Liverpool, Scotsbrig. Never saw the good Redwood again. He died within a year. I still remember him with grateful affection—the thoroughly honest soul. First station (poor Redwood's and railway's blame) had to waste four hours in reading, on the grass. Chepstow; Gloucester streets on a Saturday night. George Johnston (Ecclefechan schoolmaster), unsuccessful visit rather. Break off for Birmingham—Sunday night. To Liverpool next day—Ohe!—T. C.

To T. Carlyle, Scotsbrig,

5 Cheyne Row: Friday, Aug. 30, 1850.

My poor dear!—That was the worst journey, 'but one,' I ever read of. You can perhaps guess the exception. One good thing will come of it, I hope; and that is a certain sympathy with Quashee! You will be more disposed henceforth to grant to your black brother the compensation of unlimited pumpkins! Such is indeed the only benefit that I, 'as one solitary individual,' ever get from being made excessively miserable in any particular way; it develops a new sympathy in me for another class of human sufferers. In all other respects, I should say that being made excessively miserable is not for one's soul's good at all, but the reverse. Natures strong and good to begin with (that is, the exceptional natures), may be 'made perfect through suffering.' When one can digest it, I daresay it goes to fibre; but where the moral digestion is unhappily weak, the more miserable one is, the more one grows —'what shall I say?—bad, upon my honour!'

---

[1] Mazzini's sweep! (*supra*). [2] Carlyle himself.—J. A. F.

But you would rather be told, is the new maid come? Yes. She arrived yesterday unexpectedly early. Eliza, the young person, who has been 'doing for me,' intended to have her kitchen seductively clean for the stranger, and had just tumbled everything up, and swashed the floor with fresh water, when her successor came to hand, with plenty of nice trunks; and we had to shut her up in the spare room with some sewing (one of her accomplishments is 'needlework'), until she could find a dry place below for the sole of her foot! 'With the best intentions,' &c.! I will venture no opinion of her on such short observation, further than that she looks, though rather youthful, perfectly 'respectable,' and that her manners are distinguished! so self-possessed, and soft-voiced, and calm, as only English people can be!

The second volume of Dr. Chalmers is come, very bulky, this one weighs an ounce over the two pounds, or I would have sent it at once by post to your mother, who, I think, got the first volume. There is also come a novel, called 'Alton Locke,' which I flung aside in my worry, as not readable; but now I hear from Geraldine, whom the 'Athenæum' has invited to review it, that it is the novel of young Kingsley; and, though 'too like Carlyle,' a production of astounding merit; so I shall fall on it some evening.

For the rest, I have nothing to tell, except 'goot look' has not returned to me yet from 'the Orient;' I surely never had such a run of provoking things 'since I kent the worl!' but it will 'come all to the same ultimately,' one does hope.

From the Wednesday night, when Geraldine went off with Anthony Sterling, I had no speech with any one till Sunday, then I made a call at Miss Wynne's; no one had been here; and for me, I *cerco nessuno*. Then, again, I was silent till Tuesday evening; when Craik came, and insisted on playing at chess with me. I beat him three games in no time, and he went away heavy and displeased. The only person since was Anthony Sterling, yesterday, rather bored by his yachting expedition. His wife was to return to Knightsbridge last night, and he intended to take her to Headley; where Mrs. Prior is coming or come, on a visit of indefinite duration. The Irish business is going on towards a law-suit, perhaps the best for Anthony that could come of it. The possession of more money will only add to his troubles; but going to law for his rights will be an excitement for him, as good as any other.

Kindest regards to them all at Scotsbrig.

Ever affectionately yours,

JANE CARLYLE.

LETTER 131.

'For virtue ever is its own reward.' So had a young tragic poet written, but his critical friend objected, argued, &c.; upon which the poor poet undertook to make the line—'For virtue,' &c., 'unless something very particular occur to prevent it.'—John Mill's story.

'And he buried her *beautiful*, ma'am,' said a certain housemaid to her once. 'Cockney idea of a future state.'—Allan Cunningham.

'If so obscure a person,' &c.—Lady Waldegrave, of herself.—T. C.

To T. Carlyle, Esq., Scotsbrig.

Chelsea: Monday night, Sept. 2, 1850.

Yes indeed, dear, a letter from you on Saturday night would have been more to my purpose than the lot of newspapers, which I never look at except for 'a bird's-eye' glance at the leader, just to see how the creatures 'get through it,' and more to my purpose than even the new 'Copperfield,' which came at the same rush, and which to this hour remains uncut; the former one having given me no feeling but remorse for wasting mortal time on such arrant nonsense. But on Saturday night there came no letter: both your letters arrived together this morning, puzzling me extremely which of them to open first. It is much to be wished that one had a post that knew what it was doing again; and law-makers that knew what they were doing. If I were the Government, I should feel rather ashamed of making regulations one month and unmaking them the next; but 'folk maun do something for the bits of bairns' (as Adam Bogue[1] said when reproached with ruining himself in racehorses).

Before you receive this I hope your mother will have got the volume of 'Chalmers.' I found on inquiring of the postmaster in Piccadilly, when I posted my last letter, on my way to the library, that books of any weight could be sent by post, at the rate of sixpence to the pound; so I despatched the bulky concern to-day, with nine blue stamps, and all the newspapers at the same time, deferring the writing of my own letters to the evening, partly because I thought you had literature enough by one post, and partly because 'I felt it my duty' to go and ride all the forenoon in an

---

[1] A Haddington farmer.

13*

omnibus, instead of aggravating the sickness I was feeling by writing or indoors work.

On my return I learnt from Emma that 'a gentleman in a carriage with two servants' had been here—names are a thing she does not at all meddle with— but a 'Pendennis' on the table told me that Darwin had returned, the first of the Romans! Yesterday I had Elizabeth Pepoli for three hours. I wondered at the length of her visit, and wondered at the softness of her manner; to-day the whole thing is explained; it was our last meeting! I asked her, 'When are you going?' and she answered, 'Soon, but don't let us speak of that.' 'Well,' I said at parting, 'I shall go to you on Tuesday or Wednesday.' To-night is come a note saying, 'Don't come here, dear Jane, for you will not find me!' Alas! what a way to part! a saving of emotion certainly to both; but should we never meet again, as is most likely, some farewell words would have been a comfort for the survivor to recall.

Pepoli is in depths of tribulation at present, through 'something very particular' having occurred to prevent his virtue (in the case of old Manfredi) being 'its own reward.' (Is it not always through the virtue on which one piques oneself that one gets over the fingers in this life?) He would take a painter into his house, 'regardless of expense,' and of the comfort of his wife; and having played out that freak of princely generosity without justice, and old Manfredi being 'eventually' dead, and 'buried beautiful,' the Manfredi relations in Bologna ('if so obscure a person can be said to have relations') institute a prosecution against Pepoli, for having dishonestly appropriated, and made away with, immensely valuable pictures belonging to the old man he pretended to protect! ('The female Satyrs suckling their young' was the best of these pictures, Elizabeth says, and was sold for ten shillings to keep Manfredi in brown sugar which he licked.) The idea of figuring as a swindler in his native town has taken possession of Pepoli's whole soul, and caused the cholera; but the worst result is, that it has decided him to return to Bologna instead of settling in Ancona, where Elizabeth anticipated fewer disgusts. John Fergus is 'better, but far from well yet.'

What a dismal story is that of the Curries! Poor old man! he will surely die soon; the best that could be wished for him!

Passing along Paradise Row the other day, I found two mutes standing with their horrid black bags at Maynard's, the butcher's, door. There was a hearse too, with plenty of plumes, and many black coaches, and all the people of the street seemed turned out to look. 'Is old Mrs. Maynard dead?' I asked the omnibus conductor, surprised; for I had seen the long son at our door in the morning as usual, and had heard of no death in the family. 'Oh, no, not the old lady, it is the son George!' the handsome young man that has latterly come for orders with the cart. On the Thursday he had come and I shook my head at the window, and he touched his hat and drove on. That same day he had 'three fits,' which left him delirious; on Sunday he died, and there, on the day week that I had seen him, was he getting himself buried! His brother tells me that although he 'would work to the last,' it was 'a happy release;' that for years he had been suffering horrors from disease of the liver, but he wouldn't give in, for he was as fine a lad as ever breathed, the tall butcher said, with a quivering mouth. Just think! going round asking all the people what they wanted for dinner, and return home to die!

I think the new servant will do; she looks *douce,* intelligent, well-conditioned. Very like Lancaster Jane (if you remember her), with a dash of Ann and of Phœbie Baillie! She is not what is called 'a thorough servant,' but that will be no objection to signify, as I am not 'a thorough lady,' which Grace Macdonald defined to be one 'who had not entered her own kitchen for seven years.' I must say, however, that, so far as I have seen her yet, I have not discovered wherein she falls short of the servants who give themselves out for 'thorough.' Yet she is only twenty, and for the last two and a half years has been acting as nursemaid! However she may turn out, I am certainly under great obligations to Geraldine's old Miss Darby, for having hunted up this girl and taken much trouble to 'suit me,' in a situation that was really very desolate, my state of weakness at the time considered. But all is going on decently now again.

And so, good night, for it is time I were in bed. Love to your mother and the rest.

Ever yours affectionately,
Jane W. Carlyle.

Pray do not go ahead in milk diet too impetuously 'In every inordinate cup the ingredient is a devil'—even in an inordinate cup of innocent milk.

LETTER 132.

To T. Carlyle, Esq., Scotsbrig.

5 Cheyne Row, Chelsea: Wednesday, Sept. 18, 1850.

[1] 'If the buttons be here on Wednesday they will be in abundant time.' I should think they would! and 'don't you wish you may get them?' Why, how on earth could I have them there on Wednesday, unless, indeed, I had immediately last night, after reading your letter and swallowing my tea, dashed off in an omnibus to Regent Street, by dark; and then, having bought perhaps yellow buttons for drab ones, posted them before my return to Chelsea? One is capable of such acts of devotion to save 'a man's life, or even his watch!' But merely to expedite his buttons? hardly!

I shall go now, however, when I have written a bit; for I am able to go out again without risk. The town seemed to come momentarily alive yesterday, like a blue-bottle on an unseasonable winter's day. I was just finishing the nailing down of the library carpet—'Still that to do,' you think, 'after nearly two months of earthquaking?' Yes; and it could not have been got done sooner, under the circumstances, by the exemplary Martha Tidy herself!

> Ah, that is the mystery
> Of this wonderful history.
> And you wish that you could tell.

I have a fine misadventure about the library also to reveal to you; but that and my other various misadventures shall form a Chelsean night's entertainment, when sufficiently remote to be laughed over. So I decided some weeks ago, when I saw the part your ungrateful 'Destinies' had taken against me, that it would be better to keep my squalid difficulties to myself till I could 'take a bird's-eye view'[2] of them in the past tense, and work them up, at my ease, into a conversational 'work of art.' But I was going to say that just as I was finishing the above-mentioned job, I was surprised by the rare sound of a knock and ring, and a brisk little voice asking, 'Is your mistress within?' Emma came up with much awe in her face, and said, 'It is the Bishop of something, I don't know what.' Actually * * * * again! He had been brought up, not at his

---

[1] So Carlyle had written from Scotsbrig.—J. A. F.
[2] Phrase of old McDiarmid's, of Dumfries.

own expense, to bear witness that he had married a couple who want to be divorced, and deny having been properly married ever. 'It was a love runaway sort of match.' After an hour and half, he went his way and I returned to my carpet. In five minutes I was called down again to 'two gentlemen and a lady.' 'Don't you know their names?' 'No; but there is a coachman and a footman, and the lady is very stout.' Bunsen, Madame Bunsen, and a young German doctor. The lady was formal as usual; but Bunsen was really charming. He praised much the pamphlets; 'already saw them doing much good;' especially he delighted in 'Jesuitism'! 'Oh! his definition of Jesuitism is capital, so good, so good!' By the by, nobody that I have ever asked about it understands Bunsen recalled.

After these came my cousin John to early tea, his second visit since he was settled at Kew, three weeks ago. And, lateish, Craik, who improves in sententiousness and that universal forgiveness which springs from universal understanding. A luck I didn't wait for his maid. He now 'thinks of keeping her three months;' and she thinks of 'a little shop after.'

If I don't be off I shall be belated. Nero bids me give his kind regards, and wishes you had seen him this morning when he came to breakfast, with hair on his face all dyed bright crimson! I thought he must have done it himself to improve his looks; till I recollected that he was sent down last night to have his face washed; he had been rubbing it dry, I suppose, after his fashion, on a piece of red cloth that was lying under the table; but the effect was startling. Love to your mother and all.

Your affectionate

J. C.

LETTER 133.

Carlyle was about to return from Scotland. Mrs. Carlyle was going on a visit to the Grange.—J. A. F.

To T. Carlyle, Scotsbrig.

5 Cheyne Row: Monday, Sept. 23, 1850.

Alas, dear! I am very sorry for you. You, as well as I, are 'too vivid;' to you, as well as to me, has a skin been given much too thin for the rough purposes of human life. They could not make ball-gloves of our skins, dear, never to dream of breeches.[1] But it

---

[1] *French Revolution*, Tannery of Meudon.

is to be hoped you will feel some benefit from all this knocking about when it is over and you are settled at home, such as it is. It does not help to raise my spirits, for my own adventure, that you are likely to arrive here in my absence. You may be better without me, so far as my company goes. I make myself no illusion on that head; my company, I know, is generally worse than none; and you cannot suffer more from the fact than I do from the consciousness of it. God knows how gladly I would be sweet-tempered and cheerful-hearted, and all that sort of thing for your single sake, if my temper were not soured and my heart saddened, beyond my own power to mend them.

But you would certainly be the better for me to stand between you and this new servant, who has as little idea of going on without 'interference' as Elizabeth of going on with it. She is very willing, however, and 'not without sense;' only you must give your orders in simple unfigurative speech, and one after another. If you were to tell her, in the same breath, three things to be done, she would fly at them all at one time, and spin round on her heel simply. For living, you must confine yourself to broiled chops, or fowl quartered, one quarter boiled in soup, another broiled. Mutton broth is beyond her; and in roasting, she is far from strong. We are getting very plausible potatoes, and she boils these pretty well.

I did not find Miss Wynne on Saturday. She had been 'poorly' at Dropmore, and was not expected till Thursday; so I shall not see her at all.

I was too late for Miss Farrar after; so I went to her yesterday. Miss Farrar could not go on Wednesday after all; 'her brother was coming to town on Thursday, and she would not for the whole world go away without having seen him.' The old mother had just told John and me, before Miss —— came into the room, that she was 'detained on account of the means not being procurable before Friday!' I intended to go on Wednesday all the same before getting the inclosed this morning from Lady A.[1]

I have 'the means,' thank God, though Mrs. Farrar and her daughter did ask Mrs. White if we didn't live dreadfully poorly! I have had no money from Chapman, however. He has not come nor sent, and my house-money is utterly done, and no mistake. But then I flatter myself I have a good many things to show for it.

---

[1] Insisting on the old day. Note still extant. 'Lady William Russell and her two sons,' &c. &c.

All my little accounts are settled, except one, which I leave for you, as beyond the limits of my savings; and if you do not approve the outlay, I have a heart above slavery, and will pay it myself out of my next twelvemonth's income. But though the house-money is done, my own allowance is not. I have still five pounds—might have had more if I had not chosen to lay out what you repaid me for my ball dress on my own bedroom; a much more satisfactory investment, to my ideas! If I find myself in danger of *bankraiping* I will tell you. So do not plague yourself by sending any money for the present. I have been interrupted in this note by Mac-Diarmid and Colonel Burns. Oh, such a withered up *skite* poor Mac is become.

I am going to be very vexed at having to leave Nero.

Ever your
J. C.

LETTER 134.

To T. Carlyle, Esq., Chelsea.

The Grange: Thursday, Oct. 3, 1850.

I have put a lucifer to my bedroom fire, dear, and sat down to write, but I feel more disposed to lay my head on the table and cry. By this time I suppose you are at home; returned after a two months' absence, arrived off a long journey—and I not there! nobody there but a stranger servant, who will need to be told everything you want of her, and a mercy if she can do it even then. The comfort which offers itself under this last innovation in our life together (for it is the first time in all the twenty years I have lived beside you that you ever arrived at home and I away) is the greatest part of the grievance for my irrational mind. I am not consoled, but 'aggravated' by reflecting that in point of fact you will prefer finding 'perfect solitude' in your own house, and that if I were to do as nature prompts me to do, and start off home by the next train, I should take more from your comfort on one side than I should add to it on another, besides being considered here as beyond measure ridiculous. Certainly, this is the best school that the like of me was ever put to for getting cured of every particle of 'the finer sensibilities.'

Mrs. —— was in London yesterday and saw my maid on business of her own, and brought back word from her that you were coming last night; and the shouts of laughter, and cutting 'wits,' with which my startled look and exclamation, 'Oh, gracious!' were visited when the news was told me as we sat down to dinner, were enough to terrify one from 'showing feeling' for twelve months to come. Mrs. —— shan't snub me, however. I am quite as clever as she any day of the year, and am bound to her by no ties, human or divine. And so I showed her so plainly that I was displeased with her impertinent jesting at my expense that she made me an apology in the course of the evening.

And now what is to be done next? You say, stay where I am, as if you were not—easily said, but not at all easily done. It is quite out of the question my remaining here till the 20th, the day Lady A. has appointed for the term of my visit, doing nothing, and thinking of you at home with that inexperienced girl. Who cares one doit for me here, that I should stay here, when you, who still care a little for me, more any how than any other person living does, are again at home? And what good can 'ornament and grandeur,' and 'wits,' and 'the honour of the thing,' do to my health when 'my heart's in the Highlands, my heart is not here?' Oh dear! certainly not; I shall keep to my original programme, and come home after a fortnight—that will be next Wednesday, when you will have had plenty of time to subside from your jumbling, and will have exhausted all Emma's powers of cooking: unless you are savage enough to wish not to see my face till the 20th, and honest enough to tell me so; or, unless you prefer to accept the invitation, which Lady A. is again writing to you, to come here after you are rested. You would be bored here just at present with ——'s solemn fatherhood, and the much talk and bother about the children. But the ——s depart, sucking-baby and all, on the eighth, and after that I hear of no one coming but Thackeray and Brookfield and Lady Montague. George Bunsen and Colonel Rawlinson are coming, but only for a day or two. Do, dear, 'consult your authentic wish,' whether you will join me here, or have me back there; whichever way of it you like best, I shall like best, upon my honour. The only very good reason for my staying till the twentieth, viz. to be 'another woman in the house,' as Lady A. said, while men visitors are here in Lord A.'s absence, is done away with by the fact of Lady Montague's coming, and Miss Farrar's being to stay till the nineteenth. In going next Wednesday, I shall not put Lady A. about then the least in the world. At the same time you might be better here, perhaps till the twentieth, than in London, as Lady A. says you should have this bedroom, which is quiet enough

—at least, will be—when the —— children have ceased to 'run horses' overhead; and shall have your dinner by yourself at what hour you please.

And so I will now go and try to walk off the headache I have got by—by what do you think?—crying actually. Prosaic as this letter looks, I have not, somehow, been able to 'dry myself up' while writing it. I suppose it is the 'compress' put on me in the drawing-room that makes me bubble up at no allowance when I am alone.　　　　　　　　　　　　　　Ever your

　　　　　　　　　　　　　　　　　　　　　　　J. C.

　　　　　　　　　　　　　　　　　　October 5, 1850.

Thackeray is here—arrived yesterday, greatly to the discomfort of —— evidently, who had 'had the gang all to himself' so long. First he (Thackeray) wrote he was coming. Then Lady A. put him off on account of some Punch-offence to the ——s; then Thackeray wrote an apology to ——! then Lady A. wrote he was to come after all, and went to Winchester to meet him, and —— sulked all yesterday evening, and to-day is solemn to death. In fact he has been making a sort of superior *agapemone* here, in which he was the Mr. Price, the Spirit of Love; and no wonder he dislikes the turn that has been given to things by the arrival of the Spirit of Punch. Col. Rawlinson comes to-morrow, Kinglake with Brookfield on the 15th, and a great clerical dinner to the Bishop of Winchester comes off on Tuesday, so that you will happily escape. Poor dear little Nero! I am so glad he knew you, and showed himself 'capable of a profound sentiment of affection,' in spite of your disbelief.

LETTER 135.

To Mrs. Russell, Thornhill.

　　　　　　　　　　5 Cheyne Row, Chelsea: Dec. 31, 1850.

Don't the years get to gallop so fast, dear Mrs. Russell, that it seems no longer worth while to take note of them? Since last New Year to this one, I seem to have hardly had time enough for one good long sleep! To those, however, whom the winter finds with no money in their pockets to buy fire and food, the new winter may not look so short; I wonder if to old Mary, for example, time seems to fly in this way, with ever-increasing velocity? Do you think she has any satisfaction in her life? If so, what shame to some of us! Poor old soul! as long as the life is in her, I fancy she will like a bit of finery, especially if sent from London; and so the scarlet scarf (!) I send her, however preposterous a present you may think it, won't have been so ill-judged. I wish I were nearer her; I could give her plenty of old warm things, that poor people here hardly thank me for, and pawn generally for drink; but the carriage of such things costs more than they are all worth, and such trifles as can be easily sent by post are not adapted to the wants of a poor old woman. Yet I am sure she likes something coming from myself better than she would like the money to buy a New Year's trifle to herself. So tell her, with my kind regards, to twist this scarf several times round her old throat, and to be sure and not strangle herself with it. There is a ribbon for Margaret—the ugliest, I must say, that I ever set my eyes on; but I sent my maid to buy it, having got a little cold to-day, and this was her notion of the becoming! I must put in a cap border with it to carry it off. The sovereign please to distribute for me according to your discretion.

Things are going on well enough with us for the present. There has been no winter hitherto to give me a chance at getting myself laid up (for my cold to-day is nothing to speak of), and my head-aches have neither been so frequent nor so severe latterly. But I met with a horrid accident some weeks ago—banged my right breast against the end of the sofa, and for three weeks the pain continued, and so, not being able to get the thing forgotten, I was frightened out of my wits for the possible consequences, especially as my brother-in-law wrote from Scotsbrig that I was not to go to any doctor with it, 'London doctors being so unsafe for making a case out of everything, and any meddling with such a thing as this being, in his opinion, positively injurious.' There! what does Dr. Russell say to such views of the medical profession? The pain is quite gone now, however, and I try to think no more about it; but it may be excused to me, all things recollected, that I have suffered a good deal of apprehension from this accident. I have also been bothered to death with servants this autumn—have had three in quick succession. The first new one roasted fowls with the crop and bowels in them! and that mode of cookery was not to our taste. The second, a really clever servant and good girl, came to me with a serious disease upon her, and had to be soon sent to the hospital, where she is still, after two months; the third and last, thank Heaven, suits capitally—but I had best not praise her too much, it is 'a tempting of Providence' to 'cry before one is out of the wood.'

Kindest regards to your father and husband. Tell me about your health, and 'the smallest news will be gratefully received.'

Ever yours affectionately,

JANE CARLYLE.

LETTER 136.

To John Welsh, Esq., Liverpool.

Chelsea: Jan. 2, 1851.

'John! Sole uncle of my house and heart!' I have just one word to say to you to-day, viz. that I'll be hanged if I ever give you anything another time, if you are to go on the William Gibson tack and instantly set about making 'a suitable return.' I thank you heartily for your New Year's gift; but, only, don't do the like of that again, uncle of me! I hope the summer will plump out my poor scraggy arms into a state adapted for such transparent elegancies. And now I must simply promise you a long letter; for to-day is most unfavourable for writing one.

There arrived on us yesterday a young heroine of romance, with a quantity of trunks and a lady's-maid, who is for the moment keeping this poor house and my poor self in a state of utter disgust. I had invited her to dine one day, and, if it suited her better, to stay over the night. And she has so arranged her affairs that, if she leaves here to-day, it must be to live till next week in an hotel (at nineteen). What can one do, then, but let her remain —with protest against the lady's-maid. She is Mrs. ——'s adopted daughter, whom you may have heard of, and has just been playing the Sultana in India for a year and—— Oh dear, here is her lover come to see her, and in a quarter of an hour a prison inspector is coming to take Mr. C. and me through Pentonville Prison. I am bothered to death, my blessed uncle; so adieu. I will write again next week. Your affectionate

JANE CARLYLE.

LETTER 137.

To John Welsh, Esq., Liverpool.

Chelsea: Jan. 7, 1851.

Dear, estimable uncle of me,—Have you been reading Thackeray's 'Pendennis'? If so, you have made acquaintance with Blanche Amory; and when I tell you that my young lady of last week is the original of that portrait, you will give me joy that she, lady's-maid, and infinite baggage, are all gone! Not that the poor little —— is quite such a little devil as Thackeray, who has destested her from a child, has here represented; but the looks, the manners, the wiles, the *larmes*, 'and all that sort of thing,' are a perfect likeness.   The blame, however, is chiefly on those who placed her in a position so false that it required extraordinary virtue not to become false along with it.   She was the only legitimate child of a beautiful young 'improper female,' who was for a number of years ——'s mistress (she had had a husband, a swindler).   His mother took the freak of patronising this mistress, saw the child, and behold it was very pretty and clever.   Poor Mrs. —— had tired of parties, of politics, of most things in heaven and earth; 'a sudden thought struck her,' she would adopt this child; give herself the excitement of making a scandal and braving public opinion, and of educating a flesh and blood girl into the heroine of the three-volume novel, which she had for years been trying to write, but wanted perseverance to elaborate. The child was made the idol of the whole house; her showy education was fitting her more for her own mother's profession than for any honest one; and when she was seventeen, and the novel was just rising into the interest of love affairs, a rich young man having been refused, or rather jilted, by her, Mrs. —— died, her husband and son being already dead; and poor —— was left without any earthly stay, and with only 250*l.* a year to support her in the extravagantly luxurious habits she had been brought up in.

She has a splendid voice, and wished to get trained for the opera.   Mrs. ——'s fine lady friends screamed at the idea, but offered her nothing instead, not even their countenance.   Her two male guardians, to wash their hands of her, resolved to send her to India, and to India she had to go, vowing that if their object was to marry her off, she would disappoint them, and returned 'to prosecute the artist life.'   She produced the most extraordinary *furore* at Calcutta; had offers every week; refused them point-blank; terrified Sir —— by her extravagance; tormented Lady —— by her caprices; 'fell into consumption' for the nonce; was ordered by the doctors back to England! and, to the dismay of her two cowardly guardians, arrived here six months ago *with her health perfectly restored!* But her Indian reputation had preceded her, and the fine ladies who turned their backs on her in her extreme need now invite a girl who has refused Sudar Judges by the dozen.   She has been going about from one house to another, while no home could be found for her. The guardians had a brilliant idea—'would we take her?' 'Not for her weight in gold,' I said; but I asked her to spend a day with me, that I might see what she was grown to, and whether I could do anything in placing her with some proper person. The result of this invitation was that alarming arrival, bag and baggage, on New Year's Day!

She has saved us all further speculation about her, however, by engaging herself to someone (from ——shire) who came home in the ship with her, and seems a most devoted lover. She told me she 'had been hesitating some time betwixt accepting him, or going on the stage, or drowning herself.' I told her her decision was good, as marrying did not preclude either 'going on the stage' at a subsequent period, or 'drowning herself;' whereas had she decided on the drowning, there could have been no more of it.

I have my own notion that she will throw him over yet; meanwhile it was a blessed calm after the fly rolled her away from here on Saturday. 'Oh, my dear!' Mr. Carlyle said, 'we cannot be sufficiently thankful!' Indeed you can have no notion how the whole routine of this quiet house was tumbled heels over head. It had been for these three days and three nights not Jonah in the whale's belly, but the whale in Jonah's belly; that little creature seemed to have absorbed this whole establishment into herself.

There is a long story for you, which perhaps you can't take any interest in; I am sure, however, you would be amused with an account of our visit, the other day, to Pentonville Prison, if I had left myself time and breath to tell it. 'Oh, my!' (as old Helen used to say) 'how expensive!' prisoners costing 50l. a year each! You may fancy their accommodations are somewhat remarkable. In each cell I saw a pretty little corner cupboard, on one shelf of which was the dressing apparatus—a comb and brush, and small tooth comb! —laid on a neatly folded-up towel; a shaving jug with metal top on one side, an artistic soap-box on the other! In one cell I remarked a blue tassel, with a bit of steel chain attached to it, hung upon a brass nail. 'What is the use of that tassel?' I asked the inspector. 'That tassel, ma'am? why that tassel is—a fancy of the prisoner's own; we allow them to have their little fancies!' They all wear masks when in each other's presence, that, should they afterwards meet in society, their feelings may be spared. They have such charming bath-rooms! Each man has a good-sized court all to himself to run about in for an hour at a time; and while we were there they all 'went to school,' with books and slates under their arm, masked! If any man wishes to have the comforts of life, and be taught, and, 'have his fancies,' let him rush out and commit a felony!

We went to hear their religious teaching in the chapel. An under-chaplain stood on the altar with a bible in one hand and a red book (like a butcher's) in the other; he read a passage from the Bible, then looked in the red book for the numbers (they have no names) whose turn it was to be examined. For instance, he read about the young man who came to Jesus, and asked what he should do to be saved? Then after consulting the red book he called out, 'Numbers thirty-two and seventy-eight: What shall I do to enter into eternal life?' Thirty-two and seventy-eight answered, the one in a growl, the other in a squeal, 'Sell all that thou hast and give to the poor.'

Now, my blessed uncle, did you ever hear such nonsense? If a grain of logic was in the heads of thirty-two and seventy-eight, mustn't they have thought, 'Well, what the devil are we taken up, and imprisoned, and called criminals for, but just because we take this injunction seriously, and help you to carry it out, by relieving you of your watches and other sundries.' I should tell you too that each prisoner has a bell in his cell! One man said to some visitor, 'and if I ring my bell a fool answers it.'

Uncle dear, good-night. If you and I were the Government, wouldn't we sweep such confounded humbug out of creation!

                              Ever your affectionate
                                          JANE CARLYLE.

Love to the children.

LETTER 138.

End of July or beginning of August, 1851, we went to Malvern to the water cure, which was then, and perhaps is still, a prevalent delusion among chronic invalids. Dr. Gully, a distinguished professor of the new art, by far the most distinguished then, had pressingly again and again invited us. 'Oh, come, lodge in my house; only come and I will cure you!' Me especially, I suppose, which indeed would have suited well two ways had he succeeded (*vide* Lytton Bulwer's flaming pamphlet, and other noneenses). My own faith in water cure was nearly zero, and has not since risen higher. But I reflected with myself, 'You will have to try it some day (as you had to try that rubbing with hair gloves humbug, though with damage). No humbug can prevail among your acquaintances, but they will force you to get the means of saying, "Oh, I have tried all that and found it naught!"' So lying open for a summer jaunt, and judging humanly well of Gully, we decided to go; stayed with

him, as per bargain, a month: most humanly and hospitably entertained; drank a good deal of excellent water there, and for some
time after tried compressors, sitting baths, packings, &c. Admired
the fine air and country; found by degrees water, taken as a medicine, to be the most destructive drug I had ever tried—and thus
paid my tax to contemporary stupor, and had done with water cure.

I remember vividly enough our rolling off for Worcester; and
except (more indistinctly) our parting somewhere, and my arriving
at Scotsbrig, almost nothing more. My Jeannie (as this letter re-
kindles into light in my memory (had gone for Manchester; I for
Scotsbrig, full of gloom and heaviness, and totally out of health,
bodily and spiritual. Prussian Friedrich, and the Pelion laid on
Ossa of Prussian Dryasdust, lay crushing me with the continual
question, 'Dare I try it? dare I not?'

The portmanteau I do recollect. It had been flung off at Kendal
junction by mistake, and next afternoon arrived safe at Scotsbrig.

Mrs. Gaskell is the novelist, since deceased. Dr. Smith (Angus
Smith), a chemist of merit and man of much *naïveté* and simplicity,
is he who, now in Government pay, goes about investigating foul
atmospheres (mines, factories, cities, slums), and says, 'How foul!'
—T. C.

To Thomas Carlyle, Scotsbrig, Ecclefechan.

2 Birchfield Place, Higher Ardwick, Manchester:
Friday, Sept. 5, 1851.

Well, really! *you* don't 'beat us all for a deep thought.' If you
had lost my address, why not send a letter for me to the care of F.
Jewsbury, Fire Insurance Office, Manchester? or to the care of Mr.
Ireland, or any of the many people in Manchester you are in correspondence with, if you could not risk writing to the care of Miss
Jewsbury, Manchester, which is address enough for practical purposes. Round by Chelsea, at second-hand, was a very 'slow' proceeding—'upon my honour!' Besides, the sight of a letter addressed
to Geraldine, in John's handwriting, was calculated to give me a
serious fright. When we came in late last night from Bowden,
where we had passed the day, and I saw on the table only that letter for her, instead of the one I made sure of for myself, my heart
jumped into my mouth, I assure you; and I tore it open without
asking her leave, and was downright thankful to learn that 'my
brother had merely found his portmanteau missing.' I hope you
have recovered it by this time; it can't be that it is permanently lost?
If it be irrecoverable, however, you must just try to think how
much worse it would have been to have lost a manuscript or me?
that (so far as I am aware) it is but, after all, a question of shirts
and woollen clothes, which may all be replaced with a small expen

diture of money and patience. I shall be very happy, however, to hear that the old portmanteau is safe at Scotsbrig, for ' you are the last man in England' that should, in the course of a kind Providence, be visited with such untoward accidents. As I have by this time quite forgiven you for coming to go through the form of kissing at parting with a lighted cigar in your mouth (!), I am sadly vexed at the idea of all this new botheration for you at the end of your journey; and vexed, too, for your mother and the rest, whose pleasure in your arrival would be spoiled for them by your arriving in a state of worry.

For myself, it seems almost Grahamish, under the circumstances, to tell you that I performed my journey in the most prosperous manner—even to the successful smuggling of Nero. At the Manchester station a porter held out his hands for the basket in which I had him, that I might descend more conveniently; but I said with wonderful calm, ' Thank you—I have something here that I require to be careful of, I will keep it myself,' and the man bowed, and went for my other luggage.

I found Geraldine in a much nicer house—with large high rooms prettily furnished, really as beautiful a house as one could wish to live in; and she is the same kind little hostess as ever. With her old Peggy and a new young girl, she manages to surround me with ' all things most pleasant in life; ' and I don't know where I could be better off for the moment. The first night Dilberoglue and Dr. Smith came to tea; the next, Mrs. Gaskell and her husband, and Ireland, and young Bernays. All yesterday we spent at Bowden, with a Miss Hamilton (who has a history), and to-night we are to drink tea at Dilberoglue's, with the Greek mother and the beautiful daughter Calliope. For the rest, I keep up as much as possible the forms of Malvern life, splash in cold water, and walk before breakfast; though the Manchester atmosphere is so thick that one feels to put it aside with one's nose—oh, so thick, and damp, and dirty! Still the walk does me good. We dine at two, and I resolutely abstain from pills—continuing to wear my compressor. I went in search of one to send on to you, but unsuccessfully as yet; and I have not had leisure to make one, though I am sure I can, if none be procurable at the shops.

I wrote to Miss Gully since I came here, but there has not been time to get an answer. The more I think of these people the more I admire their politeness and kindness to us. I don't remember ever in my life before to have stayed a whole month in anybody's house, without ever once wishing to be away: Geraldine says, 'My dear, it is a fact that speaks volumes.'

I am writing under your image—Geraldine has got your large print, in a pretty gilt frame over the chimney-piece in my bedroom, facing Neukomm; and a little lower between you is—a similar sized print of Jesus Christ.

But what will you be caring for all this that I write if—the portmanteau be still in infinite space. Pray write the state of the case; long letters are a bore to write when one is in retreat, and I don't want you to take any bore on my account; but a short note concerning the portmanteau and your health I cannot dispense with.

Nero sends his dear little love, and bids me say that since you went his digestion has been much neglected, everybody stuffing him with dainties, out of kindness, and no exercise to speak of. He is afraid of ending like the king and queen of the Sandwich Islands.

My kind regards to all at Scotsbrig.

Ever yours faithfully,
JANE CARLYLE.

LETTER 139.

To Mrs. Russell, Thornhill.

The Grange, Hants: Monday, Dec. 1851.

My dear Mrs. Russell,—I must appeal to your well-known kindness to help me out of a little puzzle. I left home on a visit to Lord Ashburton's some four or five weeks ago, intending to go back on the day after Christmas; but some people were to be here this week, strangers to Lady A., and known to me, and I was requested to remain another week to make these young people's visit more agreeable to them. Thus New Year's Day finds me unprepared with any little presents for those whom I wish to remind of me at this season. There is a town (Winchester) eight miles off; but I cannot drive there to procure any things, having caught a bad cold in the first week of my visit, which confined me to the house the first three weeks as a measure of necessity, and I have gone on limiting my exercise since to a walk in the conservatory, and corridors, as a measure of precaution. Cold is so easily retaken, and it is so miserable to be ill in other people's houses. What I must ask of you then is, to be so good as to advance the usual sovereign for me, which I will repay with a Post-Office order immediately on my return, and then you must buy for Margaret and Mary a pair

I.—14

of warm stockings each, or some such thing—half-a-crown each you may lay out for them, and don't say but that I sent the stockings, or whatever it may be, from London. I am sure you will do this for me, without grudging time and trouble.

I hear very often from Liverpool since that serious illness of my uncle's. At present he is pretty well, but his life seems to hang by a mere thread now. Every little agitation, such as 'listening for the guns of the American steamer, bringing a letter from Johnnie!' produces threatenings of the same sort of attack, and another attack will probably be fatal. I wish very much to go and see him once more, and must try to manage it early in the spring. Perhaps I may be in Scotland again next year, and surely you will come and see me somewhere, if I should not be able to find courage to go to Thornhill. A young friend of mine married the Earl of Airlie last autumn, and asks me to visit her at Cortachy Castle; and there is an old gentleman, called 'the Bear' in London society, who has a beautiful place twenty miles beyond Fort Augustus, who has also invited us. And there I should really like to go, to see again the places where I went with my mother, about thirty years ago.

We have had a deal of company here since I came, Macaulay amongst the rest, whom I had never before seen at any length. I used to think my husband the most copious talker, when he liked, that was anywhere to be fallen in with; but Macaulay beats him hollow! in quantity.

You need not take the trouble of writing till after I have returned and sent the money; but then you must write me all about yourself, and about dear old Thornhill.

Kindest regards to your father and husband.

Ever yours, dear Mrs. Russell, affectionately,

JANE W. CARLYLE.

LETTER 140.

This was the year (only first year, alas!) of repairing our house; 'architect' (Helps's) was 'Mr. Morgan,' a very honest man, and with workmen honest though inexpert; he himself had no talent for managing the chaos he created here, and indeed he at length fell sick, and left it to end by collapse. My own little heroine was manager, eye, inventress, commandress, guiding head and soul of everything; and made (witness this drawing-room, and compare it with the original, *i.e.* with every other in the street) a real triumph of what without her would have been a puddle of wasteful failure. She feared no toil howsoever unfit for her, had a marked 'talent in architecture,' too—in fact, the universal talent of applying intellect, veracity, and courage to things gone awry for want of those qualities. My noble darling! few women have had such an outfit of talent, far fewer such a loving nobleness and truth of heart to urge it into action and guide it there. Meanwhile, to escape those horrors of heat and dust, I fled (or indeed was dismissed) to Linlathen, to my excellent T. Erskine's, where I morbidly and painfully stayed three weeks, gentlest and best of hospitality able to do little for me. I remember trying to bathe in the summer mornings—bad bathing coast. Most of my leisure went in translating what is now the Appendix to *Friedrich,* vol. vii. of 2nd edition.—T. C.

Mrs. Russell, Thornhill.

5 Cheyne Row, Chelsea : July 13, 1852.

Dearest Mrs. Russell,—I might be excused for forgetting my own birthday this time, and even my own name and address, and everything about me, except the one terrific fact that I am in a house under what is called 'thorough repair.' Having never had to do with London workmen, you cannot form any adequate idea of the thing. Workmen who spend three-fourths of their time in consulting how the work should be done, and in going out and in after 'beer,' were not, at least in my day, known in Scotland; and then a thorough repair complicated by the altering of chimneys and partitions, and by heat at 82° in the shade, was a wild piece of work with any sort of workmen. The builder promised to have all done in six weeks, painting included; if he get done in six months it is as much as I hope. Meanwhile I run about in the great heat, carrying my furniture in my arms from one room to another, and sleep, or rather lie about, like a dog, just where I see a cleared space. I am needed here to keep the workmen from falling into continual mistakes; but why Mr. Carlyle, who is anything rather than needed, stays on I can't imagine. Nor do I know when I shall get away, nor where I shall go. We were to have gone to Germany, but that is all knocked on the head—at least for the present. If you saw me sitting in the midst of falling bricks and clouds of lime dust, and a noise as of battering-rams, you wouldn't wonder that I should make my letter brief.

The poor little sweetbriar grew through all the east winds, and was flourishing beautifully, when heavy rains came and killed it. I am vexed, and can't help feeling the sweetbriar's unwillingness to grow with me a bad omen somehow. I wonder if you will be good-natured and unwearied enough to send me another slip to try when the right time comes?

And now to the business: will you lay out five shillings for old Mary in some judicious way for me, and will you give my little packet to Margaret, and tell them I still think of them both kindly?

I had a great hope, very vague, but quite probable, that I should have gone to Scotland this summer and seen you somewhere. Now everything is unsettled with the talk about Germany, and the fact of this house-altering.

Ever affectionately yours,
Jane Welsh Carlyle.

LETTER 141.

T. Carlyle, Linlathen, Dundee.

5 Cheyne Row: Friday night, July 24, 1852.

Oh, my! I wonder if I shall hear to-morrow morning, and what I shall hear! Perhaps that somebody drove you wild with snoring, and that you killed him and threw him in the sea! Had the boatman upset the boat on the way back, and drowned little Nero and me, on purpose, I could hardly have taken it ill of them, seeing they ' were but men, of like passions with yourself.' But on the contrary, they behaved most civilly to us, offered to land us at any pier we liked, and said not a word to me about the sixpence, so I gave it to them as a free gift. We came straight home in the steamer, where Nero went immediately to sleep, and I to work.

Miss Wilson called in the afternoon, extremely agreeable; and after tea Ballantyne came, and soon after Kingsley. Ballantyne gave me the ten pounds,[1] and Kingsley told me about his wife—that she was ' the adorablest wife man ever had!' Neither of these men stayed long. I went to bed at eleven, fell asleep at three, and rose at six. The two plumbers were rushing about the kitchen with boiling lead; an additional carpenter was waiting for my directions about ' the cupboard' at the bottom of the kitchen stair. The two usual carpenters were hammering at the floor and windows of the drawing-room. The bricklayer rushed in, in plain clothes, measured the windows for stone sills (?), rushed out again, and came no more that day. After breakfast I fell to clearing out the front bedroom for the bricklayers, removing everything into your room. When I had just finished, a wild-looking stranger, with a paper

---

[1] Borrowed, doubtless.

cap, rushed up the stairs, three steps at a time, and told me he was 'sent by Mr. Morgan to get on with the painting of Mr. Carlyle's bedroom during his absence!' I was so taken by surprise that I did not feel at first to have any choice in the matter, and told him he must wait two hours till all that furniture was taken—somewhere.

Then I came in mind that the window and doors had to be repaired, and a little later that the floor was to be taken up! Being desirous, however, not to refuse the good the gods had provided me, I told the man he might begin to paint in my bedroom; but there also some woodwork was unfinished.

The carpenters thought they could get it ready by next morning. So I next cleared myself a road into your bedroom, and fell to moving all the things of mine up there also. Certainly no lady in London did such a hard day's work. Not a soul came to interrupt me till night, when —— stalked in for half-an-hour, uncommonly dull. 'It must have taken a great deal to make a man so dull as that!' I never went out till ten at night, when I took a turn or two on Battersea Bridge, without having my throat cut.

My attempts at sleeping last night were even more futile than the preceding one. A dog howled repeatedly, near hand, in that awful manner which is understood to prognosticate death, which, together with being ' in a new position,' kept me awake till five. And after six it was impossible to lie, for the plumbers were in the garret and the bricklayers in the front bedroom! Mr. Morgan came after breakfast, and settled to take up the floor in your bedroom at once. So to-day all the things have had to be moved out again down to my bedroom, and the painter put off; and to-night I am to ' pursue sleep under difficulties ' [1] in my own bed again. They got on fast enough with the destructive part. The chimney is down and your floor half off!

After tea I ' cleaned myself,' and walked up to see Miss Farrar. She and her sister were picnicking at Hampton Court; but the old mother was very glad of me, walked half-way back with me, and gave me ice at Gunter's in passing. I am to have a dinner-tea with them next Wednesday. And to-morrow I am to give the last sitting for my picture, [2] and take tea at Mrs. Sketchley's. And now I must go to bed again—more's the pity.

I shall leave this open, in case of a letter from you in the morning.

---

[1] *Pursuit of Knowledge under Difficulties*, &c. (a poor book of that time).
[2] By Miss Sketchley (an amateur trying to become artist).

Saturday.

Thanks God too for some four hours of sleep last night.   I don't mind the uproar a bit now that you are out of it.

Love to Mr. Erskine; tell him to write to me.

Ever yours,   J. W. C.

LETTER 142.

'Dalwig,' grandson of the famed cavalry general of Friedrich the Great, was himself a Prussian officer of horse; from Silesia, where his rank and possessions were ample; as fine, handsome, intelligent, brilliant, and modest a young fellow of his kind as I ever saw.   'Reichenbach' (once Graf von Reichenbach and his neighbour and friend) brought him to us here; where he met Kate Sterling, our late John's second daughter, and one of the brightest of young women.   Dalwig, much struck with her, was evidently deliberating great things; and did, before long, apply formally to Captain Anthony Sterling, uncle and guardian, for the 'great honour and pleasure of making some acquaintance' with Kate.   To both of us, who knew him, it seemed precisely the offer that might suit beyond all, both for the noble Kate and for her friends, especially her sisters ; who were in no society here for making fit matches, but who there, in Silesia, having portions of solid amount, and being all pretty and amiable, need not fail of marrying well if they cared to marry, &c., &c. : to all which we wished cordially well, but kept, and had kept, strictly silent except to one another. Abrupt Captain Anthony, now growing elderly, and very abrupt and perverse, was not slow in answering, as if to 'a beggarly foreigner,' his emphatic No !   To which Dalwig, like a man of honour, at once bowed.   Bright Kate testified all along a maidenly indifference, maidenly nescience, but was not thought to have an averse feeling.

Poor, ardent, enthusiastic, high-minded Kate! she used to ride with me sometimes in those years ; she was to the last passionately the friend and adorer of my Jane ; perhaps there hardly was in England a brighter young creature; and her fate was cruel—this of Dalwig, the turning-point, I rather think ! Being forbidden our house (abrupt Captain Anthony being in some tiff of his own here), she frequented 'uncle Maurice's,' where no foreigners frequented, but only young 'unsound' divines much did.   One of these . . . . she did, on her own footing—' over twenty-one now !' —give her hand to : . . . . was at length declared to be consumptive, and in four or five years died. . . . . She was very beautiful, very high and heroic ; father and mother both beautifully noticeable in her, and if as changed into a still finer *tertium quid* both of person and, still more, of mind.—T. C.

T. Carlyle, Linlathen, Dundee.

Chelsea: Tuesday, July 27, 1852.

Now you are not here to paint out the horrors of every kind so eloquently, I don't care, the least in the world, about the noise, or the dust, or the tumble heels over head, of the whole house. All I am concerned about is, to get it rapidly on; which, as builders and builders' men are at present constituted, seems pretty much of an impossibility. Yesterday I wrote to Mr. Morgan to take back the third carpenter, and bestow him on somebody with more patience and a less correct eye than myself. But it's worse than useless plaguing you, in your cold, clean retirement there, with the worries from which you have just fled away. Best you should forget the sound of our hammering altogether; so I will henceforth fight my own battle with the house, without saying a word about it.

Better news for you is, that Lord Ashburton is 'greatly better, quite well since the last attack, and gone on to the place in Switzerland.' Such was the answer to a message of inquiry which I sent to Bath House on Sunday. 'His lordship had written himself' to the large housemaid. So all is right in that direction.

Poor Dalwig is gone away. He came on Saturday with Reichenbach to bid me farewell. I gave him the copy of the 'Life of Sterling' I extorted from you for Mrs. Newton, who never got it; not in memory of Kate I told him, but of myself; and he blushed and kissed my hand, and went away rather sad, but with as manly and dashing a bearing as if Kate had been ever so kind. I don't believe the girl will ever have such another chance in her whole life.

There was also here one day a Rev. Llewelyn Davies, Lincoln. Do you know such a person? He asked for me, on hearing you were absent; shook hands with me, sat talking half-an-hour with me as if we were friends; and did all this so coolly and naturally that he left me persuaded I had known him some time. Did I ever know him?[1] Clough, too, was here last night; and Miss Wilson again, to offer me her carriage 'to do any business I might have.'

She promised to drink tea with me on my return from Sherborne;[2] where I still mean to go on Friday, and stay till Monday. It is a long way to go for so short a time. But I should repent it afterwards if I did not gratify that poor dear woman's wish to see me once more.

Ever affectionately yours,
J. W. CARLYLE.

---

[1] Never; nor I.

[2] Going thither to visit good Mrs. Macready, who was now ill, and, indeed, dying.

LETTER 143.

T. Carlyle, Scotsbrig.

Chelsea: Thursday, Aug. 5, 1852.

You recollect, dear, that Macready told me of two routes, recommending that by Frome as the quickest and least fatiguing; so I rendered myself at the Paddington station on Friday morning, with my night-things in a bag on one arm and my 'blessed'[1] in a basket on the other. He gave me no trouble, kept himself hidden and motionless till the train started, and then looked out cautiously, as much as to say, 'Are we safe?' The journey to Frome was quite a rest after that morning's work (carrying down all the books from the top landing-place into the back parlour), and I descended from the train quite fresh for the thirty miles by coach.

But when I inquired about the coach to Sherborne, I was told there was none. 'A coach passing through Sherborne passed through Frome without coming to the station at eleven in the morning,' three hours before the time we were at; 'no other since many months back.' My first thought was, 'What a mercy you were not with me!' my next, that the Macreadys could not blame me for keeping them waiting; and then I 'considered,' like the piper's cow, and resolved not to stay all day and night at Frome, but to take a Yeovil coach, which started at five, and which could take me, I was told, to a wayside inn within eight miles of Sherborne, and there I hoped to find a fly 'or something.' Meanwhile I would proceed to the town of Frome, a mile from the station, and get something to eat, and even to drink, 'feeling it my duty' to keep my heart up by all needful appliances. I left my little bag at the station, where the coach came, and set my dog quite free, and we pursued our way as calmly and naturally as if we had known where we were going.

Frome is a dull, dirty-looking place, full of plumbers; one could fancy the Bennett controversy[2] must have been a godsend to it. I saw several inns, and chose 'The George' for its name's sake. I walked in and asked to have some cold meat and a pint bottle of Guinness's porter. They showed me to an ill-aired parlour, and brought me some cold lamb that the flies had been buzzing round

---

[1] Dog Nero.
[2] Something in the newspaper.

for a week—even Nero disdained to touch it. I ate bread, however, and drank all the porter ; and 'the *cha-arge*'[1] for that feeble refection was 2*s.* 6*d.* ! Already I had paid one pound eight and sixpence for the train. It was going to be a most unexpectedly costly journey to me. But for that reflection I could almost have laughed at my forlorn position there.

The inn and town were 'so disagreeable' that I went presently back to the station, preferring to wait there. One of the men who had informed me about the coach came to me, as I was sitting on a bench, and remarked on the beauty of the scene, especially of some scarlet beans that were growing in his own piece of garden. ' Ah,' he said, ' I have lived in London, and I have lived abroad ; I have been here and there, backwards and forwards, while I was in service with them as never could rest; but I am satisfied now that the only contentment for man is in growing his own VEGETABLE! Look at them beans,' he said again. ' Well! to-morrow they'll be ready, and I'll be pulling them, and boiling them, and eating them—and such a taste! No agriculture like that in Piccadilly!' Then he looked sympathisingly at me and said, ' I'm going to get you something you'll like, and that's a glass of cool, fresh, clear water;' and he went away with a jug to his garden and fetched some water from a little spring well and a great handful of mignonette. 'There! there's something sweet for you, and here's splendid water, that you won't find the like of in Piccadilly!' I asked him how it was going with Mr. Bennett? ' Huh! I hear no complaints, but I goes to neither one nor other of them, and follows my own notions. I finds agriculture the thing!' He would have been worth a hundred pounds to Dickens, that man.

I had the coach all to myself for a while; then a young gentleman got in, who did exactly the right thing by me, neither spoke to me nor looked at me till we stopped at Castle Carey (Yeovil is pronounced Youghal, Carey Carry? I grew quite frightened that I had been somehow transported into Ireland). There the young gentleman went into the inn, and said to me first, ' Excuse the liberty I take in asking, but would you take anything—a little wine

---

[1] In my first voyage to London (1824, by Leith smack), a certain very rustic-looking, but polite and quiet, old baronet, called Sir David Milne, slept in the same cabin with me; and there and on deck was an amusing human study. Courteous, solemn, yet awkward, dull; chewing away the *r* when he spoke, which indeed was seldom, and then mainly in the way of economic inquiry to passengers who knew London—what you could do there, see, eat, &c.; and to every item, the farther question: ' And what is the cha-arge (charge)?'

and water?' I thought that very polite; but I was to meet with 'something more exquisite still' before I got to Sherborne. At the 'Sparkford Inn,' eight miles from Sherborne, I got out and asked, had they a fly? 'Yes, but one of its wheels was broken, and it was gone to be mended!' 'Had they any other conveyance that was whole—a gig or cart?' 'Yes, they had a nice little gig, and I should have the loan of a cloak to keep me warm' (the evening was rather chill). So I went in, and sat down in a parlour; where an old gentleman was finishing off with bread-and-cheese. He soon made himself master of my case, and regretted he was not going back to Sherborne that night, as then he would have taken me in his carriage; and presently he offered something else more practical, viz., to try to recover my parasol (my mother's, the one she bought with the sovereign you gave her,[1] and which I had got new covered), left stupidly on the roof of the coach, and never recollected till the coach, with its four horses, had thundered past the window! If the landlady would tell the coachman about it next day, and get it there, he, the old gentleman, would bring it to Sherborne House. I went into the lobby to tell the landlady, some five or eight minutes after the coach had started, and told her in presence of a gentleman, who was preparing to start in a barouchette with two horses. He looked hard at me, but said nothing; and a minute or two after I saw him also drive past the window. Some twenty minutes after, I started myself, in a little gig, with a brisk little horse and silent driver. Nothing could be more pleasant than so pirring through quiet roads, in the dusk, with the moon coming out. I felt as I were reading about myself in a Miss Austen novel. But it got beyond Miss Austen when, at the end of some three miles, before a sort of carrier's inn, the gentleman of the barouchette stept into the middle of the road, making a sort of military signal to my driver, which he repeated with impatience when the man did not at once draw up! I sat confounded, expecting what he would do next. We had halted; the gentleman came to my side, and said, exactly as in a book: 'Madam, I have the happiness of informing you that I have reclaimed your parasol; and it lies here in my carriage ready to be restored!' 'But how on earth?' I asked. 'Madam, I judged that it would be more pleasing for you to take the parasol along with yourself than to trust to its being brought by the other gentleman; so I just gal-

---

[1] A sovereign to each of them, on returning home with a pocketful from my 'fisrt lecture.' Ah, me!

loped my horses, overtook the coach as it was leaving this court, reclaimed the parasol, and have waited here, knowing you could take no other road to Sherborne, for the happiness of presenting it to you!'—To an ostler—'Bring the parasol!' It was brought, and handed to me. And then I found myself making a speech in the same style, caught by the infection of the thing. I said: 'Sir, this day has been full of mischances for me, but I regard the recovery of my parasol so unexpectedly as a good omen, and have a confidence that I shall now reach my destination in safety. Accept my thanks, though it is impossible to give any adequate expression to my sense of your courtesy!' I never certainly made so long and formal a speech in my life. And how I came to make anything like it I can't imagine, unless it were under mesmerism! We bowed to each other like first cousins of Sir Charles Grandison, and I pirred on. 'Do you know that gentleman?' I asked my driver. 'Never saw him before.'

I found Sherborne House without difficulty; and a stately, beautiful house it was, and a kind welcome it had for me. The mistake had been discovered in the morning, and great anxiety felt all day as to my fate. I was wonderfully little tired, and able to make them all (her too) laugh with my adventures. But I must positively interrupt this penny-a-lining, and go to bed. It is true to the letter, all I have told.

My two days at Sherborne House were as happy as could possibly be with that fearfully emaciated, dying woman before my eyes. They were all doing their best to be cheerful—herself as cheerful as the others. She never spoke of her death, except in taking leave of me; when she took my head in her hand, and kissed it, and gave me her solemn blessing, and asked me to come again with you, to see William and the children, when she should be gone. That was a dreadful trial of my composure. I am so glad I went, it pleased her and all of them so much!.

The journey back by Dorchester went all right; and was less expensive, for I came by the second-class, and so saved the nine shillings my gig had cost me. It was a weary long way, however, from a quarter before nine till half after seven flying along in one shape or other, with only ten minutes' delay (at Southampton). My only adventure on the road back was falling in with a young unfortunate female in the Chelsea boat, the strangest compound of angel and devil that I ever set eyes on, and whom, had I been a great, rich lady, I should decidedly have—brought home to tea with me and tried 'to *save!*' The helpless thought that I had nothing to offer her instead alone prevented me. I could not leave her, however, without speaking to her, and my words were so moving, through my own emotion, that she rushed from me in tears to the other side of the vessel. You may feel a certain curiosity to know what I said. I only recollect something about 'her mother, alive or dead, and her evident superiority to the life she was leading.' She said, 'Do you think so, ma'm?' with a look of bitter wretchedness, and forced gaiety that I shall never forget. She was trying to smile defiantly, when she burst into tears and ran away.

I made a frantic appeal to the workmen the other day, since when we have been getting on a little more briskly. The spokesman of them, a dashing young man, whom you have not seen, answered me: 'My dear (!) madam, you must have patience, indeed you must; it will be all done—some day!' The weather is most lovely. *Monsieur le Thermomètre* pretty generally at 70°.

My health continues wonderfully good. To-day I dine at the Brookfields', for what poor Helen used to call 'a fine change.'

Ever yours affectionately,
JANE W. C.

LETTER 144.

To T. Carlyle, Esq., Scotsbrig.

Chelsea: Tuesday night, Aug. 10, 1852.

Oh, my dear, what a comfortless letter! In your last from Linlathen you said you were 'decidedly better,' and now again you seem to be again 'all nohow.' I hope it has only been the fag of the journey. Don't fret about the house; it is getting on pretty fast now, and will be satisfactory when finished. For my part, I am got quite used to the disturbance, and begin to like the—what shall I say?—excitement of it. To see something going on, and to help its going on, fulfils a great want of my nature. I have prevented so many mistakes being made, and afforded so many capital suggestions, that I begin to feel rather proud of myself, and to suspect I must have been a builder in some previous state of existence. The painter is my chief delight; he does his work so thoroughly. He is only in your bedroom as yet, but he has rubbed it all down with pumicestone, till it looks as smooth as paper. And I have never been inconvenienced by any smell! Perhaps the house may be habitable a week or two sooner than I guessed, though I hardly think the workmen will be fairly out of it sooner. I shall 'see my way' better next week. The weather is capital for drying both paint and plaster, that is one blessing! My half of the low room is kept always tidy; the bedding, and tables with their legs in the air, as if in convulsions, which show themselves above the screen, often make me laugh. When the noise is very great I practise on the piano! I do quite well, in short; and don't see how I can be spared till things are done to my mind, and the chaotic heaps of furniture restored to their proper places. Decidedly nobody but myself can do that.

I found your letter to-day on my return from Tavistock House, where I had gone to see Forster. He is staying there for a change, in the absence of the Dickenses. I had promised the Macreadys to go, and tell him about her, and found no time till to-day. I went by the boat to Paul's Wharf, like a goose, and found myself so far off my destination! Besides, a violent thunder-shower fell just as I set my foot on land, and having on a pair of those cheap boots I bought a stock of (chiefly paper, Mr. Carlyle!), my feet were wet through in two minutes. I went in a shop and bought a pair of stockings, then on till I found a good-looking shoe-shop, and bought a pair of real boots; left my dripping stockings and paper boots with the shoemaker, requesting that when they were dry, and not till then, he would pack them up and send them to the care of Forster; and so proceeded on my long walk dry-shod. Cleverly managed, don't you think? and 'regardless of expense.' Forster was very glad to see me. He is a little less helpless, but still on fish diet. I got into a Holborn omnibus after, which left me at the top of Regent Street; and then I went to Verey's, and had—a beautiful little mutton chop and a glass of bitter ale! That is the sort of thing I do! It was my second dinner at Verey's. Meat dinners at home are as nearly impossible as can be, and one sleeps ill on tea-dinners. The charge at Verey's is very moderate, and the cooking perfect. For my dinner and ale to-day I paid one-and-fivepence. The day I went to the Foundry I dined at a clean-looking shop in the Strand, where I had half a roast chichen (warm; very small indeed), a large slice of warm ham, and three new potatoes, for one shilling! It amuses me, all that, besides keeping me in health; and for the outrage to 'delicate femaleism,' I am beyond all such considerations at present. However, I see single women besides myself at Verey's—not improper—governesses, and the like. And now good-night; I am off to bed.

Wednesday.—Ah! it is a tempting of Providence always to congratulate oneself on the weather! To-day it 'is pouring hale water' (as Helen used to say), and has so poured all night. If it weren't for the paint and plaster's sake I should have no objection. I called at the London Library yesterday on my way home to get Madame de Staël's 'Mémoires' for Count Reichenbach. Mr. Donne [1] never comes out of that end room seemingly. Mr. Jones was 'absent three days for a little pleasuring.' The tall young man was on the eve of his departure; had 'found on trial of six years that the place didn't suit him.' He was going to embark in a silk manufactory at Derby—'a very good opening indeed.' Mrs. H—— M—— (did I tell you?) left your books and a card for me just before leaving town. Dilberoglue might surely call that 'glorious prudence!' Nevertheless she might have safely relied on her own powers of boring me, and on my general indisposition to intrude! God help us! I don't know of any fine people remaining except the Farrars, who can't get away for fear of their house being robbed. Mazzini was here on Sunday morning, and made my hair stand on end with his projects. If he is not shot, or in an Austrian fortress within the month, it will be more by good luck than good guiding. I rely on the promise, 'God is kind to woman, fools, and drunk people.'

Kind love to your mother and all of them. After going all that way to Sherborne for two days, who knows whether I shan't run to Scotsbrig for two days and see her when she is not thinking of me?

Ever yours,

J. W. C.

If you won't go to Germany alone, and don't much like the notion, is there no little lodging to be got by the seaside, within reach of Scotsbrig's butter and eggs, for two or three weeks,—for yourself, I mean?

LETTER 145.

T. Carlyle, Scotsbrig.

Chelsea: Saturday, Aug. 14, 1852.

'With the best intentions always unfortunate.' I was putting together my packet yesterday, when Dr. Weber [2] came, and stayed long enough to belate the whole affair. He seemed bent on coming up to the immense expectations I must have formed of him. And that excessive desire to please was just what I disliked him for. But

---

[1] Now librarian; excellent old Cochrane dead.

[2] Late travelling doctor to the Ashburtons, who are at Salzburg, &c.

he is clever and gentlemanly, and thoroughgoing, to appearance at least, when looked at in front; for the back of his head and neck, and all down, has a different character, much less bred, and less intellectual; 'the human curve'[1] not so well defined. He reminds me of a statue that had been perfectly polished in front, and left rough-hewn behind, to stand with its back to a wall. He gave me the most flourishing accounts of Lord and Lady A. And we parted after 'swearing everlasting friendship' to a certain very limited extent.

Your letter came after; and also, alas! came news, through Mr. Piper,[2] of the death of Mazzini's mother. The accounts had been written to Mrs. Hawkes in two letters. She found them on her return from town, where she had been all day, and, opening first the letter which told only of a stroke of apoplexy, she rushed off to Mazzini with the news. Having returned to her own house, she opened the second letter, which, in her agitation, she had not looked at, and found it an announcement of death, and so had again to go to Mazzini. He is dreadfully struck down, the Pipers say. I have not seen him. I wrote him a few lines last night, and took them up myself, but would not go to him, though Mrs. Piper thought it might be good for him to see me. I am sure there are too many bothering him with kindness.

Kind regards to all.

Yours affectionately,
JANE W. C.

LETTER 146.

Under way for Germany at last. My first visit. I remember too well the base miseries, and even horrors (physical, chiefly), which had now begun for me, and did not cease till the voyage did. At midnight (August 29 it must have been) I embarked at Leith on a small Rotterdam steamer (laden to the lip with iron I found, and the uneasiest of kicking little wretches); never sailed in such a craft before, or since; rested little, slept worse (except on a bench in the Rhine steamboat) till I got to Bonn. Neuberg waiting on the beach for me—Neuberg—but not any sleep there either. *Pfui!*

Hon. Byng, called Poodle Byng all his days, the Eton name he had.

'Engrush' for 'ingratiate' (a very old expression of ours).

Car il était très aimable, &c.: Robespierre—a Parisian myth which G. Lewes used to give us with first-rate mimicry, &c.

Fanny is 'Irish Fanny,' whom I recollect well; she was by nature a very good girl (and got full generously treated here, even to the

---

[1] Mazzini's phrase. Plattnauer, for fat, was 'losing the human curve.'
[2] Mazzini lodging with Piper.

saving of her life, I might say), and she did well for a year or more;
but after that sank to the common level or below it, and had to
disappear like the others.

'Beautiful enthusiasm.'—Foolish, inflated English lady, of the
elderly governess kind, who once came to us at Craigenputtock
(where we had little need of her), spoke much to *her* of a 'Ba-ing
I could love,' 'Brush the down from the cheek of,' &c.—T. C.

To T. Carlyle, Esq., Bonn.

Chelsea: Tuesday night, Sept. 1852.

When I returned from Addiscombe yesterday forenoon, I saw a
letter on the table, and cut short poor Nero's vehement leaping to
take it; and lo! it was my own letter from Rotterdam, addressed to
the London Library, St. James' Square! a fact which puzzled me
extremely. 'An old man' had brought it from there, and said 'a
shilling had been paid for it,' the second shilling the unlucky *dud*
had cost. By-and-by I noticed that the envelope had the London
Library mark on it, and then the small mystery was solved. I had
written the letter at the London Library, after some hours of wild
galloping in a street cab to ascertain about the passport: indeed that
passport affair was as pretty a version of 'Simon Brodie's Cow' as
any I have lately had on hand. To-day I have to thank you for a
letter more agreeable to receive than that one. As you have not
got 'stolen or strayed' hitherto, one may now feel a moderate
assurance that you will be safely landed at the far end of this
journey to—what shall I say?—Flaetz ! [1] Neuberg being not likely
either to lose sight of you, or to lose patience with you.

The Addiscombe programme was only once changed. We went
on the Saturday instead of the Friday, separately of course; I by
steamboat and railway. The G——s, baby and all, came about an
hour after me; and an hour after them the Poodle. Mrs. G.
was as sweet as syrup, and dreadfully tiresome, her husband
engrushing himself, *très aimable dans la société*, and the baby a 'bit
of fascination' seemingly for every one but me. The visit went off
harmoniously, but I got no better sleep in my entirely curtainless
bed there than among the bugs at number two. [2] On Monday forenoon
the G——s and I came back together by the railway. Lady A.
was to come too, and sleep at Bath House, and go to the Grange

---

[1] Flätz (Jean Paul's *Schmelze*).

[2] In Cheyne Row, where she had slept once during the repairs in Carlyle's
own house.—J. A. F.

this morning. Mr. G—— invited me to dine with them the same evening; but I preferred a chop and silence at home. He seems to be very fond of me, has a perception, I think, that I don't adore his wife, and is grateful to me for that. I was engaged to tea at the Farrars to-night; but a note came from Annie to say that her mother was lying ill with a blister on her back, and her sister brought home from a visit she had been making with her *nose* broken, and otherwise all *smashed* by a dreadful fall. Poor girl! I saw her the day before I went to Addiscombe looking so pretty.

Thursday morning.—At this point I stopped on Tuesday night, the thunder and rain becoming too loud 'for anything.' It was still raining violently when I went to bed (in your room—the bed up; for the rest, carpetless and full of lumber), so I left only one of the windows open; and what with the paint smell, and the fatigue of having nailed up all the hangings myself, and the want of sleep at number two and at Addiscombe, I took quite ill in the middle of the night—colic, and such headache! In the morning I crawled down to the sofa in the parlour, and lay there all day, till eleven at night, in desperate agony, with a noise going on around me like the crack of doom.[1] If it had not been for Fanny's kindness, who, when all else that she could do failed, fairly took to crying and sobbing over me, I think I must have died of the very horror and desolation of the thing; for the plasterers came back yesterday to finish the cornice in the new room, and the bricklayers were tramping out and in repairing the backyard; and the painter was making a rare smell of new paint in my old bedroom; besides the two carpenters, into whose head the devil put it to saw the whole day, at God knows what, without a moment's intermission, except to hammer. I have passed a good many bad days in this world, but certainly never one so utterly wretched from mere physical and material causes as yesterday. It is over now, however, that bout, and I should be thankful to have held out so long.

In the evening came a note, which I was not up to looking at till some hours after, when lo! it was a few hurry-scurry lines from John, to say that he and 'the Ba-ing' were actually engaged; they were all well, I was to tell you, and had got your letter. No newspaper reached me except the *Athenæum*, which I supposed had been overlooked at Scotsbrig. I hope poor John is 'making a good thing of it;' the 'parties' having known each other for fifteen years, it is possible they mayn't be marrying on a basis of fiction.

---

[1] Oh, heavens! How can I endure all that?

Reflecting with a half-tragical, half-comical feeling that John was just my own age, I turned to another letter still lying unopened, and found what might have been a proposal of marriage to—myself ! had you not been alive at Bonn. A man who, having wished to marry me at fifteen, and ' with the best intentions proved unfortunate,' and whom I had seen but once these twenty years, now ' thought himself sufficiently master of his emotions to dare to tell me that for nearly forty years (!) he had loved me with the same worshipful love—me, the only human soul who ever possessed the key to his locked heart !' And they say man is an inconstant animal ! Poor fellow ! I am afraid he must be going to die, or to go mad, or he would have continued to pursue the silent system, which use must have rendered easy to him.   The practical inference from all this, and a good deal more I could instance, is that the laws of nature in the matter of love seem decidedly to be getting themselves new made; ' the bloom ' not to be so ' speedily swept from the cheek of that beautiful enthusiasm.'

You may calculate on having your bedroom quite ready and the new room in a cleaned-out state, not papered ; but really that is easily to be borne after what has been to bear.   The door in the parlour has been left as it was, partly because I dreaded to let the wretches begin any new mess, and partly because I find the room can be made so warm for winter by having the door opened into the passage, and the folding-door space completely filled by the screen. Now that I see a probable end to the carpenters and bricklayers, I may tell you, without putting you quite wild, that Mr. Morgan has been here just twice since you left home, and neither time have I seen him.   The first time I was out at ' the balloon,' and the second time was yesterday, when I was on my back in an agony, and could not have stood up for anyone.   The botheration of hounding on the men of such a careless master, and the responsibility of directing them, you may partly figure.   Fanny is the best comfort I have had, so willing to fly over the moon for me, and always making light of her discomforts.   And now I must write a word of congratulation to John.

Ever affectionately yours,

J. W. C.

LETTER 147.

John Clerk (Lord Eldin ultimately), of the Scotch 'Court of Session,' a man of great faculty and singular, rather cynical, ways, and much famed in Edinburgh, was a *dilettante* in art withal, and an expensive collector of pictures. After his long-delayed advancement to the bench his faculties began to decline, and many stories of his outbreaks were current; *e.g.*, *Visitor* one day (to Lord Eldin): 'What a bit of painting you have done there, my lord ! Admirable! exquisite! Why it reminds one of Titian!' *Eldin :* 'Titian (Tishon) ? Tishon never did the like o't.' Jeffrey's story to us (twenty years before).

At Craigenputtock, foolish man-servant of ours, reporting his procedures on an errand to Edinburgh: 'Called for Mr. Inglis, ma'm, Messrs. Donald (Doandle) and Inglis, m'm.' 'Told me Inglis was not in, but Mr. Doandle yes, who was all the same as Mr. Inglis.'

To T. Carlyle, Poste Restante, Dresden.

Chelsea: Sunday, Sept. 13, 1852.

As there was already a letter gone to you, dear, and as next day was Sunday, when there would be some human quiet, I did not answer yesterday by return of post, but went instead to the city, where I had business. Indeed, it was well to get out into space yesterday, for the plasterers were rushing about like demons, finishing off, and clearing away their scaffoldings, &c., and the plumbers were once more boiling lead in the kitchen, to repair some spout on the roof, and a note I had written to Mr. Morgan, that your brother Alick 'never did the like o',' in point of sarcasm, had produced an influx of things perfectly bewildering. And the two carpenters, who have been too long together, fell to quarrelling so loud, that I had to send the painter to express my sentiments. In fact, it was a patent hell here yesterday for any 'lover of quiet things.'[1]

In the evening I had a tea-party to wind up with. Had madly invited some people to meet a man, who, after all, couldn't come, but will come next Tuesday instead. The man was Herzen,[2] whom you have had some correspondence with. He is in London for a short time, and was very bent on seeing *you;* and Saffi, who is much with him, asked leave to bring him to *me*, not as being 'all the same as Mr. Doandle,' but as the Hades through which these

---

[1] Basil Montague's account of himself.
[2] Big Russian exile and propagandist.

people pass to you—or hope to. So I said he might bring him last night, and asked Darwin, and the Reichenbachs, and Brookfield to meet him—all in this end of a room. There were six of us, and we spoke four languages, and it is all to be done over again on Tuesday. Herzen is not a German as you fancied him, but a Russian; and he is rich, which is indicated by his having given Mazzini two hundred pounds for his objects.

Chapman has told Saffi to write him three articles, one on Italian religion, two more on Italian literature; and Saffi is very thankful to you. The other Chapman, when I was in his shop the other day to get a note from him to Griffiths,[1] made me again the offer of 'very advantageous terms' for a novel of my own; so I have something to retire upon'[2] in prospect, not inferior to 'an old washer-woman.'

But meanwhile what a pity it is that you can't get any good sleep; all the rest would be made smooth for you were that one condition granted. It is not only German beds, however, that one can't get sleep in. Three nights ago in desperation I took a great dose of morphia for the same state of things, and was thankful to get four hours of something like forgetfulness by that 'questionable' means. I am not otherwise ill, however; that one horrid headache I told you of has been my only real illness since you left.

I had a long, very nice letter from John two days ago. His marriage is not to come off till November or December. He talks about it with an innocent faith that is quite touching, and already seems to be 'seeing his way' more clearly than I ever knew him to do. Thomas Erskine, too, wrote to me that 'he loved me much,' and wished he could see what God intended me for. I answered his letter, begging him to tell me 'what God intended me for,' since he knew and I didn't. It would be a satisfaction even to know it. It is surely a kind of impiety to speak of God as if He, too, were 'with the best intentions always unfortunate.' Either I am just what God intended me for, or God cannot 'carry out' His intentions, it would seem. And in that case I, for 'one solitary individual,' can't worship Him the least in the world.

I had a visit the other morning from Cooper, the Chartist; come, not to pay the five pounds he borrowed, but to 'ask for more!' You had desired him, he said, to apply to you again, if he

---

[1] Don't know.

[2] Darwin's valet: 'My father, he has now retired, sir, upon,' &c.

wĕre again in difficulty ! ! I told him that I ' had none to give him,' and he took the refusal like a man used to it, quite 'light and airy.'

Fanny is really a nice servant; a dash of Irish 'rough and ready' in her, but a good cleaner, and a good cook, and a perfect incarnation of ' The Willing Mind !' Very tidy too in her own person, under all circumstances. An awful complication revealed itself two or three days after she came, which she stood by me under with a jolliness that was quite admirable. When the new-painted kitchen was capable of being slept in, she fell to taking the bed in pieces to give it ' a good washing.' Anne, who would never be at the trouble to look to her bed, pretended, when she did finally take it down by my express order, before she went away, to have found 'nothing worth mentioning;' 'just four bugs,' and these ' very small ones,' like the girl's illegitimate child. Well ! I was sitting writing here, when Fanny came and said, ' Do step down, ma'am, and see what I have kept to show you;' and when I had gone down, not knowing what she had been at, there lay her bed all in pieces, and beside it a large basin of water, containing the drowned bodies of something like two hundred bugs ! ! The bed perfectly swarmed with these ' small beings ;' was in fact impregnated with them beyond even my cleansing powers. We gathered it all up, and carried it out into the garden to be sold to a broker, who is coming for certain rubbish of things ; and I went the same day and bought a little iron bedstead for the kitchen, for one pound two-and-sixpence. The horror of these bugs quite maddened me for many days ; and I would not tell you of them at the time, that you might not feel them prospectively biting you ; but now I think we are ' quite shut [1] of them!' The painter's consolation, that he ' knew fine houses in Belgrave Square where they were crawling about the drawing-room floors !' did not help me at all.

The poor white cat no longer gives offence to Nero; I suppose she ' couldn't stand the muddle,' like that girl who went away into infinite space two weeks ago. Darwin says, if I can put up with ' a cat with a bad heart,' I may have his. ' That minds me ' (as Helen used to say) of an Italian, living with Mazzini at present, who is beating Saffi hollow in ' the pursuit of English under difficulties;' sitting down by some Englishman the other day, he said ' fluently,' ' Now let we have a nice cat together!' (chat).

---

[1] Manchester phrase; should be 'shot,' as in Annandale.

How disappointed poor Bölte will be that I am not along with you! I will write to her one day.

Mr. Kenyon and Browning left their cards for me yesterday. I heard at Addiscombe that Macaulay was ill of some mortal disease, but the information seemed vague. Thiers is expected at the Grange the first of November, 'to stay till they come to London, and live on at Bath House after.' And now, a Jew, a Jew! for I have still some writing to do before I go out: a letter to Geraldine in the Isle of Man, and one to John. My love to Neuberg, and bid him ' be strong.'

Affectionately yours,

J. W. C.

LETTER 148.

To T. Carlyle, Poste Restante, Berlin.

20 Hemus Terrace, Chelsea: Sept. 25, 1852.

By this time, dear, you will have got my letter to Dresden. I wrote there according to your first instructions. Since then I have been rather pleased that uncertainty about your whereabout afforded me a fair excuse for observing silence. In all my life I was never in a state more unfavourable to letter-writing; so 'entangled in the details,'[1] and so continually out of temper. I have often said that I couldn't be at the trouble to hate anyone; but now decidedly I hate one man—Mr. ——! His conduct has been perfectly shameful; not a promise kept, and not even an apology made for breaking them. I have ceased to write to him, or send any messages to him. I merely pray God to 'very particularly damn him.'[2] The carpenters, bricklayers, and plasterers are all gone out of the house; there are still some odds and ends for the carpenter to do, and the bricklayer will be outside; but the only work doing for the last week has been painting. And though Mr. —— promised that two more painters should be sent to help the one already here, that promise has gone ad plures. Neither will he send back the paperhangers to finish in the staircase. With this one painter it was impossible to do all that was needed before your return. So I have

---

[1] John's phrase.

[2] Old McTurk, on paying his reapers at evening (who had taken to 'kemp,' and spoiled him much stuff), said to each, with the 2s. 6d., ' God damn you! ' and to one old woman (originator of the thing), ' And God particularly —— you, ye b——! '

had to give up the painting of the lower rooms—too thankful to
get them thoroughly cleaned once more, and refurnished. Fanny
and Mrs. Heywood were two days washing the old paint, while I
cleaned the paper; and two days more it took us to bring the furniture to its old condition. The new room is cleaned out, and has
the old furniture in it; and, though sufficiently bare-looking, will
not be uninhabitable during the winter, and when it is papered and
furnished prettily, it will be a very fine room indeed. Chalmers[1]
said, with a look of envy, that we couldn't have got a house with
such a room in it under a hundred and fifty pounds a year.

The new bedroom upstairs is still representing the 'belly of
Chaos,' all things thrown out of their old places finding refuge
there, but my old bedroom will be 'better than I deserve'[2] till the
other is ready. The bed is up there, without curtains, but the work
of rehabilitation is going on in it; so that it will be ready for sleeping in, when one can safely sleep in the house at all; which is not
the case at present, the new paint in the staircases poisoning the
whole house. And your bedroom! Ah! that has been the cruelest
cut of all. I had it painted the first thing, that it might be well
aired for you; and the presses you wished for, which they would
not make on the spot, but must have made at the workshop, were
ordered, and promised to be all painted there to save us the smell;
and, behold! after keeping me up with this delusion for six weeks,
they bring them home in raw wood—declaring they could not be
painted till they were fixed up. And so that room, where I had
been sleeping for a week, had to be again abandoned. I could not
try the sofa in the parlour again, for the passage was all in wet
paint, and I felt myself growing quite ill; got up every morning
with a sick headache, and had got back my old sickness through
the day, which I had hoped was gone for good. So there was no
sense in staying on till I took a nervous fever, or some such thing.
I went off then on a new hunt for lodgings; and found a decent
little apartment next door to Mrs. Thorburn, whose house was fully
let. I have the ground floor, and my bed is quite free of 'small
beings,' an unspeakable mercy! Indeed, it is a very comfortable
little bedroom, though feebly furnished; and the people very decent,
quiet people. I go home to breakfast every morning, and work
there very hard till dinner-time—two o'clock, and for an hour after,
or as long as I can bear the smell; and then I come back here to

---

[1] Rich man of next door; and endless builder, renovator, and decorator of
No. 4. [2] Coleridge.

early tea, and spend the evening in pure air. The quantity of work it takes to restore order at Cheyne Row, and repair the ruin of that general upturn, is perfectly incredible. Three flittings, they say, is equal to a fire; but a 'thorough repair' is equal to three fires.

Oh, dear, in case I forget Masson! Masson is quite frantic at having received no testimonial [1] from you. The election takes place on the fifth; so pray try to write to him in time. I promised to tell you his ardent wish as soon as I knew where to hit you with a letter.

I see hardly anybody;—going nowhere. Dr. H—— has called *four* times (!) without finding me; two of the times I was in the house—*au secret*. Darwin is into his new house, and now off to Shrewsbury for a little while. The Farrars are gone to Malvern. Poor Mrs. Macready is gone; died at Plymouth on the eighteenth. Miss Macready wrote me a long, most kind letter, telling me that till her last hour she 'loved me much.' Her life had become too suffering, it is best that it is over.

I should like to have seen Göthe's and Schiller's house with you. In fact your travels, though you make them out rather disagreeable than otherwise, look to me quite tempting.

I have given you a good dose of the house this time; and, besides that, I have really no news worth telling. A. Sterling came one day; returned from Scotland, and on the road to Cowes—a dreadfully corpulent black *Werter*. A letter from John would be lying for you at Dresden with mine, so I need not tell his plans. I hope I shall like this new sister-in-law. He seems to think I have as much share in marrying her as himself has.

John Welsh has been made much of at Belfast, and complimented in public by Colonel Sykes. He sent me a Belfast newspaper. Oh! I had nearly forgotten—Lady Stanley has been in town, and sent to ask when she could find me, or if I would come to her. Drank tea with her—went and came in omnibus, but having Mrs. Heywood with me by way of lady's-maid. And now, good-night. I am very tired; and the tireder I am, the less I sleep.

Yours affectionately,

JANE CARLYLE.

---

[1] London professorship; I sent him one from Berlin.

LETTER 149.

To T. Carlyle, British Hotel, Unter den Linden, Berlin.

Chelsea: Oct. 5, 1852.

I write, dear, since you bid me write again; but upon my honour it were better to leave me silent; all the thoughts of my heart just now are curses on Mr. ——. I have not a word of comfort to give; I am wearied and sad and cross; feel as if death had been dissolved into a liquid, and I had drunk of it till I was full! Good gracious! that wet paint should have the power of poisoning one's soul as well as one's body! But it is not the wet paint simply; it is the provocation of having an abominable process spun out so interminably, and the prospect of your finding your house hardly habitable after such long absence and weary travel. Never in all my life has my temper been so tried. So anxious I have been to get on, and the workmen only sent here, seemingly, when they have nowhere else to go, and Mr. —— dwindled away into a myth! Not once have I seen his face! I will have your bedroom at least in order for you, and if the smell of the staircase is too bad, you must just stay the shorter time here. Lady A. wrote to invite us to the Grange on the fifteenth, for 'a long visit,' and I have engaged to go—myself for a week or ten days; but you, I said, could stay longer it would be the better for you. We shall see how it smells when you come and need not make long programmes.

For myself I have been sleeping about at home, again, have done so since Monday. I had to give up my snug little lodging suddenly and remain here, for 'reasons which it may be interesting not to state.' As the painter (only one can I get) paints me out of one floor, I move to another; but I have slept oftenest in the back parlour, on the sofa, which stands there in permanency, and which, with four chairs and a quantity of pillows, I have made into an excellent bed. But surely it were more agreeable to write of something else.

Dr. H—— then! What Doctor H—— means I am at a loss to conjecture, but that he comes here oftener than natural is a positive fact. After the five ineffectual visits he made a sixth, which was successful. I was at home, and he stayed an hour and half!—look_ing so lovingly into my eyes that I felt more puzzled than ever. Is it to hear of Lady A. he comes? I thought, and started that topic, but he let it drop without any appearance of particular interest.

I.—15

'He is an Austrian,' I thought again, and all Austrians are born spies, Reichenbach said; he may know I am the friend of Mazzini, and be wanting to find out things of him; so then I brought in the name of Mazzini, bat that was also *no go*. When he was going away he said, 'In a few days I will do myself the honour of calling again!' I did not want him to be taking up my time in the mornings, so I said, 'It was the merest chance finding me at present in the mornings.' 'At what time then may I hope to find you?' 'In the evenings, I said, 'but it is too far for you to come then.' 'Oh, not at all.' Better fix an evening I thought, and have somebody to meet him. So I asked him for Wednesday, and had Saffi and Reichenbach here, and both were charmed with him, as well they might be, for he took such pains to please us; actually at my first request sang to us without any accompaniment. To-day he has been here again with his wife, a pretty, lady-like, rather silly young woman, whom Lady A. has taken into favour. Mrs. G—— called yesterday—of the same genus. The Captain [1] is come to town and is on his good behaviour for the moment. He says he was keeping a journal of his travels in Scotland, but when he found no letter from me at Oban, where he had begged me to write, he dropt his journal—'never wrote another word.'

I have had no accounts from John very lately—entangled in the details no doubt; indeed, I get almost no letters, not having composure or time to write any.

Geraldine has been some weeks in the Isle of Man, making love to some cousin (a doctor) she has there, and even she has fallen mute.

Last Sunday I thought I had got a letter! Oh, worth all the letters that this earth could have given me! I was tumbling two boxfuls of my papers into one large box, when the desire took me to look into my father's day-book, which I had never opened since it came to me, wrapt in newspaper, and sealed, from Templand. I removed the cover and opened it; and fancy my feelings on seeing a large letter lying inside, addressed 'Mrs. Carlyle,' in my mother's handwriting, with three unbroken seals of her ring! I sat with it in my hands, staring at it, with my heart beating and my head quite dizzy. Here was at last the letter I had hoped would be found at Templand after her death—now, after so many years, after so much sorrow! I am sure I sat ten minutes before I could open it, and when I did open it I could not see to read anything.

---

[1] A. Sterling.

Alas! it was not that wished-for letter of farewell; still it was some-thing. The deed was there, making over my property to her, and written inside the envelope were a few words: ' When this comes into your possession, my dearest child, do not forget my sister. G. W., Templand, May 1827.'

Beside the deed lay my letter, which accompanied it, and a long, long letter, also mine, most sad to read, about my marriage, some copies of letters also in my father's writing, and a black profile of him. On the whole I felt to have found a treasure, though I was dreadfully disappointed too, and could do nothing all the day after but cry.

Wednesday, 6th.—Last night I took to crying again at this point; besides it was more than time to go to bed (figuratively speaking); and now I have my *all work* to attend to. Fanny continues the best-tempered of creatures, and her health keeps pretty good through all the mess; so that decidedly one may hope she will be equal to our needs in the normal state of things.

Do you know I think I have found out, though Erskine has never written to tell me, ' what God intended me for'—a detective police-man! I should have gone far in that career had it been open to my talent![1] You may remember an ornament I have been wearing for some years on my neck, or rather you certainly remember no-thing about it. It was a large topaz set richly in gold, forming a clasp to a bit of black velvet ribbon. Well this disappeared while I was at my last lodging, and I was very sorry, as it was the first jewel I ever possessed, and was given me by my father. As I had perfect faith in the honesty of the simple people of the lodgings, I would not fancy it stolen there, and as little was it possible for me to believe anyone here had stolen it; it was gone anyhow, and for the first time in my life I let a thing I valued go, helplessly and hopelessly, without one effort to recover it, beyond searching thoroughly the two places. One day, about a week after, it came into my head in the King's Road, ' Does it not look like a decay of my faculties to so part with my clasp? How many things have I not recovered by trying the impossible?' And then I said to myself, ' It is not too late for the impossible even now;' and set myself to ' consider'—thus: I am certain it is not mislaid, either at the lodging or at home; I have searched too thoroughly. I am equally certain that in neither house would any of the people have stolen it. *Ergo*, it must have

---

[1] That is truth, too.

been lost off my neck, or out of my pocket, out of doors. Off my neck? No; I had a blue ribbon on my neck when it was lost. Out of my pocket then? Now it couldn't have leapt out of my pocket; it must have been pulled out with my handkerchief, or my purse. With my handkerchief? No, I never use one, unless I am crying, or have a cold in my head; and I don't cry on the streets, and have had no colds this twelvemonth. With my purse, then, it must have been pulled out—*ergo* in some shop. I could not be pulling out my purse, except to pay for something. Now what shops was I in last week? I could easily count them: the Post Office, Warne's, Smith's, Todd's. I asked at the Post Office, at Smith's—no result; at Todd's—the same careless answer—but suddenly a gleam of intelligence came over Mrs. Todd's face, and she exclaimed to her girl, ' *That* couldn't be *gold* surely, that thing the children were playing with!' And it was my clasp, found by Mrs. Todd under a chair in her shop, and taken for ' a thing of no value,' and given to her little boys to play with; and so well had they played with it that only the setting could be found, and that after two days' search; the topaz had been ' lost in the Green Park!' But I was so glad to have the frame at least, and am getting some hair put in it, instead of the stone. But just fancy recovering such a thing out of space in London, after a week! I wonder if my letter will be over-weight. Such weather—rain, rain, and the paint —*ecco la combinazione!* Kind regards to Neuberg, who will certainly go to Heaven without any lingering in Purgatory.

Ever affectionately yours,

J. W. CARLYLE.

LETTER 150.

To Dr. Carlyle.

5 Cheyne Row, Chelsea: Friday, Oct. 18, 1852.

My dear John,—The last letter you got from me lay here two days before it got posted. I was put in what Anthony Sterling calls ' a state of mind,' and forgot it in my pocket. It was written at Hemus Terrace, that letter, late at night, and after writing it I went to bed, and I awoke with a bad headache, and when I got up at my usual hour (six o'clock), I reeled about like ' a drunk' (as Mazzini would say). But as no coffee or attentions were there, I would go home to breakfast as usual, and, after splashing my head with cold water, succeeded in getting my clothes on. When I opened the front door it was a deluge of rain, and I had only thin silk shoes, with holes in them, and no umbrella. A beautiful out-look, with a sick headache! I rang the bell, and implored the landlady's daughter to lend me a pair of clogs and an umbrella, and these being vouchsafed me, I dragged home, thinking resolutely of the hot coffee that Fanny would have all ready for me, to be taken at the kitchen fire, and the kind sympathy that she would accompany it with. On reaching my own door I could hardly stand, and leant on the rails till it was opened. Fanny did not open it, but a Mrs. Heywood, who had been assisting in the cleaning for some days—a decent, disagreeable young woman. 'Oh,' she said, the first thing, 'we are so glad you are come! Fanny is in such a way! The house has been broken into during the night! the police are now in the kitchen!' Here was a cure for a sick headache! and it did cure it. 'Have they taken much?' I asked. 'Oh, all Fanny's best things, and a silver table-spoon, and a table-cloth be-sides!' A mercy it was no worse! In the kitchen stood two police-sergeants, writing down in a book the stolen items from Fanny's dictation; she, poor thing, looking deathly. There was no coffee, of course—no fire even—everything had gone to distrac-tion. The thieves had come in at the larder window, which Mr. Morgan had kept without a frame (!) for three weeks; the bolts on the outside of the back-kitchen door had saved the whole house from being robbed, for Fanny slept sound and never heard them. They had taken her nice new large trunk out of the back kitchen into the larder, broken off the lock, and tumbled all the contents on the floor, carrying away two shawls, two new dresses, and a variety of articles, along with the spoon, which had unluckily been left, after creaming the milk for my tea, and a table-cloth (good), which had been drying Nero; they had also drunk the milk for my breakfast, and eaten a sweet cake baked for me by Mrs. Piper; but they had not taken the half of Fanny's clothes, which are all excel-lent; nor three sovereigns, which she had lying wrapped in a bit of brown paper at the bottom of her box; nor a good many things of mine that were lying open in a basket for the laundress, and which they had also tumbled on the floor; nor many little things lying about in the back kitchen, which would have useful to them, whence I infer that they had been frightened away. Fanny, though not conscious of having heard them, said that about mid-night 'something awoke her,' and she stretched out her hand for her handkerchief which lay on a table at her bedside, and in so doing

knocked over a brass candlestick, which 'made a devil of a row '—
doubtless that had disturbed them, or we should have lost more.
As it was, Fanny's loss amounted to four sovereigns, I computed,
which, of course, I gave her, though she was not expecting, poor
thing, to be compensated, and kept declaring she was thankful it was her, and not the mistress, that had lost most. There
were dirty prints of naked feet all over the larder shelf, on which
they stepped from the window; a piece of the new shelf burnt with
a candle that had been stuck to it. A mercy the fine new house
was not set on fire! Policemen, four of them, kept coming in plain
clothes, and in uniform, for the next three days, talking the most
confounded nonsense, and then died away *reinfecta*, not a trace of
any of the *corpus delicti* found. Mr. Chalmers had a pair of heavy
steps carried over his wall, and applied to a window of number
one the same night, and a pair of bad worsted stockings left in his
conservatory; the carrying away of the steps proved there had been
more than one thief, as they were too heavy for one to take over a
high wall. The window at number one was got up a little way,
but stuck there. Almost every night since some house in the immediate neighbourhood has been entered or attempted, and still the
police go about ' with their fingers in their mouths.' Of course I
no longer went out to sleep, but occupied the sofa below, where
the paint was least noxious. Fanny was thrown into such a nervous state that I was sure she would take a nervous fever if she
were not relieved from all sense of responsibility, which could only
be through my own presence in the house. So I declined Mr. Piper's
offer to come and sleep here instead of me. Besides, as they had
seen our open condition—ladders of all lengths lying in the garden,
and all the windows to the back, except the parlour ones, absolutely without fastenings (!)—I had considerable apprehension that
they would return in great force, and Mr. Piper, his wife confessed to me, ' would be useless against thieves, as he slept like a
stone.' I sleep lightly enough for such emergency, and if I had to
wait several days before the carpenter would return to put on the
fastenings, I could at least furnish myself with a pair of loaded
pistols. Capital good ones lie at my bedside every night, the
identical pistols with which old Walter of the *Times* was to have
fought his duel, which did not come off. Bars of iron I got put in
the larder window next day, independently of Mr. Morgan. In a
day or two more these bothering ladders will be taken away, and
then, when I go to the Grange on Friday, Mr. Piper can come for

the consolation of Fanny's imagination, and sleep as sound as he likes. I took care to let all the workmen, and extraneous people about, know of my loaded pistols. The painter came and examined them one day when I was out, and said to Fanny: 'I shouldn't like to be a thief within twenty feet of your mistress, with one of these pistols in her hand. I shouldn't give much for my life; she has such a devil of a straight eye!' The workmen have all had to suffer a good deal from my 'eye,' which has often proved their foot rules and leads in error.

In writing to Isabella to-night I said nothing of all this, in case of frightening your mother, nor have I told Mr. Carlyle, in case he should take it in his head to be uneasy, which is not likely, but just possible.

And now good-night, and kind regards to the Ba-ing,[1]

Affectionately yours,

JANE CARLYLE.

---

[1] Note, p. 328.

END OF VOLUME I.

LETTERS AND MEMORIALS

OF

JANE WELSH CARLYLE

PREPARED FOR PUBLICATION

BY

THOMAS CARLYLE

EDITED BY

JAMES ANTHONY FROUDE

TWO VOLUMES IN ONE

VOL. II

NEW YORK

HARPER & BROTHERS, FRANKLIN SQUARE

1883

LETTERS AND MEMORIALS

OF

JANE WELSH CARLYLE.

LETTER 151.

Returning (middle of October, 1852), 'half dead,' out of those German horrors of indigestion, insomnia, and continual chaotic wretchedness, I fly upstairs to my poor Heroic Helper; am met by her dear warning, 'Take care of the paint!' and find that she too is still fighting—has not conquered—that beast of a task, undertaken voluntarily for love of one unworthy. Alas, alas! it pains me to the heart, as it may well do, to think of all that. Was ever any noble, delicate, and tender woman plunged into such an abyss of base miseries by her own nobleness of heart and of talent, and the black stupidities of others? She was engaged out to dinner, and, as it was already night, constrained me to go with her. Hans Place. Senior, Frederick Elliot, &c.—not a charming thing in the circumstances.

We hereupon took refuge for a week or ten days (it seems) at the Grange—nothing recollected by me there—and by November were at last settled in our own clean house. Frederick had been upon my mind since 1851, and much reading and considering going on; but even yet, after my German investments of toil and pain, I felt uncertain, disinclined, and in the end engaged in it merely on the principle *Tantus labor non sit cassus* (as the 'Dies Iræ' has it). My heart was not in it: other such shoreless and bottomless chaos, with traces of a hero imprisoned there, I did never behold, nor will another soon in this world. *Stupiditas stupiditatum, omnia stupiditas.*

Beginning of March 1853 I must have been again at the Grange for about a month. Portuguese Ambassador and other lofty insignificancies I can vaguely recollect, but their date not at all. *She* from some wise choice of her own, wise and kind it was sure to be, had remained at home.—T. C.

To Mrs. Russell, Thornhill.

5 Cheyne Row: Friday, Dec. 31, 1852.

My dear Mrs. Russell,—Here is another year; God help us all! I hope it finds you better than when I last heard of you from my friends at Auchertool. I have often been meaning to write to you

II.—1

without waiting for a New Year's Day; but in all my life I never have been so driven off all letter-writing as since the repairs began in this house. There were four months of that confusion, which ended quite romantically, in my having to sleep with loaded pistols at my bedside! the smell of paint making it as much as my life was worth to sleep with closed windows, and the thieves having become aware of the state of the premises. Once they got in and stole some six pounds' worth of things, before they were frightened away by a candlestick falling and making what my Irish maid called 'a devil of a row;' it was rather to be called 'an angel of a row,' as it saved further depredation. Another time they climbed up to the drawing-room windows, and found them fastened, for a wonder! Another night I was alarmed by a sound as of a pane of glass cut, and leapt out of bed, and struck a light, and listened, and heard the same sound repeated, and then a great bang, like breaking in some panel. I took one of my loaded pistols, and went downstairs, and then another bang which I perceived was at the front door. 'What do you want?' I asked; 'who are you?' 'It's the policeman, if you please; do you know that your parlour windows are both open?' It was true! I had forgotten to close them, and the policeman had first tried the bell, which made the shivering sound, the wire being detached from the bell, and when he found he could not ring it he had beaten on the door with his stick, the knocker also being off while it was getting painted. I could not help laughing at what the man's feelings would have been had he known of the cocked pistol within a few inches of him. All that sort of thing, and much else more disagreeable, and less amusing, quite took away all my spirit for writing; then, when Mr. C—— returned from Germany, we went to the Grange for some weeks; then when I came home, and the workmen were actually out of the house, there was everything to look for, and be put in its place, and really things are hardly in their places up to this hour. Heaven defend me from ever again having any house I live in 'made habitable!'

What beautiful weather! I was walking in the garden by moonlight last night without bonnet or shawl! A difference from being shut up for four months, as I used to be in the winter.

All is quiet in London now that we have got that weary Duke's funeral over; for a while it made our neighbourhood perfectly intolerable. I never saw streets so jammed with human beings in all my life. I saw the lying-in-state, at the cost of being crushed for four hours, and it was much like scenes I have seen in the Lyceum

Theatre, only not so well got up as Vestris would have had it. I also saw the procession from Bath House, and that too displeased me; however, when the funeral car happened to stop exactly opposite to the window I was sitting at for some eight minutes, and I saw Lord Ashburton, and several others of the Duke's personal friends standing on the terrace underneath, with their hats off, looking on the ground very sorrowful, and remembered that the last time I had seen the old Duke alive was in that very room, I could not help feeling as if he were pausing there to take eternal leave of us all, and fell to crying, and couldn't stop till it was all over. I send you some pictures of the thing which are quite accurate. It may amuse you to see what you must have read so much of in the newspapers.

And now will you give Mary and Margaret some tea or something, with my blessing, and dispose of the rest of the sovereign as you see fit?

With kindest regards to your husband and father, believe me

Ever, dear Mrs. Russell,

Yours affectionately,

JANE CARLYLE.

LETTER 152.

Sir James Stephen used to frequent us on an evening now and then—a volunteer, and much welcome always. Son is the now notable James Fitzjames. Fat Boy is Senior the younger; had been at Malvern with us for the reason below, 'too much 'ealth,' according to the Gullies.—T. C.

T. Carlyle, Esq., at the Grange.

Chelsea: Thursday, March 31, 1853.

Several letters for you; but nothing to tell, except that we have had a—what shall I say?—second fright with the cat! He or she (whichever be its honour-worthy sex) disappeared this time for a whole day and night together, and having gone away over the garden wall, returned by the front area. A clever cat this one, evidently, but of an unsettled turn of mind. The weather is beautiful now; the wind in the east, I fancy, from the roughness of my general skin; but the sun cannot be shining more brightly even at the Grange.

Sir James Stephen and his inseparable long son left a card yesterday. I saw them from the top of the street, and slackened my

steps, till they were clear off. 'The Fat Boy' also made an ineffectual call one day, surely in a moment of 'too much *'elth !'* I
was in the house, but 'engaged,' reading the last pages of 'Jeanne
de Vaudreuil,' which, if Lady A. felt down to reading a pretty
religious book, you may safely recommend to her; it is worth a
dozen 'Preciosas.'

When I was paying a bill at Wain's on Monday, he asked, with
an attempted solemnity, 'had I heard the news?' 'No, I had
heard nothing; what was it?' 'The Queen!' 'Well?' 'Premature labour.' 'Well! what of that?' 'But—accompanied with
death!' 'The child you mean?' 'No, the Queen!—very distressing isn't it, ma'am—so young a woman? Is there anything I can
have the pleasure of sending you to-day?' I hardly believed the
thing, and by going a little further satisfied myself it was 'a
false report.' But was not that way of looking at it, 'so young a
woman,' noteworthy? Mr. Wain being a model of respectable
shopkeepers. What a difference since the time of the Princess
Charlotte!

Tell Lady A. that I think there is no great harm in oranges in
the forenoon; the rubbish at dessert is what you need to be withheld from.

I should be glad if you would ask for a bouquet for me when
you are coming away.   Ever yours,

                                          J. W. C.

LETTER 153.

'Moffat House,' where brother John was now established with
his wife, is the Raehills' (Hope Johnstone) town house; a big, old-
fashioned, red ashlar edifice, stands gaunt and high in the central
part of Moffat; which the Hope Johnstones now never use, and
which, some time ago, brother John had rented as a dwelling-place,
handy for Scotsbrig, &c., being one of various advantages. 'Beattock' (ancient Roman, it is thought) is now the railway station
about a mile from Moffat.

To T. Carlyle, Chelsea.

Moffat House: Friday, July 8, 1853.

And my letter must be in the Post-Office before one o'clock!
'Very absurd!'[1] And I have had to go to Beattock in the omnibus with my cousin Helen to see her off for Glasgow, and am so

---

[1] 'Very absurd' is a phrase of John's.

tired! Don't wonder then if you get a 'John's letter'[1] from me also.

The most important thing I have to tell you is, that you could not know me here, as I sit, from a Red-Indian! That I was kept awake the first night after my arrival by a—hyæna! (Yes, upon my honour; and you complain of a simple cock!) And that yesterday I was as near as possible to giving occasion for the most romantic paragraph, of the 'melancholy accident' nature, that has appeared in any newspaper for some years!

But, first, of the hyæna. On my arrival I found an immense caravan of wild beasts, pitched exactly in front of this house; and they went on their way during the night, and the animal in question made a devil of a row. I thought it was the lion roaring; but John said 'No, it was only the hyæna!' I rather enjoyed the oddness of having fled into the country for 'quiet,' and being kept awake by wild beasts!

Well, having got no sleep the first night, owing to these beasts, and my faceache, I felt very bothered all Wednesday, and gladly accepted John's offer to tell you of my safe arrival, meaning to write myself yesterday. But it was settled that we should go yesterday to see St. Mary's Loch, and the Grey-Mare's Tail.[2] We started at nine of the morning in an open carriage, 'the Doctor,' and Phœbe—a tall, red-haired young woman, with a hoarse voice, who is here on a visit ('the bridesmaid' she was); my cousin Helen, one little boy, and myself: the other two boys preceding us on horseback. It was the loveliest of days; and beautifuller scenery I never beheld. Besides that, it was full of tender interest for me as the birthplace of my mother. No pursuit of the picturesque had ever gone better with me till on the way back, when we stopped to take a nearer inspection of the Tail. The boys had been left fishing in the Loch of the Lows. John and Miss Hutchison had gone over the hills by another road to look at Loch Skene, and were to meet us at the Tail; so there were only Phœbe, Helen, and I as we went up to the Tail from underneath.

We went on together to the customary point of view, and then I scrambled on by myself (that is, with Nero), from my habitual tendency to go a little further always than the rest. Nero grew quite frightened, and pressed against my legs; and when we came

---

[1] Too brief generally.

[2] Lofty cataract in the green wilderness left altogether to itself—the most impressive I ever looked on. (See Sir Walter Scott, &c.)

close in front of the waterfall, he stretched his neck out at it from under my petticoats, and then barked furiously. Just then, I saw John waving his hat to me from the top of the hill; and, excited by the grandeur of the scene, I quite forgot how old I was, how out of the practice of 'speeling rocks;' and quite forgot, too, that John had made me take the night before a double dose of morphia, which was still in my head, making it very light; and I began to climb up the precipice! For a little way I got on well enough; but when I discovered that I was climbing up a ridge (!), that the precipice was not only behind but on both sides of me, I grew, for the first time in my life that I remember of, frightened, physically frightened; I was not only afraid of falling down, but of losing my head to the extent of throwing myself down. To go back on my hands and knees as I had come up was impossible; my only chance was to look at the grass under my face, and toil on till John should see me. I tried to call to him, but my tongue stuck fast and dry to the roof of my mouth; Nero barking with terror, and keeping close to my head, still further confused me. John had meanwhile been descending the hill; and, holding by the grass, we reached one another. He said, 'Hold on; don't give way to panic; I will stand between you and everything short of death.' We had now got off the ridge, on to the slope of the hill; but it was so steep that, in the panic I had taken, my danger was extreme for the next quarter of an hour. The bed of a torrent, visible up there, had been for a long time the object of my desire; I thought I should stick faster there, than on the grassy slope with the precipipice at the bottom of it: but John called to me that 'if I got among those stones I should roll to perdition.' He was very kind, encouraging me all he could, but no other assistance was possible. In my life I was never so thankful as when I found myself at the bottom of that hill with a glass of water to drink. None of them knew the horrors I had suffered, for I made no screaming or crying; but my face, they said, was purple all over, with a large black spot under each eye. And to-day I still retain something of the same complexion, and I am all of a tremble, as as if I had been on the rack.[1]

It is a lovely place this, and a charming old-fashioned house, with 'grounds' at the back. It is comfortably but plainly and old-fashionedly furnished, looks as if it had been stripped of all its

---

[1] Terrible to me was the first reading of this, with memory of the horror and peril of the actual locality.

ornamental details, and just the necessaries left. There is a cook, housemaid, and lady's-maid, and everything goes on very nicely. The three boys are as clever, well-behaved boys as I ever saw, and seem excessively fond of 'the Doctor.' John is as kind as kind can be, and seems to have an excellent gift of making his guests comfortable. Phœbe's manner is so different from mine, so formal and cold, that I don't feel at ease with her yet. She looks to me like a woman who had been all her life made the first person with those she lived beside, and to feel herself in a false position when she doubts her superiority being recognised. She seems very content with John, however, and to suit him entirely.

My hand shakes so, you must excuse illegibility.

I don't know yet when I am to go to Scotsbrig.

[No room to sign.]

LETTER 154.

Mrs. Braid is the excellent, much loving, and much loved old servant Betty. Her husband Braid, an honest enough East-Lothian man, is by trade and employment a journeyman mason in Edinburgh, his wife keeping a little shop in Adam Street there by way of supplement. They have one child, 'George,' an innocent, good lad, who has learned the watchmaking business, and promises modestly in all ways to do well; but had, about this time, fallen into a kind of languid illness, from which, growing ever worse, and gradually deepening into utter paralysis, he never could recover, but was for eight or nine years the one continual care of poor Betty till he died.

Mrs. Braid, Adam Street, Edinburgh.

Moffat House, Moffat: July 13, 1853.

My dearest Betty,—I am afraid almost to tell you that I am here, without being able to say positively that I am coming to see you. When I left London, to see you was one of the chief pleasures I expected from my travels. I intended to be in Scotland some six weeks at least, and to go to Haddington and Fife. But now it seems likely I shall have to return to London, almost immediately, without having seen anyone but my husband's relations in Dumfriesshire. Mr. Carlyle remained behind at Chelsea, having never recovered (he says) from the knocking about he had last year in Scotland and Germany, while the house was repairing. He is very melancholy and helpless left alone at the best of times; and now I am afraid he is going to have a great sorrow in the death of his old mother. She has been in a frail way for years back; but within the last few days her weakness has increased so much that Dr. Carlyle thinks it probable enough she may not rally again, in which case I shall go home at once, to be some help to Mr. Carlyle. I am staying now with Dr. Carlyle's wife, while he himself is gone to see his mother; and his report to-night will decide me what to do. So in case I do not see you, dear Betty—and I fear I shall not see you—here is a ribbon, in remembrance of my birthday, with a kiss and my blessing.

Mr. Erskine writes that he saw you, and liked you very much. I am sure you would like him too.

The little view at the top of this sheet is where I live in London.

Bishop Terrot told me George was poorly when he saw you last. I hope he is recovered. If I do not write within a week, address to me, Cheyne Row, Chelsea.

Affectionately yours,
JANE CARLYLE.

LETTER 155.

Her visit to my mother I perfectly remember, and how my dear old mother insisted to rise from bed to be dressed, and go down-stairs to receive her daughter-in-law out of doors, and punctually did so. I suppose the last time she was in holiday clothes in this world! It touched me much. My Jane she had always honored as queen of us all. Never was a more perfect politeness of heart, beautifully shining through its naïve bits of embarrassments and simple peasant forms. A pious mother, if there ever was one: pious to God the Maker and to all He had made. Intellect, humour, softest pity, love, and, before all, perfect veracity in thought, in word, mind, and action; these were her characteristics, and had been now for above eighty-three years, in a humbly diligent, beneficent, and often toilsome and suffering life, which right surely had not been in vain for herself or others. The end was now evidently nigh, nor could we even wish, on those terms, much longer. Her state of utter feebleness and totally ruined health last year (1852) had been tragically plain to me on leaving for Germany. For the first time even my presence could give no pleasure, her head now so heavy.

These by my Jeannie are the last clear views I had of this nobly human mother. It is pity any such letters should be lost.

T. Carlyle, Esq., Chelsea.

Scotsbrig: July 20, 1853.

I daresay you have thought me very neglectful, dear, in not writing yesterday, to give you news of your mother; but there was nothing comfortable, or even positive, to be said yesterday; and to torture you at a distance with miserable uncertainties seemed a cruel attention. Through Saturday and Sunday your mother continued much the same as I found her on my last coming. Too weak and frail to be out of bed, but without pain or sickness; for the rest, perfectly clear in her mind, and liking us to be in the room talking to her. During the Sunday night she became very restless, and about seven on Monday morning she fell into a state which was considered by all here, the minister included, to be the beginning of the end. There was no pain, no struggle. She lay without sense or motion, cold and deathlike, hardly breathing at all. The minister prayed without her hearing him. John and Mary were sent for, with scarce a hope that they could arrive in time, and all of us sat in solemn silence awaiting the end. Had it come thus, you would have had no cause to lament, dear; a more merciful termination there could not have been to a good life. But after lying in this state from seven in the morning till a quarter after two in the day, she rallied as by miracle. Jane was wiping her lips with a wet sponge, when she (your mother) suddenly took the sponge out of Jane's hand and sponged her face all over with her own hand; then she opened her eyes, and spoke quite collectedly, as if nothing had happened; nor has she ever shown the least consciousness of having come through that fearful crisis.

When John and Mary arrived together, at a quarter after four, not expecting to find her alive, they found her a little weaker perhaps, but not otherwise worse than when they left her. She talked a good deal to me during the afternoon; said you had been as good a son to her as ever woman had; 'but indeed they had been all good bairns; and Isabella, puir bodie, was gaiy[1] distressed hersell, and it was just to say that Isabella had been often kind to her, extraordinar kind, and was ay kindest when they were alane thegither, and she had none else to depend on.' That I can well believe; and very glad I was to have those kind words to carry to Jamie and Isabella. Isabella had been crying all morning, for since Jane came your mother had hardly spoken to her. When I left your mother that night, she said in a clear, loud voice, 'I thank ye most kindly for all your attentions.' 'Oh, if I could but do you any good!' I said. 'Ye have done me good, mony a time,' she answered. I went to bed to lie awake all night, listening for noises. John slept in the mid-room. But the light of a new day found your mother better, rather than worse. It was more the recollection of the state in which

---

[1] Gaiy, pretty much.

II.—1*

she had been than her actual state that kept us in agitation all yesterday. One thing that leads me to believe her life will be prolonged
is, that she recovered out of that crisis by the natural strength that
was still in her; she must have been much stronger than anyone
thought, to have rallied after so many hours of such deathlike pros-
tration, entirely of herself.

She had been in the habit of getting what seems to me perfectly
extraordinary quantities of wine, whisky, and porter, exciting a
false strength, not to be depended on for an hour. Of late days
this system has been discontinued, and she takes now only little
drops of wine and water, two or three times a day, and about the
third of a tumbler of Guinness' porter at night. The day that John
was sent for last week, he told me himself she had 'a bottle of
wine (strong Greek wine), a quarter of a bottle of whisky (25 over
proof), besides a tumbler of porter.' A life kept up in that way
was neither to be depended on, nor I should say to be desired.
Now she is living on her own strength, such as it is; and you may
conceive what irritation is removed. I don't know whether it is to
be considered lucky or unlucky that I came at this time. Of
course I give as little trouble as possible, and make myself as
useful as possible, and I feel sure that Jamie and Isabella like me
to be here, even under these sad circumstances, and that the sight
of me coming and going in her room does your mother good rather
than harm; and then I shall be able to answer all your questions
about her when I come back, better than the others could do by
letter. As for Mary, she is the same kindly soul as I knew her at
Craigenputtock. Jamie was to have driven me over to the Gill on
Monday, and instead the empty gig was sent to bring Mary here.
She ran out of the house to meet me, and was told her mother was
at the point of death. She is still here—but goes home to-morrow,
I believe; and John goes back to Moffat to-day. He will probably
be down again to-morrow. It is a comfort to himself to come, but
he can do nothing; no doctor can do anything against old age,
which is your mother's whole disease.

I shall be home one of these days. Any little spirits for visiting
and travelling that I had left are completely worn out by what I
have found here. I only wait till things are re-established in a state
in which I can leave with comfort.

I have just been to see if your mother had awoke; she has slept
two hours. I asked her if she had any message for you, and she
said, 'None, I am afraid, that he will like to hear, for he'll be

sorry that I'm so frail.' She has had some chicken broth. I will write again to-morrow, and I beseech you not to be fancying her ill off in any way. She has no pain, no anxiety of mind, is more comfortable, really, lying in bed there 'so frail,' than we have often seen her going about after her work. She is attended to every moment of the day, gets everything she is able to take. No one can predict as to the length of her life, after what we saw on Monday; but there is nothing in her actual state or appearance to make it impossible, or even improbable, that she should live a long time yet. I would much rather not have written to-day, but I judged that my silence might alarm you even more than the truth told you. I like few things worse than writing ill news.

Ever affectionately yours,

J. W. CARLYLE.

I had a very kind letter from Jeannie Chrystal,[1] pressing me to go there for a week or two; but, as I have said, I am quite out of heart. I have had no sleep the last two nights, and shall get none now, probably, till I am in my own bed at Chelsea. It is quite affecting, James's devoted attention to me. If I am but out half an hour for a walk, he will follow me to my bedroom, no matter how early in the day, carrying (very awkwardly, you may be sure) a little tray with a decanter of wine (not the Greek wine, but wine bought for me by himself) and a plateful of shortbread. Nor can anybody be more heartily and politely kind than Isabella has been to me.

My remembrances to Fanny.

LETTER 156.

To T. Carlyle, Chelsea.

Scotsbrig: Thursday, July 21, 1853.

It is a pleasure to write to-day, dear; your mother is so well. She went to sleep last night about eight o'clock, and slept a fine natural '*pluffing*' sleep till one in the morning, when she awoke and asked for some porridge, which having taken, she went to sleep again, and slept till six in the morning. Then she opened her eyes and said, 'write a line to the doctor' by the train to tell him 'no to come back the-day; for 'atwell[2] she wasna needing

---

[1] Cousin Jeannie, of Liverpool, now wedded in Glasgow.
[2] That well; very certainly.

him.' Then off to sleep again till half after nine. I was sitting at
her bedside when she woke up then quite fresh, and her first word
was, 'Did they send a bit line to the doctor to bid him no come?'

Her going on hitherto is all confirmatory of my first impression,
that it could not be for nothing that she had come out of that
death-like trance through her own unassisted strength; but that
she was going to have a new lease of life with better health than
before. I have not seen her so well as she is to-day since I came
to the country; and Jane says she has not seen her so well since
Candlemas; and Mr. Tait [1] told me an hour ago he had not seen
her so well for eight weeks. And she has not a drop of wine or
whisky, or any of those horrible stimulants to-day, so that one is
sure the wellness is real.

It was put in my power, 'quite promiscuously,' to give her a
little pleasure this morning. I 'do all the walking of the family'
at present; carry all the letters backwards and forwards, like a
regular post-woman, of my own free will of course, for Jamie
would send to Middlebie or Ecclefechan at any time for me; but I
can be best spared to go, and I like it. Since I came here, I 'have
been known' to walk to Ecclefechan and back again twice in one
day! And most times I get an old man for company; different old
men attach themselves to me, like lovers; and I find their innocent
talk very refreshing.

This morning I went to Middlebie as usual on the chance of a
letter from you, and the post, as usual, not being come (I always
go far too soon), I walked on, as usual, and met the postman half-
way to Ecclefechan. Coming back, reading your notes, I met
three or four women, one of whom stopped me to inquire for your
mother. Then she left her companions and turned back with me,
telling me about her mother, how ill she had been last week, and
that she would 'like weel to ken what I thocht o' her looks compared wi' Mrs. Cairl's.' [2] And when we arrived at a farmhouse on
the Ecclefechan side of the mill she begged me, as a great favour,
'just to step in and take a look o' her mother, and say what I
thocht.' I did not refuse, of course; but went in, and sat awhile
beside a good patient-looking old woman in the bed, who asked
many questions about your mother, and told me much about herself. When I came in and described where I had been, it turned
out I had brought your mother the very information she had been
asking of all the rest yesterday with no result; and she had left off,

---

[1] The clergyman.   [2] Low Annandale for 'Carlyle's.'

saying, 'naebody cared for auld-folks nowadays, or some o' them would hae gaen an' asket for puir Mrs. Corrie.' And there had I come home with the most particular intelligence of Mrs. Corrie.

I must write to Thomas Erskine to-day; and to Liverpool to tell them they may look for me any day. With John hovering about 'not like one crow, but a whole flight of crows,' and Jane rubbing everything up the wrong way of the hair, my position is not so tenable as it would have been alone with your mother and Jamie and Isabella. But I could not have gone with comfort to myself, while your mother was in so critical a state. I shall probably go to Liverpool to-morrow or next day; at all events, you had best write there.

I am decidedly of opinion that one should make oneself inde-peudent of Rocna[1] and all contingencies by building the 'sound-proof' room, since so much money has already been spent on that house.

Yours ever affectionately,
JANE W. C.

LETTER 157.

A letter, perhaps two letters, seem to be lost here, which con-tained painful and yet beautiful and honestly pathetic details of her quitting Scotsbrig before the time looked for, and on grounds which had not appeared to her, nor to anybody except my brother John, to be really necessary in such a fashion. It is certain all the rest at Scotsbrig (Jamie and Isabella especially, her hosts there) were vexed to the heart, as she could herself notice; and her own feeling of the matter was sorrowful and painful, and continued so in a degree, ever after, when it rose to memory. My dear little heavy-laden, tender-hearted, 'worn and weary,' fellow pilgrim, feet bleeding by the way over the thorns of this bewildered earth. Of this weeping all the way to Carlisle, on quitting one's fatherland, I

---

[1] Ronca, inhabitant of the then dilapidated No. 6 next door, who nearly killed us with poultry and other noises! The 'sound-proof room' was a flat-tering delusion of an ingenious needy builder, for which we afterwards paid dear. Being now fairly in for 'Frederick,' and the poultry, parrots, Cochin China, and vermin like to drive one mad, I at last gave in to the seducer, set him to work on the top of the house story as floor, and got a room, large, well ventilated, but by far the noisiest in the house, and in point of bad building, scamping, and enormity of new expense and of unexpected bad behaviour in hand and heart by his man and him, a kind of infernal 'miracle' to me then and ever since; my first view of the Satan's invisible world that prevails in that department as in others.

surely remember another letter to have said (in the words of a foolish song then current)—

> And I left my youth behind
> For somebody else to find,

which gave the last sad touch to the picture. In one of her letters
to me it indubitably was. ' Sophy,' an orphan half-cousin, to whom
and to her mother Uncle John's munificence had been fatherly and
princely, was now, and still continues, Alick Welsh's good and
amiable wife.

T. C.

To T. Carlyle, Chelsea.

Liverpool: Monday, July 25, 1853.

Sophy's letter yesterday would be better than nothing, would at
least satisfy you I had come to hand, though in *assez mauvais état*.
I got your last letter, addressed to Scotsbrig, at Middlebie on my
way to the station; and it cheered me up a little for 'taking the
road.' God knows I needed some cheering. In spite of your letter
I cried all the way to Carlisle pretty well; I felt to love my poor
old country so much in leaving it that morning, privately minded
never to return. After an hour-and-half of waiting at Carlisle I
was whirled to Liverpool so fast, oh so fast! My brains somehow
couldn't subside after. The warmest welcome awaited me at Maryland Street. My uncle looked especially pleased; Nero ran up to
him alone in the drawing-room, as if to tell we were come; and
when I went in, it was standing at his knees, my uncle's hand on
his head, as if receiving his blessing.

But the front door and windows were being painted at Maryland
Street; and they were afraid of the smell annoying me, and had
settled I was to sleep at Alick's. Alick and Sophy were there to
take me home with them. I was better pleased to sleep here; it is
a much larger, better-aired house. A more comfortable, quieter
bedroom never was slept in; but I couldn't close my eyes; took two
morphia pills at three in the morning, and they produced that horrible sickness which morphia produces in some people.

All yesterday I was in bed alternating between retching and
fainting. Sophy ' came out very strong' as a nurse, and even as a
doctor; reminding me so much of her mother. I wish you would
write two lines of answer to her note; she was really uncommonly
kind to me. To-day I am recovered, having slept pretty well last
night, only ' too weak for anything.' I shall probably be home on
Thursday, hardly sooner I think; but I will write again before I

come. I told Sophy to tell you that your mother had slept twelve hours the night before I came away. She does not read herself at present, but Jane was reading the books you sent aloud to her. And Margaret Austin read aloud some of Chalmers's letters.

As Jamie and I were driving to the station on Saturday, we met Jessie Austin going to Scotsbrig to stay a little while in room of Margaret, who had gone home when Jean came.

I thought Jessie a remarkably nice-looking young woman, sweet-tempered, intelligent, and affectionate-looking, and well-bred withal. I only spoke with her five minutes in passing, but she made the most decided impression on me.

'No more at present.'

Affectionately yours

J. W. C.

Your letter to Maryland Street was brought up in the morning; but I could not read it till after noon. Thanks for never neglecting.

[Contains inclosure from Kate Sterling (dated 'Petersburg'!); do. from sister Mary, last part of letter is written on that.]

LETTER 158.

'Uncle John,' at Liverpool, died shortly after Mrs. Carlyle returned to London. 'Helen,' to whom this letter is written, died a few weeks after.

To Miss Helen Welsh, Auchtertool Manse.

Chelsea: Wednesday, Oct. 12, 1853.

Dearest Helen,—I know not what I am going to say. I am quite stupefied. I had somehow never taken alarm at my uncle's last illness. I had fixed my apprehensions on the journey home, and was kept from present anxiety by that far off one. My beloved uncle, all that remained to me of my mother. A braver, more upright, more generous-hearted man never lived. When I took leave of him in Liverpool, and he said 'God bless you, dear' (he had never called me dear before), I felt it was the last time we should be together, felt that distinctly for a few hours; and then the impression wore off, and I thought I would go back soon, would go by the cheapest train (God help me), since it gave him pleasure to see me. That we have him no longer is all the grief! It was well he should die thus, gently and beautifully, with all his loving kindness fresh as a young man's; his enjoyment of life not wearied out; all our love for him as warm as ever; and well he should die in his own dear Scotland, amid quiet kindly things. We cannot, ought not to wish it had been otherwise, to wish he had lived on till his loss should have been less felt.

But what a change for you all, and for me too, little as I saw of him. To know that kind, good uncle was in the world for me, to care about me, however long absent, as nobody but one of one's own blood can, was a sweetness in my lonely life, which can be ill-spared.

Poor dear little Maggie, I know how she will grieve about these two days, and think of them more than of all the years of patient, loving nursing, which should be now her best comfort. Kiss her for me. God support you all. Write to me when you can what you are going to do. Alas! that I should be so far away from your councils. I need to know precisely about your future in an economical sense; through all the dull grief that is weighing on me, comes a sharp anxiety lest you should be less independent than heretofore; to be relieved of that will be the best comfort you could give me at present. I never knew what money you had to live on, nor thought about it; now, it is the first question I ask. I am dreary and stupid, and can write no more just now.

Your affectionate

J. C.

When I saw your handwriting again last night, my only thought was 'how good of her to write another letter soon.' I was long before I could understand it.

LETTER 159.

After her return, 'Friedrich' still going on in continual painful underground condition, the 'sound-proof' operation was set about, poor Charley zealously but ineffectually presiding; Irish labourers fetching and carrying, tearing and rending, our house once more a mere dust-cloud, and chaos come again. One Irish artist, I remember, had been ignorant that lath and plaster was not a floor; he, from above, accordingly came plunging down into my bedroom, catching himself by the arm-pits, fast swinging, astonished in the vortex of old laths, lime, and dust! Perhaps it was with him that Irish Fanny, some time after, ran away into matrimony of a kind. Run or walk away she did, in the course of these dismal tumults, she too having gradually forgotten old things; and was never more heard of here. We decided for Addiscombe, beautifullest cottage in the world; the noble owners glad we would occupy a room or two of it in their absence. I liked it much, and kept busy reading, writing, riding; she not so much, having none of these resources, no society at all, and except to put *me* right, no interest at all. I remember her coming and going; nay, I myself came and went. Off and on we stayed there for several weeks till the hurly-burly here was over or become tolerable. Miserable hurly-burly; the result of it, zero, and 'Satan's Invisible World Displayed' (in the building trade, as never dreamt of before!).

For the Christmas month, we were at the Grange, company brilliant, &c., &c.; but sad both of us, I by the evident sinking of my mother (though the accounts affected always to show the hopeful side); she, among other griefs, by the eminently practical one of Ronca's ' Demon Fowls,' as we now named them, and the totally futile issue of that ' sound-proof room.' ' My dear,' said she, one day to me, ' let us do as you have sometimes been saying, fairly rent that Ronca's house, turn Ronca with his vermin out of it, and let it stand empty—empty and noiseless. What is 40*l*. or 45*l*. a year, to saving one's life and sanity? Neighbour Chalmers will help me; the owner people are willing; say you "yes," and I will go at once and have the whole bedlam swept away against your return!' I looked at her with admiration; with grateful assent, 'Yes, if you can' (which I could only half believe). She is off accordingly, my saving companion (beautiful *Dea ex machinâ*), and on the day following, writes to me [T. C.]:—

To T. Carlyle, Esq., The Grange.

Chelsea: Monday, Dec. 19, 1853.

I cannot write till to-morrow, but just a line that you may not be fancying horrors about me. I did get home, and did do what was to be done, but now I must go to bed. It is nothing whatever but a nervous headache, which was sure to have come after so many nights without sleep; and perhaps it was as easy to transact it on the railway as in a bed in a strange house. I shall be better to-morrow, and will then tell you how the business proceeds.

Greetings to Lady B——.[1]

Yours ever,

J. W. C.

LETTER 160.

No. 6 Cheyne Row was, if I recollect, the joint property of two brothers, ' Martin ' their name, one of whom had fallen imbecile, and could, or at least did give no authority for outlay on the house, which had in consequence fallen quite into disrepair, and been let

---

[1] Dowager Lady Bath, perhaps.

to this Ronca with his washing tubs, poultries, and mechanic sons-in-law, and become intolerable as a neighbourhood. Poor Ronca was not a bad man, though a misguided ('Irish Fanny,' a Catholic like the rest of them, was thought to have done mischief in the matter); but clear it was, at any rate that on him (alone of all London specimens), soft treatment, never so skilful, so graceful, or gentle, could produce no effect whatever. But now wise appliance of the hard, soon brought him to new insight; and he had to knuckle and comply in all points. In a few days, my guardian genius saw herself completely victorious; the Ronca annoyances, Ronca himself in three months, &c., &c. Neighbour Chalmers, great in parochialities, did his best. The very house-agent was touched to the heart by such words (one Owlton, whom I never saw, but have ever since thanked), and this tragic *canaillerie* too had an end. As all here has—all—but not the meaning and first of all! Thou blessed one, no. Farther letters on this tragic contemptibility I find none; indeed, perhaps hardly any came till my own sad re-appearance in Chelsea, as will be seen.—T. C.

To Mrs. Russell, Thornhill.

5 Cheyne Row, Chelsea: Friday night, Dec. 31, 1853.

My dear Mrs. Russell,—Ever since I received your note by Mrs. Pringle, I have been meaning to write to you, yet always waited for a more cheerful season, and now here is New Year's day at hand, and my regular letter due, and the season is not more cheerful; and besides I am full of business, owing to the sudden movements of the last two weeks, and Mr. C——'s absence, leaving me his affairs to look after, as well as my own. We went to the Grange, (Lord Ashburton's) in the beginning of December to stay till after Christmas. I was very glad to get into the country for a while, and had nothing to do but dress dolls for a Christmas-tree For the last months had quite worn me out; I had had nothing but building and painting for so long, varied with Mr. C——'s outbursts against the 'infernal cocks' next door, which made our last addition of a ' silent apartment' necessary. Alas! and the silent apartment had turned out the noisiest apartment in the house, and the cocks still crowed, and the macaw still shrieked, and Mr. C—— still stormed. At the Grange I should at least escape all that for the time being, I thought. The first two days I felt in Paradise, and so well; the third day I smashed my head against a marble slab, raised a bump the size of a hen's egg on it, and gave a shock to my nerves that quite unfitted me for company. But I struggled on amidst the eighteen other visitors, better or worse, till at the end of a fortnight I was recovered, except for a slight lump still visible, when Mr. C—— came to me one morning, all of a sudden, and told me I must go up to London myself, and take charge of some business—nothing less than trying to take the adjoining house ourselves, on the chance of letting it, and get our disobliging neighbours turned out; and, there being but six days till Christmas (the time for giving them notice to quit), of course despatch was required, especially as the owner of the house lived away in Devonshire. I thought it a most wild-goose enterprise I was sent on, and when Lady Ashburton, and the others asked him why he sent poor me instead of going himself, and when he coolly answered, 'Oh I should only spoil the thing, she is sure to manage it;' it provoked me the more, I was so sure I could not manage it. But he was quite right—before the week was out I had done better than take a house we did not need, for I had got the people bound down legally 'under a penalty of ten pounds, and of immediate notice to quit, never to keep, or allow to be kept, fowls, or macaw, or other nuisance on their premises,' in consideration of five pounds given to them by Mr. Carlyle. I had the lease of the house, and the notice to quit lying at my disposal; but the threat having served the end, I had no wish to turn the people out. You may fancy what I had suffered, through the effects of these nuisances on Mr. C——, when I tell you that, on having this agreement put in my hand by their house-agent, I burst into tears, and should have kissed the man, if he had not been so ugly. Independently of the success of my diplomacy about the cocks, I was very thankful I happened to be sent home just then, otherwise I should have got the news of my cousin Helen's death in a houseful of company. It was shock enough to get it here. I had received a long letter from herself a day or two before leaving the Grange, in which she told me she was unusually well; and the night after my return I had sat till after midnight answering it. Two hours after it had gone to the post-office came Mary's letter announcing her death. And the same day came Mr. C——, who had suddenly taken the resolution to go to Scotsbrig, and see his mother once more, John's letter indicating that she was dying fast. I hurried him off all I could, for I was terrified he would arrive to find her dead, and he was just in time. He writes he will probably be home to-morrow night. It has been a continuous miracle for me, Mrs. C——'s living till now, after the state I saw her in last July. But poor Helen Welsh! One has to think hard, that she had a deadly disease with much suffering before her, painful operations before her, had she lived, to reconcile oneself to losing her so suddenly.

Tell me, when you write, if poor Mary got her comforter. Mrs. Aitken forgot it for a long time; but on my telling her you had not received it, she sent it, she said, at once. I send the money order for the usual purposes—Mary, Margaret, who else you like.

I hope Dr. Russell is quite strong now. Kind regards to him and your father. Tell Mrs. Pringle,[1] when you see her, that I regretted being from home when she called, and that I really think my own full second cousin might have come to see me without a recommendation, and at first, instead of at last. As she left word she was going next door, there was nothing to be said or done.

If you should not receive the usual donation from my cousins for old Mary, be sure to tell me; she must not be worse off at this advanced age. But I daresay Maggie will be very desirous to continue her father's good deeds. Poor little Maggie, I am like to cry whenever I think of her, kind, patient, active, little nurse, and now transplanted to another country, her occupation gone.

Your affectionate
J. W. CARLYLE.

I send for New Year's luck a book, which I hope you have not read already.

LETTER 161.

From the Grange I must have followed in three days. The Scotsbrig letters on my mother's situation were becoming more and more questionable, indistinct too (for they tried to flatter me); evident it was the end must be drawing nigh, and it would be better for me to go at once. Mournful leave given me by the Lady Ashburton; mournful encouragement to be speedy, not dilatory. After not many hours here I was on the road. Friday morning, December 23, 1853, got to the Kirtlebridge Station; a grey dreary element, cold, dim, and sorrowful to eye and to soul. Earth spotted with frozen snow on the thaw as I walked solitary the two miles to Scotsbrig; my own thought and question, will the departing still be there? Vivid are my recollections there; painful still and mournful exceedingly; but I need not record them. My poor old mother still knew me (or at times only half knew me); had no disease, but much misery; was sunk in weakness, weariness, and pain. She resembled her old self, thought I, as the last departing moonsickle does the moon itself, about to vanish in the dark waters. Sad, infinitely sad, if also sublime. Sister Jean was there. Mary and she had faithfully alternated there for long months. It was now, as we all saw, ending; and Jean's look unforgetably sad and grand. Saturday night breath was nearly impossible; teaspoons of

---

[1] A cousin of the Welsh family—one of the Hunters.

weak whisky punch alone giving some relief. Intellect intrinsically still clear as the sun, or as the stars, though pain occasionally overclouded it. About 10 P.M. she evidently did not know me till I explained. At midnight were her last words to me, tone almost kinder than usual, and, as if to make amends, ' Good night, and thank ye!' John had given her some drops of laudanum. In about an hour after she fell asleep, and spoke or awoke no more. All Sunday she lay sleeping, strongly breathing, face grand and statue like; about 4 P.M. the breath, without a struggle, scarcely with abatement for some seconds, fled away whence it had come. Sunday, Christmas Day, 1853. My age 58; hers 83.

T. Carlyle, Scotsbrig.

Chelsea: Tuesday, Dec. 27, 1853.

Oh, my dear! never does one feel oneself so utterly helpless as in trying to speak comfort for great bereavement. I will not try it. Time is the only comforter for the loss of a mother. One does not believe in time while the grief is quite new. One feels as if it could never, never be less. And yet all griefs, when there is no bitterness in them, are soothed down by time. And your grief for your mother must be altogether sweet and soft. You must feel that you have always been a good son to her; that you have always appreciated her as she deserved, and that she knew this, and loved you to the last momeet. How thankful you may be that you went when you did, in time to have the assurance of her love surviving all bodily weakness, made doubly sure to you by her last look and words. Oh! what I would have given for last words, to keep in my innermost heart all the rest of my life; but the words that awaited me were, ' Your mother is dead!' And I deserved it should so end. I was not the dutiful child to my mother that you have been to yours. Strange that I should have passed that Sunday in such utter seclusion here as if in sympathy with what was going on there.

It is a great mercy you have had some sleep. It will surely be a comfortable reflection for you in coming home this time, that you will look out over a perfectly empty hen-court; part of it even already pulled down, as all the rest, I daresay, soon will be. There are cocks enough in all directions, as poor Shuttleworth remarked; but none will plague you like those, which had become a fixed idea, and a question, Shall I, a man of genius, or you, 'a sooty washerwoman,' be master here? If you would like to know the ultimate fate of the poultry, it was sold away to a postman, who has 'a hobby for fowls,' in Milman's Row. I let them make what profit they could of their fowls, for we had no right to deprive them of them, only the right of humanity to have the people forced to do us a favour voluntarily for a suitable compensation. I am on terms of good neighbourhood now with all the Roncas, except the old laundress herself, who 'took to her bed nearly mad,' the married daughter told me, 'at lying under a penalty.' She must leave the place,' she said, 'her husband would sooner have died than broken his word, when he had passed it—and to be bound under a penalty!' I felt quite sorry for the people as soon as I had got them in my power, and have done what I could to soothe them down.

Ever yours

J. W. C.

LETTER 162.

Mrs. Russell, Thornhill.

5 Cheyne Row, Chelsea: July 13, 1854.

Isn't it frightful, dear Mrs. Russell, what a rate the years fly at? Another birthday came round to me! and it looks but a week or two ago since I was writing to you from Moffat! [1] The days look often long and weary enough in passing, but when all 'bunched up' (as my maid expresses it) into a year, it is no time at all to look back on.

We are still in London with no present thought of leaving it. The Ashburtons have gain offered us Addiscombe to rusticate at, while they are in the Highlands. But, in spite of the beauty and magnificence of that place, and all its belongings, I hate being there in the family's absence—am always afraid of my dog's making foot-marks on the sofas or carpet; of asking the fine housemaid to do something 'not in her work,' &c., &c.; and so would, for my part, much rather stay in my own house all the year round. When Mr. C—— gets ill with the heat, however—if this year there is to be any—he may choose to go there for a few weeks, and will need me to order his dinners.

I am hoping for a considerable acquisition before long: Miss Jewsbury, the authoress of 'The Half Sisters,' &c., the most intimate friend I have in the world, and who has lived generally at Manchester since we first knew each other, has decided to come and live near me for good. Her brother married eighteen months ago, and has

---

[1] Letter lost.

realised a baby, and a wife's mother in the house besides. So Geraldine felt it getting too hot for her there. It will be a real gain to have a woman I like, so near as the street in which I have decided on an apartment for her. All my acquaintances live so far off, that it is mechanically impossible to be intimate with them.

You would be sorry to hear of poor Elizabeth Welsh's [1] accident. Ann has written me two nice long letters since, and added as few printed documents [2] as could be expected from her. From my cousins I hear very little now. Jeannie in Glasgow never was a good correspondent; I mean, always wrote remarkably bad letters, considering her faculty in some other directions. Now there is a little tone of married woman, and much made of married woman, added to the dulness and long-windedness, that irritates me into— silence. As for the others, they all seem to think I have nothing to do at my age, but send them two or three letters for one! When my dear uncle was alive, my anxiety to hear of him overcame all other considerations; and I humoured this negligence more than was reasonable. Besides, Helen wrote pretty often, poor dear, and good letters, telling me something. Now, as they are all healthy, and 'at ease in Zion,' I mean to bear in mind, more than heretofore, that I am not healthy, and have many demands on my time and thought, and am, besides, sufficiently their elder to have my letters answered.

I began to make a cap for old Mary; but it is impossible to get on with sewing at this season; so you must give her a pound of tea from me instead. Do you know I am not sure to this moment that she ever got the woollen thing I sent her through Mrs. Aitken. Mrs. Aitken forgot it, I know, and it was long after she said she had sent it to you by the carrier.

God bless you, dear Mrs. Russell. I am in a great hurry, visitors having kept me up all the forenoon. Love to your father and husband.

Yours affectionately,

JANE CARLYLE.

I inclose a cheque (!) for five shillings.

---

[1] Her eldest aunt; fell and dislocated the thigh-bone; lame ever since. Youngest aunt, Grace, is now dead (since 1867).

[2] Given to inclose tracts, &c. Poor, good Ann!

EXTRACTS.

To Mrs. Russell.

November 7, 1854.—Oh, aren't you miserable about this war?[1] I am haunted day and night with the thought of all the women of England, Scotland, and Ireland, who must be in agonies of suspense about their nearest and dearest. Thank God I have no husband, or father, or son, in that horrible war. I have some few acquaintances, however, and one intimate friend—Colonel Sterling; and I read the list of killed and wounded always with a sick dread of finding his name.

To the same.

December 30.—I have been shut up in the house almost entirely for six weeks with one of my long colds; but for that I should have been now at the Grange, where I had engaged myself to go on the 19th. The month of country, of pure air and green fields, might have done me good; but I felt quite cowardly before the prospect of so much dressing for dinner and talking for effect, especially as I was to have gone this time on my own basis, Mr. C—— being too busy with his book to waste a month at present, besides having a sacred horror of two several lots of children who were to be there, and the bother about whom drove him out of all patience last year.

For me no letter in 1854. We did not shift at all from home that year, but were constantly together. Addiscombe at Easter was intended (at least for her) but it misgave. Ditto the Grange with me through December with a day or two of January—not executable either when the time came. She was in poor fluctuating health; I in dismal continual wrestle with 'Friedrich,' the *unexecutable* book, the second of my twelve years' 'wrestle' in that element! My days were black and spiritually muddy; hers, too, very weak and dreamy, though *un*complaining; never did complain once of *her unchosen* sufferings and miserable eclipse under the writing of that sad book.

One day last year (November 8, 1854) I had run out to Windsor (introduced by Lady Ashburton and her high people) in quest of Prussian prints and portraits—saw some—saw Prince Albert, my one interview, for about an hour, till Majesty summoned him out to walk. The Prince was very good and human. Next autumn (1855) I was persuaded out to a Suffolk week, under Edward Fitzgerald's keeping, who had been a familiar of mine ever since the old battle of Naseby inquiries. Father, a blundering Irishman,

---

[1] Thrice stupid, hideous blotch of a 'Crimean War,' so called.

once proprietor of vast estates there and in Suffolk, &c. Foolish Naseby monument, his. Edward still lives in Woodbridge, or oftenest in his coasting boat, a solitary, shy, kindhearted man. Farlingay was a rough, roomy farm and house, which had once been papa's, and where Edward still had a rough and kind home when he chose. I did not fare intolerably there at all; kind people, rather interesting to me. Snatch of country welcome on the terms. The good Fitz gave me a long day's driving, and, indeed, several others shorter, which are partly in my recollection, too. I had seen Aldborough, had bathed there, and thought as a *quasi*-deserted, but not the least dilapidated, place it might suit us for a lodging.

Ugly home voyage in Ipswich steamer, &c., stuffy railway having grown so horrible to me. At Addiscombe some time after, I had three weeks, mostly of utter solitude, strange and sombre. She only going and coming as need was.—T. C.

LETTER 163.

T. Carlyle, Farlingay Hall.[1]

5 Cheyne Row, Chelsea: Aug. 14, 1855.

No, dear, I don't take your sea-bathing place, because I have a place of my own in view! Positively I fancy I have found the coming cottage.[2] I am just going off to consult Tait about it. And at all events you must go and look at it with me next Monday, before we incur any lodging expenses, which would be best laid out on a place ' all to oneself.'

I took such an amount of air and exercise yesterday as would have done for most nineteenth century ' females.' Started at eight by the boat,[3] with a good tide, and was at the station a quarter before nine. Was quite well situated in my open carriage, and reached Brighton without the least fatigue. Bathed, the first thing; and then walked along the shore to a little inn I had been told of by Neuberg and Ballantyne, as a charming, quiet place ' for even Mrs. Carlyle ' to stop at;—found it, of course, noisy, dirty, not to be even dined at by Mrs. Carlyle, and walked on still further along the cliffs to a village I had seen on the map, and was sure must be very retired. The name of it is Rottingdean. It is four miles at least from the Brighton station. I walked there and back again! and in the last two miles along the cliffs I met just one

---

[1] On visit there to Mr. Fitzgerald.

[2] A poor old vacant hut at Rottingdean, which was to be furnished, to be sure! Dear soul, what trouble she took, what hopes she had, about that! *Sunt lachrymæ rerum.*

[3] Chelsea steamboat, for London Bridge.

man! in a white smock! ¡Thus you perceive the travelling expenses to one of the quietest sea villages in England is just, per
boat and third class train, 3s. 10d.!—a convenient locality for one's
cottage at all rates. The place itself is an old sleepy-looking little ¸village close on the sea, with simple poor inhabitants; not
a trace of a lady or gentleman bather to be seen! In fact, except
at the inn, there were no lodgings visible. I asked the maid at
the inn, 'was it always as quiet as this?' 'Always,' she said in
a half whisper, with a half sigh, 'a'most too quiet!' Near the
inn, and so near the sea you could throw a stone into it, are
three houses in a row; the centre one old, quaint, and empty, small
rooms, but enough of them; and capable of being made very live-
able in, at small cost; and there are two 'decent women' I saw, who
might, either of them, be trusted to keep it. But I should fill sheets
with details without giving you a right impression. You must just
go and look. I returned to Brighton again, after having dined at
the Rottingdean on two fresh eggs, a plateful of homebaked bread
and butter, and a pint bottle of Guinness's (cha-arge 1s. 6d.) I
walked miles up and down Brighton to find the agent for that cottage—did finally get him by miracle; name and street being both
different from what I set out to seek; and almost committed myself
to take the cottage for a year at 12l. (no rates or taxes whatever) or
to take it for three months at 6l. However, I took fright about
your not liking it; and the expenses of furnishing, &c., &c., on the
road up; and wrote him a note from Alsop's shop that he might
not refuse any other offer and hold me engaged, till you had seen
and approved of it. If Tait shared this cottage, and went halves
in the furnishing, it would cost very little indeed. My only objection to it, this morning, is that one might not be able to get it another year; and then what would be done with the furniture? But
oh; what a beautiful sea! blue as the Firth of Forth it was last
night! I lay on the cliffs in the stillness, and looked at the 'beautiful Nature' for an hour and more; which was such a doing of the
picturesque as I have not been up to for years. The most curious
thing is the sudden solitude beginning without gradation just where
Kemp Town ends. It is as if the Brighton people were all enchanted
not to pass beyond their pier.

One can get any sort of lodgings in Brighton. I brought away
the card of one—very beautiful, and clean as a pin, where the lady
'received no dogs nor children; dogs she did not dislike, but she
dreaded their fleas!' An excellent sitting-room and bed-room 30s.;

sitting-room and two bed-rooms 2*l.*; but then they are such rooms as one has at home, not like Eastbourne! But Brighton is Brighton. Rottingdean is like a place in a novel.

I am stiff to-day. I had to walk to St. Paul's last night, after all my walking, before I got an omnibus, and then from Alsop's home.

And last night the results of Cremorne in the King's Road were —what shall I say? strange, upon my honour! First I heard a measured tread; and then, out of the darkness, advanced on me eight soldiers carrying, high over their heads, a bier! on which lay a figure covered with a black cloth, all but the white, white face ! And before I had recovered from the shock of that, some twenty yards further on, behold, precisely the same thing over again! I asked a working man what had happened. 'It was a great night at Cremorne, storming of Sebastopol; thirty or forty soldiers were storming,[1] when the scaffolding broke, and they all fell in on their own bayonets! The two who had passed were killed, they said, and all the others hurt.' But a sergeant, whom I accosted after, told me there were none killed and only three hurt badly.

Lord Goodrich had your ' Zouaves,'[2] and it is come back with a farewell note to me from the lady. And Lady Sandwich brought on Sunday 'Anecdotes Germaniques.' Is that one of the books you had last? Your silent room is swept and the books dusted.

I am making shocking writing; but my pen is horrid; my mind in a frightful hurry; and my hand very unsteady with yesterday's fatigues.

A letter from you was eagerly asked for last night, but it came this morning.

Those cows[3] must have been Philistines in some previous state of existence.   Ever yours,

                                        J. W. C.

Extracts from Mrs. Carlyle's Journal.

A part only of the following extracts was selected by Mr. Carlyle, and a part, sufficient merely to leave a painful impression, without explaining the origin of his wife's discomfort. There ought to be no mystery about Carlyle, and there is no occasion for mystery. The diaries and other papers were placed in my hands, that I might add whatever I might think necessary in the way of elucidation, and in this instance I have thought it right to avail myself

---

[1] Populace, soldiers, officers: was there ever seen such a transaction among men before?

[2] Some French booklet on the subject.   [3] Lowing by night!

of the permission. It has been already seen that among the acquaintances in the great world to whom Carlyle's reputation early introduced him, were Mr. and Lady Harriet Baring, afterwards Lord and Lady Ashburton. Mr. Baring, one of the best and wisest men in the high circle of English public life, was among the first to recognise Carlisle's extraordinary qualities. He soon became, and he remained to his death, the most intimate and attached of Carlyle's friends. Lady Harriet was a gifted and brilliant woman, who cared nothing for the frivolous occupations of fashion. She sought out and surrounded herself with the most distinguished persons in politics and literature, and was the centre of a planetary system, in which statesmen, poets, artists, every man who had raised himself into notice by genuine intellectual worth, revolved, while she lived, as satellites. By Lady Harriet, Carlyle was ardently welcomed. In the society which gathered about herself and her husband, he found himself among persons whom he could more nearly regard as his equals than any whom he had met with elsewhere. He was thrown into connection with the men who were carrying on the business of the world, in a sphere where he could make his influence felt among them. He was perhaps, at one time, ambitious of taking an active part in such affairs himself, and of ' doing something more for the world,' as Lord Byron said, ' than writing books for it.' At any rate his visits to Bath House and the Grange, Lord Ashburton's house in Hampshire, gave him great enjoyment, and for many years as much of his leisure as he could spare was spent in the Ashburton society.

The acquaintance which was so agreeable to himself was less pleasant to Mrs. Carlyle. She was intensely proud of her husband, and wished to be the first with him. She had married him against the advice of her friends, to be the companion of a person whom she, and she alone, at that time, believed to be destined for something extraordinary. She had worked for him like a servant, she had borne poverty and suffering. She had put up with his humours, which were often extremely trying. As long as she felt that he was really attached to her, she had taken the harder parts of her lot lightly and jestingly, and by her incessant watchfulness had made it possible for him to accomplish his work. And now his fame was established. He had risen beyond her highest expectations; she saw him feared, admired, reverenced, the acknowledged sovereign, at least in many eyes, of English literature; and she found, or thought she found, that, as he had risen she had become, what in an early letter she had said she dreaded that she might be, a ' mere accident of his lot.' When he was absorbed in his work, she saw but little of him. The work was a sufficient explanation as long as others were no better off than she was. But when she found that he had leisure for Bath House, though none for her, she became jealous and irritable. She was herself of course invited there; but the wives of men of genius, like the wives of bishops, do not take the social rank of their husbands. Women understand how to make one another uncomfortable in little ways invisible to others, and Mrs. Carlyle soon perceived that she was admitted into those high regions for her husband's sake and not for her own. She had a fiery temper, and a strong Scotch republican spirit, and she would have preferred to see Carlyle reigning alone in his own kingdom. Her anger was wrong in itself, and exaggerated in the form which it assumed. But Carlyle too was to blame. He ought to have managed his friendships better. He ought to have considered whether she had not causes of complaint; and to have remembered how much he owed to her care for him. But Carlyle was wilful, and impatient of contradiction. When his will was crossed, or resisted, his displeasure rushed into expressions not easily forgotten, and thus there grew up between these two, who at heart each admired and esteemed the other more than any other person in the world, a condition of things of which the trace is visible in this diary. The shadow slanted backwards over their whole lives together; and as she brooded over her wrongs, she came to think with bitterness of many recollections which she had laughed away or forgotten. Carlyle's letters during all this period were uniformly tender and affectionate, and in them was his true self, if she could but have allowed herself to see it. 'Oh,' he often said to me after she was gone, 'if I could but see her for five minutes to assure her that I had really cared for her throughout all that! But she never knew it, she never knew it.'—J. A. F.

October 21, 1855.—I remember Charles Buller saying of the Duchess de Praslin's murder, ' What could a poor fellow do with a wife who kept a journal but murder her?' There was a certain truth hidden in this light remark. Your journal all about feelings aggravates whatever is factitious and morbid in you; that I have made experience of. And now the only sort of journal I would keep should have to do with what Mr. Carlyle calls 'the fact of things.' It is very bleak and barren, this fact of things, as I now see it—very; and what good is to result from writing of it in a paper book is more than I can tell. But I have taken a notion to, and perhaps I shall blacken more paper this time, when I begin quite promiscuously without any moral end in view; but just as the Scotch professor drank whisky, because I like it, and because it's cheap.

October 22.—I was cut short in my introduction last night by Mr. C.'s return from Bath House. That eternal Bath House. I wonder how many thousand miles Mr. C. has walked between there and here, putting it all together; setting up always another milestone and another betwixt himself and me. Oh, good gracious! when I first noticed that heavy yellow house without knowing, or caring to know, who it belonged to, how far I was from dreaming that through years and years I should carry every stone's weight of it on my heart. About feelings already! Well, I will not proceed, though the thoughts I had in my bed about all that were tragical enough to fill a page of thrilling interest for myself, and though, as George Sand has shrewdly remarked, ' rien ne soulage comme la rhétorique.'

October 23.—A stormy day within doors, so I walked out early, and walked, walked, walked. If peace and quietness be not in one's own power, one can always give oneself at least bodily fatigue— no such bad succedaneum after all. Life gets to look for me like a sort of kaleidoscope—a few things of different colors—black predominating, which fate shakes into new and ever new combinations, but always the same things over again. To-day has been so like a day I still remember out of ten years ago; the same still dreamy October weather, the same tumult of mind contrasting with the outer stillness; the same causes for that tumult. Then, as now, I had walked, walked, walked, with no aim but to tire myself.

October 25.—Oh, good gracious alive; what a whirlwind—or rather whirlpool—of a day! Breakfast had 'passed off' better or worse, and I was at work on a picture-frame, my own invention, and pretending to be a little work of art, when Mr. C.'s bell rang like mad, and was followed by cries of ' Come, come! are you coming?' Arrived at the second landing, three steps at a time, I saw Mr. C. and Ann in the spare bedroom hazily through a waterfall! The great cistern had overflowed, and was raining and pouring down through the new ceiling, and plashing up on the new carpet. All the baths and basins in the house were quickly assembled on floor, and I, on my knees, mopping up with towels and sponges, &c.

In spite of this disaster, and the shocking bad temper induced by it, I have had to put on my company face to-night and receive. —— and —— were the party. Decidedly I must have a little of ' that damned thing called the milk of human kindness ' after all, for the assurance that poor —— was being amused kept me from feeling bored.

My heart is very sore to-night, but I have promised myself not to make this journal a ' miserere,' so I will take a dose of morphia and do the impossible to sleep.

October 31.—Rain! rain! rain! ' Oh, Lord! this is too ridiculous,' as the Annandale farmer exclaimed, starting to his feet when it began pouring, in the midst of his prayer for a dry hay time. I have no hay to be got in, or anything else that I know of, to be got in; but I have a plentiful crop of thorns to be got out, and that, too, requires good weather. To-day's post brought the kindest of let-

ters from Geraldine, enclosing a note from Lady de Capel Broke
she is staying with, inviting me to Oakley Hall. This lady's 'faith
in things unseen' excited similar faith on my part, and I would go,
had I nothing to consider but how I should like it when there. I
had to write a refusal, however. Mr. C. is 'neither to hold nor bind'
when I make new visiting acquaintances on my own basis, however unexceptionable the person may be. The evening devoted to
mending Mr. C.'s trowsers among other things! 'Being an only
child,' I never 'wished' to sew men's trowsers—no, never!

November 1.—At last a fair morning to rise to, thanks God!
Mazzini never says 'thank God' by any chance, but always
'thanks God;' and I find it sound more grateful. Fine weather
outside in fact, but indoors blowing a devil of a gale. Off into
space, then, to get the green mould that has been gathering upon
me of late days brushed off by human contact.

November 5.—Alone this evening. Lady A. in town again; and
Mr. C. of course at Bath House.

> When I think of what I is
> And what I used to was,
> I gin to think I've sold myself
> For very little cas.

November 6.—Mended Mr. C.'s dressing-gown. Much movement
under the free sky is needful for me to keep my heart from throbbing up into my head and maddening it. They must be comfortable people who have leisure to think about going to Heaven!
My most constant and pressing anxiety is to keep out of Bedlam! that's all . . . . Ach! If there were no feelings 'what
steady sailing craft we should be,' as the nautical gentleman of some
novel says.

November 7.—Dear, dear! What a sick day this has been with
me. Oh, my mother! nobody sees when I am suffering now; and
I have learnt to suffer 'All to myself.' From 'only childless' to
that, is a far and a rough road to travel.

> Oh, little did my mother think,
> The day she cradled me,
> The lands I was to travel in,
> The death I was to dee.

November.—'S'exagérer ses droits, oublier ceux des autres, cela
peut être fort commode; mais cela n'est pas toujours profitable et
on a lieu souvent de s'en repentir. Il vaudrait mieux souvent

avoir des vices qu'un caractère difficile. Pour que les femmes perdent les familles, il faut qu'elles aillent jusqu'à l'inconduite, jusqu'au désordre. Pour les y pousser, il suffit souvent qu'un homme gâte toutes ses bonnes qualités et les leurs par des procédés injustes, de la dureté et du dédain.'

It is not always, however, that unjust treatment, harshness, and disdain in her husband drives a woman *jusqu'au désordre*, but it drives her to something, and something not to his advantage any more than to hers.

To-day has been like other days outwardly. I have done this and that, and people have come and gone, but all as in a bad dream.

November 13.—Taken by —— to Lord John's lecture at Exeter Hall. The crowd was immense, and the applause terrific; the lecture 'water bewitched.' One thing rather puzzled me: at every mention of the name Christ (and there was far too much of it) the clapping and stamping rose to such a pitch that one expected always it must end in 'hip, hip, hurrah.' Did the Young Men's Christian Association take his Lordship's recognition of Christ as a personal compliment, or did it strike them with admiration that a Lord should know about Christ?

November 20.—I have been fretting inwardly all this day at the prospect of having to go and appeal before the Tax Commissioners at Kensington to-morrow morning. Still, it must be done. If Mr. C. should go himself he would run his head against some post in his impatience; and besides, for me, when it is over it will be over, whereas he would not get the better of it for twelve months—if ever at all.

November 21.—*O me miseram!* not one wink of sleep the whole night through! so great the ' rale mental agony in my own inside' at the thought of that korrid appealing. It was with feeling like the ghost of a dead dog, that I rose and dressed and drank my coffee, and then started for Kensington. Mr. C. said 'the voice of honour seemed to call on him to go himself.' But either it did not call loud enough, or he would not listen to that charmer. I went in a cab, to save all my breath for appealing. Set down at 30 Hornton Street, I found a dirty private-like house, only with Tax Office painted on the door. A dirty woman-servant opened the deor, and told me the Commissioners would not be there for half-an-hour, but I might walk up. There were already some half-score of men assembled in the waiting-room, among whom I saw

the man who cleans our clocks, and a young apothecary of Cheyne
Walk. All the others, to look at them, could not have been suspected for an instant, I should have said, of making a hundred a
year. Feeling in a false position, I stood by myself at a window
and 'thought shame' (as children say). Men trooped in by twos
and threes, till the small room was pretty well filled; at last a
woman showed herself. O my! did I ever know the full value
of any sort of woman—as woman—before! By this time some
benches had been brought in, and I was sitting nearest the door.
The woman sat down on the same bench with me, and, misery ac-
quainting one with strange bedfellows, we entered into conversation without having been introduced, and I had 'the happiness,' as
Allan termed it, 'of seeing a woman more miserable than myself.'
Two more women arrived at intervals, one a young girl of Dundee,
'sent by my uncle that's ill;' who looked to be always recapitulat-
ing inwardly what she had been told to say to the Commissioners.
The other, a widow, and such a goose, poor thing; she was bringing an appeal against no overcharge in her individual paper, but
against the doubling of the Income Tax. She had paid the double
tax once, she said, because she was told they would take her goods
for it if she didn't—and it was so disgraceful for one in a small
business to have her goods taken; besides it was very disadvantage-
ous; but now that it was come round again she would give. She
seemed to attach an irresistible pathos to the title of *widow*, this
woman. 'And me a widow, ma'm,' was the winding up of her
every paragraph. The men seemed as worried as the women,
though they put a better face on it, even carrying on a sort of sickly
laughing and bantering with one another. 'First-come lady,'
called the clerk, opening a small side-door, and I stept forward into
a *grand peutêtre*. There was an instant of darkness while the one
door was shut behind and the other opened in front; and there I
stood in a dim room where three men sat round a large table spread
with papers. One held a pen ready over an open ledger; another
was taking snuff, and had taken still worse in his time, to judge
by his shaky, clayed appearance. The third, who was plainly the
cock of that dung-heap, was sitting for Rhadamanthus—a Rhadamanthus without the justice. 'Name,' said the horned-owl-looking
individual holding the pen. 'Carlyle.' 'What?' 'Carlyle.'
Seeing he still looked dubious, I spelt it for him. 'Ha!' cried
Rhadamanthus, a big, bloodless-faced, insolent-looking fellow.
'What is this? why is Mr. Carlyle not come himself? Didn't he

II.—2*

get a letter ordering him to appear? Mr. Carlyle wrote some non-sense about being exempted from coming, and I desired an answer to be sent that he must come, must do as other people.' 'Then, sir,' I said, 'your desire has been neglected, it would seem, my husband having received no such letter; and I was told by one of your fellow Commissioners that Mr. Carlyle's personal appearance was not indispensable.' 'Huffgh! Huffgh! what does Mr. Carlyle mean by saying he has no income from his writings, when he him-self fixed it in the beginning at a hundred and fifty?' 'It means, sir, that, in ceasing to write, one ceases to be paid for writing, and Mr. Carlyle has published nothing for several years.' 'Huffgh! Huffgh! I understand nothing about that.' 'I do,' whispered the snuff-taking Commissioner at my ear. 'I can quite understand a literary man does not always make money. I would take it off, for my share, but (sinking his voice still lower) I am only one voice here, and not the most important.' 'There,' said I, handing to Rhadamanthus Chapman and Hall's account; 'that will prove Mr. Carlyle's statement.' 'What am I to make of that? Huffgh! we should have Mr. Carlyle here to swear to this before we believe it.' 'If a gentleman's word of honour written at the bottom of that paper is not enough, you can put me on my oath: I am ready to swear to it.' 'You! you, indeed! No, no! we can do nothing with your oath.' 'But, sir, I understand my husband's affairs fully, better than he does himself.' 'That I can well believe; but we can make nothing of this,' flinging my document contemptuously on the table. The horned owl picked it up, glanced over it while Rhadamanthus was tossing papers about, and grumbling about 'people that wouldn't conform to rules;' then handed it back to him, saying deprecatingly: 'But, sir, this is a very plain state-ment.' 'Then what has Mr. Carlyle to live upon? You don't mean to tell me he lives on that?' pointing to the document. 'Heaven forbid, sir! but I am not here to explain what Mr. Carlyle has to live on, only to declare his income from literature during the last three years.' 'True! true!' mumbled the not-most-important voice at my elbow. 'Mr. Carlyle, I believe, has landed income.' 'Of which,' said I haughtily, 'for my spirit was up, 'I have for-tunately no account to render in this kingdom and to this board.' 'Take off fifty pounds, say a hundred—take off a hundred pounds,' said Rhadamanthus to the horned owl. 'If we write Mr. Carlyle down a hundred and fifty he has no reason to complain, I think. There, you may go. Mr. Carlyle has no reason to complain.'

Second-come woman was already introduced, and I was motioned to the door; but I could not depart without saying that 'at all events there was no use in complaining, since they had the power to enforce their decision.' On stepping out, my first thought was, what a mercy Carlyle didn't come himself! For the rest, though it might have gone better, I was thankful that it had not gone worse. When one has been threatened with a great injustice, one accepts a smaller as a favour.

Went back to spend the evening with Geraldine when Mr. C. set forth for Bath House. Her ladyship in town for two days.

November 28.—Took the black silk —— presented me with last Christmas to Catchpool, that it might be made up. 'Did you buy this yourself, ma'am?' said Catchpool, rubbing it between her finger and thumb. 'No, it was a present; but why do you ask?' 'Because, ma'am, I was thinking, if you bought it yourself, you had been taken in. It is so poor; very trashy indeed. I don't think I ever saw so trashy a moire.'

December 4.—I hardly ever begin to write here that I am not tempted to break out into Jobisms about my bad nights. How I keep on my legs and in my senses with such little snatches of sleep is a wonder to myself. Oh, to cure anyone of a terror of annihilation, just put him on my allowance of sleep, and see if he don't get to long for sleep, sleep, unfathomable and everlasting sleep as the only conceivable heaven.

December 11.—Oh dear! I wish this Grange business were well over. It occupies me (the mere preparation for it) to the exclusion of all quiet thought and placid occupation. To have to care for my dress at this time of day more than I ever did when young and pretty and happy (God bless me, to think that I was once all that!) on penalty of being regarded as a blot on the Grange gold and azure, is really too bad. *Ach Gott!* if we had been left in the sphere of life we belong to, how much better it would have been for us in many ways!

March 24, 1856.—We are now at the 24th of March, 1856, and from this point of time, my journal, let us renew our daily intercourse without looking back. Looking back was not intended by nature, evidently, from the fact that our eyes are in our faces and not in our hind heads. Look straight before you, then, Jane Carlyle, and, if possible, not over the heads of things either, away into the distant vague. Look, above all, at the duty nearest hand, and what's more, do it. Ah, the spirit is willing, but the flesh is weak, and four weeks of illness have made mine weak as water. No galloping over London as in seven-leagued boots for me at present. To-day I walked with effort one little mile, and thought it a great feat; but if the strength has gone out of me, so also has the unrest. I can sit and lie even very patiently doing nothing. To be sure, I am always going on with the story in my head, as poor Paulet expressed it; but even that has taken a dreamy contemplative character, and excites no emotions 'to speak of.' In fact, sleep has come to look to me the highest virtue and the greatest happiness; that is, good sleep, untroubled, beautiful, like a child's. Ah'me!

March 26.—To-day it has blown knives and files; a cold, rasping, savage day; excruciating for sick nerves. Dear Geraldine, as if she would contend with the very elements on my behalf, brought me a bunch of violets and a bouquet of the loveliest most fragrant flowers. Talking with her all I have done or could do. 'Have mercy upon me, O Lord; for I am weak: O Lord, heal me, for my bones are vexed. My soul also is sore vexed: but thou, O Lord, how long? Return, O Lord, deliver my soul: O save me for thy mercies' sake.'

March 27.—Mr. C. took Nero out with him to-night, and half an hour after he opened the door with his latch-key and called in, 'Is that vermin come back?' Having received my horrified 'No!' he hurried off again, and for twenty minutes I was in the agonies of one's dog lost, my heart beating up into my ears. At last I heard Mr. C.'s feet in the street; and, oh joy! heard him gollaring at something, and one knew what the little bad something was. Ach! we could have better spared a better dog.

March 30.—Plattnauer told me how the 'grande passion' between —— and —— had gone to the dogs utterly—the general recipients of 'grandes passions.'

> Oh, waly, waly, love is bonnie
> A little while when it is new;
> But when it's auld
> It waxeth cauld,
> And melts away like morning dew.

Beautiful verse, sweet and sad, like barley sugar dissolved in tears. About the morning dew, however! I should rather say, 'Goes out like candle snuff' would be a truer simile; only that would not suit the rhyme.

April 11.—To-day I called on 'my lady' come to town for the season. She was perfectly civil, for a wonder. To-day also I lighted upon an interesting man. It was in our baker's shop. While the baker was making out my bill he addressed some counsel to a dark little man with a wooden leg and a basket of small wares. That made me look at the man to watch its effect upon him. 'I'll tell you what to do,' said this Jesuit of a baker; 'Go and join some Methodists' chapel for six months; make yourself agreeable to them, and you'll soon have friends that will help you in your object.' The man of the wooden leg said not a word, but looked hard in the baker's face with a half-perplexed, half-amused, and wholly disagreeing expression. 'Nothing like religion,' went on the tempter, 'for gaining a man friends. Don't you think so, ma'am?' (catching my eye on him). 'I think,' said I, 'that whatever this man's object may be, he is not likely to be benefited in the long run by constituting himself a hypocrite.' The man's black eye flashed on me a look of thanks and approbation. 'Oh,' said the baker, 'I don't mean him to be a hypocrite, but truly religious, you know.' 'If this man will be advised by me,' I said, ' he will keep himself clear of the *true religion* that is purposely put on some morning to make himself friends.' 'Yes,' said the poor man pithily, 'not that at *no* price!' In my enthusiasm at his answer, and the manner of it, I gave him—sixpence! and inquired into his case. He had been a baker for some time, met with an accident, and 'had to let his leg be taken,' after trying over eight years to keep it. Meanwhile his grandfather died, leaving him a small property worth 40*l.* a year, which he was still kept out of for want of a small sum of money to prove his right to it. I did not understand the law part of the story, but undertook to get some honest lawyer to look at his papers and give him advice for nothing.

April 21.—I feel weaklier every day, and my soul also is sore vexed—Oh how long! I put myself in an omnibus, being unable to walk, and was carried to Islington and back again. What a good shilling's-worth of exercise! The Angel at Islington! It was there I was set down on my first arrival in London, and Mr. C. with Edward Irving was waiting to receive me.

The past is past, and gone is gone.

May 29.—Old Mrs. D. said to me the other day when I encountered her after two years, 'Yes, ma'am, my daughter is dead: only child, house, and everything gone from me; and I assure you I stand up in the world as if it was not the world at all any more.'

Mr. B. says nine-tenths of the misery of human life proceeds according to his observation from the institution of marriage. He should say from the demoralisation, the desecration, of the institution of marriage, and then I should cordially agree with him.

June 27.—Went with Geraldine to Hampstead.

Various passages in this journal seemed to require explanation. Miss Geraldine Jewsbury, who was Mrs. Carlyle's most intimate friend, was the only person living who could give it. I sent her the book. She returned it to me with a letter, from which I extract the following passages:—

'The reading has been like the calling up ghosts. . . . It was a very bad time with her just then. No one but herself or one constantly with her knows what she suffered physically as well as morally.

'She was miserable: more abidingly and intensely miserable than words can utter. The misery was a reality, no matter whether her imagination made it or not. . . . Mr. C. once said to me of her that she had the deepest and tenderest feelings, but narrow. Any other wife would have laughed at Mr. C.'s bewitchment with Lady A.; but to her there was a complicated aggravation which made it very hard to endure. Lady A. was admired for sayings and doings for which she was snubbed. She saw through Lady A.'s little ways and *grande-dame* manners, and knew what they were worth. She contrasted them with the daily, hourly endeavours she was making that *his* life should be as free from hindrances as possible. He put her aside for his work, but lingered in the "Primrose path of dalliance" for the sake of a great lady, who liked to have a philosopher in chains. Lady A. was excessively capricious towards her, and made her feel they cared more about *him* than about *her*.

'She was never allowed to visit anywhere but at the Grange; and the mortifications and vexations she felt, though they were often and often self-made, were none the less intolerable to her. At first she was charmed with Lady A., but soon found she had no real hold on her, nor ever could or would have. The sufferings were real, intense, and at times too grievous to be borne. C. did not understand all this, and only felt her to be unreasonable.

'The lines on which her character was laid down were very grand, but the result was blurred and distorted and confused.

'In marrying she undertook what she felt to be a grand and noble life task: a task which, as set forth by himself, touched all that was noble and heroic, and inspired her imagination from its difficulty. She believed in him, and her faith was unique. No one else did. Well, but she was to be the companion, friend, helpmate—her own gifts were to be cultivated and recognised by him. She was bright and beautiful, with a certain star-like radiance and grace. She had devoted to him her life, which so many other men had desired to share. She had gone off into the desert with him. She had taken up poverty, obscurity, hardship even, cheerfully, willingly, and with an enthusiasm of self-sacrifice, on asking to be allowed to minister to him. The offering was accepted, but, like the precious things flung by Benvenuto into the furnace when his statue was molten, they were all consumed in the flames; and he was so intent and occupied by what he was bringing forth that he could take no heed of her individual treasures. They were all swallowed up in the great whole. In her case it was the living creature in the midst of the fire which felt and suffered. He gave her no human help nor tenderness.

'Bear in mind that her inmost life was solitary—no tenderness, no caresses, no loving words; nothing out of which one's heart can make the wine of life. A glacier on a mountain would have been as human a companionship. He suffered too; but he put it all into his work. She had only the desolation and barrenness of having all her love and her life laid waste. Six years she lived at Craigenputtock, and she held out. She had undertaken a task, and she knew that, whether recognised or not, she *did* help him. Her strong persistent will kept her up to the task of pain. Then they came back to the world, and the strain told on her. She did not falter from her purpose of helping and shielding him, but she became warped.—GERALDINE E. JEWSBURY.'

LETTER 164.

Mrs. Russell, Thornhill.

5 Cheyne Row, Chelsea: Thursday, July 3, 1856.

Dearest Mrs. Russell,—Your letter quite warmed my heart, and gave me a pull towards Scotland, stronger than I had yet felt. I think it in the highest degree unlikely, and certainly it will not be my own fault if I am there without seeing you. But we have no programme positively laid out yet for the summer, or rather the autumn. Mr. C. always hithers and thithers in a weary interminable way, before he can make up his mind what he would like most to do. And so, as I don't like wandering in uncertainties, with a net of 'ifs,' and 'buts,' and 'perhapses,' and 'possibles,' and 'probables' about my feet, I have got into the way of standing aside, and postponing my own plans, till he has finally got to some conclusion. His present 'most probably' is that he will go to his sister's, at a farm within a few miles of Annan, and 'enjoy perfect solitude for a time.' I mean, in that case, to stream off after 'my own sweet will;' as he would not need me with him at the Gill, and indeed there would be no room for me there, and I should only complicate his case. When he has settled to go there, or anywhere else where I am not needed, I shall proceed to scheme out a programme for myself, and I want to go to Scotland too, and I want to see you, and to see my cousins in Fife, and my old people at Haddington. But I do not take up all that practically at the present stage of the business, in case he take some new thought, with which my wishes could not so easily combine. I don't see any hope of his quitting London anyhow till the beginning of August, at soonest, which is a pity; the present month would be passed so much more pleasantly in the green country than here, where everything seems working up to spontaneous combustion. I was thinking the other night, at 'the most magnificent ball of the season,' how much better I should like to see people making hay, than all these ladies in laces and diamonds, waltzing! One grows so sick of diamonds, and bare shoulders, and all that sort of thing, after a while. It is the old story of the Irishman put into a Sedan chair without a bottom: 'If it weren't for the honour of the thing, I might as well have walked!'

I shall write, dear Mrs. Russell, whenever I know for certain what we are going to do. And, as I have great faith in the magnetic power of wishes, I pray you to wish in the meantime that I may come; as I, on my side, shall not fail to wish it strongly.

I am just going off this burning day to—sit for my picture! rather late! But I have a friend, who has constituted herself a portrait-painter, and she has a real genius for the business; and Ruskin told her she must paint a portrait with no end of pains, must give it 'twenty sittings at the least.' And I suppose she thinks I am the most patient woman she knows, and may give her these twenty sittings, out of desire for her improvement. As she is a clever, charming creature, I don't feel all the horror that might be expected of my prospect.

My kind regards to your husband and father.

Yours affectionately,

JANE W. CARLYLE.

LETTER 165.

After Addiscombe and three months more of deadly wrestling with Friedrich and the mud elements, we went to the Grange for Christmas; stayed for several weeks. Company at first aristocratic and select (Lord Lansdowne and Robert Lowe); then miscellaneous, shifting, chiefly of the scientific kind (Jowett, and an Oxonian or two among them), some of whom have left more than the shadow of an impression on me. Our last Grange Christmas, such as it proved, under presidency of that great lady. We returned in January, both of us. I at least much broken by this long course of gaieties, resumed work for 1856, and with dreary obstinacy kept pushing, pushing. The intolerable heats of July forced us north again. Ride to Edinburgh in the Lady Ashburton's royal carriage, which took fire, and at Newcastle had to be abandoned, dustiest and painfullest of rides, regardless of expense, and yet actually taking fire and falling flat like Dagon of the Philistines. Nothing good in it but the admirable bearing of that great lady under its badness. The Ashburtons off towards Ross-shire next morning. I under promise to follow thither by-and-by. Towards Auchtertool Manse we two, where after some days I left my dear woman and took refuge with my sister Mary at the Gill, near Annan, seeking and finding perfect solitude, kindness, and silence (the first time there) for a good few weeks.

Scotsbrig ten miles off, but that was now shut to me. Poor brother John had tragically lost his wife; was much cast down, and had now, most unwisely as I thought, filled Scotsbrig with his orphaned step-sons—three mischievous boys, whom to this day none of us could ever get to like. Scotsbrig accessible only on a riding call at this time.—T.C.

T. Carlyle, The Gill.

Auchtertool: July 29, 1856.

I am glad that all has gone so well with you hitherto. 'A good beginning makes a good ending,' and we have both begun more prosperously than could have been anticipated. Even the lost clogs are quite well supplied, I find, by the things I bought, and which must have been made for the wife of Goliath of Gath; and they have got me a new box of Seidlitz powders, and new chloroform from Kirkcaldy. I have needed to take neither, 'thanks God.' For the rest all goes well with me also; only no sea-bathing has been practicable yet, nor does it look as if it would ever be practicable here; the dog-cart having many other more important demands on it, as well as old John and Walter himself. There are preachings going on just now, at which Walter has to assist. Last Sunday his place was supplied at his own church by a grey-headed preacher called Douglas, who flattered himself he had been at school with you; but the Thomas Carlyle he had been school-fellow to 'had reddish hair, and a sharp face.' I am never done thanking heaven for the freshness, and cleanness, and quietness into which I have plumped down; and for my astonishingly comfortable bed, and the astonishing kindness and good humour that wraps me about like an eider-down quilt! It is next thing to being at Templand! I could almost imitate old 'Kelty,' [1] and fall to writing 'A Visit to my Relations in the Country,' followed up by 'Waters of Comfort' in verse! Of course I am sad at times, at all times sad as death, but that I am used to, and don't mind. And

---

[1] Old scribbling governess person.

for the sickness, it is quite gone since the morning I left Chelsea; and I am as content, for the time being, as it were possible for me to be anywhere on the face of this changeful earth.

Of course I will never be 'within wind' of Scotsbrig without going to see Jamie and Isabella, who have treated me always with the utmost kindness. If I had been their own sister they could not have made me feel more at home than I have always done under their roof. I never forget kindness, nor, alas! unkindness either!

My plans are still in the vague; I feel no haste to 'see my way.' My cousins seem to expect and wish me to make a long visit, and I am not at all likely to take to feeling dull nowadays beside people who really care for me, and have true hearts, and plenty of natural sense. Besides I have two invitations to dinner for next week! and have made acquaintance with several intelligent people. Meanwhile I have written to my aunt Elizabeth, who I believe is alone just now at Morningside, and also to Miss Donaldson, to announce my proximity; and it will depend on their answers whether I pay them a few hours' visit from here, or a longer one when I leave here altogether.

Give my kind regards to Mary and the rest. I am sure you will want for no attention she can show you, or she must be greatly changed from the kind soul I knew her at Craig o' Putta.

Faithfully yours,

JANE W. C.

LETTER 166.

My Jeannie has come across to Craigenvilla (fond reminiscences of Craigenputtock!), her aunts' new garden residence of their own in Edinburgh, Morningside quarter, same neat little place where the surviving two yet live (1869). They had all gone deep into conscious 'devotion,' religious philanthropy, prayer meetings, &c. &c., but were felt to be intrinsically honest-minded women, with a true affection for their niece, however pagan!

Old Betty's [1] one child, a promising young man, who had grown to be a journeyman watchmaker, was struck with paralysis; powerless absolutely, all but the head, in which sad state his unweariable, unconquerable mother watched over him night and day till he died.—T. C.

T. Carlyle, The Gill.

Craigenvilla, Morningside, Edinburgh: Thursday, Aug. 7, 1856.

Heaven and earth! I have been watching these three days for an hour's quiet to write in, but one would say there had been a con-

---

[1] Old Haddington nurse.

spiracy of things in general to prevent me. The day before yesterday I bathed at Kirkcaldy, and walked to Auchtertool after, and the fatigue was too much, and I was up to nothing but lying on the sofa all the evening, which delayed my packing till yesterday morning; and I got up at half after six, to leave time for a letter, and it was not till 'prayers' were over, and the breakfast ready, that I was ready to sit down. Immediately after breakfast the dog-cart came round to take me to the half after eleven boat. I tried writing again at Betty's; I could do nothing effectually except cry. She was so glad over me, so motherlike—and that poor dying lad, and her white worn face, and compressed lips; and the smile far more touching than any tears! Oh, it was so dreadfully sad, and yet her kisses, and the loving words about my father and mother, made me so happy! Then, when I got here to tea, my aunts were so unexpectedly tender and glad over me. I tried writing again in my bedroom, but it was lighted with gas, and I found I could not put the light out too soon to save my life. This morning, again, I got up at half-past six to write to you; but I had paper and ink, and no pen! so went to bed again, and lay till half-past seven, amidst a tearing rumble of carts, that seemed to drive over my brain.

I go home [1] to-night; and shall be there till Monday or Tuesday (address Sunny Bank till Monday, if you write), then back here, and I fear I cannot avoid staying a few days next time, in spite of the sleeping difficulties; but they are so kind, my aunts. By the end of the next week, anyhow, I hope to get to Auchtertool again. I will write from Haddington—this steel pen is too dreadful.

Yours,

J. W. C.

LETTER 167.

T. Carlyle, The Gill.

Sunny Bank, Haddington: Friday, Aug. 9, 1856.

I got here last night about seven. The carriage was waiting for me at the station, but this time empty; no kind Miss Kate in it. We came in at the back gate; and when we turned round the house I saw Miss Jess, or rather I saw a face, or rather eyes straining at the dining-room window with a look I shall remember while I live. The next moment I was in her arms; and then my 'god-

---

[1] To Haddington, to Misses Donaldson (eldest of them her 'godmother,' as was always remembered).

mother' tottered blindly forward, and took me in hers; and the
two dear old women clasped and kissed and wept over me both together, and called out 'Jeannie, Jeannie!' 'Oh, my own bairn!'
'My angel' (! !) and ever so many beautiful names. Mrs. Donaldson and Miss Eliza [1] had kindly retired to their own room, that the
meeting might transact itself in peace. A beautiful tea was waiting on the table—all so pretty and calm and good! It looked like
one of those entertainments spread for the good boys that 'went
out to *poos* their fortunes' in my godmother's fairy tales; and my
godmother herself, like the good fairy, so little, oh, so little, she
has grown! and her face so little and round, and so sweet!
And Miss Jess has been transformed by Kate's death into an active,
self-forgetting providence for the older and blinder sister. She
waits upon her, cuts her bread into mouthfuls, is gentle and
thoughtful for her, reads aloud to her (Miss Donaldson tells me),
she herself being about eighty; and instead of complaints about her
own ailments, it is all now 'Poor Jean !' and the loss she had in
Kate. The hearts of these two old women are as fresh as gowans.
It is like being pretty well up towards heaven, being here. And
what a house! so quiet and clean, and so perfectly the same as I
knew it thirty years ago! The same papers, the same carpets, the
same everything that I made acquaintance with when I was a child,
in perfect condition still. I expect to sleep in my great comfortable four-posted bed now that the first exciting night is over, and
shall stay till the middle of next week, I think. My aunts were
extremely kind, and expect me to make them a long visit on my return; but that is not possible, on account of the gas in my bedroom
(at Morningside) and the public road passing the window, where
carts grind from three in the morning. Besides that I like being
at Auchtertool, and they want me there for all the time I can stay.
Everybody is so kind to me—oh, so kind ! that I often burst out
crying with pure thankfulness to them all.

Betty said yesterday, speaking of the photograph I had sent her,
the one with the bonnet and the dog, and which, together with
yours, she has got handsomely framed and keeps in a pocket-handkerchief in a drawer! 'It has a look o' ye, but I dinna ken what
that white thing is aboot the face !' 'That is the white roses of my
bonnet, Betty.' 'A weel ! a weel ! May be sae! but as ye wur
kindly sending me yer pictur, dear, I wud hae liket better ye had
gotten't dune wi' yer bare pow !' I promised her one with the bare

---

[1] The famed Cantab. doctor's (Dr. Donaldson) mother and sister.

pow, but said, 'You know, it is a shame for me to be without a cap or a bonnet at this age.' 'Ay, ay, I dar' say, it's no very richt; but ye ken, bairn, ye wasne brocht up to dae just like ither folk; at a' rates I'll hae the bare pow if ye please; though I wudna be thocht ower greedy!' Dear, darling old Betty! She gets no rest night or day for that poor spectre of a son; and it looks to me he may live for years in this suffering, hopeless state. And the husband, though a good enough man in his way—sober and laborious, and all that—has not the refinement or the spirituality of Betty, and can be but a sorry comforter to her in her sore trouble. She called me back as I was coming away yesterday to say, 'Dear, wull ye tell Miss Donal'son, for I am sure it 'ill please her to hear it, that the Bish'p [1] is rale gude to us, puir auld manny!'

I had two bathes in the sea; neither did me any good—the first a great deal of harm, by ill luck. Just the day after I wrote—I had had no bathing—Walter took me to Aberdour; and I was to partly undress, and get a bathing gown at Aberdour House, where Mrs. Major Liddle lives. She gave me the key of the park, that Maggie and I might walk through it to the shore; but the key proved a wrong one, and, as there was no time to return for the right key, I proposed to Maggie to leap from the top of the wall, which was only high on the off-side. She positively declined; and we were at a fix, when a working man passing, I called to him, and asked him to catch us in leaping. He took me between his big thumbs, one on my left side, and the other, alas! on my right breast—that unlucky breast I am always hurting! There! I thought to myself, as I found my feet, 'There is something to serve me for six weeks again!'

I suffered a good deal for the first two or three days, and lost my just-recovered sleep. It (the pain) is going off, however, though still a nuisance, especially when I use my right arm. Remember that in estimating the virtue of this very long letter.

I inclose a note from Lady A., which was forwarded to me here this morning.

I am not sure where to address; but, as one letter was sent to Scotsbrig, I had best send this one to the Gill.

Yours faithfully,

J. W. C.

---

[1] Terrot; the Donaldsons were Episcopal.

LETTER 168.

T. Carlyle, The Gill.

Craigenvilla, Morningside: Tuesday, August 19, 1856.

Oh, dear me! I am back from Haddington; and a sad day yesterday was. The people at Haddington seem all to grow so good and kind as they grow old. That isn't the way with us in the south. It wasn't the Miss Donaldsons only that made much of me, and cried over me at parting, as if I were 'their own bairn.' Mr. Howden, Mrs. Howden, and all of them still alive, that knew my father and mother, were in tears; and poor old Mr. Lea,[1] who has otherwise lost his wits, said, 'Oh, Jeannie, Jeannie, when you come again you won't find me here!' and then he said angrily to Miss Brown, 'Are you going to let that lassie go away by herself? send the Man with her.' (The Man, meaning *his keeper*.) It would have touched you to the heart to see poor Jess Donaldson daundering about, opening drawers and presses to find something to give me. It was her chief employment all the time I was there. One day it was an Indian shawl; the next a real lace veil; the next a diamond ring, and so on, till the last hour, when after my boxes were all packed, she suddenly bethought her that I used to like old china, and took me privately to the press that contained her long-prized Indian china, and bade me take as much of it as I cared to carry; and then, when I told her my boxes were full, she said, 'Take my work-basket, dear, to pack it in; I shall never need it any more.' But inanimate objects were not all that I brought from home with me. I brought two live plants in flower-pots, one out of our own garden, and two live—oh, gracious! I picture your dismay!—'whatever' will you say or sing?—two live—ca-ca-naries! They were born in our own house, the darlings; and poor Mrs. Howden made with her own hands a black silk bag to draw over the cage, and trimmed it with braid. You may still hope that they shall get eaten by my aunt's cat, or my cousin's terrier, or, at least, by the cat or Nero at home. 'But I hope better things, though I thus speak.'[2] At all events, they shan't plague you the least in the world; and it was a luck for me yesterday in coming away that I had these live things to look after.

---

[1] A kind of ex-military *haberdasher* (I think)—shop near the entrance to her father's house.

[2] Scotch preaching phrase.

Aren't you a spoiled child, without the childness and the spoiling, to go and write in that plaintive, solemn way about 'help of some connexions of Jane's in Glasgow,' as if you were a desolate orphan 'thrown out *sang froid*[1] to charity.' If you weren't satisfied with the *duffle* you got, why couldn't you have said so straightforwardly, and told me you wished me to choose another? But I was to do it only 'if I wanted a lark,' or 'if it didn't satisfy me,' &c., &c. You know very well that if you had told me to go fifty miles to buy your dressing-gown, and that you were 'depending on me for doing it,' I shouldn't have hesitated a minute, and it could have been done now when I am on the spot without the least trouble, had you so chosen. But if it was merely to 'please my own taste' that I was to go into Edinburgh from Haddington and back again, or to give myself 'a lark,' I was right to decline. You have no notion what a disagreeable train that is; both in going and coming you have to wait at Long Niddry from half an hour to an hour, in consequence of the irregularity of the London trains, which stop there. The express don't stop. Yesterday I had to wait an hour all but three minutes. You will be glad to hear as a symptom that an enterprising man is starting anew the old Haddington stage, to go twice a week at the same price as the railway, for the comfort of passengers who have not temper to stand this irregular waiting.

My aunts received me back with the heartiest welcome; and I don't think it will be possible for me to get back to Auchtertool this week without offending them. But I have changed my room for one to the back, left vacant by Ann, who is in Dumfriesshire, and it is as quiet as Cheyne Row, except for a very singular water-cistern that runs without a minute's interruption day and night.

> 'Men shall come, and men shall go,
> But thou go'st on for ever!'

It is only a gentle sound, however, like the flow of a brook; and it rather helped me to sleep last night than otherwise.

By the way, the trash of things that bit you so must have been the new insect called 'harvest bugs,' or 'gooseberry lice,' imported, they say, in some American plants about twenty years ago; they last for six weeks, and are most tormenting. Mrs. Donaldson was covered, as with chicken-pox, from them; and I finally was dreadfully bitten, but got off easier as I resolutely refused to scratch the places; they took me chiefly on the legs, of all places.

Yours faithfully.

---

[1] Not '*de sang*,' &c. (*supra*).

LETTER 169.

T. Carlyle, Esq., The Gill.

Craigenvilla: Saturday, August 23, 1856.

Your letter of yesterday arriving at the same time with one from my aunt Ann (away in Dumfriesshire) to Grace, just as we were going to breakfast, threw us into such a little flutter of excitement that we all fell quite unconsciously into sin. I was reading my letter, and had taken a sip or two of tea and bitten into my soda-scone, and the others had done the same, when Grace suddenly shrieked out like 'a mad,'[1] 'Mercy! we have forgotten the blessing!' I started on my chair, and (to such a pitch of compliance with 'coostom in part' have I already reached) dropped instinctively the morsel out of my mouth into my hand, till I should see what steps were to be taken for making our peace. But the case was judged past remedy, and the breakfast allowed to proceed unblessed.

I was regretting to Betty that my aunts should live in such a fuss of religion. 'My dear!' said she, 'they were idle—plenty to live on, and nocht to do for't; they might hae ta'en to waur; so we maun just thole them, an no compleen.'[2] For the rest, they are more affectionate to myself than I ever found them before—really kind, almost to tenderness, especially Elizabeth, who seems much softened by her sad accident. I am glad I stayed, for henceforth I shall feel to have aunts, which is a gain to one who has no brothers or sisters, and whose 'many friends' are something like the hare's. At the same time I shall be well pleased to return to Auchtertool on Monday, where also they are adorably kind to me, and where I have more room to turn in, in all ways.

I have no friends in the north except Mr. Gillespie of Ardachy, who I dare say would give me a welcome. But it would be a deal too far to travel for any satisfaction I should get out of him, even were there no unknown wife in the case. I should prefer being 'well let alone' in Fife, till the time of our return to Chelsea, with just a week or so taken for Dumfriesshire. There they won't weary of me either, which is a main ingredient in my contentment. If I want to 'vaary the schane'[3] a little, I may go a few days to Miss

[1] 'A mad,' Mazzini's.

[2] 'They might have taken to waur,' wise Betty! This was never forgotten.

[3] 'Vaary the schane,' imitation of grandfather Walter—*supra Reminiscences*, vol. ii.

Fergus, who has returned to Kirkcaldy, and sent me a kindly ex-pressed invitation for 'a long visit.' She does not mention your name, as indeed was natural—considering. Thomas Erskine also invites us both to Linlathen, and understands you to have written that you would come.

I went to call at poor Captain Paterson's (the house is close by here), and saw the Patersons [1] and Mrs. Stirling, who went home yesterday, and 'would write to me.' I should not much dislike going with you to Linlathen, if you take it on the way to the High-lands; but I would rather stay quietly with my own people. —— ——, too, has sent me an affectionate letter about coming to —— Castle; but, though in an affectionate mood when she asked me to come, her mood might change by the time I went. And, on the whole, I am not drawn towards —— Castle, but 'quite the contrary.' 'The honour of the thing' looks too mean, and scraggy, and icy a motive, to make me go a foot length, or trouble myself the least in the world, with all those tears and kisses I brought away from Had-dington, still moist and warm on my heart, tears and kisses be-stowed on me for the sake of my dead father and mother.

I have just been interrupted by a touching visit from Mrs. And-erson (Miss Grove),[2] who has been invalided with her spine for ten years. She was carried in by her husband, and laid on the sofa; a sad, grey, resigned-looking, suffering woman. But the husband so gentle and attentive to her, that there was a certain comfort in looking at them. I have an engagement to Betty, who will have curds and cream waiting for me, and I must go now. I am to dine out to-day, for the first time, with Miss Hamilton (of Gladsmuir), who asked Grace, too.

I always forgot to tell you that I met at the Liddells, in Fife, Mr. William Swan, and that I made him a pretty little speech about 'your enduring remembrance of his father's and mother's kindness to you,' on which account I begged to shake hands with him, which had the greatest success. He was so pleased that Walter fol-lowed up my advances by inviting him to a dinner-party at the Manse, and there I presented him with your photograph, which he called 'a treasure.' So fat a man one rarely sees, but he looks kind, and has the character of being 'most benevolent,' and he evidently had a deep affection for his parents.

---

[1] 'Captain Paterson,' Erskine's brother-in-law. Mrs. Stirling is Erskine's widow sister and lady house-manager.

[2] 'Miss Grove,' once a young Haddington friend and loved *protégée*, being English, and a stranger.

Also I have a strange story to tell you about Samuel Brown's[1] illness; but that must lie over, or I shall miss the omnibus.

Good luck to the new clothes.

Yours ever faithfully,
JANE W. CARLYLE.

LETTER 170.

'Infants weeping in the porch.'

'Vagitus et ingens,
Infantumque animæ flentes in limine primo.'

Inclosures in this letter from poor Nero and servant Anne. This Anne, who had continued and did still for several years, was an elderly cockney specimen (mother still in Holborn), punctual, rational, useful, though a little selfish and discontented.

T. Carlyle, Esq., The Gill.

Auchtertool, Bedroom: Friday, August 29, 1856.

There! I have put my foot in it! I was well to a wonder; hadn't had one hour of my sickness, nor one wholly sleepless night since I left Chelsea; and the idea must needs take me, that Sunday I was in Edinburgh, to have out my humour to hear Dr. Guthrie. And so for two hours I was slowly simmered, as in one of Soyer's patent stewpans (the crush to hear him being quite as great in Edinburgh as in London). And then I had to walk to Morningside in a cutting east wind; and then, at the far end, a miserable refection of weak tea and tough toast by way of dinner, when I needed to have stimulants ' thrown into the system' (my aunts always dining on tea on Sundays, that the servant may attend both morning and afternoon 'services'). The consequence of all this bad management was a cold on my nerves, which the crossing[2] next day, and the blowy drive in the dog-cart, brought to a height. And I have been two whole days in bed 'suffering martyrs' (as poor Paulet used to say); and am still very poorly, though to-day I can sit up and write, as you see. Indeed, last night I never once closed my eyes. Nothing could be more ill-timed than this illness, two dinner-parties having gone off here in the meantime to my honour and glory; and 'gone off without effect,' so far as I was concerned. Mr. Peter Swan (the other brother) was at the yester-

---

[1] ' Samuel Brown,' doctor of great promise once; poor young man killed in Edinburgh by too much kindness! (far worse than none, if blind both.)
[2] Of the Frith.

day dinner; Walter thinking, after my speech to the younger Swan, that he could not be too hospitable to that family. Poor Walter! his poor little stipend must be dreadfully perplexed to meet all the demands his munificent spirit makes on it.

Besides these dinner-parties, we have a house choke full. Jeannie and her husband come over to see me chiefly; and Sophy from Liverpool, with 'Jackie,' a remarkably stirring little gentleman of three and a half years; and another human mite, that rejoices as yet in the name of 'Baby.' And in the dead watches of the night there will arise a sound of 'infants weeping in the porch;' and on the whole it is not now like Paradise here, as it was in my first two weeks. I should have stayed still here while the coast was clear, and only been going on my Haddington visit now. But, above all, I should not have gone and got myself all stewed into mush, hearing a popular preacher: though out of all sight the very most eloquent preacher I ever head, or wish to hear. Never was there such exquisite artistic simplicity! never such gushing affluence of imagery! It reminded me of those god-daughters of good fairies in my nursery tales, who every time they opened their blessed mouths 'pearls and rubies rolled out.' But, alas! they were the pearls and rubies of a dream! One brought away none of them in one's pocket to buy a meal of meat with, if one happened to need one.[1]

So long as it is in my head, please send me three or four autographs for my aunt Ann, to give to some friend of hers, who has applied to her to beg them of you for some philanthropic purpose or other. I have had a knot in my pocket handkerchief to remind me of this for some time.

As to Samuel Brown—'the history of Samuel Brown[2] is this:' For seven years he has, as you know, been afflicted with some derangement of the bowels, which was always expected to terminate fatally in iliac passion. Some weeks ago he seemed beyond recovery, and, indeed, they were watching him for death. At last his bowels being moved by some very strong medicine, there was passed a little bone; a bone of some sort of game—grouse they think—about half an inch long only, and this having fixed its sharp end into the bowel had caused (the doctors are positive) his whole illness. He has no recollection of ever swallowing the bone. As it left an open hole in the bowel, and he was already so weak, they did not think he would be able to struggle through the cure, but it

---

[1] Never looked at eloquent Guthrie again.　　[2] See note, p. 50.

is now a good many weeks and he is still alive (I believe), and if he escapes the danger of having the bowel closed up in the course of healing the hole in it, he will be restored to perfect health, the doctors think.[1] All this, which I was told by Susan Hunter in Edinburgh, was corroborated for me by the poor man's sister at Haddington. Isn't it a strange story? such a poor, little, little cause producing so much torment and misery.

I have written till the prespiration is running down my face—not wisely but too well.

Yours faithfully,
Jane W. C.

LETTER 171.

T. Carlyle, Kinloch Luichart, Dingwall.

Scotsbrig: Thursday, Sept. 18, 1856.

Well, I am safe here, though not without a struggle for it.

Your letter this morning is a degree more legible than the first one! But, dear me! what galloping and spluttering over the paper; as if you were writing in a house on fire, and bent on making a little look as much as possible! I have measured the distance between your lines in the letter just come, and it is precisely one inch. In the first letter, it must have been an inch and half! I call that a foolish waste of writing paper! If you have an excellent bedroom, could you not retire into it for, say, one hour, in the course of a whole week, and write composedly and leisurely? Why write in the midst of four people?

For the rest, in spite of all objections, 'for the occasion got up,' I daresay you are pretty comfortable. Why not? When you go to any house, one knows it is because you choose to go; and when you stay, it is because you choose to stay. You don't, as weakly amiable people do, sacrifice yourself for the pleasure of ' others. So pray do not think it necessary to be wishing yourself at home, and 'all that sort of thing,' on paper. 'I don't believe thee!'[2] If I were inclined to, I should only have to call to mind the beautiful letters you wrote to me during your former visit to the Ashburtons in the Highlands, and which you afterwards disavowed and trampled into the fire! !

As to Tom Gillespie, if you could have got into his hands, I am sure he would have been useful to you, and been delighted to be so. But the poor man is quite laid up, has been for long in a dan-

---

[1] He died, poor fellow.   [2] 'I don't believe thee,' my father's phrase.

gerous state. His sister, Mrs. Binnie, lives near the Caledonian Railway; and I spent the hours I had to wait for the train on Tuesday at her house, and she was speaking quite despondingly about him. So that it is no go!

Five pounds is as easily sent as two one-pounds notes; more easily indeed, for I have no one-pound notes. So I send a five-pound note to put you out of all danger of running short. It is a very unnecessary grievance that to incur! so long as one has money.

I write to Mrs. Russell to-day that I shall be at Thornhill on Monday, D.V. Isabella says I had best go from here to Annan; it will make the gig-journey shorter. I haven't the least objection to the gig-journey, 'quite the contrary.' But I daresay Jamie's time is very precious just now, so I accepted that route at once. Whether I return to Scotsbrig or not will depend on your arrangements.

Lady Ashburton is very kind to offer to take me back. Pray make her my thanks for the offer. But though a very little herring, I have a born liking to 'hang by my own head.' And when it is a question simply of paying my own way, or having it paid for me, I prefer 'lashing down'[1] my four or five sovereigns on the table all at once! If there were any companionship in the matter it would be different; and if you go back with the Ashburtons it would be different, as then I should be going merely as part of your luggage, without self-responsibility. Settle it as you like, it will be all one to me; meeting you at Scotsbrig, or in Edinburgh, or going home by myself from Thornhill.

This is September 19th, the day of my father's death.

Jamie is going to take me a little drive at one o'clock. He is such a dear good Jamie for me always!

Walter wrote me a long letter, to meet me at Scotsbrig, which I received in bed yesterday, and it gave me 'a good comforting cry;' it is so kind—oh, so kind and brotherly!

Yours faithfully,

JANE W. C.

---

[1] 'Lashing down my four or five sovereigns.' ' They tould me he was 'listed. I sought high and low; at last I found him in an upstairs room at breakfast among them, with an ounce of tay and a quarter of sugar, all lashed down on the table at one time! Says I, "Pat, you're going on at a great rate here, but," &c. &c.' Speech of an Irish peasant's father on his lost son, to Edward Irving long ago.

LETTER 172.

T. Carlyle, Kinloch Luichart, Dingwall.

Scotsbrig: Monday, Sept. 22, 1856.

Oh, dear! oh, dear! To be thrown into a quandary like this, just when I am getting ready to start for Thornhill! You are so wrong in your dates that I don't know what to make of it. '22nd' you have written at the top of your note, and it arrives here on the 22nd!

It may be all right, but also it may very probably be all wrong, and the five-pound note I sent you from Ecclefechan on Thursday, the 18th, and the long letter that accompanied it, gone to nobody knows where! Pleasant! Why can't you take money enough with you? If I had not been told to inclose notes I would have sent a post-office order on Dingwall.

Till I hear for certain that the letter and money are lost, I don't know what to write! There is no pleasure in telling you the same things over again.

I took the letter to Ecclefechan in the gig, and Jamie posted it while I bought envelopes. There was no visibility of the note in it even when held between you and the light.

Please to write immediately on receiving this, to Mrs. Russell's, Thornhill, Dumfriesshire, to say you have got the money.

Jamie is going to drive me to Annan, and it is a day of heavy showers. But I am to be met at Thornhill station, and must go.

Yours faithfully,

JANE WELSH CARLYLE.

LETTER 173.

Alas! my poor, much suffering, ever toiling, and endeavouring woman. No doubt I was very bad company, sunk overhead in the Frederick mud element.

Anne did not go at this time; but a sad, sick winter was awaiting my dear one: confined to the house for five months and utterly weak, says a note of the time! Her patience in such cases always was unsurpassable—patience, silent goodness, anxiety only for one unworthy.—T. C.

Mrs. Russell, Thornhill.

5 Cheyne Row, Chelsea: Friday, Oct. 10, 1856.

Oh, my dear! my dear! my dear!—To keep myself from going stark mad I must give myself something pleasant to do for this one hour! And nothing so pleasant suggests itself as just writing to you, to tell you how miserable and aggravated I am! Geraldine says, 'Why on earth, when I was beside a doctor I had confidence in, didn't I consult him about my health?' Why? Because when I was beside Dr. Russell, and indeed (except for a common cold) all the time I was in Scotland, nothing ailed my health! A London doctor's prescription for me long ago (the only sensible man I ever knew in the profession here—a pity he is dead), that I 'should be kept always happy and tranquil' (! ! !), had finally got itself carried into effect for ten whole weeks, and was found an efficacy! But from the day I left Scotland quite other things than happiness and tranquillity have been 'thrown into my system'! I arrived here with a furious faceache, Mr. C. having insisted on my sitting in a violent draught all the journey; that kept me perfectly sleepless all night, in spite of my extreme fatigue, and so I began to be ill at once, and have gone on *crescendo* in the same ratio that my worries have increased. Figure this: [Scene—a room where everything is enveloped in dark yellow London fog! For air to breathe, a sort of liquid soot! Breakfast on the table—'adulterated coffee,' 'adulterated bread,' 'adulterated cream,' and 'adulterated water'!] Mr. C. at one end of the table, looking remarkably bilious; Mrs. C. at the other, looking half dead! Mr. C.: 'My dear, I have to inform you that my bed is full of bugs, or fleas, or some sort of animals that crawl over me all night!' Now, I must tell you, Mr. C. had written to me, at Auchtertool, to 'write emphatically to Anne about keeping all the windows open; for, with her horror of fresh air, she was quite capable of having the house full of bugs when we returned;' and so I imputed this announcement to one of these fixed ideas men, and especially husbands, are apt to take up, just out of sheer love of worrying! Living in a universe of bugs out-side, I had entirely ceased to fear them in my own house, having kept it so many years perfectly clean from all such abominations. So I answered with merely a sarcastic shrug, that was no doubt very ill-timed under the circumstances, and which drew on me no end of what the Germans call *Kraftsprüche!* But clearly the practical thing to be done was to go and examine his bed—and I am practical, *moi!* So, instead of getting into a controversy that had no basis, I proceeded to toss over his blankets and pillows, with a certain sense of injury! But, on a sudden, I paused in my operations; I stooped to look at something the size of a pin-point; a cold shudder ran over me; as sure as I lived it was an infant bug! And, oh, heaven, that bug, little as it was, must have parents — grandfathers and grandmothers, perhaps! I went on looking then with frenzied minuteness, and saw enough to make me put on my bonnet and rush out wildly, in the black rain, to hunt up a certain trustworthy carpenter to come and take down the bed. The next three days I seemed to be in the thick of a domestic Balaklava, which is now even only subsiding—not subsided. Anne, though I have reproached her with carelessness (decidedly there was not the vestige of a bug in the whole house when we went away), is so indignant that the house should be turned up after she had 'settled it,' and that 'such a fuss should be made about bugs, which are inevitable in London,' that she flared up on me, while I was doing her work, and declared 'it was to be hoped I would get a person to keep my house cleaner than she had done; as she meant to leave that day month!' To which I answered, 'Very good,' and nothing more. And now you see, instead of coming back to anything like a home, I have come back to a house full of bugs and evil passions! I shall have to be training a new servant into the ways of the house (when I have got her) at a season of the year when it will be the most uphill work for both her and me. As to this woman, I kept her these three years because she was a clever servant, and carried on the house without any bother to me; but I never liked her as a woman; from the first week I perceived her to be what she has since on all occasions proved herself, cunning, untrue, and intensely selfish. The atmosphere of such a character was not good, and nothing but moral cowardice could have made me go on with her. But I did so dread always the bothers and risks of 'a change'! Now, however, that it is forced on me, I console myself by thinking, with that 'hope which springs eternal in the human mind,' that I may find a servant, after all, whom it may be possible to, not only train into my ways, but attach to me! What a fool I am! Oh, I should so like a Scotchwoman, if I could get any feasible Scotchwoman. These Londoners are all of the cut of this woman. I have written to Haddington, where the servants used to be very good, to know if they can do anything for me. I suppose it is needless asking you; of course, if there had been any 'treasure' procurable you would have engaged her yourself. But do you really know nobody I could get from Nithsdale? How stupid it was of Margaret not to come when I wanted her. I am sure it is harder work she must have at the Castle. Oh, my darling, I wish you were here to give me a kiss, and cheer me up a bit with your soft voice! In cases of this sort, Geraldine with the best intentions is no help. She is unpractical, like all women of genius! She was so pleased with your letter! 'My dear,' she said to me, 'how is it that women who don't write books write always so much nicer letters than those who do?' I told her it was, I supposed, because thay did not write in the 'Valley of the shadow' of their future biographer, but wrote what they had to say frankly and naturally.

Your father (a kiss to him) should write me a word about 'Providence.' Oh, be pleased all of you, Dr. Russell too, for all so busy as he is, to think of me, and love me! I have great faith in the magnetic influence of kind thoughts. And, upon my honour, I need to be soothed—magnetically, and in any possible way!

Your affectionate

JANE W. CARLYLE.

LETTER 174.

To Mrs. Austin, The Gill, Annan.

5 Cheyne Row, Chelsea: Jan 2, 1857.

My dear Mary,—The box came yesterday, all safe—not so much as one egg cracked, and just in time to have one of the fowls boiled for Mr. C.'s dinner. Mr. C. dines all by himself at present, I merely looking on, as he doesn't participate in my dislike to eating in presence of one's fellow-creatures not similarly occupied.

Since my illness, that is to say, pretty nearly ever since I returned from Scotland, I have used my privilege of invalid (and no doubt about it) to dine at the hour when nature and reason prompt me to dine, viz. two o'clock, instead of at Mr. C.'s fashionable hour of six. So my go at the fowl comes off to-day. They look famous ones; and as for the goose—heaven and earth! what a goose! Even Anne, who is so difficult to warm up to bare satisfaction point with anything of an eatable sort, stood amazed before that goose, 'as in presence of the infinite!' and, when she had found her tongue, broke forth with, 'Lord! ain't it fat, ma'm?' Thank you very much, dear Mary. Your box reminds me of the time when you came to me at some dreadful inn at Annan, where I happened to be, I don't remember why, and was doing I don't remember what, except that I was horridly sick and uncomfortable, and you came tripping in with a reticule-basket, and gave me little cakes and sweeties out of it; and that comforted my mind, if not exactly good

II.—3*

for my stomach. Dear Mary, how kind you used to be in those old times, when we were thrown so much on one another's company! That is the only feature of my existence at Craig-o'-putta that I recall with pleasure; the rest of it was most dreary and uncongenial.

The meal is welcome, for I brought but little from Scotsbrig, not thinking to need more. When I dine in the middle of the day, however, I can take my old supper of porridge, provided I feel up to the bother of making it myself. So I have my porridge, while Mr. C. takes his more unsubstantial breadberry—so I call it—Anne calls it 'Master's pap'!

We have beautiful weather again, and I get out for a drive in an omnibus. The Scotsbrig gig would be nicer, but anything is better than walking, when one feels like an eel in the matter of backbone. I go in an omnibus from the bottom of our street to the end of its line, and just come back again; thus realising some fourteen miles of shaking at the modest cost of one shilling. Mr. C.'s horse gives him the highest satisfaction; he says it is a quite remarkable combination of courage and sensibility. The Secretary, too, would do well enough if he could only give over 'sniffing through his nose.' The canaries are the happiest creatures in the house; the dog next.

Kind regards to your husband and Margaret.

Affectionately yours,

JANE CARLYLE.

LETTER 175.

Monday, May 4, 1857.—At Paris, on her way home from Nice, Lady Ashburton (born Lady Harriet Montague) suddenly died: suddenly to the doctors and those who believed them; in which number, fondly hoping against hope, was I. A sad and greatly interesting event to me and to many! The most queen-like woman I had ever known or seen. The honour of her constant regard had for ten years back been among my proudest and most valued possessions—lost now; gone—for ever gone! This was our first visit to Addiscombe after. I rode much about with Lord A. in intimate talk, and well recollect this visit of perhaps a week or ten days, and of the weeks that preceded and followed. How well I still remember the evening Richard Milnes brought down the news; the moonlit streets, and dirge-like tone of everything, as I walked up to Lady Sandwich's door and asked for the weak, devoted, aged mother. In no society, English or other, had I seen the equal or the second of this great lady that was gone; by nature and by culture *facile princeps* she, I think, of all great ladies I have ever seen.

My Jane's miserable illness now over, a visit to Haddington was steadily in view all summer. July 7.—Craik from Belfast, with his daughters, was here holidaying; had decided on flying to Edinburgh by some unrivalled and cheap excursion train, and persuaded her to go with them. I accompanied to Euston Square; had dismal omens of the 'unrivalled,' which were fully realised through the night.—T. C.

T. Carlyle, Chelsea.

Sunny Bank, Haddington: Wednesday, July 8, 1857.

Oh, mercy! Lord be thanked! 'Good times, and bad times, and all times pass over.' Last night is passed over, like an excessively bad dream; and I am sitting here in cleanness and quiet, announcing my safety so far. But it is a wonder that somebody else has not rather to announce my death by 'bad air.' Oh, my dear! you saw all those people in one box, sixteen of them! Well, imagine that they closed every window and slit, except the fourth window, commanded by Georgina[1] and me. Not one breath of air to be had all night except in holding one's head out of the window. Craik and his offsprings[2] were very attentive and kind, and I ate my cold fowl wing, and drank a little brandy and water; and the large Scotchman offered me 'his shoulder to rest on, if it would be of any service;' but what availed all that against 'a polluted atmosphere'? How it happened that everybody got through the night alive I can't explain; nay, everybody but Craik, one of his girls, and myself, slept the sleep of the just! By the way, you may tell Mr. Larkin 'snoring' is not audible in a railway train. My chief torment proceeded from the tendency to sleep produced by the atmosphere getting itself overcome by the upright position, with no rest for the head. It 'was cheap,' but I did not 'like it,'[3] and have seldom been thankfuller than when I found myself the only living creature visible at the Dunbar station, after the Craiks had streamed away. I washed my face with Eau-de-Cologne, and combed my dishevelled hair in a little, cold, tidy waiting-room; and in about an hour my train came and picked me up, and set me down at Haddington station soon after nine, where the carriage was duly waiting.

I never saw the country about here look so lovely, but I viewed it all with a calm about as morbid as was my excitement last year. Dear Miss Jess received me with open arms in a room with a bright fire, and the prettiest breakfast-table set out. Miss Donaldson does not come down till eleven. They are the same heavenly kind creatures,

---

[1] Craik. [2] Both (*supra*).
[3] Famous Dr. Reid on whisky punch.

and there is no falling off even in looks since last year. I am not going out of the house again to-day, but I cannot write, I am so wearied! oh, so dreadfully wearied! Being hindered from sleeping is quite another thing from not being able to sleep.

I hope you found a fire when you got home, and some reasonable good tea. If you could fancy me in some part of the house out of sight, my absence would make little difference, considering how little I see of you, and how preoccupied you are when I do see you.

Do you know I had yester-even a presentiment I should die before I got back? Those things Lord Ashburton brought had shivered me all through, and the first thing we met was a coffin. I was so nervous that I wanted to scream, but the physical weariness had quashed down that nonsense.

Oh! be kind to Nero, and slightly attentive to the canaries, and my poor little nettle and gooseberry bush. Moreover, tell Anne she will find Mrs. Cook's bill in my blot-book; I forgot to give it to her. I also forgot to bring my boa; tell Anne, please, to shake it every two or three days, and to leave the fur jacket exposed to the air where I placed it, and shake it and the great fur coat downstairs frequently. She let the moths get into my fur last year. A kiss to Nero.

I wonder how you are getting along.

God keep you.

Affectionately yours,
Jane W. Carlyle.

I wish you would thank Lord Ashburton for me. I couldn't say anything about his kindness in giving me those things, which she had been in the habit of wearing. I felt so sick and so like to cry, that I am afraid I seemed quite stupid and ungrateful to him.

LETTER 176.

T. Carlyle, Chelsea.

Haddington: July 14, 1857.

Good morning, dear! I wonder if you are 'quite happy and comfortable' this morning? or—what shall I say—'contrairy'? Perhaps I may have a letter by the midday post; your last came by it. But it is best, in my own writing, to take time 'by the forelock;' his pigtail is so apt to come away in one's hand! Indeed, I have less time for letter-writing here than might be thought, considering the quiet monotony of the life I lead. I am 'called' at eight by their clock; but in reality at half-past seven; and at a quarter after eight (in reality) Miss Jess and I sit down to breakfast: tea, eggs, brown bread, and honey-comb. This is Miss Jess's best talking time, and we sit till ten or so. From that till eleven I may write, or darn my stockings, or meditate on things in general, without being missed.

At eleven the carriage comes round, and both ladies go a drive of two miles along the Dunbar Road! I accompany them; and, having set them down at their own door again, I go a long drive by myself. That is my chief entertainment during the day. Nowhere in the world that I know of are there such beautiful drives; and I recognise places that I had seen in my dreams, the recollection of them having been preserved in my sleep long after it had passed out of my waking mind.

I come in just in time to change my dress and rest before dinner at three; a dinner always 'very good to eat' (as you say) and of patriarchal simplicity. Always strawberries and cream *ad libitum!* Between dinner and tea (at six) I talk to Miss Donaldson, and I take a little walk, to the churchyard or some place that I care for. After tea talking again, or I read aloud—excessively loud (I read them your Nigger Question, much to Miss Donaldson's approval and delight); and before supper (of arrowroot milk), at half-past nine, I have run down every evening to speak a few words of encouragement to my poor unlawful cousin, in her sick bed. I think she would recover if she could overcome the effects of the frightful quantity of mercury Mr. Howden has given her. My heavens, what my father would have said to him! At ten, bed !!

I am so grieved to find the fair, which used to be held to-day, has turned into a mere cattle-fair; no booths with toys and sweeties![1] and I had set my heart on buying a pair of waxen babes of the wood covered with moss (by imaginary robins), in a little oval spale-box,[2] which used to be my favorite fairing. Last night, however, I bought a—hedgehog from a wee boy. I thought I might take it home in my carpet-bag to eat the cockroaches. Perhaps I will think better of it!

I imagine Miss Jess was so inspirited by my presence, that last Sunday she 'took a notion' of going to church! She had not been there for years. Of course I had to go with her. As it was to 'the chapel' I didn't so much mind. I should not have liked to sit in a strange seat in our own church. I found the poor little

---

[1] Anglican comfits. [2] 'Spale' is joiner's shaving, *spill.*

whitewashed, bare-boarded chapel transformed into a little blossom of Puseyite taste! Painted glass windows! Magnificent organ! Airs from the opera of 'Acis and Galatea'! the most snow-white and ethereal of surplices! and David Roughead (he of the 'fertile imagination') chanting his responses behind us, and singing 'a deep bass,' and tossing off his A—mĕns! in a jaunty style, that gave me a strong desire to box his ears.

Give my compliments to Anne; the usual kiss to my 'blessed' dog.

Your affectionate

J. W. C.

LETTER 177.

T. Carlyle, Chelsea.

Sunny Bank: Thursday, July 23, 1857.

The pens you made me, dear, are all ground down on this lime-paper, and I am obliged to write now with the backs, which has a perverse effect on my ideas, and my ideas are rather awry to begin with. I feel provoked that, having 'made an effort' like this to get well, I do not succeed in doing it effectually and at once. 'Very absurd.' I ought to be thankful for ever so little amendment; above all, even if no cure should be worked on me by all this fresh air, and sweet milk, and riding in carriages, and having my own entire humour out, I ought to be thankful for the present escape from that horrid sickness, which nobody that has not felt it can know the horror of.

Though my nights are no better than they were at Chelsea—indeed, worse latterly—still it is only oppression and weariness I feel during the day; not that horrid feeling as if death were grasping at my heart. But, 'oh, my!' what a shame, when you are left alone there with plenty of smoke of your own to consume, to be puffing out mine on you from this distance! It is certainly a questionable privilege one's best friend enjoys, that of having all one's darkness rayed out on him. If I were writing to—who shall I say?—Mr. Barlow, now, I should fill my paper with 'wits,' and elegant quotations, and diverting anecdotes; should write a letter that would procure me laudation sky-high, on my 'charming, unflagging spirits,' and my 'extraordinary freshness of mind and feelings;' but to you I cannot for my life be anything but a bore.

I went and drank tea with Mrs. David Davidson, the worst-used woman I ever knew; and at seventy-eight years of age she hasn't a drop of gall in her whole composition, and is as serene as if she had never had a sorrow. She has still the same servant, Mary Jeffrys, who was with her when I was a child; she has served her with the same relish for fifty years. ' Ye dinna find us as perfect as I could wuss,' she (Mary) said to me (the house was clean as a new pin); ' but I'm as wullin as ever to work, only no just sae able.' At the door she called after me: ' Ye'll find us ay here while we're to the fore; but it's no unco lang we can expect to get bided.' I don't think either mistress or maid could survive the other a month.

To-night, again, I go out to tea, at Miss Brown's; and on Saturday night at the Sheriffs', who were at school with me. On Monday I go to Mrs. Binnie's; on Tuesday to Craigenvilla, Morningside; and on Wednesday to Auchtertool.

I have a most affectionate letter from Lady Airlie, but I hardly think I shall go so far.

Compliments to Anne. Your care of the live stock does ' credit to your head and hort.' [1]

Affectionately yours,
JANE WELSH CARLYLE.

LETTER 178.

T. Carlyle, Chelsea.

Sunny Bank: Sunday, July 26, 1857.

Thanks for your note, meant to be very soothing, I can see; but it rather soothes me the wrong way of the hair somehow—makes me feel I had been making a baby of myself, and a fractious baby. Well, never mind, as Miss Madeline Smith [2] said to old Dr. Simpson, who attended her during a short illness in prison, and begged to use ' the privilege of an old man, and speak to her seriously at parting,' ' My dear doctor, it is so good of you. But I won't let you trouble yourself to give me advice, for I assure you I have quite made up my mind to turn over a new leaf!' That is fact. Simpson told it to Terrot, who told me.

And so I have made up my mind to turn over a new leaf, and no more give words to the impatient or desponding thoughts that rise in my mind about myself. It is not a natural vice of mine, that

---

[1] Poor Lady Bulwer, quizzing (her mother-in-law), in a mad mood, where also were ' Fuz ' = Forster, &c. &c.

[2] The Glasgow murderess.

sort of egoistical babblement, but has been fostered in me by the patience and sympathy shown me in my late long illness. I can very easily leave it off, as I did smoking, when I see it to be getting a bad habit.

But about Miss Smith I have one thing to tell you which I think you will be rather glad of, as giving the death-stroke to testimonials. The Glasgow merchants are actually raising a subscription (it has reached nine thousand pounds) ' to testify their sympathy for her.' One man, a Mr. D——, has given a thousand himself—he had better marry her, and get poisoned. Not that I believe the girl guilty of the poisoning; but she is such a little incarnate devil that the murder don't go for much in my opinion of her.

Haddington has half the honour of having produced this cocatrice. I knew her great-grandmother—a decent, ancient woman, called ' Mealy Janet,' never to be seen but with a bag of flour under each arm. She was mother to the ' Mr. Hamilton, architect of Edinburgh,' and to one of the most curious figures in my childhood, Mysie Hamilton, or ' Meal Mysie ' (she continuing her mother's flour trade); she spoke with a loud *man's* voice, that used to make us children take to our heels in terror when we heard it. I remember the boys said Mysie was a —— but what that was I hadn't a notion, nor have I yet; my mother thought her a good woman, and once by way of lark, invited her to tea. I bought a pamphlet the other day containing the whole ' trial,' on the very spot where Mysie Hamilton sold her flour, now a book-shop.

I was in our own house yesterday. They have new papered the drawing-room and dining-room. But the paint we left on it is still the same, and perfectly new-looking, after some forty years. My father always had everything done effectually. There are no such doors as those painted wainscot ones that I ever saw, with their eight coats of paint and as many of varnish. The old drawing-room still looks to me a beautiful room, independent of associations. But a full-length portrait of Mr. Howden, leaning like Sir David Baird on his horse's neck, was over the mantel-piece, vulgarising everything by its gloom-like presence. I gave young Dr. Howden, who lives there still, the large photograph of Woolner's Medallion,[1] in the secret expectation it would be hung up in that dear old room which still feels mine.

> And my youth was left behind
> For some one else to find.[2]

---

[1] Of me. [2] *Supra*, my wrong recollection.

The young girl-wife who lives there is very lovely, and writes poetry—God help her!

I adhere to my programme of leaving to-morrow, &c., but have promised to stop here again on my way home. I could not help it, when I saw those dear old women crying about my going so soon.

[No room for signature. Two flower-leaves—petals—inclosed.]

LETTER 179.

Archy something, an enthusiast Annandale pedlar, gone half mad with theology and horror of mad dogs, was gratefully supping porridge and milk in a wealthy farmer's kitchen one summer evening, intending to lodge there, when a mischievous maid servant whispered to another, 'Was that the bowl the stranger dog had?' as audibly to Archy as the 'Whist, whist!' (hush) of answer was. Archy sprang to his feet, snatched his pack, and ran through the wilderness many miles incessantly towards the cottage of a brother whom he had there. In the dead of the night a knock at the window was heard: brother asking who? what? Archy answered 'I'm degenerating.'

T. Carlyle, Chelsea.

Auchtertool: Monday, Aug. 3, 1857.

Oh, heaven! or rather, oh, the other place! 'I am degenerating from a woman into a dog, and feel an inclination to bark—bow wow! wow!' Ever since I came here I have been passing out of one silent rage into another at the things in general of this house. Viewed from the invalid point of view, they are enough really to make one not only bark but bite; were it not that, in other people's houses, one has to assume the muzzle of politeness. The best intentions always unfortunate. The finest possibilities yielding zero, or worse. The maximum of bother to arrive at the minimum of comfort (so far as I am concerned). Is it possible that the change of a cook can make the difference betwixt now and last summer? or is it the increased irritability of my nerves that makes it? or are my cousins getting stupefied for want of anything to stir their souls on this hilltop? The devil knows best how it comes, but 'I, as one solitary individual,' find no satisfaction in the arrangements here, though 'there need be no reflections for want of roses,' and, 'beautiful views,' and 'pure air'! And it is not only my soul that protests but my body; I sleep shockingly, and the sickness has come back. How little Mary has escaped dying under these late and irregular hours, and bad bread, and all the rest of the 'much ado about nothing,' and 'don't you wish you may get it,' here, is a wonder to me, and I don't think much of her doctor. When I looked at him and his ways intently, the other day, with a half-thought to consult him myself about certain things, he 'left me cold,'[1]—very cold indeed, and, 'with a decided preference,' for nature! Hadn't I better be going then? Decidedly; 'being an only child,' I have 'no wish' to stay. But then, 'that damned thing called the milk of human kindness,'[2] not being yet all gone to sour curd in me, I would not show any unfeeling impatience to be gone; where I am treated (though God knows how injudiciously) most kindly according to their light and ability.

I have written to Lady Airlie declining the honour proposed to me, which looked, on consideration, something of the Irishman's bottomless-Sedan sort. Also I have declined a pressing invitation to Thornhill. My flesh quivered at the thought of going through that again, in my present weakness of body and mind. But I mean to stop some days—a week perhaps—with my aunts; who are really good, intelligent companions when they keep off their hobby, and where I am well cared for materially. They have a good, plain house, and keep early hours and to a moment, and seemed really pleased to have me. I never saw women more improved by keeping! I had been thinking to try a week's sea-bathing before you suggested it; and perhaps shall go for a week to Portobello or North Berwick. At all events, I go back, if I am spared, to Sunny Bank to start from there for London. I could not get away without promising that, and shall be very glad of another breath of my 'native air'—I shouldn't wonder if it were the last till it blows over my grave; for when one of these dear old women dies, the other will follow fast; and they, too, gone, I don't think, if I even lived long, I should ever have the courage or wish to go back more.

Yours affectionately,

JANE W. CARLYLE.

LETTER 180.

T. Carlyle, Chelsea.

Auchtertool: Monday, Aug. 10, 1857.

Oh, my dear!—I am so sorry to think of your having been all alone there with Anne 'dreadfully ill!' As it has turned out, it

---

[1] Mazzini.

[2] 'That damned thing called the "Milk of human kindness." Sea-captain thanked God he had nothing of,' &c. Spedding's story.

was better that you did not tell me; for certainly I should have at once flown off to the rescue, and arrived only to complicate your difficulties by falling 'dreadfully ill' myself. Still, the confidence in all being well (figuratively speaking), so long as I hear nothing to the contrary, is done for by this concealment. So it will be for my peace of mind to be making no further move than is not a move homeward. My consolation, under the images of your discomfort that present themselves, is of that melancholy sort produced by 'two afflictions.' [1] I have been in such a way myself for the last week, that I could have done no good to you, Anne, or myself by being 'at my post'! The physical pain has been over for three days, but followed by such horrible depression of spirits that it felt as if one degree more of it would make me hang or drown myself. I could not write to you anything but articulate moans and groans, with a sprinkling of execrations! And so I preferred letting down the valve and consuming my own smoke. The last two nights I have had better sleep; and to-day I feel a little more up to living, though still far enough from 'doing the hoping of the family.'

Walter is going to give me a drive. Since Friday I have not had any exercise. Jeannie, with her 'child of 'miracle' and its two attendants, is still expected to-morrow, and I have fixed my departure for Thursday, which is as much giving in to family proprieties as could reasonably be expected of me. I have not named any time for my stay at Morningside—will 'leave it open' (as you say); but, even should I thrive there, I don't think of more than a week. And another week at Sunny Bank will make as much 'outing' as should suffice for this year! For the rest, I may give myself the same comfort about my travels that I used to give you about your horse, when you were saying it did you 'next to no good;' I 'can't tell how much worse' I should have been had I stayed through all that heat of London. Certainly I have had nothing to suffer from heat, whatever else.

Oh, those Indian women! It seems sinful of one to complain of anything in face of their dreadful fate, and their mothers and sisters at home! [2] It is difficult to reconcile such things with the belief that God takes care of every individual He has made!—that 'God is Love!' Love? It isn't much like a world ruled by Love,

---

[1] 'Two afflictions.'—'Deux afflictions mises ensemble peuvent devenir une consolation.'

[2] Indian Mutiny, and such news of its horrors!

this. My dear, I am tempted to write a good deal of blasphemy just at this moment. 'Better not!'

Thanks for writing so often. If you saw your letters received, you would think them important to me, surely; or that I am certainly too weak and nervous 'for anything' (as they say in Lancashire). The last two or three letters I turned quite sick at the sight of, and had to catch at a chair and sit down trembling before I could open and read them. This is 'a plain unvarnished' fact. And yet I was frightened for nothing in particular that I could have put into words. If you had put a loaded pistol to me, and required me to tell on my life what was agitating me to such a degree, I could have said nothing more lucid than that I didn't know whether there mightn't be some word in the letter that I would rather hadn't been there, or that the tone of the letter might show you were ill or uncomfortable, or that, in short, I couldn't guess whether it would make me gladder or sadder. But for a rational creature to be at the point of fainting with no more reason than that! 'A poor, miserable wretch with no stamina!' (as old Sterling used to say).

Address to Craigenvilla, Morningside.

Yours affectionately,
JANE W. C.

LETTER 181.

'Child of Glory,' absurd phrase in somebody's translation from poor Zacharias Werner, much commented upon at Comely Bank (I being thought concerned) by a certain Madame Viaris, zealous and honest Pomeranian, wife of an ex-Napoleon officer, whom and their one boy she honourably supported by teaching German. Reciting or reading in a high shrieky tone the original of Werner, she exclaimed passionately, at every turn, 'But where is the Child of Glory?' and got no answer, except in assenting smiles and long-continued remembrance.—T. C.

T. Carlyle, Chelsea.

Auchtertool: Thursday, Aug. 13, 1857.

My packing is just finished, dear; my dinner will be up in five minutes; and then I am off to Kirkcaldy to catch the three o'clock train. The day is very calm, so I hope to escape sickness; anyhow I shall be glad to have saved myself from 'The Child of Glory,' and its court. And as one hopes for relief, when one is feverish in bed, from turning on the other side, so I look forward to Morningside with a certain thankfulness. At all events it is near Sunny Bank, and Sunny Bank is on the road to London.

Jeannie and her suite did not arrive till yesterday. The baby is about three finger-lengths long; the two nurses nearly six feet each. Five packing cases came before them by the carrier, and as many portmanteaus and carpet-bags in the carriage with them. ' Did you ever?' ' No, I never!' I have kept my temper with all this nonsense wonderfully, to outward appearance at least. But it is only the speedy prospect of getting far away from it that has enabled me to keep from bursting out into swearing.

I hoped to have had leisure to write at decent length yesterday afternoon or to-day; but one can't get on with anything in this infernal hubbub. So I just scribble this little note to put in the post-office on my way out to Morningside, that you may know I have ' crossed' without accident. The Morningside post leaves early I believe.

Yours affectionately,
JANE W. CARLYLE.

LETTER 182.

T. Carlyle, Esq., Chelsea.

Craigenvilla: Saturday, Aug. 15, 1857.

Now then, ' thanks God,' I am back into the regions of common sense; have a nice little ' my-foot-is-on-my-native-heath-and-my-name's-Macgregor' feeling. The lungs of my soul begin to play, after having been all but asphyxiated with tarnation folly. Such a scene of waste, and fuss, and frivolity, and vanity, and vexation of spirit, I desire not to set my foot in again on this side of time. ' All sailing down the stream of time into the ocean of eternity, for the devil's sake. Amen!' I am sure it wasn't my irritability. Looking back on it coolly from here, I am as much disgusted as when I was in it.

I was taken to the Kirkcaldy station instead of Burnt Island, Walter having business there. Of course the first person I saw there was Mr. William Swan; and he was ' crossing' too, and took me under his ample wing. The sea was as smooth as a looking-glass, and I wasn't upset the least in the world. When my cab stopped at the gate here everybody ran out to meet me—three aunts, maid, and the very cat, with whom I am in high favour; it came purring about my feet, and whipping my leg with its tail; but you needn't say a word of that to Nero. I respect his too sensitive feelings. They made me quite comfortable, and got me warm tea in no time.

We had just finished when another cab drove to the gate, out of which leaped John [1] from Richmond, and one of his mother's sisters. I rushed off to open the house-door to him, and you should have seen how he started and stared. He looked dreadfully weak still, poor fellow! and coughed much, but not so incessantly as when we parted in London. He told my aunts I looked better. They gave me nice porridge to supper, and plenty of milk—not turned, as every drop of milk and cream at Auchtertool was; and I have slept better both the nights I have been here.

By the time I get done with this, and Sunny Bank, I shall be heartily glad to get home. Betty says, 'My dear, ye just toiled yersel last year; oh, ye mauna do that again!' And I don't mean to. Nobody knows what going into Dumfriesshire is for me. Haddington I have now got used to—like the pigs—to a certain extent; but Thornhill! Oh, mercy!

Grace got hold of your proof-sheet [2] yesterday, and shut herself up in her bedroom to read it. I knocked at the door to say something, and she opened it with spectacles on, and the open sheet in her hand, looking so fierce at being interrupted. She thought I was the maid. Her opinion is, 'It will be a remarkably interesting work,—really very interesting; she can see that by even this much.' They all send you their kind regards and say, 'Tell him to come down.' Don't they wish they may get it.

Your letter has come since I began this. And, *ach!* since I began this, I have recollected to-morrow is Sunday; but you will get it on Monday morning. I sent the photograph to Isabella a week ago.

Compliments to Ann; and no end of kisses to Nero.

Yours affectionately,
J. W. C.

LETTER 183.

This is the last (and perhaps the first, and pretty much the one) bit of pure sunshine that visited my dark and lonesome, and in the end quite dismal and inexpressible, enterprise of Frederick; the rest was all darkness, solitude; air leaden coloured, frozen rain, sound of subterranean torrents, like Balder's ride to the Death Kingdom, 'needing,' as I often said, the obstinacy of ten mules for ten or thirteen years at that time of life. Except a small patch of writing by Emerson, this is the only bit of human criticism in which, across the general exaggeration, I could discover real linea-

---

[1] Her clever cousin.   [2] *Hist.*, vol. i. and ii., Friedrich.—J. A. F.

ments of the thing.   Very memorable was this of her to me, and
will for ever be.   How memorable are all these letter of 1857, and
my silent moods (deep sorrow and toil, tinted with gratitude and
hope) in those summer months!   Two china seats (little china
barrel-shaped things) in the garden here, which were always called
'Noble-men,' from a spiteful remark of Anne's about the purchase
of them.   My midnight 'smoke' there, looking up into the empy-
rean and the stars.   Ah me!—T. C.

T. Carlyle, Esq., Chelsea.

Craigenvilla, Edinburgh: Monday, Aug. 24, 1857.

Oh, my dear!   What a magnificent book this is going to be!   The
best of all your books.   I say so, who never flatter, as you are too
well aware; and who am 'the only person I know that is always in
the right!'[1]   So far as it is here before me, I find it forcible and
vivid, and sparkling as 'The French Revolution,' with the geniality
and composure and finish of 'Cromwell'—a wonderful combination
of merits!   And how you have contrived to fit together all those
different sorts of pictures, belonging to different sorts of times, as
compactly and smoothly as a bit of the finest mosaic!   Really one
may say, of these two first books at least, what Helen said of the
letters of her sister who died—you remember?—'So splendidly put
together one would have thought that hand couldn't have written
them!'

It was the sheets that hindered me from writing yesterday;
though I doubt if a letter posted at Morningside (the Scotch *Campo
Santo*) yesterday (Sunday) would have reached you sooner than if
posted to-day.   Certainly it is a devil of a place for keeping the
Sunday, this!   Such preaching and fasting, and 'touting and praying,' as I was never before concerned in!   But one never knows
whence deliverance is to come any more than misfortune.   I was
cut out of all, or nearly all, my difficulties yesterday by the simple
providential means of—a bowel complaint!   It was reason enough
for staying away from church; excuse enough for declining to be
read to; and the loss of my dinner was entirely made up for by the
loss of my appetite!   Nothing could have happened more opportunely!   Left at home with Pen (the cat), when they had gone
every one to her different ('Place of Worship,' I opened my desk to
write you a letter.   But I would just take a look at the sheets first.
Miss Jess had put a second cover on the parcel, and forwarded it by

---

[1] 'Faut avouer, ma chère, je ne trouve que moi qui aie toujours raison,'
said Madame Lafayette.

railway on Saturday night; and I had not been able to read then,
by the gaslight, which dazzles my eyes. It is one of the little
peculiarities of this house that there isn't a candle allowed in it of
any sort—wax, dip, moulded, or composite! Well, I took up the
sheets and read 'here a little and there a little,' and then I began at
the beginning and never could stop till I had read to the end, and
pretty well learnt it by heart. I was still reading when Church
came out, and so my letter got nipt in the bud. If it is so interesting for me, who have read and heard so many of the stories in
it before, what must it be to others to whom it is all new? the
matter as well as the manner of the narrative! Yes, you shall see,
it will be the best of all your books—and small thanks to it! It
has taken a doing!

I suppose you are roasting again. Here there has been no such
heat since I came north as in the last three days—mercury at 75° in
the shade yesterday. But there is plenty of east wind to keep one
from suffocating, provided one can get it without the dust. I used
to fancy Piccadilly dusty; but, oh, my, if you saw the Morningside
Road!

I must tell you a compliment paid me before I conclude. A lady
I hadn't seen for twenty years came to call for me. ' You were ill
I heard,' she said. ' Ah, yes, it is easy to see you have suffered!
an entire wreck, like myself.' Then, looking round on my three
aunts, ' Indeed, like all of us! !'

Yours affectionately,
JANE W. CARLYLE.

What of Lady Sandwich? You never mention her. Fleming[1]
at Raith! I should have been as astonished to meet *him* in Kirkcaldy, as to meet Tiger Wull's[2] 'finest blackcock that ever stepped
the streets of Greenock!'

LETTER 184.

In final settlement of heritage into equal parts, John Welsh,
senior, totally omitted her (*i.e.* her father, who was eldest, and had
been the benefactor and stay of all the family), of which I remember she wrote at the time to me, nobly sorrowful—not ignobly then
or ever, in that case or in any.—T. C.

---

[1] Fleming—Old fogie of fashion; once Charles Buller's ' attached.'

[2] 'Teeger Wull,' Tiger Will—William Dunlop, a well-known cousin of hers,
one of the strangest men of his age, with an inexhaustible sense of fun. One
friend promised another (according to Wull) ' the finest blackcock that,' &c.

T. Carlyle, Esq., Chelsea.

Sunny Bank: Friday, August 28, 1857

Here I am, dear, an incarnation of 'the bad sixpence.' Sixteen miles nearer home, anyhow. I left Edinburgh at two yesterday, was at Longniddry by half-past two, and didn't get to Haddington till four. Such complete misunderstanding exists between the little Haddington cross-train and all other trains, that one may lay one's account with having to wait always three-quarters of an hour at the least. Then the waiting-room is 'too stuffy for anything,' and the seated structure outside expressly contrived for catching cold in; so that one is fain to hang about on one's legs in space.

The bother of all this, taken together with the excitement of my rapturous welcome, kept me awake in a high fever, till my doomed hour of four o'clock this morning—or something kept me awake that the devil only knows! It was such an arrival, after all: the servants waiting outside the house, smiling and saying, 'Glad to see you back, ma'am.' Miss Jess, tumbling into my arms on the threshold, 'faintly ejaculating' (as a novelist would say), 'Our Precious!' 'Our Beloved!' and beyond her my godmother, advancing with her hands stretched out, groping the air, and calling out in an excited way, 'Is that my bairn?'

The niece and grand-niece were discreet enough to keep upstairs till 'the first flush o' meeting' was over, but were very cordial when they appeared. To their credit I must say, they might easily take offence at the preference shown me. Even in the midst of these raptures my eye sought and discovered your letter on the usual table, but I refrained from opening it (paragon of politeness that I was!) till dinner was over, for which I had already kept them waiting an hour.

They think me looking much better. Indeed, my first fortnight at Craigenvilla, with all its drawbacks of weekly fasts, inordinate reading to, gas, and water-cistern, was very good for my health, and, on the whole, pleasant to live. I cannot say which of my aunts was the kindest to me—they were all so kind. Grace knitted me a pair of such warm stockings while I was there; and Ann flowered me a most lovely collar; and Elizabeth procured a whole calf's stomach (!) for me (now in my carpet-bag) that I might have curds at home, as it was the thing I seemed to like best of all that they gave me to eat; and it was so pleasant talking about 'dear old

II.—4

long ago' with those who I felt (for the first time perhaps) had interests in common with me in it.

It was better so, surely, I thought, after our affectionate parting; far better so than if I had gone to law with them about that fraction of my grandfather's property I might have disputed, and even gained it, and put heart-burnings and resentment between my own father's sisters and me for evermore. A little true family affection is worth a great many hundreds of pounds, especially when one isn't needing pounds!

Since writing this sheet I have been to Dirleton Castle, and it is now dinner-time, and I must take my letter to the post office immediately after, or you won't hear of me till Tuesday.

Yours affectionately,

JANE W. C.

No date fixed yet, or, indeed, to be spoken of for the moment.

LETTER 185.

T. Carlyle, Chelsea.

Sunny Bank: Sunday, Aug. 30, 1857.

I am reading the sheets to them—they most likely will not live to see the finished book. You never saw more ardent listeners! My godmother, with her head bent forward, hearkening with her blind eyes, as well as her ears, might sit for a picture of Attention. And every now and then one or other asks some question or makes some remark, that shows how intelligently they listen. Miss Jess said one good thing: 'To look merely to the wording—it is so brief, so concise, that one would expect some obscurity in the narrative, or at least that it would need a great effort of attention to understand it; instead of which the meaning is as clear as glass!' And Miss Donaldson said, 'I see more than ever in this, my dear, what I have always seen in Mr. Carlyle's books, and what I think distinguishes him from all the writers of the present day—a great love of truth; and, what is more' (observe the fine discrimination!) 'a perfect detestation of lies!'

I was afraid, having to read in a voice so high pitched, my reading would not do justice to the thing; but Miss Donaldson asked me last night, 'My dear, does Mr. Carlyle read what he writes to you bit by bit?' 'Oh, dear, no! he does not like reading aloud.' 'Then I suppose you read it often over to yourself? For I was

noticing that in reading those sheets, you did it so natural-like, just
as if it was coming out of your own head!'

I was dreaming last night about going to some strange house,
among strange people, to make representations about cocks! I went
on my knees at last, weeping, to an old man with a cast-metal face
and grey hair; and while I was explaining all about how you were
an author, and couldn't get sleep for these new cocks, my auditor
flounced off, and I became aware he was the man who had three
serpent-daughters, and kept people in glass bottles in Hoffman's
Tale![1] I forgot his name, but knew it well enough in my dream.

A kiss to Nero.   Yours ever,

                                                  J. W. C.

LETTER 186.

T. Carlyle, Chelsea.

Sunny Bank: Wednesday, September 2, 1857.

Oh, my dear, my dear! you give me the idea of a sensible Christian man making himself into a spinning dervish. Oh, ' depend
upon't, the slower thou ridest, the faster thou'lt get,' &c. These
dinings 'before sunset,' teas ' about ten,'—don't I know what comes
of all that, and that what comes of it is ' eventually,' ' rale mental
agony in your own inside'?[2] hardly to be assuaged by blue pill
and castor oil at a great expense of inward life. If I hadn't been
coming home at any rate, your last letter would have determined
me to come, just to put a spoke in your wheel, that you mayn't
like a furious grinding-stone, fly all off in sand.

It will be a great nuisance to you, I know, when you have got
the bridle of time shaken off your head, about your heels, and your
face to the wind, to be again in harness with a little steady-going
animal, that looks to have her corn and her mashes regular, or lies
down in the road.

But bless you, if you hadn't had a counter-pull on you in the direction of order, and regularity and moderation, and all that stupid
sort of thing, where would you have been by this time? Tell me
that! Oh, how I wish I were home, that horrid journey over!
Eliza Donaldson says, ' Not like the journey, Mrs. Carlyle? how
odd!' I declare it is a consolation for having one's nerves 'all

---

[1] *Archivarius Lindhorst :* ' Oh, my beautiful little darling! was there ever a
prettier dream, bad or good?'

[2] Servant Helen's phrase.

gone to smithers,' to see how stolid and unlovable good health makes people, with the best intentions too.

I have broken to Miss Jess the fact that I am going next week, on Tuesday or Wednesday; and before that time I shall surely have made up my mind about the train. Never fear, but I shall go by first-class this time. Only which first-class? Haddington is most inconveniently situated as to the railway, which is the reason of those strange delays of letters. No express train stops at Longniddry. Well, well, as Nancy at Craigenputtock said of Elliot's descent from the roof, 'Pooh! his own weight will bring him down.'[1] I shall get home surely by some force of gravitation or other.

I haven't got through the American novel yet. It is a curious book; very nearly a good book but spoiled, like old Sterling's famous carriage, by pretending to be too many different things all in one. It is 'Quinland' (a novel), or it is 'Varieties of American Life.' Then it is an allegory (himself tells us that) symbolising the Marriage of Genius and Religion. Then it is a note-book of Mr. White, or White's opinions of all the authors he has studied, and all the general reflections he has ever made. Then it is an American Wilhelm Meister. Then it is Mr. White's realised Ideal of—a new Christian Bible! And, finally, one doesn't know what it is or is not; any more than whether the style is a flagrant imitation of you, or of Goethe, or of Jean Paul, or of Emerson. Happily it 'isn't of the slightest consequence' which.

Yours ever affectionately,

J. W. C.

LETTER 187.

Printing of Friedrich, first two volumes, now well advanced. Christmas was spent among the most refractory set of proof sheets I expect in this world.

To Mrs. Austin, the Gill, Annan.

5 Cheyne Row, Chelsea: Christmas Day, 1857.

My dear Mary,—I understood that your brother would write himself to-day, to announce the save arrival of your box, the contents of which were exhibited to him in succession last night. When it came to the goose, carried in on my arms like a strange new kind of baby (with that belly-band about it!), he burst into such a laugh! 'That fellow I think has got his quietus' (he said).

---

[1] Our 'jack-of-all-trades' servant.

But now he has just come down, and is off for his ride, and when I asked ' had he written to Mary?' he exclaimed wildly that he had 'fifteen hours of the most awful work of correcting proofs ahead of him, that I who had nothing to do should have written to Mary!' With all the pleasure in life! had I known in time, instead of within just half an hour of post-time—from which is to be subtracted ten minutes for putting on my things and running to the post-office! But better a line than no letter at all till to-morrow— you thinking the while that those blessed birds may be coming to harm from being too long on the road!

No, my dear! one 'Chucka' is boiling at this moment for the master's dinner (I dine on anything at two o'clock; not being up to waiting for Mr. C.'s six or seven o'clock dinners). But I had one of the eggs to my breakfast, and it was the very best and biggest I ever ate in my life! There were only two broken, and not wasted even these; I lifted up the yolks, which lay quite round and whole, in a spoon (for puddings).

I wish I had begun in time, for I had plenty of things to say; but I must keep for this time to mere acknowledgment of your present—another day I may tell you the rest.

Yours ever affectionately,

JANE CARLYLE.

LETTER 188.

She returned to me Wednesday evening, September 9, evidently a little better, says the record. Her winter was none of the best; end of the year she is marked very feckless, though full of spirit. I, deep all the while in Frederick proofs and fasheries, hoping to have all ended—of these two volumes—by the end of May, which term in effect was nearly kept.

In January 1858, we had engaged to a week at the Grange with Lord Ashburton, from which my poor Jeannie (trouble with servants, &c., superadding itself) was obliged to excuse herself and send me alone, who only stayed three days. This, her dear letter during these, which except two tragic moments—first entrance to the empty drawing-room in silence of dusk; then another evening Lady Sandwich and Miss Baring new hanging the pictures there —have left no trace whatever with me.—T. C.

T. Carlyle, Esq., at the Grange.

Cheyne Row: Monday, January 18, 1858.

My dear! 'Ye maun joost excuse us the day!' I have an aching head come to fraternise with my aching side, and between the two am 'very much detached;' can't easily sit still to write. For the rest, even Geraldine couldn't say of me that I am 'much happier for your being away.' I feel as forlorn as—'the maiden' that 'milked the cow with the crumpled horn.' My sickness and help-lessness striving to 'keep up its dignity,' and, what is more to the purpose, to keep its temper in this atmosphere of systematic inso-lence and arsenical politeness, is one of those sufferings through which I suppose man (meaning woman) is 'made perfect,' or ought to be.

Then the poor little dog, who was to have been 'company to me,' is not recovered from the illness he took before you left. He seemed coming to himself yesterday forenoon, though still he had not tasted food since the last you gave him; and I stupidly let Mr. Piper take him to Fulham. He came home—carried most of the way, not able to keep his legs—his eyes extinct, his legs stretched out cold and stiff. He has lain ever since without moving, but he now looks at me when I stroke him, and his posture is more natu-ral. You may fancy how many lucifers I lighted through the night, when I *felt* him quite cold, and couldn't hear him breathing! Poor wee Nero! how glad I should be to hear him snoring, or see-ing him over-eating himself again!

Please thank Lady Sandwich for the dear little letter I had from her this morning. I don't say 'dear' in the Lady A. sense, but really meaning it. I will write to her when I have got my head a little above all this troubled water. Also thank Lord Ashburton for the game (hare and pheasants). It gives one a taste of the pleasures of patronage, having such things to give away.

Mr. and Mrs. Lowe called to ask for me yesterday morning (Sunday) between ten and eleven, on their way to 'the Cottage.' Happily they found me in no muddle. In the middle of the day Geraldine walked in! She couldn't have managed to reappear at a more propitious moment for having her judgment commuted.

Just one packet of proofs. Though there is no sheet, I send it, in case you should stay over Wednesday. Don't hurry for me if you get good of the change. It will be all in my own interest your staying, if you come back better for it.

With Geraldine at hand, I don't suffer the same practical incon-venience from being confined to the house. I can send her on any message.

Love to Lady Sandwich.

Yours ever,
JANE WELSH CARLYLE.

For God's sake don't put such great platches of black wax on your letters, to me at least. My heart turned in my throat this morning; I thought it was some horrid news from Annandale.

LETTER 189.

Beginning of June, Friedrich quite off my hands. There were the usual speculations about sea quarters, covert from the heat, &c. (miserable feature of London life, needing to be disanchored every year, to be made comparatively a nomadic, quasi-Calmuck life). After much calculating, it is settled I am to go first to the Gill, afterwards to Germany, a second time; she, after settling home botherations, to go for Nithsdale, Mrs. Pringle, of Lann Hall, pressing to be her hostess. Evening of June 24, with four fat Glasgow gentlemen, submissively astonished at my passion for fresh air, set off, ride vigilant all night—the last time of my entering Scotland with anything of real hope, or other than affectionate gloom and pain.—T. C.

T. Carlyle, Esq., The Gill.

5 Cheyne Row, Chelsea: Friday, June 25, 1858.

' And the evening and the morning were the first day!' 'Let alone,' with a sort of vengeance. Exhausted human nature could not desire more perfect letting alone! It was wonderful to reflect, while breakfasting at nine, that you had probably already breakfasted at the Gill in Scotland. After all, railways are a great thing, only inferior to ' the Princess of China's "flying bed,"' Prince Houssain's ' flying carpet,' and Fortunatus's 'wishing cap.' Transported over night from here to there; from Chancellor's dung-heap, the ' retired cheesemonger's dogs, and two-pence worth of nominal cream,' away to ' quiet, fresh air,' and ' milk without limit,' in one night! If it weren't for the four fat men in the carriage with you, wouldn't it be like something in a fairy tale?

Don't let your enjoyment of 'the country' be disturbed by thoughts of me still 'in town.' I won't stay here longer than I find it good for me. But what I feel to need at present is, above all things human and divine, rest from 'mental worry;' and nowhere is there such fair outlook of that for me as just at home under the present conditions. 'The cares of bread'[1] have been too heavy for me lately; and the influx of 'cousins'[2] most wearing;

---

[1] Mazzini, on his *Plot* expeditions.

[2] Maggie and Mary, of Auchtertool, had been to the Isle of Wight for winter; lately home again.

and to see you constantly discontented, and as much so with me, apparently, as with all other things, when I have neither the strength and spirits to bear up against your discontent, nor the obtuseness to be indifferent to it—that has done me more harm than you have the least notion of. You have not the least notion what a killing thought it is to have put into one's heart, gnawing there day and night, that one ought to be dead, since one can no longer make the same exertions as formerly; that one was taken 'for better,' not by any means 'for worse;' and, in fact, that the only feasible and dignified thing that remains for one to do is to just die, and be done with it.[1]

Better, if possible, to recover some health of body and mind, you say. Well, yes; if possible. In that view I go with Neuberg this evening to view a field of hay.

Mrs. Welsh did not come yesterday—only a note from her to say she and John would be here on Saturday afternoon. Her journey to ¦Scotland was 'all up,' she said; but no reason given. Not a word about the dear horse.[2] So I wrote to bid her remember to bring the receipt for him on Saturday. I shall regret his being sent for, for I foresee that if he goes he will be left behind, as the shortest way of settling the matter.

I have not spoken to a soul since you left but Charlotte;[3] only Lady Airlie called yesterday, and I was out. Charlotte is as kind and attentive as possible, and her speech is remarkably sensible. She was observing yesterday morning that 'master looked rather dull at going away, and I can't say,' she added, 'that you look particularly brilliant (!) since his departure.'

I have got Mrs. Newnham's[4] little sick daughter lying out on the green to-day reading fairy tales, to her intense delight. Our green to her is grander than the Grange grounds to us.

No letters for you but one from Oxford, requiring information about India.[5] Nero is much astonished that you do not come down in the mornings to take him out. He runs upstairs and then down

---

[1] Alas! alas! sinner that I am!

[2] Poor horse 'Fritz,' beautiful, stout, and loyal, had been nearly killed (on arsenic diet) by a villain here, and was now roaming in grass near Richmond.

[3] The new maid, a fine little Chelsea creature—courageously, with excellent discernment, and with very good success, now taken on trial.

[4] An astonishingly good old cook, who sometimes officiates here—curious Chelsea specimen too.

[5] Sent that to John Mill (after long years of abeyance), who kindly granted the young man 'a few minutes' interview.'

to me, and stares up in my face, saying as plainly as possible, 'did you ever?'

Give them at the Gill my kind regards.

Yours ever,

J. W. C.

LETTER 190.

Mrs. Russell, Thornhill.

5 Cheyne Row, Chelsea: Sunday, June 27, 1858.

Dearest Mary,—It is so long since I wrote, and I have been so bothered and bewildered in the interval, that I can't recollect whether it is your turn or my own to write. But whosoever turn it is, the silence is equally needing to be broken, and if I am the delinquent, I can only say I have had plenty of excuse for all my sins of omission of late weeks. First, my dear, the heat has really been nearer killing me than the cold. London heat! nobody knows what that is till having tried it; so breathless, and sickening, and oppressive, as no other heat I ever experienced is! Then the quantities of visitors rushing about me at this season, complicated by an influx of cousins, to be entertained on special terms, have taken out, in talk, my dregs of strength and spirit!

Then Mr. Carlyle, in the collapse from the strain of his book, and the biliousness developed by the heat, has been so wild to 'get away,' and so incapable of determining where to go, and when to go, that living beside him has been like living the life of a weathercock, in a high wind, blowing from all points at once!—sensibility superadded!—so long, at least, as he involved me in his 'dissolving views.' The imaginary houses, in different parts of the kingdom, in which I have had to look round me on bare walls, and apply my fancy to furnishing with the strength I have (!) (about equal to my canary's, which, every now and then, drops off the perch on its back, and has to be lifted up), would have driven me crazy, I think, if one day I hadn't got desperate, and burst out crying. Until a woman cries men never think she can be suffering. Bless their blockheadism! However, when I cried, and declared I was not strong enough for all that any more, Mr. C. opened his eyes to the fact, so far as to decide that, for the present, he would go to his sister's (the Gill), and let me choose my own course after. And to the Gill he went last Wednesday night, and since then I have been resting, and already feel better for the rest, even without 'change of air.'

II.—4*

What my own course will be I haven't a notion! The main point in my system of rest is, to postpone not only all doing, but all making up my mind to do; to reduce myself as much as possible to a state of vacant, placid idiotcy. That is the state, I am sure, a judicious doctor would recommend for the moment. When the time comes for wishing for change and action, it will be time to decide where to go. Meanwhile I shall see what being well let alone will do for my health. All the cousins are gone now, the visitors going, no household cares (' cares of bread,' as Mazzini calls them), for, with no husband to study, housekeeping is mere play, and my young maid is a jewel of a creature. It seems to me the best chance I have had for picking up a little strength this good while.

I suppose you will be having my aunt Ann again soon. I hear from them very seldom. I should like so much if I could be set down there in ' the Princess of China's flying bed,' or on ' Prince Houssain's flying carpet,' to land at Thornhill, before the fine weather end; but the length of journey by rail terrifies me, especially the length of the journey back; Mrs. Pringle, I dare say, half expects me to visit her in August, for I have never said positively I would not, and she has pressed my coming most kindly. But to say where I will not go would require consideration and decision, as well as saying where I will go. And, as I have said, I mean to be an idiot for a time, postponing all mental effort.

Do write to me; I don't feel to know about you at all. Love to the doctor.

Your affectionate
JANE W. CARLYLE.

LETTER 191.

T. Carlyle, The Gill.

5 Cheyne Row, Chelsea: Sunday night, July 4, 1858.

Ach ! what a three days and three nights I have had, dear! Jonah in the whale's belly could not have had worse. ' Brighton' still I suppose! I was not to get off from that adventure with only one night and day of torture. I must have caught cold that day, and had it unpronounced in my nerves till Friday, when it broke out in sore throat, headache, faceache, rheumatism all over, retching and fever! Certainly I had done nothing after to give me a cold. But that was folly enough, I knew quite well that I was not fit for such an excursion; and yet I went, ' going whether I could or not.'[1] My only comfort was to be at home, and not transacting these horrors on a visit, or in a wretched sea-side lodging.

I had some sleep this morning, and the cold seems now concentrating in my head—not in my chest, which would have been a drearier prospect. Don't disturb yourself about my being ill in your absence—that is to say, about the absence part of it. Outside of myself I have nothing to complain of. Charlotte is much kinder and helpfuller than Anne was, and the comfort of talking with you now and then would have been counterbalanced in my present circumstances by 'the cares of bread.' Besides, I don't mean to be ill long, and once rid of this, won't I take care how I expose myself and over-fatigue myself again!

I can have as much society as I like, but I prefer none when I am ill; and I have these delightful volumes of Tourgueneff's to amuse me when I am up to being amused. I am gone 'into the country' 'at the shortest notice and on the cheapest terms' (as the undertakers' sign-boards have it). I have made the sideboard and large sofa change places, arranged the back parlour as a boudoir, filled up the folding doors with the screen, and look out on nothing but green leaves and the 'nobleman's seats!'[2] Moreover, the dunghill is quite suppressed; I have not felt a whiff of it since the letter was written. To be sure, the hot weather went with you; the last week has been like winter. I have a fire, so has Mrs. Hawkes, and the fur rug is again in action. I have surely more amusing things to tell you; but I must leave off for to-night. I am dead tired already. Besides, to-morrow I may have a letter from you to answer. Don't forget to tell me the address to put on the newspaper for America.

Monday.

'Nothing for Craigenputtock to-day.'[3] Awell! you waited, I suppose, for an answer, you cross thing! And if my sore throat on Friday had turned to '*the* sore throat,' as I was half expecting, you might have waited long enough, and then wouldn't you have been '*vaixed*'?

Neuberg came on Saturday evening, and, being told I couldn't see anyone, he went up to the study 'to get some books.' Half an hour after, I was going to my bedroom, and came on him, standing quite noiselessly on the landing-place, so I had to take him in and

---

[1] Groom's phrase about a horse of mine.
[2] China barrel-shaped things (*supra*), p. 71.
[3] Postmaster at Dumfries (painfully civil).

give him a cup of my tea, which was ready; and then he had the sense to go.

I am rather better to-day; had about four hours' sleep, and came down to breakfast. It is still very cold. I look forward to spending the day under my fur rug, reading Tourgueneff—nobody to be let in but Mrs. Hawkes, who will come at four o'clock. I have a nice little fire opposite me in my back-room, and the prospect of the 'nobleman's seat.'   Yours ever,

                                                                J. W. C.

LETTER 192.

NOTES OF A SITTER-STILL.

T. Carlyle, Esq., Scotsbrig.

                                        Chelsea: Sunday night, July 11, 1858.

Botkin (what a name!), your Russian translator, has called. Luckily Charlotte had been forewarned to admit him if he came again. He is quite a different type from Tourgueneff, though a tall man, this one too. I should say he must be a Cossack—not that I ever saw a Cossack or heard one described, instinct is all I have for it. He has flattened high-boned cheeks—a nose flattened towards the point—small, very black, deep-set eyes, with thin semi-circular eyebrows—a wide thin mouth—a complexion white-grey, and the skin of his face looked thick enough to make a saddle of! He does not possess himself like Tourgueneff, but bends and gesticulates like a Frenchman.

He burst into the room with wild expressions of his 'admiration for Mr. Carlyle.' I begged him to be seated, and he declared 'Mr. Carlyle was the man for Russia.' I tried again and again to 'enchain' a rational conversation, but nothing could I get out of him but rhapsodies about you in the frightfullest English that I ever heard out of a human head! It is to be hoped that (as he told me) he reads English much better than he speaks it, else he must have produced an inconceivable translation of 'Hero Worship.' Such as it is, anyhow, 'a large deputation of the Students of St. Petersburg' waited on him (Botkin), to thank him in the strongest terms for having translated for them 'Hero Worship,' and made known to them Carlyle. And even the young Russian ladies now read 'Hero Worship,' and 'unnerstants it thor—lie.' He was all in a perspiration when he went away, and so was I!

I should like to have asked him some questions; for example,

how he came to know of your Works (he had told me he had had
to send to England for them 'at extreem cost'), but it would have
been like asking a cascade! The best that I could do for him I
did. I gave him a photograph of you, and put him up to carrying
it in the top of his hat!

I don't think I ever told you the surprising visit I had from
David Aitken[1] and Bess. I was so ill when I wrote after that all
details were omitted. Charlotte had come to say one of the latch-
keys was refusing to act. I went to see what the matter was, and
when we opened the door, behold, David at the bottom of the
steps, and Bess preparing to knock! 'Is this Mrs. Carlyle's?'
she asked of myself while I was gazing dumfoundered. My
goodness!' cried I. At the sound of my voice she knew me—not
till then—though at my own door! and certainly the recognition
was the furthest from complimentary I ever met. She absolutely
staggered, screaming out, 'God preserve me, Jane! That you?'
Pleasant! David coming up the steps brought a little calm into
the business, and the call got itself transacted better or worse.

They were on their way home from Italy. Both seemed rather
more human than last time, especially David, whose face had taken
an expression of 'Peace on earth and good-will unto men.' Bess
had lost a tooth or two, was rather thinner, and her eyes hollower;
otherwise much the same.

They invited me very kindly to Minto, and he seemed really in
earnest.

July 16.

Surely, dear, the shortest, most unimportant note you can write
is worth a bit of paper all to itself? Such a mixed MS., with flaps
too, may be a valuable literary curiosity 'a hundred years hence,'
but is a trial of patience to the present reader, who, on eagerly
opening a letter from you, had not calculated on having to go
through a process like seeking the source of the Niger, in a small
way.

For the rest, you don't at all estimate my difficulties in writing a
letter every day, when I am expected to tell how I am, and when
'I's ashamed to say I's no better.' Dispense me from saying anything whatever about my health; let me write always 'Notes,' and
it would be easy for me to send you a daily letter. As easy at least

---

[1] Minister of Minto and wife (once Bess Stoddart), Bradfute's niece and
heiress.

as it is to be lively with the callers, who go away in doubt (like George Cooke) 'whether I am the most stoical of women, or whether there is nothing in the world the matter with me?'

But you want to be told how I sleep, &c. &c.; and can't you understand that having said twice, thrice, call it four times, 'I am sleeping hardly any, I am very nervous and suffering,' the fifth time that I have the same account to repeat, 'horrible is the thought to me,' and I take refuge in silence. Wouldn't you do the same? Suppose, instead of putting myself in the omnibus the other day, and letting myself be carried in unbroken silence to Richmond and back again, I had sat at home writing to you all the thoughts that were in my head? But that I never would have done; not a hundredth part of the thoughts in my head have ever been or ever will be spoken or written—as long as I keep my senses, at least.

Only don't you, 'the apostle of silence,' find fault with me for putting your doctrine in practice. There are days when I must hold my peace or speak things all from the lips outwards, or things that, being of the nature of self-lamentation, had better never be spoken.

My cold in the meanwhile? It is still carrying on, till Lonsdale coom,[1] in the shape of cough and a stuffed head; but it does not hurt me anywhere, and I no longer need to keep the house; the weather being warm enough, I ride in an omnibus every day more or less.

All last night it thundered; and there was one such clap as I never heard in my life, preceded by a flash that covered my book for a moment with blue light (I was reading in bed about three in the morning, and you can't think what a wild effect that blue light on the book had!). To-day it is still thundering in the distance, and soft, large, hot drops of rain falling. What of the three tailors?

I could swear you never heard of Madame —— de ——. But she has heard of you; and if you were in the habit of thanking God 'for the blessing made to fly over your head,' you might offer a modest thanksgiving for the honour that stunning lady did you in galloping madly all round Hyde Park in chase of your 'brown wide-awake' the last day you rode there; no mortal could predict what the result would be if she came up with you. To seize your

---

[1] Cumberland old woman (*supra*).

bridle and look at you till she was satisfied was a trifle to what she
was supposed capable of. She only took to galloping after you
when more legitimate means had failed.

She circulates everywhere, this madcap 'Frenchwoman.' She
met 'the Rev. John' (Barlow), and said, when he was offering delicate attentions, 'There is just one thing I wish you to do for me—
to take me to see Mr. Carlyle.' 'Tell me to ask the Archbishop of
Canterbury to dance a polka with you,' said Barlow, aghast, 'and
I would dare it, though I have not the honour of his acquaintance;
but take anybody to Mr. Carlyle—impossible!' 'That silly old
Barlow won't take me to Carlyle,' said the lady to George Cooke;
'you must do it then.' 'Gracious heavens!' said George Cooke;
'ask me to take you up to the Queen, and introduce you to her,
and I would do it, and "take the six months' imprisonment," or
whatever punishment was awarded me; but take anybody to Mr.
Carlyle—impossible!'

Soon after this, George Cooke met her riding in the Park, and
said, 'I passed Mr. Carlyle a little way on, in his brown wide-
awake.' The lady lashed her horse and set off in pursuit, leaving
her party out of sight, and went all round the Park at full gallop,
looking out for the wide-awake. She is an authoress in a small
way, this charming Frenchwoman; and is the wife of a newspaper
editor at Paris, who 'went into the country' (Miss F—— told me)
'and brought back a flowerpot full of earth, and, on the strength
of that, put de —— to his name of Monsieur ——.'

But the absurdest fact about her is, that, being a 'Frenchwoman,'
she is the reputed daughter of Lord F. and a Mrs. G.! It is in Lord
F.'s house that she stays here. Miss F—— also declares she was a
celebrated singer at Munich. But Miss F—— is a very loose talker,
and was evidently jealous of the sensation the lady produced by her
wit and eccentricities.

Will that suit you?

LETTER 193.

Larkin (Henry; young Londoner, then collector or cashier on the
Chelsea steamers, now partner in some prosperous metallurgic or
engineering business) had come to me some three years before this
in a loyally volunteer and interesting manner—a helper sent me by
favour of Heaven, as I often said and felt in the years coming.
He did for me all manner of maps, indexes, summaries, copyings,
sortings, miscellanea of every kind, in a way not to be surpassed
for completeness, ingenuity, patience, exactitude, and total and

continual absence of fuss.   Never had I loyaller or more effective help; nowhere was there a more honest-minded man; really of fine talent, too; clear, swift discernment, delicate sense of humour, &c.; but he preferred serving me in silence to any writing he could do (that was his own account on volunteering himself).   Till Frederick ended he was my factotum, always at hand; and still from the distance is prompt and eager to help me actually; a man to thank Heaven for, as I still gratefully acknowledge.—T. C.

T. Carlyle, Esq., The Gill.

Chelsea: July 19, 1858.

There, my dear! I send you a wonderful communication—a map of your new 'parish' and township in Australia!   I have spent an hour over the packet before I could understand what it all meant. The letter accompanying the maps was inserted between them, so that it was not discovered at first.   There are six copies of this map that I send you, and there is a large colored map on excessively thick paper, professing to be 'Plan of the Township of Carlyle, in the Parish of Carlyle, Murray District;' to which is affixed the signature of 'C. Gavan Duffy, Minister of Land and Works.' This I will not send—it would cost so much—unless you wish for it at once.   Poor Duffy appears by the letter to be very ill, but past the worst.

It is such a beautiful day, this! as clear as a bell, and not too warm.   And for quiet, I question if you be nearly as quiet at the Gill.   Charlotte is gone for her quarter's holiday, went off at eight in the morning with her nominal parents to Gravesend; and I wouldn't have Mrs. Newnham come till two o'clock, when my dinner would be needed, and there might be 'knocking at the door!'

The only sign of life in the house is the incessant chirp of a little ugly brown bird, that I rescued yesterday afternoon from some boys who were killing it; bought of them for twopence; and now I find it cannot feed itself and I have to put crowdy into its mouth (which is always gaping) with a stick.

I went in an omnibus to Putney yesterday evening, and came back outside.   It is as pleasant as a barouche and four, the top of an omnibus; but the conductors don't like the trouble of helping one up.   When I came home at six, I found Charlotte wildly excited over Mrs. Cameron, who had waited for me more than an hour, played on the piano, and written 'a long letter on three sheets of paper.'   Certainly she had spoiled three sheets in telling me she had come to carry me off to Little Holland House, and that she would send back the carriage for me at nine, and bring me home at eleven. Charlotte told her I had been very ill, and was never out late; but that made no difference—the carriage would be sent; only if I could not come, she (Charlotte) must come over to Little Holland House and tell them in time to stop the carriage—'it was a long way to send a carriage for nothing.' She did not consider it was a long way for my only servant to be sent for nothing.

While I was hesitating about sending, for of course I never dreamt of going, Mr. Neuberg came to tea; and, needing Charlotte at home, I found it too absurd that she should have to leave me to get the tea, while she went for Mrs. Cameron's whim to Holland House. So I wrote a note, and coolly gave it to the coachman to take back instead of myself.

You are very kind in pressing your present refuge on me, but I will never allow you to either 'pig in' at Scotsbrig, or to commit yourself to Providence at Dumfries. My greatest comfort all this time has been just knowing *you* situated according to your needs, in full enjoyment of air, milk, and quiet. Never fear but I will make some arrangement for myself when it becomes desirable that I should leave London. I am not yet equal to so long a journey as to Scotland, but I am improving, and taking as much exercise as is good for me; change of air too.

I am going to-morrow to Mr. Larkin's mother's, to spend the day in that beautiful garden from which he brings me such bouquets. Mr. Larkin is to come himself at twelve o'clock to take me; and the next day Mrs. Forster is to come and take me to early dinner in Montague Square. I have had even an invitation to Ristori's benefit to-night, shawls and cloaks to be in readiness the moment I left the box, &c., and brought home with closed windows; but that, of course, I screamed at the idea of. It was little Mrs. Royston who wished to take me, a box having been given her. So you see I am very kindly seen to. I have slept better these two nights, and am rather stronger, and my cough is abated; speaking I find the worst thing for it. Yours ever,

J. W. C.

LETTER 194.

I am now about setting out on my second German tour 'to visit all the battlefields of Friedrich,' which cost me a great deal of misery, but was not honestly to be avoided. She, being rather stronger, is going to stay with Miss Baring, at Bay House, Alverstoke.—T. C.

T. Carlyle, The Gill.

Chelsea: Thursday, July 29, 1858.

Oh, my dear, my dear! What did you do with the key of your bureau? There is no vestige of a passport in the upper 'little drawer next the fire,' the only drawer which is unlocked; the keys used to lie in that. I have wasted the whole morning in seeking a key to open the top part, or another drawer where the keys may be, and have found only two of your lost dog-whistles! I don't like to have the locks picked till it is hopeless finding the key. If you have it or know where you put it, and tell me by Saturday morning, there would just be time to send the passport before I start; but as I tell you, my morning is all wasted, and in the afternoon I must go up to Piccadilly to get some indispensable little items for my visit. I have been kept back these two last days by the coldness of the weather, and my extreme sensitiveness. The prospect of going a journey aud living in another person's house is doing me more harm than probably the reality will do; I could 'scream at the idea of it' sometimes, and write off, ' Oh, you must excuse me!' But again, just the more I feel nervous, the more I need to try anything that may brace my nerves; and, of course, a doctor would tell me to get rid of this incessant little dry cough ' before October.' I should not say incessant, for in the forenoons, when I hold my tongue, I hardly cough at all—at least it is quite another sort of cough, bringing up phlegm at intervals; but in the evening, especially if any one comes, it is as incessant as the chirp of my adopted sparrow. I am not getting weaker, however, except in my mind. I take exercise every day, ' chiefly in an omnibus, Mr. Carlyle!' And I try every day to do or see something cheering; I should soon fall into melancholy mania if I didn't. Last evening, for example, I had old Mrs. Larkin to tea—such a pretty little rough tea, you can't fancy, and Mrs. Larkin was so pleased. And I had Mrs. Hawkes to talk to them, and George Cook came accidentally. George Cook is very attentive and sympathetic to me. But the key, the key!

Yours affectionately,

JANE CARLYLE.

LETTER 195.

T. Carlyle, Esq., The Gill.

Bay House: Monday, Aug. 2, 1858.

All right, dear; I got through my journey much better than could have been expected, having slept even soundly (mercifully), just the last night before leaving. A fat, old, real lady in the carriage opposite me paid me delicate attentions;' lent me her smelling bottle, gave me her nosegay, put her dressing-case under my feet, &c. &c., having commenced acquaintance by asking, ' Have you been poorly long?' When she changed trains at Bishopstoke, she looked over her shoulder to say: ' I sincerely hope you may soon be better, ma'am.'

How differently one's looks impress different people! The man who drove me from the station (and charged me three-and-sixpence!) evidently took me for well enough to be going to service at Bay House, for he turned round as soon as we passed through the gate to ask, ' was he to drive round to the back door?' And then the footman who received me took me for deaf! coming close up to me when he had anything to say, and shouting it into my ear. He was the only person I saw for three hours after my arrival. The ' Miss Barings out walking;' ' would I wish to be shown to my room?' ' Certainly.' ' Would I wish any refreshment?' ' Yes, a cup of tea.' It was brought, and then all lapsed into the profoundest silence. I could have fancied a pleasanter reception; at the same time ' it was coostom in part,' [1] no harm meant.

Having had lots of time to unpack and dress myself, I was first in the drawing-room before dinner. A gentleman came in, whom I liked the look of, but no word passed between us; then Mrs. Mildmay came, and finally my hostess, who assured me she was ' delighted to see me,' and so I was installed. Another lady entered with Emily, whom I recognised as Mrs. Frederick Baring, and the gentleman was Frederick Baring, whom I had never seen before, and of whom I had got the most absurdly unjust impression. Both he and his wife are kindly, unaffected people; he, indeed, strikes me as quite a superior man. I had a good deal of talk with him yesterday, and am sorry he is gone to-day. His wife went with him, so there is now only Mrs. Mildmay and her son.

---

[1] ' Why are these mills going to-day?' (*Sunday*, in Cumberland.) ' Coostom in part.'

The railway journey made me so sleepy that I could hardly keep my eyes open till I got to bed, and in bed I slept in a wonderful manner. My room is the same where I lay three days in a sore throat, and the boy 'Jack' had to bring in my breakfast. But no association could keep me awake that night. Certainly if pure air, and quiet, and wholesome food, and freedom from all 'cares' but of dressing oneself, can cure me, I shall be cured—in a few days.

It is Louisa Baring that goes with Lord Ashburton to Scotland on Monday. I thought if Emily was going somewhere too, I might be wished to go away in less time than a week; and, at all events living on in that sort of fear of over-staying one's welcome is very disagreeable. So I thought I had best go frankly to the end of it at once, and I said to Emily, when we were walking this morning, that I had meant to stay till the end of this week; but, as Miss Baring was leaving the place so soon as Monday, perhaps it would be more convenient that I should go on an earlier day— would she kindly tell me? Emily protested against my going this week. She and Mrs. Mildmay are to be here till the twenty-fourth, and I 'had better stay over next week.' The invitation was given with cordiality enough to make me feel quite at ease for this week anyhow, the rest will disclose itself. The Baring manner is naturally so shy, and so cold, that I dare say one may easily underrate the kindness of feeling which accompanies it.

Yours ever,

JANE W. CARLYLE.

LETTER 196.

T. Carlyle, Esq., The Gill.

Bay House: Friday, August 7, 1858.

Only Friday morning, dear, yet! Heaven knows! Possibly this may not reach you till Monday. However, when it does reach you it won't bring bad news. I still have nothing but good to tell of myself. I continue to get a very tolerable allowance of sleep, and to eat my breakfast 'with the same relish.'[1] And, will you believe it? I eat two dinners every day. I do that—one at half-past one, and the other at eight; which last, I call, in my own mind, supper, and no tea after. The little nervous cough is entirely gone, and the rough cough gets rarer every dry. For the rest, I am quite com-

---

[1] A phrase of John Jeffrey's (Lord Jeffrey's brother), *quasi* pathetic: 'eats his beef-steak with,' &c.

fortable morally. I never was put more at ease on a visit. I feel
to have dropt into the regular life of the house, and to have found
my place in it, without anybody taking trouble to adjust me, or
myself taking trouble.

The only visitor now besides myself is Mrs. Mildmay yes, Geraldine's mother, a much nicer woman than one fancied her, full of
fun and good humour). She reads to us for an hour or so after
breakfast (' Chambers's Annals of Scotland'), while the rest sew.
Then we go to our rooms to write, or do anything that needs privacy. I, for my part, take always a stroll on the shore before
lunch at half-past one. At three we go out in the open carriage,
and have the pleasantest drives, being permitted to sit perfectly
silent; Miss Baring seems to think this the natural way of driving
in the open air, and she is quite right. Coming in about five, there
are the letters; each one takes her own, and retires to her own room
till dinner-time. After dinner, till eleven, we talk, and work, and
read the newspapers, and play piquet. At eleven the butler enters
with a silver tray, containing four bright crystal tumblers filled with
the purest cold water; nothing else whatever. I always take one,
and have grown to feel a need of it. You cannot think how genial
the Miss Barings are at home; what a deal of hearty laughing they
do in a day!

You will foresee that I am not going at the end of ' a week.' Miss
Baring goes to join Lord A. on Monday; but Emily has pressed me
quite cordially to remain with her and Mrs. Mildmay till she goes
into Norfolk. And, if nothing unforeseen occur to ' dash the cup of
fame from my brow,' [1] I shall remain and be thankful to. I don't
feel the least drawn to 5 Cheyne Row in your absence; indeed, I
don't mean to have anything more to do with it than I can help till
you are there. Don't think me crazy. I have written to Mrs.
Pringle this morning (the 16th) that I shall be with her, if all go
well, the end of this month; September is often a fine month in
Scotland. You may see how much better I am, from this effort of
moral courage, as well as if you were beside me. I can't be said to
need ' change of air,' after having had it so long here—don't, indeed, intend to give any ' varnish of duty ' to the journey. It may
not have the least effect in keeping off illness through the winter; it
can't in the least add to your comfort when you are only waiting
for a yacht; but it will be a pleasant way of spending the next
month, and perhaps may (if I manage myself carefully) help to keep

---

[1] Scotch preacher (*supra*).

me well through the next month; and, oh, my dear! I have suffered so much—so much, and so long—that even a month of respite looks to me a thing worth taking any trouble for and spending any money for that I can lawfully spend. When I left home I did not believe that a change could do so much for me, even for the time being. Now that I feel what it has done, I want more of it. There is no other place nearer hand where I could get any good; besides, there is no place nearer hand that I am invited to.

To be sure I might go into lodgings nearer hand; but 'horrible is the thought to me!' and in lodgings I should have the 'cares of bread.' One of the reasons I eat so heartily here is, that I have had no forethought about the things set before me. Eating the dinner one has ordered oneself is, to a sick person, as ungrateful as wearing the gown one has made oneself is to an inexpert sewer. So please don't think me crazy! and, above all, don't fetter yourself with me the least in the world. If the 'yacht'[1] turn up before I come—if your stay seems to find its natural limit before I come, go all the same. As I should try to cut the journey in two by sleeping at Liverpool, I could go straight on if you were not there to give me a rest and good speed. But it is far off yet, all that; and meanwhile it may become intolerably cold, or I may catch cold, or fall off my sleep, and so become too cowardly 'for anything.' I said to Mrs. Pringle I would go if I could, not that I would 'whether I could or not.'

Now I have just been down to lunch, and must get ready for Gosport, in the carriage. I will take this letter on chance of hastening it.   Yours ever,

JANE CARLYLE.

LETTER 197.

Dumfries.—Lord Ashburton did come by that road, and we drove together to New Abbey, &c., before his starting again next day. Rous, the house doctor.—A copiously medicinal man. 'William Harcourt,' the now lawyering, parliamenteering, &c.; loud man, who used to come hither at intervals. 'A glorious bit of colour.'—One of Leigh Hunt's little children dixit.—T. C.

T. Carlyle, Esq., The Gill.

Bay House: Monday, Aug. 9, 1858.

How curious if Lord A. be at this moment on the road to Dumfries! Miss Baring started an hour ago in full assurance of finding

---

[1] It I have quite forgotten, what or whom; only that it never came.

him waiting to go with her to-morrow. Not one word has been received from him since they parted in London, on the understanding they were to go north together on the 10th; and I thought it best to say nothing of your news that he was to be at Dumfries on the 9th. She might have felt mortified at the new arrangement being communicated only through me, and nervous about what would await her in London. Rous, no doubt, will smooth all down. But what an odd man Lord A. is! I hope it will come off all right, the meeting at Dumfries, and that it will enliven you for some days. Perhaps he will persuade you to go to Loch Luichart? Miss Baring is most anxious you should come. By the way, please to send the remaining volume of 'Tourgueneff' to her; she has taken the others, and fears there will be great dearth of literature in the Highlands.

I felt quite sorry to see her drive off this morning. She has really been most kind to me, and took leave of me quite affectionately; 'now that I had found my way to them, she hoped I would never be so hard to persuade here again.' We are now reduced to three; but Bingham Mildmay is expected. When he comes we are to go to inspect 'the camp,' and go again to 'the Island.' The camp astonished me the first time I went to walk on the shore—a field, about a quarter of a mile off, all covered over with snow-white cones. I thought for a moment it was the grandest encampment of gipsies. But there are some two thousand soldiers in these tents. Near it there is a most beautiful new fort a-building; the guns of which, if they ever come into action, will smash right through Bay House.

On Saturday we left for the island at eleven, and did not return till six,—Emily, Mrs. Mildmay, and I. At Ryde we got an open fly, and drove to a place up the shore called Spring Vale, where Sir Henry Mildmay and his wife and rosebuds were rusticating. Very human, pleasant people. They had been warned of our coming, and had dinner (No. 1) waiting for us. Then we drove to St. Clair, the property and work of art of Colonel Harcourt, and Lady Catherine (uncle of William Harcourt). There, too, Mrs. Mildmay introduced me with graceful emphasis; and I was very courteously treated and shown about. A lady said I 'had forgotten her,' that she was the Mrs. Malcolm who dined with us at Lady Sandwich's; she is sister to Colonel Harcourt. The sea being as smooth as glass that day, I wasn't in the least sick, and the whole affair passed off to the general satisfaction.

Mrs. Mildmay is going to take us to Osborne to call for Lady Caroline Barrington, the governess to 'the Royal children,' and on to Cowes to call for somebody else. In fact, she is the most good-natured of women, Mrs. Mildmay, besides being excessively amusing in herself. She is not the widow of Sir Walter's friend, but of his nephew and the heir to ——. One is so apt to lose a generation nowadays.

Did I tell you that Crocker's house is now a royal residence, has been given to little Prince Alfred, who is learning to be a sailor? I saw him this morning shaking hands with two of his tutors, and jumping into his little boat with the third—a slight, graceful little boy. The Queen came over and breakfasted with him one morning, and another time took tea with him. He keeps a little red flag flying when at home, which adds 'a glorious bit of colour' to the scene.

Your description of 'Craig-o-putta' made me feel choked; I know what that wood must be grown to. Close on the house, forming a great dark shearing-hook before the windows. I always thought the laying out of that planting detestable, and if I were living there I would set fire to it.

This paper is thick, so I will take off half a sheet to make room for poor little Charlotte's unexpected letter—worth reading.

Yours ever,
JANE W. CARLYLE.

LETTER 198.

'What ornament and grandeur!'—Indignant old sailor to me once about his new binnacle in his new-fangled steamship. 'Suet and plums' was a casual reflection of my own. Rob Austin used to be our private post-boy once a week.—T. C.

T. Carlyle, Esq., Dresden.

Lann Hall: Friday, Sept. 10, 1858.

I was sure of it; knew without being told that the bathe in the Baltic had given you cold. You ought to know by this time that just the more you feel drawn to do those rash things, the more you should keep yourself from doing them. God grant this wild-huntsman rush over Germany don't spoil all the good you got in quiet Annadale! But you had to do it; would not have finished your book in peace without having done it!

I saw Eaves about the horse before I left; but he could not go out to Richmond till the following Sunday, when he got a good ducking to settle his account for the Sunday-breaking. He had no difficulty in finding the horse, who was in capital condition, and as nimble on his feet as the Irishman's flea. He (the horse) has no end of pasture to roam about in, and has 'found a friend;' formed a romantic attachment to another horse of his own way of thinking; they are always together, both in their feeding and their playing, and evidently enjoy their liberty and their abundant grass. So you may be quite happy in your mind so far as the horse is concerned.

Charlotte is behaving herself quite well so far as I can ascertain.

The sparrow whom I did design to train to flying, and 'eventually' to *flying away*, died before my return from Bay House; but the poor little canary has recovered health and feathers under the nursing of Mrs. Huxham, in whose 'bosom it spends several hours every day;' I should think not too happy hours! [1]

For the rest, one's life here is remarkably cheerful. It is the very loveliest glen I ever saw, endeared to me by old associations. The people in it are all remarkably prosperous, and were always hospitable. They are glad to see me again, and I am glad to see them.

The practical result has been a perfect explosion of lunches to my honour and glory, all over Glen Shinnel and Glencarin. I would not be out after sunset, so these lunches are early dinner-parties; and, oh, my! what 'ornament and grandeur!' what 'suet and plooms.' I assure you, not at the Grange itself have I seen better food or better wine (champagne) than these big farmers or little lairds bring forth to one here 'in a lordly dish!' And it is so much heartier a sort of hospitality than one finds in the south! It makes one feel younger by twenty years! I catch myself laughing sometimes with a voice that startles myself as being not like my own but my mother's, who was always so much gayer than I. Indeed, it is good for me to be here; and I wish my visit had come off while you were at the Gill, that you might have tried it too. Better material accommodation you could have nowhere; and Mrs. Pringle has tact and consideration enough, I think, to have suited the moral atmosphere to the shorn lamb (?).

The question is now about your journey home? Are you going straight to London? If that is decidedly the most convenient way for yourself, of course I should not so much as suggest your returning by here; and so far as my own journey is concerned, I should rather prefer doing it 'all to myself' (as the children say).

---

[1] Far too flattering an account.

Perhaps I might choose to stay a night at Liverpool. At all events, I might need to have a window shut when you preferred it open. But if you liked to return by Leith, and to be a little longer in the country under easy circumstances, you could not do better than stop here. About your welcome you may feel the most exuberant assurance.

If you decide to go straight to London, I should know as soon as possible, that I may shape my own course accordingly. For I should not like your being *done for* by only Charlotte. I have a week's visit promised to Mrs. Russell, and I also undertook to stay a few days at Scotsbrig, in case Dr. C. and his 'poor boys' lingered on at London till the end of my time here. I will see Mary and Jane on my road back. But I need to give myself as little rough travelling as possible, not to be going and catching a cold after all these mighty efforts to strengthen myself. The Donaldsons and my aunts won't believe I can mean to go away without seeing them. To see the dear old women at Sunny Bank once more I would gladly incur the expense of the journey there; but that is the least of it. The 'tashing' myself which Betty so strongly protests against must not be ventured.

We have just had one perfectly fair, beautiful day since I came (last Wednesday), and I spent it in an excursion to—Craigenputtock! We took some dinner with us, and ate it in the dining-room, with the most ghastly sensations on my part. The tenant was at Dumfries; the wife very civil; the children confiding to a degree. Their father 'had wine,' 'whiles took ower muckle.' We called on the Austins and Corsons. Nobody knew me! or could guess at me! Peter said I 'micht hae speaket to him seven year, and he wouldna hae faund me oot.' Peter privately stroked my pelisse, and asked Mrs. Pringle, 'That'll be real silk, I'm thinking?' 'Satin,' said she. 'Aye,' said Peter, 'nae doot, nae doot, the best o't.' Rob Austin almost crunched my fingers in his big hand, and that was the only pleasant thing that befell me at my 'ancestral home.' *Ach Gott!*

I wrote already to Dresden.

Mrs. Pringle has been trying to write you a note, pressing you to come here on your way back; and now she comes with her face like to burst, asking me to 'say it all for her. She is so afraid to write to you.'

LETTER 199.

To Mr. James Austin, The Gill, Annan.

5 Cheyne Row, Chelsea: Thursday, Sept. 30, 1858.

My dear Jamie,—I never saw such a thing in all my life! I plunged into a carriage full of ill-bred, disobliging, English tourists; they would make no room for me with my beehive and all my little things! I had to force a way for myself and my belongings, and when I had got my hands freed, and turned round to shake hands with you, before I sat down, behold the door was shut, and you had disappeared, and we were in motion! I could have cried for vexation; and could not get it out of my head all the road to London—that I had come off without a word of thanks for your kindness to me, or a word of leave-taking! And I felt such a detestation of these broad-hatted women in the carriage with me, whose disobligingness had been the cause of my flurry.

I went to the guard, at Carlisle, and told him I would not go on with these people, and should like to have a carriage all to myself. He seemed quite taken with my assurance, and asked if I could put up with one lady beside me? I said, ' Yes, if she were not troublesome!' He took me to a stout gentleman (the clerk at Carlisle, I suppose) and said, ' This lady wants a carriage all to herself! but she would allow one lady with her.' The gentleman said 'it was a very natural wish; but he did not see how it could be gratified; however, if I would keep quiet beside him, he would see what was possible!' And the result was, I got a carriage with only one lady in it! Nothing like a modest impudence for getting one on in this world! So far from objecting to the quantity of my luggage, they asked ' Was that all? Had I nothing more?' and they put up my things quite softly, whereas everybody else's, I noticed, were pitched up like quoits! The result is, that not so much as one egg was broken! And much satisfaction was diffused over the house by the unpacking of that improvised hamper!

When I found how much at ease I was in my carriage, I regretted not bringing away that kitten! It might have played about! But wasn't I thankful prudence had prevailed when I found myself already the enviable mistress of a kitten exactly the same size, but black as soot! Charlotte had taken the opportunity of my absence to discover ' there were mice in the house,' and bring home a new pet to herself! The dog and it are dear friends, for a wonder. I was delighted to see it this morning trying to ride on the dog's back!

Mr. C. was waiting for me, and had firmly believed for the last quarter of an hour that it was no use, as I must certainly have been smashed to pieces! We were in fact an hour later than the regular time—in consequence of a bridge burnt down over the Trent, which occasioned a great roundabout. Besides, the train did not behave itself at all like an Express, stopping at a great many places, and for long whiles.

My house was all right; indeed, I never found it as thoroughly cleaned, or the general aspect of things as satisfactory. She is a perfect jewel, that young girl; besides all her natural work, she had crocheted, out of her own head, a large cover for the drawing-room sofa!

You will be glad to hear that a good situation is found at last for James Aitken. Carlyle seemed very grateful to you for the care you took of me. I told him about that 'close carriage' before we had been five minutes in the cab together.

Kindest love to Mary; and remember me to all those girls, visible and invisible, 'who are world-like,' their mother says, 'and have their wits.'

I will write to Mary before long.

Yours most kindly,
JANE CARLYLE.

LETTER 200.

Mrs. Russell, Thornhill.

5 Cheyne Row, Chelsea: Friday, Oct. 1, 1858.

Oh, my dear! my dear! Will you ask 'the Doctor' what is the reason that, when I travel from London to Scotland I get quite fresh to the journey's end, however weakly I may have been at starting; but when I do the same journey back again, I am tired through every fibre of me, and don't get over it for days? I do begin to believe London a perfectly poisonous place for me, and to wish that the projected Pimlico Railway may actually tear our house up, and turn us adrift in space! Such a headache I had all yesterday! and to-day still I drag myself about with difficulty. Really, it is always 'pursuit of life under difficulties' here.

I hope your picture arrived, and safely. If it didn't, I will get you another. I was too ill with my head to write along with it. Indeed I have not succeeded yet in getting my boxes all unpacked. I should be doing that 'duty nearest hand,' for the moment, if I were a thoroughly well-principled woman—such a woman as Mrs. Pringle, for example—instead of sitting here writing to you. But, my dear, it is so much pleasanter this; and I miss your kind face and kind voice so much, and writing to you is a sort of substitute for seeing and hearing you. My little visit to Mary Austin was very pleasant. But I was obliged to put on an additional box at the Gill, to hold the fresh eggs (!), 'pookit fools,' and other delicacies she loaded me with. Then Mr. Carlyle had left an enormous bundle of new clothes to come with me—the produce of the indefatigable exertions of three tailors, whom he had kept sewing for him at the Gill for four weeks! besides a large package of books. So I made the journey with six pieces of luggage, not counting my writing-case, travelling-bag, and the beeskep, which last I let nobody carry but myself. It arrived in the most perfect state. I told Mr. C. you had sent him 'improper female' honey, and I think he is greatly charmed with your immoral present. I took out some for immediate use; but I think I will not displace the rest.

When I was stepping into a carriage at the Cummertrees station that morning (Wednesday), a horrid sight turned me back. Nothing less than the baboon face of our new acquaintance the surgeon! I don't know if he recognised me; I dashed into the next carriage, and fell amongst an odious party of English tourists. My baboon friend and I exchanged glances at the different stations, where he expended his superfluous activity in fussing to and fro on the platform, till finally he left the London train at Lancaster. I wonder what impression he left at Lann Hall!

I find all extremely right here. A perfectly-cleaned house, and a little maid, radiant with 'virtue its own reward,' and oh, unexpected joy! a jet-black kitten added to the household! playing with the dog as lovingly as your cat with your dog! This acquisition of Charlotte's announced itself to me by leaping on to my back between my shoulders. A most agile kitten, and wonderfully confiding. Charlotte said yesterday, 'I think Scotland must be such a fresh, airy place! I should like to go there! You did smell so beautiful when you came in at the door last night!' She is quite a jewel of a servant. Far more like an adopted child than a London maid-of-all-work. And, upon my word and honour, her bread is a deuced deal better than that loaf of Mrs. B——'s.

A kiss to—the Doctor? or Nipp? And do tell Nipp to behave better at prayers.

Mr. C. has sent his book to your husband.   It goes in some book-seller's parcel, so there may be a little delay.

[*No room to sign*] 'J. W. C.'

LETTER 201.

I returned from second German tour.—T. C.

J. G. Cooke, Esq.

5 Cheyne Row: Wednesday, October (?) 1858.

Dear Mr. Cooke,—I am here again—the more's the pity! Once for all, this London atmosphere weighs on me, I find, like a hun-dredweight of lead.   No health, no spirits, one brings from 'the country' can bear up against it.   Come and console me, at least come and try 'to!'—on Sunday afternoon perhaps.   Mr. C. is home from his battle-fields, and as busy and private as before.   So my evenings are now sacred to reading on his part, and mortally ennuying to myself on mine.

> Quoth Burgundy, the living
> On earth have much to bear.[1]

Yours affectionately,
JANE W. CARLYLE.

LETTER 202.

Mrs. Russell, Thornhill.

5 Cheyne Row, Chelsea: November 1, 1858.

Oh, my dear! I feel so fractious this evening; should like to break something, or box somebody's ears! Perhaps it is the east wind, perhaps my dinner of only soup, perhaps original sin; what-ever it is, I must positively try to come out of it, and the best way I can think of to smooth my 'raven down' is writing some lines to you.   Your last letter was charming, dear, just the sort of letter one wants from a place familiar and deas to one; all about everything and everybody.   Since I knew Mrs. Pringle I have

---

[1] Said Burgundy, 'I'm giving
Much toil to thee, I fear.'
Eckart replied, 'The living
On earth have much to bear.'

[Tieck's *Phantasms;* the trusty Eckart of my translating!]

come to understand and enter into the late Lady Ashburton's terror and horror of what she called 'all about feelings.'

My cousin John (George's son) was here again the other day, and I never felt so hopeless about him. His countenance, his voice, manner, everything about him is changed. And yet Bence Jones tells him it will be time enough, if he get to a warm climate before the spring winds set in. He will never go, I believe, if he wait till spring. I am going to Richmond the first possible day to talk to his mother. She is the strangest woman—always trying to hide her son's danger, as if it were a crime. The fatallest symptom I see in him is the sanguineness about his recovery, the irritability on the subject of his health, which have taken place of the depression he manifested in summer, while his state gives no reason for the change of mood; on the contrary, his cough, and expectoration are greatly increased, and so, he owns, are his night-perspirations. He is paler and thinner; and, from being the shyest, most silent of men, he now talks incessantly, and excitedly, and, in this state he goes about doing his usual work, and he left here the other day after dusk! I am very grieved about him. He is the only cousin I have, that I have had any pride or pleasure in.

Upon my word, I had better give up writing for this day—nothing to tell but grievances! Well, here is one little fact that will amuse you. Just imagine, the bit of boiled ham, which you would hardly let me have, has lasted for my supper, up to last week; and I never stinted myself, only I kept it 'all to myself,' like the greedy boy of the story book. I began to think it was going to be a nineteenth century miracle. But it did end at last, and now I am fallen back on porridge and milk, which is not so nice. I don't know about Dr. Coupland; I fancied him an old man. I am curious to know what will become of the Irish tutor.

Love to the Doctor.

Yours ever affectionately,

J. C.

LETTER 203.

J. G. Cooke, Esq.

5 Cheyne Row, Chelsea: Tuesday, about Dec. 22, 1858.

Oh, my dear kind friend, what a shock for you! And what a loss! The loss of one's mother! You can hardly realise it yet, so suddenly and softly it has befallen; but I doubt if there be any other loss in life equal to it—so irreplaceable, so all-pervading. And the consolation given one, that it is a loss 'in the course of nature,' and 'common to all who live long,' only makes it the sadder, to my thought. Yes; the longer one lives in this hard world motherless, the more a mother's loss makes itself felt, and understood, the more tenderly and self-reproachfully one thinks back over the time when one had her, and thought so little of it. It is sixteen years since my mother died, as unexpectedly; and no a day, not an hour has passed since that I have not missed her, have not felt the world colder and blanker for want of her. But that is no comfort to offer you.

Come to-morrow; I shall certainly be at home, and shall take care to be alone. I feel very grateful to you, very, for liking to come to me at such a time of trouble.

Yours affectionately,
JANE W. CARLYLE.

LETTER 204.

Mrs. Russell, Thornhill.

5 Cheyne Row, Chelsea: December 30, 1858.

Oh, young woman! there you go again! again a long silence! And I will tell you how it willbe—your silence will become longer and longer, and be of more and more frequent occurrence, till you fall out of acquaintance with me again, feel shy, and distrustful with me, and speculate about 'not having the accommodation of Lann Hall to offer!' And, oh my dear, who will be to blame for that state of things but yourself? Like all very sensitive people, you need an atmosphere of the familiar to open the leaves of your soul in. The strange, the unaccustomed, blights you like a frosty night; and yet, by procrastination, which your copy-lines told you was 'the root of all evil,' you suffer the familiar to become, by little and little, that 'strange,' which has such withering effects on you. Please don't, not in my case, for Heaven's sake! The more you don't write to me, the more you will find it uphill work when you do write, and from that, to speaking about 'the accommodation of Lann Hall,' is but a step or two in a straight line. You write such nice letters when your hand is in, that they cannot be a labour to write. Then do, my dear, keep your hand in.

Meanwhile, I have sent you a New Year's gift, which, if it come to hand safe, will, I am sure, at least I hope, give you a pleasant surprise; for really it will be like seeing into our interior in a peep-show. It is the only one, of the size that exists as yet, and I had it done on purpose for you. Another, smaller, is gone, inside of a large picture-book for Mrs. Pringle's children, to Robert MacTurk, a sort of *amende honorable* for having failed to give him myself—Good God! when he had some right to expect it—long ago, when I was an extremely absurd little girl. His good feeling towards me, after all, deserves a certain esteem from me, and a certain recognition, which, I hope, has been put into an acceptable form for him in the peep-show!

But I must not be expatiating over things in general to-day; for I am in a dreadful hurry, a great many letters to be written, besides that it is my day for driving out in what our livery-stable keepers call a neat fly, viz., a second-hand brougham with one horse—an expensive luxury, which Mr. C. forces on me twice a week 'now that I am old and frail, and have a right to a little indulgence,' he says.

The fact is, I have been belated in my letters, and everything, this week, by having had to give from two to three hours every day to a man who has unexpectedly lost his mother. He has five sisters here,[1] and female friends world without end—is, in fact, of all men I know, the most popular; and such is relationship and friendship in London, that he has fled away from everybody to me, who wasn't aware before that I was his particular friend the least in the world. But I have always had the same sort of attraction for miserable people and for mad people that amber has for straws. Why or how, I have no idea.

Mrs. Pringle wrote me a long really nice letter, in answer to my acknowledgment of the intimation of her uncle's death. She is a clever woman (as the Doctor says), and has discovered now, no doubt, that the style which suits me best is the natural and simple style, and that my soul cannot be thrown into deliquium, by any hundred-horse power of upholstery or of *moral sublime*. She is nice as she is.

I will get the money order for the poor women, in passing the post-office, and inclose it for your kind offices. Kindest regards to the Doctor, for whom I have a new story about Locock. God keep you both, for me, and so many that need you.

Yours,

J. W. CARLYLE.

---

[1] Can't remember him (J. G. Cooke?).

II.—5*

LETTER 205.

Miss Barnes, a very pretty, amiable, modest, and clever young lady, was the Doctor's one daughter; is now Mrs. Simmonds, of this neighbourhood (wife of a rising barrister), and was always a great favourite with my darling.—T. C.

Miss Barnes, King's Road, Chelsea.

5 Cheyne Row: Monday, June 1859.

Dear Miss Barnes,—Your father left a message for me this morning, the answer to which I expected him to 'come and take' when he had done with our next-door neighbour. But blessed are they who expect nothing, for they shall not be disappointed.

Pray come to tea with me to-morrow evening at seven, if my husband's particular friends 'the Destinies,' *alias* 'the Upper Powers,' *alias* 'the Immortal Gods' (your father says you read Mr. C., so you will understand me), don't interfere to keep you away.

I will drop this at your door in passing for my drive, and, along with it, a piece of old, old German crockery, which had the honour to catch your father's eye and has set its heart on belonging to him. So don't let it get broken—till he have seen it at least.

All you know of me as yet is that I seem to be in the very lowest state as to penmanship. But I assure you I can write much more tidily than this, made with the back of the very worst pen in the created world!

And if you will bring with you to-morrow evening whatever stock you may have of 'faith, hope, and charity,' I have no doubt but we shall become good friends.

Yours truly,
JANE WELSH CARLYLE.

LETTER 206.

This year 1859 it was resolved, for the hot weather, that 'Frederick' should be thrown aside, and Fife and the North be our refuge for a month or two. We had secured a tolerable upper floor in the farmhouse of Humbie, close by pleasant Aberdour; we had great need, especially she had, of all the good it could do us. I went by steamer with clever little Charlotte, my horse, and Nero; remember somewhat of the dreariness, the mean confusion, ennui; got at last to Granton, where brother John from Edinburgh joined me to accompany across the Frith. Our first talk was of poor Isabella of Scotsbrig,[1] who had died a few weeks before, a permanent loss to all of us.

---

[1] Mrs. James Carlyle.

My own Jeannie, frail exceedingly, had gone by rail to Hadding-ton; in a few days more she joined Charlotte and me at Humbie; for a month after that at 'Auchtertool House' (a big, goodish house, rather in disrepair, for which no special rent, only some vol-untary for such politeness, could be accepted), for above a month more.

Fife was profoundly interesting to me, but also (unexpectedly), sad, dreary, troublesome, lonely, peopled only by the ghosts of the past. My poor darling in Humbie Wood with me; weak, weak! could not walk, durst not (really durst not) sit on the loyal willing Fritz, with me leading; got her a cuddy (donkey) from Dumfries (none to be heard of in Fife), but that also was but half successful. She did improve a little; was visibly better when I rejoined her at home. For myself I had ridden fiercely (generally in tragic humour), walked ditto late in the woods at night, &c., bathed, &c., hoping still to recover myself by force in that way, 'more like a man of sixteen than of sixty-four,' as I often heard it said by an ever-loving voice! It was the last time I tried the boy method. Final Fife (particulars not worth giving) had a certain gloomy beauty to me—strange, grand, sad as the grave!—T. C.

J. G. Cooke, Esq., Mount Street, W.

Humbie, Aberdour, Fife: Saturday.

My dear Friend,—I was very glad of your letter, not only be-cause it was a letter from you, but a sign that you had forgiven me —or, still better—that you had never been offended! I assure you, an hour or two later, when left alone and quiet in the railway car-riage, I wondered, as much as you could do, what demon inspired the tasteless jest with which I bade you goodbye! in presence too, of the most gossiping and romancing of all our mutual acquaint-ances! I was so tired that day! Oh my heavens! so tired! And fatigue, which makes an healthy human being sleepy, makes me, in my present nervous state, delirious. That is my excuse—the only one I have to make, at least—for the foolish words I took leave of you with.

Mrs. Hawkes will have told you that I arrived safe, and that I am quite content with the 'Farmhouse.' It commands the beauti-fullest view in the world, and abundance of what Mr. C. calls 'soft food' (new milk, fresh eggs, whey, &c.). The people are obliging; and the lodging very clean. Mr. C. bathes in the sea every morn-ing, lyrically recognises the 'pure air,' and the 'soft food;' and, if not essentially in better health, is in what is almost as good—that make-the-best-of-everything state, which men get into when carry-ing out their own idea; and only then!

Charlotte[1] is the happiest of girls! not that she seems to have much sensibility for the ‘Beauties of Nature,’ nor that her health was susceptible of improvement, but that the ‘kindness of Scotch people’ fills her with wonder and delight. ‘Young men that don’t so much as know her name, passing her on the road, say to her, Bonnie wee lassie!’ And the farmer here gave her ‘a little sugar rabbit,’ and said to her ‘Little girl, you are growing quite pretty since you came.’ Did I ever hear of such kind people? The horse also likes ‘the change.’ Mr. C. says ‘he is a much improved horse; is in perfect raptures over his soft food (grass and new hay) but incapable of recovering from his astonishment at the badness of the Fife roads!’ Nero bathes with his master from a sense of duty; and is gradually shaking off the selfish torpor that had seized upon him in London: he snores less, thinks of other things besides his food; and shows some of his old fondness for me. Myself is the individual of the party who has derived least benefit hitherto from the place and its advantages. Indeed, I am weaker than before I left home. But great expectations are entertained from—an ass (cuddy they call it here!) which arrived for me from Dumfriesshire last night. My own choice of animal to ride upon! Mr. C. mounted me twice on the enraptured and astonished horse. But a cuddy will suit better; as Betty remarked when she was here, ‘its fine and near the grund, dear. It’ll no be far to fa’!’ The farmer says, ‘I hope it’ll gang! Them creturs is sometimes uncommon fond to stand still!’ I am just going to try it. Geraldine sent me a note that looked like being written on a ship in a storm at sea. Such scrawling and blotting I never beheld, and the sense to match! If Mr. Mantel makes his way here, we shall give him a friendly welcome; but it is a much more laborious affair than from London to Richmond.

Yours affectionately,
Jane W. Carlyle.

LETTER 207.

Miss Barnes, King’s Road, Chelsea.

Auchtertool House, Kirkcaldy ..Aug. 24, 1859.

My dear Miss Barnes,—How nice of you to have written me a letter, ‘all out of your own head’ (as the children say), and how very nice of you to have remarked the forget-me-not, and read a

---

[1] Mrs. Carlyle’s maid.

meaning in it! It was certainly with intention I tied up some for-get-me-nots along with my farewell roses; but I was far from sure of your recognising the intention, and at the same time not young enough to make it plainer. Sentiment, you see, is not well looked on by the present generation of women; there is a growing taste for fastness, or, still worse, for strong-mindedness! so a discreet woman (like me) will beware always of putting her sentiment (when she has any) in evidence—will rather leave it—as in the for-get-me-not case—to be divined through sympathy; and failing the sympathy, to escape notice.

And you are actually going to get married! you! already! And you expect me to congratulate you! or 'perhaps not.' I admire the judiciousness of that 'perhaps not.' Frankly, my dear, I wish you all happiness in the new life that is opening to you; and you are marrying under good auspices, since your father approves of the marriage. But congratulation on such occasions seems to me a tempting of Providence. The triumphal-procession-air which, in our manners and customs, is given to marriage at the outset—that singing of *Te Deum* before the battle has begun—has, ever since I could reflect, struck me as somewhat senseless and some-what impious. If ever one is to pray—if ever one is to feel grave and anxious—if ever one is to shrink from vain show and vain babble—surely it is just on the occasion of two human beings binding themselves to one another, for better and for worse, till death part them; just on that occasion which it is customary to celebrate only with rejoicings, and congratulations, and *trousseaux*, and white ribbon! Good God!

Will you think me mad if I tell you that when I read your words, 'I am going to be married,' I all but screamed? Positively, it took away my breath, as if I saw you in the act of taking a fly-ing leap into infinite space. You had looked to me such a happy, happy little girl! your father's only daughter; and he so fond of you, as he evidently was. After you had walked out of our house together that night, and I had gone up to my own room, I sat down there in the dark, and took 'a good cry.' You had re-minded me so vividly of my own youth, when I, also an only daughter—an only child—had a father as fond of me, as proud of me. I wondered if you knew your own happiness. Well! know-ing it or not, it has not been enough for you, it would seem. Nat-urally, youth is so insatiable of happiness, and has such sublimely insane faith in its own power to make happy and be happy.

But of your father? Who is to cheer his toilsome life, and make home bright for him? His companion through half a lifetime gone! his dear 'bit of rubbish' gone too, though in a different sense. Oh, little girl! little girl! do you know the blank you will make to him?

Now, upon my honour, I seem to be writing just such a letter as a raven might write if it had been taught. Perhaps the henbane I took in despair last night has something to do with my mood to-day. Anyhow, when one can only ray out darkness, one had best clap an extinguisher on oneself. And so God bless you!

Sincerely yours,

JANE W. CARLYLE.

LETTER 208.

To George Cooke, Esq.

Auchtertool House, Kirkcaldy: Friday.

I am not at the manse, but within a quarter of an hour's walk of it, in a large comfortable house lent us by a Mr. Liddell; and we should have done well here had not Mr. C. walked and rode and bathed himself into a bilious crisis just before leaving Humbie; so that he began life under the most untoward auspices. For the first fortnight, indeed, it was, so far as myself was concerned, more like being keeper in a madhouse than being 'in the country' for 'quiet and change.' Things are a little subsided now, however, and in spite of the wear and tear on my nerves, I am certainly less languid and weak than during all my stay in the farmhouse. Whether it be that the air of Auchtertool suits me better than that of Aberdour, or that having my kind little cousins within cry is a wholesome diversion, or that it required a continuance of country air to act upon my feebleness, I am not competent to say, nor is it of the slightest earthly consequence what the cause is, so that the effect has been as I tell you.

LETTER 209.

T. Carlyle, The Gill, Annan.

York, Scawin's Hotel: Thursday, Sept. 22, 1859.

There! I have done it! You prophesied my heart would fail me when it came to the point, and I would 'just rush straight on again to the end.' But my heart didn't fail me, 'or rather' (to speak like Dr. Carlyle) it did fail me horribly! but my memory held true, and kept me up to the mark. With the recollection of the agonies of tiredness I suffered on the journey down, and for many days after, still tingling through my nerves, I took no counsel with my heart, but kept determined to not expose myself to that again, whatever else (bugs inclusive). And, so far, I have reason to congratulate myself; for I was getting ' quite ' done up by the time we reached York, and I am now very comfortable in my inn, with prospects for the night not bad! If only there be no 'small beings' (as Mazzini prettily styles them) in the elegant green-curtained bed of number 44, Scawin's.

I am sitting writing in that number, by the side of a bright little fire; which I ordered to be lighted, the first thing, on my arrival. While it was burning up, I went down and had tea in the 'ladies' coffee-room,' where was no fire, but also no ladies! They brought me very nice tea and muffins, and I 'asked for' cream!! and for an egg!!! 'And it was all very comfortable!' I think I shall order some supper when the time comes; but I haven't been able to decide what yet. There isn't a sound in the house, nor in the back court that my windows look out on. It is hardly to be hoped such quiet can last. Trains will come in during the night, and I shall hear them, anyhow; for this hotel, though not the Railway Station Hotel, is just outside the station gate. It was Eliza Liddell who recommended it to me. I never was in an inn, all by myself, before; except one night years ago, in the 'George' at Haddington, which was not exactly an inn to me; and I like the feeling of it unexpectedly well! The freedom at once from 'living's cares, that is cares of bread,' the pride of being one's own mistress and own protector, all that lifts me into a certain exaltation, 'regardless of expense.' And now I am going to ring my bell, and order a pair of candles!

Candles come! a pair of composite—not wax, 'thanks God!' I shall breakfast here in peace and quietness to-morrow morning; and leave by a train that starts at ten, and reaches London at four; and shall so avoid night air, which would not suit me at present. It has grown very cold, within the last two weeks; and I was as near catching a regular bad cold as ever I was in my life without doing it! The habit I took of waking at four at Auchtertool continued at Morningside, where there was much disturbance from carts 'going to the lime.' The morning I left was chill and damp; and I rose at six, tired of lying still, and dawdled about my room, packing, till I took what Anne used to call 'the cold shivers.'

Mrs. Binnie's warm welcome and warm dinner failed to warm me; which was a pity; for Mrs. Godby had arrived and the short visit would have been extremely pleasant, but for my chill. My tongue and throat became very sore towards night. Next day I felt quite desperate; but Mrs. Godby gave me a stiff tumbler of brandy toddy, in the forenoon, before I started; and her brother sent me, in his carriage, straight to Sunny Bank, so as to avoid the cold waiting at Long Niddry, and the other risks of the train; and on arriving at Sunny Bank, I swallowed two glasses of wine, and then, at bed-time, a stiff tumbler of whisky toddy!!! and so on, for the next two days fairly battling down the cold with 'stimulants.' I think I shall escape now, if I take reasonable care. Pity there should be 'always a something'! But for this apprehension of an overhanging illness, and these horrid 'cold shivers,' I should have enjoyed my last visit to Sunny Bank so much. They were so much better— the house so much cheerfuller with Eliza there, and so many people came to see me that I liked to see. Even when I left, this morn-ing, I did not despair of seeing them again![1]

Surely you will never be so rude to that good-humoured Lady Stanley as to fling her over after all. Besides, Alderley would make so good a resting-place for you on the long journey. I hope to get things into their natural condition before you arrive.

Ever yours,

J. W. C.

Love to Mary. I hope she liked her picture. You never saw such a pen as I am writing with!

LETTER 210.

T. Carlyle, Scotsbrig.

5 Cheyne Row, Chelsea: Monday, Sept. 26, 1859.

Two letters to be forwarded, or catch me having put pen to paper this day, I am so tired, Oh my! I never! A good sleep would have put me to rights, but that hasn't come yet. In spite of the stillness, and the good bed, and the all-my-own-way, I do noth-ing but fall asleep, and start up, and light matches, till four o'clock strikes, and after that I lie awake, wishing it were break-fast-time. What a wise woman I was to come home by myself, and get my fatigues done out before you arrived. I am not going

---

[1] Never did, alas!

out to-day, nor was I out yesterday, but on Saturday afternoon I trailed myself to Silvester's, and saw the horse—'just come in from being exercised,' 'in capital condition,' 'so fat!' Silvester said, clapping its buttock, 'and so spirity that he never——!' The stable seemed good and very clean. I think them most respectable people. And the distance is less than to ——'s.[1]

If you could conveniently bring a small bag of meal with you from Scotsbrig, it would be welcome; we have none but some Fife meal, which is very inferior to the Annandale. At all events, you could ask Jamie to send us a few stone, say four, and if Mary would give us a little jar of butter, like what she sent with me last year, it 'wud be a great advantage.'[2]

I find everything in the house perfectly safe—no bugs, no moths, grates unrusted, much more care having been taken than when Anne was left in it, with wages, and board wages, at least in the last years of Anne's incumbency. Mrs. Southern is an excellent woman, I do believe, and Charlotte is already the better for being back beside her—away from Thomson's and Muat's.[3]

Ever yours,
J. W. C.

LETTER 211.

T. Carlyle, Esq., at Alderley Park, Congleton.

5 Cheyne Row, Chelsea: Thursday, Sept. 29, 1859.

Thanks! Just one line, that you may not be fancying me past writing. But there is no time for a letter. I am shocked to find how late it is. I fell to putting down the clean drugget, in the drawing-room, 'with my own hands,'[4] that you might not on your first arrival receive the same impression of profound gloom from the dark green carpet, that drove myself towards thoughts of suicide! And, behold, the seams had given way in many places at the washing; and I have had to sit on the floor like a tailor, stitch-ing, stitching, and so the time passed away unremarked, and it now

---

[1] The *arsenic* place! My poor 'Fritz' had been suddenly taken to Salter's, Eaton Square, and for a year or more had been quite coming round then.

[2] Good East Lothian woman's speech to me, on the return from Dunbar and the plagues of Irishry, &c. &c. (? seventeen years ago): 'If the wund would fa', it wud be,' &c.

[3] Names merely—unknown.

[4] 'Signed it, with my own hand' (Edward Irving, forty years ago).

is long past my dinner-time, and no dinner so much as thought of, in spite of Charlotte's repeated questions.

I will put myself in an omnibus, and go up to Michel's in Sloane Street, and dine on a plate of soup. Woman wants but little here below—after a railway journey from Scotland especially.

I am glad you have gone to Alderley. I have slept a degree better the last two nights; but have still much to make up in that way. Don't hurry on, if you do well at the Stanleys'. Kind regards to the lady.

Yours ever,

J. W. C.

LETTER 212.

'Butcher's cart passed over Nero's throat.' Poor little foolish faithful dog! it killed him after all; was never well again. He died in some four months (Feb. 1, 1860, as the little tablet said, while visible) with a degree of pitying sorrow even from me, which I am still surprised at.

The wreck of poor Nero, who had to be strychnined by the doctor, was, and is still, memorable, sad and miserable to me, the last nocturnal walk he took with me, his dim white little figure in the universe of dreary black, and my then mood about 'Frederick' and other things.

Holmhill is half a mile from the village of Thornhill. Dr. Russell withdrawing from regular business there.—T. C.

Mrs. Russell, Thornhill.

5 Cheyne Row, Chelsea: Wednesday, October 30, 1859.

Dearest Mary,—'If you but knew how I have been situated!' (my husband's favourite phrase). First, I arrived so tired! oh so dead tired! Notwithstanding that, I actually summoned nerve to put in effect my often cherished idea of sleeping at York (half-way) alone in an inn. Odd that I should never, at this age, have done that thing before, in my life, except once, when, after an absence of eighteen years, I spent a night *incognita* in the George Inn of Haddington, where I could not feel myself a mere traveller. It was a proof that my nerves were stronger, if not my limbs, that I really carried out the York speculation, when it came to the point. It would certainly have been again a failure, however, but for a lady in Fife telling me of a comfortable inn to stop at. I was to ask, on getting out of the carriage, 'was any porter from Mrs. Scawin's here?' which I had no sooner done, than the name Scawin was shouted out in the sound of 'Sowens!' to my great shame! I feeling as if everybody knew where I was going, and that it was my first adventure of the sort!! But I was comfortably and quietly lodged; no bugs, no anything to molest me, only that the tumult in my own blood kept me awake all night; so that I arrived here as tired, next evening, as if I had come the whole road at one horrid rush. And I hadn't much time allowed me to rest; for, though Charlotte had got down all the carpets, there were still quantities of details for me to do, before Mr. C. came. And he stayed only a week behind me.

When the house was all in order for him, my cares were destined to take another turn, even more engrossing. Just the night before his arrival, Charlotte went to some shops, taking the dog with her, and brought him home in her arms, all crumpled together like a crushed spider, and his poor little eyes protruding, and fixedly staring in his head! A butcher's cart, driving furiously round a sharp corner, had passed over poor little Nero's throat! and not killed him on the spot! But he looked killed enough at the first. When I tried to 'stand him on the ground' (as the servants here say), he flopped over on his side, quite stiff and unconscious! You may figure my sensations! and I durst not show all my grief; Charlotte was so distressed, and really could not have helped it! I put him in a warm bath, and afterwards wrapped him warmly, and laid him on a pillow, and left him, without much hope of finding him alive in the morning. But in the morning he still breathed, though incapable of any movement; but he swallowed some warm milk that I put into his mouth. About midday I was saying aloud, 'Poor dog! poor little Nero!' when I saw the bit tail trying to wag itself! and after that, I had good hopes. In another day he could raise his head to lap the milk himself. And so, by little and little, he recovered the use of himself: but it was ten days before he was able to raise a bark, his first attempt was like the scream of an infant! It has been a revelation to me, this, of the strength of the throat of a dog!! Mr. C. says, if the wheel had gone over anywhere else, it would have killed him. A gentleman told me the other night that he once saw a fine large dog run over; the great wheel of one of Pickford's heavy-laden vans went over its throat!! And the dog just rose up and shook itself!! It next staggered a little to one side, and then a little to the other, as if drunk, then it steadied itself, and walked composedly home!

When I was out of trouble with my dog, I had time to feel how very relaxing and depressing the air of Chelsea was for me, as usual, after the bracing climate of Scotland. I was perfectly done, till Mr. C. insisted on setting up the carriage again, and Providence put me on drinking water out of a 'bitter cup;' that is a new invention, very popular here this year!—a cup made of the wood of quassia, which makes the water quite bitter in a minute; of course, a chip of quassia put into water would have the same effect; but nobody ever bid me take that! I thought, for three or four days, that I had discovered the grand panacea of life! I felt so hungry! and so cheerful! ! and so active! But one night I was seized with the horridest cramps! which quite took the shine out of quassia for me, though I daresay it was merely that I had quite neglected my bowels. I haven't had courage to re-commence with the 'bitter cup;' but it will come! Meanwhile I am pretty well over the bilious crisis that has befallen, to 'remind me that I am but a woman!' and a very frail one (I mean in a physical sense)!

How pleasant it will be to think of you at that pretty Holmhill! though one will always have a tender feeling towards the 'old rambling house,' where we have had such good days together. But the other place will be for the good of your health, as well as more agreeable, when you have once got over the pain of change, which is painful to good hearts, though it may be joyful enough to light ones. It will also be a comfort to my mind to think of that drawing-room getting papered all with one sort of paper!

God bless you. Love to your husband.

J. W. CARLYLE.

LETTER 213.

To Mrs. Stirling, Hill Street, Edinburgh.

5 Cheyne Row, Chelsea: October 21, 1859.

You dear nice woman! there you are! a bright cheering apparition to surprise one on a foggy October morning, over one's breakfast—that most trying institution for people who are 'nervous' and 'don't sleep!'

It (the photograph) made our breakfast this morning 'pass off,' like the better sorts of breakfasts in Deerbrook, [1] in which people seemed to have come into the world chiefly to eat breakfast in every possible variety of temper!

Blessed be the inventor of photography! I set him above even the inventor of chloroform! It has given more positive pleasure to poor suffering humanity than anything that has 'cast [2] up' in

---

[1] The Deerbrook breakfasts refer to Miss Martineau's poor novel.
[2] Turned.

my time or is like to—this art by which even the 'poor' can possess themselves of tolerable likenesses of their absent dear ones. And mustn't it be acting favourably on the morality of the country? I assure I have often gone into my own room, in the devil's own humour—ready to swear at 'things in general,' and some things in particular—and, my eyes resting by chance on one of my photographs of long-ago places or people, a crowd of sad, gentle thoughts has rushed into my heart, and driven the devil out, as clean as ever so much holy water and priestly exorcisms could have done! I have a photograph of Haddington church tower, and my father's tombstone in it—of every place I ever lived at as a home—photographs of old lovers! old friends, old servants, old dogs! In a day or two, you, dear, will be framed and hung up among the 'friends.' And that bright, kind, indomitable face of yours will not be the least efficacious face there for exorcising my devil, when I have him! Thank you a thousand times for keeping your word! Of course you would—that is just the beauty of you, that you never deceive nor disappoint.

Oh my dear! my dear! how awfully tired I was with the journey home, and yet I had taken two days to it, sleeping—that is, attempting to sleep—at York. What a pity it is that Scotland is so far off! all the good one has gained there gets shaken off one in the terrific journey home again, and then the different atmosphere is so trying to one fresh from the pure air of Fife—so exhausting and depressing. If it hadn't been that I had a deal of house-maiding to execute during the week I was here before Mr. C. returned, I must have given occasion for newspaper paragraphs under the head of 'Melancholy suicide.' But dusting books, making chair-covers, and 'all that sort of thing,' leads one on insensibly to live—till the crisis gets safely passed.

My dear! I haven't time nor inclination for much letter-writing —nor have you, I should suppose, but do let us exchange letters now and then. A friendship which has lived on air for so many years together is worth the trouble of giving it a little human sustenance.

Give my kind regards to your husband—I like him.—And believe me,

Your ever affectionate,

JANE WELSH CARLYLE.

LETTER 214.

In October, after getting home, there was a determined onslaught made on 'Frederick,' an attempt (still in the way of youth—16 rather than 60!) to vanquish by sheer force the immense masses of incondite or semi-condite rubbish which had accumulated on 'Frederick,' that is, to let the printer straightway drive me through it!— a most fond and foolish notion, which indeed I myself partly knew, durst I have confessed it, to be foolish and even impossible! But this was the case all along; I never once said to myself, 'All those chaotic mountains, wide as the world, high as the stars, dismal as Lethe, Styx, and Phlegethon, did mortal ever see the like of it for size and for quality in the rubbish way? All this thou wilt have to take into thee, to roast and smelt in the furnace of thy own poor soul till thou fairly do smelt the grains of gold out of it!' No, though dimly knowing all this, I durst not openly know it (indeed, how could I otherwise ever have undertaken such a subject?); and I had got far on with the unutterable enterprise, before I did clearly admit that such was verily proving, and would, on to the finis, prove to have been the terrible part of this affair, affair which I must now conquer *tale quale*, or else perish! This first attempt of October–February, 1859–1860 (after dreadful tugging at the straps), was given up by her serious advices, which I could not but admit to be true as well as painful and humiliating! November 1860 had arrived before there was any further printing: nothing thenceforth but silent pulling at a dead lift, which lasted four or five years more.

My darling must have suffered much in all this; how much! I sometimes thought how cruel it was on her, to whom 'Frederick' was literally nothing except through me, so cruel, alas, alas, and yet inevitable! Never once in her deepest misery did she hint, by word or sign, what she too was suffering under that score; me only did she ever seem to pity in it, the heroic, the thrice noble, and wholly loving soul!

She seemed generally a little stronger this year, and only a little; her strength, though blind *I* never saw it, and kept hoping, hoping, was never to come back, but the reverse, the reverse more and more! Except a week or two at the Grange (January 1860), which did not hurt either of us, I think we had intended to make no visits this year, or as good as none. We did, however, and for good reasons, make two—hers, a most unlucky or provoking one, provokingly curtailed and frustrated, as will be seen. This was in August, to Alderley, and she could have gone further but for blind ill luck. Beginning of July she had tried a week or thereby of lodging at Brighton, and invited me, who tried for three days, but could get no sleep for noises, and had to hurry home by myself; where also I could not sleep nor stay to any purpose, and was chiefly by brother John, who accompanied, led by sea to Thurso, for a 'long sail' first of all.

To Mrs. Russell, Thornhill.

5 Cheyne Row, Chelsea: Friday, Jan. 28, 1860.

Dearest Mary,—A letter from me would have crossed yours (with the book) on the road, if it hadn't been for a jacket! Things are so oddly hooked together in this world. The connection in this case is simple enough. I needed a little jacket for home wear, and, possessing a superfluous black silk scarf, I resolved, in a moment of economical enthusiasm, to make with my own hands a jacket out of it. For, in spite of the ' thirty thousand distressed needlewomen' one hears so much of, the fact remains that nobody can get a decent article of dress made here, unless at enormous cost. And besides, the dressmakers who can fit one won't condescend to make anything but with their own materials. So I fell to cutting out that jacket last Monday, and only finished it to-day (Friday)! and was so much excited over the unusual nature of the enterprise (for I detest sewing, and don't sew for weeks together) that I could not leave off, for anything that could be postponed, till the jacket was out of hands. But Lord preserve me, what a bother; better to have bought one ready-made at the dearest rate. I won't take a needle in my hands, except to sew on Mr. C.'s buttons, for the next six months. By the way, would you like the shape of my jacket, which is of the newest? I have it on paper, and could send it to you quite handy.

Oh my dear, I am very much afraid, the reading of that book will be an even more uncongenial job of work for me than the jacket, and won't have as much to show for itself when done. If there be one thing I dislike more than theology it is geology. And here we have both, beaten up in the same mortar, and incapable, by any amount of beating, to coalesce. What could induce any live woman to fall awriting that sort of book? And a decidedly clever woman—I can see that much from the little I have already read of it here and there. She expresses her meaning very clearly and elegantly too. If it were only on any subject I could get up an interest in, I should read her writing with pleasure. But even when Darwin, in a book that all the scientific world is in ecstasy over, proved the other day that we are all come from shell-fish, it didn't move me to the slightest curiosity whether we are or not. I did not feel that the slightest light would be thrown on my practical life for me, by having it ever so logically made out that my first ancestor, millions of millions of ages back, had been, or even had not been, an oyster. It remained a plain fact that I was no oyster, nor had any grandfather an oyster within my knowledge; and for the rest, there was nothing to be gained, for this world, or the next, by going into the oyster-question, till all more pressing questions were exhausted! So—if I can't read Darwin, it may be feared I shall break down in Mrs. Duncan. Thanks to you, however, for the book, which will be welcome to several of my acquaintances. There is quite a mania for geology at present, in the female mind. My next-door neighbour would prefer a book like Mrs. Duncan's to Homer's 'Iliad' or Milton's 'Paradise Lost.' 'There is no account ing for tastes.'

I have done my visit to the Grange,[1] and got no hurt by it; and it was quite pleasant while it lasted. The weather was mild, and besides, the house is so completely warmed, with warm water-pipes, that it is like summer there in the coldest weather. The house was choke-full of visitors—four-and-twenty of us, most of the time. And the toilettes! Nothing could exceed their magnificence; for there were four young new-married ladies, among the rest, all vie-ing with each other who to be finest. The blaze of diamonds every day at dinner, quite took the shine out of the chandeliers. As for myself, I got through the dressing-part of the business by a sort of continuous miracle, and, after the first day, had no bother with my-self of any sort. The new Lady[2] was kindness' self and gave gen-eral satisfaction. Affectionately yours,

JANE CARLYLE.

LETTER 215.

To Miss Barnes, King's Road, Chelsea.

5 Cheyne Row: Saturday, Jan. 14, 1860.

My dear Miss Barnes,—I send you a pheasant, which is a trophy as well as a dead bird! For I brought it home with me last night from one of the most stupendous massacres of feathered innocents that ever took place ' here down ' (as Mazzini expresses himself)— from seven hundred to a thousand pheasants shot in one day! The firing made me perfectly sick. Think of the bodily and men-tal state of the surviving birds when the day's sport was ended! Decidedly, men can be very great brutes when they like!

---

[1] Finished January 13.

[2] Lord Ashburton married secondly, November 17, 1858, Louisa Caroline, youngest daughter of the Right Hon. James Stewart Mackenzie.

We have been away for ten days at the Grange (Lord Ashburton's place in Hampshire), where I always thrive better than anywhere else; and where, as you see, there are many pheasants.

I went to take leave of you before we went; but saw all the blinds down, and grew sick with fright! I went into Mr. Gigner's shop and inquired was anything the matter; and he told me of your new loss. At least, it was an immense relief to me to hear that your father and yourself were not ill or worse. After that I thought a note about my insignificant movements would only bother your father; so I left him to learn my whereabouts from the 'Morning Post,' certain he would be too much preoccupied for looking after me at all. Do come soon, if I don't go to you. Do you care to have this card? It will do for an autograph if you don't want to use it.

Affectionately yours,

J. CARLYLE.

LETTER 216.

To Mr. Barnes, King's Road, Chelsea.

5 Cheyne Row: Thursday night, Feb. 1 [Nero died].

My dear good Mr. Barnes,—I cannot put into words how much I feel your kindness. It was such a kind thing for you to do! and so kindly done! My gratitude to you will be as long as my life, for shall I not, as long as I live, remember that poor little dog? Oh don't think me absurd, you, for caring so much about a dog? Nobody but myself can have any idea what that little creature has been in my life. My inseparable companion during eleven years, ever doing his little best to keep me from feeling sad and lonely. Docile, affectionate, loyal up to his last hour. When weak and full of pain, he offered himself to go out with me, seeing my bonnet on; and came panting to welcome me on my return, and the reward I gave him—the only reward I could or ought to give him, to such a pass had things come—was, ten minutes after, to give him up to be poisoned.

I thought it not unlikely you would call to-day; because your coming to-day would be of a piece with the rest of your goodness to me. Nevertheless, I went out for a long drive; I could not bear myself in the house where everything I looked at reminded me of yesterday. And I wouldn't be at home for visitors to criticise my swollen eyes, and smile at grief ' about a dog,' and besides, suppose you came, I wished to not treat you to more tears; of which you had had too much; and to-day I couldn't for my life have seen you without crying dreadfully.

Tell your little jewel of a daughter I have not forgotten her wish, for which I thank her. I wish all her wishes were as easy to fulfil.

Yours affectionately,

JANE WELSH CARLYLE.

LETTER 217.

To John Forster, Esq., Montagu Square.

5 Cheyne Row: Thursday, Jan. 1860 ? or March ?

All right, dear Mr. Forster—nothing but 'yeses' out of that man's mouth, when your proposal was stated to him. Willing, pleased yeses. I am afraid something must be going to happen to him. 'Yes,' he would go on Sunday; 'yes,' he would be there a quarter before six; yes, he would walk there, and let you send him home. Exactly as you predicted, he did not come in till half-past six by the clock. It is a pity for poor me; I daren't do anything pleasant ever. Though, like the pigs, I get used to it, and am thankful if I can but keep on foot in-doors.

I am bent on seeing her and Katie, however, before we go to the Grange.

Yours affectionately,

JANE CARLYLE.

[In T. C.'s hand :—]
Yes, Saturday;—for the brougham to fetch me, no, with thanks.
—T. C.
(Written then!—T. C.)

LETTER 218.

Autumn 1860, I made a visit of four or five weeks to Sir George Sinclair at Thurso. Early in the summer of that year, I was visited by sleeplessness; and first began to have an apprehension that I should never get my sad book on Friedrich finished, that it would finish me instead. I still remember well enough the dark, cold, vague, yet authentic-looking feeling of terror that shot athwart me as I sat smoking 'up the chimney,' huddled in rugs, dressing-gown and cape, with candle on the hob, my one remedy in sleepless cases; the first real assault of fear, pointing, as it were, to undeniable fact; and how it saddened me the whole of next day. The second day, I compared it to Luther's temptings by the devil; and thought to myself in Luther's dialect, 'Well, well, Herr Teufel, we will just go on as long as we are alive; and keep working, all the same, till thou do get us killed!' This put away the terror, but would by no means bring the sleep back. I recollect lying whole nights awake, still as a stone; getting up at six, and riding to Clapham Common, to Hammersmith region, by way of surrogate for sleep. My head had an unpleasant cloudy feeling; I was certainly far from well, far below my average of illness even. Brother John, who lived in his Brompton lodgings then, recommended strongly a sea-voyage; voyage to Thurso, for example, whither the hospitable Sir George Sinclair had been again, perhaps for the third or fourth time, eagerly inviting me. Nothing else being so feasible, and something being clearly indispensable, we both set off, John volunteering to escort me to Wick; and generously and effectively performing that fraternal service. The very first night, in spite of the tumults of the crowded Aberdeen steamer, and such a huddle of a sleeping-place as is only seen at sea, I slept deep for six or seven hours; and had not again, during this visit, nor for years, any real misery about sleep.

On the part of my generous host and household, nothing was left wanting; I was allowed to work daily some hours, invisible till three P.M. I bathed daily in the Pentland Firth in sight of the 'Old Man,' roamed about, saw 'John o' Groat's House' (evidently an old lime-kiln!), &c. &c., a country ancient, wild, and lonely, more than enough impressive to me. I was very sad, 'soul exceeding solitary;' nothing could help that. Sir George was abundantly conversible, anecdotic, far-read, far experienced, indeed a quite learned man (would read me lyrics, &c., straight from the Greek any evening, nothing pleased him better), and full of piety, veracity, and good-nature, but it availed little; I was sad and weary, all things bored me! Here at Chelsea, with my clever Jeannie for hostess, and some clever Mrs. Twistleton for fellow-guest, Sir George was reported to be charming and amusing at their little dinner, while I sat aloft and wrote. But not here could he amuse; not here, though his constant perfect goodness, and the pleasure he always expressed over me, were really welcome, wholesome, and received with gratitude. I had many invitations from him afterwards, saw him here annually once or twice; but never went to Thurso again; never could get going, had I even wished it more.

Few letters went from me in that Thurso solitude, none that I could help. From my darling herself I seemed to receive still fewer than I wrote; the tediously slow posts, I remember, were unintelligible to her, provoking to her! Here is one, beyond what I could count on, come to me last week among four of my own, printed on 'approval,' in some memoirs of Sir George, which the relations have set a certain well-known Mr. James Grant upon writing! To Miss Sinclair's poor request, I said reluctantly yes—could not say no; corrected the five letters (not without difficulty); returned my own four originals; retained (resolutely) the original of this, and a printed copy as well as this. (December 13, 1869.) —T. C.

The letter from Mrs. Carlyle to Sir George Sinclair is not dated, so far as regards the year; but evidently follows close on the fore-going. It is felicitously playful in reference to her own husband. It is as follows:—

5 Cheyne Row, Chelsea: August 1, 1860.

My dear Sir,—Decidedly you are more thoughtful for me than the man who is bound by vow to 'love and cherish me;' not a line have I received from him to announce his safe arrival in your do-minions. The more shameful on his part, that, as it appears by your note, he had such good accounts to give of himself, and was perfectly up to giving them.

Well! now that you have relieved me from all anxiety about the effects of the journey on him, he may write at his own 'reasonably good leisure.' Only I told him I should not write till I had heard of his arrival from himself; and *he knows* whether or no I am in the habit of keeping my word—to the letter.

A thousand thanks for the primrose roots; which I shall plant, as soon as it fairs! To-day we have again a deluge; adding a deeper shade of horror to certain household operations going on under my inspection (by way of 'improving the occasion' of his absence!). One bedroom has got all the feathers of its bed and pillows airing themselves out on the floor! creating an atmosphere of down in the house, more choking than even 'cotton-fuzz.' In another, uphol-sterers and painters are plashing away for their life; and a couple of bricklayers are tearing up flags in the kitchen to seek ' the solu-tion' of a non-acting drain! All this on the one hand; and on the other, visits from my doctor, resulting in ever new 'composing draughts,' and strict charges to ' keep my mind perfectly tranquil.' You will admit that one could easily conceive situations more ideal.

Pray do keep him as long as you like! To hear of him 'in high spirits' and 'looking remarkably well' is more composing for me than any amount of ' composing draughts,' or of insistence on the benefits of 'keeping myself perfectly tranquil.' It is so very dif-ferent a state of things with him from that in which I have seen him for a long time back!

Oh! I must not forget to give you the 'kind remembrances' of a very charming woman, whom any man may be pleased to be re-membered by, as kindly as she evidently remembered you! I speak of Lady William Russell. She knew you in Germany, 'a young student,' she told me, when she was Bessie Rawdon. She 'had a great affection for you, and had often thought of you since.' You were 'very romantic in those days; oh, very romantic and sentimental,' she could assure me! Pray send me back a pretty message for her; she will like so much to know that she has not remembered you 'with the reciprocity all on one side.'

I don't even send my regards to Mr. C., but—

Affectionately yours,

JANE W. CARLYLE.

LETTER 219.

T. Carlyle, Esq., Thurso Castle.

5 Cheyne Row, Chelsea: Friday, Aug. 10, 1860.

Oh my dear! If 'all about feelings' be bad in a letter, all about scenery and no feelings is a deal worse! Such a letter as that I received from you, yesterday, after much half-anxious, half-angry waiting for, will read charmingly in your biography! and may be quoted in 'Murray's Guide Book;' but for 'me, as one solitary individual,' I was not charmed with it at all! Nevertheless, I should have answered it by return of post, had I not been too ill for writing anything yesterday, except, on the strength of phrenzy, a passionate appeal to the 'retired cheesemonger,' about his dog, which, I am happy to say, like everything coming straight from the heart, went straight to the heart of the good little old cheesemonger. You will infer, from my going ahead against 'noises' on my own account, that the 'extraordinary disturbance of the nervous system,' which Mr. Barnes found me suffering under when he came, has not yielded yet to an equally extraordinary amount of 'composing mixture!' My sleep had been getting 'small by degrees, and beautifully less,' till I ended in lying awake the whole nights through! not what you call 'awake,' that is, dozing; but broad wide awake, like a hawk with an empty stomach! Still the mixture was to be persevered in, nay, increased, and I was assured that it was 'doing me a little good,' so little I myself couldn't perceive it, even through the powerful microscope of my faith in Mr. Barnes! and, in spite of his assurance that 'home was the best place for me at present,' I had wild impulses to 'take the road' (like the 'Doctor,' and with the Doctor's purposelessness!). The night before last, however (Wednesday night), I fell into a deep natural sleep, which lasted two hours, and might have lasted till the masons began, but for cheesemonger's dog, which was out that night (bad luck to it!) on a spree! and startled me awake at three of the morning with furious continuous barking—just as if my head was being laid open with repeated strokes of a hatchet! Of course I 'slept no more;' and yesterday was too ill for anything except, as I have said, writing a wild appeal to the cheesemonger. I will inclose his comforting answer which he handed in himself an hour after. It will be comforting to you also, in reference to your own future nights.

I have nothing to tell that you will take any interest in, except about the horse. He is still under the process of 'breaking,'[1] poor creature! Is 'so nervous and resolute,' so 'dreadful resolute,' that the breaker 'can't tell how long it will take to get the better of him!' I must see Silvester to-day before writing to Frederick Chapman. I saw the poor horse three days ago, just coming in from the breaker's, like a horse just returning from the 'Thirty Years' War!' Poor beast! I could have cried for him—required to turn over a new leaf in his old age! I know what that is!

'The nephew of Haggi Babda,' dropt in 'quite promiscuously' last Sunday evening, when old Jane was out at church, and I was alone, except for Geraldine, who opened the door to him, and afterwards talked social metaphysics with him! He is the fattest young large man I ever saw, out of a caravan! but in other respects rather charming. He wished me to impress on you how happy he would be to transact any commissions for you at Berlin, 'for which his connection with the embassy might give him facilities, &c., &c.' He seemed heartily in earnest about this, and a hearty admirer of your 'Frederick.' He is the best-bred, pleasantest man I have seen 'for seven years,' and the hour and half he stayed would have been delightful, if I hadn't been deadly sick all the while, and my nervous system 'in an extraordinary state of disturbance.'

Tell Sir George I have planted the cowslips, 'with my own hand,' and have not needed to water them, 'the heavenly watering-pan' (which Mariotti spoke of) having spared me the trouble. I gave them the place of highest honour (round poor little Nero's stone). I have had fires all day long for the last week—such a summer! Lady Stanley sent me her portrait. The only bit of real pleasantness, however, that has come my way has been, last Wednesday, a visit from William Dodds and his wife. They told me such things about the behaviour of the London Donaldsons, when they went down to Miss Jess's funeral!

Your situation sounds as favourable as a conditional world could

---

[1] To run in harness; but he wouldn't—couldn't—though the best-natured of horses, poor Fritz!

have afforded you. I trust in Heaven that you will go on improving in it.

You remember, no pens got mended, so you won't wonder at this scrawling.

Yours ever,
J. WELSH CARLYLE.

LETTER 220.

T. Carlyle, Thurso Castle.

5 Cheyne Row, Chelsea: Friday, Aug. 17, 1860.

Thanks for the two letters, dear! I 'did intend' to have answered them together, at full length, by to-day's post, but have been hindered sadly, and ignominiously, by—'what shall I say?'—an attack of British cholera! Don't be alarmed; it is over now! and it is still but two o'clock, and, though I was ill all night as well as all the forenoon, I don't feel disabled for writing. It is an appointment with Lady Sandwich, which I don't like to break, that takes away the remaining two and a half hours, in which I might have written a sufficient letter. She sent the coachman last night, with a note to say she had returned to Grosvenor Square, on account of a slight attack of bronchitis, and would I tell the coachman when to bring the carriage to fetch me; I appointed a quarter before three to-day, not foreseeing what the night had in reserve for me! Indeed, I had no reason to expect anything of the sort, having been sleeping better, and feeling better in every way for the last week. I rather 'happrehend' it was my own imprudence, in taking a glass of bitter ale at supper that caused this deadly sickness, and—other things. Trust me for doing the best for myself, in the circumstances. I am the last person to let myself be humbugged by a doctor; Mr. Barnes was perfectly right in ordering me, at the time you left, to put all ideas of travelling out of my head, and 'go to bed for two hours every forenoon instead.' And the mixture, which for many days failed in its intended effect, on account (he said) of the excitement I was in, got to do me palpable, unmistakable good at last, and is now discontinued by his own order. At the time you left I was hanging on the verge of nervous fever, and have made a very near miss of it! He does not disapprove of my going away now, provided I keep short of fatigue and excitement, and I am taking steps towards forming a programme. I will tell you in a day or two what direction I have decided on. I should like very well to spend a day or so at the Gill; but a stay of any length there would not suit me at all. Milk is no object, as it is not strong enough food for my present weak appetite; and solitude is positively hurtful to me. Human kindness is precious everywhere, and nobody appreciates it more than I do; but just the kinder they are, the more I should be tempted to exert myself in talking, and putting my contentment in evidence. In short, there would be a strain upon me, while I was supposed to be enjoying the height of freedom! I mean were my stay prolonged beyond the day or two during which the enthusiasm of meeting after so long absence, and having things to tell one another, holds out. I am so sorry to put you off with such a scrubby letter, but the carriage will be here before I am dressed; and here is my beef-tea—my first breakfast.

Kind love to Sir George.

Yours ever,
J. W. C.

LETTER 221.

Mrs. Russell, Thornhill.

5 Cheyne Row, Chelsea: Friday, Aug. 17, 1860.

Dearest Mary,—I haven't leisure to commence this letter with•reproaches; for the reproaches would be very long, and my time for writing is very short. In an hour hence a carriage will come to take me to a sick old lady, I myself being quite as sick and nearly as old, and there are directions to be given to divers workmen before I start. For Mr. Carlyle is absent at Thurso, and I have taken the opportunity of turning a carpenter, and a painter, and a paperhanger into his private apartment.

Yes, after repeatedly assuring you that Mr. Carlyle would not go north this summer, but restrict his travels to some sea-side place near hand, I am almost ashamed to tell you that he has gone 'north' after all, and further north than he ever was in all his life before, being on a visit to Sir George Sinclair at Thurso Castle— the northernmost point of Scotland. A trial of Brighton had been made, and had ended abruptly and ignominiously in flight back to Chelsea, to get out of the sound of certain cocks. Of all places in the world, Brighton was the last one could have expected to be infested with poultry. But one week of Brighton had only increased Mr. C.'s desire for sea, and indeed he had got into such a sleepless, excited condition through prolonged over-work, that there could be no doubt about the need of what they call 'a complete change' for him. So he looked about for a sea-residence, where he might be safe from cocks and cockneys, and decided for Thurso Castle, which could moreover be reached by sailing, which he prefers infinitely to railwaying, and whence there had come a pressing invitation for us both to spend a couple of months. Accordingly, he streamed off there a fortnight ago, I remaining behind for several reasons; first, that sailing is as much as my life is worth, and seven hundred miles of railway would have been just about as fatal. Second, if I was going to undertake a long journey, I might take it in directions that would better repay the trouble and expense. And third, the long worry and anxiety I had had with Mr. C.'s nervousness had reduced myself to the brink of a nervous fever, and my doctor was peremptory as to the unfitness of my either going with Mr. C., or rejoining him at Thurso. Indeed I was not to leave home at all in the state I was in, but to take three composing draughts a day! and go to bed for two hours every forenoon. A fortnight of this and perfect quiet in the house has calmed me down amazingly, only I feel as tired as if I were just returned from the 'thirty years' war.' And now Mr. Barnes does not object to my going away, provided I don't go to Mr. C.! and don't over-exert myself. Mr. C., who is already immensely improved by his residence at Thurso Castle, is all for everybody 'going into the country,' and has made up his mind that, like it or not, I must go 'instantly' to —the Gill (Mary Austin's), which, as it suits his milk-loving habits, he thinks would equally suit me. And I myself would like very well to turn my two or three remaining weeks of liberty to some more agreeable use than superintending the house-cleaning here! But decidedly mooning about, all by myself, at the Gill, lapping milk, which doesn't agree with me, and being stared at by the Gill children as their 'aunt!' is not the happy change for which I would go far, much as I like Mary Austin.

Now, I want to know how you are situated, whether the invitation held out to me, and which I, 'ignorant of the future,' declined for this year, be still open to me; for if I had it in my power to go on to you for a week or so from the Gill, I might give myself the air of a charmingly obedient wife, and agree to go there, without my obedience costing me any personal sacrifice. I could break the long journey by staying a few days at Alderley Park (Lord Stanley's), where I have half engaged to go in any case. But I don't know if you are settled yet, or if you are not gone somewhere for change of air yourself, or if somebody else be not located, for the

II.—6*

present, in my room, and unfortunately I am tied to time. I must be back in London—some weeks before Mr. C.; for reasons I will explain later, for they require time to explain them.

In the meanwhile you will, in any case, answer me, as briefly as you like, by return of post? for I shan't answer Mr. C. till I get your letter. And I do beseech you to be perfectly frank, to tell me if you are going anywhere, or if anybody else is coming to you, or if my room is not ready yet, or, worst of all, if you are poorly, and can't be troubled.

I understand that state so thoroughly well.

Your affectionate
JANE W. CARLYLE.

LETTER 222.

T. Carlyle, Thurso Castle.

Alderley Park, Congleton, Cheshire: Thursday, Aug. 23, 1860.

There! What do you think of this? If you knew all you would admit that I have as much 'courage' as your horse, which 'goes whether he can or not.' But the present is not a moment for entering into details, of how ill I was after my last letter, and of how my illness was complicated with household griefs, and of how it was necessary to leave for here at hardly a day's notice, or give up altogether the idea of going anywhere. All that will keep till I am in better case for writing a long letter, or even till we meet 'on our return from the thirty years' war.' Enough to say, for the present, that I am here on a most kindly pressing invitation from Lady Stanley, to stay 'a week,' and 'be nursed' (you may be sure it was pressing enough when I accepted it), and that my intention is, if I get as much better as I hope, to go on from here to the Gill, and from there, after a day or two's rest, to Holm Hill (Mrs. Russell's), where I can remain with advantage as long as I find expedient with relation to the time of your return home.

Mrs. Russell had been urging me to visit them for the last three months at intervals. And I am always much made of, and very comfortable there. And to have a doctor for one's host was a consideration of some weight with me, under the circumstances, in choosing that ultimate destination. I couldn't have travelled all the way to Dumfriesshire at one fell rush; but the invitation to Alderley broke the journey beautifully for me. It (the coming to Alderley) had been spoken of, or rather written of, by Lady S. before I last wrote to you, but I was afraid to say a word about it in case you had played me the same trick as in the case of Louisa Baring. No time had been specified then. So that when I received a letter on Monday (written in forgetfulness of the intervening Sunday), urging me to be at Chelford station on Tuesday by four o'clock, where Lady S. would send the carriage for me, it quite took away my breath. I could not possibly get myself and the house packed by Tuesday. Besides, Lady Ashburton had offered to come to tea with me on Tuesday, and been accepted, 'in my choicest mood;' so I answered that I would, D.V., be at Chelford station by four on Wednesday.

A more tired human being than myself, when I got into the train at Euston Square yesterday, you haven't seen 'this seven years.' Geraldine and Mr. Larkin escorted me there, and paid me the last attentions. I was hardly out of sight of the station when I fell back in my seat and went to sleep, and slept off and on (me, in a railway carriage!) all the way to Crewe, where I was roused into the usual wide-awakeness by seeing the van containing my portmanteau go off as for good. It came back, however, after much running and remonstrating; and I was put down at Chelford 'all right' in a pouring rain, which indeed had poured without a moment's intermission all day. The carriage was waiting with drenched coachman and footman, who I had the discomfort of thinking must wish me at Jericho, at the least, and I was soon in the hall at Alderley, into which Lady S., with the girls at her back, came running to welcome me with kisses and good words, a much more human mode of receiving visitors than I had been used to in great houses. In fact, the whole thing is very human, and very humane as well. Lord S. is still in London, Postmaster-General you will have heard—nobody here but Lady S. and the girls, which suits my nervous system, and also my wardrobe (which I had no time or care to get up) much better than company would have done. Indeed, I had made the aloneness and dulness, which Lady S. had complained of, my conditions in accepting her invitation. Mr. Barnes had been saying all he could about 'the excited state of my brain' (I too have a brain it seems?) to frighten me into 'taking better care' of myself, and 'avoiding every sort of worry, and fuss, and fatigue,' as if anybody could avoid worry, and fuss, and fatigue in this world. Worry, and fuss, and fatigue under the name of 'pleasure,' of 'amusement,' that however one certainly may avoid. So I should not have gone wilfully into a houseful of visitors.

I shall write to Mary to-day. I had the kindest little letter from her.

Love to Sir George. I have had no letter from you since—I cannot remember when.   Yours ever,

J. W. C.

F. Chapman will have written about the horse he undertook to break. Silvester says the horse is not broken, has a nasty trick that would break any brougham—turns sharp round, and stands stock still, in spite of all you can do, holding his head to one side as if he were listening. Poor dear Fritz. The breaker, who I suppose desires to be rid of it, says to Chapman it is broken, and Frederick means to try it himself.

LETTER 223.

Mrs. Russell, Holm Hill.

Alderley Park, Congleton: Saturday, Aug. 25, 1860.

My dearest Mary,—I could sit down and take a good hearty cry. I am not to get to you after all. This morning is come a letter from Mr. C., forwarded from Chelsea, giving me the astounding news that there is every likelihood of his coming home by next Wednesday's steamer. Always the way, whenever I go anywhere to please myself—plump he appears at Chelsea, and, just now, his appearance there in my absence would be (as Lord Ashburton would say) ' the devil! '

I cannot enter into an account of my household affairs just now —being long, and most ridiculous. I was keeping it as an amusing story for you when we met. I will write the story from Chelsea at my first leisure (when will that be?). But just now I am too vexed for making a good story, besides being too busy, having so many letters demanding to be written about this provoking change of plan. When I leave here, it must be straight for Chelsea, and I must go on Tuesday morning. What a pity! I was just beginning to recover my sleep in the fresh air and the absence of worries—have had actually two nights of good sleep; and they are so kind to me, and they to whom I was going would have been so kind to me! But when one has married a man of genius, one must take the consequences. Only there was no need for him to have spoken of staying at Thurso till the beginning of October, and misled me so.   Your loving friend,

J. W. C.

LETTER 224.

T. Carlyle, Thurso Castle.

Alderley Park: Sunday, Aug. 26, 1860.

Oh, dear me! this length of days needed for a letter written to or from Thurso, to get an answer in the course of post, is very trying to impatient spirits! Not on account of the slowness only, but on account of the 'change come o'er the spirit of one's dream' in the interval between the post's going out and coming in. Not once, since you went to that accursedly out-of-the-way place, has a letter from you found me in the same mood and circumstances to which it was addressed, as being the mood and circumstances in which my own letter had left me, and of course it has been the same with my letters to you. For example, your announcement that you might be home immediately, crossing my announcement that I was on the road to Scotland. Now I write to say I am turning back, and shall be at Chelsea, D.V., on Tuesday afternoon, to prepare for you, in case you do come soon, which I shall regret for your sake; a few more weeks of sound sleep would be so good for you. What will be the contents of the letter that crosses this? Something quite irrelevant I have no doubt. Perhaps assurances that you can do perfectly well at Chelsea without me, and that I am to stay in Scotland as long as I like, when I shall be reading the letter at Cheyne Row, and as sure as ever woman was of anything that you could not have done at Chelsea without me for twelve hours.

The week before my departure, which should have been devoted to setting my house in order, was devoted to British cholera, which, coming on the back of low nervous fever, reduced me to a state of exhaustion, which even 'zeal for my house' couldn't rouse to the requisite activity. Many things had been begun, but few of them finished—for instance, your bed had been all taken to pieces to look for bugs, and it had been ascertained that not one bug survived there, and the bed had been put together, but the curtains were away being cleaned.

Fancy your coming home to a curtainless bed, and 'Old Jane'[1] would have made no shift! for 'Old Jane,' my dear, I may as well tell you soon as syne, is a complete failure and humbug! Although you provokingly enough attributed the silence I systematically ob-

---

[1] I have quite forgotten.

serve on the shortcomings of servants to want of 'care about it,' I still think that until I am arrived at parting with a servant, and have to show reason why, the more I hold my peace about them, and make the best of them, the more for your comfort and for my own credit.[1] 'Old Jane' then disappointed me from the first day. Before you left I had satisfied myself that she was a perfectly incompetent cook and servant, and soon after you left I satisfied myself that she—told lies! and had no more sense of honour in her work than Charlotte. There was no need to worry you with the topic of her, which was to myself perfectly loathsome, until I had to account for replacing her. I mention her now to reconcile you to the idea of my having gone back home to wait for you. You couldn't have done without me, you see. I have engaged a woman of thirty-four, who is really promising (the woman Miss Evans wanted to have), and a remarkably nice-looking girl of sixteen to be under her.[2] She would not have taken a place of ' all work, and indeed it is very difficult to find even a respectable servant who will take it—naturally, when they can find plenty of less confused places. She, the elder woman, comes home on September 14, and I wished the girl to wait till then. I think the house will really be comfortable and orderly by-and-by—at more cost; but that, you said repeatedly, you didn't mind. At all rates, I have taken immense trouble (two journeys to Richmond included), to find respectable and competent servants. If I have failed, it will just be another instance of my ill-luck, rather than my want of zeal.

Maud[3] has been sitting in my room waiting till I am done. Excuse haste and abrupt ending. I can't write on this principle, and I shan't get a chance again before post time.

Yours,

J. W. C.

LETTER 225.

Surely this is one of the saddest of letters—the misery of it merely slowness of posts, and on both sides hardly bearable heaviness of load. Oh, my own much-suffering little woman!—T. C.

---

[1] Alas! can that need to be said?—insane that I was!

[2] Yes, I recollect these two. I had often latterly been urging 'two servants,' but she never till now would comply. The elder of these 'two' did not suit either. A conceited fool; got the name 'Perfection,' and (to the great joy of the younger, who continued worthily) had to go in a few months.

[3] Stanley.

T. Carlyle, Thurso Castle.

5 Cheyne Row, Chelsea: Sunday, Sept. 2, 1860.

This is all—'what shall I say? strange, upon my honour!' On Friday morning comes a note from Sir George (that had gone round by Alderley) to the effect that his 'dear friend's pen being more devoted to the service of unborn generations than to mine' (truly! and if the 'unborn generations' will do the answering, I shan't object!), and another expedition to John o' Groats being on foot, he writes to tell me the dear friend has been prevailed upon, &c. &c. Well! 'I am most particularly glad to hear it,' like Archivarius Lyndhorst. The more of Thurso Castle, the better for his sleep, and his head; and, as concerns myself, the more time for putting things straight here, the better for my sleep, and my head! (if so insignificant an individual can be said to have a head!) But certainly on the following morning (Saturday), there would be a few lines from the dear friend's self, snatched from his service to 'unborn generations' to tell me 'with his own hand' of his change of plan! No! On Saturday morning the postman didn't so much as call! and when I ran out at the house door to see if he could really mean it, he merely shook his head from the steps of No. 8. Late at night, however, I hear of a letter from you, received that morning by Neuberg. There had been time found or made to write to him. And he 'thought it his duty to,' not forward your letter to me, but interlard his own note with single words or whole lines of yours 'in ticks '[1]—'means to move *gradually* southward again, wishes *you* could be persuaded to start again, if able at all, and to rectify her huge error!' &c. Who was to 'persuade' me to start again? Neuberg himself, perhaps? Not you it would seem, who send not a single line to, as it were, welcome me home, though come home entirely for your sake! No matter! there is the less to be grateful for!

Meanwhile I am glad to know, even indirectly, that you are positively coming south by land, and 'gradually.' The two notes written after hearing I was at Alderley, and bound for Dumfriesshire, which were received together (on account of the misdirection), within an hour of the time the carriage was ordered to take me to the station, threw no certain light for me on your plans. When you first fixed to go to Thurso, your grand induce-

---

[1] Her own Scotch name for double commas.

ment had seemed to be that you 'could sail there, and back, and avoid all that horror of railways.' You had never once in my hearing spoken of taking Dumfriesshire on your road; on the contrary, when I spoke to you of Loch Luichart, you said: 'Oh, that was a great way off! and you shouldn't be going back by land at all!' Then the letter, forwarded to Alderley from Chelsea, written in the belief I was still at home, made no allusion whatever to any intention of taking Dumfriesshire on your road home. You could not remain there longer, without work, and, to get on with your work, you must be 'beside your reservoir of books at Chelsea.' Read that letter yourself—Mary Austin has got it (I sent it to her as my valid excuse for breaking my engagement to come, and as a valid excuse she accepted it)—and say if I was committing any 'huge error,' or error at all, in supposing it in the highest degree probable that you would sail straight from Thurso to London? And granting that high probability, there was but one course for me, under the circumstances (the curtains; the keys, which you could never have known one from another! the imbecile 'Old Jane;' the new servant to come, &c. &c.)—but one course: to go south again instead of north, on the day when my Alderley visit was to terminate: unless, after my resolution was taken, and everybody warned not to expect me in Dumfriesshire, and the new woman who had been put off warned that she must now immediately render herself at Cheyne Row—unless, after all that, I was to unsettle everything over again at the very last hour, when there was no longer time to warn anybody. On the receipt of the two little letters, which came together, taking them as an exposition of your voluntary plans, not of plans which you had been forced to adopt voluntarily by the knowledge of mine—by the dread of going home to a comfortless house, and, simultaneously with that, a kind desire not to interfere with any arrangements of mine by which my health might be benefited. No! I could not be quite certain that, were I at Chelsea instead of half-way to Scotland, you might not still wish to avoid the 'horror of railways,' and to get back to your 'reservoir of books.' At all events, you should have your free choice, and now you have had it, and I learn, *through Mr. Neuberg*, that it is to be 'in no hurry.' I am very glad of that, as I shall be in better trim for you here than had you come straight.

As to my 'starting again' (on any long expedition at least), you couldn't believe Mr. Neuberg or anyone else could persuade me to do it! I am not 'able at all,' which does not mean, however, that

. I am ill. My three days at Alderley, before the letter came, did me all the good which I was likely to get from change of scene;—after the letter came, my sleep was no better than at Chelsea. When I am worried about anything, no air nor surroundings can put me to sleep. At present your curtains are come home and put up. The bricklayers have mended the broken tiles on your dressing closet. That dreadful old woman is to be got handsomely rid of next Wednesday; and I feel rather quiet, and am getting to sleep better, and mean to lead a pleasant life in my solitude—taking these 'little excursions so long talked of.'

Lady Stanley was to write to you, the day I left, to tell you I was despatched safely south. My own letter, to say I was going home on Tuesday, would reach you last Monday I suppose. You will write when the 'unborn generations' can spare you for half an hour.

The only news I have to tell is, that the poor 'little darling!'[1] has lost the use of an arm and hand by paralysis. He came himself to tell me, with his arm in a sling, and repeatedly broke down into tears, and made me cry too. 'Oh!' he said, 'how I do miss my poor dear!'—I thought he was going to say wife—she died two years since; but, no, it was 'arm!' 'Oh, how I miss my poor dear arm!' He didn't need money, wouldn't even be paid what was owing him. It was the helplessness that was breaking his heart.

All good be with you.

Yours ever,
JANE WELSH CARLYLE.

Don't expect another letter for a long time, even should I know the address; writing is very bad for me, and I hate it at present.

LETTER 226.

T. Carlyle, Thurso Castle.

5 Cheyne Row, Chelsea: Monday, Sept. 3, 1860.

Two letters from you this morning—one redirected from Alderley. But I must let the long letter I wrote yesterday go, as it is all the same! It is too much writing to throw away, after having given myself a headache over it. Besides, after having read your two letters of this morning, I feel none the less called upon to defend myself against the charge of 'huge error,' 'rashness,' 'precip-

---

[1] Her name for a neat and good old gardener that used to work for us.

itancy,' 'folly,' and so on! I maintain that, however unfortunate my course may have been, I could not, under the circumstances, have rightly taken any other! So the letter of yesterday had best go! Nor do I deign to accept the very beggarly apology you make for my 'infatuated conduct,' that I had myself lost heart for the Dumfriesshire visits, and was glad of any excuse to be off from them; that tortuous style of thing is not at all in my line. Had I lost heart I would have said so. On the contrary, feeling myself at Alderley, half-way—all the hateful preparatory lockings up and packings well over—nothing to do but go north at Crewe instead of south, and Mary Austin and Mrs. Russell promising me the very warmest welcome, far from losing heart, I had for the first time gained heart for the further enterprise; the 'interest' had 'not fallen but risen,' I assure you, and I turned south with real mortification! There! you have provoked that out of me, which, if 'well let alone,' I should never have said.

As for your indignation at my not writing, I don't quarrel with that—only beg to remind you that 'the reciprocity is not all on one side!' I also have been feeling myself extremely neglected—for what shall I say? 'unborn generations?' Let us hope so, and not for just nothing at all!

Ever yours,

J. W. C.

LETTER 227.

Mrs. Russell, Holm Hill, Thornhill.

5 Cheyne Row, Chelsea: Sept. 7, 1860.

Dearest Mary,—I am so sorry that letter should have arrived to mislead you, for, alas! I have had no thought of starting again, since I found, on my return home, that Mr. C. had made a perfectly wrong impression on me as to his plans! When he talked of 'sailing' by such a steamer, how could I imagine he only meant sailing to Aberdeen, and afterwards making visits in Scotland? He had always declared the attraction of Thurso, for him, to be the possibility of getting there and back by sea, without any horror of 'railwaying.' And he had never once spoken of returning through Dumfriesshire! My error was quite natural, almost inevitable. But that doesn't make it the less mortifying for myself and others.

If I had ordinary powers of locomotion I should, on perceiving the real state of the case, have streamed off again—this time straight to the Gill. But indeed, my dear, I have no such thing as ordinary strength. When I told my doctor that Mr. C. urged me to do this, he fairly swore, though a very mild man by nature! It was not merely the ground to be gone over, but the fuss and flurry of so much travelling for me, that he entirely protested against. 'Quiet, quiet, quiet' was what I needed above everything else—no change could do me good that involved fatigue or fret of mind. I know he is right in that, and that no purer air nor change of scene could do me good if bought with a new unsettling of myself, and the hurry of mind inseparable from travelling, especially railway travelling, for a person whose nervous system is in such a preternatural state of excitability as mine is. I should never have had courage to think of going to you at all but for the week's rest in the middle of the journey, offered in the visit to Alderley. It has been a real disappointment to me, having had to turn back, and a great provocation to find my turning back unnecessary. But, now that I am here, I must make the best of it.

I will write you a long letter soon, and tell you several things about my household affairs which will throw more light for you on the supposed necessity for my abrupt return.

God bless you, dear.

Your ever affectionate
JANE W. CARLYLE.

LETTER 228.

'I did it, sir.'—Blusterous pedagogue, a Welsh Archdeacon Williams, head of the Edinburgh New Academy (who used to call at Comely Bank, reporting to us his dreadful illness he once had, illness miserable and fatal 'unless you can dine for three weeks without wine'—'and I did it, sir!'—T. C.

T. Carlyle, Scotsbrig.

5 Cheyne Row, Chelsea: Sunday night, Sept. 10, 1860.

Oh, my dear! was there ever such a game at cross-purposes as this correspondence of ours? It reminds me of nothing so much as the passages between 'the wee wifie, who lived in a shoe,' and her bairns, so many 'that she didn't know what to do!'

> 'She went to the market to buy them some bread;
> When she came back they were all lying dead!
> She went to the wright's to get them a coffin;
> When she came back they were all sitting laughing!'

Not one letter you have written to me since you went away has hit the right state of things! Do the best that ever you could, your 'sheep's head' and your 'coffin' have been equally out of time! Such being, I suppose, the natural result of going where an answer to one's letters cannot be received in less than six days, in a world where nothing keeps still.

Your last letter, received on Saturday morning, expressing your relief from anxieties about me, found me a more legitimate object of anxiety than I had been at all since your departure!—at least found me thinking myself so! For, thank God, this attack, if very violent while it lasted, has passed off unexpectedly soon. I suppose if I had followed Mr. Barnes's directions about lying down in the middle of the day, instead of yielding to popular clamour about 'change of air,' the thing would have been avoided altogether. On Friday morning down came Geraldine, having had a letter from you, and insisted that we should make one of those 'excursions' I had talked of. I had my 'sickness' (as I call it) worse than usual that morning, and begged to be off from any adventure; but 'a breath of Norwood air would do me so much good!' 'It would take off the sickness to sit on the hillside,' &c., &c. I didn't feel that it would, but foolishly yielded to 'reason' rather than instinct. The movement made me sicker, and sicker; still I had fortitude to order dinner (a nice little roasted chicken, and a bottle of soda-water) at the best hotel, and to force myself to eat some of it too, at an open bow-window, with such a 'beautiful view.' But, oh, how I wished myself in my bed at home, with no view to speak of! for I had grown all burning-hot and ice-cold, not a square inch of me at the same temperature, and 'my head like a mall!'

I got home, better or worse, and went to bed, and lay, or rather tossed about, all night in a high fever, with a racking headache, severe sickness, and, most questionable of all, a bad sore throat. I only waited for Mr. Barnes being up to send for him, though he had given me up as a patient. Without having had a wink of sleep, however, or anything to do me good, my fever abated of itself as the morning advanced; and, after having had some tea in bed, between seven and eight, 'all very comfortable,' from the new woman, I felt so much better that I should have held my hand from sending for a doctor if it hadn't been for the sore throat, which continued very bad, and frightened me from its unusual nature. Mr. Barnes was out, and didn't come in to get the message till three o'clock, by which time I had transferred myself to the drawing-room sofa.

Meanwhile, long before this, being still in bed, but washed and combed, and the room tidied up in expectation of Mr. Barnes, there was sent up to me the card of Madame ——! two hours after I had read your wish that I should call for her! And I heard her voice in the passage! I sent down polite regrets in the first instance; then, thinking you would be vexed at my not admitting her, I called Charlotte ('Charlotte' the second) back, and said, to tell the lady, if she wouldn't dislike coming to me in my bedroom, that I should be glad to see her 'for a minute.' If I had known that she was to flop down on the bed, and cover my face with kisses (!) the first thing, I should have thought twice of admitting her, with the sore throat I had! However, the thing was done! So I didn't say a word of sore throat to put infection in her head, and indeed I hoped it mightn't be of an infectious nature. As for the 'minute,' she prolonged it to an hour; talking with an emphasis, and an exaggeration, and a velocity, and cordiality, which left me little to do but listen, and not scream! I will tell you all I remember of her talk when we meet. She will be again in London towards the end of October. She went off with the same, or rather redoubled, embracings and kissings; I, purposely, holding in my breath; and when the door had closed, didn't I fall back on my pillows with a sense of relief!

Mr. Barnes looked into my throat, and said it was bad; but if I had 'courage to swallow the very ugliest, most extraordinary-looking medicine I had ever seen in this world, he thought he could cure it in a day or two;' and there came a bottle containing apparently bright blue oil-paint!! It did need courage, and faith, to take the first dose of that! But 'I did it, sir!' and positively, as if by magic, my throat mended in half an hour! I had a good night; the throat was a little sore only in the morning. The second dose had the same magically sudden effect, and now, after three half-glassfuls of that magical blue oil-paint, my throat is perfectly mended, and I am as well as before I knocked myself up.

Monday.—For the rest, all that has been said and written about my turning back and about my not starting again is kindly meant, but being said or written in total or in partial ignorance of the subject, quite overshoots or undershoots the mark; is, in fact, perfect nonsense, setting itself up for superior sense! 'Why not have left you to "fen" for yourself, if you had come home in my absence?' your sister Jane asks; 'if she had been me, she would have done that.' And I would have done it if I had been she perhaps.

Ever yours,   J. W. C.

LETTER 229.

T. Carlyle, The Gill.

5 Cheyne Row, Chelsea: Monday, Sept. 17, 1860.

You will open this, prepared to hear that I went to Forster's,[1] and have been very ill in consequence. If there be a choice betwixt a wise thing and a foolish one, a woman is always expected to do the foolish. Well, I didn't! Very ill I have been, but not from going out to dinner. By one o'clock that day I was quite ill enough to care no more for Fuz's wrath than for a whiff of tobacco! I had taken the influenza, and no doubt about it! So I despatched a message to Montagu Square, and another to Mr. Barnes; went to bed, and have not slept till within the last hour! So provoking! I had been so much better, and hoped to be quite flourishing on your return. *Howsomdever* an influenza properly treated, and an influenza allowed to treat itself, like all my former ones, is a very different affair I find. It has not been allowed to settle down on my chest at all, this one; and, after only three days of sharp suffer-ing, here I am in the drawing-room, looking forward with some interest to the sweet bread I am to dine on, and writing you a let-ter better or worse.

The new woman is a good nurse, very quiet and kindly, and with sense to do things without being told. I have not had my clothes folded neatly up, and the room tidied, and my wants anticipated in this way since I had no longer any mother to nurse me. In ordinary circumstances I should have felt it horrid to be lying entirely at the mercy of an utter stranger; but, being as she is, I have wished none else to come near me. Even you I rather hope may not come this week. It would worry me so, not to be able to run about when you come, and I must be cautious for some days yet—'Mrs. Prudence,' as Mr. Barnes calls me in mockery. The girl is to come to-morrow, but I don't feel to trouble my head about her. Charlotte (2nd) can be trusted to direct her in the way she should go till I am well enough to meddle. Besides I have every reason to believe her a nice girl. The old Charlotte, poor foolish thing! is still hanging on at her ' mother's,' just as untidy in her person, with nothing to do, as she used to be in her press of work. She has been much about me, and I don't know what I

---

[1] Alluding to close of last letter, omitted.

should have done without her, to cook for me, and show me some human kindness, when I was ill under 'Old Jane.' But I am glad at the same time that I had fortitude to resist her tears, and her request to be taken back as cook. I told her some day I might take her back; but she had much to learn and to unlearn first. Still it is gratifying to feel that one's kindness to the girl has not been all lost on her, for she really loves both of us passionately—only that passionate loves, not applied to practical uses, are good for so little in this matter-of-fact world.

Kindest love to dear Mary. Tell her I will make out that visit some day, on my own basis; it is only postponed. 'Thank God,' you can't get any clothes.

Yours,

J. W. C.

LETTER 230.

I seem to have got home again, September 22. Halted at Alderley a couple of days; of Annandale, the Gill, or Dumfries I remember nothing whatever, except the last morning at the Gill (which is still vivid enough), and my wandering about in manifold sorrowful reflections, loth to quit that kindly, safe *tugurium;* and also privately my making resolution (seeing the fitness of it), not to revisit Scotland till the unutterable Frederick were done—resolution sad and silent, which I believe was kept.—T. C.

Mrs. Austin, The Gill, Annan.

5 Cheyne Row, Chelsea: Thursday, Oct. 19, 1860.

My dear Mary,—The box arrived last night, 'all right.' Many thanks, Mary dear. The things from Dumfries are also all right; but I will write to tell Jane about them to-morrow. Mr. C. doesn't seem to have benefited from his long sojourn by the sea-side so much as I had hoped, and at first thought. He still goes on waking up several times in the night—when he bolts up, and smokes, and sometimes takes a cold bath! And all that is very dismal for him, to whom waking betwixt lying down and getting up is a novelty. For me, my own wakings up some twenty or thirty times every night of my life, for years and years back, are nothing compared with hearing him jump out of bed overhead, once or sometimes twice during a night. Before he went to Thurso, that sound overhead used to set my heart a-thumping to such a degree that I couldn't get another wink of sleep—and I was on the brink of a nervous fever when he left.[1] Now that my nerves have had a rest, and that I am more 'used to it,' I get to sleep again when I hear all quiet, but God knows how long I may be up to that! And when he has broken sleep, and I no sleep at all, it is sad work here, I assure you.

You will have heard of my setting up a second servant, and think perhaps that I must be more comfortable now, with two people to work and run for us; but I would much rather have made less working and less running do, and kept to my accustomed one servant. I have never felt the house my own since my maid-of-all-work was converted into a 'cook' and 'housemaid,' and don't feel as if I should ever get used to the improvement. It is just as if one had taken lodgers into one's lower story. Often in the dead of night I am seized with a wild desire to clear the house of these newcomers, and take back my one little Charlotte, who is still hanging on at her mother's, in a wild hope than one or other of them, or both, may break down, and she be reinstated in her place. Poor little Charlotte! if I had seen how miserable she was to be at leaving us, I couldn't have found in my heart to put her way, though she was so heedless, and 'thro' other,'[2] with a grain of method she could have done all the two do, as well or better than they do it, she was so clever and willing.

The new tall Charlotte (the cook) said to me one day ' little Charlotte' had been here: 'What a fool that girl is, ma'am! I said to her to-day, "You seem to like being here!" and says she, " Of course I do; I look upon this as my home." "But," says I, "you are a nice-looking, healthy girl, you will easily get another place if you try." "Oh," says she, "I know that. I may get plenty of places; but I shall never get another home!" What a poor spirit the girl has! If anybody had been dissatisfied with me, it's little that I should care about leaving them.' 'I can well believe that,' said I, with a strong disposition to knock her down. But I have no pretext for putting the woman away—although I don't like her. She is a good servant as servants go, and I can't put her away merely for being vulgar-minded, and totally destitute of sentiment; and, after all, the faults for which I parted with little Charlotte after twelve months of considering won't have been cured, but rather have been aggravated by three months' muddling at her mother's. Heigh-ho! I feel just in the case of the ' Edinburgh meat-jack:' 'Once I was happ-happ-happ-y! but now I am mee-e-ser-

---

[1] Poor loving soul!   [2] *Durcheinander* (German) as an adjective.

able!' If one's skin were a trifle thicker, all these worries would seem light. But one's skin being just no skin 'to speak of,' no wonder one falls into the meat-jack humour. God bless you and all your belongings. Kind regards to your husband.

Ever affectionately yours,
JANE W. CARLYLE.

LETTER 231.

To Miss Margaret Welsh, Auchtertool Manse.

Chelsea: December 8, 1860.

Dearest Maggie,—Having made no sign of myself for the last month, you may be fancying I have succumbed to the general doom; seeing that it has been 'the gloomy month of November, in which the people of England hang and drown themselves!' But I am neither hanged nor drowned yet (in virtue perhaps of being born in Scotland); only, all my energies having been needed to stave off suicide, I had none left for letter-writing. It is now December, and the suicidal mania should have passed off; but I can't see much difference between this December and the gloomiest November on record! the fog, and the mud, and the liquid soot (called rain in the language of flattery), have not abated; and the blood in one's veins feels so thick and dirty! But, shame of my silence must serve instead of inspiration, impossible under the circumstances; and you, dear, good little soul as you are, will not be critical!

In the first place you will be glad to hear I am 'about' anyhow. Except for one week that I had to lie on the sofa on my back, with neuralgia (differing in nothing, so far as I can see, from the old-fashioned 'rheumatiz'), I have not been laid up since you heard of me; and I have had a great fret taken off me, in the removal of that vulgar, conceited woman, and the restoration of little Charlotte. Upon my word, I haven't been as near what they call 'happy' for many a day as in the first flush of little Charlotte! She looked so bursting with ecstasy as she ran up and down the house, taking possession, as it were, of her old work, and as she showed in the visitors (not her business, but she would open the door to them all the first time, to show herself, and receive their congratulations), that it was impossible not to share in her delighted excitement! Most of the people shook hands with her! and all of them said they were 'glad to see her back'! I had trusted that she would in time humanise the other girl, and that the two would be good friends,

II.—7

when the other girl got over the prejudices the woman who had left had inspired her with! But it needed no time at all. Sarah was humanised, and the two sworn friends in the first half-hour! In the first half-hour Sarah had confided to Charlotte that, if I hadn't given the tall Charlotte warning, she (Sarah) would have given me warning, she disliked ' tall Charlotte ' so much!

It is now three weeks since the new order of things; mistress and maid have subsided out of the emotional state into the normal one, but are still very glad over one another; and if the work of the house does not get done with as much order and method as under the tall Charlotte, it is done with more thoroughness, and infinitely more heartiness and pleasantness; and the ' bread-puddings' are first rate. Sarah's tidiness and method are just what were wanted to correct little Charlotte's born tendency to muddle; while little Charlotte's willingness and affectionateness warm up Sarah's drier, more selfish nature. It is a curious establishment, with something of the sound and character of a nursery. Charlotte not nineteen till next March, and Sarah seventeen last week. And they keep up an incessant chirping and chattering and laughing; and as both have remarkably sweet voices, it is pleasant to hear. The two-ness is no nuisance to me now. As neither can awake of themselves, I don't know what I should have done about that, hadn't Charlotte's friends come to the rescue. An old man who lodges with Charlotte's ' mother ' (aunt), raps on the kitchen window till he wakes them, every morning at six, on his way to his work; and Charlotte's ' father' (uncle) raps again on the window before seven, to make sure the first summons had been attended to! to say nothing of an alarum, which runs down at six, at their very bed-head, and never is heard by either of these fortunate girls! So I daresay we shall get on as well as possible in a world where perfection is not to be looked for. I shall be glad to hear that your domesticities are in as flourishing a state!

I hope we shall go to the Grange by-and-by, and make a longer visit than last year. It is such a good break in the long, dreary, Chelsea winter, and stirs up one's stagnant spirits, and rules up one's manners! But Mr. Carlyle won't stay anywhere if he can't get work done; and though Lady Ashburton says he shall have every facility afforded him for working, I don't know how that will be when it comes to be tried. I never saw any work done in that house! Meanwhile, I have sent an azure blue *moire*, that Lady Sandwich gave me last Christmas Day, to be made, in case.

My dear, beautiful Kate Sterling (Mrs. Ross) was buried last week at Bournemouth, where she had been taken for the winter. I had long been hopeless of her recovery, but did not think the end so near, and that I should never see her sweet face again. Julia came to see me yesterday on her return, looking miserably ill. Poor Mr. Ross wrote me a sad, kind letter. I am very sorry for him; and none of the family treat him as if he had anything to do with their loss. He was not a man one would ever have wished Kate to marry, but he has been the most devoted husband, and tenderest nurse to her; and she said to her sister Lotta, the day before her death, that she had repented doing many things in her life, but she had never for one moment repented her marriage! Surely that should have made them all less hard for him! But, no!

Kindest love to Walter and Star.

Your affectionate

J. W. CARLYLE.

LETTER 232.

Mrs. Russell, Thornhill.

5 Cheyne Row, Chelsea: Dec. 31, 1860.

Dearest Mary,—If there were no other use in a letter from me just now, it will serve the purpose of removing any apprehensions you may have as to the frost having put an end to my life! 'Did you ever?' 'No, I never,'—felt such cold! But then, there being no question for me of ever crossing the threshold, and my time thrown altogether on my hands (my visitors being mostly away, keeping their Christmas in country houses, or, like myself, shut up with colds at home, or too busy with 'the festivities of the season' to get as far as Chelsea, and my two maids leaving me nothing earthly to do in the business of the house), I have time, enough and to spare, for adopting all possible measures to keep myself warm. To see the fires I keep up in the drawing-room and my bed-room! An untopographical observer might suppose we lived within a mile of a coal pit, instead of paying twenty-eight shillings a cart-load for coals! Then I wear all my flannel petticoats at once, and am having two new ones made out of a pair of Scotch blankets! And Lady Sandwich has sent me a seal-fur pelisse (a luxury I had long sighed for, but, costing twenty guineas, it had seemed hopeless!), and a Greek merchant[1] has sent me the softest

---

[1] Dilberoglue.

grey Indian shawl. And if all that can't warm me, I lie down under my coverlet of racoon skins! (My dear! if you are perishing, act upon my idea of the Scotch blankets; no flannel comes near them in point of warmth.) My doctor told me, in addition to all this outward covering, to drink 'at least three glasses of wine a day!' But I generally shirk the third. And the cough, and face-ache, which I had the first week of the frost, is gone this week, at any rate.

Have you seen that Tale of Horror, which ran through the news-papers, about the Marquis of Downshire? Everybody here believed for some days that the Marquis of Downshire had really found the skipper of his yacht· kneeling at the side of Lady Alice (his only daughter, a lovely girl of seventeen), and really pitched him into the sea, and so there was an end of him! I was dreadfully sorry, for one. Lord D. is such a dear, good, kind-hearted savage of a man; and it seemed such a fatality that he should be always killing somebody!! He had killed a school companion, without meaning it; and afterwards (they say) a coalheaver, who was boxing with him! The fact is, he is awfully strong, and his strokes tell, as he doesn't expect. But if you knew what a simple, good man he is, you wouldn't wonder that I felt sorrier for him than the skipper, who, after all, had no business to be 'kneeling' there surely! And the little darling daughter, that her young life should be clouded at the outset with such a scandal! I made all sorts of miserable re-flections about them all. And the story, all the while, a complete fabrication—equal to the proverbial story of the 'six black crows!' The story was told to Azeglio (the Sardinian Ambassador), who, to give himself importance, said, 'Oh, yes! it had been officially com-municated to him from Naples.' And the man he said it to, being Secretary of Legation, made an official despatch of the story to Lord Cowley at Paris!! Then it flew like wild-fire, and people couldn't help believing it; and, of course, all sorts of details were added—that Lady Alice was 'struggling and screaming, that Lord D. wouldn't let a boat be lowered to pick the man up,' &c. &c. One knows how a story gathers like a snowball. They went the length of stating that Lord D. was being brought home to be tried by the Peers, 'the offence having been committed on the high seas!!!' The talk now is all of prosecution of certain newspapers and certain people. But I shouldn't wonder if it all end in Lord Downshire's giving somebody a good thrashing.

Please to give my good wishes 'of the season' to all my friends at Thornhill and about, and to attend to the old women on New Year's Day. I send a cheque this time. The Japanese trays are for the new drawing-room, if you think them worth a place in it. I took them as far as Alderley on the road in autumn. They are a popular drawing-room ornament here at present. Kindest regards to the Doctor.

Your ever affectionate

JANE CARLYLE,

LETTER 233.

To Miss Barnes, King's Road, Chelsea.

5 Cheyne Row: Sunday, April 26, 1861.

Carina,—I was going to you to-day, having been hindered yester-day; but a thought strikes me. You are a Puseyite, or, as my old Scotch servant writes it, a 'Puisht,' and I am a Presbyterian; would it be proper for you to receive me, or for me to pay a visit on Sunday? I don't quite know as to you; but for me it is a thing for-bidden certainly. So I write to say that if you could have gone to the gorillas to-morrow, the gorillas would have been 'not at home.' On consulting my order of admission I find it is for all days except just the two I successively fixed upon, Saturdays and Mondays. My order is available through all the month of May, so it will still be time when you return, provided you do not indefinitely extend your programme, as you are in the habit of doing. I shall fix with the others for Tuesday, 28th, early—say to start between eleven and twelve. Will that do?

Your affectionate

JANE CARLYLE.

LETTER 234.

Mrs. Russell, Holm Hill.

5 Cheyne Row, Chelsea: Thursday, July 3, 1861.

Decidedly, dearest Mary, I am in a run of bad luck, and enter-taining for a moment any idea of pleasure seems to be the signal with me for some misfortune to plunge down.

The longer I thought of it, the more it seemed to me fair and feasible that, since Mr. C. was minded to go nowhere this summer, I should go for two or three weeks by myself where I had been so unreasonably disappointed of going last August. Mr. C. himself

said I might, 'if I thought it would be useful to me;' and there could
be no question about its being 'useful to me' to have a breath of
Scotch air and a glimpse of dear Scotch faces. So, when I had
read your cordial letter, I felt my purpose strong to carry itself out,
and only delayed answering till I had seen the baking difficulty
overcome, and could say, positively, that I would come as soon as
you pleased after your visitor had departed. Two visitors at one
time is too much happiness, I think, for any not over strong mistress of a house, who gives herself so much trouble as you do to
make everything comfortable and pleasant about one.

And, in the meantime, here is what has befallen. My nice trustworthy cook, who inspired me with the confidence to leave Mr. C.,
being certain, I thought, to keep him all right, and the house all
right, and the young girl all right, in my absence; this treasure of
a cook, my dear, who was to be the comfort of my remaining
years, and nurse me in my last illness (to such wild flights had my
imagination gone), turns out to have come into my service with a
frightful neglected disorder—what the doctors call 'strangulated
hernia,' making her life (my doctor says) 'not safe for a day!' He
could do nothing with it, he said; she must go to St. George's
Hospital, and what was possible to do for her would be done there.
But I have no hope that the woman will ever be fit for service again.
And what she could mean in going into a new service with such a
complaint I am at a loss to conceive. And I am also dreadfully at
a loss what I am to do with her. She is such a good creature, and
hasn't a relation in the world to depend upon. If the doctors take
her as an in-patient, of course it would settle the question of her
leaving here; but if they don't—! Oh, my gracious, how unlucky
it is! In any case, I see no chance for me now of getting to you.

Unless, indeed, she could be cured sufficiently to go on at service. I shall know more about it when she comes back from the
hospital, or when I have spoken with one of the surgeons there
whom I know. But unless the case is much less grave than Mr.
Barnes seemed to consider it, we shall be all at sea again. And the
best arrangement I can think of, for the moment, would be to put
my new housemaid into the kitchen, for which she is better suited
than for her present place, only that she would have the cooking
all to learn!—and to take another nice girl I know of for housemaid. But fancy the weeks and months it will take to get even
that most feasible scheme to work right, and all the while I must
be standing between Mr. C. and new bother, and looking after these

girls that they may be kept in good ways! I declare I could take a good cry, or do a little good swearing! I will stop now till the poor woman comes back from the hospital; and then tell you the news she brings.

No Matilda come yet, and I must take the letters myself now to the post-office, having nobody to send.

I will write soon.

Your much bedevilled, but always loving,

J. CARLYLE.

LETTER 235.

Mrs. Russell, Holm Hill.

5 Cheyne Row, Chelsea: Tuesday, July 16, 1861.

Dearest Mary,—Mr. Dunbar's[1] book was from you, was it not ? I used to be able to swear to your handwriting; but latterly one or two people have taken to writing exactly like you, and I need the post-mark to verify the handwriting, and the post-mark was illegible on that book-parcel. Whether from you or not, I am glad of the little book, which I am sure I shall read with pleasure ; I like that mild, gentlemanly man so much.

But I am still as far as when I last wrote from sitting down quietly to read a pleasant book. Everything is at sixes and sevens still ! My treasure of a servant, who was to 'soothe my declining years,' and enable me to go to Scotland this year, is still lying in St. George's Hospital, certain to lie there 'for some months,' and not certain to be fit for service, even of the mildest form, when the months are over! Mr. ——, the Head Surgeon, found immediately that she had got ulceration of the spine, and the rupture proceeded from that. He says she 'may get over it ; but it will be a tedious affair.' I don't think that, even if she were cured nominally, I should like to have her for kitchen servant again ; I should live in perpetual terror of her hurting herself at every turn. Meanwhile I have been puddling on with my old 'going-out-to-cook-woman,' coming daily to cook the dinner, and teach the Welsh housemaid, whom I have decided to make kitchen-woman, getting another girl for housemaid. A safe housemaid is so much easier to get here than a cook, who doesn't drink, nor steal, nor take the

---

[1] I don't recollect.

house to herself! This Welsh girl [1] has, I think, more the shaping of a good cook than of a housemaid, not being good at needlework, and utterly incapable of reading the titles on Mr. C.'s books, so that she can't bring him a book when he wants it. The girl I am getting is more accomplished, whatever else!

The present state of affairs is wretched; for Mr. C., being a man, cannot understand to exact the least bit less attendance, when we are reduced to one servant again, than he had accustomed himself to exact from the two. So I have all the valeting, and needle-womaning, and running up and down to the study for books, &c. &c. &c. to do myself, besides having to superintend the Welsh girl, and to go to St. George's (two miles off) almost every day in my life, to keep up the heart of poor Matilda, who, lying there, with two issues in her back, and nobody but myself coming after her, and her outlooks of the darkest, naturally needs any cheering that I can take her.

Mercifully the plentiful rain keeps things cooler and fresher here than is usual in summer; and I am nothing like so sick and nervous as I was last year at this time. So I am more able to bear what is laid on me—to bear amongst the rest the heavy disappointment of having to give up my visit to you, and stay here at my post, which is a rather bothering one.

God bless you. It does me good anyhow to think that, if I could have gone, the kind Doctor and you would have been so kind to me.   Your ever affectionate

                                        J. W. CARLYLE.

LETTER 236.

T. Carlyle, Esq., Chelsea.

Mrs. Stokes's, 21 Wellington Crescent, East Cliff, Ramsgate:
                            Sunday, August 4, 1861.

That is the address, if there be anything to be addressed! Fortune favors the brave! Had one talked, and thought, and corresponded, and investigated about lodgings for a month before starting, I doubt if we could have made a better business of it than we have done. Certainly in point of situation there is no better in Ramsgate or in the world: looking out over a pretty stripe of lawn

---

[1] *Irish* in reality; a little, black, busy creature, who did very well for some time; but, &c. &c. (some mysterious love-affair, I think)—and went to New Zealand out of sight.

and gravel walk on to the great boundless Ocean ! You could throw a stone from the sitting-room window into the sea when the tide is up ! Then there is not the vestige of a bug in our white dimity beds ! For the rest, I cannot say it is noiseless ! Geraldine says her room looking on the sea is perfectly so ; but I consider her no judge, as she sleeps like a top. However, the rooms looking on the sea cannot but be freer from noise than those to the back, looking on roofs, houses, stables, streets, &c.; but the bedrooms to the back are much larger, and better aired. With no sensibilities except my own to listen to them with, I can get used (I think) to the not extravagant amount of crowing and barking, and storming with the wind, and even to occasional cat-explosions on the opposite roofs ! If I can't, I can exchange beds with Geraldine; and there I can only have the noise of the sea (considerable !), the possibilities of occasional carriages passing (I have none to-day, but it is Sunday), and 'rittle-tippling' of Venetian blinds ! With a great diminution of room, however, and alarming increase of glare. The people of the house are civil and honest-looking and slow. Oh, my ! But we are not come here, Geraldine and I, to be in a hurry ! For us the place will answer extremely well for a week, that we had to engage it for, and the sea air and the 'change' will overbalance all the little disagreeables, as well as the *cha-arge*, which is considerable.

If my advice were of any moment, I would strongly advise you to come one day during the week, and see the place under our auspices, and stay one night. I could sleep on the sofa in the drawing-room; and you would not mind any trifling noises with the knowledge that it was only for one night. The mere journey and a sight of the sea and a bathe would do you good.

I am going to seek out the Bains after church. I feel much less tired to-day than I have done for weeks, months back ; and though I was awake half the night, first feeling for bugs, which didn't come! and then taking note of all the different sounds far and near, which did come !

Margaret will do everything very well for you, if you will only tell her distinctly what you want ; I mean not elaborately, but in few plain words.

Ever yours,
JANE W. C.

II.—7*

LETTER 237.

T. Carlyle, Esq., 5 Cheyne Row.

Wellington Crescent, Ramsgate: Tuesday, August 6, 1861.

[1] Very charming doesn't that look, with the sea in front as far as eye can reach ? And that seen (the East Cliff), you needn't wish to ever see more of Ramsgate. It is made up of narrow, steep, confused streets like the worst parts of Brighton. The shops look nasty, the people nasty, the smells are nasty ! (spoiled shrimps complicated with cesspool !) Only the East Cliff is clean, and genteel, and airy ; and would be perfect as sea-quarters if it weren't for the noise ! which is so extraordinary as to be almost laughable.

Along that still-looking road or street between the houses and gardens are passing and repassing, from early morning to late night, cries of prawns, shrimps, lollipops—things one never wanted, and will never want, of the most miscellaneous sort; and if that were all ! But a brass band plays all through our breakfast, and repeats the performance often during the day, and the brass band is succeeded by a band of Ethiopians, and that again by a band of female fiddlers ! and interspersed with these are individual barrel-organs, individual Scotch bagpipes, individual French horns ! Oh, it is 'most expensive ! ' And the night noises were not to be estimated by the first night ! These are so many and frequent as to form a sort of mass of voice; perhaps easier to get some sleep through than an individual nuisance of cock or dog. There are hundreds of cocks ! and they get waked up at, say, one in the morning by some outburst of drunken song or of cat-wailing ! and never go to sleep again (these cocks) but for minutes ! and there are three steeple clocks that strike in succession, and there are doors and gates that slam, and dogs that bark occasionally, and a saw mill, and a mews, &c.—in short, everything you could wish not to hear ! And I hear it all and am getting to sleep in hearing it ! the bed is so soft and clean, and the room so airy; and then I think under every shock, so triumphantly, 'Crow away,' 'roar away,' 'bark away,' 'slam away; you can't disturb Mr. C. at Cheyne Row, that can't you ! ' and the thought is so soothing, I go off asleep—till next thing ! I might try Geraldine's room ; but she

---

[1] Written on Ramsgate note-paper, with a print of the harbour, &c.

has now got an adjoining baby! Yesterday we drove to Broadstairs—a quieter place, but we saw no lodgings that were likely to be quiet, except one villa at six guineas a week, already occupied.

I sleep about, in intervals of the bands, on sofas during the day; and am less sick than when I left home, and we get good enough food very well cooked, and I don't repent coming, on the whole; though I hate being in lodgings in strange places.

I found the Bains; and saw Mrs. George [1] before she left.

Wednesday, Aug. 7, 1861.

I had just cleared my toilet-table, and carried my writing-things from the sitting-room to my bedroom window, where there was no worse noise for the moment than carpet beating and the grinding of passing carts, whereas the sitting-room had become perfectly maddening with bagpipes under the windows, and piano-practice under the floor (a piano hired in by 'the first floor, yesterday)! All which received an irritating finishing touch from the rapid, continuous scrape, scraping of Geraldine's pen (nothing more irritating, as you know, than to see 'others' perfectly indifferent to what is driving oneself wild). Had just dipped the pen in the ink when—a 'yellow scoundrel,' the loudest, harshest of yellow scoundrels, struck up under my bedroom window! And here the master power of Babbage has not reached! Indeed, noise seems to be the grand joy of life at Ramsgate. If I had come to Ramsgate with the least idea of writing letters, or doing anything whatever with my head, I might go back at once. But I came to swallow down as much sea air as possible, and that end is attained without fatigue; for lying on the sofa with our three windows wide open on the sea, we are as well aired as if we were sailing on it; and the bedroom is full of sea air all night too. It is certainly doing me good, though I can't ever get slept many minutes together for the noises. I get up hungry for breakfast, and am hungry again for dinner—and a fowl does not serve Geraldine and me two days!! I do hope you are getting decently fed. It won't be for want of assiduous will on Margaret's part if things are not as you like them.

We called for the Bains last night and invited them to tea tonight, which they thankfully accepted. They seem entirely occupied in studying their mutual health. Indeed, what else would any mortal stay here for! Mrs. Bain is quite the female of that male,—clear and clever, and cold and dry as tinder! They have

---

[1] Welsh; her uncle's wife.

'the only quiet house in Ramsgate.' Mrs. Bain is troubled with nothing but the bleating of sheep to the back; after to-day, however, there will be crying the babies in the house, and it is nothing like so airy a situation as ours. What a mercy you did not try Ramsgate!

My compliments to the maids, and say I hope to find them models of virtue and activity when I come on Saturday. Geraldine is clear for staying another week; but I had better have gone to Scotland than that.

Yours,

J. W. C.

LETTER 238.

Mrs. Russell, Holm Hill.

5 Cheyne Row, Chelsea: Tuesday, Aug. 30, 1861.

Darling! I want to hear about you; and that is lucky for you, if you be at all wanting to hear about me! For I'll be hanged if mere unassisted sense of duty, and that sort of thing, could nerve me to sit down and write a letter in these days, when it takes pretty well all the sense and strength I have left to keep myself soul and body together, doing the thing forced into my hands to do, and answering when I am spoken to. A nice woman I am! But I know you have been in such depths yourself occasionally, and will have sympathy with me, instead of being contemptuous or angry, as your strong-minded, able-bodied women would be; and accordingly strong-minded, able-bodied women are my aversion, and I run out of the road of one as I would from a mad cow. The fact is, had there been nobody in the world to consider except myself, I ought to have 'carried out' that project I had set my heart on of streaming off by myself to Holm Hill, and taking a life-bath, as it were, in my quasi-natural air, in the scene of old affections, not all past and gone, but some still there as alive and warm, thank God, as ever! and only the dearer for being mixed up with those that are dead and gone.

Ah, my dear, your kindness goes to my heart, and makes me like to cry, because I cannot do as you bid me. My servants are pretty well got into the routine of the house now, and if Mr. C. were like other men, he might be left to their care for two or three weeks, without fear of consequences. But he is much more like a spoiled baby than like other men. I tried him alone for a few days, when I was afraid of falling seriously ill, unless I had change of air. Three weeks ago I went with Geraldine Jewsbury to Ramsgate, one of the most accessible sea-side places, where I was within call, as it were, if anything went wrong at home. But the letter that came from him every morning was like the letter of a Babe in the Wood, who would be found buried with dead leaves by the robins if I didn't look to it. So, even if Ramsgate hadn't been the horridest, noisiest place, where I knew nobody, and had nothing to do except swallow sea air (the best of sea air indeed), I couldn't have got stayed there long enough to make it worth the bother of going. I had thought, in going there, that if he got on well enough by himself for the few days, I might take two or three weeks later, and realise my heart's wish after all. But I found him so out of sorts on my return that I gave it up, with inward protest and appeal to posterity.

Again a glimmer of hope arose. Lady Sandwich had taken a villa on the edge of Windsor Forest for a month, and invited us to go with her there. Mr. C. is very fond of that old lady, partly for her own sake, and partly for the late Lady Ashburton's (her daughter). He can take his horse with him there, and his books, and if he miss his sleep one night he can come straight home the next. So, on the whole, after much pressing, he consented to go. And the idea came to me, if he were all right there, might not I slip away meanwhile to you. Before however it had been communicated, he said to me one day: 'What a poor, shivering, nervous wretch I am grown! I declare if you were not to be there to take care of me, and keep all disturbance off me, nothing would induce me to go to that place of Lady Sandwich's, though I daresay it is very necessary for me to go somewhere.' Humph! very flattering, but very inconvenient. And one can't console oneself at my age for a present disappointment with looking forward to next year, one is no longer so sure of one's next year.

One thing I can do, and you can do—we can write oftener. It is a deal nicer to speak face to face from heart to heart. But we might make our correspondence a better thing than it is, if we prevented the need of beginning our letters so often with an apology for silence.

Thanks for all your news. Every little detail about Thornhill people and things is interesting to me. And, oh, many, many thanks for your kind messages to us all! God bless you, dear, and love to the Doctor.   Affectionately yours,

JANE W. CARLYLE.

LETTER 239.

The good old dowager Lady Sandwich had this autumn engaged us to go out with her to a pretty little lodge she had hired for a while in Windsor Forest, to rusticate there. It struck us afterwards, she had felt that this was likely to be her last autumn in this world, and that we, now among the dearest left to her, ought to be there. She was a brave, airy, affectionate, and bright kind of creature; and under her Irish gaieties and fantasticalities concealed an honest generosity of heart, and a clear discernment, and a very firm determination in regard to all practical or essential matters. We willingly engaged, went punctually, and stayed, I think, some twelve or more days, which, except for my own continual state of worn-out nerves, &c., were altogether graceful, touching, and even pleasant. I rode out, and rode back (my Jeannie by railway both times). Windsor Forest sounded something Arcadian when I started, but, alas! I found all that a completely changed matter since the days of Pope and his sylvan eclogues; and the real name of it now to be Windsor Cockneydom unchained. The ride out was nowhere pleasant, in parts disgusting; the ride back I undertook merely because obliged. During my stay I rode daily a great deal; but except within the park, where was a gloomy kind of solitude, very gloomy always to me, I had nowhere any satisfaction in the exercise, nor did Fritz seem to have. Alas! both he and I were getting very sick of riding; and one of us was laden for a long while past and to come far beyond his strength and years. It seems by this letter I was at times a very bad boy; and, alas! my repentant memory answers too clearly Yes. The lumbago, indeed, I have entirely forgotten, but I remember nights sleepless, and long walks, the mornings after which were courageous rather than victorious! I remember the old lady's stately and courteous appearance at dinner, affecting to me, and strange, almost painful. This little scene even to the very name had vanished from me, and Harewood Lodge, when I read it here, reads a whole series of things to me; things sad—now sad as death itself, but good too, perhaps, almost great.

Miss Barnes, King's Road, Chelsea.

Harewood Lodge, Berks: Sept. 22, 1861.

Carina! Oh, Carina! 'Did you ever?' 'No, you never!' It has been an enchantment—a bad spell! the '*quelque chose plus fort que moi*' of French criminals! I don't think a day has passed since I got your letter—certainly not a day has passed since I came here—that I haven't thought of you; and meant to write to you: only I never did it! And why? Were I to assign the only reason which occurs to me for the moment, it would seem incredible to your well-regulated mind. You could never conceive how a woman 'born of respectable parents, and having enjoyed the advantages of a liberal education' (like Judge somebody's malefactor, who, 'instead of which, had gone about the country stealing turkeys!'), should be withheld from doing a thing by just the feeling that she *ought to!* Although if she had ought *not to* she would have done it at the first opportunity! No! You have no belief in such a make of a woman, you! You are too good for believing in her! And one can't do better than believe all women born to a sense of duty 'as the sparks fly upwards' as long as one can.

For the rest, I should have enjoyed this beautiful place excessively if Eve hadn't eaten that unfortunate apple, a great many years ago; in result of which there has, ever since, been always a something to prevent one's feeling oneself in Paradise! The 'something' of the present occasion came in the form of lumbago! not into my own back, but into Mr. C.'s; which made the difference so far as the whole comfort of my life was concerned! For it was the very first day of being here that Mr. C. saw fit to spread his pocket-handkerchief on the grass, just after a heavy shower, and sit down on it! for an hour and more in spite of all my remonstrances! ! The lumbago following in the course of nature, there hasn't been a day that I felt sure of staying over the next, and of not being snatched away like Proserpine; as I was from the Grange last winter! For what avail the 'beauties of nature,' the 'ease with dignity' of a great house, even the Hero Worship accorded one, against the lumbago? Nothing, it would seem! less than nothing! Lumbago, my dear, it is good that you should know in time, admits of but one consolation—of but one happiness! viz.: 'perfect liberty to be as ugly and stupid and disagreeable as ever one likes!' And that consolation, that happiness, that liberty reserves itself for the domestic hearth! As you will find when you are married, I daresay. And so, all the ten days we have been here, it has been a straining on Mr. C.'s part to tear his way through the social amenities back to Chelsea; while I have spent all the time I might have been enjoying myself in expecting to be snatched away!

To-morrow we go finally and positively, though the lumbago is almost disappeared, and we were to have stayed at least a fortnight. Where are you, then? If you are returned to 'the paternal roof,' no need almost of this letter. But I dare say you are gadding about on the face of the earth; 'too happy in not knowing your happiness' of having a paternal roof to stay under! If your father would take me home for his daughter, and pet me as he does you, would I go

dancing off to all points of the compass as you do? No, indeed.
God bless you, anyhow! If you are returned, this letter will be
worth while, as enabling me to look you in the face more or less.

Yours affectionately,

JANE WELSH CARLYLE.

LETTER 240.

January 1, 1862.—'First foot,' perhaps explained already, is a
Scotch superstition about good or ill luck for the whole year being
omened by your liking or otherwise of the first person that accosts
you on New Year's morning. She well knew this to be an idle
babble; but nevertheless it had got hold of her fancy in a sort,
and was of some real importance to her, as other such old super-
stitions were. Thus I have seen her, if anybody made or received
a present of a knife, insist on a penny being given for it, that so it
might become 'purchase,' and not cut the friendship in two. I
used to laugh at these practices, but found them beautiful withal;
how much more amiable than strong-mindedness (which has needed
only deduction of fine qualities) in regard to such things!—T. C.

J. G. Cooke, Esq.

5 Cheyne Row: January 1, 1862.
Ach Gott!

My dear Friend,—What an adorable little proceeding on your
part! I declare I can't remember when I have been as pleased.
Not only a 'good first foot,' but salvation from any possibility of a
'bad first foot,' with which my highly imaginative Scotch mind
(imaginative on the reverse side of things in my present state of
physical weakness) had been worry itself as New Year's Day drew
near. I could hardly believe my ears when little Margaret glided
to my bedside and said, 'Mr. Cooke, ma'am, with this letter and
beautiful egg-cup (!) for you; but he wouldn't come up, as you
were in bed!' That, too, was most considerate of Mr. Cooke! The
'egg-cup' ravished my senses with its beauty and perfect adaptation
to my main passion. I think you must have had it made on purpose for me, it feels already so much a part of myself. And how
early you must have risen to be here at that hour! Dressed, perhaps, by candle-light! Good God! all that for me! Well, I am
grateful, and won't forget this. A talismanic remembrance to
stand between my faith in your kindness for me and any 'babbles'
(my grandfather's word) that may ever attempt, consciously or
unconsciously, to shake it. And so God bless you! and believe
me   Yours affectionately,

JANE WELSH CARLYLE.

LETTER 241.

Miss Barnes, King's Road, Chelsea.

5 Cheyne Row: January 24, 1862.

Oh, you agonising little girl! How could you come down upon me in that slap-dash way, demand of poor, weak, shivery me a positive 'yes' or 'no' as if with a loaded pistol at my head? How can I tell what I shall be up to on the 18th? After such a three months of illness, and relapses, how can I even guess? If I am alive, and able to stand on my hind legs, and to look like a joyful occasion, I shall be only too happy to attend that solemnity. But in my actual state it would be a tempting of Providence to suppress the *if* in my acceptance of your 'amiable invitation.'

As for Mr. C.—my dear, I must confide to you a small domestic passage. I told him what your father had said weeks ago, and he expressed himself as terrified—as was to be expected—at the idea of his being included in anything joyful! and I thought he had forgotten all about it, three or four days after, when he came into my room with evidently something on his mind, and said, 'My dear, there is a small favour I want from you. I want you to not let me be asked to Miss Barnes's marriage, for it would be a real vexation to me to refuse that bonnie wee lassie what she asked, and to her marriage I could not go; it would be the ruin of me for three weeks!' And that is no exaggeration, I can say, who know his ways better than anyone else. He added that, 'the rational thing to be done,' was, that you should 'bring your husband, when you had married him, to spend an evening with him (Mr. C.) in his own house, among quiet things' (me and the cat?).

Your affectionate
JANE W. CARLYLE.

LETTER 242.

Mrs. Russell, Holm Hill.

5 Cheyne Row, Chelsea: Feb. 28, 1862.

Oh, my dear, what a horrid thing![1] It still makes my flesh creep all over whenever I think of it! and I think of it a great deal oftener than there is occasion for, since, thank God, he is now on foot

---

[1] Some accident which had befallen Dr. Russell.

again! But I have seen that safe! I can appreciate to the full
the crash of its lid, smack down on human fingers! Mercy! what
a piece of capital good stuff the Doctor must have been made of
originally, that his fingers should have stuck together through such
an accident, instead of being all pounded into mush! That is not
what surprises me most, however, in the business. What surprises
me most is, that the Doctor being a doctor, and a good, skilful one,
should have gone about after, braving such a hurt, as though he
had never in his life heard of lockjaw, or gangrene, or fever! I
don't wonder that you were terrified. I wonder rather that you
are not, now when your nursing is no more needed, in a brain fever
yourself. The longer I live, the more I am certified that men, in
all that relates to their own health, have not common sense!
whether it be their pride, or their impatience, or their obstinacy, or
their ingrained spirit of contradiction, that stupefies and misleads
them, the result is always a certain amount of idiocy, or distraction
in their dealings with their own bodies! I am not generalising from
my own husband. I know that he is a quite extravagant example
of that want of common sense in bodily matters which I complain
of. Few men (even) are so lost to themselves as to dry their soaked
trowsers on their legs! (as he does) or swallow five grains of mercury in the middle of the day, and then walk or ride three hours
under a plunge of rain! (as he does) &c. &c. But men generally,
all of them I have ever had to do with—even your sensible husband
included, you see—drive the poor women, who care for them, to
despair, either by their wild impatience of bodily suffering, and the
exaggerated moan they make over it, or else by their reckless defiance
of it, and neglect of every dictate of prudence! There! You may
tell the Doctor what I say! It won't do him the slightest good
against next time; but it is well he should know what one thinks of
him—that one does not approve of such costly heroism at all!

I have nothing new to tell you which is lucky; as the things that
have happened this long time back have been of a disastrous sort.

I go out now occasionally for a drive—walking tires me too much.
I have even been twice out at dinner last week, and was at a wedding
besides! The two dinners were of the quietest: at the one (Miss
Baring's), nobody but Lord Ashburton, who had come up from the
Grange for a consultation; at the other (Lady Sandwich's), nobody
but the Marchioness of Lothian, who, having lived thirty years in
Scotland, is as good as a Scotchwoman. But the wedding [1] was an

---

[1] Barnes's.

immense affair! It was my doctor's little daughter, who was being married, after a three years' engagement; and as soon as she was engaged, she had made me promise to attend her wedding. I had rather wished to see a marriage performed in a church with all the forms, the eight bridesmaids, &c. &c. But I had renounced all idea of going to the church, for fear of being laid up with a fresh cold; and meant to attend only the breakfast party after, in which I took less interest. But imagine how good the people here are to me. Our rector, in whose church (St. Luke's) the marriage was to take place, being told by his wife I wished to go, but durstn't for fear of the coldness of the church, ordered the fires to be kept up from Sunday over into Tuesday morning! besides a rousing fire in the vestry, where I sat at my ease till the moment the ceremony began! I was much pressed afterwards to acknowledge how superior the English way of marrying was to the Scotch, and asked how I had liked it. I said my feelings were very mixed. 'Mixed?' the rector asked, 'mixed of what?' 'Well,' I said, 'it looked to me something betwixt a religious ceremony and a—pantomime!' So it is. There were forty-four people at the breakfast!

Your ever affectionate
J. W. CARLYLE.

LETTER 243.

Mrs. Russell, Holm Hill.

5 Cheyne Row, Chelsea: Thursday, June 5, 1862.

Dearest Mary,—I cannot count the letters I have written to you in my head within the last six weeks, they have been so many; I have written them mostly before getting out of bed in the morning, or while lying awake at night. But in the day-time, with pen and ink at hand, I have been always, always, always too sick or too bothered to put them on paper, have indeed been writing to nobody, if that be any excuse for not writing to you. The beginning of warm weather is as trying for me, in a different way, as winter was, and so many sad things have happened.

Just when the freshness of one sorrow was wearing off, there has come another. First Elizabeth Pepoli, then Lady Sandwich, then Mrs. Twisleton: [1] the three people in all London whose

---

[1] A very beautiful and clever little Boston lady, wife of Hon. Edward Twisleton, and much about us for the six or seven years she lived here. I well remember her affecting funeral (old Fiennes Castle, in Oxfordshire), and my ride thither with Browning, &c.

friendship I had most dependence on. Nobody will believe the
loss Lady Sandwich is to us. They say 'a woman of eighty! that
is not to be regretted.' But her intimate friends know that this
woman of eighty was the most charming companion and the loyal-
est, warmest friend; was the only person in London or in the world
that Mr. C. went regularly to see. Twice a week he used to call
for her; and now his horse makes for her house whenever he gets
into the region of Grosvenor Square, and does not see or understand the escutcheon that turns me sick as I drive past. Dear little
Mrs. Twisleton, so young, and beautiful, and clever, so admired in
society and adored at home, is a loss that everyone can appreciate!
And the strong affection she testified for me, through her long terrible illness, has made her death a keener grief than I thought it
would be.

I should have been thankful to be away from here—anywhere—
at the bottom of a coal-pit, to think over this in quiet, safe from
the breaking in of all the idlers 'come up' to that great vulgar
show of an 'Exhibition,' and safe from the endless weary chatter
about it. Nothing could keep me here for an hour but Mr. C.'s
determination to stay;—since at the top of the house he is safe
enough from tiresome interruptions, simply refusing to see anybody, which, alas! makes it all the more needful for me to be civil.
Here he will stay and work on; (what an idea you have all got in
your heads, that, having published a third volume he must be at
ease in Zion, when two more volumes are to come, and one wholly
unwritten;) and to leave him in the present state of things is what
I cannot make up my mind to. If I go on in this way, however, I
shall die, and just before it comes to that extremity I shall probably
muster the necessary resolution.

Mr. C.'s comfort under the confusion of the Exhibition is that
'It is to be hoped it will end in total bankruptcy.' They say the
guarantees will be called on to pay twenty-five per cent.

Kindest love to the doctor; a hearty kiss to yourself.

Yours affectionately,
JANE W. CARLYLE.

LETTER 244.

We were with the Ashburtons, she first, for a week or more, then
both of us for perhaps a week longer. *Ay de mi!* (October 29,
1869.)

To Thomas Carlyle, Chelsea.

West Cliff Hotel: Wednesday, July 2, 1862.

Thanks, dear! especially for telling me about Mrs. Forster. I had been so vexed at myself for not begging you to go again and send me word.

Lady A. came and sat awhile in my room last night, and, speaking of Miss Bromley's departure, I took occasion to say that, ' As she and I came on the same day, I felt as if I ought to have also gone on the same day.' The answer to which was a very cordial 'Nonsense, my dear friend!' I was expected to stay as long as they did, ' or ' (when I shook my head at that) ' as long at all events as I could possibly make it convenient.' There was no doubt whatever about her present wish being to that effect. And then came up the old question as a new one, ' Did I think he would come? It would be such a pleasure to Bingham, now that he could move about.' I said, you might perhaps be persuaded to come for a very short visit, but, &c. &c. That was it! A short visit was evidently what she wanted, and she *does* want that; but she did not see her way through a long one, in the circumstances I could see, and I don't wonder. She would write herself to-day, and urge you to come on Saturday and stay till Monday—' You might surely do that!'

Now that is just what you must do. Even two days of sea will benefit you; and it can be had at little sacrifice of anything. You don't need to trouble about clothes; what you could bring in your carpet-bag would be enough; there is no elaborate dressing for dinner here; and the tide is convenient, and there is a horse! And Lady A. says she can give you ' a perfectly quiet room:'—indeed, mine is quiet as the grave from outside noises; not a cock nor a dog in all Folkestone I think! And the cookery, which is objected to as all too English, would suit you:—constant loins of roast mutton, and constant boiled chickens! Now pray take no counsel with flesh and blood, but come straight off on Saturday morning, according to the invitation that will reach you (I expect) along with this. And in all likelihood we will go home together on Monday.

If you don't come, I will stay away as long as ever they will keep me, just to spite you!

Look up in your topographical book for Saltwood Castle. Lady A. asked, when we were there to-day, if I thought you would be able to tell us about it; and I said, 'Of course you would:' Salt-wood Castle, near Folkestone.

There is here too a review of 'Frederick' in the 'Cornhill,' which would amuse you! Adoring your genius, but absolutely horror-struck at your 'scorn,' which is 'become normal.' How you dare to utter such blasphemy against Messrs. Leibnitz and Maupertius ! ! I could not help bursting out laughing at the man's sacred horror, as if he had been speaking of Milton's Devil!

Yours ever,

J. W. C.

Horrible paper! I have no other.

LETTER 245.

Mrs. Russell, Holm Hill.

5 Cheyne Row, Chelsea: July 20, 1862.

Dearest Mary,—When you wrote last you were going somewhere —to see your cousin, I think. Is that visit paid? and what other visits have you to pay? And how are you? I fear but poorly from your late letters; but are you well enough to feel any pleasure in— in—in seeing me if I should come?

Look here! I am not sure about it! But Mr. C. said something this morning that I am determined to view as permission for me to go away by myself—where I please and when I please for a very little while. We had got into words about an invitation to the Marquis of Lothian's, in Norfolk. I had written a refusal by his (Mr. C.'s) desire, and Lady Lothian had written to me a second letter, holding out as inducements for altering his mind that there was a wonderfully fine library at Blickling Park, and that Lord Lothian's health prevented company; and Mr. C., tempted a little by the library and the no company, had suggested I might write that if the weather got unbearable! and if he got to a place in his work where he could gather up some papers and take them with him! and if—if—if ever so many things, he might perhaps—that is, we might perhaps—come 'by and by'! ! ! I had said 'by no means. I have written a refusal by your desire; I shall gladly now write an acceptance by your desire; but neither yes nor no, or yes and no both in one, I can't and won't write; you must do that sort of thing yourself!' And then he told me, 'Since I was so im-patient about it,' I had better go by myself. To which I answered that it wouldn't be there that I would go by myself, nor to the Trevelyans, nor the Davenport Bromleys; but to Scotland to Mrs. Russell. 'Then go to Mrs. Russell—pack yourself up and be off as soon as you like.'

Now it wasn't a very gracious permission, still it was a permission —at least I choose to regard it as such; and if I had been quite sure how you were situated—whether you were at home, without other visitor, well enough to be bothered with me, &c. &c., I should have said on the spot, 'Thanks! I will go then on such a day!'

I know to my sorrow that, if I should be long absent, things would go to sixes and sevens, and I should find mischievous habits acquired in the kitchen department, which it would take months to reform—if ever. But my week at Folkestone with the Ashburtons passed off with impunity;—and their (the servants') moralities might surely hold out for a fortnight or so; which would give plenty of time to see you, and look about on the dear old places, and go round by Edinburgh for a kiss of old Betty.

You see how it is, however, for I have told you exactly what passed;—and you see it is not a very settled question. Without further speech with Mr. C. I can't just say, 'I am coming if you will have me!' But if you say you will have me, can have me soon, without inconvenience; then I will myself open the further speech and ascertain if he means to stand to his word, and look favourably on my going for a week or two.

I say forgive me coming to you, year after year, with these indecisions. Next to being undecided oneself the greatest misery is to be mixed up with undecided people. I myself know always mighty well what I want; and buts and ifs and possiblys are not words in my natural vocabulary, for all so often as I am obliged to use them. If I plague you with my uncertainties, believe me I plague myself quite as much or more.

Affectionately yours,

J. CARLYLE.

LETTER 246.

Mrs. Russell, Holm Hill.

5 Cheyne Row, Chelsea: Saturday, Aug. 2, 1862.

Dearest Mary,—Your letter of this morning had the same effect that a glass of port wine, administered in my babyhood, was recorded to have had on a less dignified organ: 'Port wine' (I was said to have said to my mother, with the suddenness of Balaam's ass) 'mak's inside a' cozy!' So indeed did your cordial letter mak' heart a' cozy. On the strength of the coziness, I said right out to Mr. C., sitting opposite: 'How long had you to wait at Carlisle for the train that put you down at the Gill at seven in the morning?' No opening could have been better. He was taken quite by surprise; and, before he had time to consider my going as a question, he found himself engaged in considerations of the best way to go. After that he could not well go back upon his implied assent.[1] The only 'demurrer' he could put in, with a good grace, was to ask: 'What did I mean to do with my foot?' I meant it to get well, I said, in a few days; of course I shouldn't think of going from home on one leg. This related to a bruised, or sprained, or someway bedevilled foot, that I came by the very day I had written to you, as if, I almost felt, with a shudder at the time, it was the monition of Providence that I should go on no such journey. I was returning from Islington where I had been to ask after the lamed foot (!) of the little lady who was my honorary nurse[2] last winter. The Islington omnibus put me down within some eighth part of a mile of my own house. I had one rather dark street to pass through first—taking the shortest way—and it was near eleven o'clock at night. I didn't care for being alone so late; but I didn't want to be seen by any of the low people of that street alone. So I stepped off the pavement to avoid passing close to a small group standing talking at a door; when I had cleared these only people to be seen in the whole street, I was stepping back on to the pavement, when, the curbstone being higher than I noticed in the shadow, I struck the side of my right foot violently against it and was tripped over, and fell smack down, full length on the pavement.[3]

Considering how easily I might have broken my ribs, it is wonderful that the fall did me no harm. I scrambled up directly; but the foot I had struck on the curbstone before falling was dreadfully sore, and it was made worse, you may believe, by having to use it, after a sort, to get myself home. How I got home at all, even in holding on to walls and railings, I can't think. But once at home on a chair, I couldn't touch the ground with it on any account. Mr. C. had to carry me to bed, at the imminent risk of knocking my head off against the lintels. So I wouldn't be carried by him any more, my head being of more consequence to me than my foot.

---

[1] Alas! how little did I ever *know* of these secret wishes and necessities—now or ever!

[2] Mrs. Dilberoglue (?).   [3] I remember, and may well.

It was dreadfully swelled for a couple of days; but to-day, though I still cannot get a shoe on, or walk, it is so much better that I am sure it will be all right presently. In a few days I hope to be able to write that I am road-worthy, and I will only wait for that. It is a most provoking little accident, for delays are so dangerous. I should have wished after my experiences of late summers to go to you at once, before any ' pigs' have time to 'run through.'

And now I needn't be saying more but that God grant nothing may prevent our meeting this time.

Love to the Doctor.

Affectionately yours,

JANE CARLYLE.

LETTER 247.

To Thomas Carlyle, Esq., Chelsea.

Holm Hill, Thornhill: August 13, 1862.

Oh, my dear, I wish they hadn't started that carpet-lifting and chimney-sweeping process so immediately, but left you time to recover my loss (if any) in the usual 'peace and quietness'! That chimney in my bedroom had to be swept, however, before winter came; and no time so good as when I was on my travels. You don't complain: but your few lines this morning make the impression on me of having been written under 'a dark brown shadd!' I told Maria if she observed you to be mismanaging yourself, and going off your sleep and all that sort of thing, to tell me, and I should be back like a returned sky-rocket.

For myself, I am all right. I was in bed before eleven o'clock struck, with a stiff little tumbler of whisky toddy in my head, and I went to sleep at once, and slept on, with only some half-dozen awakenings, till the maid brought in my hot water at eight o'clock! My foot, as well as my 'interior,' is benefited by the good night. It was too lame for anything yesterday. But there was no temptation to use it much yesterday; it rained without intermission. To-day is very cloudy, but not wet as yet; and we are going for a drive in the close carriage. Dr. Russell has both an open and a close carriage, the lucky man! Indeed he has as pretty and well-equipped a place here as any reasonable creature could desire. But Mrs. Russell has never ceased to regret the tumble-down old house in Thornhill, 'where there was always something going on!' 'Looking out on the trees and the river here makes her so melancholy,'

II.—8

she says, that she feels sometimes as if she should lose her senses! The wished-for, as usual, come too late! Ease with dignity, when the habits of a lifetime have made her incapable of enjoying it!

Would you tell Maria to put a bit of paper round the little long-shaped paste-board box, in my little drawer next the drawing-room, containing the two ornamental hair-pins, and send them to me by post;—they are quite light; I want them to give away. Also if you were to put a couple of good quill-pens of your own making in besides the hair-pins, 'it would be a great advantage.' I have written to say a word expressly about the tobacco. Oh, please, do go to bed at a reasonable hour, and don't overwork yourself, and consider you are no longer a child!

Faithfully yours,

J. W. C.

LETTER 248.

To Mrs. Austin, The Gill, Annan.

Holm Hill, Thornhill, Dumfries: Thursday, Aug. 14, 1862.

Oh, my little woman, how glad I was to recognise your face through the glass of the carriage window, all dimmed with human breath! And how frightened I was the train would move, while you were clambering up like a school-boy to kiss me! And how I grudged the long walk there and back for you, and the waiting. Still you did well to come, for it (your coming) quite brightened up my spirits for the last miles of my journey, which are apt to be mortally tiresome. I had meant to wave my handkerchief from the window when we passed the Gill, but I found no seat vacant except the middle one; and disagreeable women, on each side of me, closed the windows all but an inch, so to make any demonstration had been impossible. The more my gladness to catch sight of your very face. And Jane and her husband and daughter were waiting for me at Dumfries, having heard of my coming from Dr. Carlyle. 'So the latter end of that woman' (meaning me) 'was better than the beginning.'

Dr. Russell was waiting for me—had been waiting more than an hour, like everyone else—with his carriage, in which I was conveyed through ways, happily for me, clothed in darkness, so that the first object I saw was Mrs. Russell at the door of their new home. It is a most beautiful house and place they have made of old Holm Hill. And I do not see Templand from the windows as I feared I should. The trees have grown up so high.

The first night I couldn't sleep a bit for agitation of mind, far more than fatigue of body. The next night I slept; last night again not. So to-day I feel rather ghastly. Then it has rained pretty much without intermission. Yesterday we took a very short drive between showers, and that was the only time I have crossed the threshold; besides the bad weather I brought away with me a recently sprained foot, which makes walking both painful and imprudent.

Under these circumstances I have not yet formed any plan for my future travels; but shall tell you in a few days whether I will pay you a little visit on the road home, or run down from here, and back again. I will certainly not let that brief meeting stand for all, unless you forbid me to come. But I have all along looked to be guided by circumstances in this journey.

My stay is to be determined by the accounts I get of Mr. C. from himself, and (still more dependably) from my housemaid Maria; and my road back, whether as I came or by Edinburgh, to be decided on when I shall have heard from Lady Stanley and another English friend on the North Western line. But I would not leave you wondering what was become of me, or if it had been really me or my wraith you had seen.

In a few days, then, you will hear further. Meanwhile

Your affectionate

J. W. C.

LETTER 249.

To Mrs. Austin, The Gill, Annan.

Holm Hill: Saturday, Aug. 30, 1862.

My dear, ever kind Mary,—In the first place, God bless you and yours. Secondly, I am 'all right' or pretty nearly so. Thirdly, I forward the proof-sheet of Mrs. Oliphant's book which I promised, and something else which was not promised—a photograph of my interesting self, taken by a Thornhill hairdresser, and not so very bad, it strikes me, as photographs go. This last blessed item of my sending is intended as a present to your husband, 'all to himself,' as the children say.

A letter from Mr. C. to me was forwarded from Scotsbrig to the Doctor, and given to me at the station, and another letter from Mr. C. awaited me at Thornhill; a very attentive Mr. C. really!

I have no time to spare for writing more than the absolutely needful. Six letters by post this morning, most of them needing immediate answer, and we are to drive to Morton Castle before dinner.

God keep you all, well and mindful of me till I come again.

Yours affectionately,

JANE CARLYLE.

LETTER 250.

To T. Carlyle, Esq., Chelsea.

Craigenvilla: Tuesday, Sept. 2, 1862.

Oh, you stupid, stupid Good! not to know my handwriting when you see it at this time of day. It was I who directed that photograph and posted it at Thornhill. I just turned my handwriting a little back, and sent it, without a word, to puzzle you, forgetting that the post-mark would betray where it came from. It was done by a Thornhill hairdresser; Mrs. Russell and I got taken one day for fun, and if I had dreamt of coming out so well I would have dressed myself better, and turned the best side of my face.

My departure from Nithsdale was like the partings of dear old long ago, before one had experienced what ' time will teach the softest heart, unmoved to meet, ungrieved to part,' as the immortal Mr. Terrot once wrote. And then the journey through the hills to that little lonely churchyard [1]—all that caused me so many tears, that to-day my eyes are out of my head, and I am sick and sore. And, of course, sleep was out of the question after such a day of emotion—when so ill to be caught at the best of times—and I have had just one hour of broken slumber (from five till six), and I was up at six yesterday morning. So I mustn't go after Betty to-day; she would be too shocked with my looks. Grace and I will take a short drive in an omnibus (for a change). Neither must I sit writing to you, in detail, for my head spins round, and I could tell you nothing worth the effort of telling it. I left a letter to be posted at Thornhill yesterday.

So Garibaldi—or, as a man in the carriage with me last evening was calling him, Garri Bauldy—is wounded and captured already —luck, I should say, to the poor fellows he was leading to destruction! Mazzini will be thankful he must have reached Garibaldi; it is to be hoped he is not taken also, but he went with his eyes perfectly open to the madness.

---

[1] Crawford, where her mother's grave is.

Grace was waiting at the train for me, and instantly found me under my hat and feather in the dark. She said it was by a motion of my hand.

They are all most kind. Elizabeth not so poorly as I expected to find her; Grace and Ann younger-looking than last time—hair raven black, far blacker than mine. Good-bye! I hope to sleep to-night; for I will have a dose of morphia now that I am near Duncan and Flockhart, and then I will be up to a better letter than this. I have left Grace to make out the 'old goose,'[1] and tell me the needful.   Your ever

J. W. C.

LETTER 251.

Mrs. Russell, Holm Hill, Thornhill.

Craigenvilla, Morningside: Tuesday, Sept. 2, 1862.

My darling!—Nature prompts me to write just a line, though I am not up to a letter to-day, at least to any other letter than the daily one to Mr. C., which must be written dead or alive. Imagine! after such a tiring day, I never closed my eyes till after five this morning! and was awake again for good, or rather for bad, before six struck! My eyes are almost out of my head this morning; and tell the Doctor, or rather don't tell him, I will have a dose of morphia to-night!—am just going in an omnibus to Duncan and Flockhart's for it. It will calm down my mind for once—generally my mind needs no calming, being sunk in apathy. And this won't do to go on!

Mr. C. writes this morning that he had received a letter in the handwriting of Dr. Russell (!) (my own handwriting slightly disguised), and 'had torn it open in a fright!! thinking that the Doctor was writing to tell I was ill! and found a photograph of me, really very like indeed,' but not a word 'from the Doctor' inside! He took it as a sign that I was off! (why, in all the world, take it as that?) 'but it would have been an additional favour had the Doctor written just a line!'

Grace was waiting at the station for me, much to my astonishment; and discovered me at once, under the hat and feather, actually! She said by 'a motion of my hand'! The drains are all torn up at Morningside, and she was afraid I would not get across the rubbish in my cab without a pilot. They are all looking well, I

---

[1] Some foolish letter to me.

think—even Elizabeth. Many friendly inquiries about you, and love to be sent.

Oh, my dear, my dear! My head is full of wool! Shall I ever forget these green hills, and that lonely churchyard, and your dear, gentle face!

Oh, how I wish I had a sleep!

Your own friend,

JANE CARLYLE.

The roots are all in the garden.

LETTER 252.

To T. Carlyle, Esq., Chelsea.

Craigenvilla, Morningside (Edinburgh): Thursday, Sept. 4, 1862.

'Two afflictions make a consolation'—of a sort! The disappointment of not receiving the usual good words from you this morning comforted my conscience at least for having failed in my own writing yesterday. I could figure you eating your breakfast at Cheyne Row, without any letter from me, with no particular pang of remorse; when I was eating my breakfast here with only the direction on 'Orley Farm' for a relish to my indifferent tea! It was partly the morphia that hindered me yesterday, and partly the rain. The morphia, which answered the end capitally, and procured me the only really sound sleep I have had since I went on my travels, made me feel too listless for writing before going to Betty's; and the walk through the rain to the cab when we returned made me too tired for writing after in time for the Morningside post.

Well, I have seen Betty, and Betty has seen me. Poor dear! It wasn't so 'good a joy' as it might have been; for Ann and Grace in their kindness would not let me go by myself, and the three of us were too many for the wee house and for Betty's nerves, which aren't what they were. But she made the best of that as of everything else. 'It's weel they're so kind to ye, dear; and it's richt,' she said, during a minute we were alone together. She gave me the 'stockns' (beautiful fine white ones), and a little packet of peppermint lozenges were lying beside them, 'in case I ever cam'.' Dear, kind soul! her heart is the same warm loyal heart; but these seven years of nursing have made terrible alterations in her; her hair is white as snow, and her face is so fined away that it looks as if one might blow it away like powder. I don't think she can stand much longer of it. George (poor patient 'Garg'!) is neither better nor worse; his mind not weakened at all, I think (which is wonderful). Old Braid keeps himself in health by much working in his garden, which is prolific. 'Sic a crapp o' gude peas, dear! Oh, if I could have sent Mr. Carlyle a wee dish o' them to cheer him up when he was alane, poor man!' 'Oh, dear!' she said, again catching my arm excitedly, 'wad onybody believe it? He—yer gudeman—direcks "Punch" till us every week, his ain sell, to sic as us!' Mr. Braid did not know me when I went in at the door the first; and when I taxed him with it he said, 'How should I ken ye? Ye lookit like a bit skelt o' a lassie, wi' that daft wee thing a-tap o' yer heed!'

I mean to get home, please God, at the beginning of next week. I cannot fix the day just yet, being 'entangled in details' with the Auchtertool people. I have seen nobody here but the Braids—indeed, there is nobody I much care to see. A most uninteresting place Edinburgh is become. I would like to spend an hour at Haddington in the dark! But I 'don't see my way' to that. I was glad to hear that Scotsbrig Jenny was getting over her bad fit. Grace has just come in, and sends her regards.

Yours ever,

JANE CARLYLE.

LETTER 253.

To T. Carlyle, Chelsea.

Craigenvilla (Edinburgh): Friday, Sept. 5, 1862.

Thanks, dear; here is a nice little letter this morning, which has had the double effect of satisfying my anxieties and delivering me from 'prayers.' I ran up to my room with it, and shut myself in, and when I issued forth again, prayers were over! What luck! My aunts are as kind to me as they can be—all three of them—and they exert themselves beyond their strength, I can see, to make my visit pleasant to me; but still I am like a fish out of water in this element of religiosity, or rather like a human being *in* water, and the water hot.

I am glad you have heard from my lady at last. I was beginning to not understand it; to fear either you or I must have in some way displeased her. If you could bring yourself to go to the Grange at once I shouldn't at all mind your being away when I arrived; should rather like to transact my fatigues and my acclimatising 'in a place by myself.' And we might still have the 'sacred week' of idling and sightseeing (an exceptional week in our mutual life, it would be) after your return.

I find I cannot get off from Auchtertool. I shouldn't dislike a couple of days there (though many days couldn't be endured) if it weren't for that ' crossing.' But, like it or not, I must just ' cross and recross'! Maggie is returned. Walter has put off joining Alexander at Crawford; they are all expecting me, and the only expedient by which I could have avoided visiting them without giving offence to their kind feelings, viz., inviting them all to spend a day with me here, cannot be ' carried out'—for ' reasons it may be interesting not to state.' After all I have no kinder relative or friend in the world than poor Walter. Every summer, when invitations were not so plenty, his house, and all that is his, has been placed at my disposal. It is the only house where I could go, without an invitation, at any time that suited myself; and, considering all that, I must just ' cross' to-morrow, in the intention, however, of staying only two days. I should have gone to-day but for a letter of Walter's—' mis-sent to Liberton '— and so not reaching me in time.

I am now going off to town with Grace to get her photograph taken—' for Jeannie's book,' she says; but I doubt the singleness of the alleged motive. I shall call for Mrs. Stirling—who else? Alas, my old friends are ' all wed away'![1]

I return the letter, which seems to me perfectly serious and rather sensible; only what of Shakespeare? Shakespeare ' never did the like o't!'

Address here; I shall find it (the letter) on my return from Auchtertool, if I am not here before it. It was thunder and lightning and waterspouts yesterday; terrible for laying the crops, surely.

Yours ever,
JANE W. CARLYLE.

LETTER 254.

Mrs. Russell, Holm Hill.

Auchtertool Manse: Monday, Sept. 8, 1862.

So long as I am in Scotland, my darling, I cannot help feeling that my head-quarters is Holm Hill! though I go buzzing here and there, like a ' Bum-bee ' in the neighbourhood of its hive. Everywhere that I go I am warmly welcomed, and made much of; but

---

[1] *Flowers of the Forest.*

nowhere that I go do I feel so at home, in an element so congenial to me, as with you and the Doctor! At Craigenvilla, though treated as a niece, and perhaps even a favourite niece, I am always reacting against the self-assumption, and the religiosity (not the religion, mind!); and here, though I am 'cousin'—their one cousin, for whom their naturally hospitable and kindly natures are doubly hospitable and kindly—still I miss that congeniality which comes of having mutually suffered, and taken one's suffering to heart! I feel here as if I were 'playing' with nice, pretty, well-behaved children! I almost envy them their light-hearted capacity of being engrossed with trifles! And yet, not that! there is a deeper joy in one's own sorrowful memories surely, than in this gaiety that comes of 'never minding'! Would I, would you, cease to regret the dear ones we have lost if we could? Would we be light-hearted, at the cost of having nothing in one's heart very precious or sacred? Oh, no! better ever such grief for the lost, than never to have loved anyone enough to have one's equanimity disturbed by the loss!

I came here on Saturday; was to have come on Friday, but had to wait for a letter of Walter's 'mis-sent to Liberton.' I go back to Morningside to-morrow forenoon, unless it 'rains cats and dogs!' And then to London after one day's rest! And after all my haste —at least haste after leaving Holm Hill—the chances are I shall find Mr. C. just gone to the Grange. He had 'partly decided on going next Tuesday (to-morrow).' And, if I wasn't home in time to go with him, he had engaged I would join him there! Don't he wish he may get me! He will have to stay considerably longer than the 'one week' he talks of, before I shall feel disposed to 'take the road' again! In fact, I should greatly like a few days 'all to myself,' to sleep off my fatigues, and get acclimatised, before having to resume my duties as mistress of the house.

Alex. Welsh came to Crawford the 'next day,' as predicted; but 'his Reverence' never joined him there. And Alex., finding the fishing as bad as possible, went on to spend a few days with the Chrystals in Glasgow, before returning to Liverpool.

God keep you, dearest friend; after the Doctor, there is nobody you are so precious to as to me! I will write from Chelsea.

Your loving

J. CARLYLE.

II.—8*

LETTER 255.

Mrs. Russell, Holm Hill.

5 Cheyne Row: Tuesday night, Sept. 30, 1862.

Dearest of Friends,—I am writing two lines at this late hour, because I don't want the feeling of closeness that has outlived the precious three weeks we were together to die out through length of silence. For the rest, I am not in good case for writing a pleasant letter, having had no sleep last night, and the bad night not having been compensated, as my bad nights at Holm Hill were, strangely enough, by a good day. And I am bothered, too, with preparations for a journey to-morrow. What a locomotive animal I have suddenly become! Yes, it is a fact, my dear, that to-morrow [1] I am bound for Dover, to stay till Monday with that lady we call 'the flight of Skylarks,' [2] who was wanting me to come home by her place in Derbyshire. She is now at Dover, in lodgings, for the benefit of sea air; and has invited me there since I wouldn't go to Wooton Hall, and Mr. C., who thought I ought to have come home by her, wishes me to go. And I am sure I have no objections; for I like her much, and I like the sea much. But I 'am not to be staying away this time,' he says, ' and leaving him long by himself again.' No fear! I must return to London on Monday, or I should not see Charlotte Cushman (who is now in Liverpool and returns here on Thursday) before her departure for Rome. Indeed, charming as I think the 'flight of Skylarks,' I should not be unsettling myself again if only I had kept the better health and spirits I brought back from Scotland. It was too much to hope, however, that I could keep all that long. The clammy heavy weather we have had for the last week has put me all wrong somehow. I am sick at stomach, or at heart (I can't tell which), and have a continual irritation in my bits of 'interiors,' and horrid nights, for all which, I daresay, the sea is the best medicine. I shall tell you how it has answered when I come back.

Love to the Doctor.   Your own
                                         J. W. C.

---

[1] Went October 1.
[2] Miss Davenport Bromley; her great-grandfather at ' Wooton,' in Staffordshire, was the ' Mr. Davenport' who gave shelter to Rousseau.

LETTER 256.

T. Carlyle, Esq., Chelsea.

1 Sidney Villas, Dover: Wednesday afternoon, Oct. 1, 1862.

I may take a reasonable sheet of paper, dear! for, besides being not 'too tired for writing,' I have abundance of time for writing, 'the Larks'[1] being all far up out of sight, beyond the visible sky! looking for me there. My journey was successful, and I stepped out at Dover worth half a dozen of the woman I left Chelsea. Curious what a curative effect a railway journey has on me always, while you it makes pigs and whistles of! Is it the motion, or is it the changed air? 'God knows!'

The first thing that befell me at Dover was a disappointment— no Larks waiting! not a feather of them to be discovered by the naked eye. The next thing that befell me was to be deceived and betrayed and entirely discomfited by—a sailor. After looking about for the Larks some ten minutes, and being persecuted as long by pressing proposals from cabmen and omnibus conductors, I was asking a porter how far it was to Sidney Villas. The porter not knowing the place, a sailor came forward and said he knew it, that it 'was just a few steps; I would be there in a minute if I liked to walk, and he would carry my trunk for me.' And, without waiting to have the question debated, he threw my trunk over his shoulder and walked off. I followed, quite taken by assault. And we walked on and on, and oh, such a distance!—certainly two miles at least, the sailor pretending to not hear every time I remonstrated, or assuring me 'I couldn't find a prettier walk in all Dover than this.' At last we reached Sidney Villas; and when I accused my sailor of having basely misled me that he might have a job, he candidly owned, 'Well, things are dear just now, and few jobs going,' wiping the sweat from his brow at the same time, and looking delighted with the shilling I gave him. I thought it was all gone to the devil together when the man who answered the bell denied that Miss Bromley was there. On cross-questioning, however, he explained that she did reside there, but was not at home— was 'gone to the railway to meet a lady '—and his eye just then squinting on my portmanteau, he exclaimed, with sudden cordiality, 'Perhaps you are the lady?' I owned the soft impeachment

[1] See note, p. 178.

and was shown to the bedroom prepared for me, and have washed and unpacked. Meanwhile Miss B.'s maid, who had gone to one station while Miss B. went to the other to make sure of me, returned and gave me a cup of tea, and then went off to catch the poor dear Larks, who was waiting for me at the wrong station. There being a third station (the one at which I landed), it hadn't occurred to either mistress or maid to ask at which of the three stations the three o'clock train stopped.

Larks come with feathers all in a fluff. 'So dreadfully sorry,' &c. &c. Dinner not till seven, and to be enlivened by the presence of Mr. Brookfield, whom she had met while looking for me. 'Seven!' and I had only one small cup of tea and one slice of etherial bread and butter. But we ' must make it *do.*'

This house is within a stone-cast of the sea, and also, alas! of the pier; so that there is as much squealing of children at this moment as if it were Cheyne Row. Nothing but a white blind to keep out the light of a large window. But with shutters and stillness, and all possible furtherance, I was finding sleep impossible at home; so perhaps it may suit the contradictory nature of the animal to sleep here without them.

Now, upon my word, this is a fairly long letter to be still in the first day of absence. It will, at least, show that I am less ghastly sick and with less worry in my interior than when I left in the morning.

Yours anyhow,

J. W. CARLYLE.

LETTER 257.

T. Carlyle, Esq., Chelsea.

1 Sidney Villas, Dover: Friday, Oct. 3, 1862.

Oh, my dear! I ' did design ' to write you a nice long letter today. But 'you must just excuse us ' again. I am the victim of ' circumstances over which I have no control.' I must put you off with a few lines, and lie down on the sofa of my bedroom, and try to get warm, or it will be the worse for me. You see I am taking every day a warm sea-bath, hoping to derive benefit from it —'cha-arge' half-a-crown. But, never mind, if I can stave off an illness at the beginning of winter, I shall save in doctor's bills! Well, my bath to-day made me excessively sleepy, and I lay down to sleep, and in five minutes I was called down to luncheon, and after luncheon I must go with Miss Bromley to call for Lady Doyle, with whom Miss Wynne, just arrived from Carlsbad, had been yesterday—might still be to-day. Our call executed, it was proposed we should drive on to Shakespeare's Cliff, and when there, we were driven away 'over the heights'—a most alarming road—all this time in an open carriage; and now that we are come in there is not a fire anywhere—never is any fire to warm myself at—and so I am not at all in right trim for letter-writing. And common prudence requires I should lie down and get into heat.

For the rest it is all right. I have slept very fairly both nights in spite of—'many things!' Miss B. is kind and charming, the place is 'delicious,' and I am certainly much better for the change. But, for all that, I am coming home without fail at the time I fixed; not from any 'puritanical' adherence to my word given, but that by Monday I shall have had enough of it and got all the good to be got. Miss B. has pressed me earnestly to stay till Monday week; but no need to bid *me*—'be firm, Alicia!'

What a pity about poor Bessy! She says she 'was always a worshipper of genius, and recollects one day in particular when Mr. Carlyle poured out such a stream of continuous eloquence that she was forcibly reminded of the lady who spoke pearls and diamonds in the fairy tale.' She is very proud of her book and photograph. That absurd corkmaker sends me his photograph. I will bring his letter for you; inclosed in mine it is over-weight.

[*No room to sign*] 'J. W. C.'

LETTER 258.

Mrs. Russell, Holm Hill.

5 Cheyne Row, Chelsea: Monday, October 20, 1862.

Now Mary, dear! pray don't let the echoes of your voice die out of my ears, if you can help it! It makes the difference betwixt feeling near and feeling far away; the difference betwixt writing off-hand, as one speaks, and writing cramped apologies. You may not have anything momentous to tell; but I am not difficult to interest, when it is you who are writing. Just fill a small sheet with such matter as you would say to me, if I were sitting opposite you, and I shall be quite content.

Neither have I myself anything momentous to tell, except, I was going to say, that I had got a new bonnet, or rather my last win

ter's bonnet transformed into a new one; but it suddenly flashes
over me, that is by no means the most momentous thing I have to
tell; a new bonnet is nothing in comparison to a new—maid! Ah,
my dear! Yes, I am changing my housemaid; I have foreseen
for long, even when she was capering about me, and kissing my
hands and shawl, that this emotional young lady would not wear
well ; and that some fine day her self-conceit and arrogance
would find the limits of my patience. Indeed, I should have lost
patience with her long ago, if it hadn't been for her cleverness
about Mr. C.'s books, which I fancied would make him extremely
averse to parting with her, as cleverness of that sort is not a common gift with housemaids. But not at all—at least not in prospect; he says she is ' such an affected fool,' and so heedless in
other respects that it is quite agreeable to him ' that she should
carry her fantasticalities and incompetences elsewhere!' She had
calculated on being indispensable, on the score of the books, and
was taking, since soon after my return from Scotland, a position
in the house which was quite preposterous—domineering towards
the cook, and impertinent to me! picking and choosing at her work
—in fact, not behaving like a servant at all, but like a lady, who, for
a caprice, or a wager, or anything except wages and board, was
condescending to exercise light functions in the house, provided
you kept her in good humour with gifts and praises.

When Mr. C.'s attention was directed to her procedure, he saw
the intolerableness as clearly as I did; so I was quite free to try
conclusions with the girl—either she should apologise for her impertinence and engage (like Magdalen Smith) ' to turn over a new
leaf,' or she should (as Mr. C. said) ' carry her fantasticalities and
incompetences elsewhere!' She chose, of course, the worser part;
and I made all the haste possible to engage a girl in her place, and
make the fact known, that so I might protect myself against
scenes of reconciliation, which, to a woman as old and nervous as
I am, are just about as tiresome as scenes of altercation. All sorts
of scenes cost me my sleep, to begin with; and are a sheer waste of
vital power, which one's servant at least ought really not to cost
one!

I am going to try a new arrangement—that of keeping two
women (experienced, or considering themselves so) to do an amount
of work between them which any good experienced servant could
do singly having hitherto proved unmanageable with me. I have
engaged a little girl of the neighbourhood (age about fifteen) to be

under the Scotchwoman. She is known to me as an honest, truthful, industrious little girl. Her parents are rather superior people in their station. The father is a collector on the boats. She is used to work, but not at all to what Mr. C.'s father would have called the ' curiosities and niceties ' of a house like this. So I shall have trouble enough in licking her into shape. But trouble is always a bearable thing for me in comparison with irritation. The chief drawback is that the mother is sickly, and this child has been her mainstay at home; and though both parents have willingly sacrificed their own convenience to get their child into so respectable a place, my fear is that after I have had the trouble of licking her into shape, the mother, under the pressure of home difficulties, may be irresistibly tempted to take her home again. Well, there is an excellent Italian proverb, ' The person who considers everything will never decide on anything!' Meanwhile, Elizabeth looks much more alive and cheerful since she had this change in view; and I shall be delivered from the botheration of two rival queens in the kitchen at all events. That I shall have to fetch the books, and do the sewing myself, will perhaps—' keep the devil from my elbow.'

I had a letter from my Aunt Ann the other day, the first I have had from any of them since I was at Craigenvilla, in spite of entreaties and remonstrances on my part. She tells me that the maidservant whom Grace ' converted ' some years ago is still praying earnestly for Mr. Carlyle. She has been at it a long while now, and must be tired of writing to my aunts to ask whether they had heard if anything had happened through her prayers. I will send you Ann's letter; burn it before, or having read it—as you like. Does it amuse you to read letters (good in their way) not addressed to yourself? Tell me that; for if it does, I could often, at the small cost of an extra stamp, send you on any letter that has pleased myself, without putting you to the trouble of returning them. I am afraid you will not have so many visitors to enliven you in the winter; and then you will take to thinking it was livelier at Thornhill, with your window looking on the street. Oh my dear! I wonder how the Doctor is so angelically patient with your hankering after the old house, when he has made the new one so lovely for you. Yet I can understand all that about the old house. I can, who am a woman!

LETTER 259.

To Mrs. Austin, The Gill, Annan.

5 Cheyne Row, Chelsea: Thursday, Oct. 23, 1862.

Blessings on you, dear! These eggs have been such a deliverance. Can you believe it of me? I have been in such a worry of mind of late days, that were it asked of me, with a loaded pistol at my breast, whether or not I had written again after receiving your letter, I could not tell! So in case I did not, I write to-night, while I have a little breathing-time.

Lord Ashburton, whom we had been led to suppose out of danger, made no progress in convalescence and then began to sink. Lady A., who has had the news of her mother's death since his illness, was alone to nurse him day and night. Her sister, who had gone to her at Paris, was obliged to hurry back to London, to attend to her own husband, who is confined to bed. She told me I was the only other person whom her sister (Lady A.) would like to have beside her. Would I write and ask if I might come? It was a serious undertaking for me, at this season, who had never crossed the Channel, and suffering so from sailing, and whose household affairs were in such a muddle; a servant to go away and no one yet found to replace her—but what else could I do but go to her if she would have me? Mr. C., too, thought I could do nothing else. So I wrote and offered to come immediately, and you may think if I have not been perfectly bewildered while waiting her answer— 'seeing servants,' as the phrase is, all the while. This morning I had a few hurried lines from her—No—I was not to come, 'it could do her no good and would knock me up;' for the rest, she was 'past all human help,' she said, 'and past all sympathy.' And the poor dear soul had drawn her pen through the last words. So like her, that she might not seem unkind, even in her agony of grief and dread she thought of that.

Their doctor's last two letters to me were very despondent, and neither to-day nor yesterday has there been any word from him, as there would have surely been, could he have imparted a grain of hope. We dread now that the next post will bring the news of our dear Lord Ashburton's death. Carlyle will lose in him the only friend he has left in the world, and the world will lose in him one of the purest-hearted, most chivalrous men that it contained. There are no words for such a misfortune.

Meanwhile one's own poor little life struggles on, with its daily petty concerns, as well as its great ones. About these eggs, which mustn't be neglected, if the solar system were coming to a stand— I do not think, dear, it was the fewness of the eggs that kept them safe so much as the plentifulness of the hay. Depend on it, your woman's plan of making the eggs all touch each other was a bad one. We have still eggs for a week—and then? I know of two hens in the neighbourhood that have begun to lay, but they do it so irregularly, so I mustn't trust to them. I don't think it would be safe to send the butter and eggs in the same box; a coarse basket would do as well as a box for the eggs—the difficulty of getting them sent doesn't seem to be the carriage so much as things to pack them in. If we were but nearer, I might send what the Addiscombe gardener calls the empties back again at trifling cost. I must inquire what it would cost to send empty baskets, as it is; I could take them myself to the office.

Oh dear me! what a pleasure it is when one is away from home and has no servants to manage, and no food to provide. Mr. C. gets more and more difficult to feed, and more and more impatient of the imperfections of human cooks and human housewives. I sometimes feel as if I should like to run away. But the question always arises, where to?

Kind regards to Jamie and the girls. What a pleasant time I had with you all, those nice evening drives!—Carlaverock Castle! How like a beautiful dream it all is, when I look back on it from here!

Your affectionate
JANE CARLYLE.

LETTER 260.

Mrs. Russell, Holm Hill.

5 Cheyne Row, Chelsea: Thursday, Nov. 21, 1862.

Dearest Mary,—The last of the four notes I inclosed, which had come a few hours before I wrote to you, made us expect the worst; and as the day went on, we could not help expecting the worst with more and more certainty. The same night we were talking very sadly of Lord Ashburton, almost already in the past tense; Mr. C. saying, 'God help me! since I am to lose him, the kindest, gentlest, friendliest man in my life here! I may say the one friend I have in the world!' and I, walking up and down in the room, as my way is when troubled in mind, had just answered, 'It's no use going to

bed and trying to sleep, in this suspense!' when the door opened
and a letter was handed me. It was from Paris, a second letter
that day! I durstn't open it. Mr. C. impatiently took it from me,
but was himself so agitated that he couldn't read it, when he had
it. At last he exclaimed, '"Better!" I see the one word "better,"
nothing else! look there, is not that "better"?' To be sure it was!
and you may imagine our relief! and our thankfulness to Lady A.
and Mrs. Anstruther for not losing a moment in telling us! The
letters go on more and more favourable. The doctors say 'they
cannot understand it.' When do these grand doctors understand
anything? But no matter about them, so that he is recovering,
whether they understand it or not!

I may now tell you of my household crisis, which has been
happily accomplished. Maria has departed this scene, and little
'Flo'(!) has entered upon it; not a little dog, as you might fancy
from the name, but a remarkably intelligent, well-conditioned girl
between fourteen and fifteen, who was christened 'Florence'—too
long and too romantic a name for household use! She is so quick
at learning that training her is next to no trouble. And Mr. C. is
so pleased with the clever little creature, that he has been much
less aggravating than usual under a change. Maria wished to make
me a scene at parting (of course). But I brutally declined partici-
pating in it, so she rushed up to the study with her tears to Mr. C.,
who was 'dreadfully sorry for the poor creature.' The 'poor creature' had been employing her mind latterly in impressing on Elizabeth, who is weak enough to believe what mischief-makers tell her,
rather than the evidence of her own senses, that she was going to
be overworked (!) with only an untrained girl instead of a fine lady
housemaid for fellow-servant, and in making herself so charming
and caressing for Elizabeth that her former tyrannies were forgotten; and Elizabeth, who had looked quite happy at the idea of
Maria's going 'and a girl under her,' turned suddenly round into
wearing a sullen look of victimhood, and declining silently to give
me the least help in training the girl! All the better for the girl;
and perhaps also all the better for me!

But it is a disappointment to find that my Scotch blockhead is
no brighter for having her 'Bubbly Jock' taken off her! Such a
woman to have had sent four hundred miles to one! Mr. C. always
speaks of her as 'that horse,' 'that cow,' 'that mooncalf!' But
upon my honour, it is an injustice to the horse, the cow, and even
the mooncalf! For sample of her procedure: there is a glass door

into the back court consisting of two immense panes of glass; the cow has three several times smashed one of these sheets of glass, through the same carelessness, neglecting to latch it up! three times, in the six months she has been here! and nobody before her ever smashed that door! Another thing that nobody before her ever did, in all the twenty-eight or nine years I have lived in the house, was to upset the kitchen table! and smash, at one stroke, nearly all the tumblers and glasses we had, all the china breakfast things, a crystal butter-glass (my mother's), a crystal flower vase, and ever so many jugs and bowls! There was a whole washing-tub full of broken things! Surely honesty, sobriety, and steadiness must have grown dreadfully scarce qualities, that one puts up with such a cook; especially as her cooking is as careless as the rest of her doings. No variety is required of her, and she has been taught how to do the few things Mr. C. needs. She can do them when she cares to take pains; but every third day or so there comes up something that provokes him into declaring, 'That brute will be the death of me! It is really too bad to have wholesome food turned to poison.' But I suppose she understands herself engaged by the half-year, though I never had any explanation with her, as to the second half-year. And so, Heaven grant me patience!

What a pack of complaints! but, my dear, there is nobody but you that I would think of making them to! and it is a certain easing of nature to utter them; so forgive the mean details.

Love to the Doctor.

Your ever affectionate

JANE CARLYLE.

LETTER 261.

To Mrs. Austin, The Gill, Annan.

5 Cheyne Row, Chelsea: Nov. 1862.

Dearest Mary,—The box of eggs came yesterday. Another perfect success; not a single egg broken or cracked! The barrel arrived to-day; and Mr. C. has already eaten a quarter of one of the fowls, and found less fault with his dinner than he is in the habit of doing now. In fact, I look forward to his dinner-time with a sort of panic, which the event for most part justifies. How I wish this long, weary book were done, for his own sake and for everybody's near him. It is like living in a madhouse on the days when he gets ill on with his writing.

I have a new woman coming as cook next Tuesday, and intense
as has been Mr. C.'s abhorrence of the present 'mooncalf,' 'cow,'
'brute-beast,' I look forward with trepidation to having to teach
the new-comer all Mr. C.'s things, which every woman who comes
has to be taught, whether she can cook in a general way or not.
If the kitchen were only on the same floor with the room! but I
have to go down three pairs of stairs to it, past a garden-door kept
constantly open in all weathers; and at this season of the year, with
my dreadful tendency to catch interminable colds, running up and
down these stairs teaching bread-making, and Mr. C.'s sort of soup,
and Mr. C.'s sort of puddings, cutlets, &c. &c., is no joke. My
one constant terror is lest I should fall ill and be unable to go down
to the kitchen at all. I dream about that at nights. Really

> If I were dead,
> And a stone at my head,
> I think I should be *be*-tter.[1]

There is the anxiety about dear Lord Ashburton too; that has
been going on now some five weeks; sometimes relieved a little,
then again worse than ever. I have a note in my pocket at this
moment which Mr. C. does not know of, leaving scarce a hope of
his recovery. As it was not from the doctor, but from Lady A.'s
niece, who expresses herself very confusedly, and might have made
the case worse than it is, I decided not to unsettle Mr. C. at his
writing with a sight of it; and it has felt burning in my pocket all
day; and every knock at the door makes my heart jump into my
throat, for it may be news of his death.

As this letter won't reach you any sooner for being posted to-
night, I will keep it open till to-morrow in case of another from
Paris. And if I have more to say I had better keep that till to-
morrow too. I write with such a weight on my spirits to-night.
                 But always
                     Most affectionately yours,
                             JANE CARLYLE.

A note has just come from Lady Ashburton's sister in London,
forwarding a telegram just received: 'My Lord has passed a better
night. Dr. Quain thinks him no worse.' So there is still hope—
for those who have a talent for hoping.

---

[1] Old beggar's rhyme on entering:
> 'I'm a poor helpless craiture,
> If I were, &c. . . . . better (baiture!)'

LETTER 262.

To Mrs. Russell.

5 Cheyne Row: December 15, 1862.

I should not be at all afraid that after a few weeks my new maid would do well enough if it weren't for Mr. C.'s frightful impatience with any new servant untrained to his ways, which would drive a woman out of the house with her hair on end if allowed to act directly upon her! So that I have to stand between them, and imitate in a small, humble way the Roman soldier who gathered his arms full of the enemy's spears, and received them all into his own breast.[1] It is this which makes a change of servants, even when for the better, a terror to me in prospect, and an agony in realisation—for a time.

LETTER 263.

Mrs. Braid, Edinburgh.

5 Cheyne Row, Chelsea: Christmas Day, 1862.

Dearest Betty,—Here we are, you and I, again at the end of a year. Still alive, you and I, and those belonging to us still alive, while so many younger, healthier, more life-like people, who began the year with us, have been struck down by death. Can we do better, after thanking God that we are still spared, than embrace one another across the four hundred miles that lie between, in the only fashion possible, that is on paper.

'Merry Christmases,' and 'Happy New Years,' are words that produce melancholy ideas rather than cheerful ones to people of our age and experience. So I don't wish you a 'mirth,' and a 'happiness,' which I know to have passed out of Christmas and New Year for such as us for evermore; passed out of them along with so much else; our gay spirits, our bright hopes, living hearts that loved us, and the fresh, trusting life of our own hearts. It is a thing too sad for tears, the thought how much is past and gone, even while there is much to be cared for. And that is all the dismals I am going to indulge in at this writing.

For the rest, we have been in great anxiety about Lord Ashburton. It is six weeks past on Monday that he has been hanging betwixt life and death, at an hotel in Paris, where he was taken ill of

---

[1] Oh heavens, the comparison! it was too true.

inflammation of the lungs, on his way to Nice; and all the time I have been receiving a letter from Lady A.'s sister by her directions, or from their travelling physician, Dr. Christison (son of that Robert Christison, who used to visit at my uncle Benjamin's in your time), every day almost, sometimes two letters in one day; such constant changes there have been in the aspect of his illness! The morning letter would declare him 'past all human help,' and in the evening would come news of decided 'improvement,' so that we couldn't have been kept in greater suspense if we had been in the same house with him. The last three days there has been again talk of 'a faint hope,' 'a bare possibility of recovery.' And their London physician, who has been five times telegraphed for to Paris, called here to-day immediately on his return, directed by Lady A., to go and tell us of his new hopes. When I was told Dr. Quain was in the drawing-room, I went in to him with my heart in my mouth, persuaded he had been sent to break the news of Lord A.'s death. My first words to him (he had never been in the house before) were, 'Oh, Dr. Quain, what has brought you here?'—a reception so extraordinary that he stood struck speechless, which confirmed me in my idea, and I said, violently, 'Tell me at once! you are come to tell me he is dead?' 'My dear lady, I am come to tell you no such thing, but quite the contrary! I am come by Lady Ashburton's desire to explain to you the changes which again have raised us into hope that he may recover.' Then, in the reaction of my fright, I began to cry. What a fool that man must have thought me! Poor Lady A., who is devotedly attached to her husband, has nursed him day and night, till she is so worn out that one could hardly recognise her (her sister writes). Next to her and their child, it is to us, I believe, that he would be the greatest loss. He is the only intimate friend that my husband has left in the world—his dearest, most intimate friend through twenty years now.

I told you in my last—did I not?—that I had got a little girl of fifteen in place of my fine-lady housemaid; and that the East Lothian woman, instead of coming out in a better light when left to her own inspirations, was driving Mr. C. out of his senses with her blockheadisms and carelessness; and that, much as I disliked changes in the dead of winter, there was no help for it, but to send that woman back to a part of God's earth where she had been 'well thought of' (Jackie Welsh had said), and where she 'could get plenty of good places' (the Goose herself said). A sorry account of the style of service now going in East Lothian, I can only say.

I hope I shall be more comfortable now—for a while, at least. The little girl is extremely intelligent, and active, and willing; is a great favourite with her master, thank Heaven! and has never required a cross word from me during the six weeks or so that she has been in the house. The other is a girl of twenty-four, with an excellent three years' character, whom I confess I chose out of some dozen that offered, more by character than outward appearance; she is only on a month's trial as yet. I rather hope she will do; but it is too soon to make up my mind in the four days she has been with me.

I inclose a post-office order for a sovereign to buy what you need most, and wear it for the sake of your loving

JANE W. CARLYLE.

Best regards to your husband and dear George.

LETTER 264.

Dr. Russell, Holm Hill.

5 Cheyne Row, Chelsea: Jan. 6, 1863.

My dear Dr. Russell,—At last I send you the promised photograph. It goes along with this note. You were meant to have it on New Year's Day; but I needed to go out for a sheet of millboard, and then to cut it to the proper size; and all that, strange to say, took more time than I had at my disposal. You wonder, perhaps, what a woman like me has to take up her time with. Here, for example, is one full day's work, not to say two. On the New Year's morning itself, Mr. C. 'got up off his wrong side,' a by no means uncommon way of getting up for him in these overworked times! And he suddenly discovered that his salvation, here and hereafter, depended on having, 'immediately, without a moment's delay,' a beggarly pair of old cloth boots, that the street-sweeper would hardly have thanked him for, ' lined with flannel, and new bound, and repaired generally!' and ' one of my women '—that is, my one woman and a half—was to be set upon the job! Alas! a regular shoemaker would have taken a whole day to it, and wouldn't have undertaken such a piece of work besides! and Mr. C. scouted the idea of employing a shoemaker, as subversive of his authority as master of the house. So, neither my one woman, nor my half one, having any more capability of repairing ' generally ' these boots than of repairing the Great Eastern, there was no help for me but to sit down on the New Year's morning, with a great ugly beast of a man's boot in my lap, and scheme, and stitch, and worry over it till night; and next morning begin on the other! There, you see, were my two days eaten up very completely, and unexpectedly; and so it goes on, 'always a something' (as my dear mother used to say).

The accounts from Paris continue more favourable. But they sound hollow to me somehow.

Love to Mary.

Your ever affectionate
JANE CARLYLE.

LETTER 265.

The following letter has been forwarded to me by a gentleman who modestly desires that his name may not be mentioned.—J. A. F.

To J. T.

5 Cheyne Row, Chelsea: Feb. 11, 1863.

I wish, dear sir, you could have seen how your letter brightened up the breakfast-time for my husband and me yesterday morning, scattering the misanthropy we are both given to at the beginning of the day, like other nervous people who have 'bad nights.' I wish you could have heard our lyrical recognition of your letter— its 'beautiful modesty,' its 'gentleness,' and 'genuineness;' above all I wish you could have heard the tone of real feeling in which my husband said, at last, ' I do think, my dear, that is the very nicest little bit of good cheer that has come our way for seven years!' It might have been thought Mr. C. was quite unused to expressions of appreciation from strangers, instead of (as is the fact) receiving such almost every day in the year—except Sundays, when there is no post. But, oh, the difference between that gracious, graceful little act of faith of yours, and the intrusive, imper-tinent, presumptuous letters my husband is continually receiving, demanding, in return for so much 'admiration,' an autograph per-haps! or to read and give an opinion on some long, cramped MS. of the writer's; or to—find a publisher for it even! or to read some idiotic new book of the writer's [that is a very common form of letter from lady admirers]—say a translation from the German (!) and 'write a review of it in one of the quarterlies!' 'It would be a favour never to be forgotten!' I should think so indeed.

Were I to show you the 'tributes of admiration' to Mr. C.'s genius, received through the post during one month, you, who have consideration for the time of a man struggling, as for life, with a gigantic task—you, who, as my husband says, are 'beautifully modest,' would feel your hair rise on end at such assaults on a man under pretence of admiring him; and would be enabled perhaps, better than I can express it in words, to imagine the pleasure it must have been to us when an approving reader of my husband's books came softly in, and wrapped his wife in a warm, beautiful shawl, saying simply—'There! I don't want to interrupt you, but I want to show you my good-will; and that is how I show it.'

We are both equally gratified, and thank you heartily. When the shawl came, as it did at night, Mr. C. himself wrapped it about me, and walked round me admiring it. And what think you he said? He said, 'I am very glad of that for you, my dear. I think it is the only bit of real good my celebrity ever brought you!'

Yours truly,

JANE W. CARLYLE.

The letter which called out so many praises was this:—

'Mrs. Thomas Carlyle. Madam,—Unwilling to interrupt your husband in his stern task, I take the liberty of addressing you, and hope you will accept from me a woollen long shawl, which I have sent by the Parcel Delivery Co., carriage paid, to your address. If it does not reach you, please let me know, and I shall make inquiries here, so that it be traced and delivered. I hope the pattern will please you, and also that it may be of use to you in a cold day.

'I will also name to you my reason for sending you such a thing. My obligations to your husband are many and unnameably great, and I just wish to acknowledge them. All men will come to acknowledge this, when your husband's power and purpose shall become visible to them.

'If high respect, love, and good wishes could comfort him and you, none living command more or deserve more.

'You can take a fit moment to communicate to your husband my humble admiration of his goodness, attainments, and great gifts to the world; which I wish much he may be spared to see the world begin to appreciate.

'I remain, &c.,
'J. T.'

LETTER 266.

To Mrs. Austin, The Gill, Annan.

5 Cheyne Row: Thursday, Feb. 26, 1863.

I promised you a voluntary letter, Mary dear; and after all the waiting you are going to get a begging letter, which is nothing like so pleasant for either the writer or the receiver. But those London hens! they are creatures without rule or reason. I had just made an arrangement with a grocer, who keeps a lot of them, to let me have at least seven new-laid eggs a week; and the very day the bargain was concluded the creatures all struck work again, 'except one bantam!' So we are eating away at yours, without any hope of reinforcement from this neighbourhood. Jane, in a letter to Mr. C., kindly offered to send a second supply from Dumfries! but, as she does not lay them 'within herself' (as an old lady at Haddington used to say), it seems more natural that I should apply to you who do! We have still enough to last about a week. There! I have done my begging at the beginning of my letter, instead of reserving it for a postscript, the common dodge, which deceives nobody. And now my mind is free to tell any news I may have.

You would hear of my incomparable small housemaid having turned out an incomparable small demon. People say these wonderfully clever servants, whether old or young, are always to be suspected. Perhaps; still a little cleverness is much nicer than stupidity to start with. Anyhow I don't need to live in vague apprehensions about either of my present servants on the ground of cleverness.

But I am well enough content with them as servants go. I have arranged things on a new footing, which I am in hopes ('hope springing eternal in the human mind') may work better than the old one; I have made the cook, who came in place of the Scotch one, a general or upper servant; she does all the work upstairs, the valeting, &c., besides the cooking; and the new girl is a sort of kitchen-maid under her. On this plan there cannot be the same room for jealousies and squabbles for power, which have tormented me ever since I kept two.

I had a visit the other day which turned me upside down with the surprise of it! I was putting on my bonnet to go out early in the day, when Mary came to say there was 'a lady at the door, who would like if I would see her for a few minutes.' The hour being unusual for making calls, and the message being over-modest for a caller, I thought it might be some 'good lady' with a petition, a sort of people I cannot abide, so I asked: 'Is she a lady, do you think?' 'Well—no, ma'm—I think hardly;' said Mary. 'She wouldn't give her name; but she said she came from fishshire, or something like that!' 'Fishshire?—could it be Dumfriesshire?' I said with a veritable inspiration of genius. 'Show her up,' and I heard a heavy body passed into the drawing-room. I hastened in and saw, standing in the middle of the floor, a figure like a haystack, with the reddest of large fat faces, the eyes of which were straining towards the door. The woman was dressed in decent country clothes and bore no resemblance to any 'lady' 'in the created world,' but looked well-to-do. I stared; I didn't know the woman from Adam (as the people here say)!

But she spoke—'Eh! !' she said; 'Lord keep me! Is that you?' —and there was something strangely familiar in the voice. I stared again and said—'Nancy?'—'Atweel and it's just Nancy,' answered the haystack! and then followed such shaking of hands, as if we had been the dearest friends. Do you know who it was? Not the little Nancy we used to call 'piggy' at Craigenputtock, but the great coarse Nancy with the beard. She who said she 'never kenned folk mac sic a wark aboot a bit lee as we did!' She left Craigenputtock to marry an old drunken butcher at Thornhill, who, happily for her, died in a few years, and then (as she phrased it) she 'had another chance,' and she just took it, as she 'thocht it might be her last,' that is, she married again a very respectable man of her own age, who is something in the Duke's mines at Sanquhar. She bore him one son, who is well educated, and clerk in the Sanquhar bank. He had been at Holm Hill on some bank business just before I was there last year, and Mrs. Russell had him to tea, and said he was a 'nice gentlemanly lad.' Well done, Nancy, beard and all the rest of it! Her man had been married before, as well as herself, and had a son, who is a haberdasher 'on his own account' in this neighbourhood, and he had married, and his wife was being confined; and Nancy had been sent up for to 'take care of her.' She met one of the Miss W——s on the road before leaving home, and made her 'put down my address on a bit of paper;' and so there she was—the first day she crossed the threshold after being in London five weeks! I was really glad to see the creature! she looked so glad to see me; except for the shock my personal appearance manifestly was to her! I gave her wine and cake, and a little present, and she went away in a transport.

I slept away from home last night. I had gone to a place called
Ealing, some seven miles out of London, to visit Mrs. Oliphant—
she who wrote the ' Life of Edward Irving '—and it was too far to
come back at night. Indeed I never go out after sunset at this
season. She is a dear little homely woman, who speaks the broadest
East Lothian Scotch, though she has lived in England since she was
ten years old! and never was in East Lothian in her life, except
passing through it in a railway carriage! ! ! But her mother was an
East Lothian woman. I wish to heaven I had any place out of
London, near hand, that I could go to when I liked; I am always
so much the better for a little change. Life is too monotonous,
and too dreary in the valley of the shadow of Frederick the Great!
I wonder how we shall live, what we shall do, where we shall go,
when that terrible task is ended.

Kindest regards to Jamie and the bonnie lassies.

Your affectionate

-   JANE WELSH CARLYLE.

LETTER 267.

To Miss Grace Welsh, Edinburgh.

5 Cheyne Row, Chelsea: Monday, March 2, 1863.

My dear Grace,—You say you have sent me ' them,' and you
have only sent me *it;* and you say ' the head ' is thought a good
likeness, and I have got only a standing figure. Was it an involun-
tary omission on your part, or did you fall away from your good
intention to send ' them '? Revise it if you did, for I want very
much to see the likeness of the young man which is considered the
best. I should like much to see the young man himself; for me as
for you, a certain melancholy interest attaches to the last of so
large and so brave a family.[1] Don't wait till you have time and
heart to write me another nice long letter; but put ' the head ' in
an envelope, and send it at once.

Mr. C. was again laid hold of by Mr. A—— the other day in the
King's Road, and escorted by him all the way to Regent Street.
' Really a good, innocent-hearted man! very vulgar, but he can't
help that, poor fellow!' I have never once met him in the street
since I made up my mind to speak to him, and invite him to call

---

[1] Robert Welsh's second son: he too is dead; died shortly before her own
departure out of vale of sorrow.

for me, which Mr. C. hadn't the grace to do. I used never to walk out without meeting him; but this winter I have taken my walk early in the forenoon—when he is busy, I suppose; just once I saw him pass the butcher's door when I was giving him directions about a piece of beef. He had a pretty young lady with him, on whom he was 'beaming' benevolence and all sorts of things.

I was away a day and night last week at Ealing, visiting Mrs. Oliphant. Even that short 'change of air and scene' did me good. On the strength I got by it I afterwards went to a dinner party at the Rectory, and am to dine out again to meet Dickens, and nobody else. The people send their carriage for me, and send me home; so in this mild weather the enterprise looks safe enough.

Such a noise about that 'Royal marriage!' I wish it were over. People are so woefully like sheep—all running where they see others run, and doing what they see others do. Have you heard of that wonderful Bishop Colenso? Such a talk about him too. And he isn't worth talking about for five minutes, except for the absurdity of a man making arithmetical onslaughts on the Pentateuch, with a bishop's little black silk apron on!

Dear love to you all.   Your affectionate

JEANNIE W. CARLYLE.

LETTER 268.

Miss Grace Welsh, Craigenvilla, Morningside, Edinburgh.

5 Cheyne Row, Chelsea: March 17, 1863.

My dear Grace,—I am wanting to know if your pains keep off. I hardly dare to hope it in these trying east winds, which are the worst sort of weather for that sort of ailment. The last ten days have been horrid with us; all the worse for coming after such a summery February. My own head has been in a very disorganised state indeed. The cold first came into my tongue, swelling it, and making it raw on one side, so that for days I had to live on slops, and restrict my speech to monosyllables; then it got into my jaws and every tooth in my mouth; and that is the present state of me. I am writing with my pocket-handkerchief tied over my lower face, and my imagination much overclouded by weary gnawing pain there. Decidedly a case for trying your remedy, and I mean to; have been thinking of realising some chlorodyne all the week. But either it has been too cold for me to venture up to the druggist's in Sloane Square, or I have had to go somewhere else.

It is a comfort to reflect, anyhow, that I have not brought these aches on myself by rushing 'out for to see' the new Princess, as the rest of the world did, or to see the illuminations. I had an order sent me from Paris for seats for myself and 'a friend' in the balcony erected at Bath House—the best for seeing in the whole line of the procession. But, first, I have no taste for crowds; and, secondly, I felt it would be so sad, sitting there, when the host and hostess were away in such sickness and sorrow; and, thirdly, I was somewhat of Mr. C.'s opinion: That this marriage, the whole nation was running mad after, was really less interesting to every individual of them than setting a hen of one's own on a nest of sound eggs would be!

The only interest I take in the little new Princess is founded on her previous poverty and previous humble, homely life. I have heard some touching things about that from people connected with the Court. When she was on her visit to the Queen after her engagement, she always wore a jacket. The Queen said, 'I think you always wear a jacket; how is that?' 'Oh,' said little Alexandra, 'I wear it because it is so economical. You can wear it with any sort of gown; and you know I have always had to make my own gowns. I have never had a lady's-maid, and my sisters and I all made our own clothes; I even made my bonnet!' Two or three days after the marriage she wrote to her mother: 'I am so happy! I have just breakfasted with Bertie' (Albert, her husband); 'and I have on a white muslin dressing-gown, beautifully trimmed with pink ribbon.' Her parents were not so rich as most London shop-keepers; had from seven hundred to a thousand a year. That interests me; and I also feel a sympathy with her in the prospect of the bother she will have by-and-by.

You have never found the missing photograph? I am so sorry about it. Please write, ever so little; but I want to know if you keep free of pain. I am not up to a long letter. I am glad you are going to the Bridge of Allan. It will do Ann good for certain, and you probably; and you will be able to judge of Grace's [1] health with your own eyes, which are better than other people's reports.

I have seen nothing of Mrs. George [2] lately, though, of course, she would be in at the show. Love to you all.

Your affectionate
JANE W. CARLYLE.

---

[1] One of Robert Welsh's daughters who also died.
[2] Welsh (of Richmond).

LETTER 269.

Mrs. Russell, Holm Hill.

5 Cheyne Row, Chelsea: Friday, March 21, 1863.

Yes, my dear, the Doctor was right; the cold in my mouth was symptomatic of nothing but just cold in the mouth! I was afraid myself, for some days, it might turn to a regular influenza; the only time I ever had the same sort of thing as bad before being in the course of that dangerous influenza I had a good many years ago, when I had first to call in Mr. Barnes. But I have got off with the ten days of sore tongue and faceache, which is almost cured by the west wind we have had for the last two days.

My aunt Grace has 'suffered martyrs' (as a French friend of mine used to express it) from faceache, and pains of the head, during this last winter; and cured herself (she believes) in a day by the new pet medicine chlorodyne. She was in an agony that could no longer be borne, and invested half-a-crown in a small bottle of chlorodyne; and took ten drops every two hours, till she had taken as many as fifty; and then fell into a refreshing sleep, and (when she wrote) had had no return of the pain for three weeks. I haven't much faith in medicines that work as by miracle; and am inclined to believe that her pain, having reached its height, had been ready to subside of itself when the chlorodyne was taken. Still, as there might be some temporary relief, more or less, in the thing, I, too, invested in a small phial, and took ten drops when I was going to bed one night; and the only effect traceable in my case was a very dry dirty mouth next morning. To the best of my taste, it was composed of chloroform, strong peppermint, and some other carminatives. Has the Doctor used it? The apothecary here told me it was not sold much by itself, but that a great deal was used in the doctors' prescriptions.

Did I tell you that Mr. C.'s horse came down with him one day, and cut its knees to the bone, and had been sold for nine pounds! It cost fifty, and was cheap at that. My aunt Grace writes, that 'Mrs. Fergusson is still praying diligently for Mr. C., and that perhaps it was due to her prayers that Mr. C. was not hurt on that occasion!!'

Your ever affectionate

J. W. CARLYLE.

LETTER 270.

Mrs. Braid, Green End, Edinburgh.

5 Cheyne Row, Chelsea: May 22, 1863.

My own Betty,—I am wearying for some news of you.   I never could lay that proverb ' No news is good news' sufficiently to heart. Whenever I am feeling poorly myself (and I should be almost ashamed to say how often that is the case), I fall to fancying that you are perhaps ill, and nobody to tell me of it, and I so far away! It is so stupid of Ann and Grace, who take so much fatigue on themselves, in visiting about in their 'district,' and attending all sorts of meetings, that they don't take a walk out of their district now and then to see how you are going on, and tell me when they write.   Some news of Betty would make a letter from them infinitely more gratifying than anything they can say about Dr. Candlish, and this and the other preacher and pray-er; and would certainly inspire me with more Christian feelings.   But, once for all, it is their way, and there is no help for it.

When I came in from a drive one day lately, I was told ' a person' was waiting for me; and, on opening the dining-room door, where the ' person' had been put to wait, I saw, sitting facing me, Helen D——, the Sunny Bank housemaid.   It was such a surprise! I never liked Helen so well as Marion, the cook; but anyone from dear old Sunny Bank was a welcome sight to me now.   She has been for some years in charge of some children, at a clergyman's in Hampshire, and was passing through London with the children and their father, who was returned from India, on their way to an aunt's near Peebles.   She would go on to Haddington, she said, ' just to look in on them all, but she wouldn't like to stay there now—oh, no!'   She was grown very stout and consequential.   I took her into my bedroom to show her my picture of Sunny Bank, which hangs there, and another of the Nungate Bridge; and, while looking about, she suddenly exclaimed, ' I declare there is Mrs. Braid!'   You, too, are framed in a gilt frame, and hung on the wall.   The likeness must be very good that she knew you at once, for she had only seen you twice, she said, ' when you came to breakfast.'   Her fine talk will astonish the Haddington people when she ' looks in upon them.'   She spoke very respectfully of Miss Donaldson; ' Miss Jess,' she said, ' hadn't the same balance of mind that Miss Donaldson had!' But she was no favourite with Miss Jess, and knew it.

Poor Jackie Welsh has lost her aunt, who had been more than a mother to her all her life; and she seems quite crushed to the earth with her grief. No wonder; she is so much in need of some one to sympathise with her, and nurse her in her frequent illnesses; and that one aunt was the only person on earth that she felt to belong to, and that belonged to her. Her mother is still alive; but her mother has never done anything for her but what she had better have left alone—brought her into being! And now she (the mother) is past being any good to anybody—quite frail and stupefied.

Oh, Betty! do you remember the little green thing that I left in your care once while I was over in Fife? And when I returned you had transplanted it into a yellow glass, which I have on my toilet-table to this hour, keeping my rings, &c., in it. Well! I must surely have told you long ago that the little thing, with two tiny leaves, from my father's grave, had, after twelve months in the garden at Chelsea, declared itself a gooseberry-bush! It has gone on flourishing, in spite of want of air and of soil, and is now the prettiest round bush, quite full of leaves.[1] I had several times asked our old gardener if there is nothing one could do to get the bush to bear, if it were only one gooseberry; but he treated the case as hopeless. 'A poor wild thing. No; if you want to have gooseberries, ma'am, better get a proper gooseberry-bush in its place! The old Goth! He can't be made to understand that things can have any value but just their garden value. He once, in spite of all I could beg and direct, rooted out a nettle I had brought from Crawford Churchyard, and with infinite pains got to take root and flourish. But, I was going to tell you, one day Lizzy, my youngest maid, came running in from the garden to ask me had I seen the three little gooseberries on the gooseberry-bush? I rushed out, as excited as a child, to look at them. And there they were— three little gooseberries, sure enough! And immediately I had settled it in my mind to send you one of them in a letter when full grown. But, alas! whether it was through too much staring at them, or too much east wind, or through mere delicacy in 'the poor wild thing,' I can't tell; only the result, that the three bits of gooseberries, instead of growing larger, grew every day less, till

---

[1] It still stands there, green and leafy, and with berries; how strange and memorable to me now!

they reached the smallness of pin-heads, and then dropped on the ground! I could have cried when the last one went.

You remember my little Charlotte? I had a visit from her yesterday; and she looks much more sedate and proper than when I had to put her away. She is 'third housemaid at the Marquis of Camden's,' and lives in the country, which is good for her. She sent her compliments to 'Betty.'

My present pair of girls go on very peaceably. They are neither of them particularly bright; but they are attentive, and willing, and well behaved. I often look back with a shudder over the six months of that East Lothian Elizabeth! Her dinners blackened to cinders! her constant crashes of glass and china! her brutal manners! her lumpish insensibility and ingratitude! And to think that that woman must have been considered above the average of East Lothian servants, or Jackie Welsh wouldn't have sent her to me. What an idea it gives one of the state of things in East Lothian!

And now good-bye, Betty, dear. There is a long letter for you; which will, I hope, soon draw me a few lines from you in return. I am anxious to know how yourself, and your husband, and George have stood these cold spring weeks. My kind regards to them.

> Your ever affectionate
> JANE WELSH CARLYLE.

LETTER 271.

Mrs. Russell, Holm Hill.

5 Cheyne Row, Chelsea: June 3, 1863.

I had something to tell you which did not find room in my last letter. The name of Mrs. Oliphant's publisher is Blackett; and he has a smart wife, who came with him to dinner at Mrs. Oliphant's when I was there. They were very (what we call in Scotland) 'up-making' to me, and pressed me to visit them at Ealing, which I hadn't the least thought of doing. Well, some weeks ago, Mr. C. was just come in from his ride, very tired, and, to do him justice, very ill-humoured, when Mary put her head in at the drawing-room door and said, 'Mrs. Blackett wished to know if she could see me for a few minutes?' I went out hurriedly, knowing Mr. C.'s temper wouldn't be improved by hearing of people he didn't want coming after me. I told Mary to take the lady into the dining-room (where was no fire), and before going down myself put a shawl about me, chiefly to show her she musn't stay. On entering the room, the lady's back was to me; and she was standing looking out into the (so-called) garden; but I saw at once it wasn't the Mrs. Blackett I had seen. This one was very tall, dressed in deep black, and when she turned round, she showed me a pale beautiful face, that was perfectly strange to me! But I was no stranger to her seemingly, for she glided swiftly up to me like a dream, and took my head softly between her hands and kissed my brow again and again, saying in a low dreamlike voice, 'Oh, you dear! you dear! you dear! Don't you know me?' I looked into her eyes in supreme bewilderment. At last light dawned on me, and I said one word—'Bessy?' 'Yes, it is Bessy!' And then the kissing wasn't all on one side, you may fancy. It was at last Bessy—not Mrs. Blackett, but Mrs. B——, —who stood there, having left her husband in a cab at the door, till she had seen me first. They were just arrived from Cheshire, where they had gone to see one of his sons, who had been dangerously ill, and were to start by the next train for St. Leonards. They had only a quarter of an hour to stay. He is a good, intelligent-looking man; and while he was talking all the time with Mr. C., Bessy said beautiful things about him to me, enough to show that if he wasn't her first love, he was at least a very superior being in her estimation. They pressed me to come to them at St. Leornards, and I promised indefinitely that I would.

About a fortnight ago, Bessy walked in one morning after breakfast. She 'had had no peace for thinking about me; I looked so ill, she was sure I had some disease! Had I?' I told her 'None that I could specify, except the disease of old age, general weakness, and discomfort.' Reassured on that head, she confided to me that 'I looked just as Mrs. B—— had looked when she was dying of cancer!!' And she had come up, certain that I had a cancer, to try and get me away to be nursed by her, and attended by her husband. Besides she had heard there was so much small-pox in London; 'and if I took it, and died before she had seen me again, she thought she would never have an hour's happiness in the world again!' Oh, Bessy, Bessy! just the same old woman—an imagination morbid almost to insanity! 'Would I go back with her that night anyhow?' 'Impossible!' 'Then when would I come? and she would come up again to fetch me!' That I would not hear of; but I engaged to go so soon as it was a little warmer. And to-day I have written that I will come for two or three days on Monday next. She is wearing mourning for the mother and eldest brother of her husband, who have both died since her marriage.

And now I mustn't begin another sheet.

Your ever affectionate

J. W. CARLYLE.

LETTER 272.

To Mrs. Austin, The Gill, Annan.

5 Cheyne Row, Chelsea: Sunday, July 5, 1863.

My dear little woman,—Every day, since I got your letter, I have put off answering it till the morrow, in hope always that the morrow would find me more up to writing an answer both long and pleasant. But, alas! I had best not wait any longer for ' a more convenient season,' but just write a stupid little note, according to my present disability; as a time when my head will be clearer, and my heart lighter, and my stomach less sick, is not to be calculated on.

I went some three weeks ago to St. Leonards, the pleasantest place I know; and stayed from Monday to Saturday, in circumstances the most favourable to health that could be desired. The finest sea air in the world—a large, airy, quiet house close on the shore; a carriage to drive out in twice a day; a clever physician for host, who dieted me on champagne and the most nourishing delicacies; and for hostess, a gentle, graceful, loving woman, who, besides being full of interest for me as a heroine of romance, has the more personal interest for me of having been my—servant, about thirty years ago; and of having been sincerely mourned by me as —dead!

Well, I returned from that visit quite set up; and the improvement lasted some two or three days. Then I turned as sick as a dog one evening, and had to take to bed; and the sickness not abating after two days, during which time, to Mr. C.'s great dismay, I could eat nothing at all (nothing in the shape of illness ever alarms Mr. C. but that of not eating one's regular meals), Mr. Barnes was sent for, who ordered mustard blisters to my stomach, and unlimited soda-water ' with a little brandy in it.' In about a week I was on foot again—but weak as a dishclout! And that is my condition to the present hour. I don't see much chance of bettering it here—and Mr. C. seems determined to stick to his ' work' all this summer and autumn, as he did the last. It is very bad for him, and very bad for the work. He would get on twice as fast if he would give himself a holiday. But there is no persuading him, as you know; 'vara obstinate in his own wae!'[1] And as I was away last autumn a whole month by myself, I cannot have the face to leave him again this year, unless for a few days at a time, when I am hardly missed till I am back again. Besides, the present servants are not adapted to being left to their own devices. They do very well with overlooking and direction; and the week I was at St. Leonards nothing went wrong; but, for that long, they could have their orders for every day; and as I did not tell them for certain what day I should be back, there was a constant wholesome expectation of my return.

Mr. Carlyle has got his tent up in the back area, and writes away there without much inconvenience, as yet, from the heat. He has changed his dinner hour to half-past three instead of seven; then he sleeps for an hour, and then goes for his ride in the cool of the evening.

The horse Lady Ashburton sent him is a pretty, swift little creature, and very sure-footed, which is the first quality for a horse whose rider always goes at a gallop. But Mr. C. draws many plaintive comparisons between this horse and poor old Fritz, as to moral qualities. This one 'shows no desire to please him whatever; only goes at its best pace when its head is turned towards its own stable! Fritz was always endeavouring to ascertain his wishes and to gain his approbation; it was a horse of very superior sense and sensibility, and had a profound regard for him.'

Kindest love to you all.

Your ever affectionate
JANE CARLYLE.

LETTER 273.

Mrs. Russell, Holm Hill.

5 Cheyne Row, Chelsea: Wednesday night, Sept. 16, 1863.

How absurd of you, my dearest Mary, to make so many apologies about a trifling request like that! Why, if you had asked for twenty autographs, Mr. C. would have written them in twenty minutes, and would have written them for you with pleasure. Certainly, my dear, as I have often said before, faith is not your strong point!

---

[1] Cumberland man's account of the Scotch.

Well, we have done our 'outing,' as the people here call going into the country; and it is all the 'outing' we are likely to do till next summer (if we live to see next summer), unless Lord Ashburton should be well enough, and myself well enough, to make another expedition to the Grange during the winter.

I had some idea of going to Folkestone, where Miss Davenport Bromley has a house at present, and pressed me to come and take some tepid sea-water baths. But my experience of the wretchedness of being from home, with this devilry in my arm, has decided me to remain stationary for the present. In spite of the fine air and beauty of the Grange, and Lady Ashburton's superhuman kindness, I had no enjoyment of anything all the three weeks we stayed: being in constant pain, day and night, and not able to comb my own hair, or do anything in which a left arm is needed as well as a right one! I think I told you I had had pain more or less in my left arm for two months before I left London. It was trifling in the beginning; indeed, nothing to speak of, when I did not move it backwards or upwards. I did not think it worth sending for Mr. Barnes about it at first, and latterly he was away at the sea-side for some weeks, having been ill himself. There was nobody else I liked to consult; besides, I always flatter myself that anything that ails me more than usual is sure to be removed by change of scene, so I bore on, in hope that so soon as I got to the Grange the arm would come all right. It did quite the reverse, however; for it became worse and worse, and I was driven at last to consult Dr. Quain, when he came down to see Lord A. He told me, before I had spoken a dozen words, that it wasn't rheumatism I had got, but neuralgia (if any good Christian would explain to me the difference between these two things I should feel edified and grateful). It had been produced, he said, by extreme weakness, and that I must be stronger before any impression could be made on it. Could I take quinine? I didn't know; I would try; so he sent me quinine pills from London, to be taken twice a day if they gave me no headache, which they don't do, and an embrocation of opium, aconite, camphor, and chloroform (I tell you all this that you may ask your Doctor if he thinks it right, or can suggest anything else); moreover, I was to take castor oil every two or three days. I have been following these directions for a fortnight, and there is certainly an improvement in my general health. I feel less cowardly and less fanciful, and feel less disgust at human food; but although the embrocation relieves the pain while I am applying it, and for a few minutes after, it is as stiff and painful as ever when left to itself.

Yours ever affectionately,

JANE CARLYLE.

Of all these dreary sufferings and miseries, which had been steadily increasing for years past, I perceive now, with pain and remorse, I had never had the least of a clear notion; such her invincible spirit in bearing them, such her constant effort to hide them from me altogether. My own poor existence, as she also well knew, was laden to the utmost pitch of strength, and sunk in perpetual muddy darkness, by a task too heavy for me—task which seemed impossible, and as if it would end me instead of I it. I saw no company, had no companion but my horse (fourteen miles a day, winter time, mainly in the dark), rode in all, as I have sometimes counted, above 30,000 miles for health's sake, while writing that unutterable book. The one bright point in my day was from half an hour to twenty minutes' talking with her, after my return from those thrice dismal rides, while I sat smoking (on the hearthrug, with my back to the jamb, puffing firewards—a rare invention!) and sipping a spoonful of brandy in water, preparatory to the hour of sleep I had before dinner. She, too, the dear and noble soul, seemed to feel that this was the eye of her day, the flower of all her daily endeavour in the world. I found her oftenest stretched on the sofa (close at my right hand, I between her and the fire), her drawing-room and self all in the gracefullest and most perfect order, and waiting with such a welcome; ah, me! ah, me! She was weak, weak, far weaker than I understood; but to me was bright always as stars and diamonds; nay, I should say a kind of cheery sunshine in those otherwise Egyptian days. She had always something cheerful to tell me of (especially if she had been out, or had had visitors); generally something quite pretty to report (in her sprightly, quiet, and ever-genial way). At lowest, nothing of unpleasant was ever heard from her; all that was gloomy she was silent upon, and had strictly hidden away. Once, I remember, years before this, while she suffered under one of her bad influenzas (little known to me how bad), I came in for three successive evenings, full of the 'Battle of Molwitz' (which I had at last got to understand, much to my inward triumph), and talked to her all my half hour about nothing else. She answered little ('speaking not good for me,' perhaps); but gave no sign of want of interest—nay, perhaps did not quite want it, and yet confessed to me, several years afterwards, her principal thought was, 'Alas, I shall never see this come to print; I am hastening towards death instead!' These were, indeed, dark days for us both, and still darker unknown to us were at hand. One evening, probably the 1st or 2nd of October, 1863—but for long years I had ceased writing in my note books, and find nothing marked on that to me most memorable of dates—on my return from riding, I learned rather with satisfaction for her sake that she had ventured on a drive to the General Post Office to see her cousin, Mrs. Godby, 'matron' of that establishment; and would take tea there. After sleep and dinner, I was still without her; 'Well, well, I thought, what a nice little story will she have to tell me soon!' and lay quietly down on the sofa, and comfortably waited—still comfortably, though the time (an hour or more) was longer than I had expected. At length came the welcome sound of her wheels; I started up—she rather lingered in appearing,—I rang, got no clear answer, rushed down, and, oh, what a sight awaited me! She was still in the cab, Larkin speaking to her (Larkin lived next door, and for him she had sent, carefully saving me!) Oh, Heavens! and, alas! both Larkin and I were needed. She had had a frightful street-accident in St. Martin's, and was now lamed and in agony! This was the account I got by degrees.

Mrs. Godby sent a maid-servant out with her to catch an omnibus; maid was stupid, unhelpful, and there happened to be some excavation on the street which did not permit the omnibus to come close. Just as my poor little darling was stepping from the kerbstone to run over (maid merely looking on), a furious cab rushed through the interval; she had to stop spasmodically, then still more spasmodically try to keep from falling flat on the other side, and ruining her poor neuralgic arm. In vain, this latter effort; she did fall, lame arm useless for help), and in the desperate effort she had torn the sinews of the thigh-bone, and was powerless to move or stand, and in pain unspeakable. Larkin and I lifted her into a chair, carried her with all our steadiness (for every shake was misery) up to her bed, where, in a few minutes, the good Barnes, luckily found at home, made appearance with what help there was. Three weeks later, this letter gives account in her own words.

The torment of those first three days was naturally horrible; but it was right bravely borne, and directly thereupon all things looked up, she herself, bright centre of them, throwing light into all things. It was wonderful to see how in a few days she seemed to be almost happy, contented with immunity from pain, and proud to have made (as she soon did) her little bedroom into a boudoir, all in her own likeness. She sent for the carpenter, directed him in everything, had cords and appliances put up for grasping with and getting good of her hand, the one useful limb now left. It was wonderful what she had made of that room, by carpenter and housemaid, in a few hours—all done in her own image, as I said. On a little table at her right hand, among books and other useful furniture, she gaily pointed out to me a dainty little bottle of champagne, from which, by some leaden article screwed through the cork, and needing only a touch, she could take a spoonful or teaspoonful at any time, without injuring the rest: 'Is not that pretty? Excellent champagne (Miss Bromley's kind gift), and does me good, I can tell you.' I remember this scene well, and that, in the love of gentle and assiduous friends, and their kind little interviews and ministrations, added to the hope she had, her sick room had comparatively an almost happy air, so elegant and beautiful it all was, and her own behaviour in it always was. Not many evenings after the last of these two letters, I was sitting solitary over my dreary Prussian books, as usual, in the drawing-room, perhaps about 10 P.M., room perhaps (without my knowledge) made trimmer than usual, when suddenly, without warning given, the double door from her bedroom went wide open, and my little darling, all radiant in graceful evening dress, followed by a maid with new lights, came gliding in to me, gently stooping, leaning on a fine Malacca cane, saying *silently* but so eloquently, ' Here am I come back to you, dear!' It was among the bright moments of my life—the picture of it still vived with me, and will always be. Till now I had not seen her in the drawing-room, had only heard of those tentative pilgrimings thither with her maid for support. But now I considered the victory as good as won, and everything fallen into its old course again or a better. Blind that we were! This was but a gleam of sunlight, and ended swiftly in a far blacker storm of miseries than ever before.

That ' bright evening' of her re-entrance to me in the drawing-room must have been about the end of October or beginning of November, shortly following these two letters, ' Monday evening, November 23' (as I laboriously make out the date); ' the F——s,' F—— and his wife, the pleasantest, indeed almost the only pleasant evening company we now used to have; intelligent, cheerful, kindly, courteous, sincere (they had come to live near us, and we hoped for a larger share of such evenings, of which probably this was the first? Alas, to me, too surely it was in effect the last!) Cheerful enough this evening was; my darling sat latterly on the sofa, talking chiefly to Mrs. F——; the F——s gone, she silently at once withdrew to her bed, saying nothing to me of the state she was in, which I found next morning to have been alarmingly miserable, the prophecy of one of the worst of nights, wholly without sleep and full of strange and horrible pain. And the nights and days that followed continued steadily to *worsen*, day after day, and month after month, no end visible. It was some ten months now before I saw her sit with me again in this drawing-room—in body weak as a child, but again composed into quiet, and in soul beautiful as ever, or more beautiful than ever, for the rest of her appointed time with me, which indeed was brief, but is now blessed to look back upon, and an unspeakable favour of Heaven. I often think of that last evening with the F——s, which we hoped to be the first of a marked increase of such, but which to me was essentially the last of all; the F——s have been here since, but with her as hostess (in my presence) never more, and the reflex of that bright evening, now all pale and sad, shines, privately incessant, into every meeting we have.

Barnes, for some time, said the disease was 'influenza, merely accidental cold, kindling up all the old injuries and maladies,' and promised speedy amendment; but week after week gave dismally contrary evidence. 'Neuralgia!' the doctors then all said, by which they mean they know not in the least what; in this case, such a deluge of intolerable pain, indescribable, unaidable pain, as I had never seen or dreamt of, and which drowned six or eight months of my poor darling's life as in the blackness of very death; her recovery at last, and the manner of it, an unexpected miracle to me. There seemed to be pain in every muscle, misery in every nerve, no sleep by night or day, no rest from struggle and desperate suffering. Nobody ever known to me could more nobly and silently endure pain; but here for the first time I saw her vanquished, driven hopeless, as it were looking into a wild chaotic universe of boundless woe—on the horizon, only death or worse. Oh, I have seen such expressions in those dear and beautiful eyes as exceeded all tragedy! (one night in particular, when she rushed desperately out to me, without speech; got laid and wrapped by me on the sofa, and gazed silently on all the old familiar objects and me). Her pain she would seldom speak of, but, when she did, it was in terms as if there were no language for it; 'any honest pain, mere pain, if it were of cutting my flesh with knives, or sawing my bones, I could hail that as a luxury in comparison!'

And the doctors, so far as I could privately judge, effected approximately to double the disease. We had many doctors, skilful men of their sort, and some of them (Dr. Quain, especially, who absolutely would accept no pay, and was unwearied in attendance and invention) were surely among the friendliest possible; but each of them—most of all each new one—was sure to effect only harm, tried some new form of his opiums and narcotic poisons without effect; on the whole I computed, 'Had there been no doctors, it had been only about half as miserable.' Honest Barnes admitted in the end, 'We have been able to do nothing.' We had sick-nurses, a varying miscellany, Catholic 'Sisters of Mercy' (ignominiously dismissed by her third or fourth night, the instant she found they were in real substance Papist propagandists. Oh, that '3 A.M.' when her bell awoke me too, as well as Maggie Welsh, and the French nun had to disappear at once, under rugs on a sofa elsewhere, and vanish altogether when daylight came!) Maggie Welsh had come in the second week of December, and continued, I think, at St. Leonards latterly, till April ended. December was hardly out till there began to be speech among the doctors of sea-side and change of air: the one hope they continued more and more to say; and we also thinking of St. Leonards and our Dr. B—— and bountiful resources there, waited only for spring weater, and the possibility of flight thither. How, in all this tearing whirlpool of miseries, anxieties, and sorrows, I contrived to go on with my work is still an astonishment to me. For one thing, I did not believe in these doctors, nor that she (if let alone of them) had not yet strength left. Secondly, I always counted 'Frederick' itself to be the prime source of all her sorrows as well as my own; that to end it was the condition of new life to us both, of which there was a strange dull hope in me. Not above thrice can I recollect when, on stepping out in the morning, the thought struck me, cold and sharp, 'She will die, and leave thee here!' and always before next day I had got it cast out of me again. And, indeed, in all points except one I was as if stupefied more or less, and flying on like those migrative swallows of Professor Owen, after my strength was done and coma or dream had supervened, till the Mediterranean Sea was crossed! But the time altogether looks to me like a dim nightmare, on which it is still miserable to dwell, and of which I will after this endeavour only to give the dates.—T. C.

LETTER 274.

To Miss Grace Welsh, Edinburgh.

5 Cheyne Row, Chelsea: Tuesday, Oct. 20, 1863.

Thank you a thousand times, dearest Grace, for your long, most moving letter. It is not because of it that I write to-day, for I was meaning to write to-day at any rate; indeed, it rather makes writing more difficult to me: I have cried so over it, that I have given myself a bad headache in addition to my other lamings. But a little letter I will write by to-day's post, and a bigger one when I am more able.

I wrote a few lines to Mrs. Craven, in answer to her announcement of that dear girl's angel death. I told her of my accident, and was trusting to her telling you; but as I told her I had kept you in ignorance of it in the beginning, lest Elizabeth and you and Ann,[1] with your terrible experience of such an accident, might be alarmed and distressed for me more than (I hoped) there would prove cause for; she thought, perhaps, I wished you to remain unaware of it, even when I reported myself progressing more favourably than could have been predicted. I need not go into the *how* of the fall; I will tell you all 'particulars' when I gain more facility in writing; enough to say that exactly this day three weeks I was plashed down on the pavement of St. Martin-le-Grand (five miles from home) on my left side (the arm of which couldn't break the fall), and hurt all down from the hip-joint so fearfully, and on the already lamed shoulder besides, that I couldn't stir; but had to be lifted up by people who gathered round me (a policeman among them) and put into a cab. Elizabeth can fancy my drive home (five miles), and the getting of me out of the cab and upstairs to bed! Wasn't I often thinking of her all the time?

'My' doctor came immediately, and found neither breakage of the leg nor dislocatioon; but the agony of pain, he said, would have been less had the bone broken: I thought of Elizabeth, and doubted that! Still, for three days and three sleepless nights it was such agony as I had never known before; after that, the pain went gradually out of the leg, unless when I moved it, for some bed

---

[1] Poor Elizabeth had slipped and fallen on the street; dislocated her thighbone; got it wrong set; then, after long months of misery, undergone a setting of it 'right'—but is lame to this day.

operations, &c., &c.   But the arm, with its complication of sprain and neuralgia, has given me a sad time, till these last two days that it has returned almost to the state it was in before the fall.   A week ago Mr. Barnes made me get out of bed for fear of 'a bad back,' and *sit on end* on a sofa in my bedroom, like Miss Biffin (the little egg-shaped woman that used to be shown; and two days ago he compelled me to walk a few steps, supported with his arms, and to do the same thing at least twice a day.   It has been a case of 'lacerated sinews;' and he said the tendency of the muscles was to contract themselves after such a thing, and if I did not force myself to put down my foot now and then, I should never be able to walk at all!   Such a threat, and his determined manner, enabled me to make the effort, which *costs*, I can tell you,   But, at whatever cost of pain and nervousness, I have to-day passed through the door of my bedroom (which opens into the drawing-room luckily), using one of the maids as a crutch; so you see I am already a good way towards recovery, for which I feel, every moment, deep thankfulness to God.   To have experienced such agony, and to be delivered from it comparatively, makes one feel one's dependence as nothing else does.

For the rest, as dear Betty is always saying, 'I have mony mercies.'   My servants have been most kind and unwearied in their attentions; my friends more like sisters or mothers than commonplace friends.   Oh, I shall have such wonderful kindnesses to tell you of when I can write freely!   My third cousin, Mrs. Godby, and several others, wished to stay with me; but the 'nursing' I needed was of quite a menial sort; I should still have sought it from my servants, and a lady-nurse would only have given them more to do, and been dreadfully in the way of Mr. C.   My great object, after getting what waiting on I absolutely needed, has been that the usual quiet routine of the house should not be disturbed around Mr. C., who thinks, I am sure, that he has been victimised enough in having to answer occasional letters of inquiry about me.   And now I must conclude for the present.   I am so sorry for poor Robert's fingers.   Be sure to send me the copy of Grace's [1] words to her mother.   Oh, poor souls! what woe, and what mercy!

Your loving niece,
JANE W. CARLYLE.

---

[1] The poor niece's.

LETTER 275.

Mrs. Russell, Holm Hill, Thornhill.

5 Cheyne Row, Chelsea: Monday, Oct. 26, 1863.

Dearest Mary,—Though I still write to you in pencil I have progressed. I walk daily from my bedroom to the drawing-room, after a fashion; my sound arm round Mary's neck, and her arm round my waist. I think there is more nervousness than pain in the difficulty with which I make this little journey. For the rest, I don't lie much on my sofa, but sit on end. I cannot, however, sit up at table to write with pen and ink; I must write with cushions at my back, and with the paper on my knees; in which circumstances a pencil is less fatiguing than pen and ink, as well as less destructive to my clothes.

The unlucky leg will in a week or two, I hope, be all right. I have no pain whatever in it now, except when I try to use it; and then the pain is not great, and gets daily a trifle less. But my arm is still a bad business; especially at night I suffer much from it. It spoils my sleep, and that again reacts upon it and makes it worse. I cannot satisfy myself how much of the pain I am now suffering is the effect of the fall—how much that of the old neuralgia; and Mr. Barnes can throw no light on that for me, or suggest any remedy: at least he doesn't. It seems to me he regards my leg as his patient, and my arm as Dr. Quain's patient, which he has nothing to do with; and he is rather glad to be irresponsible for it, seeing nothing to be done! He did once say in a careless way that plain bark and soda, 'one of the most nauseous mixtures he knew of in this world,' was better than 'my quinine;' but when I asked, would it have as good an effect on my spirits as the quinine had had, he said, 'Oh, I can't promise you that; it would probably make you sick and low; better keep to your lady-like quinine!'

Ask the Doctor if he sees any superiority in plain bark and soda? I don't care how nauseous a medicine is if it do me good.

Another of my uncle Robert's daughters has died of consumption. Grace (my aunt) has written me a long, minute account of her death-bed—one of the saddest things I ever read in my life. It quite crushed down the heart in one for days. The poor young woman's sufferings, and the deaf mother's, and, oh, such a heap of misery is set before one so vividly; and then the consolation! It is a comfort to know that the dying girl was supported through her terrible trial by her religious faith and hope; a comfort, and the only comfort possible, conceivable—if it had stopped there. But you know my feelings about religious excitement—ecstatics; I cannot regard that as a genuine element of religion. Was not Christ Himself, on the cross, calm, simple? Did He not even pray that, if it were possible, the cup might pass from Him? Was there ever in the whole history of His life a trace of excitement? The fuss and excitement that seem to have gone on about this poor young death-bed, then, jars on my mind; the working up of the sufferer herself, and the working up of themselves (the onlookers) into a sort of hysterical ecstasy is almost as painful to me as the rest of the sad business; I feel it to be a getting-up of a death-bed scene to be put into a tract! And in the heart of it all such an amount of real terrible anguish; and the grand solemn faith that could bear all, and triumph over all, harrassed by earthly interference and excitations! I will send the letter; perhaps you will find all this wrong in me; we could never agree about the ' revivals.' Never mind; we love one another all the same.

My kindest regards to the Doctor.

Your affectionate
JANE CARLYLE.

Send back Grace's letter.

LETTER 276.

To Miss Margaret Welsh, Liverpool.

Chelsea: November 2, 1863.

Dearest Maggie,—The very sight of your letter was a relief to me, for I knew that unless dear Jackie had been a little better you couldn't have written as much! Next time do write a mere bulletin, or I can't press you to ' be quick!' From the account you give, I draw far better hope about him than, I dare say, you meant to give in writing it. But there seems to be so much vitality in the poor little fellow; his caring to be read to, his little speech, all that sounds as if there were a good basis of life at the bottom of all this illness. God grant he may soon be pronounced convalescent!

I am very convalescent! I can move about the room with a stick, and the pain in my arm has been considerably less for the last few days, when I make no attempt to move it more than it likes. I attribute the improvement to a new medicine, recommended to me by

Carlyle's friend, Mr. Foxton, who had been cured by it. Before taking it I asked the advice of Dr. B—— at St. Leonards (a man of real ability), and he sent me a proper prescription, and directions about using it. It is called Iodide of Potash, and is taken with quantities of fluid; and along with it have to be taken pills of Valeriate or Quinine. If it cures me, and you ever need curing, you shall have the prescription.

In the beginning of the arm-business, some four months ago now, I fancied I had given my arm an unconscious sprain, as the pain in attempting to move it preceded any aching or shooting, independent of attempting to move it. The Doctor persuaded me 'it was all neuralgia.' Since my accident that sprained feeling has been dreadful, till within the last few days. And though Mr. Barnes always declared 'it was all rheumatism,' it has been impossible to persuade me that the same blow received on my shoulder and hip-joint at the same time, and damaging the sinews in my thigh, would not damage the sinews in my arm also. 'That stands to reason' (as old Helen used to say).

Of course, if rheumatism is about in one, it will gather to any strained part; and so there has been plenty of rheumatic pain, besides the pain from the hurt. But I am certain it is more than rheumatism that hinders me from lifting my arm. And having a faculty of remembering things long after date, I remembered the other day that I took to using the dumb-bells for two or three days, to make myself stronger *par vive force*, when I was feeling so weak and ill early in summer (it must have been just before I noticed the stiffness of my arm), and that I left them off because my arms felt too weak to use them, and ached after. It would be a comfort to my weak mind to be assured that I, then and there, sprained some sinew in my arm, and all the rest would have followed in the course of nature; and I might give up vague terrors about angina pectoris, paralysis, disease of the spine, &c. &c. Best stop.

Yours affectionately,

J. W. C.

LETTER 277.

Mrs. Simmonds, Oakley Street, Cheslea.

5 Cheyne Row: Nov. 3, 1863.

My darling,—I am so thankful that you are all right. And to think of your writing on the third day after your confinement the most legible—indeed, the only legible—note I ever had from you in my life.

Now about this compliment offered me, which you are pleased to call a 'favor' (to you), I don't know what to say. I wish I could go and talk it over; but, even if I could go in a cab one of these next dry days, I couldn't drive up your stairs in a cab! I should be greatly pleased that your baby bore a name of mine. But the God-motherhood? There seems to me one objection to that, which is a fatal one—I don't belong to the English Church; and the Scotch Church, which I do belong to, recognises no Godfathers and God-mothers. The father takes all the obligations on himself (serves him right!). I was present at a Church of England christening for the first time, when the Blunts took me to see their baby christened, and it looked to me a very solemn piece of work; and that Mr. Maurice and Julia Blunt (the Godfather and Godmother) had to take upon themselves, before God and man, very solemn engagements, which it was to be hoped, they meant to fulfil! I should not have liked to bow and murmur, and undertake all they did, without meaning to fulfil it according to my best ability. Now, my darling, how could I dream of binding myself to look after the spiritual welfare of any earthly baby? I, who have no confidence in my own spiritual wel-fare! I am not wanted to, it may perhaps be answered—you mean to look after that yourself without interference. What are these spoken engagements then? A mere form; that is, a piece of hum-bug. How could I, in cold blood, go through with a ceremony in a church, to which neither the others nor myself attach a grain of ver-acity? If you can say anything to the purpose, I am very willing to be proved mistaken; and in that case very willing to stand God-mother to a baby that on the third day is not at all red!

Yours affectionately,
JANE CARLYLE.

LETTER 278.

Mrs. Simmonds, 82 Oakley Street, Chelsea.

5 Cheyne Row: Friday, Nov. 27, 1863.

Dear Pet,—I am not the least well, and should just about as soon walk overhead into the Thames as into a roomful of people! At the same time, I wish to pay my respects to the baby on this her next grand performance after getting herself born, and to place in her small hands a talisman worthy of the occasion, and suitable to a baby born on 'All Saints' Day' (whatever sort of day that may be).

As I shouldn't at all recommend running a long pin into the creature, I advise you to wear the brooch in its present form till the baby is sufficiently hardened, from its present pulpy condition, to bear something tied round its throat, without fear of strangulation! And then you may remove the pin, and attach the talisman to a string in form of a locket. But what is it? 'What does it do' (as a servant of mine once asked me in respect of ' a lord'). What it is, my dear, is an emblematic mosaic, made from bits of some tomb of the early Christians, and representing an early Christian device: the Greek cross, the palm leaves, and all the rest of it. Worn by the like of me, I daresay it would have no virtue to speak of; but worn by a baby born on All Saints' Day! it must be a potent charm against the devil and all his works one would think, for it is a perfectly authentic memorial of the early Christians.

I hope you didn't go and drop the 'Jane' after all! Bless you and it.

Affectionately yours,
JANE BAILLIE WELSH CARLYLE.

LETTERS 279-282.

FOUR SHORT LETTERS.

About the beginning of January (1864) there were thought to be perceptible some faint symptoms of improvement or abatement; which she herself never durst believe in; and indeed to us eager on-lookers they were faint and uncertain—nothing of real hope, except in getting to St. Leonards so soon as the season would permit.

Early in March, weather mild though dim and wettish, this sad transit was accomplished by railway; I escorting, and visiting at every stage; Maggie Welsh and our poor patient in what they called a 'sick carriage,' which indeed took her up at this door, and after delays and haggles at St. Leonards, put her down at Dr. B——'s; but was found otherwise inferior to the common arrangement for a sick person (two window-seats, with board and cushion put between), though about five or six times dearer, and was never employed again. She was carried downstairs here in the bed of this dreary vehicle (which I saw well would remind her, as it did, of a hearse, with its window for letting in the coffin); she herself, weak but clear, directed the men. So pathetic a face as then glided past me at this lower door I never saw nor shall see! And the journey—and the arrival. But of all this, which passed without accident, and which remains to myself unforgetable enough, and sad as the realms of Hades, I undertook to say nothing.

Her reception was of the very kindest; her adjustment, with Maggie and one of our maids (in fine, airy, quiet rooms, in the big house, with the loving and skilful hosts), I saw in a few hours completed to my satisfaction, far beyond expectation. She herself said little; but sat in her pure, simple dress, &c., looking, though sorrowful, calm and thankful. At length I left the house (or indeed they almost pushed me out, 'not to miss the last train,' which I saved only by half a moment by hot speed and good luck), and got home in a more hopeful mood than I had come away. Solely, in my last cab (from Waterloo Station), I had stuck my cap (a fine black velvet thing of *her* making) too hurriedly into my pocket, and it had hustled out, and in the darkness been left. Loss irrecoverable, not noticed till next morning, and which I still regret. 'Oh, nothing!' said she, cheerily and yet mournfully, at our next meeting. 'I will make you a new cap when I am able to sew again.' But I think, in effect, she never sewed more.

Maggie's daily bulletin was indistinct and ambiguous, but strove always to be favourable, or really was so. I sat busy here; generally wrote to my poor darling some daily line; got from her now and then some word or two, but always on mere practical or household matters; seldom or never any confirmation of Maggie's reading of the omens. In the last week of March (as covenanted) I made my first visit (Friday till Monday, I think). Forster and Mrs. F. went with me, but did not see her. I stayed at Dr. B——'s, they at a hotel, where was dining, &c. Whether this was my first visit to her there I strive to recollect distinctly, but cannot. I seem to have even seen but little of her, and certainly learned nothing intimate; as if she rather avoided much communication with me, unwilling to rob me of the doctor's confident prognostications, and much unable to confirm them. Her mood of fixed, quiet sorrow, with no hope in it but of enduring well, was painfully visible. I had just got rid of my vol. v., deeply disappointed latterly on finding that there must be a sixth. Hades was not more lugubrious than that book too now was to me; and yet there was something in it of sacred, of Orpheus-like (though I did not think of 'Orpheus' at all, nor name my darling an 'Eurydice'!) and the stern course was to continue—what else?

In the end of April brother John came to me. Before this it had been decided (since the B——'s, who at first pretended that they would, now evidently would not, accept remuneration from us) that a small furnished house should be rented, and a shift made thither; which was done and over about the time John came. I was to remove thither with my work (so soon as liftable). He by himself made a preliminary visit thither; then perhaps another with me; and at his return I could notice (though he said nothing) that he meant to try staying with us there; which he did, and surely was of use to me there.

Early in May this (Chelsea) house was left to Larkin's care (who at last came into it, letting his own); and all of us had reassembled in the poor new hospice ('117 Marina, St. Leonards'), studious to try our best and utmost there. Maggie Welsh had to return to Liverpool (to nurse a poor little child-nephew who was dying). I did not find Maggie at St. Leonards; but the good Mary Craik (Professor's Mary, from Belfast), by my Jeannie's own suggestion, was written to, came directly, and did as well; perhaps more quietly, and thus better.

In those seven or eight months of martyrdom (October 1863— May 1864) there is naturally no record of the poor dear martyr's own discoverable; nothing but these small, most mournful notes written with the left hand, as if from the core of a broken heart, and worthy to survive as a voice *de profundis*. Maggie's part, which fills the last two pages, I omit. The address is gone, but still evident on inference.

T. Carlyle, Esq., Chelsea.

St. Leonards: Friday, April 8, 1864.

Oh, my own darling! God have pity on us! Ever since the day after you left, whatever flattering accounts may have been sent you, the truth is I have been wretched—perfectly wretched day and night with that horrible malady. Dr. B. knows nothing about it more than the other doctors. So, God help me, for on earth is no help!

Lady A. writes that Lord A. left you two thousand pounds—not in his will, to save duty—but to be given you as soon as possible. 'The wished for come too late!' Money can do nothing for us now.

Your loving and sore suffering
JANE W. CARLYLE.

To-day I am a little less tortured—only a little; but a letter having been promised, I write.

T. Carlyle, Esq., Chelsea.

St. Leonards: April 19, 1864.

It is no 'morbid despondency;' it is a positive physical torment day and night—a burning, throbbing, maddening sensation in the most nervous part of me ever and ever. How be in good spirits or have any hope but to die! When I spoke of going home, it was to *die* there; here were the place for *living*, if one could! It was not my wish to leave here. It was the B——s' own suggestion and wish that we should get a little house of our own.

Oh, have pity on me! I am worse than ever I was in that terrible malady. I am,

Yours as ever,
JANE CARLYLE.

T. Carlyle, Esq., Chelsea.

St. Leonards-on-Sea: April 25, 1864.

Oh, my husband! I am suffering torments! each day I suffer more horribly. Oh, I would like you beside me! I am terribly alone. But I don't want to interrupt your work. I will wait till we are in our own hired house; and then if am no better, you must come for a day.

Your own wretched

J. W. C.

To the Misses Welsh, Edinburgh.

St. Leonards-on-Sea:[1] end of April, 1864.

My own dear Aunts,—I take you to my heart and kiss you fondly one after another. God knows if we shall ever meet again; and His will be done! My doctor has hopes of my recovery, but I myself am not hopeful; my sufferings are terrible.

The malady is in my womb—you may fancy. It is the consequence of that unlucky fall; no disease there, the doctors say, but some nervous derangement. Oh, what I have suffered, my aunts! what I may still have to suffer! Pray for me that I may be enabled to endure.

Don't write to myself; reading letters excites me too much. And Maggie tells me all I should hear. I commit you to the Lord's keeping, whether I live or die. Ah, my aunts, I shall die; that is my belief!

JANE CARLYLE.

LETTER 283.

With a violent effort of packing and scheming (e.g., a box of books with cross-bars in it, and shelves which were to be put in, and make the box a press, &c. &c.), in all which Larkin and Maggie Welsh assisted diligently, I got down to Marina on one of the first days of May. Dreary and tragic was our actual situation there, but we strove to be of hope, and were all fixedly intent to do our best. The house was new, clean, light enough, and well aired; otherwise paltry in the extreme—small, misbuilt every inch of it; a despicable, cockney, scamped edifice; a rickety bandbox rather than a house. But that did not much concern us, tenants only for a month or two—nay, withal there were traces that the usual inhabitants (two old ladies, probably very poor) had been cleanly,

---

[1] Probably still in Dr. B——'s house there. The next letter is expressly dated from the new hired house. Maggie still there, but just about to leave.

neat persons, sensible, as we, of the sins and miseries of their scamped, despicable dwelling-place, poor, good souls!

In a small back closet, window opposite to door, and both always open, I had soon got a table wedged to fixity, had set on end my book-box, changing it to a book-press, and adjusted myself to work, quite tolerably all along, though feeling as if tied up in a rack. One good bedroom there was in the top story, looking out over the sea—this was naturally hers; mine below and to rearward was the next best, and, by cunning adjustments curtains improvised out of rugs and ropes were made to exclude the light in some degree and admit freely the air currents. We made with our knives about a dozen little wedges as the first thing to keep the doors open or ajar at our will, their own being various in that respect! To put up with the house was a right easy matter, almost a solacement, in sight of the deep misery of its poor mistress, spite of all her striving.

The first day she was dressed waiting my arrival, and came painfully resolute down to dinner with us, but could hardly sit it out; and never could attempt again. With intellect clear and even inventive, her whole being was evidently plunged in continual woe, pain as if unbearable, and no hope left; in spite of our encouragements no steady hope at all. On the earth I have never seen so touching a sight! She drove out at lowest three or four times a day—ultimately long drives (which John took charge of to Battle, to Bexhill regions seeking new lodgings—alas, in vain!). Her last daily drive from four to half-past five was always with me, my day's work now done. She was evidently thankful, but spoke hardly at all; or, if she did for my sake, on some indifferent matter, naming to me some street oddity, locality, or the like; those poor efforts now in my memory are the saddest of all, beautiful to me, and sad and pathetic to me beyond all the rest. On setting her down at home I directly stepped across to the livery stable, and mounted for a rapid obligato ride of three hours: rides unlike any I have ever had in the world; more gloomy and mournful even than the London ones, though by no means so abominable even, one's company here being mainly God's sky and earth, not cockneydom with its slums, enchanted aperies and infernalries. I rode far and wide, saw strange old villages (a pair of storks in one) saw Battle by many routes (and even began to understand the Harold-William duel there. Strange that no English soldier, scholar, or mortal ever yet tried to do it). Battle, town and monastery, in the calm or in the windy summer gloaming, was a favourite sight of mine; only the roads were in parts distressing (new cuts, new cockney scamped edifices, and railways and much dust). Crowhirst and its yew, that has seen (probably) the days of Julius Cæsar as well as William the Conqueror's, and ours. But that is not my topic. In the green old lanes with their quaint old cottages, good old cottagers, valiant, frugal, patient, I could have wept. In the disastrous, dust-covered, cockneyfying parts my own feeling had something of rage in it, rage and disgust. It was usually after nightfall when I got home. Tea was waiting for me; and silently my Jeannie (as I at length observed) to preside over it (ah, me! ah, me!), directly after which she went up to bed. Hastings, St. Leonards, Battle, Rye, Winchelsea, Beachy Head, intrinsically all a beautiful region (when not cockneyfied, and turned to cheap and nasty chaos and the mortar tubs), and yet in the world is no place I should so much shudder to see again.

We have various visitors—Forster, Twisleton, Woolner—and none of these could she see; not even Miss Bromley, who came twice for a day or more, but in vain—except the last time, just one hurried glimpse. Nothing could so indicate to what a depth of despair the ever gnawing pain and boundless misery had sunk this once brightest and openest of human souls. The B——s continued with unwearied kindness doing, and hoping, and endeavouring; but that also, even on the Doctor's part much more on her own, began to seem futile, unsuccessful; good old Barnes came once (fast falling into imbecility and finis, poor man), said: 'Hah! intrinsically just the same; however, the disease will burn itself out!'

About the middle of June (lease was to end with that month, and her own house, especially her own room there, had grown horrible to her thoughts) she moved that we should engage the house till end of July; which was done. But, alas! before June ended things had grown still more intolerable; sleep more and more impossible, and she wished to be off from the July bargain—would the people have consented? (which they would not)—so that the question what to do became darker and darker. 'If your room at Chelsea had a new paper?' somebody suggested; and Miss Bromley had undertaken to get it done. This of the 'new paper' went into my heart as nothing else had done, 'so small, so helpless, faint;' and to the present hour it could almost make me weep! It was done, however, by-and-by; and under changed omens. Thank God.

But in the meanwhile, hour by hour, things were growing more intolerable. Twelve successive nights of burning summer, totally without sleep; morning after the eleventh of them she announced a fixed resolution of her own, and the next morning executed it. Set off by express train, with John for escort, to London; would try Mrs. Forster's instead of her own horrible room; but would go (we could all see) or else die. Miss Bromley, who had again come, she consented to see in passing into the train; one moment only, a squeeze of the hand, and adieu. With a stately, almost proud step, my poor martyred darling took her place, John opposite her, and shot away.

At the Forsters' she had some disturbed sleep, not much; and next morning ordered John to make ready for the evening train to Dumfries (to sister Mary's, at the Gill), and rushed along all night, 330 miles at once—a truly heroic remedy of nature's own prescribing, which did by quick steps and struggles bring relief.

The Gill, sister Mary's poor but ever kind and generous *human* habitation, is a small farmhouse, seven miles beyond Annan, twenty-seven beyond Carlisle, eight or ten miles short of Dumfries, and, therefore, twenty-two or twenty-four short of Thornhill, through both of which the S. W. Railway passes. Scotsbrig lies some ten miles northward of the Gill (road at right angles to the Carlisle and

Dumfries Railway): passes by Hoddam Hill, even as of old—and at Ecclefechan, two miles from Scotsbrig, crosses the Carlisle, Moffat or Calendonian Railway—enough for the topography of these tragic things.—T. C.

T. Carlyle, Esq., 117 *Marina, St. Leonards-on-Sea.*

The Gill: July 15, 1864.

Oh, my dear, I am quite as amazed as you to find myself here, so promiscuous! I had given up all idea of Scotland when I left St. Leonards; felt neither strength nor courage for it; but postponed projects till I saw what lay for me at Palace-Gate House. I found there much kindness, and much state, and a firm expectation that I was merely passing through! And if they had wanted me ever so much to stay, there was not a bed in the house fit to be slept in from the noise point of view! Cheyne Row full of Larkins; and my old room in the same state: horrible was the idea to me! The Blunts perhaps out of town; London very hot! I did sleep some human sleep in my luxurious bedroom, all crashing with wheels; but only the having had no sleep the night before made me so clever! I could not have slept a second night. No, there was nothing to be done but what I did—turn that second night to use, travel through it, and not try for any sleep until there was some chance of getting it; that night on the road was nothing like so wretched as those nights at Marina. I drank four glasses of champagne in the night! and took a good breakfast at Carlisle. John was dreadfully ill-tempered: we quarrelled incessantly, but he had the grace to be ashamed of himself after, and apologise. On the whole, it was a birthday of good omen. My horrible ailment kept off as by enchantment.

Mary is all that one could wish as hostess, nurse, and sister. She has had something of the sort herself, and her sympathy is intelligent.

I am gone in for milk diet: took porridge and buttermilk in quantity last night, and slept, with few awakenings, all night; had a tumbler of new milk at eight, and got up to breakfast at nine. I am very shaky, you will see, but, oh, so thankful for my sleep and ease—would it but last! John went to Dumfries yesterday afternoon; and all who had been about me being gone, I felt like a child set down out of arms, but am contriving to totter pretty well so far. John was to be here to-day some time.

I am very sorry for you with those idiot servants. Mary [1] proved

---

[1] Servant now (privately) in a bad way, as turned out!

herself of no earthly use to me, besides being sulky and conceited. Mary Craik is your only present stay; kiss her for me, dear, kind, good girl. I will write to her next. I am so sorry at having had to leave her in such a mess.

James Austin had already got a nice carriage for Mary to drive me about in. Oh, they are so kind, and so polite!

Your own

J. W. C.

EXTRACTS FROM LETTERS.

Mrs. Carlyle's letters, during the remainder of the summer, are a sad record of perpetually recurring suffering. The carriage broke down in her second drive with her sister-in-law, and she was violently shaken. Mrs. Austin gave her all the care that love had to bestow; but in a farmhouse there was not the accommodation which her condition required, and her friend Mrs. Russell carried her off to Holm Hill, where she would be under Dr. Russell's immediate charge. A series of short extracts from the letters to her husband will convey a sufficient picture of her condition in body and mind. The most touching feature in them is the affection with which she now clung to him. Carlyle's anxiety, at last awake, had convinced her that his strange humours had not risen from real indifference. John Carlyle, the doctor, with whom she had travelled, had been rough and unfeeling.—J. A. F.

To T. Carlyle.

Holm Hill, July 23, 1864.—I have arrived safe. They met me at the station, and are kind as so many are. John offered to accompany here, but I declined. Fancy him telling me in my agony yesterday that if I had ever done anything in my life this would not have been; that no poor woman with work to mind had ever such an ailment as this of mine since the world began![1] Oh, my dear, I think how near my mother I am! How still I should be laid beside her.[2] But I wish to live for you, if only I could live out of torment.

July 25.—Mary Craik will go to-day, and you will be alone with town maids; and if I were there I could but add to your troubles. We are sorely tried, and God alone knows what the end will be. It is no wonder if my stock of hope and courage is quite worn out.

---

[1] Poor John! well-intending, but with hand unconsciously rough, even cruel, as in this last instance, which she never could forget again.

[2] Oh, Heaven!

July 27.—I could not write yesterday; I was too ill and desperate. Again, without assignable cause, I had got no wink of sleep.
I am terribly weak. If I had not such kind people beside me I
should be wretched indeed. I do not feel so agitated by the sights
about here as I used to do. I seem already to belong to the
passed-away as much as to the present; nay, more.

God bless you on your solitary way.

July 28.—When will I be back? Ah, my God! when? for it is
no good going back to be a trouble to you and a torment to myself.
I must not look forward, but try to bear my life from day to day,
thankful that for the present I am so well cared for.

August 2.—I am cared for here as I have never been since I lost
my mother's nursing; and everything is good for me: the quiet
airy bedroom, the new milk, the beautiful drives; and when all
this fails to bring me human sleep or endurable nervousness, can
you wonder that I am in the lowest spirits about myself? So long
as I had a noisy bedroom or food miscooked even, I had something
to attribute my sleeplessness to; now I can only lay it to my diseased nerves, and at my age such illness does not right itself.

August 5.—Except for this wakefulness I am better than when I
left Marina, and it is unaccountable that I should be so well in
spite of getting less sleep than I ever heard of anyone, out of a
medical book, getting and living with. I was weighed yesterday,
and found a gain of five pounds since April. If sleep would come
I think I should recover—the first time I have had this hope seriously; but if it won't come I must break down sooner or later,
being no Dutchman nor Jeffrey;[1] and I fear not for my life, but
for my reason. It is almost sinfully ungrateful, when God has
borne me through such prolonged agonies with my senses intact,
to have so little confidence in the future; but courage and hope
have been ground out of me. Submission! Acknowledgment
that my sufferings have been no greater than I deserved is just the
most that I am up to.

Oh, my dear, I am very weary! My agony has lasted long! I
am tempted to take a long cry over myself—and no good will come
of that.

August 22.—I have no wholly sleepless nights to report now. I
don't sleep well, by any means; but to sleep at all is such an im-

---

[1] In Cabanis, case of a Dutch gentleman who lived twenty years without
sleep! which I often remembered for my own sake and hers. Jeffrey is Lord
Jeffrey; sad trait of insomnia reported by himself.

provement. I continue to gain flesh. A—— declares that in the last ten days I have gained four pounds! But that must be non-sense.

August 26.—Walking is hardly possible for me at present, the change of the weather having produced rheumatic pains and stiff-ness in my knees. I did the best I could for myself in buying a good supply of woollen under-garments—not new dresses, not a single new dress, nor anything for the outside. The mercury of my mental thermometer has not risen to care for appearances, only to the hope of living long enough to need new flannels. I did once turn over the idea of a new bonnet, the one I have having lasted me three years! But I sent it to the daughter of your old admirer, Shankland the tailor, and she took out the 'clures' and put in a clean cap for tenpence!

August 29.—The thought of how I am ever to make that long journey back which I made here in the strength of desperation, troubles me night and day; and what is to become of me when I am back, with my warm milk and my nursing and my doctoring taken away? Oh, I am frightened—frightened! a perfect coward am I become—I, who was surely once brave! But I cannot, must not, stay on here through the winter. Besides the unreasonable-ness of inflicting such a burden on others, it would be too cold and damp for me here in the valley of the Nith. So, dear, though I would fain spare you this and all troubles with me, I must go to the subject of the papering [of her room in Cheyne Row], and you must forgive what may strike you as weakly fanciful in my desire to have 'a new colour about me.' You must consider that I was carried out of those rooms to be shoved into a sort of hearse, and (to my own feelings) buried out of that house for ever; and that I have not had time yet, nor got strength enough yet, to shake off the associations that make those rooms terrible for me. To give them somewhat of a different appearance is the most soothing thing that can be done for me.[1]

August 30.—No sleep at all last night; had no chance of sleep, for the neuralgic pains piercing me from shoulder to breast like a sword. I am profoundly disheartened. Every way I turn it looks dark, dark to me. I had dared to hope, to look forward to some years of health—no worse, at least, than I had before. I cannot write cheerfully. I am not cheerful.

---

[1] Poor, forlorn darling! All this was managed to her mind—all this yet stands mournfully here, and shall stand.

September 6.—Oh, that it was as easy to put tormenting thoughts out of one's own head as it is for others to bid one do that! I wish to heaven you were delivered from those paper-hangers. I did not think it would have been so long in the wind. I, the unlucky cause, am quite as sorry for the botheration to you as —— expresses herself, though I have more appreciation of the terrible half-insane sensitiveness which drove me on to bothering you, Oh, if God would only lift my trouble off me so far that I could bear it all in silence, and not add to the troubles of others!

September 7.—I cannot write. I have passed a terrible night. Sleeplessness and restlessness and the old pain (worse than it has ever been since I came here); and, in addition to all that, an inward blackness of darkness. Am I going to have another winter like the last? I cannot live through another such time: my reason, at least, cannot live through it. Oh, God bless you and help me!

September 9.—I am very stupid and low. God can raise me up again; but will He? Oh, I am weary, weary! My dear, when I have been giving directions about the house then a feeling like a great black wave will roll over my breast, and I say to myself, whatever pains be taken to gratify me, shall I ever more have a day of ease, of painlessness, or a night of sweet rest, in that house, or in any house but the dark narrow one where I shall arrive at last.

September 16.—Oh, if there was any sleep to be got in that bed wherever it stands! [alluding to a change in the position of her bed at Chelsea.] But it looks to my excited imagination, that bed I was born in, like a sort of instrument of red-hot torture; after all those nights that I lay meditating on self-destruction as my only escape from insanity. Oh, the terriblest part of my suffering has not been what was seen, has not been what could be put into human language!

September 26, 1864.—Oh, my dear! I thank God I got some little sleep last night! for I had been going from bad to worse, till I had reached a point that seemed to take me back to the time just before I left Marina, and to give to that time additional poignancy. I had the quite recent remembrance of some weeks of such comparative ease and well-ness! Oh, this relapse is a severe disappointment to me, and God knows, not altogether a selfish disappointment! I had looked forward to going back to you so much improved, as to be, if not of any use and comfort to you, at least no trouble to you, and no burden on your spirits![1] And now God

---

[1] Oh, my poor martyr darling!

knows how it will be! Sometimes I feel a deadly assurance that I am progressing towards just such another winter as the last! only what little courage and hope supported me in the beginning, worn out now, and ground into dust, under long fiery suffering!

Dr. Russell says, as Dr. B—— said, that the special misery will certainly wear itself out in time; if I can only eat and keep up my strength, that it may not wear out me! But how keep up my strength without sleep?

Oh dear! you cannot help me, though you would! Nobody can help me! Only God: and can I wonder if God take no heed of me when I have all my life taken so little heed of Him?

John is coming to-day to settle about the journey. When I spoke so bravely about going alone, I was much better than I am at present. I am up to nothing of the sort now, and must be thankful for his escort, the best that offers. He says Saturday is the best day. But I don't incline to arriving on a Sunday morning, so I shall vote for Friday night. But you will hear from me again and again before then.

Your ever affectionate
J. W. CARLYLE.

LETTER 284.

Thomas Carlyle, Chelsea, London.

Holm Hill: Wednesday, Sept. 28, 1864.

Again a night absolutely sleepless, except for a little dozing between six and seven. There were no shooting pains to keep me awake last night, although I felt terribly chill, in spite of a heap of blankets that kept me in a sweat; but it was a cold sweat. I am very wretched to-day. Dr. Russell handed me the other night a medical book he was reading, open at the chapter on 'Neuralgia' that I might read, for my practical information, a list of 'counter-irritants.'

I read a sentence or two more than was meant, ending with 'this lady was bent on self-destruction.' You may think it a strange comfort, but it was a sort of comfort to me to find that my dreadful wretchedness was a not uncommon feature of my disease, and not merely an expression of individual cowardice.

Another strange comfort I take to myself under the present pressure of horrible nights. If I had continued up till now to feel as much better as I did in the first weeks of my stay here, I should have dreaded the return to London as a sort of suicide. Now I again want a change—even that change! There lies a possibility, at least, of benefit in it; which I could not have admitted to myself had all gone on here as in the beginning.

I am very sorry for Lady Ashburton, am afraid her health is irretrievably ruined. Pray do write her a few lines.[1]

It has been a chill mist, from the water all the morning, but the sun is trying to break through.

God send me safe back to you, such as I am.

Ever yours,
J. W. C.

LETTER 285.

Thomas Carlyle, Chelsea, London.

Holm Hill: Thursday, Sept. 29, 1864.

This, then, is to be my last letter from here. Where will the next letter be from, or will there be a next? Blind moles! With our pride of insight too! we can't tell even that much beforehand.

If I had trusted my power of divination yesterday I should have renounced all hope of seeing you this week. I had to go to bed at five in the afternoon, in a sort of nervous fever from want of sleep. The irritation, too, unbearable! That clammy, deathly sweat, in which I had passed the previous night, as if I had been dipped in ice-water, then placed under a crushing weight of frozen blankets, seemed to have taken all warm life out of me. So I gave up and went to bed. At night I took one of Dr. B——'s blue pills (the larger dose had ceased to be beneficial) and about twelve I fell asleep, thank God! and went on sleeping and waking till half-past seven. It was healing sleep, besides being a good deal of it. My first reflection this morning was: And there are beggars—nay, there are blackguards, or both in one—who get every night of their lives far better sleep than even this, which is such an unspeakable mercy to me. *Ach!* it is no discovery that much in this world quite surpasses one's human comprehension.

I have been thrown out of my reckoning. I had calculated that on the principle of a bad night, and a less bad, the less bad would fall to-night; and that I should have some sleep in me to start with. But two waking nights coming together changes the order; and to-night, in the course of nature (second nature), no rest is to be expected.

---

[1] Is again in vigorous health.

Tell Mary I now take coffee to breakfast (John takes tea); and to have a little cream in the house that one may fall soft.

And now good-bye till we meet. Oh, that I had been a day and night (and the night a good one) in the house! No mortal can imagine the thoughts of my heart in returning there, where I was *buried* from! and my life still unrenewed! only the hope, often overcast, that it is in the way of being renewed.

Your ever affectionate
JANE CARLYLE.

My little maid asked me this morning, when about to draw on my stockings: 'What d'ye think? wouldn't it be a good thing to hae the taes (toes) clippet again, afore ye gang away?' I shall so miss that kind, thoughtful girl !

LETTER 286.

Saturday, October 1, 1864, a mild, clear (not sunny) day. John brought her home to me again to this door—by far the gladdest sight I shall ever see there, if gladness were the name of any sight now in store for me. A faint, kind, timid smile was on her face, as if afraid to believe fully; but the despair had vanished from her looks altogether, and she was brought back to me, my own again as before.

During all this black interval I had been continuing my ' comatose flight' without intermission, and was not yet by four months got to land. To extraneous events my attention was momentary, if not extinct altogether; for months and years I had not written the smallest letter or note except on absolute compulsion. But here was an event extraneous to ' Frederick,' which could not be extraneous to ' Frederick's' biographer, never so worn out and crushed into stupefaction. This again woke me into life and hope, into vivid and grateful recognition, and was again a light, or the sure promise of a light from above on my nigh desperate course. (Oh, what miserable inapplicable phrasing is this! or why speak of myself at all?)

My poor martyred darling continued to prosper here beyond my hopes—far beyond her own; and in spite of utter weakness (which I never rightly saw) and of many fits of trouble, her life to the very end continued beautiful and hopeful to both of us—to me more beautiful than I had ever seen it in her best days. Strange and precious to look back upon, those last eighteen months, as of a second youth (almost a second childhood with the wisdom and graces of old age), which by Heaven's great mercy were conceded her and me. In essentials never had she been so beautiful to me; never in my time been so happy. But I am unfit to speak of these things, to-day most unfit (August 12, 1869), and will leave the little series of letters (which were revised several days ago) to tell their own beautiful and tragical story.

Mrs. Russell, Holm Hill, Thornhill, Dumfriesshire.

5 Cheyne Row, Chelsea: Monday, Oct. 3, 1864.

Oh, my darling! my darling! God forever bless you—you and dear Dr. Russell, for your goodness to me, your patience with me, and all the good you have done me! I am better aware now how much I have gained than I was before this journey; how much stronger I am, both body and mind, than I was on my journey to Scotland. I felt no fatigue on the journey down, but I made up for it in nervous excitement! On the journey up, all my nervousness was over when I had parted with you two. Even when arrived at my own door (which I had always looked forward to as a most terrible moment, remembering the hearse-like fashion in which I was carried away from it) I could possess my soul in quiet, and meet the excited people who rushed out to me, as gladly as if I had been returned from any ordinary pleasure excursion!

Very excited people they were. Dr. C. had stupidly told his brother he might look for us about ten, and, as we did not arrive till half after eleven, Mr. C. had settled it in his own mind that I had been taken ill somewhere on the road, and was momentarily expecting a telegram to say I was dead. So he rushed out in his dressing-gown, and kissed me, and wept over me as I was in the act of getting down out of the cab (much to the edification of the neighbours at their windows, I have no doubt); and then the maids appeared behind him, looking timidly, with flushed faces and tears in their eyes; and the little one (the cook) threw her arms round my neck and fell to kissing me in the open street; and the big one (the housemaid) I had to kiss, that she might not be made jealous the first thing.

They were all astonished at the improvement in my appearance. Mr. C. has said again and again that he would not have believed anyone who had sworn it to him that I should return so changed for the better. Breakfast was presented to me, but though I had still Holm Hill things to eat, I had not my Holm Hill appetite to eat them with. All Saturday there was nothing I cared to swallow but champagne (Lady Ashburton had sent me two dozen, first-rate, in the winter); so I took the B—— blue pill that first night, as Dr. Russell had advised. And, oh, such a heavenly sleep I had! awoke only twice the whole night! It is worth while passing a whole night on the railway to get such blessed sleep the night after. Last night, again, I slept; not so well as the first night, of course, but wonderfully well for me; and this morning my breakfast was not contemptible. But it is a great hardship to have lost my warm milk in the morning. I thought by paying an exorbitant price it might have been obtained; but no; the stuff offered me yesterday at eight o'clock it was impossible to swallow. And my poor ' interior,' perfectly bewildered by all the sudden changes put on them, don't seem to have any clear ideas left; so I am driven back into the valley of the shadow of pills!

I had a two-hours' drive yesterday in Battersea Park and Clapham Common. When one hasn't the beauties of nature, one must content one's self with the beauties of art. To-day my drive must be townward; so many things wanted at the shops! There is hardly a kitchen utensil left unbroken; all broken by ' I can't imagine who did it! ' Still, it might have been worse; there seems to have been no serious mischief done.

Wasn't it curious to have your eternal ' Simpson ' given me for fellow-traveller?

Oh, my darling, if I might continue just as well as I am now! But that is not to be hoped. Anyhow, I shall always feel as if I owed my life chiefly to your husband and you, who procured me such rest as I could have had nowhere else in the world.

Your own
JANE W. C.

LETTER 287.

Mrs. Russell, Holm Hill, Thornhill, Dumfriesshire.

5 Cheyne Row, Chelsea: Thursday, Oct. 6, 1864.

Dearest,—At Holm Hill, at this hour, I should have just drunk my glass of wine, and been sitting down at the dining-room table to write the daily letter to Mr. C. The likest thing I can do here is to sit down at the drawing-room table and write to you. I feel the same sort of responsibility for myself to you, as to him, and to you only, of all people alive! and feel, too, the same certainty of being read with anxious interest. Oh, my dear Mary, it is an unspeakable blessing to have such a friend as you are to me! Often, when I have felt unusually free from my misery of late, it has seemed to me that I could not be grateful enough to God for the mercy; unless He inspired me with a spiritual gratitude, far above the mere tepid human gratitude I offered Him! And just so with you: I feel as if I needed God's help to make me humanly capable of the sort of sacred thankfulness I ought to feel for such a friend as yourself ! I wanted to say to you and your dear husband something like this when I came away, but words choked themselves in my throat at parting.

I have been wonderfully well since I came home; have slept pretty well—not as on the first night (that was sleep for only the angels, and for the mortal who had travelled from three to four hundred miles through the night!), but quite tolerably for me, every night till the last. The last was very bad. But I had the comfort of being able to blame something for it, and that was my own imprudence.

I wearied myself putting pictures to rights, which were hung up all crooked (Dr. Russell will sympathise with me), and then worried myself with the shortcomings of my large beautiful housemaid, who justifies (and more) all Mr C.'s tirades against her! This creature, with her goosishness, and her self-conceit, is unendurable after little Mary.

Only think! I get my new milk again, at eight, as usual! Our Rector's wife keeps a cow for her children, and I have a key to her grounds; and, going through that way, it is not three minutes' walk for my cook to take a warm tumbler and fetch it back full of real milk, milked into it there and then. I get plenty of cream, quite good, paying for it exorbitantly; but no matter, so that I get it. My eight stones eleven-and-a-half would soon have had a hole made into it without the milk and cream.

I go out in a nice brougham, with a safe swift horse, whom I know, every day from one till three. And, when I come in, I have added your little tumbler full of excellent champagne to the already liberal allowance of drink! ! ! It is to make up for the difference in the purity of the air! !

The letters Dr. Russell forwarded were from Dr. B—— and Maria (the maid). I send them back, the doctor's for Dr. Russell, and Maria's for you, to amuse you with the girl's presumption! My ' eternal good.' Help us! if Maria is to preach to me! Here is a letter from Grace Welsh, too. Everybody ' praying for me.' Burn them all—I mean the letters—when you have done with them.

God bless my darling.

JANE W. CARLYLE.

LETTER 288.

'Curiosities and niceties of a civilised house.'—Old phrase of my father's.

'Elise's.'—Madame Elise, she often told me, was an artist and woman of genius in her profession; and of late years there had sprung up a mutual recognition, which was often pleasant to my dear one.—T. C.

Mrs. Russell, Holm Hill, Thornhill, Dumfriesshire.

5 Cheyne Row, Chelsea: Monday, Oct. 10, 1864.

Dearest,—Nature prompts me to begin the week with writing to you, though I have such a pressure of work ahead as I can't see daylight through, with no help in putting to rights; for my large, beautiful housemaid is like a cow in a flower-garden amongst the 'curiosities and niceties' of a civilised house! Oh, thank God, for the precious layer of impassivity which that stone weight of flesh has put over my nerves! I am not like the same woman who trembled from head to foot, and panted like a duck in a thunderstorm, at St. Leonards whenever a human face showed itself from without, or anything worried from within. Indeed, my nerves are stronger than they have been for years. Just for instance, yesterday, what I went through without having the irritation increased, or my sleep worsened! As soon as I was in the drawing-room George Cooke came—the same who wrote to tell you of my accident. Now this George Cooke is a man between thirty and forty; tall, strong, silent, sincere; has been a sailor, a soldier, a New Zealand settler, a 'man about town,' and a stockbroker! The last man on earth one would have expected to make one 'a scene.' But lo! what happened? I stood up to welcome him, and he took me in his arms, and kissed me two or three times, and then he sank into a chair and—burst into tears! and sobbed and cried for a minute or two like any schoolboy. Mercifully I was not infected by his agitation; but it was I who spoke calmly, and brought him out of it! He accompanied me in my drive after, and when I had come home, and was going to have my dinner, a carriage drove up. Being nothing like so polite and self-sacrificing as you, I told Helen to say I was tired, and dining, and would see no one. She returned with a card. 'Please, ma'am, the gentleman says he thinks you will see him.' The name on the card was Lord Houghton, a very old friend whom you may have heard me speak of as Richard Milnes. ' Oh, yes! he might come up.' Nobody could have predicted sentiment out of Lord Houghton! but, good gracious! it was the same thing over again. He clasped me in his arms, and kissed me, and dropped on a chair—not crying, but quite pale, and gasping, without being able to say a word.

When the emotional stage was over, and we were talking of my saty at Holm Hill, I mentioned the horrid thing that befell just when I was leaving—the death of Mrs. ——. ' Where?' said Lord Houghton. ' At —— Hall.' He sprang to his feet as if shot, and repeated, ' Dead? dead? dead?' till I was quite frightened. ' Oh, did you know her?' I asked. ' I am sorry to have shocked you.' ' Know her? I have known her intimately since she was a little girl! I was to have gone to visit her this month.'

He told me she had had a romantic history. She was granddaughter to a brother of the —— who was Secretary of State at Naples. The family got reduced, but struggled bravely to keep up their rank in Naples; chiefly helped by this girl who was 'most brave and generous.' They afterwards came to England, and here, too, it was a struggle. ' The girl ' went on a visit, and at her friend's house Mr. —— saw her, fell in love with her, and proposed to her. ' The girl ' shuddered at him. He was a coarse, uncultivated man, perfectly unlike her, and she would not hear of such a marriage; but the father and mother gathered round her, and implored, and reasoned, and impressed on her that with so rich a husband she would be able to lift them out of all their difficulties, and make their old age comfortable and happy, till at length she gave in. Having once married the man, Lord H. said, she made him a good wife and he was a good husband.

After these two enthusiastic meetings, I was sure I should get no sleep. But I slept much as usual during the last week; not at all as I slept the first night, but better than my fraction of sleep during the last weeks with you.

My bedroom is extremely quiet ; my comfort well attended to by—myself. I miss little Mary for more things than ' the clipping o' the taes,' bless her! I was at Elise's, to get the velvet bonnet she made me last year, stripped of its finery. White lace and red roses don't become a woman who has been looking both death and insanity in the face for a year. I told her (Elise) that I had seen two of her bonnets on a Mrs. H—— in Scotland. ' Oh, yes, she has every article she wears from here!' ' You made her court dress, didn't you, that was noticed in the " Morning Post "?' ' Yes,

yes, I dressed the whole three.   Mrs. H's dress cost three hundred pounds! but she doesn't mind cost.'

Dear love to the Doctor.

Your affectionate
J. CARLYLE.

LETTER 289.

John Forster, Esq., Palace-Gate House, Kensington.

5 Cheyne Row, Chelsea: October 1864.

Dearest Mr. Forster,—Now that Mr. C. has me here before his eyes, in an upright posture, he considers it not only my business, but my wifely duty to answer all inquiries about me, myself. I have then the melancholy pleasure of informing you and dear 'Small Individual' that I am returned to this foggy scene of things with no intentions of further travels for the present. I not only 'stood' the long night journey (they always bid me travel by night) very well, but, as on the journey down, it procured me one night of heavenly sleep; and, as nervous illness is more benefited by change than anything else, I felt, for the first week after my return, even better than in the first weeks of my stay in Scotland. The almost miraculous improvement is now wearing off. I have again miserable nights, and plenty of pain intermittently. Still I am a stone heavier (!); and, in every way, an improved woman from what I was when you *did not* see me at Marina. But you will soon be here to take a look at me, and judge for yourself. I hope you won't be so shocked as my carpenter, who told me yesterday: 'I am very sorry indeed, ma'am, to see you fallen so suddenly into infirmity! There is a sad change since I saw you last!' And me a stone heavier!

Best love to her.

Yours ever affectionately,
JANE CARLYLE.

LETTER 290.

To Mrs. Austin, The Gill, Annan.

5 Cheyne Row: Tuesday, Oct. 18, 1864.

Oh, little woman! you will come to our aid, if possible; but if impossible, what on earth are we to do for eggs? At this present Mr. C. is breakfasting on shop-eggs, and doesn't know it; and I am every morning expecting to hear in my bed an explosion over some one too far gone for his making himself an allusion about it. All the people who kept fowls round about have, the maids say, during my absence ceased to keep them, and the two eggs from Addiscombe three times a week are not enough for us both; I, 'as one solitary individual,' needing three in the day—one for breakfast, one in hot milk for luncheon, and one in my small pudding at dinner. When I left Holm Hill, Mrs. Russell was in despair over her hens; thirty of them yielded but three eggs a day. Yours, too, may have struck work; and in that case never mind. Only if you could send us some, it would be a mercy.

Only think of my getting here every morning a tumbler of milk warm from the cow, and all frothed up, just as at the Gill and at Holm Hill, to my infinite benefit. The stable-fed cow does not give such delicious milk as those living on grass in the open air; but still it is milk without a drop of water or anything in it, and milked out five minutes before I drink it. Mr. C. says it is a daily recurring miracle. The miracle is worked by our Rector's wife, who keeps two cows for her children, and she has kindly included me as 'the biggest and best child;' and with a key into their garden my cook can run to their stable with a tumbler and be back at my bedside in ten minutes. Indeed, it is impossible to tell who is kindest to me; my fear is always that I shall be stifled with roses. They make so much of me, and I am so weak. The Countess of Airlie was kneeling beside my sofa yesterday embracing my feet, and kissing my hands! A German girl[1] said the other day, 'I think, Mrs. Carlyle, a many many peoples love you very dear!' It is true, and what I have done to deserve all that love I haven't the remotest conception. All this time I have been keeping better—getting some sleep, not much nor good; but some, better or worse, every night, and the irritation has been much subsided. Yesterday afternoon and this afternoon it is troubling me more than usual. Perhaps the damp in the air has brought it on, or perhaps I have been overdone with people and things; I must be more careful. I have always a terrible consciousness at the bottom of my mind that at any moment, if God will, I may be thrown back into the old agonies. I can never feel confident of life and of ease in life again, and it is best so.

I cannot tell you how gentle and good Mr. Carlyle is! He is busy as ever, but he studies my comfort and peace as he never did

---

[1] Reichenbach's daughter, probably.

before. I have engaged a new housemaid, and given warning to the big beautiful blockhead who has filled that function here for the last nine months; this has been a worry too. God bless you all.

Your affectionate

JANE W. CARLYLE.

Ever so few eggs will be worth carriage.

LETTER 291.

For years before this there had been talk from me of a brougham for her; to which she listened with a pleased look, but always in perfect silence. Latterly I had been more stringent and immediate upon it; and had not I been so smothered under 'Frederick,' the poor little enterprise (finance now clearly permitting) would surely have been achieved. Alas, why was not it? That terrible street accident, for instance, might have been avoided. But she continued silent when I spoke or proposed, with a noble delicacy all her own; forebore to take the least step; would not even by a shake of the head, or the least twinkle of satire in her eyes, provoke me to take a step. Those ' hired flys' so many per week, which were my lazy *succedaneum*, had to be almost forced upon her, and needed argument. It was in vain that I said (what was the exact truth), ' No wife in England deserves better to have a brougham from her husband, or is worthier to drive in it. Why won't you go and buy one at once?' After her return to me the propriety and necessity was still more evident; but her answer still was (and I perceived would always be) that fine, childlike silence, grateful, pleased look, and no word spoken.

Whereupon at length—what I ever since reckon among the chosen mercies of Heaven to me—I did at last myself stir in the matter, and in a week or little more (she also, on sight of this, skilfully co-operating, advising me, as she well could) the long talked of was got done. God be forever thanked that I did not loiter longer! She had infinite satisfaction in this poor gift; was boundlessly proud of it, as her husband's testimony to her; believed it to be the very saving of her, and the source of all the health she had, &c. &c. The noble little soul! So pitiful a bit of tribute from me, and to her it was richer than kingdoms.

Oh, when she was taken from me, and I used in my gloomy walks to pass that door where the carriage-maker first brought it out for her approval, the feeling in me was (and at times still is) deeper than tears; and my heart wept tragically loving tears, though my gloomy eyes were dry! And her mare, named 'Bellona!' There is a bitter-sweet in all that, and a pious wealth of woe and love that will abide with me till I die. No more of it here (August 14, 1869).—T. C.

Mrs. Russell, Holm Hill, Thornhill, Dumfriesshire.

5 Cheyne Row, Chelsea: Monday, Oct. 31, 1864.

Dearest,—I am not tied to two hours now for my drive, which was long enough to stay out in a 'fly,' costing, as it did, six shillings! I have now set up a nice little Brougham, or Clarence (as you call it), all to myself, with a smart grey horse and an elderly driver (in Mr. C.'s old brown surtout)! I was at half-a-dozen coachmakers' yards seeking that carriage, examining with my own eyes, on my own legs! Of course, I took advice as to the outside quality. Mr. Fairie and the livery-stable man, who has kept Mr. C.'s horse these dozen years, both approved my choice, and considered it a great bargain. Sixty pounds, and perfectly new, and handsome in a plain way.

It needs no unbleached linen to protect it, being dark blue morocco and cloth inside, which won't dirty in a hurry; and it is all glass in front like Mrs. Ewart's, so you will see finely about you when I drive you to see the lions here. That prospect is one of my pleasures in the new equipage. I have nothing to show you like the drive to Sanquhar; but the parks here are very beautiful, and I never drive through them now without fancying you at my side and seeing them with your fresh eyes. Mr. C. expects to actually finish his book about New Year, and then—please God that I keep well enough for it—we go to Lady Ashburton's, at a new place she has got in Devonshire, where it will be warmer than here, and evidently I can't have too much change! When we come back, and the weather is fit for the journey, the Doctor and you must come.

It has been moist, even rainy, of late; and damp seems to suit me worst of anything. My appetite defies quinine to bring it back, and the *irritation* has been more distressing. Still, I am no worse, on the whole, than when I left you; and I force myself to take always the new milk and the custard at twelve. There is a weighing-machine at our green-grocer's, at the bottom of the street, but I dare not get myself weighed.

I don't like that photograph of Mary at all. The crinoline quite changes her character and makes her a stranger for me. I want the one that is, as I have always seen her, a sensible girl with no crinoline. I would like her, if she would get herself done for me, as she is on washing mornings—in the little pink bed-gown and blue petticoat. I send a shilling in stamps for the purpose, but don't force her inclinations in the matter.

My friend Mr. Forster was at Müller's trial the last day—saw him receive his sentence, and said he behaved very well. When the sentence was pronounced he bowed to the judge, and walked away with the turnkey. But at the little door leading down from the court he stopped, and said to the turnkey that he wished to say a few words to the judge; and the turnkey led him back; and he said something which could not be heard, on account of his keeping his hand at his mouth to steady it. Forster said the only sign of emotion he had given, all through the business, was a quivering of his lips. When told to speak out he removed his hand, and said courteously to the judge: 'I have had a most fair trial! but I cannot help saying some of the worst things said by the witnesses against me are gross falsehoods.' Then he seemed to break down, and hurried out. I am certain, had it not been that every juryman felt his personal safety on the railway compromised by the acquittal of this man, he would not have been condemned to death on the evidence. It is clear to everybody he had no premeditation of murder, and that Mr. Briggs threw himself out of the carriage, and probably caused his own death thereby. The poor wretch, returning from his visit to his 'unfortunate,' having taken a second-class ticket, had seen Mr. Briggs with his glittering watch-chain get into the first-class carriage, and jumped in after him, thinking the chain would take him to America. It was to take him to a far other land! Curious that he got off, that night, without the discovery of his ticket being second-class. The train had been very late, and, contrary to all use and wont, the tickets were not asked for in the carriages.

I send you a nice letter from Thomas Erskine, the author of many religious books—which I never read, except the first ('Evidences of Christianity'). He is a fine old Scotch gentleman, such as are hardly to be found extant now. Also one from Lady A.

Love to the Doctor. Has the 'young man' from Laich been to call for you?

Tell me about the poor woman in Thornhill who was to have the operation. Mrs. Beck, was that the name?

Kind regards to Mrs. Ewart, and compliments to —— Mrs. Macgowan.

Your loving
JANE CARLYLE.

Dr. Carlyle left for Lancashire this morning. He will be back in Dumfries shortly, and said he would go up to tell you about me.

LETTER 292.

Mrs. Russell, Holm Hill, Thornhill, Dumfriesshire.

5 Cheyne Row, Chelsea: Saturday, Nov. 12, 1864.

Dearest Mary,—At the beginning of this cold, during the time I was constantly retching, and could swallow nothing, I got a moral shock which would, I think, have killed me at St. Leonards; and all it did to me, I think, was to astonish and disgust me. I told you I was parting with my big beautiful housemaid because she was an incorrigible goose, and destructive and wasteful beyond all human endurance. As a specimen of the waste, figure three pounds of fresh butter at twenty pence a pound regularly consumed in the kitchen, and half a pound of tea at four shillings made away with in four days! Then, as a specimen of the destruction—figure all, every one of my beautiful, fine, and some of them quite new, table napkins actually ' worn out' of existence! Not a rag of them to be found; and good sheets all in rags; besides a boiler burst, a pump-well gone irrecoverably dry, a clock made to strike fourteen every hour, and all the china or crockery in the house either disappeared or cracked! To be sure, the housemaid was not alone to bear the blame of all the mischief, and the cook was to be held responsible for the waste of victuals at least. But Mary—the one who attended me at St. Leonards—though the slowest and stupidest of servants, had so impressed me with the idea of her trustworthiness, and her devotion to me, that I could accuse her of nothing but stupidity and culpable weakness in allowing the other girl, seven years her junior, to rule even in the larder! Accordingly I engaged an elderly woman to be cook and housekeeper, and Mary was to be housemaid, and wait on me as usual. Helen (the housemaid) meanwhile took no steps about seeking a place, and when I urged her to do so, declared she couldn't conceive why I wanted to part with her. When I told her she was too destructive for my means, she answered excitedly: ' Well! when I am out of the house, and can't bear the blame of everything any longer, you will then find out who it is that makes away with the tea, and the butter, and all the things!' As there was nobody else to bear the blame but Mary, and as I trusted her implicitly, I thought no better of the girl for this attempt to clear herself at the expense of

II.—11

nobody knew who; especially as she would not explain when questioned. When I told slow, innocent Mary, she looked quite
amazed, and said: 'I don't think Helen knows what she is saying
sometimes; she is very strange!'

Well, Mary asked leave to go and see her family in Cambridge-
shire before the new servant came home, and got it, though very
inconvenient to me. When she took leave of me the night before
starting, she said in her half-articulate way: 'I shall be always
wondering how you are till I get back.' She was to be away
nearly a week. Mrs. Southam, who sat up at night with me last
winter, my Charlotte's mother, came part of the day to help
Helen. She is a silent woman, never meddling; so I was surprised when she said to me, while lighting my bedroom fire, the
day my cold was so bad: 'Helen tells me, ma'am, you are parting with her?' 'Full time,' said I; 'she is a perfect goose.'
'You know best, ma'am,' said the woman; 'but I always like ill to
see the innocent suffering for the guilty!' 'What do you mean?'
I asked; 'who is the innocent and who is the guilty?' 'Well,
ma'am,' said the woman, 'it is known to all the neighbours round
here; you will be told some day, and if I don't tell you now, you
will blame me for having let you be so deceived. Mary is the worst
of girls! . . . . and all the things you have been missing
have been spent on her man and her friends. There has been constant company kept in your kitchen since there was no fear of your
seeing it; and whenever Helen threatened to tell you, she frightened her into silence by threats of poisoning her and cutting her
own throat!'

Now, my dear, if you had seen the creature Mary you would just
as soon have suspected the Virgin Mary of such things! But I have
investigated, and found it all true. For two years I have been
cheated and made a fool of, and laughed at for my softness, by this
half-idiotic-looking woman; and while she was crying up in my
bedroom—moaning out, 'What would become of her if I died?'
and witnessing in me as sad a spectacle of human agony as could
have been anywhere seen; she was giving suppers to men and
women downstairs; laughing and swearing—oh, it is too disgusting!

God bless you, dearest.

JANE CARLYLE.

LETTER 293.

Mrs. Russell, Holm Hill, Thornhill, Dumfriesshire.

5 Cheyne Row, Chelsea: Monday, Dec. 20, 1864.

Dearest Friend,—If it is as cold, and snows as hard, there as here, you will be fancying me broken down if I don't write and tell you I am taking all that very easily; driving out every day from two to three hours, as usual. The cold is not so trying for me as the damp, I find. My horse has not stood it nearly so well! I had him roughened the first day of the frost and snow, but nevertheless he managed to get a strain in one of his hind legs, and is now in great trouble, poor beast, with a farrier attending him, and his leg 'swollen awful!' He is a beautiful grey horse, given me, whether I would or no, by Lady Ashburton; but young, and, I am afraid, too sensitive for this world! 'Whenever he is the least put out of his way, he goes off his food,' the groom says. Nobody can say when he will be fit for work again—if ever. Meanwhile I get a horse from the livery stables.

The most spirited thing I have done since you last heard of me was driving to Acton with—Madame Eiise! to see her beautiful place there, and take a dinner-tea with her, and back with her, arriving at home as late as six o'clock! It was a pleasant little excursion. Elsie, as a woman, with a house and children, is charming. It is a magnificent house, with a dinning-room about three times the size of the Wallace Hall dining-room, and a drawing-room to match; both rooms fitted up with the artist-genius she displays in her dresses! It is an old manor house, with endless passages; and at every turn of the passage there is a bust—Lord Byron, Sir Walter Scott, Pope, Milton, Locke.

The drawing-room opens into a conservatory that would take Mrs. Pringle's into a small corner of it. There is an immense garden round the house, with greenhouses, and a green field beyond the garden, with sheep in it—clean sheep! A middle-aged, ladylike governess took charge of the three children: perfect little beauties! and the nurse and other maids had the air of 'a great family' about them. They all treated 'Madame' as if she had been a princess! A triumph of genius!

The only drawback to my satisfaction was a dread of catching cold. The immense rooms had immense fires in them. But their size, and the knowledge that they were only lived in from Saturday till Monday in a general way, give me a sense of chill; and then be-abroad so late at this season was very imprudent. I went to bed with a pain in my shoulder and much self-upbraiding; but got some sleep, and no harm was done.

Do you know that bottle of whisky you gave me has been of the greatest use! Things affect one so differently at different times? Whisky seemed to fever me at Holm Hill. Here it calms me, and helps me to sleep I take a tablespoonful raw when I get desperate about sleeping, and invariably, hitherto, with good effect. I take no quinine, nor other medicine, at present, except the aperient pills. Half a one I have to take every night. The potash-water I like very much with my wine and my milk, and take from one to two bottles of it every day.

I have not been weighed again; but I don't think I can have lost any more, as I eat better since the new cook took me in hand. She continues to be a most comfortable servant: such courtesy! such equability of temper! such obligingness! and all that so cheap! for the weekly bills are less than when I had ignorant servants. The house-maid is also a good servant, but not so agreeable a one. The droop at the corners of her mouth, indicating a plaintive, even peevish, nature, does not belie her I think. When Mr. C. finds fault, instead of going to do what he wants, she cries and sulks. When are you going to give me little Mary? My compliments to her and to Lady Macbeth.

My grateful and warm love to your husband. To yourself a hundred kisses. I will write soon again.

Your true friend,
JANE CARLYLE.

LETTER 294.

Mrs. Russell, Holm Hill, Thornhill, Dumfriesshire.

5 Cheyne Row, Chelsea: Dec. 27, 1864.

Oh, darling, I have been wanting to write to you every day for a week, but the interruptions have been endless, and the unavoidable letters many. On Christmas Day I thought I should have a quiet day for writing, Mr. C. being to dine at Forster's. But a young German lady of whom I am very fond 'could not let me be left alone,' and came at eleven in the morning and stayed till nine at night; and then our Rector—bless him!—came when he left church and sat with me till eleven.

I wonder how you would have taken a thing that befell me last Wednesday? I was waiting before a shop in Regent Street for some items of stationery; and a young woman, black-eyed, rosy-cheeked, with a child in her arms, thrust herself up to the carriage window and broke forth in a paroxysm of begging: refusing to stand aside even when the shopman was showing me envelopes. Provoked at her noise and pertinacity, I said: 'No, I will give you not a single penny as an encouragment to annoy others as you are annoying me.' If there be still such a thing as the evil eye, that beggar-woman fixed the evil eye on me, and said slowly, and hissing out the words: 'This is Wednesday, lady; perhaps you will be dead by Christmas Day, and have to leave all behind you! Better to have given me a little of it now!' and she scuttled away, leaving me with the novel sensation of being under a curse.

Would you have minded that after the moment? I can't say I took it to heart. At the same time, I was rather glad when, Christmas being over, I found myself alive and just as well as before.

Dr. B—— writes that his wife had been dreaming about me again. Bessie is a most portentous dreamer. If I had been told this between the Wednesday and Christmas Day, it would really have frightened me, I think.

My dear, I have got five drops of my heart's blood congealed and fastened together to encircle your wrist, as a memorial of my last visit and as a New Year's blessing. I am hesitating whether to send it by post or by railway. I never lost, or knew personally of anything being lost by post except the Whigham butterfly, so I had best risk it; there is such confusion of parcels by rail at this time of year. Only I will not register it, as I always think that just points out to the covetous postman what is worth stealing.

Please to send a single line or an old newspaper by return of post, that I may be sure the thing has not misgone.

Ever your affectionate
JANE CARLYLE.

LETTER 295.

Sunday night, January 5, 1865, went out to post-office with my last leaf of 'Frederick' MS. Evening still vivid to me. I was not joyful of mood; sad rather, mournfully thankful, but indeed half killed, and utterly wearing out and sinking into stupefied collapse after my 'comatose' efforts to continue the long flight of thirteen years to *finis*. On her face, too, when I went out, there was a silent, faint, and pathetic smile, which I well felt at the moment, and better now! Often enough had it cut me to the heart to think what she was suffering by this book, in which she had no share, no interest, nor any word at all; and with what noble and perfect constancy of silence she bore it all. My own heroic little woman! For long months after this I sank and sank into ever new depths of stupefaction and dull misery of body and mind; nay, once or twice into momentary spurts of impatience even with her, which now often burn me with vain remorse : Madame Elise, e.g.—I sulkily refused to alight at the shop there, though I saw and knew she gently wished it (and right well deserved it); Brompton Museum (which she took me to, always so glad to get me with her, and so seldom could). Oh, cruel, cruel! I have remembered Johnson and Uttoxeter, on thought of that Elise cruelty more than once; and if any clear energy ever returned to me, might some day imitate it.—T. C.

To Mrs. Austin, The Gill, Annan.

5 Cheyne Row, Chelsea: Feb. 1865.

My dear,—The box is come, and this time the eggs have been a great success, not a single one broken! Neither were the cakes broken to any inconvenient degree. Already they are half eaten, by myself. Mr. C. wouldn't take a morsel because 'there was butter in them—a fatal mistake on the part of poor Mary!' I told him I believed it was not butter but cream, and no 'mistake' at all; as the cakes you made for me in that way at the Gill agreed with me quite well. It was so kind of you to take immediate note of my longing! My dear little woman, you not only do kind things, but you do them in such a kind way! Many a kind action misses the grateful feelings it should win by the want of graciousness in the doing.

I continue improving; but a week of terrible pain has given me a good shake, and I don't feel in such good heart about the Devonshire visit as I did. Still it stands settled at present that we go on the 20th, God willing. For how long will depend on how Mr. C. gets on with his sleep, &c.

I shall take my housemaid with me as lady's-maid; for I shudder at the notion of being at the mercy of other people's servants when I am so weak and easily knocked down. She is a very respectable woman, the new housemaid, and both she and Mrs. Warren (the cook) were as kind to me as kind could be when I was laid up. I never was so well cared for before, and with so little fuss, since I left my mother's house. It is a real blessing to have got good, efficient, comfortable servants at last, and I may say I have earned it by the amount of bad servants I have endured.

I have a great deal to do to-day, and little strength; so good-bye. I will write soon again.

Affectionately yours,
JANE CARLYLE.

LETTER 296.

Mrs. Braid, Green End, Edinburgh.

5 Cheyne Row, Chelsea: Feb. 14, 1865.

My own dear Betty! Oh, I am sorry for you! sorrier than I can say in words! I know what a crushing sorrow this will be for you. I, who know your affectionate, unselfish heart, know that the consolations, which some would see for you in poor suffering George's death, will be rather aggravations of the misery! That you should have found at last rest from the incessant, anxious, wearing cares, that have been your lot for years and years—oh, so many years— will be no relief, no consolation to you! This rest will be to you, at first and for long, more irksome, more terrible than the strain on body and mind that went before. He that is taken from you was not merely your own only son, but he was too the occupation of your life, and that is the hardest of all losses to bear up under! Oh, Betty darling, I wish I were near you! If I had my arm about your neck, and your hand in mine, I think I might say things that would comfort you a little, and make you feel that, so long as I am in life, you are not without a child to love you. Indeed, indeed, it is the sort of love one has for one's own mother that I have for you, my dearest Betty! But here I am, four hundred miles away; and with so little power of locomotion compared with what I once had! And the words fall so cold and flat on paper!

I have been dangerously ill; about three weeks ago I got a chill, at least so the doctor said, and the result was inflammation of the bowels. I was in terrible agony for some days, and confined to bed for a week. I am still very feeble even for me; but there is no return of the miserable nervous illness, which kept me so ruined for more than a year. I cannot write much.

Give my thanks to Mrs. Duncan,[1] who seems a most kind, nice woman. I will write to her when I am a little more able. My kind regards to your husband.

Your own bairn,
JEANNIE WELSH CARLYLE.

---

[1] Not known to me.

LETTER 297.

Seaforth (near Seaton, Devonshire) is the Dowager Lady Ashburton's pretty cottage, who waited for us at the station that Wednesday evening, and was kindness itself. It was Wednesday, March 8, 1865, when we made the journey. The day was dry and temperate; we had a carriage to ourselves, and she (though far weaker than I had the least idea of—stupid I!) made no complaint, nor, indeed, took any harm; though at the end (Lady Ashburton having brought an open carriage unfit for the coldish evening of a day so bright), we had to wrap our invalid in quite a heap of rugs and shawls, covering her very face and head; in which she patiently acquiesced, nor did she suffer by it afterwards.

I think we stayed above a month; and in spite of the noise, the exposure, etc., she did really well, slept wonderfully, and was charming in her cheerful weakness. She drove out almost or altogether daily. Sir Walter and Lady Trevelyan were close neighbors, often fellow-guests. Sir Walter and I rode almost daily, on ponies ; talk innocent, quasi-scientific even, but dull, dull! My days were heavy laden, but had in them something of hope. My darling's well-being helped much. Ah, me! ah, me! We drove to Exeter one day (Lady A., a Miss Dempster, and we two); how pretty and cheery her ways that day! Lady A. came up to London with us. From a newspaper we learned the death of Cobden (which may serve to date if needed).—T. C.

Mrs. Russell, Holm Hill.

Seaforth Lodge, Seaton, Devonshire: March 10, 1865.

Dearest,—I was to have written before I went on my travels, but adverse circumstances were too powerful. First, the nausea, which I think I complained of in my last letter, kept increasing, so that I had no heart to do anything that could be let alone till the last possible moment; and my last days were cramped full of shopping, and packing, and leave-taking, and settling with workmen about repairs, and white-washing to be done in my absence; so that any moment left me to bless myself in was devoted to lying quite down on the sofa, rather than letter-writing.

When we started on Wednesday morning, with, on my part, no sleep 'to speak of,' and five hours of railway before us, besides a carriage drive after, my mood was of the blackest. But George Cooke was at the station to look after our luggage; and, halfway, the sun broke out, and it was new country for me part of the way, and very beautiful. And the sheep, bless them, were not only white as milk, but had dear wee lambs skipping beside them! And the river, that falls into the sea near here, was not muddy and sluggish, like all the rivers (very few indeed) I had seen since I left dear Nith—but clear as crystal, and bright blue. And, at the end, such a lovely house, on a high cliff overlooking the bluest sea. And such a lovely and loveable hostess! So truly 'the latter end of that woman was better than the beginning.' I am glad to find the in-sane horror I conceived of the sea, all in one night at St. Leonards, has quite passed away. I love it again as I had always done till then; and rather regret that no sound of it reaches over the cliff.

But there is something I want to say to you, more interesting to me than the picturesque,—something that my heart is set on—about your coming to see London. I know you would make no diffi-culty for my sake, if for nothing else. It is that calmly obstinate husband of yours, who carries his love of home to such excess, that is the 'lion in the way' for my imagination. Yet, if he knew how much good I expect to get of having you in London with me, and what efforts I will make to repay him for his efforts, he, who is so kind, so obliging to the poorest old women of the country-side, will surely not resist my entreaties. You are to understand that, besides the pleasure of the thing to me, your coming at the time I ask would be doing me a real service; Mr. C. is going on his travels shortly after our return to London from this place—some two or three weeks hence, if all goes right here, and I am to be left alone at Chelsea. Accompanying him would not suit me at all; indeed, several of the houses he is going to could not receive us both at a time, as we need two bedrooms. And then I should prefer doing my outing (as the Londoners call it) in autumn. So I shall be alone, needing company; and of all company, I should like best the Doctor's and yours. Then, when he is away, I have plenty of house-room, which is not the case when he is at home, seeing that he occupies two floors of the house 'all to himself!' And I have my time all to myself to show you about London, and my carriage to take you wherever you liked. Oh, my dear, it would be so nice! I have heard you say the Doctor could leave the bank [1] for a fortnight whenever he liked. Well! if he could not stay longer than a fortnight, he might bring you up; and see and do all that could be seen and done in one fortnight, and then leave you for a good while longer. You would have no difficulty in going back along the road you had come; or I might find some-

---

[1] Dr. Russell's special employment for years back was superintendence of a country bank; but his gratis practice of *medicine*, and of every helpful thing in that region, continued and continues (1869).

II.—11*

one going that direction to take charge of you; or, if you were very good, and stayed long enough, I would go and take charge of you myself, and stay, not three months next time (!) but a week or two. Oh, my darling, it would make me so glad! Surely, surely, you and the Doctor will not refuse me. Mr. Carlyle spoke of writing to you himself to press your staying with us till he returns. [1]

[*Not signed*] J. W. C.

LETTER 298.

Mrs. Russell, Holm Hill.

5 Cheyne Row: May 4, 1865.

Darling,—When I came in to-day, and saw a letter from you on the table, I felt myself make as near an approximation to a blush as my sallow complexion is capable of. It was a little 'coal of fire' heaped on my head! For days back I had been thinking how neglectful I must seem to you, making no answer to that kindest of letters and of invitations, written, too, when you were ailing, and 'looking at the dark of things!' You had still managed to look at the bright of *me*, since you could believe that my presence would 'cheer you' instead of boring you. But it was not that I was really not caring to write, nor yet that I was giving way to physical languor (though that has been considerable). It was that for the last week or two I have been kept in a whirl of things which made it out of the question for me to sit down quietly, and make up my mind what to say.

Mr. C. has been sitting to Woolner for his bust; and it seems he 'is as difficult to catch a likeness of as a flash of lightning' is; so that it is a trying business for both sitter and sculptor. I have had to drive up to Woolner's every two or three days, and climb steep endless stairs to tell what faults I see. And in connection with this bust, there has been such a sitting to photographers as never was heard of! Woolner wants a variety of photographs to work from, and the photographer wants a variety to sell! and Mr. Carlyle yields to their mutual entreaties. And then, when they have had their will of him, they insist on doing me (for my name's sake). And Mr. C. insists too, thinking always the new one may be more successful than former ones; so that, with one thing and another, I have been worried from morning till night, and post-

---

[1] Alas! they never came.

poned writing till I should have got leisure to think what was to be written. But I must not put off any longer, since you are getting uneasy about me.

I am not worse—indeed, as to the sickness and the sleeplessness I am rather better in both respects—but I am weak and languid, have little appetite, and am getting thinner. The best thing for me would be to get away; and away to you, rather than anywhere else! I know that well enough in both my heart and my head; but one cannot do just what one likes best, and even what is best for one. I could not go with Mr. C. for several reasons. First, having made up his mind to go off ' at his own sweet will,' and having understood that I was to stay behind, he would now find it a great incumbrance to take me with him. Second, I have invited Dr. B—— and Bessy to pay me a visit so soon as I have a bedroom for them; and they have promised to come for a few days.[1] About the end of May is the doctor's leisurest time at St. Leonards. Third, Mr. C. wants the dining-room papered, and fitted up with bookcases from the study at the top of the house; which is too long a climb for him now that ' Frederick ' is done. That he expects me to ' see to ' in his absence. And how long it will take me to ' see to it ' will depend on the workmen.

For the rest, I am uncertain how long he will be away; if ' months ' (as he speaks of), there might still be time for me, after I had finished my business here, to rush off to Holm Hill, and stay as many weeks with you as I stayed *months* last year. I should so like it! And Mr. C. wouldn't object, though he would find it very absurd to be taking such a long journey so soon again. I put out a *feeler* the other night; Miss Dempster was pressing him to visit her when he should be in Forfarshire (he is going to Linlathen amongst other places), and I said: ' I shall perhaps be nearer you than he will be! Lady Airlie was pressing me so hard to-day to come to Cortachy Castle, that there is no saying but I will follow him north.' ' Indeed!' he said, not with a frown, but a smile. And I added, ' If he stays away long I may at least get the length of Dumfriesshire.' But till I get my workmen out of the house, and know something definite of Mr. C.'s plans, I can determine nothing. Will you let me leave it open? I like so ill to say positively, and absolutely, ' No, I cannot come this year!' Because, you see, having a character for standing by my word to keep up, I could not, after an absolute ' no ' said now, avail myself of any

---

[1] They never came.

facilities for going to you which may turn up later. So may I leave the question open?

How absurd! In telling you on the other sheet how I was bodily, I quite forgot to mention my most serious ailment for the last six weeks. My right arm has gone the way that my left went two years ago, gives me considerable pain, so that I cannot lie upon it, or make any effort (such as ringing a bell, opening a window, &c. &c.) with it; and if anyone shakes my hand heartily, I—shriek! Geraldine Jewsbury is always asking, 'Have you written to Dr. Russell yet about your arm?' But what could anyone do before for the other arm? All that was tried was useless except quinine; and quinine destroys my sleep. I must just hope it will mend of itself as the other did.   Your ever-attached friend,

JANE W. CARLYLE.

LETTER 299.

To-day (August 9, 1866) I have discovered in drawers of pedestal these mournful letters of my darling in 1865. They had lain torn in my writing-case, till their covers were all lost, and there is now no correct dating of them. I have tried to save the sequence and be as correct as I could. Here are the cardinal dates. About May 20 I went to Dumfries, thence to the Gill; and she, here at home (courageous little soul!), began doing this room (the very beauty of which now pains and amazes me).

Beginning of May her right arm took ill, as her left had done last year, and she painfully went and came between Streatham and here for some time (perhaps near a fortnight), writing with her left hand. June 17, she passed me (little guessing of her in the rail) and went to Holm Hill; very ill then too, still left hand; and thence in July to Nithbank, and after about ten or twelve days (middle or farther of July) went home somewhat better; got her roomdone, recovered her right hand, and went to Folkestone to Miss Bromley's for a few days (which proved her last visit, little as I then anticipated). Her beautiful figure and presence welcoming me home (end of August) will never leave my memory more. —T. C.

T. Carlyle, Esq., The Hill, Dumfries.

5 Cheyne Row, Wednesday, May 24, 1865.

I wonder if you will get this letter to-morrow, should it be put in the pillar to-night? Dear! dear! should no word reach you till Friday morning, you will be 'vaixed,' and perhaps frightened besides.

The figure I cut on Monday morning was not encouraging. When I had cried a very little at being left by myself, I lay on the sofa till mid-day, not sleeping, but considering what to do for the best with this arm, which had got to a pitch, and was reducing me to the state of last year in point of sleep. And the result of my considerations was, first, a note to Dr. B——, urging him and Bessy to keep their promise of spending a couple of days with me as soon as possible ; and next, in the meantime, a call at Quilter's to order the old quinine pills and a bottle of castor oil. If I am to be kept awake all night at any rate by the pain, I may as well have recourse to the only prescription which did any good to the other arm—even at the cost of sleep. That first day I also called at the carpenter's, to *lever* himself, for he ' had great things to do.' Then on to luncheon at the Gomms'. Do you remember I was engaged to luncheon there? They have a beautiful, large, old-fashioned, cool house. And the luncheon was a sonnet done into dainties. I brought away Lord Lothian's book on America, but have not yet read a word of it, nor of anything else—not even of Mrs. Paulet's novel, nor my own ' Daily Telegraph.' On my return, I came upon Geraldine in Cheyne Row ; and she ' could not leave me ' till ten at night, I ' looked such a ghost.'

On Tuesday I had to take Mrs. Blunt to make calls at Fulham ; and then I ' did the civil thing ' to Mrs. F——. F—— was in, and talked much of your ' gentleness and tenderness of late,' and the ' much greater patience you had in speaking of everybody and everything.' And I thought to myself, ' If he had only heard you a few hours after that walk with him, in which you had made such a lamblike impression!' He expressed a wish to read Mrs. Paulet's novel, and I have sent it to him. A very curious, clever, ' excessively ridiculous, and perfectly unnecessary' book is Mrs. Paulet's novel, so far as I have read in the first volume. And Mrs. Paulet herself I don't know what to make of, for I have seen her. In my saintly forgiveness and beautiful pity I left a card for her yesterday; and she came a few hours after ; and Geraldine, too, came ; and I was not left alone till half-past ten, when it was too late to write.

This morning (I don't know by what right) I expected a letter from you, which did not come till the afternoon. And positively I was almost well pleased there was no letter—to answer, for I had ' indulged in a cup ' of castor oil, and was—oh, so sick; and besides, that matter had unexpectedly taken to ' culminating ' again. Last night there had come from Jessie Hiddlestone a very nice letter, not accepting my rejection on the score of the ' situation ' being ' too dull for her,' but assuring me that she would not ' be the least dull and discontented,' and 'altogether' throwing a quite different and rosier colour on the project. I will inclose the letter, and you will read it, and tell me if you think I was right in being moved thereby to engage her ; for that is what I have done this forenoon, in the middle of my sorrows of castor oil !

For the rest I have no doubt you will get better, and do well there for a time. Perhaps I shall take flight myself if my terrible nights continue too long for endurance and this wearing pain lasts. It is pulling me down sadly ; and neuralgia has such an effect on the spirits.

One thing I have to say, that I beg you will give ear to. I have not recovered yet the shock it was to me to find, after six months, all those weak, wretched letters I wrote you from Holm Hill 'dadding about' in the dining-room ; and should you use my letters in that way again I shall know it by instinct, and not write to you at all ! There !

Please return Jessie Hiddlestone's letter.

Your ever affectionate
JANE W. CARLYLE.

LETTER 300.

To T. Carlyle, Esq., The Hill, Dumfries.

5 Cheyne Row, Chelsea: Saturday, May 27, 1865.

I think, dear, you must have lost a day this week—must have—stop ! No ! I should have said—gained a day ! You bid me 'not bother myself writing to-morrow, but send a word on Saturday.' And the to-morrow is Saturday. This day on which I am not to 'bother myself writing' is Saturday. I posted a letter to you yesterday at the right time. That night post is later than you think. It was past nine when Fanny put in the pillar the letter you received the following evening at eight.

My quinine and castor oil have quite failed of doing the good to my right arm which they formerly did to my left. The pain gets more severe and more continuous from day to day. Last night it kept me almost entirely awake. I often wonder that I am able to keep on foot during the day, and take my three hours' drives, and talk to the people who come to relieve my loneliness, with that arm always in pain, as if a dog were gnawing and tearing at it ! But anything rather than the old nervous misery, which was not to be called pain at all ! positive natural pain I can bear as well as most people. But I wish Dr. B—— would come! Perhaps he can deal with a reality like this, though he could 'do nothing against hysterical mania!'[1] I got the thing he mentioned, Veratrine liniment, yesterday, from Quilter; and Geraldine rubbed it in for an hour last night. But, as I said, last night was the worst!

George Cooke said you desired him to 'come often, and look after me!' 'Perfectly unnecessary;' I mean the desiring! Couldn't you fetch up Noggs[2] to Dumfries? So much walking in such hot weather must be tiring.

All good be with you.

Yours ever,

J. W. C.

LETTER 301.

T. Carlyle, Esq., The Gill.

Thursday, June 1, 1865.

Dearest,—'You must excuse us the day.' I really cannot use my hand without extreme pain; and Geraldine has not come in to write for me.

I am just going off to Dr. Quain; since Dr. B—— is postponed into the vague. I have been quite wild with the pain, the last two nights and days. To-morrow I will go to these good Macmillans whom you sneered at as my 'distinguished visitors.' None of the more 'distinguished' have come to me with such practical help and sympathy. They are just the right distance off. I can have my carriage come and take me home any day to look after the house; and for a drive as usual.

I think you will be better at the Gill than the Hill, in spite of the grand house, if you can only sleep through the railway; and do not indulge too far in curds and cream for dinner.

God bless you.

Your lamed
GOODY.

---

[1] His phrase to me one day at St. Leonards—in that desperate time.
[2] My saucy little Arab (gift of Lady Ashburton).

LETTER 302.

T. Carlyle, Esq., The Gill.

Streatham Lane:[1] Saturday, June 3, 1865.

Dearest,—You are so good about writing that you deserve to be goodly done by; so I write a few lines to-day 'under difficulties,' though you gave me an excuse for putting off, in saying you could not hear till Tuesday. But I must study brevity, the soul of wit, for the cost of physical pain at which I write is something you can hardly conceive!

When I got your letter telling me to hold my hand, it was too late! I had set my heart on doing one more stroke of work (my sort of work), fitting up one more room before I died.[2] It was all very well to say 'give the room a good cleaning.' But no amount of mere cleaning could give that room a clean look, with that *oory*, dingy paint and paper. To put clean paper without fresh paint would only have made the dirtiness of the paint more flagrant. And if the painting was not done whilst you were away, when was there a chance of doing it? I knew I couldn't sleep in wet paint; but I looked to finding a bed somewhere: and the offer of one here came most opportunely.

The day before leaving home I went to Dr. Quain, who did me at least the good of being extremely kind, and eager to help me. He said I had 'much fever;' and gave me a prescription for that, and two other prescriptions. And when I returned from here, I was to tell him, and he would 'run over.' I said to him that Dr. B—— had declared I had no organic disease, but only a strong predisposition to gout! 'Quite right,' he said, 'that is the fact.' 'Then,' I asked, 'perhaps this affair in my arm, so much more painful than what I had in the left arm, is gout?' 'I have not the least doubt that it is!!' was his answer. Pleasant!

Well! I came here about five yesterday; and the good simple people welcomed me most honestly; and Mr. Macmillan sang Scotch songs, which would have charmed you, all the evening, the governess playing an accompaniment. At eleven I retired to my beautiful bedroom, the largest, prettiest, freshest bedroom I ever was put to sleep in! And then they left me to the society of a watchdog, chained under my window!!! It barked and growled

---

[1] Mr. Macmillan's house (fine old-fashioned suburban villa there).
[2] Alas! and this was it: often have I remembered that word.

and howled in the maddest manner till they set it loose at seven in the morning. Of course I never closed my eyes for one minute all the night! and I got up in the morning a sadder and a wiser woman! How to get away without hurting feelings? I was the wretchedest woman till I got it settled softly, that when the carriage comes for me to-day to take me home for an inspection of the work, it should not bring me back, but leave me to sleep or wake in my own quiet bed; and to come out to-morrow to spend the day, and sleep here or there after, as I liked best. The dog to be ' removed to a greater distance.' So address to Cheyne Row.

Dr. Quain said I must go as soon as possible to Scotland, ' as it had agreed so well with me last year.' I said I shuddered at the length of the journey; he reminded me that I had done it with impunity last year when I was weaker than now. I suppose it will come to that before long! I need have no doubt about my welcome.

Since you are not disturbed by that railway which drove me mad, you will do well at Mary's; she is so kind and unfussing. But you must not exceed in milk diet, &c.! You must have mutton!

And oh, take care with Noggs on these hilly roads! Oh, my dear, I am not up to more; my arm is just as if a dog had got it in its teeth, and were gnawing at it, and shaking at it furiously.

Love to Mary. Your ever affectionate
JANE CARLYLE.

LETTER 303.

T. Carlyle, Esq., The Gill.

5 Cheyne Row, Chelsea: Wednesday, June 7, 1865.

Dear Mr. Carlyle,—You will be disappointed to see my hand-writing, instead of Jane's; but to-day it is not a matter of choice, but of necessity; for the pain and swelling in her hand and fingers make them entirely helpless; and she has to feed herself with the left hand. She has just come in from Mrs. Macmillan's; and has been selecting a paper for the dining-room. She incloses the three patterns, which we all think the prettiest of those submitted to us; and she says, Will you please to say which of the three *you* like the best? I think Jane is a shade better than when she went last Friday; but still to-day she is very poorly, and pulled down by the pain, which seems to increase. She would sleep if it were not for that; she does manage to sleep a little. Everything, she says, is most charmingly comfortable; and the dog has been reduced to silence.

My great hope is in Scotland; and she seems to look forward to going, which in itself is a good thing. Please to address your next letter to Streatham Lane, as they are delayed by coming here first.

> I am, dear Mr. Carlyle,
>
> Yours very respectfully,
>
> GERALDINE E. JEWSBURY.

LETTER 304.

In pencil, with the left hand, and already well done.—T. C.

T. Carlyle, Esq., The Gill.

> Streatham: Monday, June 12, 1865.

Dearest,—I will write before returning home. There will be neither peace nor time there. Thanks! I never needed more to be made much of. I must tell you about my hand: you think the swelling more important than it is; the two middle fingers were much as now for some weeks before you left, but with the thumb and forefinger I could still do much; now the forefinger is as powerless and pained as the other two; that is all the difference, but a conclusive one, for one can do nothing with only a thumb! I could sometimes sit down and cry. The pain—the chief pain— that which wakes me from my sleep is in the shoulder and fore- arm. Even hopeful Dr. Quain does not tell me I shall soon get back my hand, only tells me blandly I must learn to write with my left; and it was he who told me to take a black-lead pencil. I went to him on Friday by appointment when I had finished the antifebrile powders. I think they have quieted me. He gave me a bumper of champagne; was kind as kind could be; desired me to try the quinine once more; said Dr. B——'s prescription was an ' admirable suggestion, and well worth my trying, but, as it would cause me a good deal of pain and feverishness, I had better wait till after my journey to Scotland.' He does me real good by his kindness.

My visit here has been a great success, so far as depended on my host and hostess; and I am certainly better in my general health for all the nourishing things they have put into me by day and by night. It is a place you might fly to in a bilious crisis. Quiet as heaven, when the dog is in the wash-house.

Bellona (my mare) has given me a fine fright. You would never believe she was not safe to be left. It has been the nearest miss of herself and the carriage being all smashed to pieces! She has escaped miraculously without scratch. The carriage has not been so fortunate. I am not up to writing the narrative to-day.

Love to my dear kind Mary.

Your loving but unfortunate

J. W. C.

LETTER 305.

T. Carlyle, Esq., The Gill.

Railway Hotel, Carlisle: Saturday, June 17, 1865.

Here I am! as well as could be expected, after travelling all night, choked in dust—an unprotected female with one arm! It is no sudden thought striking me! My mind has been made up to 'try a change,' ever since my last interview with Dr. Quain, and to try it with as little delay as possible. But I would not tell you I was coming; because it was important that I should travel by night; and for you to meet me at Carlisle would have necessitated your sleeping there (an impossibility!) or else your starting from the Gill at an unearthly hour. Kindest not to place you in the dilemma!

Up to the last moment, I schemed about taking the Gill on my road to Dumfries and appointing you to meet me. But I was sure to be awfully tired, just every atom of strength needed to carry me on to Thornhill without increasing my fatigues by the smallest demand or by any avoidable 'emotion of the mind.' To stay here a couple of hours, and have breakfast and rest; and then on past Cummertrees, with shut eyes, to the place of my destination, seemed the wisest course. To this, since my arrival here, has been added the sublime idea to throw out a note for you, and a sixpence at Cummertrees; as it had suddenly flashed on me that no letter from me could reach you by post till Tuesday. So soon as I am rested, I will make an appointment with you to meet at Dumfries, if you would rather not come on to Holm Hill.

To think that I shall fly past within a quarter of a mile of you presently; and you will have no perception of my nearness!

Yours ever.

A kiss to Mary.

J. W. C.

LETTER 306

The 'Saturday' in this letter must refer to the visit she proposed making us at the Gill. Jamie of Scotsbrig particularly invited. Mournfully I ever recollect the day; bright and sunny; Jamie punctually there; I confidently expecting. Fool! I had not the least conception of her utter feebleness, and that she was never to visit 'The Gill' more! Train passed. I hung about impatiently till the gig should return from Cummertrees Station—with her, I never doubted. It came with John instead, to say she had been obliged to stop at Dumfries, and I must come thither by the next train: 'be exact; there will be a two and a half or three hours for us there still.' I went (with John, Jamie regretfully turning home). She was so pleasant, beautifully cheerful, and quiet, I enjoyed my three hours without misgiving. Fool! fool!—and yet there was a strange infinitude of sorrow and pity encircling all things and persons for me—her beyond all others, though being really myself as if crushed flat after such a 'flight' of twelve or thirteen years, latterly on the Owen 'comatose' terms. I was stupefied into blindness! The time till her train should come was beautiful to me and everybody. Cab came for her, I escorting (the rest walked, for it was hardly five minutes off). Train was considerably too late. An old and good dumb 'Mr. Turner,' whom she recognised and rembered kindly after forty years, was brought forward at her desire by brother John. Her talk with Turner (by slate and pencil, I writing for her)—ah me! ah me! It was on the platform-seat, under an awning; she sat by me; the great, red, sinking sun flooding everything: day's last radiance, night's first silence. Grand, dumb, and unspeakable is that scene now to me. I sat by her in the railway carriage (empty otherwise) til the train gave its third signal, and she vanished from my eyes. —T. C.

T. Carlyle, Esq., The Gill.

Holm Hill: Wednesday, June 28, 1865.

I cannot make it Friday, dear—at least, could not without rudeness to a nice women who has always been kind to me. I am engaged to dine with my sort of cousin, Mrs. Hunter, on Friday, having been invited for Thursday, and asked to have the day changed to Friday. And last year, when she had got up a dinner for me, I had to send an excuse at the last hour, being too ill. To-morrow you will now be hardly expecting me. So let us say Saturday; if that does not suit there will be time to tell me. 'The wine I drink?' Oh, my! That it should be come to that. But surely you ought not to be without wine, setting aside me.

Don't be bothering, making plans embracing me. The chief good of a holiday for a man is just that he should have shaken off home cares—the foremost of these a wife. Consider that, for the present summer, you have nothing to do with me, but write me nice daily letters, and pay my bills. I came on my own hook, and so I will continue, and so I will go! To be living *in family* in some country place is just like no holiday at all, but like living at home 'under difficulties.' Shall I ever forget 'the cares of meat' at Auchtertool House?[1] ever forget the maggots generated by the sun in loins of mutton on the road from Kirkcaldy, and all the other squalid miseries of that time, for which I, as housewife, was held responsible, and had my heart broken twenty times a day? Well, my worried arm is pain enough for the present, without recalling past griefs. To-day, however, I feel rather easier. And I had more and better sleep last night. Thanks to exhaustion! for the preceding night I had not closed my eyes at all.

It is such a pity but I could have a little bodily ease. For I was never more disposed to be content with 'things in general.' I could really feel 'happy,' if it were not for my arm, and the perfectly horrid nights it causes me.

Jessie Hiddlestone is in Thornhill, awaiting my orders—the most promising-looking servant we have had since her mother. I am greatly pleased with her, and so glad I had faith in breed and engaged her. Many were eager to have her. But she was 'prood to go back to the family.' 'The family?' Where are they?

My dear, your observation of handwritings is perfectly amazing. You take Geraldine's writing for mine, Mr. Macmillan's for Geraldine's. And now I send you a charming, witty, grateful little letter of Madame Venturi's, with vignette[2] of Venturi sawing; and you seem to have taken it for Mrs. Paulet's. You could not possibly have read the letter, or you could not have made such a mistake; so I advise you to read it now, with a key: 'The Gorilla' means George Cooke, 'M' stands for Mazzini, the sawyer Venturi.

. Since you wish to know, I have gone back to sherry. And now good-bye till Saturday, unless I hear to the contrary. My left hand had taken the cramp, so this is the writing of the housemaid, who takes the opportunity to assure you that she means to be a very good girl, and try to please you, for the sake of her mother, who liked you so well.   J. CARLYLE.

[Madame Venturi had been Miss Ashurst, of a well-known London parentage. She had (and has) fine faculties, a decidedly artis-

---

[1] In 1859: 'Cares of bread.'—Mazzini's phrase.
[2] Maid's writing begins.

tic turn, which led her much to Italy, &c. Venturi was a Tyrolese Venetian (ex-Austrian military cadet, and also Garibaldist to the bone, consequently in a bad Italian position), who had fallen in love at first sight, &c., &c.; and was now fitting up a modest English house for wife and self. Within a year he died tragically—as will be seen.—T. C.]

LETTER 307.

T. Carlyle, Esq., The Gill, Annan.

Nith Bank, Thornhill: Tuesday.

Dearest,—A regular wet day. No drive possible. Well, the image of driving you have just set before my imagination—you driving me with Noggs in London—is quite enough for one day. It melts the marrow in my bones! Nor is there much relief in turning to that other picture—little Mary flying through the air in one of his 'explosions' and breaking her skull! If you were to put an advertisement in the newspapers that the horse of Thomas Caryle was for sale, there would be competition for the possession of it.

The housemaid, while combing my hair this morning, fell to telling me of 'ever so many young drapers, an' the like,' that of her knowledge had 'run frae Thornhill to the station to get a bare look o' Mr. Carlyle! And when Mr. Morrison' (the minister of Durrisdeer) 'cam' to his dinner yesterday, the first word oot o' his heed, on the very door-steps, was: "Is Mrs. Carlyle still here?" He never asket for Mrs. Ewart or the ither ladies, but only for you, mem!' I endeavoured to inform her mind by telling her, 'Yes; people liked to see any lady much spoken of, whether for good or ill. If Dr. Pritchard[1] had been at the station, all Thornhill together would have run to see him.' 'Oddsake!' said the girl, 'I daresay they would; I daresay ye're richt; but I never thocht o' that afore.'

Geraldine writes that never was such 'emotion' excited by a speech as by this of Mill's. 'Public Opinion' came addressed to you at Nith Bank in Mrs. Warren's[2] hand. How she came to know the name Nith Bank I am puzzled to know.

I took the quinine and iron yesterday twice, and slept rather sounder than otherwise. But I had a badish headache all morning. Nevertheless I took another dose before breakfast, as Dr. Russell had ordered, and the headache is wearing off.

I adhere to the intention of Dumfries for Friday, if it suit you and Mary.   Affectionately,

JANE.

---

[1] Glasgow prisoner in those weeks.   [2] Servant here.

LETTER 308.

Monday, July 24.—Early in the forenoon I was waiting at Dumfries for her train Londonward; got into her carriage (empty otherwise), and sate talking and encouraging as I could to Annan (which would hardly be an hour). Servant Jessie was in the same train; also Jamie Aitken, junior, for Liverpool. I felt in secret extremely miserable; agitated she, no doubt, and even terrified, but resolute —and *the lid shut down.* I little thought it would be her last railway, journey.—T. C.

T. Carlyle, Esq.

5 Cheyne Row, Chelsea: Thursday, July 27, 1865.

All goes well still, dearest, and this time nothing serious is *manquing.* The second night, as I expected, I slept ' beautiful.' Three hours without a break, to begin with. When I woke from that, I not only didn't know where I was, but didn't know who I was! As I got out of bed (by force of habit) to look at my watch, I was saying to myself, ' It can't be me that has made this fine sleep. It must be somebody else.' It was a full minute, I am sure, before I could satisfy myself that I hadn't been changed into somebody else. Then I slept piecemeal till seven o'clock, when I was startled erect by what seemed the house falling. Jessie came at my call, looking very guilty, and explained that it was she, who had been coming downstairs very softly, for fear of waking me, and, having new shoes on, had ' slid and sossed down on her back,' just opposite my bed-head. Luckily she was none the worse for the fall. A greater contrast than that young woman is to Fanny cannot be figured. So quick, so willing, so intelligent; never needs to be told a thing twice; and so warmly human! My only fear about her is that she will be married-up away from me. Mrs. Warren calls her ' my dear,' and they get on charmingly together.

The person who addressed the newspaper to you at ' Coming Trees' was Fanny, who had called to ask if I would ' see a lady' for her, and Mrs. Warren being busy asked her to address the newspaper.

On Tuesday Bellona, who had been warned a week before, came round at one; and after some shopping I called at Grosvenor Street, and found Miss Bromley at home—a satisfaction which I owed to the youngest of the three pugs, ' Jocky,' who was ' suffering from the heat.' She was delighted to see me; most anxious I should come to her at Folkestone; and told me, to my great joy, that Lady A. had not started on the 21st; wasn't going till Thurs-day (to-day); was staying at Bath House, but gone that morning to Bath for one day. I left a card and message at Bath House on the road home. Yesterday (Wednesday) I drove to Bath House, the first thing when I went out at one, and found the lady looking lovely in a spruce little half-mourning bonnet; and she would, 'if it was within the bounds of possibility,' come to me in the evening 'between ten and eleven;' and I went in her carriage with her (my own following) to Norfolk Street (Mrs. Anstruther's) to see baby, who is going with her mother to Germany after all. I left her there, and got into my own carriage, and went and bought my birthday present with the sovereign—at least, I paid out fifteen shillings of it. On what? My dear, the thing I bought was most appropriate, and rather touching. I drove to the great shop in Con-duit Street, where the world is supplied with 'trusses,' 'laced stockings,' and mechanical appliances for every species of human derangement, and bought a dainty little sling for my arm. The mere ribbon round my neck hurt my neck, and drew my head down. This fastens across the back, and is altogether a superior contrivance. I don't believe in Dr. Russell's prediction any more than you do. At all rates, there was no call on him to state so hopeless a view of the question when I was not asking his opinion at all. It could do no harm to leave me the consolation of hope. But I will hope in spite of him. Indeed, it seems to me that ever since he said I should never get the use of my hand, nor get rid of the pain there, that a spirit of protest and opposition has animated the poor hand, and set it on trying to do things it had for some time ceased from doing.

Lady A. did come last night—came at half after eleven, and stayed till near one! Mrs. Anstruther was left sitting in the car-riage, and sent up to say 'it was on the stroke of twelve;' and then, with Lady A.'s permission, I invited her up; and if it hadn't been for her I don't think Lady A. would have gone till daylight! She said in going, 'My regards—my—what shall I send to him?' (you). 'Oh,' I said, 'send him a kiss!' 'That is just what I should like,' she said; 'but would he not think it forward?' 'Oh, dear, not at all!' I said. So you are to consider yourself kissed. I am going up to Bath House now. She goes at night.

Lady Stanley writes to ask how I am, and to beg that you will come that way.

What a long letter! I ought to have said that all this did not

give me a bad night. Of course I did not sleep as on the preceding night, but better than I ever did at Holm Hill; and the pain in
my arm is really less since I came home.

Yours affectionately,

JANE CARLYLE.

LETTER 309.

T. Carlyle, Esq.

5 Cheyne Row, Chelsea: Sunday, July 30, 1865.

I will write to-night, dearest, while the way is open to me.
To-morrow I shall be busy from the time I get up till Bellona,
comes for me; and after driving there is no time, as I take the three
hours at least every day. It is such ' a privilege ' (as Maria's mother
would say) to have a carriage and a Bellona 'all to oneself,' independent of all agricultural operations. I don't feel it too warm
a bit when I haven't to walk on the hot pavement, though they are
celebrating the thermometer at 85° in the shade. But anyhow Miss
Bromley is irresistibly pressing; and I have promised to go to her
about the twelfth, whether my work here is done or not. She will
write to you, to urge your joining me, which you will do—won't
you?—if I, on surveying the premises, can promise you a tolerably
quiet bedroom. Of course I shall take Jessie, as I can't put my
clothes off and on yet without help. I think of staying about a
fortnight.

I am sorry you gave up the sailing and Thurso. Sailing agrees
with you, and you had good sleep at Thurso. 'The good, the
beautiful, and the true' came last evening, to inquire how I was
after my journey, and to tell me, who knew nothing and cared less,
how he had written letters of introduction for Dr. Carlyle, and sent
them to the captain of some steamer, &c. &c., and how his wife
had set her heart on having a lock of your hair and mine set in a
brooch, and he had promised her to try and complete her wishes.
And it ended—for happily everything does end—in his begging and
receiving the last pen you used, to be kept under a glass case.
I have seldom seen a foolisher hero-worshipper. But the greatest
testimony to your fame seems to me to be the fact of my photograph
—the whole three, two of them very ugly (Watkins's)—stuck up in
Macmichael's shop-window. Did you ever hear anything so preposterous in your life? And what impertinence on the part of Watkins! He must have sent my three along with your nine to the

II.—12

wholesale man in Soho Square, without leave asked. But it proves the interest or curiosity you excite; for being neither a 'distinguished authoress,' nor 'a celebrated murderess,' nor an actress, nor a 'Skittles' (the four classes of women promoted to the shop-windows), it can only be as Mrs. Carlyle that they offer me for sale.

I continue to sleep on the improved principle, and my arm continues less painful, and my hand, if not more capable, is at least more venturesome.

I saw Dr. Quain on Saturday, and he 'approved highly of my present course of treatment—that is, taking neither quinine nor anything else.' I told him what Dr. Russell had said, and his answer was, 'How could he know? That is what nobody could say but God Almighty.'

I drove to Streatham Lane to-day, and saw the Macmillans; also Mr. and Mrs. George Craik.[1] Mr. Macmillan is greatly delighted with him as a junior partner. They did not look at all ill-matched. His physical sufferings have made up in looks the ten years of difference. He has got an excellent imitation leg, and walks on it much better than American James.

God keep you.   Your affectionate
                                              JANE.

LETTER 310.

Mrs. Russell, Holm Hill.

5 Cheyne Row: Aug. 7, 1865.

Dearest,—Just a line to say that all goes well with my health. I continue to sleep better—almost to sleep well; and the pain is greatly gone out of my arm, and I use my hand a little; this charming penmanship is from my right hand.

But I have no time for elaborate writing. I was never busier in my life; about three thousand volumes have had to pass through my hands, and be arranged on the shelves by myself; nobody else could help me. The new room is getting finished, and will strike Mr. C. dumb with admiration when he comes.

                              Yours affectionately,
                                      JANE CARLYLE.

LETTER 311.

Brother John and I, as I now recollect, were in and about Edinburgh, Stowe, Newbattle (I *solus* for a call); then Linlathen both,

---

[1] Miss Mulock once, now a current authoress of *John Halifax*, &c. &c.

for some days; whence to Sterling of Keir (dreary rail journey, dreary all, though in itself beautiful and kind); thence to Edinburgh (John's bad lodging there, &c.), after which back to Dumfriesshire—to Scotsbrig, I suppose. Before this I had been three days at Keswick with my valued old friend, T. Spedding; walked to *Bassenthwaite Ha's.* (Seen five-and-forty years ago and not recognisable!) Nothing could exceed my private weariness, sadness, misery, and depression. Little thought it was, within few months, to be all sharpened into poignancy and tenderest woe, and remain with me in that far exceeding if somewhat nobler form. —T. C.

T. Carlyle, Esq.

5 Cheyne Row, Chelsea: Friday, Aug. 12, 1865.

Dearest,—It all came of you being moving, and me sitting still! I didn't know exactly when and where a letter would find you, and was occupied enough to avail myself of the shabby excuse for spending no time in writing. Besides, the time is always much longer for the person on his travels than for the one at home. And your right address did not reach me in time for that day's post. It came to hand at tea-time, as did yesterday's newspaper. So I could only answer at night to be ready for the post of yesterday. To-day I send a line or two, remembering that Sunday you can get nothing.

Jessie and I are alone just now, Mrs. Warren having petitioned for 'her holiday.' No age exempts people here from the appetite for holidays. She left on Wednesday afternoon, and does not return till Sunday, in time to see me off on Monday. As that new journey comes near, I shudder at it considerably. *'Stava bene!'*

If you cannot be at the trouble to go out to Betty's, do send her a line, telling where and when she can come to you. She will read in the newspapers that you are in Edinburgh, and break her poor old heart over it if she gets no sight of you.[1] She has already had one bad disappointment in not seeing me when I was so near.

We had a great thunderstorm last evening, and the air to-day is delightfully fresh. I had poor little Madame Reichenbach at tea with me, and her husband came late to take her home; and the thunder burst, and the rain fell; and the lamp was burning dim; and the dingy little countess from time to time made little moaning speeches in English—unintelligible, 'upon my honour!'—and Reichenbach, as usual, sat with crossed arms, and knitted brows, silent as the tombs! And to let them walk home in such pouring

---

[1] I did go.

wet seemed too cruel; and they had no shilling to take a cab; and I would gladly have paid a cab for them, but, of course, dared not! And, 'altogether, the situation was rather exquisite!'[1]

And now I must conclude, and prepare for Bellona. That poor beast behaves quite well at present. Of course, old Silvester never quits the box. I couldn't have the heart to complain about his having grown old.

I will send my address—or stop! 'Tuesday next!'—perhaps better send it now:

"Care of Miss Davenport Bromley,
            '4 Langhorne Gardens, West Cliff, Folkestone.'
                        Yours lovingly,
                                JANE CARLYLE.

LETTER 312.

T. Carlyle, Esq., Scotsbrig.

Folkestone: Saturday, Aug. 19, 1865.

Dearest,—It will be surest to direct to Scotsbrig; one might easily fail of hitting you on the wing at Edinburgh! But I wish you could have brought yourself to go for a few days to the Lothians;[2] their patience and perseverance in asking you deserved a visit! And it is rather perverse, this sudden haste to get home while I am not there to receive you! Don't you think it is? For your own sake, however, I do entreat you to break the long journey by either stopping at Alderley, or making out that visit to Foxton.[3] Alderley, which you know, and are sure of a fine quiet bedroom at, would be best. It is such a pity to arrive at home entirely fevered, and knocked up with that journey, as always happens; and then you take it to be 'London' that is making you ill!

Then, if you stayed a few days at Alderley, I could stay out the fortnight I undertook for here, and be home in time to give you welcome. I should go home on Monday week (Monday, 28th) in the course of nature. I suppose this place is good for me; I have slept so much—more than in any other week for the last three years! But I don't feel stronger for all this sleep, nor more able to

---

[1] 'Pang which was exquisite.' Foolish phrase of Godwin's in his *Life of Mary Wollstonecraft.*

[2] To Newbattle, where I spent a day.

[3] Frederic, my old German fellow-tourist: his cottage 'near Rhayader' was of route too intricate for me.

eat, or to walk. One day that I tried walking, about as far as from Cheyne Row to the hospital, I had to come home ignominiously in a donkey-cart. But the drives don't tire me, especially since Miss Bromley has had her own carriage and horses sent down. Nor need there be any reflections for want of 'simmering stagnation!' There is not a human creature to speak to out of our own house; and in it the pugs have the greatest share of the conversation to themselves!

I cannot forgive Thomas Erskine for taking up and keeping up with such a woman as that Mrs. ——. Letting you be driven out by Mrs. ——!

I am so glad you went to see dear Betty; it will be something good for her to think of for a year to come!

Do write distinctly the when, and the how, of your home-coming. What do you think? I have exactly two sovereigns in the world! enough to pay the servants here, and my railway fare home, and no more! ! Yet I have not been extravagant that I am aware of. I had to pay Silvester before I went to Scotland sixteen pounds eleven shillings and four pence; and to ditto after my return five pounds seventeen shillings. And Freure [1] couldn't get on without 'something towards the work;' and I paid him ten pounds.

	£	s.	d.
	16	11	4
	10	0	0
	5	17	0
	32	8	4

making up in all one half of my house-money. Then your being away makes no difference in the rent, taxes, servants' wages, keep, &c. And for my being away myself, I certainly have to pay to other people's servants more than it would cost me for individual 'living's cares!'

I had indeed, besides the house-money, my own fifteen pounds, of which the two sovereigns above mentioned are the sad remains. But, when these pounds came to hand, I owed for my summer bonnet and cloak; and I had some little presents to buy to take with me to Scotland, besides a gown for myself. The only part of my own money I can be said to have spent needlessly was a guinea and a half for—you would never guess what!—for a miniature of

[1] The Chelsea carpenter.

you!! Such a beauty! Everyone who sees it screams with rapture over it—even Ruskin!

But my hand will do no more.

Miss Bromley bids me say, 'that fourfooted animal sends his respects' (' and put that in inverted commas, please!'). She is good as possible to me.

Yours lovingly,
JANE CARLYLE.

LETTER 313.

Mrs. Russell, Holm Hill.

4 Langhorne Gardens, Folkestone: Aug. 23, 1865.

I am going to make an attempt at putting on paper the letter that has been in my head for you, dear, ever since I came to this place. I had even begun to write it two or three days ago, when at the first words my conscience gave me a smart box on the ear, reminding me that I hadn't written one word to Mrs. Ewart since I left her, after all her kindness to me, whereas to you I had written once and again; so my pen formed, quite unexpectedly for myself, the words 'Dear Mrs. Ewart,' instead of 'Dearest Mary.' To be sure there have been leisure hours enough since. Life here is made up of 'leisure hours'; but just the less one does, as I long ago observed, the less one can find time to do. I get up at nine, and it takes me a whole mortal hour to dress, without assistance. At ten we sit down to breakfast, and talk over it till eleven. Then I have to write my letter to Mr. Carlyle; then I make a feeble attempt at walking on the cliff by the shore, which never fails to weary me dreadfully, so that I can do nothing after, till the first dinner (called luncheon), which comes off at two o'clock; then between three and four we go out for a drive in an open barouche, with a pair of swift horses, and explore the country for three or four hours. On coming home we have a cup of tea, then rest, and dress for the second dinner at eight (nominally, but in reality half-past eight). At eleven we go to bed, very sleepy generally with so much open air. There is not a soul to speak to from without. But Miss Bromley and I never bore one another: when we find nothing of mutual interest to talk about, we have the gift, both of us, of being able to sit silent together without the least embarrassment. She is adorably kind to me, that 'fine lady!' and in such an unconscious way, always looking and talking as if it were I that was kind to her, and she the one benefited by our intimacy. And then she has something in her face, and movements, and ways, that always reminds me of my mother at her age.

I am sorry that Mr. Carlyle, after all his objections to my returning to London in August, should have taken it in his head to return to London in August himself. I find it so pleasant here; and am sleeping so wonderfully, that I feel no disposition to go back to Chelsea already; Miss Bromley having taken her house for five weeks, and being heartily desirous that I should stay and keep her company. But a demon of impatience seems to have taken possession of Mr. C., and he has been rushing through his promised visits as if the furies were chasing him. Everything right, seemingly, wherever he went; the people all kindness for him; the bedrooms quiet and airy; horses and carriages at his command; and, behold, it was impossible to persuade him to stay longer than three days with Mr. Erskine, of Linlathen; ditto with Stirling, of Keir; and just three hours (for luncheon) at Newbattle with the Lothians; and by this time he is back at Scotsbrig (if all have gone right), to stay 'one day or at most two,' preparatory for starting for Chelsea. It is really so unreasonable, this sudden haste—after so much dawdling —that I do not feel it my duty to rush home 'promiscuously' to receive him. I promised to stay here a fortnight at the least, and the fortnight does not complete itself till Monday next; so I have written to him that I will be home on Monday—not sooner—and begging him to break the journey, and amuse himself for a couple of days at Alderley Park, and then he would find me at home to receive him; since he won't do as Miss Bromley and I wish—come here for a little sea-bathing to finish off with.

It really is miraculous how soundly I have slept here, though I take two glasses of champagne, besides Manzanilla, every day at the late dinner. It couldn't have been sound, that champagne of poor, kind Mrs. ——'s, or it wouldn't have so disagreed with me. Here it always does me good. And the pain is entirely gone out of my arm; I can't move it any better yet, but that is small matter in comparison. I can do many things with my hand: write (as you see)—knit—I have knitted myself a pair of garters—I can play on the piano a little, and do a few stitches with a very coarse needle.

Kindest love to the Doctor.

Your ever affectionate

JANE CARLYLE.

LETTER 314.

To Miss Welsh, Edinburgh.

5 Cheyne Row: Monday, Oct. 1865.

My dear Ellzabeth,—I am very glad indeed of the photograph, and grateful to you for having had it done at last, knowing how all such little operations bore you. It it very satisfactory as a portrait too—very like and a pleasant likeness—'handsome and lady-like' (the epithets that used to be bestowed on you in old times). Photography is apt to be cruel on women out of their teens; but this one is neither old-looking nor cross-looking. So thank you again with all my heart.

We have had a severe time of it with heat since our return to London. Plenty of people found it 'delicious,' but Mr. C. and I —and, indeed, the whole household, not excepting the cat—suffered in our stomachs, and even more in our tempers. It was quite curious to hear the cat squabbling with her cat companions in the garden—just as the cook and housemaid squabbled in the kitchen, or Mr C. and I in the 'up stairs;' a general overflow of bile producing the usual results of irritability and disagreement. Now the weather is again favourable to the growth of the domestic virtues, and also, sad to say, to the development of rheumatism.

I paid a visit the other day, which interested me, to ' Queen Emma.' She is still in the house of Lady Franklin (the widow of that ' Sir John' that everybody used to sail away to 'seek'). When Lady Franklin made a journey to the Sandwich Islands, amongst other out-of-the-way places, she was received with great kindness by the 'royal family,' and is now repaying it by having 'the Queen' and her retinue to live with her; though *our* Queen has placed *her* apartments at Clarges' Hotel at the Sandwich Island Queen's disposition. We (Geraldine Jewsbury and I) were taken by Lady Franklin into the garden where the Queen was sitting writing, and ' much scandalized to receive us in a little hat, instead of her widow's cap,' which she offered to go in and put on. She is a charming young woman, in spite of the tinge of black—or rather green. Large black, beautiful eyes, a lovely smile, great intelligence, both of face and manner, a musical, true voice, a perfect English accent. Lady Franklin introduced me as ' the wife of Mr. Carlyle, a celebrated author of our country.' 'I know him, I have read all about him, and read things he has written,' answered the Queen of the Sandwich Islands! In fact, the young woman seemed remarkably informed on 'things in general.' The funniest part of the interview, for me, was to hear Geraldine addressing Queen Emma always as 'Your Majesty,' in a tone as free and easy as one would have adopted to one's cat.

Do you remember Joseph Turner who was deaf and dumb? I saw him on the platform at Dumfries and spoke to him, and he has written to me—such a nice letter. I will send it when I have answered it. I cannot conceive how he should have known my father, he was too young.

I hope Ann has gone or is going to Dumfriesshire. It always does her good, that trip; and many people are glad of her coming. I saw her old friend Mrs. Gilchrist at Thornhill. How changed from the time she helped me to make woollen mattresses at Craigenputtock! The history she gave me of her accidents was most pitiful. I didn't like the daughter's looks much; but she had the room as clean as a pin, and spoke kindly enough, though roughly, to her mother.

Good-bye, dear Elizabeth!

Yours affectionately,

JANE W. CARLYLE.

LETTER 315.

To Mrs. Austin, The Gill, Annan.

5 Cheyne Row: Wednesday, Oct. 11, 1865.

My dear little woman,—It is 'a black and a burning shame' that I should not have told you before now that the butter is good, very good! And Mr. C. eats it to his oat-cakes in preference to the Addiscombe fresh butter, which is the best in the world. The girl—or I should say young woman (her age being thirty)—whom I brought from Thornhill is an admirable hand at oat-cakes, and is fond of being praised, as most of us are when we can get it! so is willing to do the cake-making of the family, though it isn't 'in her work.' And I seldom eat loaf-bread now, having taken it into my head that the oat-cakes do instead of rhubarb pills. She is a capital servant, that Jessie; and pleases Mr. Carlyle supremely, attending to all his little 'fykes and manœuvres' (as she calls it in her private mind) with a zeal and punctuality that leaves him nothing to wish. But to me she leaves a good deal to wish. Not in her work: she is

II.—12*

clever and active, and has an excellent memory; but, as a woman, I might wish her different in some respects. With a face that captivates everyone by its 'brightness and sweetness,' she is, I find, what the clergyman at Morton, who had known her from a child, told me she was, and I would not believe him till I tried, 'a—*vixen*. And when Mrs. Russell told me she was—'Oh, well, about that, I should say she was as truthful as the generality of servants nowadays!' even that mild account was stretching a point in her favour. But as long as Mr. C. finds her all right, the rest don't signify. He has been off his sleep again, listening for 'railway whistles,' which have been just audible—nothing more—for years back; but he never discovered them till his experiences at Dumfries made him morbidly sensitive to that sound. The last week he has slept better; and in other respects he is better, I think, than before he went to Scotland; can walk further, and looks stronger.

For me, my neuralgia continues in abeyance—no pain in my arm, or hand, or anywhere. And though a certain stiffness remains, I can do myself, without help, almost everything I need to do, and some things not needed. For example, I made myself yesterday a lovely bonnet! My sleep has been greatly improved ever since my return from Scotland; for the bad nights I have had lately were not my own fault, but produced by listening to Mr. C. jumping up to smoke, to thump at his bed, and so on.[1]

God bless you dear. Kind regards to them all.

Your affectionate

JANE W. CARLYLE.

LETTER 316.

Some wretched people who had settled next door had brought poultry and other base disturbances; against which, for my sake, the noble soul heroically started up (not to be forbidden), and with all her old skill and energy gained victory, complete once more. For me—for me! and it was her last. The thought is cuttingly painful while I live.

The omnibus at Charing Cross. Oh, shocking! How well do I remember all this, and how easily might I have avoided it!—T. C.

To Mrs. Austin, The Gill, Annan.

5 Cheyne Row: Wednesday, Dec. 1865.

Oh, my dear! I am so vexed that you should not have had your kind sending acknowledged sooner. It arrived when I was under

---

[1] Alas, alas; watchful for two! How sad, sad that now is to me!

a cloud, last Saturday, confined to bed in a perfect agony of sick headache!

I had had nothing of that sort for many years, and it was really strange to me, the thought, how many such days I had passed formerly without being killed by them! But I am sure I couldn't live through many such at the present date. The headache and sickness lasted only one day and night, but the effects of it have not yet passed. I am as weak and nervous as if I had just come through a course of mercury! And that is why I have let several posts pass without returning you our thanks; but expressing them meanwhile in an approving consumption of the eggs and fowls. One was boiled on Monday (excellent!), the other is to be roasted to-day, according to my views about variety of food being requisite to the welfare of the human stomach—a consideration which Mr. C. makes light of, but exemplifies in his own person very convincingly the truth of.

I could very well account for that crisis the other day; several things had conspired to throw me on my back. First, my black mare, who enjoys the most perfect health generally, got her foot hurt by a runaway cart, and has had to remain in the stable for more than a week, in a state of continual poultices! Not choosing to pay for another horse, I agreed to go for exercise in an omnibus with Mr. C.—the first time I had entered an omnibus since the evening I had my fall—the beginning of all my woes! I felt very nervous at the notion, but I was to go to the end of the line and sit still while the horses were changed, and then come back again, so as to avoid any walking or hanging about in the streets. But Mr. C., as usual dawdled till we found ourselves too late for going the whole way, and I had to get down at Charing Cross in a busy thoroughfare—and Mr. C. had to run after omnibuses to stop them —and I was like to cry with nervousness to find myself left alone in an open street—and couldn't run after him as he kept calling to me to do—couldn't run at all! and was besides paralysed at the sight of carriages so near me, so that I was terribly flurried, and felt quite ill when I had to go out to dinner with Mr. C. the same evening. Then I am sure the champagne they gave us was bad— that is, poisonous; and for two nights before, I had had next to no sleep, owing to a terrible secret on my mind. One morning, when I looked out of my dressing-room window to see what sort of day it was, imagine the spectacle that met my eyes: a rubbishy hen-hutch, erected over night, in the garden next to ours—next! think of that!—and nine large hens and one very large cock sauntering under our windows!!! I should have fainted where I stood had I been in the habit of fainting; but that I never was. As Mr. C. said nothing, I could not guess whether he had made the discovery or not. The crowing which occurred several times during the night, as well as abundantly in the morning, certainly did not awake him, his mind being, at present, intent on 'railway whistles.' But when he should have once opened his eyes to the thing, and as the days should lengthen, the crowing would increase. Ah! my heaven, what then?—no wonder that I lay awake thinking 'What then?' I have not time to give a detailed account of all that followed. Enough to say the poultry is all to evacuate the premises at Christmas, and meanwhile the cock is shut up in a dark cellar from darkening till after our breakfast. And Mr. C. clasped me in his arms and called me his 'guardian angel;' and all I have to pay for this restoration of peace and quietness is giving a lesson three times a week, in syllables of two letters, to a small Irish boy! Rhyme that if you can!

Excuse this ill-written letter. I am not quite recovered from the crush of that poultry affair on my mind, although the secret load is removed.

I will write soon when more up to writing. This is merely thanks and a kiss for the fowls and eggs. Oh, if one never saw a fowl but like these—dead!

Love to them all.   Your ever affectionate

JANE W. CARLYLE.

Jessie, the Thornhill girl, is going on quite satisfactorily, since I ceased treating her too kindly—snubbing, and riding with a curb-bridle, is what she needs. All her former mistresses warned me of that, but I wouldn't believe them, the girl looked so sweet and affectionate—the humbug! Mercifully, Mr. C. sees no fault in her.

[*Remainder, a small fragment, is lost.*]

LETTER 317.

Nothing nobler was ever done to me in my life than the unseen nobleness recorded in this letter. When I look out on that garden, all so trim and quiet now (old rubbish tenants gone forever), and think what she looked out on, and resolved to do—oh, these are facts that go beyond words! Praise to thee, darling! praise in my heart at least, so long as I continue to exist.—T. C.

Mrs. Russell, Holm Hill.

5 Cheyne Row: Dec. 25, 1865.

Dearest Mary,—I was unwilling to leave your husband's letter unanswered for a single day, or I wouldn't have chosen Friday morning for writing to him, when I was busy packing your box, and had besides to write a business letter to the Haddington lawyer,[1] and to give a lesson in syllables of two letters to a small boy,[2] all before one o'clock, when I should go for my drive. After my return, between four and five, there is no time to catch the general post, which closes for Chelsea at half-past four. So, having so much to do in haste, I could only do it all badly.

Then you may be perplexed by the four pieces of cork. My dear, Mr. Carlyle has admirers of all sorts and trades; and one of them, a very ardent admirer, is by trade a cork-cutter, and he sent me, as a tribute of admiration, a box containing some dozens of bottle-corks, large and small, and half-a-dozen pairs of cork soles, to put into my shoes, when shaped with a sharp knife. It is not by many, or any, chances that I have to wet my feet; so there is small generosity in bestowing two pairs on you or the Doctor.

I hope you read that tale going on in the 'Fortnightly'—'The Belton Estate' (by Anthony Trollope). It is charming, like all he writes; I quite weary for the next number, for the sake of that one thing; the rest is wonderfully stupid.

When I wrote to the Doctor, 'my interior' (as Mr. C. would say) was in wild agitation, not severe but annoying, and reminding me of the inflammatory attack I had last winter. Nevertheless, I took my daily three hours' drive, and some tea after, and put on my black velvet gown, and went to 'Lady William's'[3] eight o'clock dinner. I hadn't dined with her for some three weeks, so I must be getting better when I could muster spirit for such a thing. Rolled up in fur, and both windows up, and warm water to my feet, I caught no cold, and it is always pleasant there, and I always sleep well after. I met the man who is said to have made the Crimean War, Lord Stratford de Redcliffe, and found him a most just-looking, courteous, agreeable, white-headed, old gentleman.

---

[1] About some trifle of legacy from poor 'Jackie Welsh,' I think (*supra*).

[2] Part of her task with those new neighbours, and their noises and paltrinesses. Good Heaven!

[3] Lady William Russell, who much liked and admired her.

When I told you I had been off my sleep, I told you—did I not? —that I had been worried off it. Better when one can put one's finger on the cause of one's sleeplessness. The cause this time, or rather the causes, were: first, a bilious fit on the part of Mr. Carlyle, who was for some days 'neither to hold nor to bind'—a condition which keeps my heart jumping into my mouth when it should be composing itself to rest. Then it happened that in these nervous days I had Agnes Veitch, my old Haddington playmate (Mrs. Grahame) coming to dinner, and seeing that he had made up his mind to find her dreadfully in his way, I ordered my brougham at eight o'clock to take her home to St. John's Wood, and that she mightn't think it was sending her off too early, I went along with her, to give her another hour of my company. Prettily imagined, you will allow. Having deposited her safely at her own door, I was on my way back, crossing Oxford Street, when I saw a mad or drunk cart bearing down upon me at a furious rate, and swerving from side to side, so that there was no escaping. My old coachman is a most cautious, as well as skilful driver; but this was too much. I shut my eyes, and crossed my arms tight, and awaited the collision. Instead of, as I expected, running into the carriage, the wild thing ran into the black mare, threw her round with a jerk that broke part of the harness, and then rushed on. Men gathered round, and Silvester descended from his box, to knot up the broken straps; my beautiful Bellona (so named for her imputed warlike disposition) standing the while as quiet as a lamb. Then we went on our way again, thanking God it was no worse. But it was found, on reaching the stables, that poor Bellona had got her foot badly hurt. The mad wheel seemed to have bruised it and snipped out a piece of skin. She was not at all lame, and was quite willing to go out with me next day; but the next again, her leg was much swelled, and for more than a fortnight she had to be attended by the veterinary surgeon, who forbade her going out, and said if the bruise had been an inch nearer the hoof she would have been a ruined Bellona. Also, he said, 'a more sweet-natured horse he had neved handled!' After much poulticing, the inward suppuration came outward; and she is now all right, being of an admirable constitution, this one; never, even through the poulticing time, losing her excellent appetite and excellent spirits. But it was worrying to not know when she could be taken out, and meanwhile to be putting Mr. C. to the cost of a livery-horse as well.

But the grand worry of all, that which perfected my sleeplessness, was an importation of nine hens, and a magnificent cock, into the adjoining garden! For years back there has reigned over all these gardens a heavenly quiet—thanks to my heroic exertions in exterminating nuisances of every description. But I no longer felt the hope or the energy in me requisite for such achievements. Figure then my horror, my despair, on being waked one dark morning with the crowing of a cock, that seemed to issue from under my bed! I leapt up, and rushed up to my dressing-room window, but it was still all darkness. I lay with my heart in my mouth, listening to the cock crowing hoarsely from time to time, and listening for Mr. C's foot stamping frantically, as of old, on the floor above. But, strangely enough, he gave no sign of having heard his enemy, his whole attentions having been, ever since his visit to Mrs. Aitken, morbidly devoted to—railway whistles. So soon as it was daylight I looked out again, and there was a sight to see—a ragged, Irish looking hen-house, run up over night, and sauntering to and fro nine goodly hens, and a stunning cock! I didn't know whether Mr. C. remained really deaf as well as blind to these new neighbours, or whether he was only magnanimously resolved to observe silence about them; but it is a fact, that for a whole week he said no word to enlighten me, while I expected and expected the crisis which would surely come, and shuddered at every cock-crow, and counted the number of times he crowed in a night—at two! at three! at four! at five! at six! at seven! Oh, terribly at seven!

For a whole week I bore my hideous secret in my breast, and slept 'none to speak of.' At the week's end I fell into one of my old sick headaches. I used always to find a sick headache had a fine effect in clearing the wits. So, even this time, I rose from a day's agony with a scheme of operation in my head, and a sense of ability to 'carry it out.' It would be too long to go into details—enough to say my negotiations with 'next door' ended in an agreement that the cock should be shut up in the cellar, inside the owner's own house, from three in the afternoon till ten in the morning; and, in return, I give the small boy of the house a lesson every morning in his 'Reading made Easy,' the small boy being 'too excitable' for being sent to school! It is a house full of mysteries—No. 6! I have thoughts of writing a novel about it. Meanwhile, Mr. C. declares me to be his 'guardian angel.' No sinecure, I can tell him. So I might fall to sleeping again if I could. But I couldn't all at once. Getting back to even that much sleep I had been having must be gradual, like the building of Rome.

Jessie is going on quite well since I decided to take the upper hand with her, and keep it   I don't think Mrs. Warren likes her any better, but I ask no questions.   Best 'let sleeping dogs lie.' She (Jessie) is much more attentive to me since I showed myself quite indifferent to her attentions, and particular only as to the performance of her work.   She is even kindly and sensitive with me occasionally.   But she can't come over me ever again with that dodge.   She let me see too clearly into her hard, vain nature that I should place reliance or affection on her again.   I do not regret having taken her—not at all.   As a servant, she is better than the average; as a woman, I do not think ill of her; but I mistook her entirely at the first, and see less good in her than perhaps there is, because I began by seeing far more good in her than she had the least pretension to.   At my age, and with my experience, it would have well beseemed me to be less romantic.   I have paid for it in the disappointment of the heartfelt hopes I had invested in my hereditary housemaid.

Good-bye, dear!

Your ever affectionate
JANE CARLYLE.

LETTER 318.

Mrs. Russell, Holm Hill, Thornhill, Dumfriesshire.

5 Cheyne Row, Chelsea: Saturday, Dec. 30, 1865.

Just a line, dearest, to inclose the poor little money-order.   I have no time for a letter—indeed, my hurry is indescribable, for I have been fit for nothing this week, and all my New Year writing is choked into the last day of it.

Wrap up five shillings, please, and address it to John Hiddlestone, and give it or transmit it to Margaret, who will save you the trouble of seeking out himself.   And you remember there was to be five shillings to that unlucky Mrs. Gilchrist—into her own hand. The other ten shillings please give where you see it most needed.

A woman who had had something from me through you (an old post-woman, Jessie said) came to Jessie, when she was coming away, and begged her to tell me that 'she had been sometimes at Templand, and had once taken tea with Mrs. Welsh in her own parlour, and if I would do something more for her, that being the case!' Jessie had properly told her that it was no business of hers to interfere, and that she could tell myself. No; I do not recognise the claim. Let her have what she has been used to have, and no more. She ought to have appealed to me through you, not through my prospective servant.

My sickness and my sleeplessness have culminated in a violent cold or influenza. Blue pill, castor oil, morphia—I have not been idle, I assure you; and now the evil thing is blowing over, and I expect to be able to keep my engagement to dine with Dr. Quain on the 3rd of January!

I hope you got my long letter—that it was not confiscated for the sake of the buttons! Will you tell me how you manage to get baskets all the way to our door without a farthing to pay? Nobody else can manage it. Even when the carriage is paid, there is still porterage from the station to the place of delivery, which cannot be prepaid—sixpence, or eightpence, or a shilling, according to the bulk. I really want to understand. Had you any porterage, from the station to Holm Hill, to pay for my box? A good New Year to the doctor. I would be his 'first foot' if I had a 'wishing carpet.'

Tell me how poor little Mrs. Ewart is.

Your ever affectionate
JANE CARLYLE.

LETTER 319.

To Miss Grace Welsh, Edinburgh.

5 Cheyne Row, Chelsea: Jan. 23, 1866.

My dear Grace,—Have you any more news of Robert?[1] I weary to hear how he is, though without hope of hearing he is better. From the first mention of his illness, I have felt that it was all over with the poor lad for this life!

One thinks it so sad that one's family should die out! And yet, perhaps, it is best (nay, of course it is best, since God has so ordered it!) that a family lying under the doom of a hereditary, deadly malady should die out, and leave its room in the universe to healthier and happier people! But, again, hereditary maladies are not the only maladies that kill; and plenty of mothers have, like Mrs. George and Mrs. Robert, seen their children, one after

---

[1] Uncle Robert's only surviving son, who had returned from sea in a dangerous state of health.

another, swept from the earth without consumption having anything to do with it.   It is hard, hard to tell by what death, slow or
swift, one would prefer to lose one's dearest ones, when lose them
one must!

Figure what has just befallen that dear, kind Dr. B——, who
saved my life (I shall always consider) by taking me under his care
at St. Leonards.   Of all his sons, the most promising was Captain
P—— B——, risen to be naval captain while still very young.   Oh,
such a handsome, kindly, gallant fellow!   He had married a beautiful girl with a little fortune, and they were the happiest pair!   A
year ago he was made 'Commander'—a signal honour for so young
a man! and just three weeks ago his wife was confined of her
second baby, in her mother's house at St. Leonards, the captain
being away to bring home a ship from somewhere in the West
Indies.   Well! four days ago, in reading his morning newspaper,
Dr. B—— read the 'Death of that distinguished officer, Captain
P—— B——, from fever, after three days' illness!'   It is too
terrible to try to conceive the feelings of a warm-hearted, proud
father under a shock like that!   Not a word of warning!

I think that going down of the 'London' has sent all the blood
from my heart!   Ever since I read its touching details I have felt
in a maze of sadness, have had no affinity for any but sorrowful
things, and can find in my whole mind no morsel of cheerful news
to tell you!   Perhaps I am even more stupid than sad; and no
shame to me, with a cold in my head, dating from before Christmas!   It is the only illness I have had to complain of this winter,
and is no illness 'to speak of;' but, none the less, it makes me very
sodden and abject; and, instead of having thoughts in my head, it
(my head) feels to be filled with wool!   Fuzzly is the word for how
I feel, all through!   But I continue to take my three hours' drive
daily, all the same.   Since I returned from Folkestone in September, I have only missed two days! the days of the snowstorm a
fortnight ago; when it was so dangerous for horses to travel, that
the very omnibuses struck work.   And besides the forenoon drive,
I occasionally, with this wool in my head, go out to dinner ! ! !
With a hot bottle at my feet, and wrapt in fur, I take no hurt, and
the talk stirs me up.   Dr. Quain told me I 'couldn't take a better
remedy, if only I drank plenty of champagne'—a condition which
I, for one, never find any difficulty in complying with!

My chief intimates have been away all this winter, which has
made my life less pleasant—Lady Ashburton on the Continent, and

Miss Davenport Bromley waiting in the country till the new paint smell should have gone out of her house. But there are always nice people to take the place of those absent. It made me laugh, dear, that Edinburgh notion, that because Mr. C. had been made Rector of the University, an office purely honorary, we should immediately proceed to tear ourselves up by the roots, and transplant ourselves there!

After thirty years of London, and with such society as we have in London, to bundle ourselves off to Edinburgh, to live out the poor remnant of our lives in a new and perfectly uncongenial sphere, with no consolations that I know of but your three selves, and dear old Betty! *Ach!* 'A wishing carpet' on which I could sit down, and be transported to Craigenvilla, for an hour's talk with you all, two or three times a week, and—back again!—would be a most welcome fairy gift to me! But no 'villa at Morningside' tempts me, except your villa! And for Edinburgh people—those I knew are mostly dead and gone; and the new ones would astonish me much if they afforded any shadow of compensation for the people I should leave here! No, my dear, we shall certainly not go 'to live in Edinburgh;' I only wish Mr. C. hadn't to go to deliver a speech in it, for it will tear him to tatters.

Love to you all.   Affectionately,

J. W. C.

LETTER 320.

To Mrs. Russell, Holm Hill.

5 Cheyne Row: January 29, 1866.

The town is no longer 'empty.' All my most intimate friends are come back, except Lady Ashburton, who, alas! will still remain on the Continent, and give no certain promise of return. Her rheumatism is better; but there are family reasons for her avoiding England at present, which she considers imperative, though her friends find them chimerical enough. Miss Davenport Bromley is back; the Alderley Stanleys, the Airlies, the Froudes, &c. &c. We were much surprised by the Lothians coming to London some two or three weeks ago. They had not stirred from New-battle Abbey for two years! The poor young Marquis came the whole journey in one day. Some hope of electricity had been put into his head, and they had been trying it on him. He said he 'did not think it had done him any harm as yet; but that was the most he could say.' He is the saddest spectacle I have seen for long. His body more than half dead, his face so worn with suffering, and the soul looking out of him as bright as in his best days. I had not seen him since before my own illness; and I was shocked with the change, especially in his voice, which, from being most musical, had become harsh and husky. She, poor soul, bears up wonderfully; but is so white and sad, that I cannot look at her without dreading for her the fate of her mother.

The house (ours) goes on peaceably enough on the whole; not without cries of ill temper, of course. But I have got Jessie pretty well in hand now. It is mortifying, after all my romantic hopes of her, to find that kindness goes for nothing with her, and that she is only amenable to good sharp snubbing. Well, she shall have it! At the same time, I make a point of being just to her and being kind to her, as a *mistress* to a *servant*. So she got the 'nice dress' at Christmas, along with Mrs. Warren; but I put no affection into anything I do for her, and let her see that I don't. It was a lucky Christmas for her. Mr. Ruskin always gives my servants a sovereign apiece at that season. 'The like had never happened to her before,' she was obliged to confess. She went to the theatre one night with some Fergussons, and has acquaintances enough. So I hope she is happy, though I don't like her.

Has the Doctor seen young Corson, who had to leave Swan and Edgar's with a bad knee? He came here several times to see Jessie. Love to the Doctor.   Yours ever,

J. C.

How is Mrs. Ewart?

LETTER 321.

Miss Ann Welsh, Edinburgh.

5 Cheyne Row: Monday, March 27, 1866.

My dear Aunts,—It is long since I have written, and I have not leisure for a satisfactory letter even now; but I want you to have these two admissions in good time, in case you desire to hear poor Mr. C.'s address, and don't know how to manage it. If you don't care about it, or can't for any other reason use the admissions, or either of them, please return them to me forthwith; for the thing[1] comes off this day week and there is a great demand for them.

Mr. C. was too modest, when asked by the University people how many admissions he wished reserved for himself, and re-

---

[1] Carlyle's address to the students as Lord Rector.—J. A. F.

quired only twenty for men and six for women, or, as I suppose they would say in Edinburgh, 'ladies.' Four have been given away to ladies who have shown him great kindness at one time or other; and the two left he sends to you, in preference to some dozen other ladies who have applied for them directly or indirectly. So you see the propriety of my request to have one or both returned if you are prevented from using them yourselves.

I am afraid, and he himself is certain, his address will be a sad break-down to human expectation. He has had no practice in public speaking—hating it with all his heart. And then he does *speak ;* does not merely read or repeat from memory a composition elaborately prepared—in fact, as in the case of his predecessors, printed before it was ' delivered'!

I wish him well through it, for I am very fearful the worry and flurry of the thing will make him ill. After speculating all winter about going myself, my heart failed me as the time drew near, and I realised more clearly the nervousness and pain in by back that so much fuss was sure to bring on. I did not dread the bodily fatigue, but the mental. We were to have broken the journey by stopping a few days at Lord Houghton's, in Yorkshire, and after giving up Edinburgh, I thought for a while I would still go as far as the Houghton's, and wait there till Mr. C. returned. But that part of the business I also decided against, only two days since, preferring to reserve Yorkshire till summer, and till I was in a more tranquil frame of mind.

Mr. C. is going to stay while in Edinburgh at Thomas Erskine's, our dear old friend; not, however, because of liking him better than anyone else there, but because of his being most out of the way of —railway whistles! It was worth while, however, to have talked of accompanying Mr. C., to have given so much enthusiastic hospitality an opportunity for displaying itself.

One of the letters of invitation I had quite surprised me by its warmth and eagerness, being from a quarter where I hardly believed myself remembered—David Aitken and Eliza Stoddart! They had both grown into sticks, I was thinking. But I have no time to gossip.

Do send me soon some word of Robert,[1] though I know too well there can no good news come.

Affectionately yours,
J. W. CARLYLE.

---

[1] Her dying cousin.

LETTER 322.

T. Carlyle, Esq., T. Erskine, Esq., Edinburgh.

Cheyne Row: Good Friday, March 30, 1866.

Dearest,—What with your being on the road, and what with the regulations of Good Friday, I don't know when this will reach you. Indeed I don't know anything about anything. I feel quite stupefied. I should have liked to have seen your handwriting this morning, though none the less obliged to Mr. Tyndall, who makes the best of your having had a bad night. What a dear, warm-hearted darling he is! I should like to kiss him! I did sleep *some* last night —the first wink since the night before you left. Last evening I felt quite smashed, so willingly availed myself of the feeble pen of Maggie,[1] who had walked in ' quite promiscuous.' She was back at Agnes Baird's, and had fixed to leave for Liverpool on Saturday. For decency's sake I asked her to come here instead and stay over Sunday, which she agreed to do. She will be company to James.[2] He didn't come back to sleep last night, having accepted an invitation from somebody (McGeorge?) at Islington, with whom he was going to spend Good Friday out of town somewhere. He had ' not quite' concluded about his office—' all but;' had failed in all attempts to find a lodging, but this McGeorge ' would help him in looking,' he thought. I pressed him to keep his bed here till he was suited, but he ' would be nearer his office at McGeorge's.' He is to come on Sunday morning, however, to spend the day; and I promised to take him to Richmond Park or somewhere before dinner. At parting, for the present, he tried to make a good little speech about ' my kindness to him.' ·Pity he is so dreadfully inarticulate, for his meaning is modest and affectionate, poor fellow.

The sudden intimation of Venturi's death, sleepless as I was at the time, stunned me for the rest of the day like a blow on the head. He was taken ill in the night at the house of Herbert Taylor,[3] but would not allow his wife to raise anyone, or to make any disturbance, and at five in the morning he was dead. There was an examination, that satisfied the doctors he had died of heart disease, and that he must have been suffering a great deal, while De Musset and other doctors of his acquaintance had treated any complaint of illness he made as ' imaginary, the result of his unsat-

---

[1] Maggie Welsh.   [2] Aitken, now attempting business in the City.
[3] John Mill's *step*son-in-law.

isfactory life.' Poor Emilie is, as you may imagine, 'like death.' Mr. Ashurst was trying to prevent a coroner's inquest, but he feared it would have to be—to-day.

Good-bye! Keep up your heart the first three minutes, and after that it will be all plain sailing.

Ever yours,

J. C.

LETTER 323.

T. Carlyle, Esq., T. Erskine's, Esq., Edinburgh.

5 Cheyne Row, Chelsea: April 2, 1866.

Dearest,—By the time you get this you will be out of your trouble, better or worse, but out of it please God. And if ever you let yourself be led or driven into such a horrid thing again, I will never forgive you—never!

What I have been suffering, vicariously, of late days is not to be told. If you had been to be hanged I don't see that I could have taken it more to heart. This morning after about two hours of off-and-on sleep, I awoke, long before daylight, to sleep no more. While drinking a glass of wine and eating a biscuit at five in the morning, it came into my mind, 'What is *he* doing, I wonder, at this moment?' And then, instead of picturing you sitting smoking up the stranger-chimney, or anything else that was likely to be, I found myself always dropping off into details of a regular execution! —Now they will be telling him it is time! now they will be pinioning his arms and saying last words! Oh, mercy! was I dreaming or waking? was I mad or sane? Upon my word, I hardly know now. Only that I have been having next to no sleep all the week, and that at the best of times I have a too 'fertile imagination,' like 'oor David.'[1] When the thing is over I shall be content, however it have gone as to making a good 'appearance' or a bad one. That you have made your 'address,' and are alive, that is what I long to hear, and, please God! shall hear in a few hours. My 'imagination' has gone the length of representing you getting up to speak before an awful crowd of people, and, what with fuss, and 'bad air,' and confusion, dropping down dead.

Why on earth did you ever get into this galley?

J. W. C.

---

[1] A lying boy at Haddington, whom his mother excused in that way.

LETTER 324.

T. Carlyle, Esq., Edinburgh.

5 Cheyne Row, Chelsea: Tuesday, April 3, 1866.

I made so sure of a letter this morning from some of you—and 'nothing but a double letter for Miss Welsh.' Perhaps I should—that is, ought to—have contented myself with Tyndall's adorable telegram, which reached me at Cheyne Row five minutes after six last evening, considering the sensation it made.

Mrs. Warren and Maggie were helping to dress me for Forster's birthday, when the telegraph boy gave his double-knock. 'There it is!' I said. 'I am afraid, cousin, it is only the postman,' said Maggie. Jessie rushed up with the telegram. I tore it open and read, 'From John Tyndall' (Oh, God bless John Tyndall in this world and the next!) 'to Mrs. Carlyle.' 'A perfect triumph!' I read it to myself, and then read it aloud to the gaping chorus. And chorus all began to dance and clap their hands. 'Eh, Mrs. Carlyle! Eh, hear to that!' cried Jessie. 'I told you, ma'am,' cried Mrs. Warren, 'I told you how it would be.' 'I'm so glad, cousin! you'll be all right now, cousin,' twittered Maggie, executing a sort of leap-frog round me. And they went on clapping their hands, till there arose among them a sudden cry for brandy! 'Get her some brandy!' 'Do, ma'am, swallow this spoonful of brandy; just a spoonful! For, you see, the sudden solution of the nervous tension with which I have been holding in my anxieties for days—nay, weeks, past—threw me into as pretty a little fit of hysterics as you ever saw.

I went to Foster's nevertheless, with my telegram in my hand, and 'John Tyndall' in the core of my heart! And it was pleasant to see with what hearty good-will all there—Dickens and Wilkie Collins as well as Fuz—received the news; and we drank your health with great glee. Maggie came in the evening; and Fuz, in his joy over you, sent out a glass of brandy to Silvester! Poor Silvester, by-the-by, showed as much glad emotion as anybody on my telling him you had got well through it.

Did you remember Craik's paper? I am going to take Maggie to the railway for Liverpool. I suppose I shall now calm down and get sleep again by degrees. I am smashed for the present.

J. W. C.

LETTER 325.

T. Carlyle, Esq., Edinburgh.

5 Cheyne Row, Chelsea: Wednesday, April 4, 1866.

Well! I do think you might have sent me a 'Scotsman' this morning, or ordered one to be sent! I was up and dressed at seven; and it seemed such an interminable time till a quarter after nine, when the postman came, bringing only a note about—Cheltenham, from Geraldine! The letter I had from Tyndall yesterday might have satisfied any ordinary man or woman, you would have said. But I don't pretend to be an ordinary man or woman; I am perfectly extraordinary, especially in the power I possess of fretting and worrying myself into one fever after another, without any cause to speak of! What do you suppose I am worrying about now?—because of the 'Scotsman' not having come! That there may be in it something about your having fallen ill, which you wished me not to see! this I am capable of fancying at moments; though last evening I saw a man who had seen you 'smoking very quietly at Masson's;' and had heard your speech, and—what was more to the purpose (his semi-articulateness taken into account)—brought me, what he said was as good an account of it as any *he* could give, already in 'The Pall Mall Gazette,' written by a hearty admirer of long standing evidently. It was so kind of Macmillan to come to me before he had slept. He had gone in the morning straight from the railway to his shop and work. He seemed still under the emotion of the thing;—tears starting to his black eyes every time he mentioned any moving part!!

Now just look at that! If here isn't, at half after eleven, when nobody looks for the Edinburgh post, your letter, two newspapers, and letters from my aunt Anne, Thomas Erskine, and 'David Aitken besides.' I have only as yet read your letter. The rest will keep now. I had a nice letter from Henry Davidson yesterday, as good as a newspaper critic. What pleases me most in this business —I mean the business of your success—is the hearty personal affection towards you that comes out on all hands. These men at Forster's with their cheering—our own people—even old Silvester turning as white as a sheet, and his lips quivering when he tried to express his gladness over the telegraph: all that is positively delightful, and makes the success 'a good joy' to me. No appearance of envy or grudging in anybody; but one general, loving, heartfelt

II.—13

throwing up of caps with young and old, male and female! If we could only sleep, dear, and what you call *digest*, wouldn't it be nice?

Now I must go; I promised to try and get Madame Venturi out with me for a little air. She has been at her brother's, quite near Forster's, since the funeral. The history she herself gave me of the night of his death was quite excruciating. He took these spasms which killed him, soon after they went to bed; and till five in the morning the two poor souls were struggling on, he positively forbidding her to give an alarm. Mrs. Taylor had a child just recovering from scarlet fever, and sent from home for fear of infecting the others. When Emilie would have gone to the Taylors' bedroom to tell them, he said, 'Consider the poor mother! If you rouse her suddenly, she will think there has come bad news of her child! It might do her great harm.' 'And I thought, dear, there was no danger,' she said to me. 'The doctors had so constantly said he had no ailment but indigestion.' It was soon after this that he 'threw up his arms as if he had been shot; and fixed his eyes with a strange wondering look, as if he saw something beautiful and surprising; and then fell to the floor dead!' I am so glad she likes me to come to her, for it shows she is not desperate.

Oh, dear, I wish you had been coming straight back![1] for it would be so quiet for you here just now: there isn't a soul left in London but Lady William, whom I haven't seen since the day you left. I am afraid she is unwell.

Good-bye! We have the sweeps to-day in the drawing-room, and elsewhere.   Affectionately yours,

JANE W. CARLYLE.

LETTER 326.

Read near Cleughbrae, on the road to Scotsbrig. Came thither, Saturday, April 7.

T. Carlyle, Esq., Scotsbrig.

5 Cheyne Row: Friday, April 6, 1866.

Dearest,—Scotsbrig, I fancy, will be the direction now.

I am just getting ready to start for Windsor, to stay a day and night, or two nights if the first be successful, with Mrs. Oliphant. Even that much 'change of air' and 'schane'[2] may, perhaps,

---

[1] Oh, that I had—alas, alas!
[2] Old grandfather Walter's 'vaary the schane.'

break the spell of sleeplessness that has overtaken me. It is easier to go off one's sleep than to go on to it. I did rather better last night, however, after an eight o'clock dinner with the Lothians. The American, Mason, was there—a queer, fine old fellow, with a touch of my grandfather Walter in him. Both Lord and Lady, and the beauty, Lady Adelaide, were so kind to me. It made me like to ' go off,' to hear the young Marquis declaring ' how much he wished he could have heard your speech.' He looked perfectly lovely yesterday, much more cheerful and bright than I have seen him since he came to London. They seemed to take the most affectoinate interest in the business.

Lady William, too, charged me with a long message I haven't time for here. I found her in bed in the middle of newspapers, which she had been ' reading and comparing all the morning; and had discovered certain variations in!' I am to dine with her on Sunday, after my return from Windsor. Miss Bromley is come back; she came yesterday, and I am to dine with her on Tuesday. I needn't be dull, you see, unless I like!

Will you tell Jamie the astonishing fact that I have eaten up all the meal he sent me, and cannot live without cakes. *Ergo!* Also take good care of Betty's tablecloth![1] She writes me it was her mother's *spening.* She was awfully pleased at your visit. ' What am i, O der me, to be so vesated!' Here is an exuberant letter from Charles Kingsley. Exuberant letters, more of them than I can ever hope to answer. Lady Airlie offers to come and drink tea with me on Sunday night. ' Can't be done'—must write in this hurry to put her off. Even I have my hurries, you see. Kind love to Jamie and the rest.

Yours ever,

J. W. C.

LETTER 327.

T. Carlyle, Esq., Scotsbrig.

5 Cheyne Row: Tuesday, April 10, 1866.

Alas, I missed Tyndall's call! and was ' vaixed!' He left word with Jessie that you were ' looking well; and every body worshipping you!' and I thought to myself, ' A pity if he have taken the habit of being worshipped, for he may find some difficulty in keeping it up here!'

---

[1] A gift of poor Betty's—never to arrive.

Finding the first night at Windsor (Friday night) a great success, I gladly stayed a second night; and only arrived at Cheyne Row in time for Lady William's Sunday dinner. It couldn't be 'quiet' that helped me to sleep so well at Mrs. Oliphant's; for all day long I was in the presence of fellow-creatures. The first evening, besides two Miss Tullochs living in the house, there arrived to tea and supper (!) a family of Hawtreys, to the number of seven!—seven grown-up brothers and sisters!! The eldest, 'Mr. Stephen,' with very white hair and beard, is Master of Mathematics at Eton; and has a pet school of his own—tradesmen's sons, and the like—on which he lays out three hundred a year of his own money. He complimented me on your 'excellent address,' which he said 'We read aloud to our boys.' I asked Mrs. Oliphant after, what boys he meant? She said it would be the boys of his hobby school; they were the only boys in the world for Mr. Stephen! On the following day arrived Principal Tulloch, and wife, on a long visit. Mrs. Oliphant seems to me to be eaten up with long visitors. He (the Principal) had been at the ' Address,' and seen you walking in your wideawake with your brother, just as himself was leaving Edinburgh.

Frederick Elliot and Hayward (!) were at Lady William's. Hayward was raging against the Jamaica business—would have had Eyre cut into small pieces, and eaten raw. He told me *women* might patronize Eyre—that women were naturally cruel, and rather liked to look on while horrors were perpetrated. But no *man* living could stand up for Eyre now! 'I hope Mr. Carlyle does,' I said. 'I haven't had an opportunity of asking him; but I should be surprised and grieved if I found him sentimentalising over a pack of black brutes!' After staring at me a moment: 'Mr. Carlyle!' said Hayward. 'Oh, yes! Mr. *Carlyle!* one cannot indeed swear what he will *not* say! His great aim and philosophy of life being " The smallest happiness of the fewest number!" '

I slept very ill again, that night of my return; but last night was better, having gone to bed dead weary of such a tea-party as you will say could have entered into no human head but mine! Sartosina,[1] Count Reichenbach, and James Aitken!! there was to have been also Lady Airlie!!! You have no idea how well Reichenbach and James suit each other! They make each other quite animated,

---

[1] A tailor's daughter, in the Kensington region, a modest yet ardent admirer, whom, liking the tone of her letter, she drove to see, and liked, and continued to like.

by the delight each seems to feel in finding a man more inarticulate than himself! They got towards the end into little outbursts of laughter, of a very peculiar kind!   Yours ever,

JANE CARLYLE.

Send me a proof [1] as soon as you can.

LETTER 328.

I still in Edinburgh on that fated visit. I called on Mrs. Stirling; the last time I have seen her. This letter was dated only ten days before the utter *finis*.

The sudden death mentioned here, minutely and sympathetically described in a letter to me, was that of Madame Venturi's (born Ashurst's) Italian husband,[2] with both of whom she was familiar. —T. C.

To Mrs. Stirling, Hill Street, Edinburgh.

5 Cheyne Row, Chelsea: Wednesday, April 11, 1866.

My dear Susan Hunter,—No change of modern times would have surprised me more disagreeably than your addressing me in any other style than the old one. The delight of you is just the faith one has—has always had—in your constancy. One mayn't see you for twenty years, but one would go to you at the end with perfect certainty of being kissed as warmly and made as much of as when we were together in the age of enthusiasm.

I was strongly tempted to accompany Mr. C. to Edinburgh and see you all once more. But, looked at near hand, my strength, or rather my courage, failed me in presence of the prospective demand on my 'finer sensibilities.' Since my long, terrible illness, I have had to quite leave off seeking emotions, and cultivating them. I had done a great deal too much of that sort of work in my time. Even at this distance I lost my sleep, and was tattered to fiddle-strings for a week by that flare-up of popularity in Edinburgh. To be sure the sudden death of an apparently healthy young man, husband of one of my most intimate friends, had shocked me into an unusually morbid mood; to say nothing of poor Craik struck down whilst opening his mouth to reprove a pupil. I had got it into my head that the previous sleeplessness and fatigue, and the fuss and closeness of a crowded room, and the novelty of the whole thing, would take such effect on Mr. C. that when he stood up to speak

---

[1] *Correcting* to the Edinburgh printer of the Address. A London pirate quite *forestalled* me and it.

[2] See page 290.

he would probably drop down dead! When at six o'clock I got a telegram from Professor Tyndall to tell me it was over, and well over, the relief was so sudden and complete, that I (what my cook called) 'went off'—that is, took a violent fit of crying, and had brandy given me.

I am very busy and cannot write a long letter; but a short one, containing the old love and a kiss, will be better than 'silence,' however 'golden.'   Your very affectionate

J. W. CARLYLE.

LETTER 329.

T. Carlyle, Esq., Scotsbrig.

5 Cheyne Row: Thursday, April 12, 1866.

Dearest,—I sent you better than a letter yesterday—a charming 'Punch,' which I hope you received in due course; but Geraldine undertook the posting of it, and, as Ann said of her long ago, 'Miss can write books, but I'm sure it's the only thing she's fit for.' Well, there only wanted to complete your celebrity that you should be in the chief place of 'Punch';[1] and there you are, cape and wideawake, making a really creditable appearance. I must repeat what I said before—that the best part of this success is the general feeling of personal goodwill that pervades all they say and write about you. Even 'Punch' cuddles you, and purrs over you, as if you were his favourite son. From 'Punch' to Terry the greengrocer is a good step, but, let me tell you, he (Terry) asked Mrs. Warren—'Was Mr. Carlyle the person they wrote of as Lord Rector?' and Mrs. Warren having answered in her stage voice, 'The very same!' Terry shouted out ('Quite shouted it, ma'm!'), 'I never was so glad of anything! By George, I am glad!' Both Mrs. Warren and Jessie rushed out and bought 'Punches' to send to their families; and, in the fervour of their mutual enthusiasm, they have actually ceased hostilities—for the present. It seems to me that on every new compliment paid you these women run and fry something, such savoury smells reach me upstairs.

Lady Lothian was here the day before yesterday with a remarkably silly Mrs. L——. I was to tell you that she (Lady L.) was very impatient for your return—'missed you dreadfully.' I was to 'come some day before luncheon, and then we could go—some-

---

[1] It came to Scotsbrig, with this letter, late at night; how merry it made us all: oh, Heaven! 'merry!'

where.' To Miss Evans[1] is where we should go still, if you would let us.

Don't forget my oatmeal.

There is a large sheet from the Pall Mall Bank, acknowledging the receipt of seventy pounds 'only.' I don't forward any nonsense letters come to you. This one inclosed has sex and youth to plead for it—so, Yours ever,

J. W. C.

My kindest regards to Mary,[2] for whom I have made a cap, you may tell her, but couldn't get it finished before you left.

LETTER 330.

T. Carlyle, Esq., Scotsbrig.

5 Cheyne Row: Friday, April, 13, 1866.

Oh, what a pity, dear, and what a stupidity I must say! After coming safely through so many fatigues and dangers to go and sprain your ankle, off your own feet! And such treatment the sprain will get! Out you will go with it morning and night, along the roughest roads, and keep up the swelling Heaven knows how long! The only comfort is that 'Providence is kind to women, fools, and drunk people,' and in the matter of taking care of yourself you come under the category of 'fools,' if ever any wise man did.

There came a note for you last night that will surprise you at this date as much as it did me, though I daresay it won't make you start and give a little scream as it did me.[3] It—such a note!—is hardly more friendly than silence, but it is more polite. I wish I hadn't sent him that kind message. Virtue (forgiveness of wrong, 'milk of human kindness,' and all that sort of 'damned thing') being 'ever its own reward, unless something particular occurs to prevent,' which it almost invariably does.

There! I must get ready for that blessed carriage. I have been *redding up* all morning. Ever yours,

J. W. CARLYLE.

It would be good to send back Mill's letter, that Reichenbach might tell Löwe[4] of it.

---

[1] Famous 'George Eliot' (or some such pseudonym).　　　[2] Sister.

[3] A note from John Mill—response about some trifle, after long delay.

[4] Löwe (German, unknown to me) wanted to translate something of Mill's, and had applied, through Reichenbach, to me on the matter.

LETTER 331.

T. Carlyle, Esq., Scotsbrig.

5 Cheyne Row: Tuesday, April 17, 1866.

Oh, my dear, these women are too tiresome! Time after time I have sworn to send on none of their nonsense, but to burn it or to let it lie, as I do all about '————,' and there is always ' a something' that touches me on their behalf. Here is this Trimnell! She was doomed, and should have been cast into outer darkness (of the cupboard) but for that poor little phrase, ' as much as my weak brains will permit.' And the Caroline C—— (who the deuce is she that writes such a scratchy, illegible hand?) sends her love to Mrs. Carlyle, and proposes to ' to talk to her about Amisfield and Haddington.' 'Encouraged by your brother to beg,' &c. &c., complicates the question still further. Yes, it is the mixing up of things that is ' the great bad.'[1]

I called at the Royal Institution yesterday to ask if Tyndall had returned. He was there; and I sat some time with him in his room hearing the minutest details of your doings and sufferings on the journey. It is *the* event of Tyndall's life! Crossing the hall, I noticed for the first time that officials were hurrying about; and I asked the one nearest me, ' Is there to be lecturing here to-day?' The man gave me such a look, as if I was *deeranged*, and people going up the stairs turned and looked at me as if I was *deeranged*. Neuberg ran down to me and asked, ' Wouldn't I hear the lecture?' And by simply going out when everyone else was going in I made myself an object of general interest. As I looked back from the carriage window I saw all heads in the hall and on the stairs turned towards me.

I called at Miss Bromley's after. She had dined at Marochetti's on Saturday, being to go with them to some spectacle after. The spectacle which she saw without any going was a great fire of Marochetti's studio—furnaces overheated in casting Landseer's ' great lion.'

How dreadful that poor woman's[2] suicide! What a deal of misery it must take to drive a working-woman to make away with

---

[1] Reichenbach's phrase.

[2] A poor neuralgic woman, near Scotsbrig—a daughter of old Betty Smail's (mentioned already?—' head like a *mall*,' &c.).

her life! What does Dr. Carlyle make of such a case as that? No idleness, nor luxury, nor novel-reading to make it all plain.[1]

Ever yours,

J. W. C.

LETTER 332.

T. Carlyle, Esq., Scotsbrig.

5 Cheyne Row, Chelsea: Thursday, April 19, 1866.

I read the Memoir[2] 'first' yesterday morning, having indeed read the 'Address' the evening before, and read in some three times in different newspapers. If you call that 'laudatory,' you must be easily pleased. I never read such stupid, vulgar janners.[3] The last of calumnies that I should ever have expected to hear uttered about you was this of your going about 'filling the laps of dirty children with comfits.' Idiot! My half-pound of barley-sugar made into such a legend! The wretch has even failed to put the right number to the sketch of the house—'No. 7!' A luck, since he was going to blunder, that he didn't call it No. 6, with its present traditions. It is prettily enough done, the house. I recollect looking over the blind one morning and seeing a young man doing it. 'What can he be doing?' I said to Jessie. 'Oh, counting the windows for the taxes,' she answered quite confidently; and I was satisfied.

I saw Frederick Chapman yesterday, and he was very angry. He had 'frightened the fellow out of advertising,' he said; and he had gone round all the booksellers who had subscribed largely for the spurious Address, and required them to withdraw their orders. By what right, I wonder? Difficulty of procuring it will only make it the more sought after, I should think. 'By making it felony, ma'am, yourselves have raised the price of getting your dogs back.'[4]

I didn't write yesterday because, in the first place I was very sick, and in the second place I got a moral shock,[5] that stunned me *pro tempore.* No time to tell you about that just now, but another day.

---

[1] Alas! that was a blind, hasty, and *cruel* speech of poor, good John's!
[2] By London *pirate*.
[3] Capital Scotch word.
[4] London dog-stealers pleaded so, on the Act passed against them.
[5] What I could never guess.

I have put the women to sleep in your bed to air it. It seems so long since you went away.

Imagine the tea party I am to have on Saturday[1] night. Mrs. Oliphant, Principal Tulloch and wife and two grown-up daughters, Mr. and Mrs. Froude, Mr. and Mrs. Spottiswoode!

Did you give Jane the things I sent?[2] When one sends a thing one likes to know if it has been received safe.

Yours ever,

J. W. C.

LETTER 333.

The last words her hand ever wrote. Why should I tear my heart by reading them so often? They reached me at Dumfries, Sunday, April 22, fifteen hours after the fatal telegram had come. Bright weather this, and the day before I was crippling out Terregles way, among the silent green meadows, at the moment when she left this earth.

Spottiswoodes, King's Printer people. I durst never see them since. Miss Wynne, I hear, is dead of cancer six months ago.

'Very equal,' a thrifty Annandale phrase.

'Scende da carrozza' (Degli Antoni).

'Picture of Frederick.' I sent for it on the Tuesday following, directly on getting to Chelsea. It still hangs there; a poor enough Potsdam print, but to me priceless.

I am at Addiscombe in the room that was long 'Lady Harriet's;' day and house altogether silent, Thursday, August 5, 1869, while I finish this unspeakable revisal (reperusal and study of all her letters left to me). Task of about eleven months, and sad and strange as a pilgrimage through Hades.—T. C.

T. Carlyle, Esq., The Hill, Dumfries.

5 Cheyne Row, Chelsea : Saturday, April 21, 1866.

Dearest,—It seems 'just a consuming of time' to write to-day, when you are coming the day after to-morrow. But 'if there were nothing else in it' (your phrase) such a piece of liberality as letting one have letters on Sunday, if called for, should be honoured at least by availing oneself of it! All long stories, however, may be postponed till next week. Indeed, I have neither long stories nor short ones to tell this morning. To-morrow, after the tea-party, I may have more to say, provided I survive it! Though how I am to entertain, 'on my own basis,' eleven people in a hot night 'without refreshment' (to speak of) is more than I 'see my way'

---

[1] Oh, Heaven!

[2] I did, and told her so in the letter *she* never received. Why should *I* ever read this again! (*Note of* 1866.)

through! Even as to cups—there are only ten cups of company-china; and eleven are coming, myself making twelve! 'After all,' said Jessie, 'you had once eight at tea—three mair won't kill us!' I'm not so sure of that. Let us hope the motive will sanctify the end; being 'the welfare of others!' an unselfish desire to 'make two Ba-ings happy:' Principal Tulloch and Froude, who have a great liking for one another! The Spottiswoodes were added in the same philanthropic spirit. We met in a shop, and they begged permission to come again; so I thought it would be clever to get them over (handsomely with Froude and Mrs. Oliphant) before you came. Miss Wynne offered herself, by accident, for that same night.

The Marchioness was here yesterday, twice; called at four when I hadn't returned, and called at five. She brought with her yesterday a charming old Miss Talbot, with a palsied head, but the most loveable babyish old face! She seemed to take to me, as I did to her; and Lady Lothian stayed behind a minute, to ask if I would go with her some day to see this Miss Talbot, who had a house full of the finest pictures. You should have sent the Address to Lord Lothian or Lady. I see several names on the list less worthy of such attention.

Chapman is furious at Hotten; no wonder! When he went round to the booksellers, he found that everywhere Hotten had got the start of him. Smith and Elder had bought five hundred copies from Hotten! And poor Frederick did not receive his copies from Edinburgh till he had 'telegraphed,' six-and-thirty hours after I had received mine.

I saw in an old furniture-shop window at Richmond a copy of the Frederick picture that was lent you—not bad; coarsely painted, but the likeness well preserved. Would you like to have it? I will, if so, make you a present of it, being to be had 'very equal.' I 'descended from the carriage,' and asked, 'What was that?' (meaning what price was it). The broker told me impressively, 'That, ma'am, is Peter the Great.' 'Indeed! and what is the price?' 'Seven-and-sixpence.' I offered five shillings on the spot, but he would only come down to six shillings. I will go back for it if you like, and can find a place for it on my wall.

Yours ever,

J. W. C.

On the afternoon of the day on which the preceding letter was written, Mrs. Carlyle died suddenly in her carriage in Hyde Park. A letter of Miss Jewsbury's relating the circumstances which attended and followed her death has been already published in the 'Reminiscences.' I reprint it here as a fit close to this book.— J. A. F.

To Thomas Carlyle.

' 43 Markham Square, Chelsea: May 26, 1866.

' Dear Mr. Carlyle,—I think it better to write than to speak on the miserable subject about which you told me to inquire of Mr. Silvester.[1] I saw him to-day. He said that it would be about twenty minutes after three o'clock or thereabouts when they left Mr. Forster's house; that he then drove through the Queen's Gate, close by Kensington Gardens, that there, at the uppermost gate, she got out, and walked along the side of the Gardens very slowly, about two hundred paces, with the little dog running, until she came to the Serpentine Bridge, at the southern end of which she got into the carriage again, and he drove on till they came to a quiet place on the Tyburnia side, near Victoria Gate, and then she put out the little dog to run along. When they came opposite to Albion Street, Stanhope Place (lowest thoroughfare of Park towards Marble Arch), a brougham coming along upset the dog, which lay on its back screaming for a while, and then she pulled the check-string; and he turned round and pulled up at the side of the foot-path, and there the dog was (he had got up out of the road and gone there). Almost before the carriage stopped she was out of it. The lady whose brougham had caused the accident got out also, and several other ladies who were walking had stopped round the dog. The lady spoke to her; but he could not hear what she said, and the other ladies spoke. She then lifted the dog into the carriage, and got in herself. He asked if the little dog was hurt; but he thinks she did not hear him, as carriages were passing. He heard the dog squeak as if she had been feeling it (nothing but a toe was hurt); this was the last sound or sigh he ever heard from her place of fate. He went on towards Hyde Park Corner, turned there and drove past the Duke of Wellington's Achilles figure, up the drive to the Serpentine and past it, and came round by the road where the dog was hurt, past the Duke of Wellington's house and past the gate opposite St. George's. Getting no sign (noticing only the two hands laid on the lap, palm uppermost the right hand, reverse way the left, and all motionless), he turned into the Serpentine drive again; but after a few yards, feeling a little surprised, he looked back, and, seeing her in the same posture, became alarmed, made for the streetward entrance into the Park a few yards westward of gatekeeper's lodge, and asked a lady to look in; and she said what we know, and she addressed a gentleman who confirmed her fears. It was then fully a quarter past four; going on to twenty minutes (but nearer the

---

[1] Mrs. Carlyle's coachman.

quarter); of this he is quite certain. She was leaning back in one corner of the carriage, rugs spread over her knees; her eyes were closed, and her upper lip slightly, slightly opened. Those who saw her at the hospital and when in the carriage speak of the beautiful expression upon her face.

'On that miserable night, when we were preparing to receive her, Mrs. Warren [1] came to me and said, that one time, when she was very ill, she said to her, that when the last had come, she was to go upstairs into the closet of the spare room and there she would find two wax candles wrapt in paper, and that those were to be lighted and burned. She said that after she came to live in London she wanted to give a party; her mother wished everything to be very nice, and went out and bought candles and confectionery, and set out a table, and lighted the room quite splendidly, and called her to come and see it when all was prepared. She was angry; she said people would say she was extravagant, and would ruin her husband. She took away two of the candles and some of the cakes. Her mother was hurt and began to weep. She was pained at once at what she had done; she tried to comfort her, and was dreadfully sorry. She took the candles and wrapped them up, and put them where they could be easily found. We found them and lighted them, and did as she desired.

'G. E. J.'

What a strange, beautiful, sublime and almost terrible little action; silently resolved on, and kept silent from all the earth for perhaps twenty-four years! I never heard a whisper of it, and yet see it to be true. The visit must have been about 1837; I remember the soirée right well; the resolution, bright as with heavenly tears and lightning, was probably formed on her mother's death, February 1842.—T. C.

Mrs. Carlyle was buried by the side of her father, in the choir of Haddington Church. These words follow on the tombstone after her father's name:—

HERE LIKEWISE NOW RESTS

JANE WELSH CARLYLE,

SPOUSE OF THOMAS CARLYLE, CHELSEA, LONDON.

SHE WAS BORN AT HADDINGTON, 14TH JULY, 1801, ONLY DAUGHTER OF THE ABOVE JOHN WELSH, AND OF GRACE WELSH, CAPLEGILL, DUMFRIESSHIRE, HIS WIFE. IN HER BRIGHT EXISTENCE SHE HAD MORE SORROWS THAN ARE COMMON; BUT ALSO A SOFT INVINCIBILITY, A CLEARNESS OF DISCERNMENT, AND A NOBLE LOYALTY OF HEART, WHICH ARE RARE. FOR FORTY YEARS SHE WAS THE TRUE AND EVER-LOVING HELPMATE OF HER HUSBAND, AND BY ACT AND WORD UNWEARIEDLY FORWARDED HIM, AS NONE ELSE COULD, IN ALL OF WORTHY, THAT HE DID OR ATTEMPTED. SHE DIED AT LONDON, 21ST APRIL, 1866; SUDDENLY SNATCHED AWAY FROM HIM, AND THE LIGHT OF HIS LIFE, AS IF GONE OUT.

---

[1] The housekeeper in Cheyne Row.

INDEX.

THOMAS CARLYLE'S WORKS

PUBLISHED BY

HARPER & BROTHERS.

REMINISCENCES BY THOMAS CARLYLE.

Edited by JAMES ANTHONY FROUDE. 12mo, Cloth, Illustrated by Thirteen Portraits, 50 cents; 4to, Paper, 20 cents.

FREDERICK THE GREAT.

History of Friedrich II., called Frederick the Great. Portraits, Maps, Plans, &c. 6 vols., 12mo, Cloth, $7 50.

OLIVER CROMWELL.

Letters and Speeches of Oliver Cromwell. 2 vols., 12mo, Cloth, $2 50.

THE FRENCH REVOLUTION.

History of the French Revolution. 2 vols., 12mo, Cloth, $2 50.

PAST AND PRESENT.

Past and Present, Chartism, and Sartor Resartus. 12mo, Cloth, $1 25.

THE EARLY KINGS OF NORWAY.

The Early Kings of Norway; also an Essay on the Portraits of John Knox. 12mo, Cloth, $1 25.

MY IRISH JOURNEY.

Reminiscences of my Irish Journey in 1849. With a Portrait. 12mo, Cloth, $1 00; 4to, Paper, 10 cents.

☞ HARPER & BROTHERS will send any of the above works by mail, postage prepaid, to any part of the United States, on receipt of the price.

THOMAS CARLYLE.

A HISTORY OF THE FIRST FORTY YEARS OF HIS
LIFE, 1795–1835. By JAMES ANTHONY FROUDE, M.A.
With Portraits and Illustrations. 2 vols. in one, 12mo,
Cloth, $1 00; 2 vols., 4to, Paper, 15 cents each.

It is a marvellously interesting work.—*Boston Evening Transcript.*

It is of the deepest interest and most profitable reading, and it discloses the author of "Sartor Resartus" as he never appeared to either friend or enemy.—*Detroit Free Press,* Michigan.

Mr. Froude has prepared a true and straightforward story of Carlyle's life, and in interest and importance it will stand next to such biographies as Trevelyan's "Life of Macaulay" and Lockhart's "Scott."—*Calvert's Magazine,* N. Y.

The work of the moment is certainly the first two volumes of Froude's life of Carlyle, which deal with the first forty years of the philosopher's life.—*Literary World,* Boston.

Froude's work is one that every student of English Literature must possess.—*N. Y. Commercial Advertiser.*

Mr. Froude has handled his subject with great spirit and in his usual masterly style. Letters by Carlyle and extracts from his note-book are freely interspersed throughout the volume. After reading them one feels strangely familiar, more at ease, as it were, with the dyspeptic old man whose trenchant pen has left such a marked impression on the literature of the nineteenth century. From beginning to end the book is thoroughly interesting.—*Sunday Press,* Albany, N. Y.

The book is a biography in a better sense than any similar work that we have lately read. Its strength lies in the fact that Mr. Froude has been eminently judicial throughout. His intimate friendship with and love for Carlyle might well have tempted him to a work of fulsome admiration, with the dark, unwholesome side of Carlyle's nature untouched, or at least glossed over. He seems, however, to have caught much of the rugged honesty of his subject, and has pictured Carlyle just as Carlyle pictured others, with all his faults and with all his virtues side by side. In this way we have the real man presented to us, not a one-sided, imperfect creation of the biographer.—*Boston Post.*

Mr. Froude's skilful hand has so arranged his materials that they bring, vividly bring, before the mind of the reader the individual, conjugal, and literary lives of both, and the interest in Mrs. Carlyle will hardly be second to that felt for her illustrious husband. The correspondence of their courtship is in its way one of the richest series of letters we have seen, while the freely expressed views of both on public men and the tendencies of society are vivid and magnetic in their effects upon the minds of their readers.—*Morning Herald,* Rochester.

PUBLISHED BY HARPER & BROTHERS, NEW YORK.

☞ HARPER & BROTHERS *will send the above work by mail, postage prepaid, to any part of the United States, on receipt of the price.*

CARLYLE'S REMINISCENCES.

REMINISCENCES BY THOMAS CARLYLE. Edited by
J. A. Froude. With Copious Index. 4to, Paper, 20 cents;
12mo, Cloth, with Thirteen Portraits, 50 cents.

These papers do in fact throw a great deal of light on Carlyle's life and character, and they will be read with eagerness. * * * Few of his most finished and elegant compositions vibrate with such intense and characteristic energy of emotion
and conviction as marks these pages.—*N. Y. Sun.*

The "Reminiscences" consist of sketches, and they give us an insight into the
man's labors and domesticity such as the world has rarely enjoyed respecting any
literary man. * * * This work is one of the notable events in literary history. It
will instruct and delight the studious reader.—*Louisville Courier-Journal.*

They display Carlyle's remarkable power of depicting character by a few rapid
strokes, and they are full of interesting information as to the circumstances of his
own life. * * * There are occasional outbursts of pathetic sentiment which it would
be difficult to match in English literature.—*St. James's Gazette, London.*

To lovers and students of Carlyle these "Reminiscences" are of the first value.
In the form of sketches of James Carlyle, Edward Irving, Jeffrey, and Jane Welsh
Carlyle—his father; his friend; his literary patron; his wife, consoler, and guardian angel—we have, in fact, a most vivid autobiography. We see Carlyle struggling with poverty, with scepticism, with the "mud-gods," with unpopularity,
with dyspepsia, until he triumphed over all except the last. * * * As for style, this
work gives Carlyle at his best.—*Academy, London.*

The graphic power of the book is as remarkable as in any of Carlyle's most
famous works.—*Athenæum, London.*

There can be no doubt of its permanent vitality.—*Spectator, London.*

If to unveil the inner life of a man truly great hitherto little known except
through his books; to paint vivid pictures of that man's family and associates—
many of them great; to tell the brave struggle which he held with poverty and
obscurity up and on to fame; to set down in the bold capitals of genius the very
face, gait, and action of his times as they touched him in the realm where he belonged—if this be a real value to the world, then Carlyle's "Reminiscences" have
much worth.—*Literary World, Boston.*

Reading these interesting posthumous papers of a great thinker, is almost like
reading *In Memoriam* rolled out in sinewy prose, its fine cadences roughened and
set to the wailing music of the loud Highland winter blast, but softened here
and there, and made sadly harmonious, by a deep human sorrow breathed as
through the very flutes of Arcady.—*Hartford Times.*

This book is very precious. It is bright with the significant art which sharpens
all his descriptions; it is honest as the utterances of his own soul to himself; it
is such a work as a man can write but once, and which even the fullest revelations
of personal letters can hardly equal as truthful outpourings of the heart. * * * The
style is clear, pure, forcible English of the best kind. * * * The "Reminiscences"
practically cover his whole life. Hardly a notable person with whom he came in
contact is unnoticed. A book with greater variety of incidents which contribute to
the unique growth of a single life has hardly ever been written.—*Boston Herald.*

PUBLISHED BY HARPER & BROTHERS, NEW YORK.

☛ HARPER & BROTHERS *will send the above work by mail, postage prepaid, to any
part of the United States, on receipt of the price.*

CONWAY'S CARLYLE.

THOMAS CARLYLE. By M. D. Conway. Illustrated. 12mo, Cloth, $1 00.

Mr. Conway's book is the most interesting that has yet been called forth by the death of Carlyle. His facilities for obtaining a just impression of the man, perhaps, exceeded those of any one else. He enjoyed years of intimate companionship with him in his own home, and the character of his mind is such that he is intensely appreciative of Carlyle's peculiar genius. The book is, to those who admire Carlyle, like a conversation with a mutual friend who was closely associated with a departed friend. The style is specially easy and fluent, and the well-known facts acquire a new significance when presented in this attractive form.—*Providence Journal.*

A thoroughly valuable and entertaining volume. * * * Mr. Conway writes with an intimate personal knowledge of his subject. * * * We believe he has come nearer to the real nature, aims, and life-work of the author of "Sartor Resartus" than most who have been moved by Carlyle's death to present their opinions to the world.—*Boston Traveller.*

He certainly succeeds in presenting the tender side of Carlyle's nature, while not ignoring its ruggedness. He lived on terms of close intimacy with him, accompanied him in his little tours about the country, and reports his conversations at first hand.—*Portland Transcript.*

We have no sort of doubt that the final judgment of Carlyle will settle down somewhere around the points of the portrait here presented, and that Mr. Conway's appreciative but discriminating estimate may be taken as a safe guide thereto. We have seen no sketch of Carlyle which gives a more nearly complete and well-balanced idea of the man, as a man, and his place in the intellectual life of his time.—*Congregationalist*, Boston.

Mr. Conway enjoyed exceptional opportunities for knowing Carlyle, and he has made an exceptionally pleasant and interesting book.—*Boston Journal.*

An admirable sketch, written in a sympathetic spirit, and containing many interesting notes of the author's intercourse with Carlyle. It ought to do good service by correcting the one-sided impression which has been produced by the "Reminiscences."—*St. James's Gazette*, London.

We have here no mere compilation, but the recollections of one who loved Carlyle, and has power to unveil some part of the lovable nature that was in the man. The glimpses of the home at Chelsea given here are more vivid and lifelike than anything else that has been published in that kind.—*Spectator*, London.

Few men had the good fortune to see so much of Thomas Carlyle in the close intimacy of private talk and association as Mr. Moncure Conway. * * * The welcome result is the transferring to paper many valuable remarks made by Carlyle in conversation, and the putting on record many incidents and traits that were otherwise doomed to oblivion.—*Westminster Review*, London.

We get much of the inner thought of the great man here, with pictures of his every-day existence that are truly inspiring. It is an admirable free-hand sketch, and is likely to be accepted as authentic and reliable.—*Boston Commonwealth.*

PUBLISHED BY HARPER & BROTHERS, NEW YORK.

WYLIE'S CARLYLE.

THOMAS CARLYLE. The Man and his Books. Illustrated by Personal Reminiscences, Table-Talk, and Anecdotes of Himself and his Friends. By W. H. WYLIE. 4to, Paper, 20 cents.

There is much in Mr. Wylie's volume that we have found a welcome reminder of what was best in Carlyle.—*Spectator*, London.

Contains a really graphic account of Carlyle's life at Craigenputtock and his correspondence with Goethe; and the best estimate we have yet seen of the signal historical service done by Carlyle in rehabilitating the defaced image of Cromwell.—*Academy*, London.

If this book is to be taken as an example of the kind of work we are to expect in the biographies of Carlyle, Carlyle will have been, on the whole, more fortunate than his fellow victims. Mr. Wylie's book is really a thoughtful and remarkably accurate performance.—*Athenæum*, London.

He has got together most of the facts of Carlyle's life, and has exposed them in a very readable piece of literary work. * * * This book gives, on the whole, a very fair and sufficient account of Mr. Carlyle's life.—*Pall Mall Budget*, London.

A timely volume of reminiscences, table-talk, and anecdotes of the sage and his friends. It is a very interesting sketch of Carlyle's life and work.—*Montreal Witness*.

A valuable contribution to literature.—*Brooklyn Times*.

A remarkable compilation of facts concerning Carlyle. * * * The author has been indefatigable in collecting material, and not a fact is lost. An acquaintance with Carlyle gives him opportunity to put in numerous little asides, and to give some conversations as they fell from the mouth of the sage.—*Saturday Evening Gazette*, Boston.

The narrative is rendered attractive, as well as instructive, by the happy mingling of personal incident, anecdote, and table-talk with the ordinary biographical data.—*New England Methodist*, Boston.

Contains a great deal of personal and literary information regarding Carlyle.—*Philadelphia News*.

A book that every lover of Carlyle should obtain.—*Home Farm*, Augusta, Me.

Will be read with much interest.—*Portland Press*.

A most interesting book.—*Brooklyn Union and Argus*.

This work was prepared before the death of its distinguished subject, and not written hastily since that event. It abounds in personal recollections, and is perhaps the best description of the famous Scotchman at present to be had.—*Christian Intelligencer*, N. Y.

A Boswellian collection from Carlyle's own lips, from reports, letters of his friends, and from the public press, of the incidents of his life and his notable words. It presents the rough, self-willed, extravagant, powerful man in a grateful light.—*Zion's Herald*, Boston.

An admirable study of a man who made his impression on the age.—*Lutheran Observer*, Boston.

A very entertaining work.—*Chicago Journal*.

PUBLISHED BY HARPER & BROTHERS, NEW YORK.

☞ HARPER & BROTHERS *will send the above work by mail, postage prepaid, to any part of the United States, on receipt of the price.*